Techniques for Optimizing Applications: High Performance Computing

Rajat P. Garg and Ilya Sharapov

Sun Microsystems, Inc.
901 San Antonio Road
Palo Alto, CA 94303
U.S.A. 650-960-1300

Part No. 806-6380-10
June 2001, Revision 01

Send comments about this document to: docfeedback@sun.com

Sun Microsystems, Inc.
901 San Antonio Road
Palo Alto, CA 94303
U.S.A. 650-960-1300

Send comments about this document to: docfeedback@sun.com

The publisher offers discounts on this book when ordered in bulk quantities. For more information, contact: Corporate Sales Department, Phone: 800-382-3419; Fax: 201-236-7141; E-mail: corpsales@prenhall.com; or write: Prentice Hall PTR, Corp. Sales Dept., One Lake Street, Upper Saddle River, NJ 07458.

Editorial/production superviser: *Laura E. Burgess*
Cover design director: *Jerry Votta*
Cover designer: *Kavish & Kavish Digital Publishing & Design*
Manufacturing manager: *Alexis R. Heydt*
Marketing manager: *Debby vanDijk*
Acquisitions editor: *Gregory G. Doench*

Sun Microsystems Press
Marketing manager: *Michael Llwyd Alread*
Publisher: *Rachel Borden*

10 9 8 7 6 5 4 3 2 1

ISBN 0-13-093476-3

Sun Microsystems Press
A Prentice Hall Title

Please
Recycle

Adobe PostScript

Please
Recycle

Contents

Acknowledgments xxxiv

Preface xxxvi

Who Should Read This Book xxxvii

How This Book Is Organized xxxviii

Additional Resources xli

Code Examples xlii

Typographical Conventions xlvi

Part I. Getting Started

1. **Introduction 1**

Performance Components 2

Hardware 2

Software 3

Optimization Process Overview 4

Serial Optimization 6

Parallel Optimization 8

2. **Overview of Sun UltraSPARC Solaris Platforms 11**

UltraSPÀRC-Based Desktop and Server Product Line   11

UltraSPARC-Based Workstations   13

UltraSPARC-Based Servers   14

Sun Technical Compute Farm   16

Solaris Operating Environment   17

Sun WorkShop and Forte Developer Tools   19

HPC ClusterTools Software   22

Summary   23

3. **Application Development on Solaris   25**

Development Basics   26

Standards Conformance   28

Binary Compatibility   29

Source Code Verification Tools   32

Checking C Programs   32

Checking Fortran Programs   34

Additional Source Code Analysis Tools   37

64-bit Development and Porting   38

Fortran Porting   45

Language Interoperability   48

Fortran 95 and Fortran 77   48

C and Fortran   50

Linking Mixed Languages   53

Summary   54

Part II.   Optimizing Serial Applications

4.   Measuring Program Performance   59

Measurement Methodology   60

    Benchmarking Guidelines   60

    Measurement Tools   62

Program Timing Tools   63

    Timing Entire Program   63

    Timing Program Portions   65

    Fine-Grained Timing Measurement   71

Program Profiling Tools   74

    Profiling With `prof` and `gprof`   74

    Profiling With `tcov`   77

    Profiling Tools in Forte Developer 6   79

Process and System Monitoring Tools   84

    `/proc` Tools   84

    Process Tracing Tools   86

    System Monitoring Tools   89

Hardware Counter Measurements   92

    Monitoring Tools   93

    Hardware Counter Overflow Profiling   95

    Code Instrumentation With `libcpc` Calls   100

Summary   103

5. Basic Compiler Optimizations 105

Compilation Overview 106

    Structure of Sun Compilers 108

Using Sun Compilers 110

    `-fast` and `-xtarget` Options 112

    Basic Guidelines 116

`-xarch` 118

    Specifying Target Architecture 118

    Generation of Conditional Move Instructions 121

    Creating 64-bit Binaries 124

`-xchip` 125

`-xO` Optimization Level 129

`-xinline`, `-xcrossfile` 132

`-xdepend` 135

`-xvector` 137

`-xsfpconst` 139

`-xprofile=collect`, `use` 144

`-xprefetch` 148

Summary 152

6. Advanced Compiler Optimizations 155

IEEE Floating-Point Arithmetic 156

    Binary Storage Format 158

    Trap Handling and `-ftrap` 160

    Gradual Underflow and `-fns` 163

`-fsimple` 166

`-dalign` 171

`-xsafe=mem` 175

Pointer Alias Analysis Options   178

    `-xrestrict`   178

    `-xalias_level`   181

`-stackvar`   189

Compiler Directives and Pragmas   192

    `pragma pipeloop`   192

    `pragma opt`   200

    `pragma prefetch`   201

    `pragma pack`   205

    `pragma align`   207

    Pointer Alias Analysis Pragmas   208

Summary   210

7.   Linker and Libraries in Performance Optimization   211

Linking Overview   212

    Static and Dynamic Linking   213

    Structure of an ELF Binary   214

Solaris Linker Usage   216

    Linking Static and Dynamic Libraries   216

    Weak Symbol Binding   220

    Linker Mapfiles   223

Linking Optimized Math Libraries   226

Creating Architecture-Specific Libraries   229

    `$PLATFORM` and `$ISALIST` Linker Tokens   230

    `$ORIGIN` Token   234

Runtime Linker in Profiling and Debugging   235

    Interposing Libraries   235

    Using `LD_PROFILE` and `LD_DEBUG`   238

Summary   242

8.   **Source Code Optimization   243**

Overview of Memory Hierarchy   244

Memory Levels   244

Memory Organization of UltraSPARC-Based Systems   247

Memory Hierarchy Optimizations   248

Cache Blocking   249

Reducing Cache Conflicts   256

Reducing TLB Misses   260

Page-Coloring Effects   263

Memory Bank Interleaving   268

Inlining Assembly Templates   270

Optimal Data Alignment   273

Restructuring for Better Data Alignment   274

Double-Word Load and Store Generation   275

Cache Line Alignment   278

Preventing Register Window Overflow   282

Aliasing Optimizations   285

Aliasing in Fortran Programs   285

Pointer Aliasing in C Programs   287

Summary   291

9. **Loop Optimization 293**

Loop Unrolling and Tiling 294

Loop Interchange 300

Loop Fusion 302

Loop Fission 305

Loop Peeling 309

Loops With Conditionals 311

Strength Reduction in Loops 314

    Division Replacement 315

    Operations on Complex and Real Operands 317

Summary 320

Part III.   **Optimizing Parallel Applications**

10. **Parallel Processing Models on Solaris 323**

Parallelization Overview 324

    Parallel Scalability Concepts 324

    Parallel Architectural Models 328

    Parallel Programming Models 329

Multithreading Models 331

    Compiler Auto-Parallelization 333

    OpenMP Compiler Directives 334

    Explicit Multithreading Using P-threads 336

Multiprocessing Models 339

    UNIX `fork/exec` Model 339

    MPI Message-Passing Model 343

Hybrid Models 346

Summary 349

11. **Parallel Performance Measurement Tools** **351**

Measurement Methodology   352

Timing a Parallel Program and Its Portions   354

Parallel Performance Monitoring With Forte Developer 6 Tools   362

Trace Normal Form Utilities   367

Analyzing and Profiling MPI Programs With the Prism Environment   376

Parallel System Monitoring Tools   379

    Binding a Program to a Set of Processors   379

    Measuring Performance on a Per-CPU Basis   381

    Monitoring Kernel Lock Statistics   383

Hardware Counter Tools for Parallel Performance Monitoring   385

`cpustat` and `cputrack` Tools   385

`busstat` Tool   388

Summary   391

12. **Optimization of Explicitly Threaded Programs** **393**

Programming Models for Multithreading   394

    Master-Slave Model   395

    Worker-Crew Model   396

    Pipeline Model   397

Multithreading in the Solaris Operating Environment   399

    Thread Models   399

    Compiling Threaded Applications   401

True and False Data Sharing   406

Synchronization and Locking   413

Thread Stack Size   422

Thread Creation Issues   427

    Pool of Threads   428

Pool of Threads With Spin Locks   433

Summary   437

13.   Optimization of Programs Using Compiler Parallelization   439

Parallelization Support in Sun Compilers   440

Parallelization Model   440

Runtime Settings   444

Automatic Parallelization   445

Explicit Parallelization   448

OpenMP Support in Fortran 95 Compiler   454

OpenMP Programming Styles   457

Section Parallel Style   457

Single Program Multiple Data (SPMD) Style   460

OpenMP Performance Considerations   467

Synchronization Issues   467

Data Scoping   470

Memory Bandwidth Requirement   475

OpenMP and P-threads   478

Parallel Sun Performance Library   479

Linking the Library   479

Runtime Issues   481

64-bit Integer Arguments   482

Fortran SUNPERF Module   483

Summary   485

14.   **Optimization of Message-Passing Programs**   487

Programming Models and Performance Considerations   488

Workload Distribution   489

Pipeline Method   494

Loop Parallelization Methods   499

Communication Metrics   502

Sun MPI Implementation   503

Building and Running MPI Programs   505

Dynamic Process Management   509

MPI I/O   512

Sun MPI Environment Variables   515

Diagnostic Information   515

Dedicated and Timeshared System Execution   516

Optimized Collectives   519

Point-to-Point Communication   523

General Performance   529

Sun Scalable Scientific Subroutine Library   530

MPI, OpenMP, and Hybrid Approaches   534

MPI and OpenMP Approaches   534

Hybrid Approach   535

Summary   538

Part IV.   **Appendices**

A.   **Commands That Identify System Configuration Parameters**   543

Hardware Parameters   544

System Configuration   549

Parameters of Installed Software and Hardware   552

Summary of Commands   554

B. Architecture of UltraSPARC Microprocessor Family 555

UltraSPARC I and II Processors 555

UltraSPARC III Processor 557

UltraSPARC IIi Processor 561

UltraSPARC IIe Processor 562

C. Architecture of UltraSPARC Interconnect Family 563

Ultra Port Architecture Interconnect 563

Gigaplane Interconnect 565

Gigaplane XB Crossbar Interconnect 566

Fireplane Interconnect 568

D. Hardware Counter Performance Metrics 571

CPU Counters 572

System ASIC Counters 575

E. Interval Arithmetic Support in Forte Developér 6 Fortran 95 Compiler 579

Interval Arithmetic Basics 580

Solution of Nonlinear Problems 583

F. Differences in I/O Performance 589

Reading a File with `read/lseek` 590

Reading a File with `fread/fseek` 592

Mapping a File to Memory 594

References 597

Index 607

Figures

FIGURE 1-1   Application Development and Optimization Stages   5

FIGURE 1-2   Serial Optimization Process   7

FIGURE 1-3   Parallel Optimization Process   9

FIGURE 3-1   Sample `appcert` Output   31

FIGURE 4-1   Distribution of `gethrtime` Call Overhead Over 100,000 Invocations   70

FIGURE 4-2   Forte Developer 6 Sampling Collector Window   81

FIGURE 4-3   Function Profile Data Generated by Forte Developer 6 Performance Analyzer   81

FIGURE 4-4   Load Object View in Forte Developer 6 Performance Analyzer   82

FIGURE 4-5   Annotated Source File in Forte Developer 6 Performance Analyzer   82

FIGURE 4-6   Annotated Disassembly in Forte Developer 6 Performance Analyzer   83

FIGURE 4-7   Counter Overflow Profiling Data Collection Facility in Forte Developer 6 Update 1 Sampling Collector   96

FIGURE 4-8   Portion of the `dbx` Window Showing the Command to Enable Overflow Profiling of `FM_pipe_completion` Event   97

FIGURE 4-9   Inclusive and Exclusive Hardware Counter Event Profiles Displayed With Forte Developer 6 Update 1 Performance Analyzer   98

FIGURE 5-1   Architecture of Sun Optimizing Compilers (Forte Developer 6 Update 1 Release)   108

FIGURE 5-2   Performance Benefit of the `-xarch=v8plus` Option—Runs on an Ultra 80 System (Forte Developer 6 Compiler)   121

FIGURE 5-3   Performance Improvement Due to the Use of Conditional Move Instruction of `-xarch=v8plus` on an Ultra 60 (Forte Developer 6 Update 1 Compiler)   123

FIGURE 5-4   Time Spent in Subroutine When Compiled With `-xchip=super2` and `-xchip=ultra2`— Runs on an Ultra 80 System (Forte Developer 6 Compiler)   127

FIGURE 5-5   Matrix-Matrix Multiplication Runtimes on a Sun Blade 1000 System for Different Optimization Levels of Forte Developer 6 Compiler   131

FIGURE 5-6   Forte Developer 6 Compilation Times for the `dblat3.f` Module With Different Optimization Levels on a Sun Blade 1000 System   132

FIGURE 5-7   Effect of Function Inlining—Runtimes on an Ultra-80   134

FIGURE 5-8   Performance Impact of `-xdepend` Option—Runs on Ultra 60 (Sun WorkShop 5.0 Compiler)   136

FIGURE 5-9   Effect of `-xvector` for Various Vector Sizes—Runs on Ultra 60 (Forte Developer 6 Update 1 Compiler)   139

FIGURE 5-10   Different Performance for Single- and Double-Precision Data—Runtimes on an Ultra 60 (Forte Developer 6 Update 1 Compiler)   143

FIGURE 5-11   Effect of `-xsfpconst` on Single-Precision Program—Runtimes on an Ultra 60 (Forte Devloper 6 Update 1 Compiler)   144

FIGURE 5-12   Speedup Due to Profile Feedback Optimization on an Ultra 60 (Sun WorkShop 5.0 Compiler)   146

FIGURE 5-13   Performance Effect of `-xprefetch` Option—Runs on an Ultra 60 (Forte Developer 6 Update 1 Compiler)   150

FIGURE 5-14   Performance Effect of `-xprefetch` Option—Runs on an Enterprise 10000 (400 MHzUltraSPARC II Processors With 8 MB Level 2 Cache; Forte Developer 6 Update 1 Compiler)   151

FIGURE 5-15   Performance Effect of `-xprefetch` Option—Runs on a Sun Blade 1000 (Forte Developer 6 Update 1 Compiler)   151

FIGURE 6-1   Bit Layout of Single-Precision and Double-Precision Floating-Point Numbers in IEEE Format   158

FIGURE 6-2   Performance Impact of Gradual Underflow—Runs on an Ultra 80 (Forte Developer 6 Compiler)   165

FIGURE 6-3   Performance Effect of `-fsimple=1` and `-fsimple=2` Options—Runs on a Sun Ultra 60 (Forte Developer 6 Update 1 Compiler)   168

FIGURE 6-4   Strength Reduction Optimization Performed With `-fsimple=2` on a Sun Ultra 60 (Forte Developer 6 Update 1 Compiler)   170

FIGURE 6-5   Effect of `-dalign` Option on Time Spent in a Subroutine Call—Runs Performed on an Ultra 60 (Forte Developer 6 Update 1 Compiler)   174

FIGURE 6-6   Performance Impact of `-xsafe=mem`—Runtimes on Ultra 60 (Sun WorkShop 5.0 Compiler)   176

FIGURE 6-7   Runtime for the Program Compiled With and Without `-xrestrict` on a Sun Blade 1000 (Forte Developer 6 Compiler)   181

FIGURE 6-8   Results for a Program Compiled With Different Levels of the `-xalias_level` Option on a Sun Blade 1000 (Forte Developer 6 Update 1 Compiler)   187

FIGURE 6-9   Improvement Due to `-stackvar` Usage—Runs on an Ultra 60 System (Forte Developer 6 Update 1 Compiler)   191

FIGURE 6-10   Modulo Scheduling of a Five Iteration Loop Using a Three-Stage Pipeline— Adapted With Permission From [Tirumalai96]   193

FIGURE 6-11   Impact of `pragma pipeloop`—Runs on an Ultra 60 (Forte Developer 6 Update 1 Compiler)   198

FIGURE 6-12   Enabling Data Prefetching With `pragma prefetch` on Sun Blade 1000 (Forte Developer 6 Update 1 Compiler)   204

FIGURE 7-1   Megaflop Rates for `v8` and `v8plus` Versions of `libsunperf` dgemm Implementation—Runs on a 360MHz Ultra 60 (Forte Developer 6 Update 1 Compiler)   233

FIGURE 8-1   Blocked and Unblocked Matrix Multiplication   250

FIGURE 8-2   Cache Line Mappings for Different Stride Values   257

FIGURE 8-3   Data Cache Hits Are Close to Zero for Array Stride N = 2,048—Hit Ratio Improves Once the Stride Doesn't Cause Cache Conflicts   258

FIGURE 8-4   Stride of 2,048 Results in the Worst Performance—Runs on an Ultra 60 (Forte Developer 6 Compiler)   259

FIGURE 8-5   Runtimes for Array Summation with Various Strides—Runs on Ultra 60 (Forte Developer 6 Compiler)   262

FIGURE 8-6   TLB Misses and Level 2 Cache Miss Rate for Array Summation   262

FIGURE 8-7   Effects of Memory Interleaving on STREAM COPY Bandwidth on an Enterprise 4500 System   270

FIGURE 8-8   Effect of Inlining the Prefetch Instruction—Runs on a Sun Blade 1000 (Forte Developer 6 Compiler)   273

FIGURE 8-9   Performance Benefit of Using a Single-Load (and Store) Instruction for Two 4-Byte Entries   278

FIGURE 8-10   Data Split Across Level 1 D-Cache Line (Subblocks in Case of UltraSPARC I and II) Boundaries—Aligned Data Exhibits Better Spatial Locality and Results in More Efficient Cache Usage   278

FIGURE 8-11   Total Number of `TICK` Counts (or Cycles) Measured in the Inner Loop with and without Cache-Line Alignment—Measurements Were Performed on Sun Blade 1000 (Forte Developer 6 Compiler)   281

FIGURE 8-12   Function Call Overhead in Microseconds Before and After Register Window Overflow
Traps—Runs on an Ultra 60 (Forte Developer 6 Compiler)   284

FIGURE 8-13   Runtime Improvements With Source Modification to Eliminate Structure Pointer Aliasing—
Times on an Ultra 60 for Functions `setvals` and `setvalsmod` Compiled With the
`-xalias_level=any` and `-xalias_level=strong` Settings (Forte Developer 6 Update
1 Compiler)   291

FIGURE 9-1   Performance Effect of Different Loop Tilings—Runs on Sun Blade 1000 (Forte Developer 6
Update 1 Compiler)   296

FIGURE 9-2   Benefit of Interchanging the Loop Order—Runs on a Sun Blade 1000 (Forte Developer 6
Update 1 Compiler)   300

FIGURE 9-3   Loop Fusion Technique—Runs on a Sun Blade 1000 (Forte Developer 6 Update 1
Compiler)   303

FIGURE 9-4   Loop Fission Technique—Runs on a Sun Blade 1000 (Forte Developer 6 Update 1 .
Compiler)   306

FIGURE 9-5   Loop Peeling Technique—Runs on a Sun Blade 1000 (Forte Developer 6 Update 1
Compiler)   309

FIGURE 9-6   Loops With Conditionals—Runs on a Sun Blade 1000 (Forte Developer 6 Update 1
Compiler)   312

FIGURE 9-7   Strength Reduction Example—Runs on a Sun Blade 1000 (Forte Developer 6 Update 1
Compiler)   316

FIGURE 9-8   Performance of Operations With Complex Operands—Runs on a Sun Blade 1000 (Forte
Developer 6 Update 1 Compiler)   320

FIGURE 10-1   Illustration of Amdahl's Law   326

FIGURE 11-1   Analyzing an OpenMP Program With Forte Developer 6   364

FIGURE 11-2   Performance Analyzer Information for a Particular Function   364

FIGURE 11-3   Analyzing a Threaded Application With Forte Developer 6   366

FIGURE 11-4   Functions Sorted by Exclusive Time Spent in Synchronization   367

FIGURE 11-5   Timeline Display on a Per-Thread Basis in the `tnfview` Tool   374

FIGURE 11-6   Latency Histogram Generated by the `tnfview` Tool for Pairs of Events That Measure Time
in the `pthread_mutex_lock` Function   375

FIGURE 11-7   Latency Table Generated by the `tnfview` Tool for Pairs of Events That Measure Time in the
`pthread_mutex_unlock` Function   375

FIGURE 11-8   Debugging an MPI Application With Prism   377

FIGURE 11-9   Viewing TNF Data Collected by Prism   378

FIGURE 11-10   Measurements of `addr_pkts` Counter Values Measured Using the `busstat` Tool on an Enterprise 4500 System   390

FIGURE 12-1   Bound and Unbound Thread Mapping to LWPs   400

FIGURE 12-2   Effect of False Sharing   413

FIGURE 12-3   Comparison of `cas` Versus `pthread_mutex` for Atomic `fetch_and_add` Operation on Enterprise 10000 System   420

FIGURE 12-4   Effect of Different Thread Stack Sizes   425

FIGURE 13-1   Master-Slave Model and Thread-Pool Approach in Microtasking Library   442

FIGURE 13-2   Stair-Stepping Effect   451

FIGURE 13-3   Performance Effect of Different OpenMP Schedule Types   456

FIGURE 13-4   Schematic for the ADI Column Sweeps Example Program   461

FIGURE 13-5   Scaling of `dgemm` Call in Sun Performance Library (Forte Developer 6 Update 1 Version)   484

FIGURE 14-1   Unipartition, Multipartition, and Transpose-Partition Schemes for Domain Decomposition of Structured Grid Computations   492

FIGURE 14-2   Pipeline Method to Parallelize Methods With Data Dependencies   495

FIGURE 14-3   Speedup of Pipelined Tridiagonal Solver on a 12-Processor Enterprise 4500 System   498

FIGURE 14-4   Scaling for Different Loop Parallelization Methods With MPI   502

FIGURE 14-5   Effect of `MPI_OPTCOLL` Environment Variable on `MPI_BARRIER()` Performance in the SYNCH1 Benchmark on a 12-CPU Enterprise 4500 System   520

FIGURE 14-6   Effect of `MPI_SHM_REDUCESIZE` Environment Variable   522

FIGURE 14-7   Point-to-Point Message Passing Over Shared Memory in Sun MPI Implementation (Reproduced with permission from *Sun HPC ClusterTools 3.1 Performance Guide*)   524

FIGURE 14-8   COMMS1 Ping-pong Bandwidth Measured as a Function of `MPI_SHM_CYCLESIZE` and `MPI_SHM_CYCLESTART` Environment Variables on an Enterprise 4500 System   528

FIGURE 14-9   Schematic of Parallelization Using MPI at Process Level and OpenMP at Loop Level   537

FIGURE E-1   Iteration of a Floating-point Newton Method   584

FIGURE E-2   Iteration of an Interval-based Newton Method   585

FIGURE E-3   Empty Intersection Indicates No Roots in Interval $X0$ 586

FIGURE E-4   Two Disjointed Intervals in the Intersection May Contain Roots--No Roots are Located in the Removed Interval   587

Tables

TABLE P-1   Desktop Reference Systems for Serial Measurements. xliv

TABLE P-2   Server Reference Systems for Parallel Measurements   xlv

TABLE 2-1   Clock Frequency Ranges of Various Members of UltraSPARC Microprocessor Family (Data are Current as of Year 2000)   12

TABLE 2-2   Overview of UltraSPARC Desktop Products—As of Year 2000   13

TABLE 2-3   Overview of UltraSPARC Server Products—As of Year 2000   14

TABLE 2-4   Overview of Netra Server Products—As of Year 2000   16

TABLE 2-5   Compiler Versions Included in Different Sun WorkShop and Forte Developer Releases   20

TABLE 2-6   Product Names in Forte Developer and Sun WorkShop Releases   20

TABLE 2-7   Product Components in Forte Developer 6   21

TABLE 3-1   Compiler Standards and Specifications   28

TABLE 3-2   Fortran Error Checking with -Xlist Options   34

TABLE 3-3   Data Type Sizes in Bits for ILP32 and LP64 Models   39

TABLE 3-4   File Suffixes for Fixed and Free Fortran 95 Source Code Forms   49

TABLE 3-5   Sizes of Data Types in Fortran and C   50

TABLE 4-1   Tools Described in This Book   63

TABLE 5-1   Some Optimizations Performed in the SunIR Optimizer Stage   109

TABLE 5-2   Some Optimizations Performed in the Code Generator Stage   110

TABLE 5-3   Synopsis of Compiler Options Discussed in Chapters 5 and 6   111

TABLE 5-4   Options in the -fast Macro   113

TABLE 5-5	Values of -xarch Set by -xtarget=native or -native 115
TABLE 5-6	Target Architectures Specified by the -xarch Option 118
TABLE 5-7	Fragments of Assembly Listings Produced With -xchip=super2 and -xchip=ultra2 Options—Load-Use Separation is Insufficient for -xchip=super2 and Sufficient for -xchip=ultra2 126
TABLE 6-1	Synopsis of Different Levels of the -xalias_level Option 183
TABLE 6-2	Distribution of ld Instructions as a Function of -xalias_level (Program Compiled on Sun Blade 1000 With -fast -xalias_level=*value*) 188
TABLE 6-3	Syntax of pragma pipeloop 195
TABLE 6-4	Syntax of pragma opt 201
TABLE 6-5	Alias Disambiguation Pragmas Supported in Forte Developer 6 Update 1 C Compiler 209
TABLE 8-1	Improvements in CPU and Bus Frequencies 244
TABLE 8-2	Sizes and Access Times (in CPU Clock Cycles) for Different Memory Levels on UltraSPARC Processors 248
TABLE 8-3	Comparison of Blocked and Unblocked Matrix Multiplication 251
TABLE 8-4	Comparison Between Interleaved and Noninterleaved 5-Point Stencil Calculations on an Ultra 60 System (Solaris 8) for Different Page-Coloring Algorithms 265
TABLE 8-5	Data Alignment Compiler Options and Pragmas 274
TABLE 13-1	Parallelization Compiler Options and Environment Variables in Sun Fortran and C Compilers 441
TABLE 13-2	Distributing 16 Iterations Between Four Threads Using Different Scheduling Types of Sun Style Directives 449
TABLE 13-3	Distributing 16 Iterations Between Four Threads Using Different Scheduling Types of Cray Style Directives 452
TABLE 13-4	Comparison Between SPMD (MPI, OpenMP) and Loop-Parallelization Styles for the Column ADI Sweep Example on a 4099x4201 Grid 466
TABLE 13-5	Synopsis of OpenMP 1.1 Fortran Data Scoping Constructs 470
TABLE 13-6	Measured Bandwidth for STREAM COPY Kernel on 14-CPU Enterprise 4500 477
TABLE 14-1	Effect of MPI_SPIN Environment Variable on Job Throughput 517
TABLE 14-2	COMMS3 Saturation Bandwidth on 12-CPU Enterprise 4500 System 527
TABLE A-1	Selected Solaris Commands to Determine System Parameters 554
TABLE B-1	Pipeline Stages in UltraSPARC III Processor 557

TABLE B-2   Latencies (in Clock Cycles) of Selected Instructions and Operations on UltraSPARC II and III
             Processors   560

TABLE C-1   Characteristics of UPA Compared to Prior Generation Interconnects Used in Sun
             Systems   567

TABLE D-1   Derived Performance Metrics From UltraSPARC CPU Counters   573

TABLE D-2   Events Supported on Address Controller, SBus, and PCI on UltraSPARC II Based
             Systems   576

TABLE D-3   Derived Performance Metrics From System ASIC Counters on UltraSPARC II Based
             Systems   578

Code Samples

CODE EXAMPLE 3-1   Errors in a C Program   33

CODE EXAMPLE 3-2   Errors in a Fortran Program   35

CODE EXAMPLE 3-3   Improper Access on an Array Element   37

CODE EXAMPLE 3-4   Checking Data Type Sizes   39

CODE EXAMPLE 3-5   Program Showing 64-bit Integer Arithmetic Performance Advantage   41

CODE EXAMPLE 3-6   Improper Pointer-Integer Conversion   42

CODE EXAMPLE 3-7   Using `-xtypemap` For 64-bit Porting of a Fortran Program   43

CODE EXAMPLE 3-8   Data Type Sizes Affected by the `-xtypemap` Option   45

CODE EXAMPLE 3-9   C Program Calling a Fortran Subroutine   52

CODE EXAMPLE 3-10   Fortran Subroutine Listing   52

CODE EXAMPLE 4-1   Example of `gethrtime` Usage   65

CODE EXAMPLE 4-2   Enabling Microstate Accounting From a Program   66

CODE EXAMPLE 4-3   Wrapper for `gethrtime` Function   68

CODE EXAMPLE 4-4   Calling `gethrtime` in Fortran 90 Program   68

CODE EXAMPLE 4-5   Program Measuring the Overhead of `gethrtime` Call   69

CODE EXAMPLE 4-6   Example of `etime` Function in Fortran   70

CODE EXAMPLE 4-7   Inline Template for Reading the `TICK` Register   72

CODE EXAMPLE 4-8   Example of Reading `TICK` Counter From a C Program   72

CODE EXAMPLE 4-9   Input File for `dblat3` Driver   75

CODE EXAMPLE 4-10   Portion of gprof Output   76

CODE EXAMPLE 4-11   Program to Show Hardware Counter Overflow Profiling   95

CODE EXAMPLE 4-12   Source Code Annotated With Overflow Profiling Data for the FM_pipe_completion
Counter on UltraSPARC-III   98

CODE EXAMPLE 4-13   Program Making libcpc Calls   100

CODE EXAMPLE 5-1   Test Program That Illustrates -xarch Usage   119

CODE EXAMPLE 5-2   Program That Generated a Conditional Move Instruction When -xarch=v8plus Option is
Used for Compilation   122

CODE EXAMPLE 5-3   Program to Show Effect of xchip Option   128

CODE EXAMPLE 5-4   Matrix-Matrix Multiplication   130

CODE EXAMPLE 5-5   Program That Makes a Function Call That Will Be Inlined   133

CODE EXAMPLE 5-6   Subroutine That Can Be Inlined   133

CODE EXAMPLE 5-7   Matrix-Matrix Multiplication   135

CODE EXAMPLE 5-8   Program Computing Logarithm of an Array Which Benefits From -xvector
Optimization   137

CODE EXAMPLE 5-9   Floating-Point Constants Treated as Doubles   140

CODE EXAMPLE 5-10   Profile Feedback Optimization   145

CODE EXAMPLE 5-11   Program That Benefits From -xprefetch Optimization   149

CODE EXAMPLE 6-1   Suppression of IEEE Warning Message   156

CODE EXAMPLE 6-2   Hexadecimal Representation of Floating-Point Numbers   159

CODE EXAMPLE 6-3   Five IEEE Floating-Point Exceptions   161

CODE EXAMPLE 6-4   Gradual Underflow Example   164

CODE EXAMPLE 6-5   Effect of -fsimple Optimizations   167

CODE EXAMPLE 6-6   Strength Reduction Optimization With -fsimple=2   169

CODE EXAMPLE 6-7   Example of Algebraically Equivalent Operations Producing Different Results   170

CODE EXAMPLE 6-8   Example of -dalign Optimization   172

CODE EXAMPLE 6-9   Program That Benefits From -xsafe=mem Optimization   175

CODE EXAMPLE 6-10   Benefits of the -xrestrict Option for a C Program   178

CODE EXAMPLE 6-11   Example Program for Testing -xalias_level Settings   184

CODE EXAMPLE 6-12   Advantage of Placing Local Function Variables on the Stack With `-stackvar`   189

CODE EXAMPLE 6-13   Program Illustrating the Effect of `pragma pipeloop`   199

CODE EXAMPLE 6-14   Example of `pragma prefetch` Usage   203

CODE EXAMPLE 6-15   Example of `pragma pack` Usage   205

CODE EXAMPLE 6-16   Alignment Control With `pragma align`   207

CODE EXAMPLE 6-17   Example of Large Alignment in Assembly   208

CODE EXAMPLE 7-1   Allocation of a Large Array   215

CODE EXAMPLE 7-2   `pragma weak` Marks Symbols for Weak Binding   221

CODE EXAMPLE 7-3   Linker Mapfile Generated by Forte Developer 6   224

CODE EXAMPLE 7-4   Functions With Global (Default) Symbol Scope   224

CODE EXAMPLE 7-5   Driver for `dgemm` Calls   230

CODE EXAMPLE 7-6   Computing Megaflop Rate for `libsunperf` Implementation of `dgemm`   232

CODE EXAMPLE 7-7   Function for Intercepting `dgemm` Calls From `libsunperf`   236

CODE EXAMPLE 7-8   Example of `malloc` Call   241

CODE EXAMPLE 8-1   Cache Blocking Example   252

CODE EXAMPLE 8-2   Performance Impact of Data Cache Conflict   257

CODE EXAMPLE 8-3   Program Showing TLB Misses Caused by Large Strides   260

CODE EXAMPLE 8-4   Program Illustrating Array Interleaving   266

CODE EXAMPLE 8-5   Assembly Template for Prefetching   271

CODE EXAMPLE 8-6   Fortran Program That Makes an Assembly Call From a Template   271

CODE EXAMPLE 8-7   Taking Advantage of Double-Word Load and Store Instructions   276

CODE EXAMPLE 8-8   Cache Line Alignment on UltraSPARC III   279

CODE EXAMPLE 8-9   Program Making Recursive Calls to Illustrate the Overhead of the Register Window Overflow   282

CODE EXAMPLE 8-10   Aliasing in Fortran   285

CODE EXAMPLE 8-11   Pointer Aliasing Optimizations   288

CODE EXAMPLE 8-12   Modifications That Lead to Performance Improvement by Decreasing Pointer Aliasing   289

CODE EXAMPLE 9-1   Different Tiling Strategies   296

CODE EXAMPLE 9-2   Subroutines With No Tiling and With 4 by 3 Tiling   298

CODE EXAMPLE 9-3   Loop Interchange   300

CODE EXAMPLE 9-4   Loop Fusion   303

CODE EXAMPLE 9-5   Loop Fission   307

CODE EXAMPLE 9-6   Loop Peeling   309

CODE EXAMPLE 9-7   Optimizing a Loop With a Conditional Statement   312

CODE EXAMPLE 9-8   Strength Reduction in Loops   316

CODE EXAMPLE 9-9   Operations on Complex and Real Operands   318

CODE EXAMPLE 10-1   Serial Program for Pi Computation   332

CODE EXAMPLE 10-2   OpenMP Version of Pi Computation   334

CODE EXAMPLE 10-3   P-thread Version of Pi Computation   336

CODE EXAMPLE 10-4   UNIX `fork/exec` Version of Pi Computation   339

CODE EXAMPLE 10-5   MPI Version of Pi Computation   343

CODE EXAMPLE 10-6   Hybrid MPI-OpenMP Version of Pi Computation   346

CODE EXAMPLE 11-1   Difference Between the Time Reported by `gethrtime` and `gethrvtime` Timers   356

CODE EXAMPLE 11-2   Difference Between `gethrtime` and `gethrvtime` Timers in Multithreaded Programs   357

CODE EXAMPLE 11-3   Modified OpenMP Example   362

CODE EXAMPLE 11-4   Modified Threaded Example   365

CODE EXAMPLE 11-5   Program to Show TNF Utilities   369

CODE EXAMPLE 11-6   Program for `cpustat` Measurements   385

CODE EXAMPLE 12-1   Creating a Thread With a Set of Attributes   402

CODE EXAMPLE 12-2   Creating Threads in a Fortran Program   405

CODE EXAMPLE 12-3   Example of False Data Sharing   406

CODE EXAMPLE 12-4   Pseudo-Code for a Simplified Mutex Lock Using an `ldstub` Instruction   415

CODE EXAMPLE 12-5   `fetch_and_add` Function Implemented Using `cas` Instruction   417

CODE EXAMPLE 12-6   Example Program to Compare `cas` With the `pthread_mutex_lock` Function   417

CODE EXAMPLE 12-7   Example Program to Show Effect of Different Thread Stack Sizes   423

CODE EXAMPLE 12-8   Overhead of the Repeated Thread Create-Join   428

CODE EXAMPLE 12-9   Pool of Threads Approach   430

CODE EXAMPLE 12-10   Pool of Threads Using Spin Lock Function   433

CODE EXAMPLE 12-11   `swap.il` inline template.   436

CODE EXAMPLE 13-1   Automatic Parallelization of Program Loops   446

CODE EXAMPLE 13-2   Stair-Stepping Effect   450

CODE EXAMPLE 13-3   Fortran Program That Relies on Uninitialized Variable   452

CODE EXAMPLE 13-4   Runtime Scheduling for OpenMP   455

CODE EXAMPLE 13-5   `!omp Parallel Sections` Directive   457

CODE EXAMPLE 13-6   MPI Version of ADI Column Sweep   461

CODE EXAMPLE 13-7   STREAM COPY Kernel   475

CODE EXAMPLE 13-8   Type-Independent `gemm` Call   483

CODE EXAMPLE 14-1   Forward Elimination and Backward Substitution Routines in Pipelined Tridiagonal Solver Program   495

CODE EXAMPLE 14-2   Loop Parallelization Methods in MPI   499

CODE EXAMPLE 14-3   Dynamic Process Spawning in MPI (Parent Process)   509

CODE EXAMPLE 14-4   Dynamic Process Spawning (Child Process)   511

CODE EXAMPLE 14-5   Program Illustrating MPI I/O Calls   513

CODE EXAMPLE 14-6   Effect of `MPI_SHM_REDUCESIZE` Environment Variable   521

CODE EXAMPLE 14-7   Distributed Matrix-Matrix Multiplication With S3L   531

CODE EXAMPLE A-1   Example of `prtconf` Call Made From a Program   547

CODE EXAMPLE A-2   Checking `processor_ID`   548

CODE EXAMPLE A-3   Usage of `sysconf` to Determine Number and Status of CPUs   550

CODE EXAMPLE E-1   Directed Rounding for Interval Data Type   580

CODE EXAMPLE E-2   Interval-specific Functions   581

CODE EXAMPLE E-3   `sqrt` Function Operating on an Interval   581

CODE EXAMPLE E-4   Order Relations for Intervals   582

CODE EXAMPLE E-5   Interval Newton Solution of a Nonlinear Equation   587

CODE EXAMPLE F-1   Reading File With `read` System Call   590

CODE EXAMPLE F-2   Reading File With `fread` System Call   592

CODE EXAMPLE F-3   Reading File After `mmap` System Call   594

Acknowledgments

Working on this book has been a truly rewarding experience and a source of great pleasure for us. When we started writing it in January of 2000, we did not realize how much time and energy it would consume. The book could not have been completed without the help and support of many people.

First of all, we express out gratitude to Omar Hassaine of Sun High End Services Engineering Group who initiated the project, helped decide the scope of the book, and got it approved as a Sun BluePrints publication. Omar also carefully reviewed the initial manuscript and provided many helpful comments.

We are thankful to our managers, John Gustafson (Ilya's manager) and Joel Williamson (Rajat's manager) for allowing us to work on the book and combining it with other projects in a flexible manner. Both of them reviewed the manuscript repeatedly as it evolved. Their feedback immensely helped in improving the organization and flow of the book.

Special words of acknowledgment are due to Eugene Loh of Sun High Performance Computing Engineering Group, who took great interest in the project. Eugene was one of the primary technical reviewers; the detail to which he provided comments on the manuscript was truly impressive, and he demonstrated remarkable expertise of the subject matter. As a result of his cogent suggestions, many sections of the book were rewritten and new topics were added. We are truly grateful to him as his comments proved to be invaluable in improving the presentation style and technical content of the book.

A number of our colleagues at Sun reviewed different versions of the manuscript or its portions. Among them are Chansup Byun, Nawal Copty, Richard Friedman, Morgan Herrington, Martin Itzkowitz, William Walster, and Brian Whitney. Their numerous comments, corrections, and criticisms were highly appreciated contributions. Their feedback was crucial for ensuring that the book fits the needs of our readers and provides accurate technical information. Any errors and omissions remaining in the book are the sole responsibility of the authors.

Ruud Van Der Paas, Melinda Shearer, and Partha Tirumalai were kind enough to spend time with us brainstorming on the scope and utility of the project. We further thank Partha for sharing his vast knowledge of compiler optimizations and computer architecture with us during the course of many discussions and e-mail exchanges.

Many other members of the growing High Performance Computing community at Sun shared their expertise with us in personal communication or through publications and presentations. We would like to mention the following people who directly or indirectly contributed to the project: Chris Atwood, Mike Boucher, Roch Bourbonnais, Alan Charlesworth, Peter Damron, Rod Evans, Kurt Goebel, Sanjay Goil, Mike Gorman, Darryl Gove, Xiangyun Kong, Michael Koster, Robert Krawitz, Manish Malhotra, Jim Mauro, Larry Meadows, Prakash Narayan, Lisa Noordergraaf, Frederic Pariente, Dominic Paulraj, Barbara Perz, Ferenc Rakoczi, Krishna Ramachandran, Youn-Seo Roh, Greg Ruetsch, Pramod Rustagi, Alexey Starovoytov, and Jian-Zhong Wang.

It was a pleasure to work with the cooperative and helpful members of the Sun BluePrints Publications Program. Rex Casey picked up the reins as the technical editor in the middle of the project and managed it with energy, enthusiasm, and admirable professionalism. We thank him for keeping the project on schedule. We are grateful to Julie Snow for her patience and high-quality copy-editing work that has helped improve the readability of the book. Barbara Jugo managed the entire production process very smoothly. David Deeths, Mark Garner, and John S. Howard reviewed the initial manuscript and provided many useful technical and stylistic comments. We also thank Timothy Marsh, Terence Williams, and Jeff Wheelock for their contributions. Our gratitude is also due to Linda Cavanaugh, the initial technical editor of the book, who has moved on from Sun since starting this book on its way.

Finally, we would like to thank our families who were very supportive during this project. Rajat thanks his wife, Sapna, for her love, encouragement, and patience during the 18-month journey and promises to make up for the many weekends spent in the office instead of at home.

Ilya thanks his wife, Karina, and daughter, Marta, for their patience and support during this project.

We dedicate this book to our parents for their unwavering love and guidance, and for enriching our lives with their wisdom.

Rajat P. Garg (rajat.garg@eng.sun.com), Sunnyvale, California

Ilya Sharapov (ilya.sharapov@eng.sun.com), Menlo Park, California

Preface

This book is a practical guide to optimizing performance of computationally intensive applications on Sun UltraSPARC platforms. It offers techniques for improving performance of applications that are predominantly compute-intensive or CPU-bound.

We wrote this book with a general enough scope so that it would be useful to as many developers of technical applications on Sun platforms as possible. Also, we made the material practical by showing developers how to use each optimization method.

For information on related topics such as system configuration and tuning, or improving the I/O and network performance, we refer readers to other resources.

This book differs from other books and technical documents written about performance optimization of high performance computing (HPC) applications. In many cases, other resources either give a detailed description of a product or provide general recommendations that are sometimes difficult to apply to practical tasks. In addition, some older resources are not as useful because of changes in technology.

Though many of the techniques we offer apply to other platforms, we limited the scope of this guide to Sun compilers and UltraSPARC-based Solaris systems. We address new features in Sun compilers and in the Solaris Operating Environment, and we show readers how to use these products to get maximum performance on Sun hardware.

Who Should Read This Book

This guide is primarily for developers of technical or HPC applications for Solaris. This audience includes both independent software vendor (ISV) developers and non-commercial developers.

Developers creating or optimizing applications in the following fields may benefit from reading this book:

- Mechanical computer-aided engineering (MCAE)
- Electronic design automation (EDA)
- Computational chemistry
- Bioinformatics
- Operations research
- Financial modeling
- Reservoir simulation and seismic modeling
- Mechanical computer-aided design (MCAD) modeling
- Graphics rendering and imaging
- Climate and weather modeling

This book may also be helpful to technical application end-users in understanding the principles of HPC and how an application utilizes system resources.

We assume the reader has:

- familiarity with development basics in UNIX environments
- a working knowledge of programming in C and Fortran languages
- familiarity with computer architecture
- experience in parallel programming
- a basic knowledge of SPARC assembly (desirable)

Unless otherwise noted, topics in this book are not limited to a programming language, parallelization method, or software version. However, emphasis is on techniques relevant to applications written in Fortran 77, Fortran 90, and C, because these languages are most commonly used in HPC and technical applications.

Most topics can be applied to C++ programs; however, we do not address performance optimization issues for object oriented programming. We refer readers to other resources.

How This Book Is Organized

This book presents information so that it follows logical stages of the process for application development and optimization. We pay special attention to issues related to parallel applications and to using appropriate performance monitoring tools. Wherever applicable, sections are illustrated with code examples that show benefits of methods described.

Part I - Getting Started

Chapter 1 "Introduction," introduces optimization for HPC applications. We describe the basics of the optimization process and illustrate it with flow charts for serial and parallel optimization.

Chapter 2 "Overview of Sun UltraSPARC Solaris Platforms," describes the available "tools of trade" for HPC developers using Solaris platforms. It gives an overview of Sun hardware and software products for technical computing. Also, the chapter introduces software development tools.

Chapter 3 "Application Development on Solaris," considers development and porting issues on Sun platforms. It includes sections on binary compatibility between platforms, standards conformance, code verification tools, language interoperability, and 64-bit porting issues.

Part II - Optimizing Serial Applications

Chapter 4 "Measuring Program Performance," focuses on tools that measure application performance. Accurate measurement of performance is crucial in tuning. We describe accurate timers available on Solaris, profiling tools, Forte Developer 6 Performance Analyzer, hardware performance counter access tools on UltraSPARC processors, and other system monitoring tools.

Chapter 5 "Basic Compiler Optimizations," introduces basic compiler optimizations and how to use compiler flags correctly. Options covered in this chapter are safe and generally can be applied without knowledge of any specifics of the application. The impact of using these flags is illustrated with examples, and analysis of the generated code with and without the options is presented.

Chapter 6 "Advanced Compiler Optimizations," extends Chapter 5 and gives an overview of techniques that enable aggressive compiler optimizations. These often result in additional performance gains but may also lead to incorrect answers or spurious side-effects. Also, we cover performance related compiler pragmas and directives, which can be inserted in a program. Information about a program can be passed to the compiler, allowing additional optimizations.

Chapter 7 "Linker and Libraries in Performance Optimization," highlights optimized libraries and features of the Solaris linker that can be used for application optimization. We describe the platform-specific optimized math libraries whose use can result in significant performance gains. We show linker techniques that allow linking of these platform-specific libraries in a portable fashion.

Chapter 8 "Source Code Optimization," provides an overview of tuning techniques at the source code level. The techniques were selected from the point of view of better utilizing the underlying architectural features of UltraSPARC systems. We pay special attention to memory hierarchy utilization such as cache blocking and reducing the translation lookaside buffer (TLB) misses. We present ways of simplifying the code to allow better compiler optimizations, such as alias disambiguation in C programs, to take place.

Chapter 9 "Loop Optimization," focuses on optimizing loops, one of the most commonly used constructs in scientific and HPC programs. We discuss ways in which developers can help the compiler control loop fusion and fission, as well as perform loop peeling. We show examples of register-tiling and consider loops with branches.

Part III - Optimizing Parallel Applications

Chapter 10 "Parallel Processing Models on Solaris," introduces concepts of parallel programming and different parallelization models available on Solaris/SPARC systems: automatic compiler parallelization, directives-based parallelism, explicit multithreading, UNIX `fork`/`exec`, message passing model, and hybrid programming (combined directives and message-passing).

Chapter 11 "Parallel Performance Measurement Tools," details the tools for performance measurement and monitoring of parallel programs. Similar to Chapter 4, we focus on accurate timers for timing parallel programs, tools for measuring synchronization and communication overheads, tools for measuring hardware counters, and tools for multiprocessor system monitoring.

Chapter 12 "Optimization of Explicitly Threaded Programs," provides an overview of explicit multithreading of programs using P-threads and Solaris threads. An overview of thread scheduling models in Solaris and their relevance to HPC programs is given and techniques for decreasing synchronization overheads are described.

Chapter 13 "Optimization of Programs Using Compiler Parallelization," covers support and optimization techniques for automatic and directive-based parallelization in Sun compilers. Special emphasis is given to tuning OpenMP programs using the Fortran 95 compiler. OpenMP programming styles and data-scoping issues are illustrated with examples. Comparisons between OpenMP and P-threads approaches are presented.

Chapter 14 "Optimization of Message-Passing Programs," describes message-passing models and how to tune MPI programs. We present an overview of message-passing programming models, compiling and linking programs using Sun MPI, and using Sun MPI environment variables. This chapter describes approaches for optimizing point-to-point and global communication with Sun MPI, using the S3L scientific library and using a hybrid OpenMP/MPI model.

Part IV - Appendices

Appendix A "Commands That Identify System Configuration Parameters," lists useful Solaris commands that identify system configuration parameters.

Appendix B "Architecture of UltraSPARC Microprocessor Family," gives an overview of architectural features of the UltraSPARC microprocessor family.

Appendix C "Architecture of UltraSPARC Interconnect Family," describes the architecture of interconnect technologies for UltraSPARC systems.

Appendix D "Hardware Counter Performance Metrics," shares some useful performance metrics that can be derived from hardware counters on UltraSPARC systems.

Appendix E "Interval Arithmetic Support in Forte Developer 6 Fortran 95 Compiler," gives an overview of interval arithmetic support in the Forte Developer 6 Fortran 95 compiler.

Appendix F "Differences in I/O Performance," considers the performance of different I/O techniques.

Additional Resources

To keep the scope of this book manageable, we intentionally omitted many subjects related to performance optimization. Our criteria was to omit subjects that were not applicable to a wide range of applications. Many of these subjects are presented in other documentation for Sun products. The following is a list of publications you may find useful for more narrowly focused subjects:

- *Numerical Computation Guide*
- *Fortran Programming Guide*
- *Fortran User's Guide*
- *Analyzing Program Performance with Sun Workshop*
- *C User's Guide*
- *Forte 6 update 1 C User's Guide Supplement*
- *Linker and Libraries Guide*
- *Sun Performance Library Reference*
- *Multithreaded Programming Guide*
- *Programming Utilities Guide*
- *64-bit Developer's Guide*
- *Solaris Tunable Parameters Reference Manual*
- *Sun HPC ClusterTools 3.1 Performance Guide*
- *Sun MPI 4.1 Programming and Reference Guide*
- *Prism 6.1 User's Guide*
- *Sun HPC ClusterTools 3.1 Installation Guide*

All these publications are available online at http://docs.sun.com. We strongly recommend that developers visit this site, because nearly all published Sun documentation is available there. Printed versions are available from Sun Documentation Center at Fatbrain:
http://www1.fatbrain.com/documentation/sun

The following publications are related to UltraSPARC microprocessors:
- *UltraSPARC I and II User's Manual*
- *UltraSPARC IIi User's Manual*

These publications are available at:
http://www.sun.com/microelectronics/manuals

Other sites of great use for developers are http://www.sun.com/developers/ and http://soldc.sun.com/, which contain current information for the Sun developer community.

A description of Sun product lines is available at http://www.sun.com/desktop and http://www.sun.com/servers. Sun products and solutions for the HPC are listed at http://www.sun.com/hpc.

For specialized books and additional theoretical information on application optimization, we refer readers to other sources. There are many excellent books on topics such as optimizing compilers, software tuning techniques, and efficient parallelization. The following are some helpful resources:

- J. Hennessy, D. Patterson - *Computer Architecture: A Quantitative Approach*, Second Edition; Morgan Kaufmann Publishing, 1996
- K. Dowd, Ch. Severance - *High Performance Computing*, Second Edition; O'Reilly & Associates, 1998
- D. E. Culler, J. P. Singh, A. Gupta - *Parallel Computer Architecture: A Hardware Software Approach*, Morgan Kaufmann Publishing, 1999
- S. S. Muchnick - *Advanced Compiler Design and Implementation*; Morgan Kaufmann Publishing, 1997.
- S. Kleinman, D. Shah, B. Smaalders - *Programming with Threads*; SunSoft Press, A Prentice Hall Title, 1996.
- W. Gropp, E. Lusk, A. Skjellum - *Using MPI: Portable Parallel Programming with Message-Passing Interface (Scientific and Engineering Computation Series)*; Second Edition, MIT Press, 1999.
- R. Chandra, L. Dagum, D. Kohr, D. Maydan, J. McDonald, R. Menon - *Parallel Programming in OpenMP*; Morgan Kaufmann Publishing, 2000.

More resources are listed in the References section at the end of this book.

Readers interested in "hands on" training should check with the Sun Educational Services to determine if a class is scheduled and enrollment is open.

Code Examples

Many sections in this book are illustrated with code examples that show benefits of optimization techniques and coding practices. The code examples can be downloaded from the Sun BluePrints site:

`http://www.sun.com/blueprints/tools`

A `makefile` is provided for each chapter so that the examples can be run with a single `make` command.

Unless otherwise noted, all examples and results presented in this book use Forte Developer 6 compilers and the HPC 3.1 ClusterTools release. The results for serial runs were obtained on Sun Ultra 60, Sun Ultra 80, and Sun Blade 1000 systems. The results for parallel runs were performed on Sun Enterprise 4500, Sun Enterprise 10000 servers, and a Sun technical compute farm. The system parameters are listed in TABLE P-1 and TABLE P-2, respectively. More information about Sun platforms is in Chapter 2.

The examples used in this book were run in C shell. We show the system prompt with:

```
example%
```

The shell prompt for the commands that require superuser privileges is shown as:

```
#
```

TABLE P-1 Desktop Reference Systems for Serial Measurements

System Parameters	System Illustration

Sun Ultra 60
2 360 MHz UltraSPARC-II CPUs
4 MB level 2 cache
1 GB memory
Solaris 8

Sun Ultra 80
4 450 MHz UltraSPARC-II CPUs
4 MB level 2 cache
2 GB memory
Solaris 8

Sun Blade 1000
2 750 MHz UltraSPARC-III CPUs
(prefetch cache enabled)
8 MB level 2 cache
1 GB memory
Solaris 8

TABLE P-2   Server Reference Systems for Parallel Measurements

System Parameters

Sun Enterprise 4500
12 400 MHz UltraSPARC-II CPUs
8 MB level 2 cache
12 GB memory
Solaris 8

Sun Enterprise 10000
64 333 MHz UltraSPARC-II CPUs
4 MB level 2 cache
32.5 GB memory
Solaris 8

Sun Technical Compute Farm
A cluster of R420 systems each
with:
4 450 MHz UltraSPARC-II CPUs
4 MB level 2 cache
4 GB memory
Solaris 8

Typographical Conventions

The following table describes the text fonts used in this book:

Typeface of a symbol	Description	Example
AaBbCc123	Commands, options, function calls, and file names mentioned in the text body; Screen output and code listing.	Use `-lmopt` to link with the optimized math libraries.
AaBbCc123	Terms introduced for the first time. Titles of books and manuals.	The *translation lookaside buffer* (TLB) provides a hardware cache for the virtual to physical page address translation. See *Sun MPI 4.1 Programming and Reference Guide* for more details.
AaBbCc123	Commands as they are typed	`example% ` **`cc -V`**

PART I Getting Started

## CHAPTER 1

Introduction

This chapter provides an introduction to high performance computing (HPC) and describes how application performance optimization fits in with this subject. HPC usually refers to large numerically intensive or scientific computations that efficiently utilize resources of underlying platforms.

Depending upon the purpose of an application and how it's used, three principles of performance optimization are common:

- Solve a problem faster
- Solve a larger problem in the same time
- Solve the same size problem in same time but with fewer system resources

Improved performance can mean getting results faster. In HPC applications, the performance time usually makes a crucial difference to users. For example, it's a considerable difference to automobile design engineers if they can repeat a simulation overnight versus over several days, during which engineers would have to wait for results before modifying their design.

Another goal in improving performance can be to solve a larger problem within a given time. For example, meteorologists need to complete simulations of their weather modelling in a given period. Improved performance allows meteorologists to use larger data sets within the same processing time for more accurate weather forecasting.

If both the problem size and processing time are held constant, an optimized application requires fewer resources to complete a computational run.

To take full advantage of system resources, an application should be carefully optimized for its platform or a range of platforms. Even though optimization is a difficult and often tedious process, it is usually more cost-effective than investing in additional system resources.

Performance Components

Run times of some computations would be prohibitively large if hardware and software components were not used synergistically to provide higher performance. In this section, we briefly describe key components of HPC platforms and how these components contribute to application performance.

Hardware

Central processing units (CPUs) and memory systems form the core of any computer system. The performance of these components often determines the run time of a numerically intensive program.

A key parameter of a CPU is its clock speed, which sets a bound on how quickly the CPU performs basic operations. Modern reduced instruction set computer (RISC) processors offer instruction level parallelism (ILP), or the ability to execute several instructions in one cycle (superscalar execution).

An efficient memory system sustains efficient CPU usage and provides data needed for computing at very high rates. Most modern platforms have multiple levels of memory. Cache forms an important component of memory structure that provides fast access to data when it's requested by a CPU. Numerically intensive programs that reuse data frequently can take advantage of cache memory.

Magnetic disks offer an inexpensive but relatively slow medium for data storage. Computational programs often operate on large amounts of data that are either permanently stored on a disk or are generated at run time and are written to scratch files. Because disk access times are very high compared to time required to access memory, care should be taken to eliminate any unnecessary disk operations.

System performance can be greatly improved with multiple processors (commonly referred to as a parallel system). A parallel system can either simultaneously execute parts of a program (reducing its run time), or can execute multiple programs concurrently (increasing throughput).

Parallel systems require specialized memory architecture that allows CPUs to exchange information or operate on the same data. These systems require support from the operating system to manage resource allocation and to control program distribution between different processors.

Distributing programs across multiprocessor systems provides additional parallel processing, but the environment and programming for it become increasingly complex. Clusters of multiprocessor systems require specialized software that enables communication and coordinates computations between cluster nodes.

Software

Programs are comprised of assembly instructions understood by a CPU. For example, load data from a memory location to a CPU register or add contents of two registers.

Although programs or their parts can be, and in some cases are, written in assembly language, by far most applications are written in high level languages such as C or Fortran. A corresponding compiler translates the program from a high level language to assembly instructions, which are subsequently transformed into object files by the assembler.

Compilers perform multiple tasks such as checking syntax of source code, applying optimization techniques, and generating code that efficiently utilizes CPU properties and platform memory structure.

Compilers and operating system software typically include optimized libraries that efficiently implement commonly used functions. Using these implementations in applications automatically takes advantage of optimization work performed by the library designers.

Parallelizing compilers take advantage of multiprocessor systems. In addition, some mathematical libraries implement parallel versions of commonly used functions.

Performance monitoring tools form another software component that help identify bottlenecks in a computer system. These tools can be stand-alone applications or can be part of operating systems or compilers.

Optimization Process Overview

In FIGURE 1-1, we present fundamental stages of the optimization process: programming and porting, serial optimization, and parallel optimization. Each stage corresponds to chapters in this book, except for the first stage. The first stage of development, choosing algorithms and data structures, is not covered in this book. Instead, we refer readers to standard texts such as [Golub98], [Kumar94], [Press92], and [Press93].

Flow charts for single CPU optimization and parallel optimization stages are presented in FIGURE 1-2 and FIGURE 1-3, respectively. We cover these in detail later but first outline some preliminary considerations to consider prior to starting application optimization.

An important decision an engineer must make is what platform or range of platforms an application should target. This decision includes choosing the operating system version and determining if the application should be built in 32-bit or 64-bit mode. A more restrictive target allows more focused optimization, but limits the range of platforms that can run the program. After a program produces correct results, it is ready for optimization. Select a set of test cases to validate that the program continues to deliver correct results, and use it repeatedly in the course of optimization.

Also select a set of cases for performing timing runs. A different set of test cases than those used to validate the program may be needed. Test cases for timing could be several benchmarks that adequately represent program usage. Use benchmarks to measure baseline performance so that there are reliable data to use later for comparisons of optimized code to original code. In this manner, the effect of optimization can be measured.

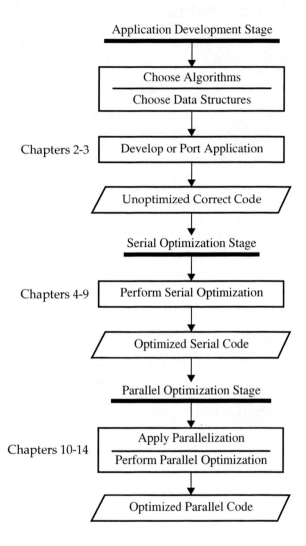

FIGURE 1-1   Application Development and Optimization Stages

Serial Optimization

Serial optimization is an iterative process that involves repeatedly measuring a program followed by optimizing its performance critical portions. FIGURE 1-2 summarizes optimization tasks and gives a simplified flow chart for the serial optimization process. Each stage corresponds to chapters in this book.

Once baseline performance measurements have been obtained, the optimization effort should be started by compiling the entire program with safe options. Next, link optimized libraries. (Linking is a simple way to bring highly optimized implementations of standard operations into a program.)

After compiling with safe options and linking optimized libraries, verify that the results preserved the correctness of the program. This step includes verifying that the program makes calls to the right Application Programming Interfaces (APIs) in optimized libraries. Also, we recommend that a program's performance be measured to verify that it has improved.

The next step is to identify performance critical parts of the code. Source code profiling can be used to determine which parts of the code take the longest to run. The parts identified thus are excellent targets to focus optimization efforts on, and the resulting improvements in performance can be significant. Another helpful technique for identifying performance critical portions of code is to monitor system activity and system resource usage. To assist with planning subsequent optimization efforts, monitor CPU hardware counters during each run. For example, large cycles per instruction (CPI) averages indicate areas to target for improving performance. Similarly, measurements showing high CPI averages and low cache hit rates (which often go together) after rigorous optimization may indicate inefficiency in the algorithm.

There are a variety of techniques that can be used to improve performance of critical code portions identified in the previous step. These include selectively applying compiler options and pragmas as well as numerous approaches for modifying source code to better optimize a program for its target platform. Some techniques discussed in this book include software pipelining, alias analysis, memory hierarchy optimizations, data alignment, and loop optimizations. As we will see in later chapters, the applicability of various techniques strongly depends on the application being optimized. Issues relevant to scope and applicability of these techniques are covered in this book.

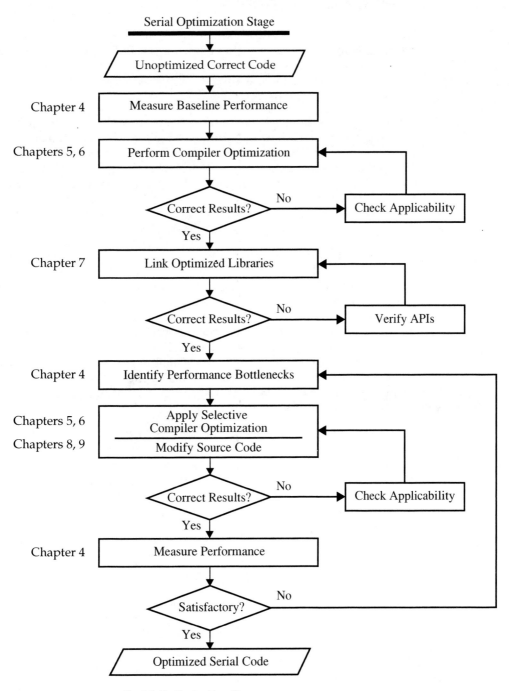

FIGURE 1-2 Serial Optimization Process

Parallel Optimization

After an application is optimized for serial processing, its run time can be further reduced by allowing it to run on multiple processors. Techniques most commonly used for parallelization are explicit threading, compiler directives, and message passing. Each of these techniques is covered in this book. In FIGURE 1-3, we illustrate the process for parallel optimization.

The first step is to choose a model, identify what parts of the program should be parallelized, and determine how to partition computational workload among different processors. Partitioning computational workload is crucial to performance, as it determines the resulting communication, synchronization, and load-imbalance overheads in a parallelized program. Generally, a "coarse-level" division of work is recommended because it minimizes communication between parallel tasks. But in some cases, a coarse level approach leads to poor load balance; a finer level of workload partitioning may lead to better load balance and application performance.

After a parallelization model is chosen and implemented, the next step is optimizing its performance. Similar to serial optimization, this process is iterative and involves repeated measurements followed by applying one or more optimization techniques to improve program performance. Parallel applications, regardless of model used, require communication between concurrent processes or between concurrent threads. Take care to minimize communication overhead and to ensure efficient synchronization in the parallel implementation. Decrease the load imbalance between parallel tasks, because it degrades scalability of the program. Also, consider issues such as process migration, scheduling, and cache coherency. Use compiler libraries to implement parallel versions of commonly used functions in both multithreaded and multiprocess applications.

Computational bottlenecks of a well parallelized program can be very different from bottlenecks in a serial version of the program. In addition to overheads specific to parallelization (such as communication, synchronization, and load-imbalance overheads), serial portions of a parallelized program can severely limit parallel speedup. In such situations, attention should be paid to the serial portions in order to improve overall performance of the parallel application. For example, consider the direct solution of N linear equations. The computational cost scales as $0(N^3)$ in the matrix decomposition stage and as $0(N^2)$ in the forward-backward substitution stage. Consequently, the forward-backward substitution stage is barely noticeable in the serial program. The developer parallelizing the program justifiably focuses on the matrix decomposition stage. Possibly, as a result of the parallelization work, the matrix decomposition stage becomes more efficient than the forward-backward substitution stage. The overall performance and speedup of the direct solver program now becomes limited by the performance of the forward-backward substitution stage. To further improve performance, the forward-backward substitution stage should become the focus of optimization and possibly parallelization work.

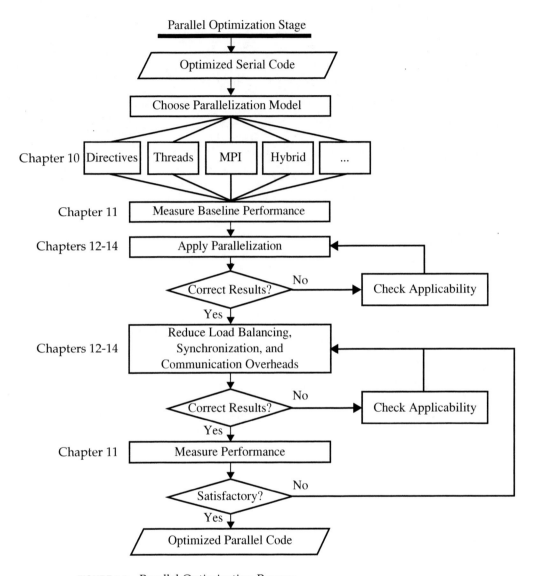

FIGURE 1-3 Parallel Optimization Process

Optimizing applications for parallel processing is a complex and rapidly changing area, which makes it a challenge to cover it comprehensively. In this book, we describe methods and models viewed as most efficient; however, we acknowledge that future trends may change in favor of other methods and models.

## CHAPTER 2

Overview of Sun UltraSPARC Solaris Platforms

This chapter gives an overview of Sun's hardware and software products for high performance computing (HPC). It provides a brief description of the UltraSPARC™-based desktop and server product lines, as well as the Solaris™ Operating Environment. This chapter also introduces the corresponding development tools, including Sun compilers, debuggers, high-performance libraries, and the Sun HPC ClusterTools™ software.

UltraSPARC-Based Desktop and Server Product Line

Sun has a diverse desktop and server product line based on UltraSPARC microprocessors and targeted to a wide range of applications and customers. The UltraSPARC microprocessor line is a family of high-performance superscalar 64-bit SPARC™ processors providing a full implementation of the SPARC V9 architecture [Weaver94]. The implementations include an extended instruction set with support for special instructions, called the Visual Instruction Set (VIS), which speeds the performance of graphics and multimedia applications. The processor line is available in three broad categories that target different applications:

- *S-Series*: The members of this family are designed for highest performance, scalability, and RAS (reliability, availability and serviceability) features. Current implementations are UltraSPARC-I, II and III processors.

- *I-Series*: The I-series is optimized for price-to-performance ratio, and features a highly integrated design (memory and PCI controllers are included on-chip) to lower the overall processor cost. Current implementation is the UltraSPARC-IIi processor.

- *E-Series*: The E-series processors are designed for embedded applications in telecommunications and network infrastructure markets. The design points are cost-to-power consumption constraints required by embedded applications. UltraSPARC-IIe is the first implementation of the E-series processor line.

The UltraSPARC processor development cycles follow the philosophy of new pipeline architectures for odd-numbered releases while process and clock rate improvements are in even-numbered releases of the family members. For example, the UltraSPARC-II processor uses the same pipeline architecture as the UltraSPARC-I processor, but it has an improved process technology. By contrast, the UltraSPARC-III processor uses a new microarchitecture compared to UltraSPARC-I and UltraSPARC-II processors.

The following table lists the clock frequency ranges of the processors in the three series.

TABLE 2-1   Clock Frequency Ranges of Various Members of UltraSPARC Microprocessor Family (Data are Current as of Year 2000)

Processor	Clock Frequency Range
UltraSPARC-I (S-series)	143-200 MHz
UltraSPARC-II (S-series)	250-480 MHz
UltraSPARC-III (S-series)	600-900 MHz
UltraSPARC-IIi (I-series)	270-480 MHz
UltraSPARC-IIe (E-series)	400-500 MHz

To support UltraSPARC-based product lines, various interconnect and system interface technologies have also been developed. UltraSPARC I and II processors (S-series) use the following three interconnect technologies, depending on the system product line:

- Ultra Port Architecture (UPA) interconnect
- Gigaplane interconnect
- Gigaplane XB crossbar interconnect

At the time of this writing, the first systems using UltraSPARC-III processors have been announced. These systems use the Sun Fireplane interconnect architecture which is a new interconnect technology developed for UltraSPARC-III processor-based systems.

I-series and E-series processors (UltraSPARC-IIi, UltraSPARC-IIe) integrate a memory controller, a PCI I/O bus controller, and a graphics interface on the CPU. Systems using these processors are architected to require no external interconnect technology.

A listing of some useful commands to identify and display system configuration parameters is given in Appendix A. An overview of the architectural features of UltraSPARC processors is included in Appendix B. Architectural details of the various interconnects are described in Appendix C.

We will now briefly describe various UltraSPARC-based desktop and server class products suitable for high performance and technical computing applications. Refer to Sun's internet website `http://www.sun.com` for up-to-date detailed descriptions of the features, configurations, and available models of the various product lines.

The UltraSPARC-based product lines of relevance to HPC are broadly classified into three categories: workstations, server systems, and cluster systems.

UltraSPARC-Based Workstations

Sun offers a wide range of workstations, from low-end, single-CPU Ultra 5 and Ultra 10 systems, to high-end, multi-CPU Ultra 80 and Sun Blade™ 1000 workstations. The family of UltraSPARC-based workstations is binary compatible with UltraSPARC-based servers, so applications developed on the workstations can be deployed without modifications on the servers[1].

Sun workstations can be used for computationally intensive analysis and graphically intensive simulations. The high performance and scaling of these platforms, as well as the high performance of graphics for 2-D and 3-D applications, made these products successful in markets such as electronic design automation, mechanical computer aided engineering and design, and genomic research.

The following table lists the UltraSPARC-based workstations.

TABLE 2-2   Overview of UltraSPARC Desktop Products—As of Year 2000

Product Name	Processor	Interconnect	CPU Speed	Number of CPUs
Ultra 1	UltraSPARC I	UPA	143 MHz (1995) 167 MHz (1995) 200 MHz (1995)	1
Ultra 2	UltraSPARC I,II	UPA	167 MHz (1995) 200 MHz (1995) 300 MHz (1998)	1,2
Ultra 30	UltraSPARC II	UPA	250 MHz (1996) 300 MHz (1996)	1
Ultra 5	UltraSPARC IIi	On-chip	270 MHz (1997) 333 MHz (1997)	1

1. Applications that use new UltraSPARC III instructions can run on UltraSPARC III systems only.

TABLE 2-2   Overview of UltraSPARC Desktop Products—As of Year 2000 *(Continued)*

Product Name	Processor	Interconnect	CPU Speed	Number of CPUs
Ultra 10	UltraSPARC IIi	On-chip	300 MHz (1997) 333 MHz (1998) 360 MHz (1999) 450 MHz (1999)	1
Ultra 60	UltraSPARC II	UPA	300 MHz (1998) 360 MHz (1999) 450 MHz (1999)	1,2
Ultra 80	UltraSPARC II	UPA	450 MHz (1999)	1-4
Sun Blade 1000	UltraSPARC III	FirePlane	600 MHz (2000) 750 MHz (2000) 900 MHz (2000)	1,2

Refer to `http://www.sun.com/desktop` for more information about Sun workstations.

UltraSPARC-Based Servers

Sun server offerings range from single-CPU systems to 64-CPU SMP systems. The server products are divided into three categories: workgroup servers, midrange servers, and high-end server systems. The following table provides a listing of the UltraSPARC-based servers, with the processor type and numbers used in the available configurations.

TABLE 2-3   Overview of UltraSPARC Server Products—As of Year 2000

Product Name	Processor	Interconnect	CPU Speed	Number of CPUs	Server Type
Enterprise 3000	UltraSPARC I,II	Gigaplane	167 MHz (1995) 200 MHz (1995) 250 MHz (1997)	1-8	Midrange
Enterprise 4000	UltraSPARC I,II	Gigaplane	167 MHz (1995) 200 MHz (1995) 250 MHz (1997)	1-14	Midrange
Enterprise 5000	UltraSPARC I,II	Gigaplane	167 MHz (1995) 200 MHz (1995) 250 MHz (1997)	1-14	Midrange
Enterprise 6000	UltraSPARC I,II	Gigaplane	167 MHz (1995) 200 MHz (1995) 250 MHz (1997)	1-30	Midrange

TABLE 2-3 Overview of UltraSPARC Server Products—As of Year 2000 *(Continued)*

Product Name	Processor	Interconnect	CPU Speed	Number of CPUs	Server Type
Enterprise 10000	UltraSPARC II	Gigaplane XB	250 MHz (1995) 336 MHz (1998) 400 MHz (1999)	1-64	High-end
Enterprise 450	UltraSPARC II	UPA	250 MHz (1998) 300 MHz (1998) 400 MHz (1999) 480 MHz (2000)	1-4	Workgroup
Enterprise 250	UltraSPARC II	UPA	300 MHz (1998) 400 MHz (1999)	1,2	Workgroup
Enterprise 5S	UltraSPARC IIi	On-chip	360 MHz (1998)	1	Workgroup
Enterprise 10S	UltraSPARC IIi	On-chip	440 MHz (1998)	1	Workgroup
Enterprise 3500	UltraSPARC II	Gigaplane	336 MHz (1998) 400 MHz (1999)	1-8	Midrange
Enterprise 4500	UltraSPARC II	Gigaplane	336 MHz (1998) 400 MHz (1999)	1-14	Midrange
Enterprise 5500	UltraSPARC II	Gigaplane	336 MHz (1998) 400 MHz (1999)	1-14	Midrange
Enterprise 6500	UltraSPARC II	Gigaplane	336 MHz (1998) 400 MHz (1999)	1-30	Midrange
Enterprise 220R	UltraSPARC II	UPA	360 MHz (1999) 450 MHz (1999)	1,2	Workgroup
Enterprise 420R	UltraSPARC II	UPA	450 MHz (1999)	1,2	Workgroup
Sun Fire 280R	UltraSPARC III	FirePlane	750 MHz (2000) 900 MHz (2000)	1,2	Workgroup

Refer to Sun's internet website `http://www.sun.com/servers` for the latest information as product lines are constantly evolving.

The above systems are targeted towards different applications and have been optimized accordingly for different price to performance ratios. The systems also vary tremendously in the amount of available memory, disk, physical configuration, attached devices, network connection, bundled system and application software, and available support options.

We should also mention the Netra™ server product family comprised of special purpose UltraSPARC-based systems targeted to telecommunications, network service providers, and other industries. The high level of redundancy in the architecture of Netra systems provides the ability to isolate and recover from hardware failures without losing data. The high-availability features of these servers make them relevant to the HPC markets.

TABLE 2-4   Overview of Netra Server Products—As of Year 2000

Product Name	Processor	Interconnect	CPU Speed	Number of CPUs
Netra t 1120 Netra t 1125	UltraSPARC-II	UPA	300 MHz (1998) 440 MHz (1998)	1,2
Netra ft 1800	UltraSPARC-II	UPA	300 MHz (1998)	1-4 per CPU set
Netra t1	UltraSPARC-IIi	On-chip	360 MHz (1999) 440 MHz (1999)	1
Netra t 1400 Netra t 1405	UltraSPARC-II	UPA	440 MHz (1999)	1-4

Sun Technical Compute Farm

For greater capacity, desktop and server systems can be clustered together, for example, using any TCP-capable commodity network. In addition, Sun offers a preconfigured solution, Sun™ Technical Compute Farm (TCF), which is a cluster of rack-mounted systems.

The Sun TCF is based on Sun Enterprise™ 420R server modules, and includes Sun StorEdge™ A5200 fibre-channel storage arrays, networking equipment, and management software. Each Sun Enterprise 420R node can have up to four 450 MHz UltraSPARC-II CPUs and up to 4 GB of memory. An advantage of the TCF over the SMP systems is that the size of the cluster can be incrementally increased to a very high CPU count. In addition, it can offer better throughput and lower local memory latency, although inter-node access time is high.

The Sun TCF is equipped with queueing software that guarantees high resource utilization. This system is well suited for EDA and bioinformatics markets where users often run large numbers of concurrent serial jobs. For these type of applications, the Sun TCF can provide a better price to performance ratio than high-end servers.

Refer to http://www.sun.com/desktop/suntcf for more information about this product.

Solaris Operating Environment

The Solaris Operating Environment is an established operating environment known for its availability, scalability, and security features. The design and the performance of the operating system plays an important role in the success of Sun products and solutions.

The Solaris Operating Environment (2.0) was introduced in 1992 as an extension of the SunOS 5.0 kernel, the first version after the SunOS transition from BSD to System V Release 4. Subsequent releases follow the versions of SunOS 5.x. The SunOS versions 4.x are sometimes referred to as Solaris 1.x, though at the time of their release, the name Solaris was not used.

Starting with version 2.5.1, the full release information of the operating system can be found in /etc/release file:

```
example% cat /etc/release
                        Solaris 8 s28_38shwp2 SPARC
        Copyright 2000 Sun Microsystems, Inc.  All Rights Reserved.
                        Assembled 21 January 2000
```

The version of the underlying SunOS kernel version can be displayed with the uname command:

```
example% uname -sr
SunOS 5.8
```

Additional commands that can be used to get information about the versions of the software and hardware parameters of the system are described in Appendix A of this book.

Solaris kernel is multithreaded and has supported symmetric multiprocessing since the 1992 release of Solaris 2.1. The first version that supported UltraSPARC processors was Solaris 2.5, released in 1995. This version did not support multiprocessor UltraSPARC systems, and was used in Ultra 1 workstations that were released the same year. The subsequent release of Solaris 2.5.1 provided support for SMP UltraSPARC systems with up to 64 processors. It was used in Sun Enterprise 3000, 4000, 5000, and 6000 servers, as well as in the Enterprise 10000 at the time of its release in 1997.

Solaris 2.6, released in 1997, allowed dynamic reconfiguration for the high-end Sun Enterprise 10000 server and provided support for large files (larger than 2GB). This version was used in Enterprise 450 servers and in Ultra 5, 10, and 60 workstations when they were introduced.

In 1998, Sun released Solaris 7, the fully 64-bit version of the operating system. This release marked the departure from 2.x numbering for Solaris versions. The 32-bit binaries produced with earlier versions of Solaris were fully compatible with Solaris 7 and could run on either its 64-bit or 32-bit kernel. Sun Enterprise servers 3500, 4500, 5500, 6500, and Ultra 80 workstations were equipped with the Solaris 7 Operating Environment at the time of their customer availability.

Solaris 8, the current version of the OS, was released in February of 2000. UltraSPARC-III-based systems, Sun Blade 1000 and Sun Fire™ 280R, use the Solaris 8 Operating Environment. The Solaris 8 Operating Environment provides additional reliability, availability, and serviceability (RAS) features, and new tools which allow monitoring CPU and bus statistics. These and other tools that monitor system activity and application performance will be discussed in Chapters 4 and 11.

Each new release of Solaris is binary compatible with the previous versions. A dynamic application that does not use private or deprecated OS symbols will run on new releases of the operating system without recompilation. The tool `appcert(1)` can be used to detect private symbols and the static linking of the system libraries that can limit portability of applications between the Solaris versions. We will discuss the usage of this tool in Chapter 3.

The Solaris kernel is multithreaded and the threads are scheduled to the CPUs by the kernel scheduler, or the dispatcher, which implements different scheduling classes. The timeshare class is the default, with the priorities of the kernel threads changing depending on recent CPU usage. The interactive class is a special case of the timeshare class for programs that use graphics to ensure that the program that has the window focus gets increased priority. The system scheduling class is used by kernel threads, which have higher priority than the user threads in timeshare or interactive classes. Finally, the threads in the real time class have fixed priorities higher than the priorities of the system class. In this book, we will focus on the applications submitted in the timeshare scheduling class either on a dedicated or shared system. The issues specific to the programming for the other scheduling classes are beyond the scope of this book.

Since its early days, the SunOS (release 2.0 in 1985) implemented a virtual file system framework that allows different types of file systems to be mounted on the same node. The SunOS also introduced the network file system (NFS) which later became a part of the System V Release 4 (SVR4) standard.

Solaris also implements the `/proc` pseudo file system, which maps active processes to the directories under `/proc`. Many of the process tracing and monitoring tools described in Chapter 4 use the `/proc` file system.

Solaris supports the dynamic linking of libraries. In Chapter 7, we will describe some of the features of the Solaris linker that can be used to improve the performance of applications.

For detailed information and documentation about the Solaris Operating Environment, we refer the reader to [Mauro00], [Winsor99], and the Solaris collection at `http://docs.sun.com` and Sun Solaris site at `http://www.sun.com/solaris`.

___

Sun WorkShop and Forte Developer Tools

The Forte™ Developer integrated development environment is a successor to the Sun WorkShop™ product line. It provides a set of tools for creating high-performance applications for Solaris-based platforms. The development environment includes optimizing compilers, a source code browser and management facilities, and a debugger that support the development of multithreaded applications.

The optimizing compilers in the Forte Developer suite are available for C, C++, Fortran 77, and Fortran 95. Fortran 90 applications can be compiled with the Fortran 95 compiler. Each of the four compilers has a front-end parser that is specific to the particular language, and transforms the source code into intermediate representation. All four compilers use a common optimizer (`iropt`) and code generator (`cg`). Sun compilers also have capabilities that allow directive-based and automatic parallelization. We will focus on the optimization features of Sun compilers in Chapters 5 and 6. In Chapter 13 we will discuss compiler-based parallelization.

The first release of development tools that allowed optimizations for UltraSPARC processors was Sun WorkShop 3.0. This release included the 4.2 version of C, C++, and Fortran 77 compilers, as well as version 1.2 of the Fortran 90 compiler. Sun WorkShop 3.0 was released in 1997 following the introduction of the UltraSPARC-based product line.

The next version of Sun WorkShop, version 5.0, was released in 1999. It supported 64-bit binaries for Solaris 7, and included version 5.0 of C, C++, and Fortran 77, and version 2.0 of Fortran 90 compilers. This release improved the code generation for UltraSPARC and supported data prefetching. Additional features included support for large files, new routines in the Sun Performance Library, as well as implementation of ANSI/ISO features in the C++ compiler.

Following the acquisition of Forte in 1999, Sun renamed Sun WorkShop products to Forte Developer, with Forte Developer 6 released in May 2000. This product included version 5.1 of the C, C++, Fortran 77, and Fortran 95 compilers. The new features of Forte Developer 6 included optimizations for UltraSPARC-III processors, support for OpenMP and interval arithmetic in the Fortran 95 compiler, and new performance analysis tools.

The following release of development tools was Forte Developer 6 update 1 in October 2000. This release included versions 5.2 of C, C++, Fortran 77, and Fortran 95, provided improved support for UltraSPARC-III CPU, and included new optimization features. In addition, the C++ compiler included in this release had improved compilation time and binary size characteristics. Even though Forte Developer 6 update 1 is considered a new version of the Forte Developer product, it does not require a new license, and can be used with a license for Forte Developer 6.

As we can see, the numbering of the compiler versions does not follow the versions of development environment releases. TABLE 2-5 shows the versions of compilers included in recent Sun WorkShop and Forte Developer releases.

TABLE 2-5 Compiler Versions Included in Different Sun WorkShop and Forte Developer Releases

	C	C++	Fortran 77	Fortran 90/95
Sun WorkShop 3.0	4.2	4.2	4.2	1.2
Sun WorkShop 5.0	5.0	5.0	5.0	2.0
Forte Developer 6	5.1	5.1	5.1	6.0
Forte Developer 6 update 1	5.2	5.2	5.2	6.1

The transition from the Sun WorkShop 5.0 product to the Forte Developer 6 product also introduced changes in the names of the individual development packages. TABLE 2-6 summarizes the transition.

TABLE 2-6 Product Names in Forte Developer and Sun WorkShop Releases

Sun WorkShop Products	Forte Developer Products
Sun WorkShop Professional C	Forte C
Sun Visual WorkShop C++	Forte C++ Enterprise Edition
Sun Visual WorkShop C++ Personal Edition	Forte C++ Personal Edition
Sun Performance WorkShop Fortran	Forte for High Performance Computing
Sun Performance WorkShop Fortran Personal Edition	Forte Fortran Desktop Edition
Sun WorkShop University Edition	Forte Developer University Edition

We should point out that there is overlap in the components offered in different products. As an example, we will list the components of Forte Developer 6 products.

Forte C software includes the C compiler, the integrated programming environment, and multithreading development tools. The Forte C++ package also includes the C++ compiler. Forte Fortran Desktop Edition 6 provides the compilers for Fortran 77, Fortran 95, and C together with the integrated programming environment. In addition, Forte for High Performance Computing 6 includes the C++ compiler, TeamWare software, and the tools for development of multithreaded applications. The University Edition is the most complete set of the Forte Developer products, and includes all of the previously listed components.

The following table summarizes the component distribution in the Forte Developer products. For additional information, refer to http://www.sun.com/forte.

TABLE 2-7   Product Components in Forte Developer 6

Forte Developer products	C	C++	f77	f95	IDE	MT tools
Forte C	X				X	X
Forte C++ Enterprise Edition	X	X			X	X
Forte for HPC	X	X	X	X	X	X
Forte Fortran	X		X	X	X	
Forte University Edition	X	X	X	X	X	X

Sun WorkShop and Forte Developer products provide a window-based environment for building, running, and debugging applications. The source code of the programs can be viewed from a text editor window with the editor selected by the developer. Forte Developer 6 supports use of the vi, XEmacs, GNU Emacs, NEdit, and Vim editors.

In addition to the compilers and the debugger, Forte Developer products include performance monitoring tools. We will focus closely on these tools, particularly on Analyzer, in Chapters 4 and 11.

Finally, Forte Developer and Sun WorkShop include TeamWare source code management tools that coordinate the development of an application by a group of programmers.

Sun compilers and related tools are typically supported for the three latest Solaris versions at the time of the release. For example, Forte Developer 6 tools are supported for Solaris 2.6, Solaris 7, and Solaris 8.

Since optimization algorithms are constantly improved and new optimization features are added, the latest released Sun compilers should be used for performance- critical applications, along with the compiler patches. At the time of this writing, patches are available at http://access1.sun.com/forte.

HPC ClusterTools Software

Sun HPC ClusterTools™ software is an integrated tool suite that provides high-performance clustering capabilities designed specifically for technical compute-intensive environments. It is a middleware solution that allows one to facilitate and manage a workload on Sun SMP systems as well as on clusters of SMP systems. Additionally, it provides the software development environment for analyzing, debugging, and monitoring the performance of Message Passing Interface (MPI) applications on Sun systems.

The HPC Software 1.0 package was released in 1997 and included Load Sharing Facility (LSF) workload management software from Platform Computing Corporation, and the public domain versions of the Message Passing Interface (MPI) and Parallel Virtual Machine (PVM) libraries.

Later the same year, following the acquisition of the Thinking Machines Corporation parallel development unit, Sun released HPC Software 2.0. This release supported single SMP and cluster of SMP systems with up to 256 processors, and included the optimized version of Sun MPI and Sun MPI I/O, which supported parallel I/O capabilities. The HPC Software 2.0 included the Prism programming environment for developing, executing, debugging, and visualizing programs, and the Sun Scalable Scientific Subroutine Library (S3L) which provided scalable parallel functions and tools for scientific and engineering applications. It could be configured with the Load Sharing Facility (LSF), which provided resource management, including distributed batch scheduling. Or, it could be configured with the Run Time Environment (RTE), which delivered tools for parallel application configuration, monitoring, and execution. HPC Software 2.0 also included Sun™ High Performance Fortran (HPF), which was later discontinued from the Sun product line, and had support for Sun™ Parallel File System (PFS).

Sun HPC ClusterTools 3.0 software was released in 1999. It extended the Sun HPC software product by providing the support for 64-bit applications with the Solaris 7 Operating Environment. It improved the performance of Sun MPI both within a single server, and across multiple servers. HPC ClusterTools 3.0 introduced a new component, Sun Cluster Runtime Environment (CRE), which provided job-launching and load-balancing capabilities for parallel applications running on up to 256 processors and as many as 64 nodes. As an option, it also provided the Load Sharing Facility (LSF) that allowed one to run applications across as many as 1,024 processors.

In addition to the features listed above, the Sun HPC ClusterTools version 3.1, released in 2000, improved the functionality of the Prism debugger to enable one to debug multithreaded and mixed applications. In this release, one-sided communication for use within a single node was also implemented in Sun MPI. The Sun Cluster Runtime Environment in Sun HPC ClusterTools 3.1 supported MPI jobs of up to 1,024 processes, running across as many as 64 nodes. The HPC ClusterTools 3.1 software is supported on UltraSPARC-based systems running Solaris 2.6, Solaris 7, or Solaris 8 operating environments.

HPC ClusterTools software is an important component of the Sun product line for HPC markets. We will describe the Prism™ environment in Chapter 11 of this book. We will also discuss the Sun MPI implementation, which is a part of Sun ClusterTools package, in Chapter 14.

Information about the latest features in the Sun HPC ClusterTools product can be found at `http://www.sun.com/software/hpc`.

Summary

In this chapter, we gave an overview of Sun's HPC enabling hardware and software products. Sun has a diverse UltraSPARC-based product line that is suited for high volume, computationally-intensive applications that arise in areas such as EDA, MCAE, bioinformatics, oil and gas, financial analysis, and other HPC markets. The product line spans from low-end desktop systems, to high-end SMP servers, and also includes tightly coupled cluster systems. Since all current Sun systems are based on UltraSPARC processors running the Solaris Operating Environment, there is binary compatibility across the entire spectrum of systems. Systems are continuously evolving to provide massive scalability, high levels of reliability, and minimal downtime. At the time of this writing, UltraSPARC-III processor-based systems are being introduced on desktop systems, to massively parallel multiprocessor computers.

The hardware products are complemented on the software side by the Solaris Operating Environment, Forte development tools (compilers, debuggers, high performance libraries, performance tools), and Sun HPC ClusterTools software.

The remainder of this book describes how to use these software products in application porting, performance measurement, compiling, linking, source tuning and parallelization to attain optimal application performance on UltraSPARC systems.

Refer to Sun's internet website at `http://www.sun.com`, online documentation at `http://docs.sun.com`, and references such as [Cockcroft98] and [Mcdougall99] for detailed information about Sun's products.

## CHAPTER 3

Application Development on Solaris

The Solaris Operating Environment provides a flexible and mature framework for application developers. A significant number of tools and products have been developed over the years to enable application developers to produce high-performance, high-quality software with minimal investments on UltraSPARC Solaris-based systems. The availability of integrated development tools such as advanced debuggers, performance analyzers, optimizing compilers, correctness checking utilities, source maintenance utilities, and high-performance libraries make Solaris an attractive and highly productive development environment. Standards conformance and binary compatibility between Solaris releases and across SPARC hardware platforms ensures the portability and interoperability of applications.

In this chapter, we provide guidelines for application development on Solaris, covering topics of specific interest to HPC developers who are writing or porting their software to Solaris. We address issues related to binary compatibility, standards conformance, language interoperability, and 64-bit porting. We also describe various developer tools, including tools for source code verification.

Development Basics

This section gives a brief overview of some issues specific to development on, or porting to, the Solaris Operating Environment. We assume that the reader has a good knowledge of standard UNIX commands and tools, as well as some experience using compilers, debuggers, and tools such as make(1S) and sccs(1). We do not explain how to use these tools and their features, but instead outline steps that ease the initial development setup on Solaris.

- We recommend that the developer's version of the Solaris Operating Environment be used on the system. The choice to install the developer's version can be made when the operating system is being installed on a computer. In the development version, tools such as /usr/ccs/bin/make and /usr/ccs/bin/sccs and files in /usr/include, which are essential for software development, get installed with the rest of the operating system. Solaris commands that show parameters of the software installed on the system are listed in Appendix A.

- The Sun compilers, for example, those in the Forte™ Developer 6 release, are installed by default under the /opt/SUNWspro directory. It is recommended that if these are installed in a different location, the <location>/opt/SUNWspro directory structure be preserved for easier maintenance, upgrades, and patch installation. The version of the compiler and available flags can be checked with the following commands.

```
example% cc -V
cc: Sun WorkShop 6 2000/04/07 C 5.1
usage: cc [ options] files.  Use 'cc -flags' for details
example% cc -flags | more
```

Another useful option is the verbose option: -v for the Fortran 95, Fortran 77, and C++ compilers, and -# for the C compiler. This option gives detailed information about the compilation process.

- Updates to the compiler should be implemented through the *patch* process. Patches can be downloaded from http://sunsolve.sun.com, or from http://access1.sun.com, and installed using the patchadd(1M) command. For example, the following command installs the patches 107355-01 and 107390-01.

```
# patchadd -M /var/spool/patch 107355-01 107390-01
```

The list of patches installed on a system can be generated with the showrev -p command. The system administrator should be notified if the recommended patches are not installed.

- Extensive online documentation is available for the compilers and other tools at `http://docs.sun.com`. Hard copies of documentation can be ordered from the Sun Documentation Center at Fatbrain.com: `http://www1.fatbrain.com/documentation/sun`.

  The documents in the HTML form are linked from `/opt/SUNWspro/WS6U1/lib/locale/C/html/index.html` page. Specific notes for a particular compiler release can be seen in the ASCII files in `/opt/SUNWspro/READMEs` directory.

  The compiler man pages can be accessed by setting

```
example% setenv MANPATH /opt/SUNWspro/man:$MANPATH
```

  or by specifying the path to the man pages directly, for example

```
example% man -M /opt/SUNWspro/man cc
```

  Additional information is available at the Solaris Developer Connection internet site `http://soldc.sun.com`.

- The Solaris environment and Forte Developer 6 tools contain numerous high-performance libraries for use in applications. While there are restrictions on distribution of some of these libraries by developers of commercial products in their applications, most can be shipped with third-party application packages. A list of libraries that can be redistributed is included in `/opt/SUNWspro/READMEs/runtime.libraries` along with licensing restrictions.

- A utility of particular use in building large programs is `dmake(1)` (distributed make). It allows concurrent processing of `makefile` targets on a number of build servers. This can considerably decrease the compilation time of a large application. For example, on an 8-CPU, E4500 system, to launch 8 compilation jobs in parallel, one might use

```
example% dmake -j 8
```

  If the build is distributed over multiple systems, all of them must be listed in the `~/.rhosts` file to enable remote login without password access. Naturally, access via the `.rhosts` file should be enabled only on trusted hosts. The resources used by `dmake` are controlled by `~/.dmakerc` and `/etc/opt/SPROdmake/dmake.conf` files.

Standards Conformance

The Solaris Operating Environment is comprised of numerous components that include kernel, file system, networking, resource management, and clustering. The various components have been architected and implemented in conformance with industry and trade standards, and with accepted practices in the area of operating system software. It is beyond the scope of this book to list all of the standards to which the Solaris Operating Environment, as a whole, conforms. Instead, we only address the primary standards that have been adhered to in the Solaris 8 release.

The command

```
example% man -s 5 standards
```

lists the manual page for standards(5) - Headers, Environments, and Macros. It gives a description of the major standards supported in a particular Solaris release.

Based on the output of above command on a Solaris 8 system, we can see that it conforms to the various standards and extensions in Open Group UNIX98, POSIX.1, and POSIX.2 (IEEE 1003.1 and 1003.2) specifications. It also conforms to the X/Open Common Applications Environment XPG3, XPG4, and SUSv2 standards.

Listing all of the standards that the various development tools, language compilers (Fortran 95, Fortran 77, C, C++), and parallelizing libraries (OpenMP, MPI) adhere to is also beyond the scope of this book, and only the primary ones are mentioned here for completeness.

The Sun compilers conform to, or are compatible with, the standards and specifications listed in the following table.

TABLE 3-1   Compiler Standards and Specifications

Compiler	Standard
Fortran 95	ANSI X3.198-1992, ISO/IEC 1539:1991, ISO/IEC 1539:1997
Fortran 77	ANSI X3.9-1978, ISO 1539-1980, FIPS 69-1, BS 6832, MIL-STD-1753.
C	ANSI/ISO 9899-1990, ISO/IEC 9899:1990, FIPS 160
C++	ISO 14882:1998

The floating-point arithmetic for the compilers is based on IEEE standard 754-1985, and international standard IEC 60559:1989. The Fortran 95 compiler also fully supports the OpenMP version 1.1 standard for Fortran.

The Sun MPI 4.1 library (part of HPC ClusterTools 3.1 release) supports the MPI 1.1 standard and a subset of the MPI-2 standard.

Binary Compatibility

Binary compatibility allows one to use the same software and data regardless of changes to the architecture or operating system. It provides an investment protection for the customer, guaranteeing that applications can be used after upgrading hardware or an operating environment. It also assures that the binaries developed and built on low-end workstations will run on high-end servers.

Sun Microsystems has a strong commitment to the binary compatibility between its products. The SPARC hardware is designed with this compatibility in mind. Each new SPARC instruction set architecture extends the previous ones, therefore, an application built for a particular SPARC architecture will run (though sometimes suboptimally) on subsequent architectures if they don't use deprecated features in SPARC architecture. For example, a program compiled with -xarch=v8 compiler option for SPARC V8 platform will run on a SPARC V9 implementation such as the UltraSPARC processor. The isalist(1) command, introduced in the Solaris 2.6 release, can be used to list all of the instruction sets available on a particular platform.

```
example% isalist
sparcv9+vis sparcv9 sparcv8plus+vis sparcv8plus sparcv8
sparcv8-fsmuld sparcv7 sparc
```

This information can also be obtained from an application with the SI_ISALIST command of sysinfo(2) call.

The Solaris Operating Environment provides backward binary compatibility for applications, meaning that each release of Solaris can run applications that were built on preceding versions of Solaris if they strictly conform to Solaris application binary interface (ABI), do not use private Solaris symbols, and link the system libraries dynamically.

To ensure that the application is properly built and will run on subsequent Solaris releases, developers can use the appcert(1) tool which is freely available from the Sun web site. This tool is coshipped with Solaris 8, or can be downloaded from http://www.sun.com/developers/tools/appcert. Information about using appcert can be found in the on-line article *Operating Environments: Building Longevity into Solaris Operating Environment Applications* available at the Sun BluePrints OnLine page http://www.sun.com/blueprints/online.html.

This is a tool that statically checks the application symbols against the Solaris ABI and reports potential stability and compatibility problems related to the use of private (non-ABI), or deprecated symbols. In its analysis of the symbols of an application, appcert uses the model files for all the system libraries for Solaris releases from 2.3 to 8. It also detects static linking of system libraries which limit portability between Solaris versions. Note that starting with Solaris 7, the 64-bit kernel does not offer the static versions of system libraries.

To illustrate how appcert can be used, we can test if the Solaris 8 ls(1) command can run on Solaris 7. Compatibility with previous releases implies that binaries developed on Solaris 7 will run on Solaris 8, but the reverse is not necessarily true. In fact, the Solaris 8 ls command will not run on Solaris 7, and this can be verified using the appcert tool. We can use the command

```
example% appcert -c 5.7 -b 5.8 /bin/ls
```

where -b option specifies the Solaris version that was used for building the binary, and -c specifies the target Solaris version for which the application is being checked. This generates its output both in ASCII and HTML, showing that Solaris 8 ls cannot be used on Solaris 7 because it uses a private symbol _fputwc_xpg5 in /usr/lib/libc.so.1 that is not available in Solaris 7. The following figure shows a sample appcert HTML report.

FIGURE 3-1 Sample appcert Output

In addition to appcert, which is a static ABI verification tool, Solaris 8 offers apptrace(1) which dynamically traces the application function calls to Solaris shared libraries. Usage of this tool is described in Chapter 4.

Source Code Verification Tools

Any porting or optimization work should primarily focus on improving the performance of the application while preserving the correctness of the computations. It is recommended that one selects an extensive set of test cases that validate the correctness of the program, and use the set repeatedly in the course of optimization work.

There are several types of errors that can change the behavior of a correct program. Programs with semantic errors in the source code may compile and run correctly with some compilers, but may give different results when ported to another compiler, or when compiled with different optimization options. A different type of error results from inappropriate use of optimization or parallelization. For example, aliasing, if not treated carefully, may result in data corruption during optimization, or an attempt to parallelize the program without protecting shared data will lead to erroneous results.

In this section, we present an overview of the tools that validate the correctness of the source code of a program. The effects of different optimization techniques and parallelization on program correctness will be addressed later in the book.

In addition to having the dbx(1) debugger, which allows monitoring the correctness of execution, Forte Developer software provides a number of tools that can detect potential runtime errors by analyzing source code prior to compilation.

Checking C Programs

The C programs can be checked with the lint(1) tool which gives warnings about incorrect or error-prone code that the compiler does not necessarily flag. A detailed description of lint usage is provided in the *C User's Guide* and in [Darwin88]. In addition to lint, one can use cc -v option, which forces the C compiler to perform semantic checks.

We illustrate the action of these tools with an example of a poorly written C program.

CODE EXAMPLE 3-1   Errors in a C Program

```
/* example_bad_c.c */
/* cc example_bad_c.c -o example_bad_c */
#include<stdio.h>
int main(){
    int i[2];
    int j=i[2]+2;
    int m=j;
    printf("j = %d \n", j);
}
```

```
example% cc example_bad_c.c -o example_bad_c
example% example_bad·c
j = 2
```

Even though the program compiles and gives a seemingly correct result, there are a number of potential problems with this code that may cause compilation or runtime failure when another version of the compiler or optimization level is used.

The error-prone statements in this program can be shown with

```
example% cc -v example_bad_c.c
"example_bad_c.c", line 7: warning: Function has no return
statement : main
```

and a more complete list can be obtained with `lint`

```
example% lint example_bad_c.c
(4) warning: array subscript cannot be > 1: 2
(7) warning: Function has no return statement : main
set but not used in function
    (5) m in main
function falls off bottom without returning value
    (7) main
function returns value which is always ignored
    printf
```

We should also mention that Forte Developer 6 introduced the `-errwarn=<value>` C compiler option which instructs the compiler to treat the specified warnings as errors.

Checking Fortran Programs

Checking the correctness of Fortran code is done differently. In addition to printing the error and warning messages to `stderr`, Fortran compilers (`f77`, `f95`) have a number of options that check the code for specific violations.

The `-Xlist` option instructs the Fortran compiler to perform global program checking. Compiling with this option creates a file with `.lst` extension that gives a line-numbered listing of the source code annotated with error messages and warnings. The following table shows various suboptions to `-Xlist` available in Forte Developer 6 Fortran 95 and Fortran 77 compilers.

TABLE 3-2   Fortran Error Checking with `-Xlist` Options

Xlist Option	Availabilty	Action
`-Xlist` (no suboption)	f77, f95	Show errors, listing, and cross-reference table.
`-Xlistc`	f77	Show call graphs and cross-routine error.
`-XlistE`	f77, f95	Show cross-routine errors.
`-Xlisterr[nnn]`	f77, f95	Suppress error *nnn* in the report. This option can be useful if certain practices are not considered as real errors and corresponding messages should not be listed. If *nnn* is not specified, all error messages are suppressed.
`-Xlistf`	f77, f95	Perform just `-Xlist` error checking without generating object files. Can be used for faster processing.
`-Xlistfln`*dir*	f77	Put the source file analysis result .fln files into the *dir* directory.
`-Xlisth`	f77	Halt the compilation if errors are detected.
`-XlistI`	f77, f95	List and cross-check include files. The default is not to show include files.
`-XlistL`	f77, f95	Show listing and cross-routine errors.
`-Xlistln`	f77, f95	Set the page length for pagination to *n* lines.
`-Xlisto` *name*	f77, f95	Rename the `-Xlist` output report file. Output will be put to the *name*.lst file.
`-Xlists`	f77	Suppress unreferenced identifiers from the cross-reference table.
`-Xlistv`*n*	f77	Set level of checking strictness. *n* can be one of 1,2, 3, or 4. Level 1 corresponds to least strict checking. Level 4 is the strictest. Default value is `-Xlistv2`.

TABLE 3-2   Fortran Error Checking with -Xlist Options *(Continued)*

Xlist Option	Availabilty	Action
-Xlistw[*nnn*]	f77	Set width of output line to *nnn* columns. Default is 79.
-Xlistwar[*nnn*]	f77, f95	Suppress warning *nnn* in the report.
-XlistX	f77, f95	Show cross-reference table and cross-routine errors.

Let us examine a poorly written Fortran program.

CODE EXAMPLE 3-2   Errors in a Fortran Program

```
C example_bad_fortran.f
C f77 example_bad_fortran.f -o example_bad_fortran
      dimension n(5)
      j=n(10)+2
      call example_bad_fortran_foo(j,j)
      end
      subroutine example_bad_fortran_foo(j)
      print*,j
      end
```

```
example% f77 example_bad_fortran.f -o example_bad_fortran
example% example_bad_fortran
   2
```

Like the previous C example, this program compiles and gives the expected result, but it also does it purely by chance.

If we compile this example with

```
example% f77 -Xlistv4 example_bad_fortran.f
```

a file example_bad_fortran.lst gets created in the current directory. Its top portion lists the errors and warnings for this program.

```
example% head -20 example_bad_fortran.lst
example_bad_fortran.f                    Thu May  4 19:39:34 2000
page 1
FILE  "example_bad_fortran.f"
     1          program example_bad_fortran
     2          dimension n(5)
     3          j=n(10)+2
```

```
**** WAR  #424:  array "n" is set to zero value by default
     3          j=n(10)+2
                   ^
**** WAR  #120:  subscript expression on "n" out of bounds
     4          call example_bad_fortran_foo(j,j)
                                               ^
**** ERR  #589:  wrong number of arguments to
"example_bad_fortran_foo"
                 See: "example_bad_fortran.f" line #7
     5          end
     6
     7          subroutine example_bad_fortran_foo(j)
     8          print*,j
     9          end
```

We should also mention two options that allow one to check the code for specific
problems that commonly cause runtime errors. Option -C can be used to check for
references to elements out of declared array bounds, and -u forces the compiler to
generate errors when a program attempts to use uninitialized variables. Checking
for this particular error can be very important if the -stackvar option is used for
compilation (the usage of -stackvar is discussed in Chapters 6 and 13). We
illustrate these options with the same example.

```
example% f77 -C example_bad_fortran.f
example_bad_fortran.f:
 MAIN example_bad_fortran:
"example_bad_fortran.f", line 3: Error: subscript number 1 out of
range on "n"
        example_bad_fortran_foo:
example% f77 -u example_bad_fortran.f
example_bad_fortran.f:
 MAIN example_bad_fortran:
"example_bad_fortran.f", line 2: Error: attempt to use undefined
variable "n"
"example_bad_fortran.f", line 3: Error: attempt to use undefined
variable "j"
        example_bad_fortran_foo:
"example_bad_fortran.f", line 7: Error: attempt to use undefined
variable "j"
```

Fortran programs compiled with -C perform the array bound checks at run time if there is not enough information about array references at compilation time.

CODE EXAMPLE 3-3   Improper Access on an Array Element

```
c example_test_bounds.f
c f77 -C example_test_bounds.f -o example_test_bounds
      integer a(5), i
      do i=1,5
         a(i)=i
      enddo
      call example_test_bounds(a,7)
      end

      subroutine example_test_bounds(a,n)
      integer a(5), n
      print*, a(n)
      return
      end
```

```
example% f77 -C example_test_bounds.f -o example_test_bounds
example% example_test_bounds
Subscript out of range on file example_test_bounds.f, line 12,
procedure example_test_bounds.
Subscript number 1 has value 7 in array a.
 Abort
```

It is recommended to use the -C option for debugging and testing purposes only, as it can impact the performance of the program.

Additional Source Code Analysis Tools

In addition to lint and cc -v, Forte Developer 6 provides a set of tools that allow the analysis of the C source code. In particular, cflow(1) generates a flow graph, cxref generates a file cross-reference table, and cscope(1) allows browsing through C source files for specified elements of code. The ctrace tool is a simple debugger that allows monitoring the sequential execution of C programs.

The cb(1) tool, or the C beautifier, is packaged with the compiler. It performs format spacing and indentation of syntactically correct C source code. Another formatter, indent(1), reformats a C program according to numerous options that this command can take.

In many cases, a C or Fortran source file contains a large number of functions or subroutines. This can complicate the source code analysis of a particular function. A multiroutine C or Fortran file can be split with csplit(1) or fsplit(1) commands, respectively. The csplit tool is a part of the OS release and is located in /usr/bin while the fsplit is distributed with the compilers.

We should also mention the preprocessors cpp(1) and fpp(1) for C and Fortran programs respectively. The location of cpp is /usr/lib. The fpp command is located in the compiler bin directory. The Fortran compilers can use either cpp or fpp, depending on the setting of the -xpp option.

64-bit Development and Porting

Some scientific and engineering applications operate on data sets that are well in excess of 4 GB, the limit of the virtual memory size for 32-bit applications. At the same time, modern servers can also have physical memory exceeding 4 GB. For example, the Sun Enterprise™ 10000 server can have up to 64 GB of physical memory. 64-bit computing allows programs to operate on data sets larger than 4 GB and address all the physical memory available on large systems.

Solaris 7 and later versions can be booted on UltraSPARC systems with either 32-bit or 64-bit kernels. The 64-bit kernel can run applications that address a 64-bit virtual memory space. In these Solaris releases, to check which kernel is running and which instruction sets are available, one can use the isainfo(1) and isalist(1) commands.

```
example% isainfo -v
64-bit sparcv9 applications
32-bit sparc applications
```

The 64-bit kernel is fully compatible with 32-bit binaries, which still constitute a vast majority of applications.

The 64-bit C (and C++) applications use the LP64[1] model, which is different from ILP32 used by 32-bit applications. The following table shows the data type sizes used in ILP32 and LP64. The two types that have different sizes are longs and pointers.

TABLE 3-3   Data Type Sizes in Bits for ILP32 and LP64 Models

C data types	ILP32	LP64
char	8	8
short	16	16
int	32	32
long	**32**	**64**
long long	64	64
pointer	**32**	**64**
enum	32	32
float	32	32
double	64	64
long double	128	128

The following test program displays the sizes of data types used by ILP32 and LP64 models.

CODE EXAMPLE 3-4   Checking Data Type Sizes

```
/* example_sizes.c */
/* 32 bit: cc -xarch=v8plus example_sizes.c -o example_sizes
   64 bit: cc -xarch=v9  example_sizes.c -o example_sizes */
#include <stdio.h>
int main(int argc, char *argv[])
{
   printf("size of pointer is   %lu bytes\n", sizeof (void *));
   printf("size of char is      %lu bytes\n", sizeof (char));
   printf("size of short is     %lu bytes\n", sizeof (short));
   printf("size of int is       %lu bytes\n", sizeof (int));
   printf("size of long is      %lu bytes\n", sizeof (long));
   printf("size of long long is %lu bytes\n", sizeof (long long));
   return (0);
}
```

1. I,L, and P stand for int, long, and pointer respectively. ILP32 implies 32-bit sizes of int, long, and pointers, while LP64 requires that the sizes of longs and pointers are 64-bit. Another data type model used in the industry, ILP64, is not used in Solaris/SPARC systems.

64-bit applications can be built with Sun WorkShop 5.0 or Forte Developer 6 by specifying the -xarch=v9[a,b] compiler options. Other -xarch settings produce 32-bit binaries. We will describe the -xarch compiler option in detail in Chapter 5.

The result of running this program compiled with -xarch=v8plus and with -xarch=v9 is as follows.

```
example% cc -xarch=v8plus example_sizes.c -o example_sizes
example% example_sizes
size of pointer is    4 bytes
size of char is       1 bytes
size of short is      2 bytes
size of int is        4 bytes
size of long is       4 bytes
size of long long is 8 bytes
example% cc -xarch=v9  example_sizes.c -o example_sizes
example% example_sizes
size of pointer is    8 bytes
size of char is       1 bytes
size of short is      2 bytes
size of int is        4 bytes
size of long is       8 bytes
size of long long is 8 bytes
```

The conversion to 64-bit might be needed for one or more of the following reasons:

- A need for more than 4 gigabytes of virtual address space.

- A need to use files larger than 2 gigabytes. A 32-bit application can use the large file interface if it is compiled with -D_FILE_OFFSET_BITS=64 (see *Large Files in Solaris: A White Paper* at http://www.sun.com/software/white-papers/ wp-largefiles/largefiles.pdf. 64-bit binaries provide large file support with no special compilation.

- Performance advantage of using instructions that operate on 64-bit registers to perform efficient 64-bit integer arithmetic.

- Application uses a library that has only a 64-bit version has to be 64-bit.

The following simple example shows the performance benefits of faster 64-bit integer arithmetic on Solaris 64-bit kernel.

CODE EXAMPLE 3-5   Program Showing 64-bit Integer Arithmetic Performance Advantage

```
/* example_inttest.c
32-bit: cc -o example_inttest example_inttest.c -xO4 -xarch=v8plus
64-bit: cc -o example_inttest example_inttest.c -xO4 -xarch=v9 */
#include <sys/types.h>
#include <sys/time.h>
#include <inttypes.h>
#define ARRSZ 2097152
int main( int argc, char *argv[])
{
    longlong_t arr1[ ARRSZ], arr2[ ARRSZ], res[ ARRSZ];
    int i;
    hrtime_t st, et, tt;
    float secs;
    for (i= 0; i < ARRSZ; i++) {
        arr1[i]= i;
        arr2[i]=( i * 2);
        res[i]=0;
    }
    st= gethrtime();
    for (i= 0; i < ARRSZ; i++) {
        res[i]=( arr2[i] + arr1[i]);
    }
    et= gethrtime();
    tt = et - st;
    secs = (( float) tt / (float) 1000000000);
    printf(" RUNTIME: %6.2f Seconds \n", secs);
    return 0;
}
```

We build the program in 32-bit and 64-bit modes. Note the use of −xarch=v9 option which specifies generation of a 64-bit executable.

```
example% cc -o example_inttest example_inttest.c -xO4 \
        -xarch=v8plus
example% example_inttest
 RUNTIME:   0.28 Seconds
example% cc -o example_inttest example_inttest.c -xO4 -xarch=v9
example% example_inttest
 RUNTIME:   0.17 Seconds
```

Note, the above example is a contrived case. The actual benefits in any application depend on the extent of 64-bit integer arithmetic usage.

To convert a 32-bit application to 64-bit, compile it with -xarch=v9 and check for proper matches between the data types. Errors often arise when variables are declared as data types of the same size in ILP32 model, but whose size is different in LP64 model. For example, the following pairs of data types are of the same size for 32-bit applications, but are different for 64-bit ones.

- int and pointer in C programs
- int and long in C programs
- long in C and INTEGER in Fortran

An assumption that the sizes of these types are equal prevents an application from working when built in 64-bit. For more information about 64-bit porting, refer to the *Solaris 64-bit Developer's Guide*.

The source code verification tool lint(1) shipped with Sun WorkShop and Forte Developer software can be used to detect potential problems related to porting 32-bit applications to 64-bit. The option -errchk=longptr64 checks portability from ILP32 to LP64 environments.

The following program assumes that int and pointer data types are of the same size. As a result it works properly when compiled as a 32-bit binary but breaks in 64-bit version.

CODE EXAMPLE 3-6   Improper Pointer-Integer Conversion

```
/* example_bad_LP64.c */
/* 32 bit: cc -xarch=v8plus example_bad_ILP64.c -o
example_bad_LP64
   64 bit: cc -xarch=v9 example_bad_LP64.c -o example_bad_LP64 */
#include <stdio.h>
int main()
{
    int i;
    char *ptr="a";
    printf("before conversion: a = %c \n", *ptr);
    i=(int)ptr;
    ptr=(char *)i;
    printf("after conversion: a = %c \n", *ptr);
    return 0;
}
```

```
example% cc -xarch=v8plus example_bad_ILP64.c -o example_bad_LP64
example% example_bad_LP64
before conversion: a = a
after conversion: a = a
```

```
example% cc -xarch=v9 example_bad_LP64.c -o example_bad_LP64
example% example_bad_LP64
before conversion: a = a
Segmentation Fault
```

The conversion between pointer and integer types can be detected with lint

```
example% lint -errchk=longptr64 example_bad_LP64.c
(8) warning: conversion of pointer loses bits
(9) warning: cast to pointer from 32-bit integer
```

In building Fortran programs that have 64-bit address space, the implicit size of
Fortran data types must be kept in mind. The following example illustrates the use
of the malloc(3F) function in a Fortran 77 program. In 64-bit, the return value of
malloc is a 64-bit quantity, while the default declaration of malloc returns
integer*4 or 32-bit. One can use the compiler option -xtypemap to change the
implicit default sizes of integer to 64-bit and then the program works correctly. We
discuss the use of this option in the following section.

CODE EXAMPLE 3-7   Using -xtypemap For 64-bit Porting of a Fortran Program

```
c   example_ptrtst.f77
c   32-bit: f77 example_ptrtst.f -o example_ptrtst
c   64-bit: f77 -xtypemap=real:32,double:64,integer:64 \
c                  -xarch=v9 example_ptrtst.f -o example_ptrtst
      parameter(n=1000)
      integer malloc
      external malloc
      integer*4 isum, xadj(*) ! explicitly size declaration
      pointer (xadj_p, xadj)
      xadj_p = malloc(sizeof(isum)*n)
      do i=1,n
         xadj(i) = 1
      enddo
      isum = 0
      do i=1,n
         isum = isum + xadj(i)
      enddo
      write(6,*) 'isum= ',isum
      end
```

```
example% f77 -xarch=v9 example_ptrtst.f -o example_ptrtst
example% example_ptrtst
*** TERMINATING example_ptrtst
```

```
*** Received signal 11 SIGSEGV
Segmentation Fault
example% f77 -xtypemap=real:32,double:64,integer:64 -xarch=v9 \
        example_ptrtst.f -o example_ptrtst
example% example_ptrtst
 isum=    1000
```

Changing the default size of integer, as shown in the previous example, can have many implications for the I/O and various library calls (for example, MPI library, Sun Performance Library™), and must be used carefully. For example, if a 32-bit application was used to create unformatted (or binary) files in which implicitly typed integer variables were used, the 64-bit application that uses the option -xtypemap (as in the previous example) will not be able to correctly read in those files. In such cases, explicit typing of the variables is needed in the program.

Care is also needed if library calls are made. For example, if the application uses calls to MPI library and is compiled with -xtypemap=...integer:64, the integer arguments (including the constants) need to be cast explicitly to integer*4 or integer(KIND=4).

```
integer len,tag,ierr
real*4 a(1000)
...
...
call mpi_send(a, len, MPI_REAL, 1, tag, MPI_COMM_WORLD, ierr)
```

When compiling with -xtypemap=...integer:64 -xarch=v9, the above should be changed to

```
integer*4 len,tag,ierr
real*4 a(1000)
...
...
call mpi_send(a, len, MPI_REAL, 1_4, tag, MPI_COMM_WORLD, ierr)
```

to explicitly control the size of parameters passed to MPI interfaces. If this is not possible, temporaries might need to be used to convert back and forth between 8-byte and 4-byte integer quantities. We will discuss the usage and features of Sun MPI in Chapter 14. We return to the usage of -xtypemap option in the next section about Fortran porting.

We conclude this section by mentioning that the 32-bit and 64-bit versions of the same application can be packaged together with isaexec(3C) wrapper. This utility chooses between versions of the application depending on the running kernel of

Solaris transparently to the user. The drawback of this approach is that two distinct sets of binaries have to be available, doubling the storage requirements for the application.

For more information about the issues related to 64-bit porting, refer to the *Solaris 64-bit Developer's Guide.*

Fortran Porting

In this section, we briefly touch upon some issues that are relevant to porting Fortran applications to the Solaris platform. A detailed description of this subject can be found in the *Fortran Programming Guide.*

We already mentioned the `-xtypemap` option available in the Fortran compilers. It can be used for controlling the default size of data types when porting from 64-bit computers such as CRAY or CDC vector supercomputers. For example, to specify all implicitly typed `real` variables to be 64-bit (or `real*8`), all implicitly typed `integer*4` variables to be `integer*8`, and `double precision` to be `real*16`, one can use the following setting for -xtypemap

```
example% f77 -xtypemap=real:64,double:128:integer:64
```

The size of the `complex` data type changes according to changes in the size of the underlying `real` or `double precision` type.

If the size of `double precision` variables were to be left at 8 bytes, then `double:64` should be used. The -xtypemap flag only changes the sizes of implicitly typed variables. If the size of a variable is explicitly declared, say `integer*4`, then a setting of `integer:64` in -xtypemap will not change it.

In the following example, if the -xtypemap option is not specified, the variables r, r4, and implicitly typed s are treated as `real*4`. We can see the corresponding precision loss in the output of the program (see Chapter 6 for a discussion of the precision of the floating-point numbers).

CODE EXAMPLE 3-8 Data Type Sizes Affected by the -xtypemap Option

```
c example_xtypemap.f
c f77 example_xtypemap.f -o example_xtypemap \
c     (-xtypemap=real:64,double:64,integer:64)
      real r
      real*4 r4
```

CODE EXAMPLE 3-8 Data Type Sizes Affected by the -xtypemap Option

```
      real*8 r8
c

      r =0.123456789012345
      r4=0.123456789012345
      r8=0.123456789012345
      s =0.123456789012345
c

      print*,'r = ', r
      print*,'r4= ', r4
      print*,'r8= ', r8
      print*,'s = ', s
      end
```

```
example% f77 example_xtypemap.f -o example_xtypemap
example_xtypemap.f:
 MAIN:
example% example_xtypemap
 r =    0.123457
 r4=    0.123457
 r8=    0.12345678901234
 s =    0.123457
```

When we compile this program with the -xtypemap=real:64... setting, only the variable r4 whose data type size is explicitly set stays real*4. Both r and implicitly typed s are treated as real*8.

```
example% f77 example_xtypemap.f -o example_xtypemap \
        -xtypemap=real:64,double:64,integer:64
example_xtypemap.f:
 MAIN:
example% example_xtypemap
 r =    0.12345678901234
 r4=    0.123457
 r8=    0.12345678901234
 s =    0.12345678901234
```

The possible values for the arguments to -xtypemap are

```
real:32
real:64
double:64
double:128
integer:32
integer:64
integer:mixed
```

The last option is only available in Fortran 77 and implies that while 8-byte storage is allocated for the implicitly typed integer variable, only 4-byte arithmetic takes place. It is preferred that integer:64 is used instead.

The use of the -xtypemap flag is preferred over the -r8 and -dbl flags in the Fortran compilers (see the documentation for Forte Developer 6 Fortran compilers).

Some other things to be careful of when porting from other platforms relate to the use of non-standard language and system-specific features. Specifically, different data representations and alignments across systems cause most porting problems. The following items are relevant to porting from other systems:

- By default, the Sun Fortran compilers follow the IEEE 754 floating-point arithmetic standard by which an exception is raised on overflow or divisions by zero, but no trap or SIGFPE is delivered. If the user wishes to stop the program on overflows or divide by zero, the option -ftrap=common should be used when compiling the program. We will discuss this subject in detail in Chapter 6.

- The default sizes of various data types (real, complex, integer, logical) are as described in the Fortran standard, except when explicitly controlled by the use of options such as -xtypemap.

- It is recommended that character variables not be mixed with other variables in common blocks or equivalenced with other variables, because of potential alignment problems. It is also recommended that the variables listed in common blocks are arranged from the largest types to the smallest.

- A well-written program should not depend on default initialization of variables for correct execution. Instead, all variables should be explicitly initialized as much as possible. A common initialization problem occurs when a program that assumes default initialization (zero value) is compiled with the -stackvar compiler option (see Chapters 6 and 13); with -stackvar, the variable is put on the stack and will usually have a garbage initial value. Additionally, on different systems the default initial values could be different (zero, NaN) and this causes problems when the program is ported from one system to the other.

- Programs being ported from vector or scientific mainframes (CRAY, CDC) often have vectorizing optimizations in the source code that are obsolete for RISC-based optimizing compilers (such as Sun compilers for SPARC platform), and may hinder Sun compiler optimizations.

- The results of the program should not depend on the type of arithmetic performed in the hardware for correctness. For example, the arithmetic performed on old VAX systems or scientific computers, such as older CRAY systems, is different from the IEEE standard arithmetic that is implemented in SPARC processors. Even with IEEE arithmetic, the results on different processors may differ (mainly as the result of the use of the "guard bits" to increase the precision of scratch computations). See the *Numerical Computation Guide* for understanding the fine aspects of implementation dependencies in IEEE arithmetic.

Language Interoperability

In this section, we will describe some issues relevant to interoperability of programs written in different languages.

Fortran 95 and Fortran 77

Since a large number of scientific and HPC applications are written in Fortran 77, a significant effort was put into the design and implementation of the Sun Fortran 95[1] compiler to preserve compatibility with the Sun Fortran 77 compiler. In addition to the Forte Developer 6 Fortran 95 compiler fully conforming to the Fortran 95 standard, extensions and features were added to make it interoperate better with Forte Developer 6 Fortran 77 and earlier releases of Sun Fortran compilers. A detailed description of these extensions is given in the Appendix C of the *Fortran User's Guide*. Some important ones are listed below:

- The Fortran 95 compiler supports directives in the program. The accepted formats for the directives are Sun style (CDIR$, !DIR$), Cray style (CMIC$, !MIC$), OpenMP style (C$OMP), and pragmas (C$PRAGMA). The Fortran 95 standard has no specific discussion on directives.

- There is support for both *free* and *fixed* source form. The fixed source form is compatible with Fortran 77 standard and restricts the use of the first six characters of a line. The free form does not have this restriction. The interpretation of the fixed and free source form depends on:
  - The usage of -fixed and -free compiler options.
  - The usage of FIXED and FREE directives.
  - The file suffixes.

1. Programs conforming to the Fortran 90 standard can be compiled with f95 command. The f90 command available in Forte Developer software is a link to f95.

The following table summarizes the supported file suffixes by the Fortran 95 compiler in the fixed and free forms.

TABLE 3-4 File Suffixes for Fixed and Free Fortran 95 Source Code Forms

Suffixes	Source Form
.f, .for, .ftn, .F	fixed
.f90, .F90, .f95, .F95	free

The two forms can be mixed in the compile line, same program file, and same program unit according to the following rules:

- In the same compile line, some source files can be in fixed form, while some can be in free form.
- In the same program file, free and fixed forms can be mixed by using directives.
- In the same program unit, the tab form (lines start with the tab character) can be mixed with either the free or the fixed form.

- Both Forte Developer Fortran 95 and Fortran 77 compilers allow 99 continuation lines. The Fortran 95 standard requires only 19 lines in the fixed form and 39 for the free form.

- The Fortran 95 compiler also supports the −e option which allows source lines in fixed format up to 132 characters.

- The Forte Developer 6 Fortran 95 compiler supports Cray pointers, while the standard does not require that.

- Some I/O extensions that are part of Sun Fortran 77 compilers have also been added to the Fortran 95 compiler. For example, as in Fortran 77, the OPEN(...,FORM='BINARY') treats the file as binary data without record mark. (See *Fortran User's Guide* for a list of I/O extensions.)

In general, as a result of the above extensions, Fortran 77 source that conforms to ANSI standard Fortran, and uses standard features used in older systems (like VMS) will compile with the Fortran 95 compiler. One major difference is the limits in array dimensions. While the Fortran 77 compiler allows 20 array subscripts, only seven are allowed in the Fortran 95 compiler.

Forte Developer 6 update 1 compilers introduced the option −xlang which can be used at link stage to specify the set of languages used in the program.

```
example% f77 a.f
example% f95 b.f90
example% f77 a.o b.o -xlang=f95
```

If the option -xlang is not used to mix f77 and f95 compiled objects, one needs to link with libf77compat library using the f95 compiler at the link step. For example,

```
example% f77 -c a.f
example% f90 -c b.f90
example% f90 a.o b.o -lf77compat
```

The final linking should be done with the f95 compiler even if the main program is a Fortran 77 program.

The Fortran 77 libraries are compatible with Fortran 95 libraries. For example, dtime(3F), can be called from Fortran 95 source and compiled with the f95 compiler.

C and Fortran

In large computational applications written in Fortran, it is common to have some parts, for example preprocessing or graphics, written in C or C++. Different languages can be mixed, and the object files produced by C and Fortran compilers can be used for generating a binary. There are, though, some issues specific to interfacing C and Fortran programs that require special attention.

The data types of the variables passed between Fortran and C should match in size. The following table lists selected data types and their sizes in Fortran 77, Fortran 95, and C.

TABLE 3-5   Sizes of Data Types in Fortran and C

Fortran 77	Fortran 95	C[1]	Size (Bytes)
INTEGER	INTEGER	int	4
INTEGER*2	INTEGER (KIND=2)	short	2
INTEGER*4	INTEGER (KIND=4)	int	4
INTEGER*8	INTEGER (KIND=8)	long long	8
LOGICAL	LOGICAL	int	4
LOGICAL*1	LOGICAL (KIND=1)	char	1
LOGICAL*2	LOGICAL (KIND=2)	short	2
LOGICAL*4	LOGICAL (KIND=4)	int	4
LOGICAL*8	LOGICAL (KIND=8)	long long	8

TABLE 3-5   Sizes of Data Types in Fortran and C *(Continued)*

Fortran 77	Fortran 95	C[1]	Size (Bytes)
REAL	REAL	float	4
REAL*4	REAL (KIND=4)	float	4
DOUBLE PRECISION	DOUBLE PRECISION	double	8
REAL*8	REAL (KIND=8)	double	8
REAL*16	REAL (KIND=16)	long double	16
COMPLEX	COMPLEX	Struct{float r, i;}	8
COMPLEX*8	COMPLEX (KIND=4)	Struct{float r, i;}	8
COMPLEX*16	COMPLEX (KIND=8)	Struct{double r, i;}	16
DOUBLE COMPLEX	DOUBLE COMPLEX	Struct{double r, i;}	16
COMPLEX*32	COMPLEX (KIND=16)	Struct{long double r, i;}	32

1. The C `long` data type is 4 bytes or 8 bytes long in ILP32 and LP64 models respectively. These models were discussed in the section on 64-bit porting in this chapter

The C functions that return one of the built-in data types are analogous to Fortran functions. Like `void` C functions, the Fortran subroutines do not return a value. The Fortran compiler appends the trailing underscore to the names of functions and subroutines. To call a C function from Fortran, one should either append an underscore to the function name in the C program

```
void foo_(...);
```

or use `PRAGMA C` in the Fortran declaration of the function. For example,

```
EXTERNAL FOO !$PRAGMA C(FOO)
```

Functions can pass data between C and Fortran by reference. It is also possible to pass data by value from Fortran to C using `%VAL()` construct.

The arrays in C are numbered starting from 0, and the default numbering of Fortran arrays starts from 1, but this behavior can be overridden and the ranges of Fortran arrays can be set explicitly. In addition, the memory layout of multidimensional arrays is different for C and Fortran. In C arrays, the last dimension is the one that changes most rapidly, while for Fortran arrays, the opposite is true.

Passing character strings between C and Fortran functions is not recommended as they are treated differently in two languages. For all character function arguments, Fortran compilers add an extra integer argument that contains the length of the string.

Another important distinction between C and Fortran is that, unlike Fortran, C is a case-sensitive language.

In the following example, a Fortran subroutine is called from C.

CODE EXAMPLE 3-9   C Program Calling a Fortran Subroutine

```
/* example_C.c
   cc -c example_C.c -o example_C.o */
int main(){
   int a[3][3], i, j, k=1;
   for (i=0; i<3; i++){
      for (j=0; j<3; j++){
         a[i][j]=k;
         k++;
      }
   }
   printf("Printing array from C: \n");
   printf("a[0][0] = %d, a[0][1] = %d, a[0][2] = %d, \n",
          a[0][0], a[0][1], a[0][2]);
   printf("a[1][0] = %d, a[1][1] = %d, a[1][2] = %d, \n",
          a[1][0], a[1][1], a[1][2]);
   printf("a[2][0] = %d, a[2][1] = %d, a[2][2] = %d, \n",
          a[2][0], a[2][1], a[2][2]);
   fortran_call_(a);
   return 0;
}
```

CODE EXAMPLE 3-10 Fortran Subroutine Listing

```
c example_F.f
c f77 example_F.f example_C.o
      subroutine fortran_call(a)
      integer a(3,3)
      print*, 'Printing from Fortran:'
      do i=1,3
         write(6,1) (i,j,a(i,j),  j=1,3)
      enddo
```

CODE EXAMPLE 3-10 Fortran Subroutine Listing

```
1     format('a(',i1,',',i1,') = ',i1, ', a(',i1,',',i1,') = ',
      &      i1, ',   a(', i1, ',', i1, ') =', i1 )
      end
```

Note that we appended an underscore to call it properly. Also note the different layout of the array.

```
example% cc -c example_C.c -o example_C.o
example% f77 example_F.f example_C.o -o example_C_F
example% example_C_F
Printing array from C:
a[0][0] = 1, a[0][1] = 2, a[0][2] = 3,
a[1][0] = 4, a[1][1] = 5, a[1][2] = 6,
a[2][0] = 7, a[2][1] = 8, a[2][2] = 9,
 Printing from Fortran:
a(1,1) = 1,   a(1,2) = 4,   a(1,3) =7
a(2,1) = 2,   a(2,2) = 5,   a(2,3) =8
a(3,1) = 3,   a(3,2) = 6,   a(3,3) =9
```

Linking Mixed Languages

When objects produced by Sun C and Fortran compilers are used together, they should be linked with the Fortran compiler as the link driver. That ensures that all the necessary Fortran libraries are linked in.

While there is no problem with mixing C and Fortran because libc needed for C programs is linked in when a Fortran compiler is used as a link driver, there is a potential problem for mixing Fortran with C++, which requires using C++ as a link driver. As we already mentioned, Forte Developer 6 update 1 solved this problem by introducing the -xlang option to specify all the languages used in the link. For example, the following command allows one to link object files generated with Sun Fortran 95 and C++ compilers.

```
example% CC fortran95_object.o Cplusplus_object.o -xlang=f95 \
         -o mixed_binary
```

Summary

Solaris provides numerous tools, utilities, and libraries that create a robust environment for application developers. The APIs in Solaris, various tools, and language compilers all conform to industry standards such as UNIX98 and ANSI/ISO, ensuring high software quality and reliability.

The `appcert` tool can be used to ensure binary compatibility of applications across different Solaris releases and SPARC systems. We recommend that developers check application binaries with `appcert` to detect usage of private or deprecated system calls and symbols that could cause compatibility problems.

There are many static program checking tools. For C, the use of `lint` and the `cc -v` option is recommended to detect program errors. For checking correctness of Fortran programs, the `-Xlist`, `-C`, and `-u` options should be tried on the program source. These perform global program checking, array-subscript out of bounds checks, and checks on use of uninitialized variables, respectively.

If applications need more than 4 GB of virtual memory or need 64-bit integer arithmetic, they should be ported from 32-bit to 64-bit mode. Solaris 7 and later releases of Solaris support 64-bit programs. The C data model used in Solaris 64-bit is `LP64`, while the 32-bit operating system uses the `ILP32` data model. These data model differences have implications on program functioning when porting to 64-bit. The option `-errchk=longptr64` in `lint` can be used for catching many of the common data model related errors.

The Sun WorkShop 5.0 and Forte Developer 6 compilers provide the `-xarch=v9` option for the 64-bit mode. In porting Fortran programs to 64-bit, one must be careful of the implications of changing the default size of integers (by use of `-xtypemap` flag). For many libraries, the APIs are only defined for `integer*4` or smaller size integers (such as MPI library). In such cases, explicit size-typing in combination with `-xtypemap` flag can be used.

The Fortran 95 compiler has been designed to be maximally compatible with the Fortran 77 compiler. A lot of flexibility has been added in terms of the file suffixes and handling of fixed and free source formats. Linking of objects compiled with Fortran 95 and 77 compilers should be done with `-xlang` option or using the `f95` driver with the `-lf77compat` library added to the link command.

A program can combine parts written in Fortran and in C or C++. The important language features that should be kept in mind when mixing Fortran and C include different memory layout of multidimensional arrays and the trailing underscore added to the Fortran function names by the compiler. Programs that combine Fortran 95 and C++ should be linked with the `-xlang` option available for Forte Developer 6 update 1 compilers.

PART II   Optimizing Serial Applications

## CHAPTER 4

Measuring Program Performance

In working on performance optimization of an application, it is essential to use various tools and techniques that suggest what parts of the program need to be optimized, compare the performance before and after optimization, and show how efficiently the system resources are being utilized by the tuned code. In most cases, the optimization process starts with timing and profiling an application to identify the most heavily used parts of the program, followed by subsequent tuning and timing to assess results. This process should be repeated because as a result of program tuning, some bottlenecks are removed and the optimization work might need to be focused on other parts of the program.

In this chapter, we describe various tools available in the Solaris Operating Environment for measuring aspects of program performance for a CPU-bound application. The discussion is centered around highlighting the most useful features for measuring performance. We do not attempt to provide an exhaustive description of these tools. For information about these tools, refer to the documentation that is available online at `http://docs.sun.com`.

The chapter starts with a description of tools for program timing and profiling. It follows with a description of the Forte Developer 6 (and Forte Developer 6 update 1) Sampling Collector and Performance Analyzer tools. We also cover utilities that measure overheads of system calls and quantify operating system activities (such as paging and swapping), as well as tools that provide information about hardware performance counters. The discussion is limited to using these tools and utilities to measure the performance of serial (single-process, single-threaded) programs. Measuring the performance of parallel programs is the subject of Chapter 11. Even if the reader is only interested in measuring the performance of parallel programs, our recommendation is to read this chapter in its entirety before reading Chapter 11.

Measurement Methodology

The first step in the application tuning process is quantifying its performance. This step is usually achieved by establishing a baseline performance and setting expectations appropriately for how much performance improvement is reasonable. There are many metrics of application performance: wall-clock time for a single job (also called turnaround time), wall-clock time for multiple jobs (throughput measurements), MFLOPS (million floating-point operations per second) rating, memory usage, I/O utilization, MIPS (million instructions per second), network usage, and others. Hence, based on the characteristics of the application, it is important to decide what metric to use.

For scientific programs, the metrics of most interest are usually the wall-clock time for a single job, and those which relate application performance to theoretical peak CPU performance. For example, MFLOPS or CPI (cycles per instruction) attained in a program compared to their theoretical peak values on a given computer system. These measurements help analyze the attained performance in an application (or a part of it) with respect to the idealized performance of a computer system.

Benchmarking Guidelines

The most important guideline in designing application performance analysis experiments is that measurements should be reproducible within an expected tolerance range. With this in mind, we recommend adherence to the following general rules:

- Datasets used in benchmarks should be carefully selected and should adequately represent the use of an application. Benchmark measurements should be done using the same datasets and setup environment. The program source at the level of its functionality, algorithms, and data structures should preferably be kept unchanged during the tuning experiments. The exception to this guideline occurs when during the tuning process, a superior algorithm or data structure is discovered. It is also desirable that only one variable (for example, compiler flag or system setting) be changed from one experiment to another. This facilitates correlating the effects of a change in performance to changes made in performance variables. Wherever possible, data obtained with different tools or techniques must be cross-checked. For example, if one run uses `ptime` tool to measure the total runtime, and a different experiment uses `cputrack` tool (using UltraSPARC hardware performance counters) to measure "Cycle Count," then the two results should be cross-checked because Cycle-Count × Cycle-time = RunTime should hold if the measurements are accurate. `ptime` tool and `cputrack` tool are described later in this chapter.

- Similar to measurements in other fields of engineering, uncertainty also applies to computer program performance measurements. The very step of trying to measure a computer program intrudes on its execution and possibly affects it in uncertain ways. Hence, it is quite important to ascertain, as accurately as possible, the impact of using performance measurement tools on the execution and runtime of a program. Some measurement and tracing tools, such as `truss`, are heavily intrusive and can significantly change the runtime behavior of a program. We recommend to first obtain a repeatable runtime of a program without using performance measurement tools (except the timing tool). Then, measure the runtime again while using a performance tool to measure the degradation in runtime as a result of using the tool.

- When possible, benchmarks should be run from `/tmp` (`tmpfs` *filesystem*) or from a locally mounted UFS file system. Running an application from an NFS-mounted file system introduces unreproducible network effects in the runtime, and must be avoided. Further, all of the I/O operations performed in `/tmp` actually take place in the physical memory, which can considerably decrease the I/O overhead in a benchmark run (assuming the physical memory is large enough to accommodate files generated by the program). Note, however, that `tmpfs` is volatile, and valuable data should be saved in a persistent file system (such as UFS or NFS) after a benchmark is complete.

- The paging and swapping activity must be carefully monitored while the benchmark is being run, as these can completely skew the measurements. Refer to the section on System Monitoring Tools later in this chapter to learn about the tools available for this purpose. It is also recommended that the system be set up using the suggested values for `/etc/system` parameters as described in the *Solaris Tunable Parameters Reference Manual* and [Mauro00].

- All measurements for *program turnaround* should be performed on a system with no other user program or application running; that is, a benchmark must be run in a dedicated fashion. For very fine-grained performance measurements, variations introduced even by the operating system daemon programs may not be acceptable. In such situations, use of a multiprocessor system is desirable with one processor left idle to handle the operating system activities.

- System characteristics should be recorded and saved. We recommend to save the `/etc/system` and `/etc/release` files, as well as the outputs of commands that show system parameters such as `uname(1)` and `prtdiag(1M)`. A partial list of the commands that can be used to identify system configuration is provided in Appendix A.

Measurement Tools

Before analyzing the performance of an application, one must identify the parameters that should be measured and select a set of tools suitable for the measurements.

Performance measurement tools can be divided into three groups based on the functions they perform:

- Timing tools measure time spent in a user program or in its portions. They include both command line tools and functions that can be used in a program.

- Profiling tools use timing results to identify the most heavily used parts of an application. Profiling information can be collected at the level of function calls, basic blocks, source code lines, or assembly instructions.

- Monitoring tools measure the usage of various system resources to identify bottlenecks that occur during the run. This information can be subsequently used for tuning specific parts of an application.

Another way of categorizing performance measurement tools is based on the requirements of their use:

- Tools that can operate on optimized binaries don't require any preparatory work for their use. This group includes tools that measure program run time, monitoring tools, and some of the profiling tools. Measurements collected with these tools cannot be directly attributed to the source lines of a program.

- Tools that require recompilation can generate measurements at the source level of a program. Some tools from the previous group can offer additional functionality for applications recompiled with certain options.

- Tools that require source code instrumentation include timing and probing function calls that can be used for fine-grain analysis of selected parts of a program.

Measurement tools can also be grouped into two broad categories:

- Tools measuring serial performance collect measurements on a per-process or system-wide basis without regard to parallelism in the computation.

- Tools measuring parallel performance can provide additional information specific to parallel runs. This can include synchronization overhead measurements and load balancing analysis.

This chapter focuses on tools for analyzing serial performance. Measurement tools for parallel applications are discussed in Chapter 11. In this guide, we group tools by the function they perform. For each tool or measurement technique, we also mention the specific requirements of its use. The following table lists the tools discussed in these two chapters. Some of the tools are listed more than once depending on their functionality and usage.

TABLE 4-1   Tools Described in This Book

	Tools Discussed in Chapter 4	Tools Discussed in Chapter 11
No recompilation required	time, timex, Forte Developer Performance Analyzer, /proc tools, vmstat, kstat, cpustat, cputrack, busstat	Forte Developer Performance Analyzer, Trace Normal Form tools (using libraries), Prism, mpstat, lockstat, cpustat, cputrack, busstat
Recompilation required	prof, gprof, tcov, Forte Developer Performance Analyzer	Prism, Forte Developer Performance Analyzer
Source change and recompilation required	gethrtime, etime, dtime, TICK measurements, libcpc calls	gethrtime, gethrvtime, Trace Normal Form Tools (code instrumentation), libcpc calls

Program Timing Tools

The fundamental step in benchmarking and performance tuning a program is accurately measuring the amount of time spent in running it. Typically, one is interested in the overall time spent running a program, as well as the time spent in portions of the program. In this section, we will discuss tools for timing the entire program, as well as tools to measure time at the routine or program section level.

Timing Entire Program

For entire program timing, one should use tools that will accurately measure the elapsed (wall-clock) time from the beginning of the program execution. For programs running on a dedicated system and spending most of the time computing, the wall-clock time and CPU time [Dowd98] should be approximately equal in value. Discrepancies between the two will usually occur in cases when a program is running on a timeshared system or an application is I/O bound, or a program is paging (or swapping) due to insufficient memory on the system.

The three Solaris timing utilities we discuss are `time(1)`, `timex(1)`, and `ptime(1)`. Both `time` and `timex` are based on a commonly used method in UNIX, namely, sampling the state of the CPU at each clock interrupt, approximately 100 times a second [Cockcroft98b]. While `time` only reports timing information, `timex` also provides process data and system activity information (options -o, -s). This information can be obtained for parent, as well as all children processes (options -p, -f). The elapsed time reported by `timex` is accurate to roughly 1/100th of a second.

In Solaris, an alternative method of measurement is *Microstate Accounting* [Mauro00]. Microstate accounting works by taking a high-resolution timestamp on every state change, system call, page fault, and scheduler change in the kernel. It is turned off by default to keep overhead to a minimum, but can be turned on programmatically by means of APIs provided under the `/proc` utilities in the Solaris Operating Environment (versions 2.6, 7 and 8). The timer `ptime` also turns on microstate accounting, and can be used for reproducible high-precision timing of programs.

A simple example illustrates the accuracy of the three commands. Note, that we used the full path `/bin/time` for the first command to distinguish it from the built-in `time` utility in the `csh(1)` shell.

```
example% /bin/time sum bench.tar
6007 36660 bench.tar

real        0.9
user        0.8
sys         0.0
example% timex sum bench.tar
6007 36660 bench.tar

real        0.91
user        0.82
sys         0.08
example% ptime sum bench.tar
6007 36660 bench.tar

real        0.905
user        0.809
sys         0.091
```

The `real` time reported is the elapsed time for the run. The `user` time is the time a CPU was active running the program. For a parallel run on a multi-CPU system, the `user` time can exceed the `real` time because the combined `user` time for multiple CPUs is reported by the timing tools. Finally, the `sys` or system time is the time spent by the system calls on behalf of the program.

One can see an increased precision in the measurement with `ptime` command. We recommend its usage over `time` and `timex` utilities.

There are many subtleties of whole program timing measurements. We refer the reader to [Cockcroft98b], [Dowd98] and [Mauro00] for additional details.

Timing Program Portions

In this section, we will illustrate two timing functions that have been used extensively in the examples presented in this book for measuring time spent in program sections or portions. These are the `gethrtime(3C)` and `etime(3F)` functions.

`gethrtime` returns the current real time measured in nanoseconds. This measurement represents the time elapsed since some arbitrary point in the past; therefore, one should take a difference of two consecutive `gethrtime` measurements. On the UltraSPARC processor, the `gethrtime` values are derived from the `TICK` register, which maintains a count of the CPU clock cycles. The clock cycles are converted to nanoseconds based on the processor clock speed. In the next section we will illustrate how to directly access the `TICK` register for fine-grained program measurements.

It is recommended that prior to usage of `gethrtime`, microstate accounting in the Solaris kernel be enabled. This can be explicitly done programmatically (as illustrated in the following example) or by using `ptime` to measure the elapsed time of the program in which `gethrtime` is being used.

The following is an example usage of `gethrtime` function.

CODE EXAMPLE 4-1   Example of `gethrtime` Usage

```
/* example_gethrtime.c */
/* cc example_gethrtime.c -o example_gethrtime */
#include <sys/time.h>
#include <sys/types.h>
#include <stdio.h>
#include <unistd.h>

int main(int argc, char*argv[])
{
    hrtime_t start, end;
    int i, iters = 500000;

    start = gethrtime();
    for (i = 0; i < iters; i++)
```

```
            (void)getpid();
   end = gethrtime();
   (void)printf("Avg getpid() time = %lld nsec\n", (end - start)
/ iters);
   return 0;
}
```

The function[1] `init_micro_acct()` listed in the following program can be used to initialize microstate accounting in the program directly.

CODE EXAMPLE 4-2   Enabling Microstate Accounting From a Program

```
/* example_msacct.c; enable MS Acct. from inside the program */
/* cc example_msacct.c -o example_msacct */
#include <stdio.h>
#include <stdlib.h>
#include <errno.h>
#include <sys/stat.h>
#include <fcntl.h>
#include <sys/time.h>
#define _STRUCTURED_PROC 1
#include <sys/procfs.h>

void init_micro_acct();

int main(int argc, char*argv[])
{
 hrtime_t start, end;
 int i, iters = 500000;
 init_micro_acct();
 start = gethrtime();
 for (i = 0; i < iters; i++)
        (void)getpid();
 end = gethrtime();
 printf("Avg getpid() time = %lld nsec\n", (end-start)/iters);
 return 0;
}

void init_micro_acct()
{ /* SunOS 5.5 or higher */
    int     ctlfd;
```

1. The function `init_micro_acct()` has been extracted from the file `timing.c` which is included in the distribution of the Forte Developer 6 release and can be obtained from the directory `/opt/SUNWspro/WS6/examples/analyzer/omptest`.

CODE EXAMPLE 4-2   Enabling Microstate Accounting From a Program *(Continued)*

```
    long    ctl[2];
    char    procname[1024];

    sprintf(procname, "/proc/%d/ctl", getpid());
    ctlfd  = open(procname, O_WRONLY);
    if(ctlfd < 0) {
        fprintf(stderr, "open %s failed, errno = %d\n",
                            procname, errno);
    }
    ctl[0] = PCSET;;
    ctl[1] = PR_MSACCT;
    if (write(ctlfd, ctl, 2*sizeof(long)) < 0) {
        fprintf(stderr, "write failed, errno = %d\n", errno);
    }
    close(ctlfd);
    printf("Enabling microstate accounting.\n" );
    return;
}
```

Compiling the two programs `example_gethrtime.c` and `example_msacct.c`
using Forte Developer 6 update 1 C compilers, and running on an Ultra 2
workstation (using 300 MHz UltraSPARC-II processor, Solaris 8 Operating
Environment), generates the following output.

```
example% cc example_gethrtime.c -o example_gethrtime
example% cc example_msacct.c -o example_msacct
example% example_msacct
Enabling microstate accounting.
Avg getpid() time = 2956 nsec
example% example_gethrtime
Avg getpid() time = 1744 nsec
example% ptime example_gethrtime
Avg getpid() time = 2987 nsec
real        1.527
user        1.051
sys         0.451
```

As expected, the times measured by `example_msacct` and `ptime`
`example_gethrtime` are approximately equal and different from the case when
microstate accounting is not enabled.

One can create a wrapper function to call `gethrtime` from Fortran programs, as in the following example.

CODE EXAMPLE 4-3   Wrapper for `gethrtime` Function

```
/* example_gethrtime_wrapper.c */
/* cc -c example_gethrtime_wrapper.c */
#include <sys/time.h>

double timingfunc_()
{ hrtime_t  t0;
   double ai;
   t0 = gethrtime();
   ai = t0*1.e-9;
   return(ai);
}
```

In the Forte Developer 6 Fortran 90 compiler, the function `gethrtime` has been incorporated in the Fortran library and can be called directly from Fortran programs as shown in the following example.

CODE EXAMPLE 4-4   Calling `gethrtime` in Fortran 90 Program

```
! example to show use of gethrtime in fortran 90; use Forte 6 (or
later)
! f90 example_gethrtimef90.f90 -o example_gethrtimef90
 integer*8 gethrtime, time1, time2
 external gethrtime
 real (KIND=8) :: sum=0.0
 real (KIND=8), dimension(100000) :: x
 time1 = gethrtime()
 do i=1,100000
    x(i) = i
    sum = sum + x(i)
 enddo
 time2 = gethrtime()
 write(*,*) 'Time= ',(time2-time1)*1.e-9
 end program
```

```
example% f90 example_gethrtimef90.f90 -o example_gethrtimef90
example% example_gethrtimef90
 Time=  0.019694168
```

The following example shows that the gethrtime call has low overhead and, therefore, can be used as a reliable and reproducible timing utility. This program has two consecutive gethrtime calls within a loop. Since there are no commands between the gethrtime calls, the difference in the return values is the overhead of the call itself.

CODE EXAMPLE 4-5   Program Measuring the Overhead of gethrtime Call

```
/* example_gethrtime_test.c */
/* cc example_gethrtime_test.c -o example_gethrtime_test */
#include <sys/time.h>
#include <stdio.h>
#include <unistd.h>
int main(int argc, char*argv[])
{
    hrtime_t start, end;
    int i, iters = 100000;
    for (i = 0; i < iters; i++) {
        start = gethrtime();
        end = gethrtime();
        (void)printf("%lld nanoseconds \n", (end - start));
    }
    return 0;
}
```

When we run this program on a 360 MHz Ultra 60 system, it produces 100,000 measurements of gethrtime overhead. The median value of 208 nanoseconds (75 CPU cycles) approximately corresponds to the function call overhead. The figure shows the distribution of 99,900 (or 99.9%) of these results that fall in the range between 180 ns and 230 ns. Out of the remaining 100 measurements, 91 are between 231 ns and 264 ns, and five are between 300 ns. and 600 ns. Finally, four measurements (0.004%) show considerably different results in the range between 25 ms and 29 ms (milliseconds). This may be caused by an interrupt or a page fault that happened between the two gethrtime calls. If a process is descheduled between gethrtime() calls, the delay will be much larger.

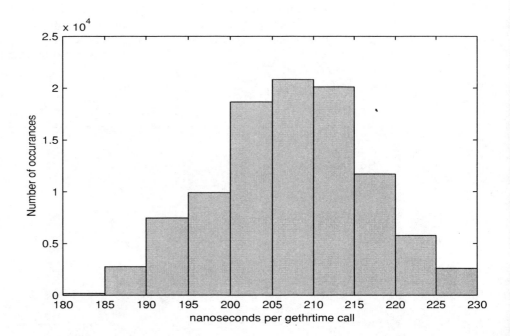

FIGURE 4-1   Distribution of `gethrtime` Call Overhead Over 100,000 Invocations

In Fortran programs, a library function `etime` is quite useful for measuring CPU (user and system) times spent in a portion of a program. It has been used extensively in the examples presented in later chapters. The function takes a two-element `REAL*4` array as an argument, and on return, fills it with the user and system CPU times; the returned value is the sum of the two. The following is a simple example of its usage.

CODE EXAMPLE 4-6   Example of `etime` Function in Fortran

```
C example_etime.f
C f77 example_etime.f example_gethrtime_wrapper.o \
C    -o example_etime
      real*4 x(4*1024*1024),sum
      real*4 tarray(2), etime, start, finish
      real*8 starthr,finishhr,timingfunc
      external timingfunc

      sum=0.0
      start = etime(tarray)
      starthr = timingfunc()
      do i=1,4*1024*1024
```

```
         x(i) = 0.5*i
         sum = sum + x(i)
      enddo
      finish = etime(tarray)
      finishhr = timingfunc()
      write(*,*) 'etime:      CPU time= ',finish-start
      write(*,*) 'gethrtime: CPU time= ',finishhr-starthr
      end
```

```
example% cc -c example_gethrtime_wrapper.c
example% f77 example_etime.f example_gethrtime_wrapper.o \
         -o example_etime
example_etime.f:
 MAIN:
example% example_etime
 etime:      CPU time=    0.635986
 gethrtime: CPU time=    0.63846762804314
```

The Sun Fortran library also supports the `dtime` function, which can be used to get elapsed CPU time since its last call. Thus, in case of `dtime` function, there is no need to take the difference between two successive calls (as is needed when `etime` is used). We recommend that `etime` and `dtime` should not be used for high-resolution timing, instead, `gethrtime` should be used for more accurate measurement. The `etime` and `dtime` functions are also not thread-safe (see Chapter 11). We close the section with a note that Fortran 95 programmers can also use the Fortran 95 intrinsic function CPU_TIME() for timing measurement.

Fine-Grained Timing Measurement

The SPARC V9 architecture [Weaver94] includes the `TICK` register which provides an accurate, low-overhead mechanism for fine-grained measurements of time in terms of processor cycles. In this section, we will describe accessing the `TICK` register directly in user programs, with a significantly lower overhead than incurred by the timers discussed in the previous section. For example, as we saw, `gethrtime` typically incurs an overhead of approximately 75 CPU cycles, while, as we show below, the `TICK` register can be accessed in just a few cycles. The `TICK` register can be used to time very small sections of code (at the granularity of tens of instructions) with a high degree of accuracy.

The use of `TICK` register by user (that is, nonprivileged user) code requires the NonPrivileged Trap (NPT) bit to be disabled in the processor. If this bit is set, then an attempt to read the `TICK` register by user code will lead to a trap, and usually the code will abort. In Solaris Operating Environment version 8, this bit is disabled, allowing user programs to access the TICK register via the use of the rd %tick instruction (see [Weaver94] for a description of the rd instruction).

We will illustrate the use of TICK register for fine-grained timing measurements with a simple example. A convenient way to access it from user program is by using inline assembly templates. Inline templates will be also discussed in Chapter 8. The following examples show the code for readtick.il and example_ticktest.c.

CODE EXAMPLE 4-7   Inline Template for Reading the TICK Register

```
.inline readtick,1
rd       %tick, %o1
stx      %o1, [%o0]
.end
```

CODE EXAMPLE 4-8   Example of Reading TICK Counter From a C Program

```
/* example_ticktest.c */
/* cc -xarch=v8plusa example_ticktest.c \
     -o example_ticktest readtick.il -lm  */
#include <stdio.h>
#include <stdlib.h>
#include <math.h>
#include <sys/types.h>

extern void readtick(void *);
#pragma no_side_effect(readtick);

#define N (128*1024*1024)
int main()
{
  uint64_t cnt1=0, cnt2=0, ovr=0, total=0, tld;
  int i, j=1, *x;
  x = &j;

  for (i=0;i<10;i++) {
    readtick((void *)&cnt1);
    readtick((void *)&cnt2);
    ovr += cnt2 - cnt1;
  }
  ovr = floor(ovr*1.0/10);

  for (i=0;i<N;i++){
      readtick((void *)&cnt1);
```

```
      *x += i;
      readtick((void *)&cnt2);
      total += cnt2 - cnt1;
  }
  tld = floor(total*1.0/N - ovr);
  printf("Overhead of readtick %lld\n",ovr);
  printf("Cost in processor cycles %lld\n",tld);
  return 0;
}
```

Running the above program on an Ultra 60 system, we obtain the following results.

```
example% example_ticktest
Overhead of readtick 6
Cost in processor cycles 7
```

We see that the overhead of the call to the TICK register on the above machine is measured to be about 6 CPU clock cycles.

Note, in the use of -xarch flag in the previous example, it is essential to use v8plus[a,b] or v9[a,b] in order to assemble the code that uses the rd %tick instruction. This is because the TICK register is defined in the V9 architecture version, and these values enable compiler's code generator to follow (partly or wholly) the SPARC V9 *Application Binary Interface* (ABI) specifications. The use of the compiler option -xarch and the difference between the meanings of different values that can be passed to it are discussed in Chapter 5.

We conclude this section by noting that UltraSPARC processors also provide two *Performance Instrumentation Counter* (PIC) registers that can be used to measure a variety of hardware events (for example, CPU clock cycles, instruction counts, and cache misses). Fine-grained measurements of hardware performance counters in user code are discussed later in this chapter.

Program Profiling Tools

Profiling shows which functions account for larger parts of application runtimes. To obtain meaningful results for an application, profiling should be used on *multiple* and *representative* test cases. A poorly chosen benchmark might not exercise the important functionality of the program, and as a result, may point to the wrong parts of the code as performance bottlenecks. We strongly suggest collecting the profiles of different benchmark runs and, if possible, consulting the developers or users of the code to find out which runs show more typical computational behavior of the application.

This section covers various profiling tools available in Solaris and Forte environments. The tools that are discussed include prof(1), gprof(1), tcov, and the Performance Analyzer and Sampling Collector tools in Forte Developer 6. While prof, gprof, and tcov are described for completeness, the reader may go directly to the discussion on Forte Developer 6 tools. The Forte Developer 6 tools provide richer functionality than prof, gprof, and tcov, and are the recommended tools for profiling applications on Solaris platforms. Additional details on all of these tools can be obtained from *Analyzing Program Performance With Sun WorkShop*, available as part of Forte Developer 6 Collection on http://docs.sun.com.

Profiling With prof and gprof

There are two similar profiling tools in Solaris, prof(1) and gprof(1), that can be used with programs compiled with -p or -pg options respectively. These are based on Program Counter (PC) sampling at periodic intervals and instrumentation of the executable to obtain function call counts. We will discuss gprof only, since it provides all of the information that prof does, and additionally generates the dynamic execution call graph of the application. Later, we will also show how to use Forte Developer 6 Performance Analyzer and Sampling Collector tools to profile an application without extra recompilation.

When a program compiled with -pg is run, it creates a file gmon.out in the run directory upon completion. The command gprof can be used to generate the profiling report for the run.

```
example% gprof <executable> [<path to gmon.out>]
```

If no path to `gmon.out` is specified, by default, it is picked from the directory where `gprof` was invoked as shown here.

```
example% cc -pg foo.c -o foo
example% foo
example% gprof foo
```

The output (which is rather long, and is usually redirected to a file) consists of three parts. The first part lists the functions sorted according to the time they consume, together with their descendants (*inclusive time*). This feature is not available in `prof(1)`. The second part lists the *exclusive time* for the functions (time spent executing the function) together with the percentage of total runtime and the number of calls. The final part gives an index of all calls performed in the run.

We will illustrate the usage of `gprof` on the standard distribution of BLAS3 subroutines and on the testing driver available from `http://www.netlib.org`. First, we compile the routines and the driver with the `-pg` option.

```
example% f77 -c -fast -xarch=v8plus -stackvar -pg dgemm.f \
        dsymm.f dsyr2k.f dsyrk.f dtrmm.f dtrsm.f lsame.f
example% ar rv libgbl3b.a dgemm.o dsymm.o \
        dsyr2k.o dsyrk.o dtrmm.o dtrsm.o lsame.o
example% f77 -fast -xarch=v8plus -stackvar -pg dblat3.f \
        libgbl3b.a -o dblat3
```

Then, we run the driver program with the test data in file `DBLAT.in` as follows.

CODE EXAMPLE 4-9 Input File for `dblat3` Driver

```
'DBLAT3.SUMM'      NAME OF SUMMARY OUTPUT FILE
6                  UNIT NUMBER OF SUMMARY FILE
'DBLAT3.SNAP'      NAME OF SNAPSHOT OUTPUT FILE
-1                 UNIT NUMBER OF SNAPSHOT FILE (NOT USED IF .LT. 0)
F         LOGICAL FLAG, T TO REWIND SNAPSHOT FILE AFTER EACH RECORD.
F         LOGICAL FLAG, T TO STOP ON FAILURES.
T         LOGICAL FLAG, T TO TEST ERROR EXITS.
16.0      THRESHOLD VALUE OF TEST RATIO
4                  NUMBER OF VALUES OF N
60 55 50 60        VALUES OF N
4                  NUMBER OF VALUES OF ALPHA
0.6 0.7 0.8 0.9    VALUES OF ALPHA
4                  NUMBER OF VALUES OF BETA
1.1 1.2 1.3 1.4    VALUES OF BETA
DGEMM   T PUT F FOR NO TEST. SAME COLUMNS.
```

```
DSYMM   T PUT F FOR NO TEST. SAME COLUMNS.
DTRMM   T PUT F FOR NO TEST. SAME COLUMNS.
DTRSM   T PUT F FOR NO TEST. SAME COLUMNS.
DSYRK   T PUT F FOR NO TEST. SAME COLUMNS.
DSYR2K  T PUT F FOR NO TEST. SAME COLUMNS.
```

```
example% dblat3 < DBLAT.in
```

Upon completion of the run, the file gmon.out, which can be used to create the profile, is put in the current directory.

```
example% ls gmon.out
  720 gmon.out
example% gprof dblat3 > dblat3.gprof
```

Now we can see, in the second part of the output, an ordered list of the functions that consume the most time in this run. The following example shows the top part of the list.

CODE EXAMPLE 4-10   Portion of gprof Output

```
granularity: each sample hit covers 2 byte(s) for 0.01% of 98.88
seconds
```

% time	cumulative seconds	self seconds	calls	self ms/call	total ms/call	name	
66.4	65.70	65.70	186116	0.35	0.35	dmmch_	[4]
15.2	80.72	15.02	20448	0.73	0.73	dmake_	[8]
10.9	91.51	10.79	16924	0.64	0.64	dgemm_	[9]
3.2	94.67	3.16	1	3160.02	19807.49	dchk1_	[7]
0.8	95.46	0.79	2	395.00	4865.47	dchk3_	[10]
0.7	96.18	0.72	1	720.00	33455.41	dchk5_	[6]
0.6	96.79	0.61	1572	0.39	1.17	dtrsm_	[12]
0.5	97.25	0.46	1572	0.29	0.97	dtrmm_	[13]
0.4	97.68	0.43	1	430.00	33488.58	dchk4_	[5]
0.4	98.08	0.40	1554	0.26	0.89	dsyrk_	[14]
0.3	98.40	0.32	16384	0.02	0.02	lderes_	[17]
0.3	98.70	0.30	1	300.00	2171.84	dchk2_	[11]

The granularity of the sampling is shown in the output before the sorted list.

Only a brief description of `gprof` usage was given in this section. The interested reader is referred to the online manual *Analyzing Program Performance With Sun WorkShop*, [Graham82], and [Dowd98] for additional details. These references include discussion on issues related to accuracy, limitations in profiling of shared objects, profiling of modules with static functions, `gprof` fallacy, quantization, and sampling errors.

`gprof` is a common UNIX profiling tool available on various platforms. We included its description for completeness, but recommend using the Forte Developer tools for profiling applications on Solaris platforms.

Profiling With `tcov`

Another profiling tool with functionality which is extended in Forte Developer tools is `tcov(1)`. Readers who are not interested in legacy tools can skip this section and proceed directly to "Profiling Tools in Forte Developer 6" on page 79.

The crucial subroutines identified with profiling can be large, in which case a more refined tool is needed to point to the lines in the source code that may account for most of the application runtime.

In the previous example, the two top subroutines `dmmch` and `dmake` are used by the driver `dblat3.f` to check the results of the tests and to set up the matrices respectively. The first essential routine on the list is `dgemm`, and if we wanted to improve the performance of the BLAS 3 implementation tested by `dblat`, we would focus on the `dgemm` call. The file `dgemm.f` has 641 lines, so we would need some help to identify the source lines to focus on.

To get the source line profile information, we can use the `tcov(1)` tool which shows how many times each line in the source file was invoked during execution. It is essentially a *basic block* profiling tool. A basic block is a portion of program with only one entrance and one exit. It is a concept of immense value to the compiler optimization process owing to the guarantee of program control flow in the basic block (see [Dowd98], [Muchnick97] for more information). The basic block profiling tools generate useful information about program execution that can be used by the compiler to refine the optimization heuristics, especially in improving branch prediction, function inlining, and code rearrangement to improve instruction cache usage. We should point out that `tcov` suppresses optimization, changing the basic block structure compared to that in the optimized executable.

Here, we will discuss usage of `tcov` to generate source-line execution frequency data. To use the tool, we need to compile and link the `dgemm.f` file with `-xprofile=tcov`.

```
example% f77 -fast -xarch=v8plus -stackvar -c dgemm.f \
        -xprofile=tcov
example% ar rv libgbl3b.a dgemm.o
example% f77 -fast -xarch=v8plus -stackvar dblat3.f \
        libgbl3b.a -o dblat3 -xprofile=tcov
```

Running the program compiled with `-xprofile=tcov` creates a directory `<executable_name>.profile` with collected data.

```
example% dblat3 < DBLAT.in
example% ls dblat3.profile
total 18        18 tcovd
```

Now `tcov(1)` can be used to generate the profile data.

```
example% tcov -x ./dblat3.profile dgemm.f
```

This creates a file `dgemm.f.tcov` in the current directory, annotated with the number of times each line in `dgemm.f` was executed. By examining this file, we can see that the body of the loop with label 350 was executed the largest number of times.

```
                     DO 350 L = LL, LL+LSEC-1
75241920 ->          F11 = F11 + T1( L-LL+1, I-II+1 ) *
            $         T2( L-LL+1, J-JJ+1 )
            . . .
```

It is worth noting that tcov lists the top ten basic block sites at the end of the file. tcov(1) can also be used to collect cumulative statistics when different runs are performed. In the trivial case of running the same test for the second time and re-generating the file dgemm.f.tcov, we can see that the numbers corresponding to the source lines have doubled.

```
                    DO 350 L = LL, LL+LSEC-1
150483840 ->        F11 = F11 + T1( L-LL+1, I-II+1 )*
            $        T2( L-LL+1, J-JJ+1 )
            . . .
```

We should point out that the even though there is an obvious correlation between the number of times the line was executed and the time spent in the corresponding instructions, these measures are not necessarily proportional.

Profiling Tools in Forte Developer 6

The Forte Developer 6 and Forte Developer 6 update 1 environments provide a set of tools that greatly extend the functionality of traditional UNIX profiling utilities. These tools allow users to collect extensive performance information for optimized programs without additional recompilation or code instrumentation.

The Sampling Collector and the Performance Analyzer tools perform event-based data collection, in which data that are specific to an event are collected with a corresponding callstack. The event-specific data and the callstack are used to attribute inclusive and exclusive metrics to the various functions in the program. Some typical metrics are user CPU time, wall-clock time, system CPU time, and system wait time. By clicking Metrics in the Analyzer window, which can be invoked from the Tools menu of Sun WorkShop environment, one can obtain the complete list of available metrics.

The event-specific data are composed of a high-resolution timestamp, a thread ID, and the lightweight process (LWP) ID of the calling thread. In the Forte Developer 6 release, the supported collection modes are clock-based profiling, synchronization wait tracing, and address space profiling. The functionality for hardware counter overflow profiling has also been incorporated in Forte Developer 6 update 1 release for UltraSPARC-III-based systems[1] and is discussed later in the chapter. In this section, we will discuss clock-based profiling.

---

1. The UltraSPARC-III processor generates an interrupt on hardware counter overflows and thus facilitates tools for data collection based on hardware counter overflows.

The callstack is a series of program counter (PC) addresses of the functions on the program runtime stack. The first PC is called the leaf PC, and is the address of the next instruction to be executed within the function that is at the bottom of the stack. The content of the next PC location in the callstack is the address of the instruction that calls the function containing the leaf PC (i.e. this address lies within the calling function), and so on, in the function call chain. The callstack mechanism is used to attribute exclusive or inclusive metrics from the collected performance data to the functions on the callstack. For example, the exclusive metrics are associated with the function in which the leaf PC is located and the inclusive metrics are associated with the functions that lie above the leaf function on the stack.

The callstack provides an extremely efficient mechanism of attributing performance data and metrics to various functions in the application being measured. Most of the time, this mechanism yields very accurate results that correspond well to the call graph of the program, but there are situations where the Analyzer output requires careful interpretation. Some examples of these situations are: function calls between shared objects, inlined functions, static functions, some kernel traps, and tail-call optimization. In the case of inlined functions, the inclusive metrics are attributed as exclusive to the function in which the inlining has taken place and nothing is attributed to the function that was inlined. A detailed discussion of these special situations is beyond the scope of this guide. For further information, refer to the online manual *Analyzing Program Performance With Sun Workshop*.

The most common and useful data collection mode is clock-based profiling. These data enable one to obtain profiling information in a manner similar to that generated by `prof` and `gprof`, but without the limitations of these tools. In this mode, the callstack is collected at regular intervals. Since the data are collected on a per LWP basis for multithreaded programs, one can generate per-thread profiling information (these features are further discussed in Chapter 11). The profiling interval can be controlled by the user and can be set in the collector window prior to the program run. The default sampling interval for clock-based profiling is 10 milliseconds. It can be modified manually up to a resolution of 1 millisecond, but for such high resolution (interval less than 10 ms), the system must first be rebooted with the following setting in the `/etc/system` file.

```
set hires_tick=1
```

We can reuse the program described in the previous sections to illustrate these tools.

The Sampling Collector can be invoked from the `workshop` GUI. Forte Developer 6 update 1 allows one to invoke the tool from the command line, which will be discussed later in the section.

To invoke the Sampling Collector from the GUI, one should choose the Sampling Collector item from the Windows menu in workshop integrated development environment. In the Sampling Collector window, we enable clock-based profiling and start the run.

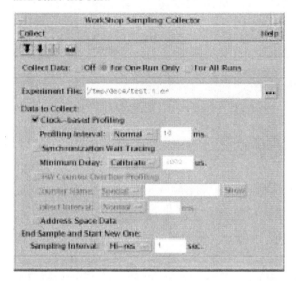

FIGURE 4-2   Forte Developer 6 Sampling Collector Window

The data are collected in the .test.1.er directory (which is hidden because its name starts with a dot). To interpret the profiling data collected in this directory, we use the Analyzer tool from the tools selection in the main workshop menu. The data are represented as a graphic profile of the run.

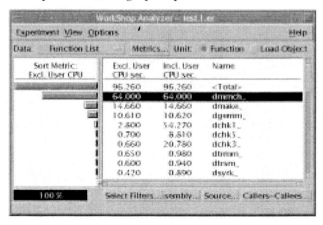

FIGURE 4-3   Function Profile Data Generated by Forte Developer 6 Performance Analyzer

By selecting Load Object, we can view the runtime spent in the executable and in the shared libraries used in the application. Since this small example provides definitions for all of the computational functions it uses in a static library, the output shows that the computations in this run were made in the `dblat3` executable.

For large dynamically linked applications, this feature of the tool can give valuable information about the distribution of the runtime between the application libraries and system or compiler libraries.

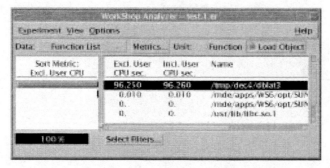

FIGURE 4-4   Load Object View in Forte Developer 6 Performance Analyzer

One can also obtain program disassembly annotated with estimated times using the Analyzer tool. Further, if the source is compiled with the `-g` option[1], the original source listing can also be annotated with the estimated times and compiler commentary. The compiler commentary is generated by the compiler on the optimizations performed during the compilation process. A fragment of the annotated source and disassembly listings are shown in the following figures for the `dblat3.f` example program; the utility of these features is obvious from these figures.

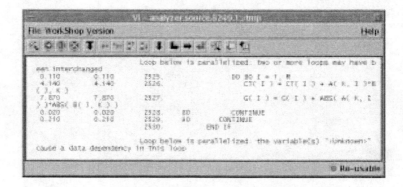

FIGURE 4-5   Annotated Source File in Forte Developer 6 Performance Analyzer

1. Note, with Forte Developer 6 compilers, the `-g` option can be used with high-level compiler optimization options.

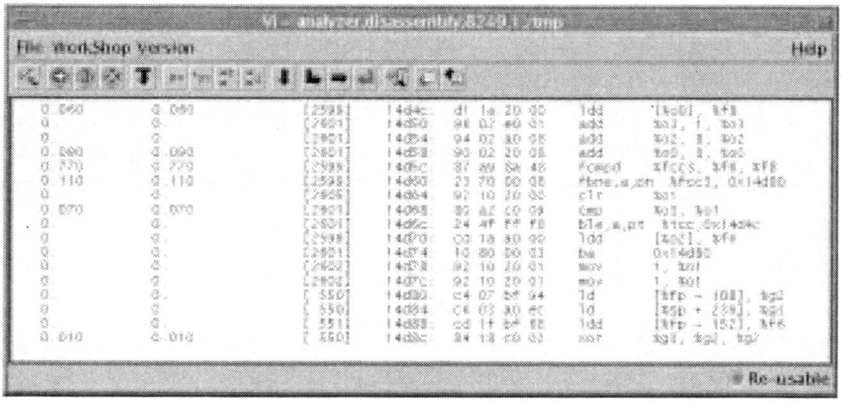

FIGURE 4-6   Annotated Disassembly in Forte Developer 6 Performance Analyzer

The results of several runs can be accumulated by the Analyzer tool to generate a composite profile of multiple runs. This a useful feature, as one can obtain the cumulative profile of the application based on runs for different datasets and identify routines that consistently show at the top of the profile distribution. Also, similarly to gprof, the Performance Analyzer output contains the caller-callee information for the run.

In Forte Developer 6 update 1, the data collection can be performed outside of the workshop and dbx environment using the standalone utility collect(1). collect is invoked from the command line and provides functionality similar to its graphical counterpart for gathering performance data. The data can be subsequently analyzed using the standalone analyzer(1) tool or in the workshop environment. For example, the following commands will gather clock-based profiling data (with default clock resolution) and launch analyzer.

```
example% collect a.out
example% analyzer test.1.er
```

The LoopTool available in Sun WorkShop and in Forte Developer 6 was not included in Forte Developer 6 update 1. Instead, we recommend using the Analyzer and Collector tools for the analysis of loop performance in the applications.

Process and System Monitoring Tools

In this section, we will give a brief overview of some tools and utilities in the Solaris Operating Environment that are useful in tracing an application, determining process resource usage, and monitoring system activity during program execution.

/proc Tools

In Solaris 2.5.1 (and later), the process file system (a System V feature) can be used to monitor processes and obtain nearly all process related statistics that are tracked by the operating system. See proc(4) for the man page on the /proc file system. The man page defines a set of utilities, located in /usr/proc/bin, that use the /proc file system. We have already described the ptime utility for high-precision timing measurement. Some other useful utilities are described below.

- pmap prints the address space of the program as shown in the following example.

```
example% du -ak * > /dev/null &
[2] 6274
example% pmap -x 6274
6274:   du -ak ACTS ACTS,v2.2 ACTS,v2.3 GSP,v4.11 GSP,v4.7 GSP,v4.8
GSP,v4.9 G
Address   Kbytes Resident Shared Private Permissions      Mapped
File
00010000       8        8      8       - read/exec           du
00020000       8        8      -       8 read/write/exec     du
00022000      16       16      -      16 read/write/exec
  heap ]
7FA80000     656      656    656       - read/exec        libc.so.1
7FB32000      32       32     16      16 read/write/exec  libc.so.1
7FB3A000       8        8      -       8 read/write/exec
  anon ]
7FB70000      16       16     16       - read/exec        libc_psr.so.1
7FB90000       8        8      8       - read/exec        libdl.so.1
7FBA0000       8        8      8       - read/write/exec
  anon ]
7FBB0000     120      120    120       - read/exec        ld.so.1
7FBDC000       8        8      -       8 read/write/exec   ld.so.1
FFBEA000      24       24      -      24 read/write/exec
```

```
  stack ]
--------  ------  ------  ------  ------
total Kb    912     912     832      80
```

Note that the output shows the total memory used in the process as divided in heap, stack, shared libraries, shared memory segments, and anonymous memory. In Chapter 7, we will return to the discussion of process structure and the use of the pmap command to monitor it. In Solaris 8, pmap output also tags shared memory segments obtained via the *intimate shared memory* (ISM) mechanism that was introduced in Solaris 2.6 (see [Mauro00]).

- pldd lists the dynamic shared objects linked to the process including any libraries explicitly attached using dlopen(3DL).

- pstack prints a hex+symbolic stack trace for each LWP in the process.

```
example% pstack 3264
3264:   nobranchopt
 7ee9a024 getpid    (0, ffbeee60, 0, 0, 0, 0) + 8
 7fb84764 etime_   (12f9b8, 7fb9a9f8, 7fb9a1ec, 7f800, 100, 127838)
+ 164
 00010f30 MAIN_     (21400, 216a0, a8828, 1b58, 6ae, a7ff0) + 228
 00010ce8 main      (1, ffbef004, ffbef00c, 21400, 0, 0) + 30
 00010ca0 _start    (0, 0, 0, 0, 0, 0) + f8
```

Repeated pstack calls can be quite useful in debugging and performance monitoring of large programs.

- pflags prints the /proc tracing flags, the pending and held signals, and other /proc status information for each LWP in the process.

In Solaris 8, several of the /proc utilities can operate on the core files generated when a process abnormally exits. The following output is generated when we examine the core file dumped in a test program that aborts due to segmentation violation.

```
example% pstack core
core 'core' of 11696:   a.out
 00010bc8 main      (1, ffbefc8c, ffbefc94, 20c00, 0, 0) + 210
 00010990 _start    (0, 0, 0, 0, 0, 0) + 108
example% pmap core
core 'core' of 11696:   a.out
00010000      8K read/exec        /tmp/garg/a.out
00020000      8K read/write/exec  /tmp/garg/a.out
7FA80000    664K read/exec        /usr/lib/libc.so.1
7FB36000     24K read/write/exec  /usr/lib/libc.so.1
```

```
7FB3C000      8K read/write/exec    /usr/lib/libc.so.1
7FB80000     16K read/exec
/usr/platform/sun4u/lib/libc_psr.so.1
7FBA0000      8K read/write/exec
7FBB0000      8K read/exec  ·        /usr/lib/libdl.so.1
7FBC0000    128K read/exec           /usr/lib/ld.so.1
7FBE0000      8K read/write/exec     /usr/lib/ld.so.1
FF44E000   7816K read/write/exec       [ stack ]
 total      8696K
```

Some other tools in /usr/proc/bin are ptree, pwait, pcred, psig, prun, pfiles. Refer to the proc(1) man pages and online documentation for details.

Process Tracing Tools

We will now turn attention to commonly used application tracing utilities available in Solaris. We start with truss(1) and sotruss(1). The truss command can be used to trace system calls being made in a process, command, or user executable. It can trace child processes, and it can count and time system calls and signals.

```
example% truss -c du -ak /usr/openwin > /dev/null
syscall             seconds    calls   errors
_exit                   .00        1
write                   .00       65
open                    .00        4      1
close                   .01     1584
chdir                   .04     1583
brk                     .00        4
stat                    .00        1
fstat                   .00        3
ioctl                   .00        1      1
execve                  .00        1
fcntl                   .01     1581
mmap                    .00        8
munmap                  .00        2
llseek                  .26    11708
getdents64              .09     2421
lstat64                 .25    10128
fstat64                 .05     1582
open64                  .02     1581
                    -------   ------   ----
```

```
sys totals:               .73    32258       2
usr time:                 .16
elapsed:                 4.12
```

The -c option produces a count of traced system calls, faults and signals. Two other useful options are -f and -t. The -f option enables tracing of the forked processes. This is quite useful in situations where application binaries are invoked with shell or perl(1) scripts which is commonly done for many large commercial applications.

The -t option allows tracing specified system calls only. For example, one can trace brk(2) and open(2) calls as follows

```
example% truss -t open,brk ls
open("/dev/zero", O_RDONLY)                       = 3
open("/usr/lib/libc.so.1", O_RDONLY)              = 4
open("/usr/lib/libdl.so.1", O_RDONLY)             = 4
open("/usr/platform/SUNW,Ultra-2/lib/libc_psr.so.1", O_RDONLY) =
4
brk(0x000249C8)                                   = 0
brk(0x000269C8)                                   = 0
brk(0x000269C8)                                   = 0
brk(0x0002E9C8)                                   = 0
...
```

We can also use truss to stop a process after a particular system call. This can be helpful in debugging a large application as the debugger can be attached to the stopped process. The -T option to truss allows the process to be stopped after a system call.

```
examplBy default, the Sun Fortran compilers follow the IEEE 754
floating point arithmetice% truss -T getpid example_gethrtime
```

The previous command stops example_gethrtime executable after the getpid() system call. We can now attach the debugger (dbx) to the stopped process. The stopped process is restarted with the prun(1) command.

Another command for tracing is sotruss(1) (available in Solaris 2.6 and later). It can be used to trace specific library calls in shared objects that are used while executing a command. Each line of the trace output reports bindings that occur between dynamic objects as each procedure call is executed in the command being traced. Tracing shared library function calls can generate a lot of output due to the typically high frequency of occurrence of library calls. For example, the first few lines of output of sotruss ls appear as follows.

```
example% sotruss ls
ls              ->          libc.so.1:*atexit(0x7fbca8bc, 0x24000, 0x0)
ls                ->          libc.so.1:*atexit(0x13ad4, 0x7fa36000,
0x7fbca8bc)
ls                ->          libc.so.1:*setlocale(0x6, 0x13b2c,
0x7fa38588)
ls              ->          libc.so.1:*textdomain(0x13b30, 0x7fa399bc,
0x7fa36000)
ls            ->          libc.so.1:*time(0x0, 0x7fa39a38, 0x7fa36000)
ls              ->          libc.so.1:*isatty(0x1, 0x7fa39a38, 0x0)
ls            ->          libc.so.1:*getopt(0x1, 0xffbeef2c, 0x13b40)
ls                ->          libc.so.1:*malloc(0x100, 0x0, 0x0)
ls                ->          libc.so.1:*malloc(0x9000, 0x0, 0x0)
ls                ->          libc.so.1:*lstat64(0x2448c, 0xffbeedd0,
0x7fa36000)
...
```

The apptrace(1) tool, which is another tracing utility similar to truss(1) and sotruss(1), was introduced in Solaris 8. This program traces the application function calls to Solaris shared libraries and displays output that is often easier to read than truss(1) output.

The following is an example of apptrace(1) applied to date(1) command.

```
example% apptrace date
date      -> libc.so.1:atexit(func = 0x7fbca8bc) = 0x0
date      -> libc.so.1:atexit(func = 0x115cc) = 0x0
date      -> libc.so.1:setlocale(category = 0x6, locale = "") = "C"
date      -> libc.so.1:textdomain(domainname = "SUNW_OST_OSCMD") =
"SUNW_OST_OSCMD"
date       -> libc.so.1:getopt(argc = 0x1, argv = 0xffbef114,
optstring = "a:u") = 0xffffffff errno = 0 (Error 0)
date      -> libc.so.1:time(tloc = 0x21cbc) = 0x3910c745
date      -> libc.so.1:nl_langinfo(item = 0x3a) = "%a %b %e %T %Z %Y"
date      -> libc.so.1:localtime(clock = 0x21cbc) = 0x7f8bc89c
date      -> libc_psr.so.1:memcpy(s1 = 0xffbef084, s2 = 0x7f8bc89c,
n = 0x24) = 0xffbef084
date      -> libc.so.1:strftime(s = "Wed May  3 17:41:41 ", maxsize
= 0x400, format = "%a %b %e %T %Z %Y", timeptr = 0xffbef084) = 0x1c
```

```
date      -> libc.so.1:puts(Wed May  3 17:41:41 PDT 2000
s = "Wed May  3 17:41:41 ") = 0x1d
date      -> libc.so.1:exit(status = 0)
```

Finally, we will illustrate the whocalls(1) utility, which can be used to trace calls to a particular system function. The tool prints (to standard output) the arguments to the function and a stacktrace every time it is called in the execution of the binary. For example, tracing memcpy calls in the date command produces:

```
example% whocalls memcpy date
memcpy(0xffbeeeb4, 0x7f9ba3e0, 0x24)
        /usr/bin/date:main+0x1c4
        /usr/bin/date:_start+0xdc
Tue Nov 28 12:29:19 PST 2000
```

System Monitoring Tools

Virtually all HPC applications heavily utilize the computational resources available on the system. For that reason, when pinpointing performance bottlenecks of an application, it is advisable to monitor system activity during the run.

Solaris offers a number of tools and utilities that gather system-wide statistics. In this section, we will briefly describe a few of the most commonly used monitoring tools.

vmstat(1M) produces statistics associated with the virtual memory, disk, faults, and CPU activity. This command is useful for monitoring the memory size used on the system, paging activity, and CPU activity, which is shown as a percentage of user, system, and idle states. On a multi-CPU system, CPU statistics are shown as system-wide averages. vmstat(1) takes the sampling interval length and number of samples as arguments.

```
example% vmstat 1 5
 procs     memory            page            disk          faults      cpu
 r b w   swap   free  re  mf pi po fr de sr f0 s0 s1 s6   in   sy
cs us sy id
 0 0 0 678200 471400   2   6  9  1  1  0  0  0  0  0  0  195  983
292  1  1 99
 0 0 0 550912 392376   0   8  0  0  0  0  0  0  0  0  0  247 1001
369 50  0 50
```

```
 0 0 0 550912 392376   0    2  0  0  0  0  0  0  1  0  0  284 1008
395 50   0 50
 1 0 0 550912 392376   0    6  0  0  0  0  0  0  0  0  0  304 1567
423 51   2 48
 0 0 0 550912 392376   0   10  0  0  0  0  0  0  0  0  0  355 1393
430 48   3 48
```

The first line of the output gives an average of the virtual memory activity since the system was booted. The output gives information on the process state (runnable, blocked, waiting), amount of virtual memory (total swap and free memory), paging statistics (page reclaims, minor page faults, page-ins, page-outs, page scan rate), disk activity, context switches, and CPU time distribution between user, system and idle. In Solaris 8, there is a new option to vmstat that gives detailed paging activity for executables, file systems, and anonymous memory.

```
example% vmstat -p 2
memory          page       executable    anonymous     filesystem
   swap    free  re mf fr de sr epi   epo  epf  api  apo  apf
fpi fpo fpf
 12546424 11846664 0 0  0    0  0    0     0    0    0    0    0
0    0   0
  9404192 10198944 0 21259 0 0   0    0     0    0    0    0    0
0    0   0
  9402264 9875312 0 15046 0  0   0    0     0    0    0    0    0
0    0   0
  9400416 9623664 0 19362 0  0   0    0     0    0    0    0    0
0    0   0
  9398328 9314488 0 16705 0  0   0    0     0    0    0    0    0
0    0   0
```

kstat(1M) is a new tool in Solaris 8 that monitors kernel activity. It examines the available statistics maintained by the kernel and displays those requested in the command. A useful option to list all of the available kernel subsystems for which statistics can be obtained is -l. In the following output, only a subset of output generated by the kstat command is shown.

```
example% kstat -l | more
cpu_info:0:cpu_info0:class
cpu_info:0:cpu_info0:clock_MHz
cpu_info:0:cpu_info0:cpu_type
cpu_info:0:cpu_info0:crtime
cpu_info:0:cpu_info0:fpu_type
cpu_info:0:cpu_info0:snaptime
```

```
cpu_info:0:cpu_info0:state
cpu_info:0:cpu_info0:state_begin
....
```

To obtain statistics on a particular subsystem or kernel module, one can use the `-n`
`<name>` option as follows.

```
example% kstat -n cpu_info0
module: cpu_info                    instance: 0
name:   cpu_info0                   class:    misc
        clock_MHz                   450
        cpu_type                    sparcv9
        crtime                      59.762911294
        fpu_type                    sparcv9
        snaptime                    276136.940064239
        state                       on-line
        state_begin                 961714495
```

Some useful modules are `system_pages`, which shows statistics on virtual memory,
`fpu_traps`, which shows the floating point traps taken by the system, and
`counters` (hardware counters). The typical usage of `kstat` is to run it prior to
executing the program, run the program, and run `kstat` again. This provides a
measure of kernel statistics for the executed program.

In addition to the tools described above, we should mention other popular tools that
monitor system activity:

- `mpstat(1M)` reports per-processor statistics for a multiprocessor system.

- `lockstat(1M)` analyzes kernel locks and reports `prof(1)` style statistics. Both
  `mpstat` and `lockstat` will be discussed in Chapter 11.

- `iostat(1M)` summarizes the I/O information including I/O errors.

- `netstat(1M)` provides data on network status and shows the contents of
  network related data structures maintained by the operating system.

- `prstat(1M)`, introduced in Solaris 8, is a tool that reports process statistics
  similar to the UNIX `top` command. It can be used in combination with the `ps(1)`
  command.

- `sar(1,1M)` is often used to generate system activity reports [Cockcroft98].

Hardware Counter Measurements

The UltraSPARC I, II, and III microprocessors have two on-chip hardware performance counters that allow runtime measurements of various hardware events such as cache references, cache misses, pipeline stalls, branch misprediction statistics, D-TLB (Data Translation Lookaside Buffer) misses, and I-TLB (Instruction Translation Lookaside Buffer) misses. For more information, see the *UltraSPARC I and II User's Manual* and the *UltraSPARC III Programmer's Reference Manual*. Hardware performance counters provide a low overhead, non-intrusive measurement of processor events which can be extremely useful in understanding the dynamic runtime behavior of applications, and in guiding the performance tuning process. Hardware counters have appeared in many other processors, and it has been demonstrated that useful tools or analyses of program behavior can be based on the data gathered using the counter facilities on modern microprocessors (see [Zagha96] for example).

The counters on UltraSPARC processors can be configured to count either system or user events. Currently, however, only two types of events can be measured at the same time. The UltraSPARC III processor is able to generate an interrupt on counter overflow which can be used for conditional sampling of performance data. This could not be done in UltraSPARC I and II processors. For example, using this feature, one could profile a program based on E-cache misses, and identify parts of the application causing E-cache misses beyond a certain threshold. The reader should also consult Appendix D which includes formulas for several metrics, that can be derived using hardware counter measurements on UltraSPARC processors.

Effective use of hardware counters to gather application-relevant performance statistics requires support in the operating system. Solaris 8 provides kernel level support and a set of APIs that allow easy access to these counters, and facilitates building performance measurement tools that make use of counter data. Two new libraries, libcpc(3LIB) and libpctx(3LIB), are provided for this purpose.

The functions in libcpc(3LIB) can be used by an application to access performance counters and gather its own performance data. This library virtualizes the hardware performance counter registers to 64-bit quantities, even though the underlying hardware (UltraSPARC processors) only supports 32-bit counter values before overflowing.

A separate library, libpctx(3LIB), provides functions that use the features of proc(4) interfaces to control a target process and, together with APIs in libcpc, allow tools to be constructed that can trace the performance counter data in other applications. An example of such a utility is cputrack(1), which is described later in this section.

For single-threaded single process programs, measurements on Solaris 8 systems indicate that typically, the overhead introduced by libcpc and libpctx functions (or tools derived from them) is less than 5% of the total runtime of the application.

Monitoring Tools

cpustat(1M) and cputrack(1M) are two tools introduced in Solaris 8 that display CPU performance counter statistics. cpustat(1M), which has to be run with superuser privileges, provides system-wide statistics. For example, the external cache hits and references can be monitored with the following command.

```
# /usr/sbin/cpustat -c EC_ref,EC_hit 1 5
   time cpu event      pic0      pic1
  1.011   0  tick  39656024  39646522
  1.011   2  tick  23723302  23712463
  2.011   0  tick  38522992  38512199
  2.011   2  tick  24155293  24145503
  3.011   0  tick  39670701  39660697
  3.011   2  tick  23045828  23035946
  4.011   0  tick  29874630  29862918
  4.011   2  tick  32887100  32876583
  5.011   0  tick  31724782  31715364
  5.012   2  tick  31291190  31278142
  5.012   2 total 314551842 314446337
```

The generated data can then be used (in a post-processing step) to compute the external cache hit rate as described in Appendix D. The external cache hit rate provides information on cache utilization, and generally has a direct bearing on program performance. In Chapter 8, we will describe the technique of cache blocking and elaborate on the correlation between cache utilization and program performance.

It is possible to get the equivalent statistics for a particular process with the cputrack(1) command, which does not require superuser privileges. Its output is easier to read than cpustat, especially on a multi-CPU system where processes migrate from one CPU to another.

```
example% cputrack -fev -c EC_ref,EC_hit -T 1 a.out
    time    pid lwp       event      pic0       pic1
   0.008  16393   1   init_lwp          0          0
   1.031  16393   1       tick   62049671   62039135
   2.031  16393   1       tick   61585868   61584568
   3.021  16393   1       tick   61377297   61375344
   4.021  16393   1       tick   61969271   61967598
   5.021  16393   1       tick   61940547   61938693
```

The tool busstat(1M), also introduced in Solaris 8, reports performance statistics related to the system bus. UltraSPARC-based systems have special application specific integrated circuit (ASIC) chips that implement the interconnect architecture and provide the interface to the microprocessor and other devices on the system. Many of these ASIC chips and devices have performance counters built into them in a manner similar to the counters on the UltraSPARC processor. To display all of the devices that support performance counters, one can use busstat -l. One can use busstat -e to show supported events for a particular device. The following example displays the memory bank stalls on the system sampled every 10 seconds.

```
# busstat -a -w ac0,pic0=mem_bank0_stall,pic1=mem_bank1_stall 10
time  dev   event0                pic0   event1              pic1
10    ac0   mem_bank0_stall       1234   mem_bank1_stall      5678
20    ac0   mem_bank0_stall       5678   mem_bank1_stall     12345
30    ac0   mem_bank0_stall      12345   mem_bank1_stall     56789
```

For additional information on the usage of the counter-based tools, refer to the man pages for cpustat(1M), cputrack(1M), and busstat(1M). In Chapter 11, we will present a case study on using these tools to analyze performance problems in a multithreaded program on an Enterprise 4500 system.

Hardware Counter Overflow Profiling

The Forte Developer 6 update 1 version of the Performance Analyzer and Sampling Collector tools includes support for hardware counter overflow profiling on UltraSPARC-III-based Solaris systems. We will illustrate this feature with a simple example on a Sun Blade 1000 system. Consider the following program.

CODE EXAMPLE 4-11 Program to Show Hardware Counter Overflow Profiling

```
/* example_ovfl.c */
/* cc -g example_ovfl.c
(using Forte 6 update 1 C compiler)*/
#include <stdio.h>
#include <stdlib.h>
#define N (500019+1)
#define TIMES 100
int main(int argc, char **argv) {
  int i,j,k,nl,nll;
  double sum = 0.0, b[N], a[N];
  double t1=0.0,t2=0.0;
  sum = 0.0;
  for (j = 0; j < TIMES; j++) {
    for (i=0; i < N; i++) b[i] = 0.3 + 0.001*j + 0.00001*i;
    for (i=0; i < N; i++) a[i] = 0.1 + 0.003*(j-1) + 0.0004*i;
    for (k = 0; k < N-1; k++) sum = sum + a[k]*b[k];
  }
  printf("sum = %14.7e\n", sum);
}
```

We compile[1] the program using Forte Developer 6 update 1 C compiler.

```
example% cc -g example_ovfl.c
```

---

1. Note, while no compiler optimization (other than what is turned on by default) is used here, the use of hardware counter overflow profiling in the Analyzer and Collector tools is not dependent on compiler optimization levels.

Now, the tool is started by typing `workshop` on a Sun Blade 1000 system. The following is a screenshot of sampling collector:

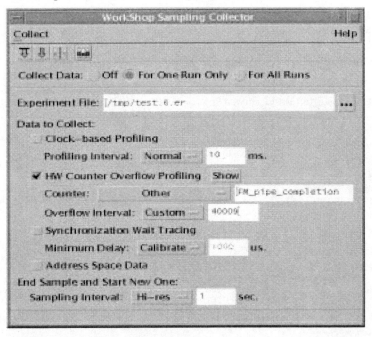

FIGURE 4-7 Counter Overflow Profiling Data Collection Facility in Forte Developer 6 Update 1 Sampling Collector

By selecting HW Counter Overflow Profiling, the user can enable or disable counter profiling. Note, the clock-based profiling is disabled once hardware counter profiling is selected. The tool supports two types of counters: standard counters and other counters. Standard counters represent metrics that are most useful in performance analysis. On UltraSPARC-III systems, the standard counters in the collector tool provide information on CPU cycles, instructions executed, data-cache read and write misses, external cache misses, instruction cache misses, instructions missed in external cache, instruction cache stall cycles, data cache and external cache stall cycles, and store queue stall cycles. Other counters can be used to instrument the remaining hardware counters on the processor.

We will show the use of the other counter feature to measure the `FM_pipe_completion` (floating-point multiples) counter values on UltraSPARC-III processor. Once the user selects Other, a list of supported counters is printed in the debugger window. In order to select `FM_pipe_completion`, the user needs to type the following at the `dbx` prompt (as shown in the following screenshot).

```
collector hwprofile counter FM_pipe_completion 40009
```

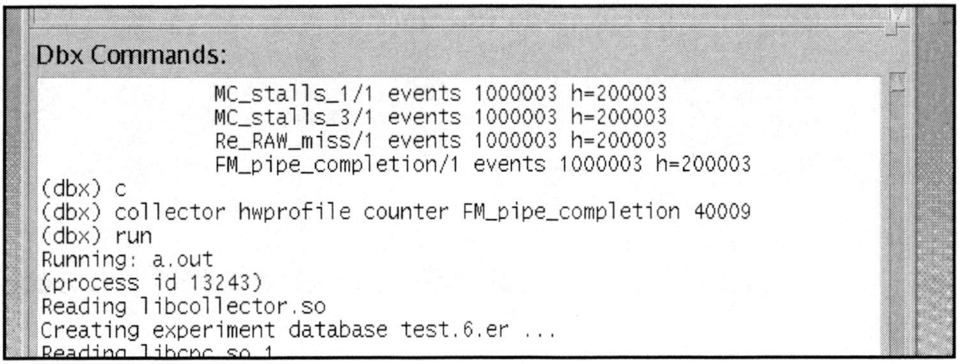

```
Dbx Commands:
                   MC_stalls_1/1 events 1000003 h=200003
                   MC_stalls_3/1 events 1000003 h=200003
                   Re_RAW_miss/1 events 1000003 h=200003
                   FM_pipe_completion/1 events 1000003 h=200003
(dbx) c
(dbx) collector hwprofile counter FM_pipe_completion 40009
(dbx) run
Running: a.out
(process id 13243)
Reading libcollector.so
Creating experiment database test.6.er ...
Reading libcnc so 1
```

FIGURE 4-8 Portion of the dbx Window Showing the Command to Enable Overflow
Profiling of FM_pipe_completion Event

The above setting enables profiling of FM_pipe_completion counter at intervals of
40009. Any other values desired by the user can be entered in the Collector window
(see figure above). The preset values of various counters can be listed in the dbx
window by clicking Show in the Collector window. Note that depending on the
overflow value selected and the program's characteristics, there is a risk of
misleading correlations (see [Zagha96]). For example, say every 200th floating-point
multiplication operation is profiled in a program which has a loop with one
statement block having 175 multiples and another statement block with 25 multiples
in every iteration. All the counts might get attributed by the profile to the second
block of statements. While the preset values have been selected to generate
statistically valid profiles, a careful user may want to run the experiments with
different overflow values to ensure that the generated profiles are statistically
correct.

Returning to our example, the generated experiment record is analyzed with the
Analyzer tool as shown in the following graphic.

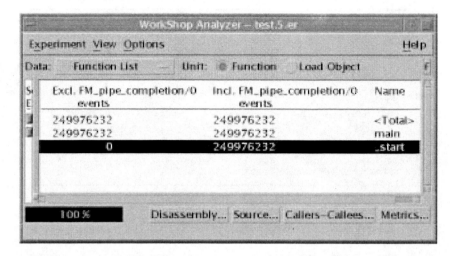

FIGURE 4-9 Inclusive and Exclusive Hardware Counter Event Profiles Displayed With Forte Developer 6 Update 1 Performance Analyzer

The screenshot shows the inclusive and exclusive metrics for the counter events. These counts are equal to the overflow intervals multiplied by the number of overflows. In the above example, the overflow interval for FM_pipe_completion was set to 40009, which implies the following:

Number of overflows = 249976232/40009 = 6248.

When the counter selected is cycles, the metrics are inclusive and exclusive times (obtained by dividing the number of cycles with processor clock frequency).

To see how the floating-point multiples were distributed at the program statement level, we use the source code annotation feature (enabled with the Source button in the Analyzer window). The annotated source code can be saved in a separate file which is listed in the following example (note, the file was reformatted to fit on the page):

CODE EXAMPLE 4-12 Source Code Annotated With Overflow Profiling Data for the FM_pipe_completion Counter on UltraSPARC-III

```
Source file: /tmp/example_ovfl.c
Object file: /tmp/example_ovfl.o
Load Object: /tmp/a.out

Excl.                   Incl.
FM_pipe_completion/0    FM_pipe_completion/0
events                  events
                        1. /* example_ovfl.c */
```

CODE EXAMPLE 4-12   Source Code Annotated With Overflow Profiling Data for the
FM_pipe_completion Counter on UltraSPARC-III *(Continued)*

```
                          2. /* cc -g example_ovfl.c
                          3. (using Forte 6 update 1 C compiler)*/
                          4. #include <stdio.h>
                          5. #include <stdlib.h>
                          6.
                          7. #define N (500019+1)
                          8. #define TIMES 100
                          9.
                          10. int main(int argc, char **argv) {
                          11.
                          12.    int i,j,k,nl,nll;
0          0              13.    double sum = 0.0, b[N], a[N];
0          0              14.    double t1=0.0,t2=0.0;
                          15.
0          0              16.    sum = 0.0;
0          0              17.    for (j = 0; j < TIMES; j++) {
99942482   99942482       18.     for (i=0;i< N;i++)
                                     b[i]=0.3+0.001*j+0.00001*i;
100022500  100022500      19.     for (i=0;i<N;i++)
                                     a[i]=0.1+0.003*(j-1)+0.0004*i;
0          0              20.      for (k=0;k<N-1;k++)
50011250   50011250       21.          sum = sum + a[k]*b[k];
                          22.    }
                          23.
0          0              24.    printf("sum = %14.7e\n", sum);
                          25.
0          0              26. }
```

The values of FM_pipe_completion counter are shown followed by the source
line. Note that for line 21, the measured value is 50011250. This is in agreement with
the actual value of 50001900 floating-point multiples for this loop.

Code Instrumentation With `libcpc` Calls

Earlier in this section, we showed the usage of `cpustat` and `cputrack` tools to access the counters on UltraSPARC processors. We will now illustrate the use of `libcpc(3LIB)` interfaces to obtain performance counter data for sections of a user program. This can be valuable in understanding how the time is spent in the critical routines, loops, and blocks of the application. In general, it is recommended to use Forte 6 update 1 Analyzer and Collector tools to obtain hardware counter profiles, as they provide this information without the need for source code modification. However, these tools are statistical in nature and may suffer from sampling size related errors. Instrumentation with `libcpc` interfaces allows direct measurement of hardware counters around selected blocks of source code. Further, the Forte Developer 6 update 1 counter-based tools only work on UltraSPARC III-based systems, whereas `libcpc`-based measurements can be performed on any current UltraSPARC-based system (running Solaris 8).

The example program[1] calculates the dot product of two vectors, and by default measures `FA_pipe_completion` (floating-point adds) and `FM_pipe_completion` (floating-point multiplies) in the loop containing the dot product. These two events are only available on the UltraSPARC III processor. By setting `PERFEVENTS` to other strings (a list of which can be obtained via `cputrack -h`), other events can be counted. For example:

```
example% setenv PERFEVENTS pic0=Load_use,pic1=Load_use_RAW
```

will measure the cycles expended in load-use stalls and load-use stalls due to read-after-write (RAW) hazards on an UltraSPARC-II-based machine.

The program performs the measurements with `cpc_take_sample(3CPC)` calls from `libcpc`, and compares the measured events to theoretically counted events, thus verifying the accuracy of the counters in this simple micro-benchmark.

CODE EXAMPLE 4-13 Program Making `libcpc` Calls *(1 of 3)*

```
/* example_libcpc.c */
/* cc -fast -fsimple=2 -xchip=ultra3 -xarch=v8plusa \
   example_libcpc.c -lcpc -o example_libcpc */
#include <stdio.h>
#include <stdlib.h>
#include <sys/types.h>
#include <inttypes.h>
#include <libcpc.h>
#include <errno.h>
```

1. This program is the same as the one used in the previous section to illustrate hardware counter overflow profiling in Forte Developer 6 update 1 tools.

```
#define N (500019+1)
#define TIMES 100

int main(int argc, char **argv) {
  int i,j,k,nl,nll;
  double sum = 0.0, b[N], a[N];
  double t1=0.0,t2=0.0;
  int cpuver, iter;
  char *setting = NULL;
  cpc_event_t event;
  long long fltadd=0, fltmult=0, fltaddtheo=0, fltmulttheo=0;

  if ((cpuver = cpc_getcpuver()) == -1) {
    printf("no performance counter hardware \n");
  } else {
    printf("hardware identifier %d\n",cpuver);
  }

  if ((setting = getenv("PERFEVENTS")) == NULL)
    setting = "pic0=FA_pipe_completion,pic1=FM_pipe_completion";

  if (cpc_strtoevent(cpuver,setting,&event) != 0)
    printf("Cannot measure %s on this processor\n",setting);
  setting = cpc_eventtostr(&event);

  if (cpc_bind_event(&event, 0) == -1)
    printf("cannot bind lwp %d %s\n",_lwp_self(),
           strerror(errno));

  nl = N-1;
  fltaddtheo = ((long long)TIMES)*(N-1);
  fltmulttheo = (((long long)TIMES)*(N-1));

  {cpc_event_t before, after;
  sum = 0.0;
  for (j = 0; j < TIMES; j++) {
    for (i = 0; i < N; i++)
        b[i] = 0.3 + 0.001*j + 0.00001*i;
    for (i = 0; i < N; i++)
        a[i] = 0.1 + 0.003*(j-1) + 0.0004*i;
    if (cpc_take_sample(&before) == -1) exit(-1);
      for (k = 0; k < N-1; k++)
          sum = sum + a[k]*b[k];
```

```
        if (cpc_take_sample(&after) == -1) exit(-1);
        fltadd += (after.ce_pic[0] - before.ce_pic[0]);
        fltmult += (after.ce_pic[1] - before.ce_pic[1]);
    }
    }


    printf("Measured Flt Adds %lld\n",fltadd);
    printf("Measured Flt Mults %lld\n",fltmult);
    printf("Theoretical Flt Adds %lld\n",fltaddtheo);
    printf("Theoretical Flt Mults %lld\n",fltmulttheo);
    printf("sum = %14.7e\n", sum);
}
```

Compiling this program and running on a Sun Blade 1000, we obtain the following output.

```
example% example_libcpc
hardware identifier 1002
Measured Flt Adds 50002200
Measured Flt Mults 50001900
Theoretical Flt Adds 50001900
Theoretical Flt Mults 50001900
sum =  1.8451251e+10
```

Summary

In this chapter, we described the tools for serial program performance measurement on the Solaris Operating Environment. Measurement of program performance is a crucial first step in improving its performance on a given platform. Keeping the benchmark datasets and program environment unchanged during measurement and tuning stages is essential to ensure reproducible and consistent measurement results. It is also important to remember that the use of various tools introduces overheads, hence one must try to ascertain *a priori* (to the extent possible) the overheads and the impact of the tools on program runtime behavior.

The recommended timer on Solaris for measuring wall-clock time is ptime. Measurement of portions of programs can be done using gethrtime or etime (for Fortran programs). The TICK register can be accessed to perform highly accurate, low overhead measurements of very small sections of the program. Once the runtime information of the whole program, or parts of it have been obtained, one can apply gprof or prof to obtain function profile and call-graph information. Data on source line (or block) execution frequency can be obtained with tcov, which is a basic block profiling tool. gprof, prof, and tcov all require recompilation and relinking of an application. The Performance Analyzer and Sampling Collector tools in Forte Developer 6 can be used to obtain program profile and disassembly annotated with performance metrics and compiler commentary without recompiling and relinking. Additionally, with recompilation and relinking using the -g flag, annotated source can also be obtained with these tools to see profiling data attributed to individual source lines and commentary on compiler optimizations.

The /proc utilities in Solaris can be used to obtain process resource usage information such as memory usage, runtime stack, number of LWPs, and number of file descriptors. Tracing tools such as truss, sotruss, and apptrace can be used to trace system calls and shared library overheads, and to quantify how the application interacts with the operating system. System monitoring tools like vmstat and kstat provide data on virtual memory usage and detailed kernel statistics in the system. vmstat, in particular, must be run occasionally during the benchmark to ensure that any undesirable paging or swapping activity is not taking place in the system.

Solaris 8 introduced cpustat, cputrack, and busstat tools and libcpc APIs to obtain the data collected by the hardware counters on UltraSPARC processors and the various ASICs used in the memory interconnect subsystems. The Forte Developer 6 update 1 tools allow hardware counter overflow profiling on UltraSPARC-III-based systems.

We close the chapter by reiterating that only a brief flavor of the utilities available under Solaris was presented. The tools and techniques outlined here were selected based on their applicability to tuning HPC applications. There are a variety of other tools and utilities (each suited for a different purpose) in Solaris, and we refer the reader to [Cockcroft98], [Mauro00], and the online documentation for information about tools that were not discussed herein. Tools that can be used for measuring the performance of parallel programs will be discussed in Chapter 11.

## CHAPTER 5

Basic Compiler Optimizations

In the next two chapters, we will look at compiler techniques for optimizing application performance. The compiler is perhaps the most powerful tuning tool in the hands of a high performance computing applications developer, and its effective use can provide substantial performance increase in a portable and nonintrusive fashion. We will describe compiler options available in Sun compilers for SPARC platforms that developers can use to improve the performance of their program.

As a general guideline for getting better compiler-driven performance, we strongly recommend use of the latest released compiler version for compiling the program (Forte Developer 6 update 1 compilers at the time of this writing). Detailed information on the features and options available in a particular version of a compiler can be obtained from the documentation available online at `http://docs.sun.com`.

We begin the chapter by giving an overview of the architecture of Sun's compilers and providing guidelines for effectively using them. Then, we discuss the components and usage of `-fast` option that combines various optimizations. This is followed by a description of some of the most effective "safe" options in Sun compilers for improving the performance of serial (single-threaded, single-process) programs. The compiler options discussed in this chapter are "safe" in the sense that they do not affect the numerical results of computations. As with any other optimization approach, these options should be used selectively, and not all of the flags described here will improve the performance of every application.

Compilation Overview

A *compiler* takes as input a program written in one language (called the *source* language) and translates it into another functionally equivalent program in a different language called the *target* language. While theoretically the source and target can be any languages, commonly, the source language is a high-level programming language (such as C, Fortran, C++), and the output is *relocatable object code* for a specific machine architecture (such as SPARC). The output may also be assembly language code, in which case it is further processed by an assembler program to produce relocatable object code. The object codes are concatenated together by *link-editor* to produce the executable program that will run on the target machine. We will discuss linker concepts in Chapter 7.

There are typically two stages in the compilation of an input program: *analysis* and *synthesis*. The analysis stage (also called *compiler front-end* stage) processes the input program and converts it into a source language-independent representation, called *intermediate representation* (IR). The synthesis stage (also called *compiler back-end* stage) converts the IR into a sequence of machine specific instructions called the object code. Breaking the compiler into front-end and back-end components gives the flexibility of having a common back end for different language-specific front ends, as well as the ability of generating code for multiple target architectures for programs written in a common high-level language.

The analysis stage of the compiler is typically further divided into three steps: *lexical analysis*, *syntax analysis,* and *semantic analysis*. In lexical analysis (also called *scanning*), the input program is read from left to right (and top to bottom) and is divided into lexical units called *tokens*. Tokens are collectively meaningful to the syntax analysis step. The syntax analysis step (also called *parsing*) examines tokens from the scanning step, associates a specific grammar rule with it (depending on the language of the source program), and groups different tokens together accordingly. The output of the syntax analysis step is a *parse tree representation* of the input program. The parse tree representation is passed onto the semantic analysis step, which checks whether the semantic rules of the programming language are obeyed. For example, if a nonpointer variable is dereferenced (in a C language program), then an error will be generated in the semantic analysis step. For a semantically correct parse tree representation, the semantic analyzer generates an intermediate representation which is passed on to the compiler back end. The intermediate representation can have a variety of forms, but the main requirements are that it should be easy to generate for programs in different high-level languages, and it should also be easy to translate into the target machine language.

The synthesis stage of the compiler is divided into two steps: *code optimization* and *code generation*. The code optimization step takes the generated IR and applies a variety of optimization techniques with the objective of producing efficient object code. Its output is optimized IR, which is then processed by the code generator which performs additional platform-specific optimizations and generates the machine code or assembly code for the target architecture.

From the above description, it may appear that these stages occur sequentially and the output of one stage is passed to another stage. In reality, the different phases of the front-end stage (lexical, syntax and semantic analysis, and intermediate representation generation) usually occur simultaneously while the compiler is reading the program source. The code optimization step is usually multipass and it is typically the most time-consuming step in the compilation process. During this step, the compiler makes several passes through the IR and literally applies hundreds of different optimization algorithms to generate more space-time efficient object code. It is also worth noting that as the program proceeds through the compilation stages, the later stages have lesser and lesser knowledge of the source program language, and increasing knowledge of the target architecture.

Other activities that take place simultaneously to all of the preceding steps include *symbol table management*, *error handling*, and *operating system interface*. A symbol table collects the attributes (such as name, type, scope, and size) of the various symbols in the program, and organizes them in a way that allows these attributes to be easily set and retrieved. The error handling facility is responsible for handling the errors that occur during various phases of compilation. For example, a syntax error in a program is considered to be a fatal error, usually leading to the termination of program compilation. The operating system interface provides the different compiler phases with the facility to interact with the user environment and perform tasks such as file input/output and generation of compilation logs and user messages.

Only a brief overview of compilation process was given above with the aim of establishing a context in which architecture and features of Sun's optimizing compilers will be discussed in this and the next chapter. Readers interested in more information on compiler theory and implementation are referred to [Aho85], [Bennett90], and [Muchnick97].

Structure of Sun Compilers

The structure and organization of Sun's optimizing compilers fit into the framework we have described above. The different front ends (for C, C++, Fortran 77, Fortran 90/95) generate a common intermediate representation, called *SunIR*. The back end processes SunIR and generates object code for different architectures (for example, SPARC architecture and Intel x86 architecture based systems running the Solaris operating system). In this book, we will only discuss features of the Sun compilers for the SPARC architecture. FIGURE 5-1 shows a schematic of the architecture of the Sun compilers. The functionality provided by various components is as follows:

- *Front ends* – Different languages are processed by different front-end components. The front ends implement features of different languages as prescribed in language standards and specifications (see Chapter 3).

- *Fast code generator* – Facilitates compile-edit-debug cycle of program development by providing quick compilation turnaround for program changes. The fast code generator short-circuits the optimizing back end in favor of decreased compile time (see FIGURE 5-1).

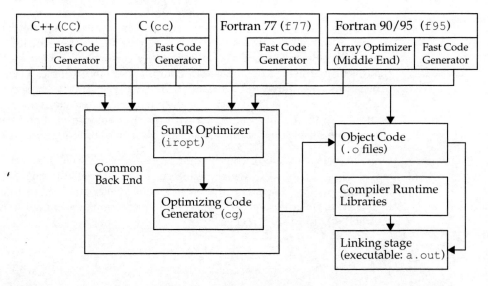

FIGURE 5-1   Architecture of Sun Optimizing Compilers (Forte Developer 6 Update 1 Release)

- *Fortran 90/95 array optimizer* – The Forte Developer 6 and Forte Developer 6 update 1 Fortran 90/95 compilers have a target independent array optimization module that performs a variety of performance optimizations on array constructs. This module is also called Fortran 90/95 Middle End.

- *SunIR optimizer* – The `iropt` performs a number of traditional local and global optimizations on the SunIR representation of a program generated by front ends. It also performs loop transformations, alias and inlining analysis, loop dependence analysis, and analysis for generation of parallel code. We will discuss the parallelization support in Sun compilers in Chapter 13. TABLE 5-1 lists some of the optimizations performed by the `iropt` stage. Refer to a compiler text such as [Muchnick97] for an explanation of these optimization techniques.

- *Optimizing code generator* – The `cg` reads in the optimized SunIR generated by `iropt` and performs machine specific optimizations (such as register allocation, software pipelining, and others) and outputs object code. TABLE 5-2 lists some of the optimizations performed in code generation stage (refer to [Muchnik97] for an explanation of these techniques). The object code is in ELF format on Solaris-SPARC systems, and can be linked by the Solaris linker to generate a final executable. The structure of ELF files will be discussed in Chapter 7.

- *Compiler runtime libraries* – A number of runtime libraries are provided that are used at the linking stage to build a final executable. These implement language intrinsics, mathematical functions, the microtasking library for parallelization (discussed in Chapter 13), language interoperability support functions, debugging support functions, and other features. The user can view the available libraries in `/opt/SUNWspro/lib` and the subdirectories underneath it.

TABLE 5-1   Some Optimizations Performed in the SunIR Optimizer Stage

Optimization Category	Optimizations
Traditional	Common subexpression elimination, constant folding and propagation, invariant code motion, strength reduction, dead code elimination.
Alias Analysis	Type-based disambiguation, ANSI-alias analysis, pointer tracking.
Loop and Cache Transformations	Loop fusion, fission, peeling, tiling, unrolling, interchange, blocking, scalar replacement.
Interprocedural	Inlining, interprocedural analysis.
Parallelization	Data dependence analysis, parallel profitability analysis for automatic and explicit parallelization.
Other Optimizations	Profile feedback, optimizations specific to compiler pragmas and directives.

TABLE 5-2   Some Optimizations Performed in the Code Generator Stage

Optimization Category	Optimizations
General	Peephole, value numbering.
Blocks and regions	Local and global scheduling.
Loops	Software pipelining (moduloscheduling).
Cache and memory	Prefetch generation (automatic and based on compiler directive or pragma).
Registers	Register allocation.
Branches	I-cache alignment, delay slot filling.
Other Optimizations	Inline assembly templates, optimizations specific to compiler pragmas and directives.

Using Sun Compilers

As we stated in the opening of this chapter, an optimizing compiler is perhaps the most important portable performance enhancing tool available to a high performance program developer (see [Boucher99]). Optimal and correct utilization of an optimizing compiler for a large program requires an understanding of the different optimizations, knowledge of the compiler options enabling these optimizations, and careful experimentation to find out what combinations of compiler options improve what parts of the program.

In the previous section, we described the structure of Sun compilers and listed some of the numerous compiler optimization techniques implemented in different compiler stages. Many of the optimization techniques are based on complex mathematical algorithms and have different effects on different programs. While one program may speed up considerably as a result of applying a specific compiler technique, the same technique may lead to performance degradation in another program. Incorrect usage of an optimization can lead to incorrect results.

One useful approach to view an optimizing compiler from a usage perspective is to look at the properties of the optimizations that a compiler performs [Barber92]. Three properties outlined in [Barber92] are:

- *Applicability* – Different optimizations have different levels of applicability to user programs. Some optimizations benefit most programs, as the situations to which they apply occur frequently. Optimizations that occur at different levels of −xO<*n*> option in Sun compilers are a good example. Note that the applicability of an optimization should not be confused with the quantity of performance improvement one obtains on a given program with a specific technique.

- *Utility* – Optimizations differ in the amount of performance improvement as a result of using them. The performance improvement depends on the machine architecture and the characteristics of the program being compiled. For example, in a floating point loop intensive cache-resident program, software pipelining (performed at -xO3 and higher) usually results in far more speedup than mere loop unrolling.

- *Cost* – The cost (as measured in compile time and compile memory requirements) varies from one optimization to another. For example, global and interprocedural optimizations (such as inlining) are typically more expensive than local optimizations (such as loop transformations).

One other important property we add to this list from a compiler usage point of view is:

- *Complementary optimizations* – Specific combinations of optimizations can often result in significantly more performance improvement than those used in isolation. For example, in floating-point-intensive C programs intended to be run on UltraSPARC platforms, the combination of double-word alignment (-dalign), UltraSPARC specific code generation (-xarch=v8plusa), pointer alias analysis (-xrestrict), and software pipelining (-xO3 and higher levels) usually results in better performance than when these options are used in isolation. Similarly, on UltraSPARC III systems, the use of -xchip=ultra3 along with -xprefetch is recommended for optimal placement of data prefetch instructions. This rationale has been used in Sun compilers to design macro options such as -fast, -xtarget and others to provide users with a simple means of invoking combinations of complementary optimization techniques. The discussion on UltraSPARC III-based systems presented in this book assumes that the prefetch cache (see Appendix B) on the UltraSPARC III processor is in an enabled state.

Sun compilers provide numerous options to enable or disable a variety of features and optimizations. On the basis of the preceding discussion and experience derived from tuning a variety of HPC applications, we have selected a handful of these options to be described in detail in this and the next chapter. These options encapsulate the most important performance enhancing optimizations implemented in Sun compilers. TABLE 5-3 summarizes these options.

TABLE 5-3   Synopsis of Compiler Options Discussed in Chapters 5 and 6

Compiler Option[1]	Covered in Chapter	Synopsis
-fast, -xtarget	5	Macros for generating optimized code.
-xarch, -xchip	5	Target architecture and chip specific optimizations.
-xO1 ... xO5	5	Traditional local and global optimizations, loop transformations, software pipelining, inlining and other optimizations.

TABLE 5-3   Synopsis of Compiler Options Discussed in Chapters 5 and 6 *(Continued)*

Compiler Option[1]	Covered in Chapter	Synopsis
-xinline, -xcrossfile	5	Inlining within and across modules.
-xdepend	5	Dependency analysis and optimization.
-xvector	5	Use of vectorized mathematical library functions.
-xsfpconst	5	Float constant treatment in C programs.
-xprofile	5	Profile feedback optimization.
-xprefetch	5	Data prefetching.
-ftrap, -fns	6	IEEE trap handling and roundoff properties.
-fsimple	6	Arithmetic simplification and aggressive floating-point optimizations.
-xrestrict, -xalias_level	6	Pointer alias analysis in C programs.
-dalign	6	Double-word memory alignment.
-xsafe	6	Speculative memory load generation.
-stackvar	6	Allocation of variables on runtime stack.

1. Some of the options can be used either with or without the x prefix. For example -x04 is equivalent to -04.

-fast and -xtarget Options

The -fast option is a good starting point for compiler optimization of well-behaved programs. This option is a macro, and it combines many complementary optimizations that experience has shown benefit a wide range of programs.

The following table shows the options that -fast expands to in different releases of Sun compilers for SPARC platforms. Detailed descriptions of most of these options, as well as examples illustrating their action, are provided in this and following chapters.

TABLE 5-4   Options in the -fast Macro

	C	FORTRAN 77	FORTRAN 90
Sun WorkShop 3.0	-xO4 -single -fns -fsimple=1 -ftrap=%none -libmil -native	-O4 -dalign -depend -fns -fsimple=1 -ftrap=%none -libmil -native -xlibmopt	-O3 -dalign -fns -ftrap=common -f -native -xlibmopt
Sun WorkShop 5.0	-xO4 -single -fns -fsimple=1 -ftrap=%none -xlibmil -native	-O4 -dalign -depend -fns -fsimple=1 -ftrap=%none -libmil -native -xlibmopt	-O4 -dalign -f -depend -fns -fsimple=1 -ftrap=common -libmil -native -xlibmopt
Forte Developer 6	-O5 -single -xmemalign=8s -fns -fsimple=2 -ftrap=%none -xlibmil -native -xprefetch=no -xvector=no	-O5 -dalign -depend -xpad=local -fns -fsimple=2 -ftrap=%none -libmil -native -xlibmopt -xvector=yes	-O5 -dalign -depend -xpad=local -fns -fsimple=2 ' -ftrap=common -f -libmil -native -xlibmopt -xvector=yes
Forte Developer 6 update 1	-O5 -single -xmemalign=8s -fns -fsimple=2 -ftrap=%none -xalias_level=basic -xbuiltin=%all -xlibmil -native -xprefetch=no -xvector=no	-xO5 -dalign -depend -xprefetch -xpad=local -fns -fsimple=2 -ftrap=%none -libmil -native -xlibmopt -xvector=yes	-O5 -dalign -depend -xprefetch -xpad=local -fns -fsimple=2 -ftrap=common -f -libmil -native -xlibmopt -xvector=yes

In this section, we list a few caveats specific to -fast that are sometimes overlooked by programmers.

- Sun compilers evaluate the options in one pass from left to right, and one or more options comprising the -fast macro can override the preceding flags. For example:

```
example% f77 -fast -nodepend foo.f
```

will suppress the dependency analysis in foo.f; however,

```
example% f77 -nodepend -fast foo.f
```

will not because of the inclusion of -depend option in the expansion of -fast.

- Since -dalign is part of -fast, and the alignment of the data should be consistent in the application, one should make sure that if some of the routines are compiled with -fast, the rest of the routines are also compiled with -dalign.

- Arithmetic optimizations invoked by the -fns and -fsimple options allow non IEEE-compliant arithmetic performed by an application. These options are discussed in Chapter 6.

- If -fast is used at the compilation stage, it should be used for linking as well.

- As shown in the table, the components of -fast change between compiler release. It is recommended to specify the options explicitly if parts of the program are compiled with different compiler versions.

- A user should experiment with the components of -fast by enabling or disabling combinations of those options.

Careful attention should be paid to the -native option that is a part of the -fast macro. The -native option is equivalent to -xtarget=native. The -xtarget option specifies the target system for compilation. Each value of -xtarget expands into a specific set of values for the -xarch, -xchip, and -xcache options. For example, -xtarget=ultra1/200 option sets -xarch=v8, -xchip=ultra, and -xcache=16/32/1:512/64/1. See the *Fortran User's Guide* or *C User's Guide* for a complete list of -xtarget values and corresponding expansions.

There are a few caveats for using `-xtarget` or `-native` options:

- If an UltraSPARC system is chosen with `-xtarget`, Sun WorkShop 5.0 and 3.0 compilers set the value of `-xarch` to `v8`. In Forte Developer 6, however, if the code is compiled on an UltraSPARC system, the value `-xarch=v8plus[a,b]` is used and the following warning is printed to alert the user of the nonportability of the resulting binary.

```
Warning: -xarch=v8plusa is not portable
```

The following Forte Developer 6 update 1 warning is more informative.

```
Warning: -xarch=native has been explicitly specified, or
implicitly specified by a macro option, -xarch=native on this
architecture implies -xarch=v8plusa which generates code that does
not run on pre-UltraSPARC processors
```

The following table summarizes the `-xarch` setting invoked by `-xtarget` or `-native`.

TABLE 5-5   Values of `-xarch` Set by `-xtarget=native` or `-native`

	UltraSPARC I, UltraSPARC II	UltraSPARC III
Sun WorkShop 3.0 Sun WorkShop 5.0	v8	v8
Forte Developer 6 Forte Developer 6 Update 1	v8plusa	v8plusb[1]

1. Note: currently, code compiled using `-xarch=v8plusb` option can execute only on UltraSPARC III-based systems.

- The `-native` option selects the target platform used in the compiler's code generator stage to be same as the platform that the code is compiled on; this may be different from the intended platform on which the program will be run.

Because of these potential problems, setting the `-xarch` value explicitly is strongly recommended, particularly for optimizing the code for the UltraSPARC CPU and for compiling 64-bit applications.

```
example% f77 -fast -xarch=v8plusa <program1>
example% f77 -fast -xarch=v9a <program2>
```

Basic Guidelines

We will now outline some general guidelines to follow when using Sun compilers to generate high-performance code (we assume Forte Developer 6 or Forte Developer 6 update 1 compiler versions). Refer to the *Fortran User's Guide* and the *C User's Guide* for additional information. Recommendations pertaining to using specific compiler options and combinations of various options are described in later sections (and in Chapter 6) along with the description of individual options.

- *Optimal compiler options* – For large applications, determining optimal compiler options is an iterative process and requires multiple experiments with different settings of optimization levels and options. During each experiment, the guidelines described in Chapter 4 for performance measurement must be followed. Also, the correctness of results must be verified in every experiment.

- *Order of flags* – The placement of different compiler options should be guided by the fact that the later options take precedence over earlier ones. We illustrated this in the previous section when discussing -fast usage.

- *Cross-compilation* – Often, code is compiled on one platform and targeted to be run on another system or class of systems. It is important that during cross-compilation, the target architecture is explicitly specified to prevent the compiler from selecting the platform on which the code is being compiled as the target platform. The compiler utility fpversion(1) displays the specifications of the native platform. For example, on a Sun Blade 1000 system:

```
example% fpversion
A SPARC-based CPU is available.
Kernel says CPU's clock rate is 750.0 MHz.
Kernel says main memory's clock rate is 150.0 MHz.
Sun-4 floating-point controller version 0 found.
An UltraSPARC chip is available.
Use "-xtarget=ultra3" code-generation option.
Hostid = 0x808DFB03.
```

So, if the program is being compiled on an Ultra 60 and targeted to be run on Sun Blade 1000, -xtarget=ultra3 should be explicitly used. For example:

```
example% f90 -fast -xtarget=ultra3 -xarch=v8plusa <program>
```

- *Default settings* – Compilers assume default settings for all options to provide good performance for a broad range of programs across Sun's different hardware platforms. It is very important to know the default values and their performance implications for your program. For example, the default setting of the optimization option -xO is -xO3 for Fortran, and -xO2 for C. Most programs benefit from higher optimization settings of -xO4 or -xO5.

- *Compilation time and memory usage* – The tools discussed in Chapter 4 can be used to measure the time expended and memory used in the compilation of a program. To obtain compilation times and memory usages for different compiler stages, the option -xtime can be used. For example:

```
example% f90 -fast -openmp -xtime lu.f
f90comp: time U:0.33s+S:0.17s=0.50s REAL:0.7s 70%. core T:23000k
D:12720k. io IN:2b OUT:8b. pf IN:0p OUT:0p.
iropt: time U:0.33s+S:0.05s=0.38s REAL:0.3s 99%. core T:5568k
D:4024k. io IN:0b OUT:0b. pf IN:0p OUT:0p.
cg: time U:0.93s+S:0.12s=1.05s REAL:1.1s 91%. core T:10040k
D:7584k. io IN:1b OUT:1b. pf IN:1p OUT:0p.
```

Above, f90comp is the Fortran 90 front-end stage. iropt and cg (as discussed in the previous section) are the SunIR optimizer and code generator stages, respectively. If compilation aborts due to insufficient memory, then either the optimization should be lowered, or virtual memory resources should be increased on the system. See the *Fortran User's Guide* for a discussion on increasing swap space and shell limits to facilitate compilation in case of insufficient memory availability.

- *Suggested option combinations* – The following are some of the commonly used combinations of optimizing options:
  - For programs sensitive to floating point numerics and where strict IEEE 754 conformance is desirable, the following combination can be used.

```
example% <f90|f77|cc> -fast -xarch=v8plus -fsimple=0 <program>
```

  - In C programs, if pointer arguments to functions do not alias each other, then the combination of -fast with -xrestrict is recommended as follows.

```
example% cc -fast -xarch=v8plus -xrestrict <program>
```

  - For C programs that follow ISO C 1999 pointer dereferencing rules, the std setting of -xalias_level can be experimented with as follows.

```
example% cc -fast -xrestrict -xalias_level=std <program>
```

  - The -stackvar option of Sun Fortran compilers should be used to force the compiler to allocate local variables on the stack as shown in this example:

```
example% <f77|f90> -fast -xarch=v8plusa -stackvar <program>
```

- To best utilize the benefits of data prefetching on UltraSPARC II and UltraSPARC III-based systems, -xprefetch must be used in combination with -xchip, -xdepend, and -xO4 or higher. The -xprefetch option is a part of the -fast macro in Forte Developer 6 update 1 Fortran compilers. The following C compilation command generates prefetches for code targeted to run on UltraSPARC III systems.

```
example% cc -fast -xdepend -xchip=ultra3 -xprefetch <program>
```

-xarch

The target architecture instruction set used by the compiler can be specified with the -xarch option. In this section, we will examine this option in detail and discuss how it can be used to enhance program performance.

Specifying Target Architecture

Sun compilers offer the following values of -xarch for SPARC platforms: v7, v8a, v8, v8plus, v8plusa, v9, and v9a. In addition, Forte Developer 6 introduced values v8plusb and v9b.

TABLE 5-6 Target Architectures Specified by the -xarch Option

-xarch=	Instruction Set Architecture	Platform Requirements
v7	SPARC-V7 ISA. Does not use fsmuld or integer mul and div	Any SPARC architecture
v8a	SPARC-V8 ISA without fsmuld	MicroSPARC I architecture or higher
v8	SPARC-V8 ISA	SuperSPARC or higher
v8plus	32-bit subset of SPARC-V9 ISA without the Visual Instruction Set (VIS)	UltraSPARC
v8plusa	32-bit subset of SPARC-V9 ISA including the Visual Instruction Set 1.0	UltraSPARC
v8plusb	32-bit subset of SPARC-V9 ISA including the Visual Instruction Set 1.0 and UltraSPARC III extensions	UltraSPARC III only

TABLE 5-6   Target Architectures Specified by the `-xarch` Option *(Continued)*

-xarch=	Instruction Set Architecture	Platform Requirements
v9	SPARC-V9 ISA without the Visual Instruction Set	UltraSPARC, 64-bit operating system
v9a	SPARC-V9 ISA including the Visual Instruction Set 1.0	UltraSPARC, 64-bit operating system
v9b	SPARC-V9 ISA including the Visual Instruction Set 1.0 and UltraSPARC III extensions	UltraSPARC III, 64-bit operating system

The architectures are binary compatible from earlier to later versions. That is, a program compiled with `-xarch=v8` will run on an UltraSPARC CPU that implements V9 architecture, but will not run on a V7 implementation of SPARC.

The best performance of a 32-bit floating point application on UltraSPARC processors will be achieved if it is compiled with `-xarch=v8plus[a,b]`. These options allow the compiler to use the V9 instruction set in the 32-bit addressing mode. In addition, the `v8plusa` setting allows the use of the VIS instructions. For information, see the *UltraSPARC I and II User's Manual*. The value `v8plusb` can be used in Forte Developer 6 for generating the code specifically optimized for UltraSPARC III CPU.

The `-xarch` flag is often used in combination with other optimization options and can considerably impede the performance if its value is set to an early architecture version. For example, the `v8` setting limits the number of the floating point registers used to 16 while the `v8plus` architecture allows the use of all 32 registers available in the V9 architecture.

Floating point programs that use many intermediate values in computationally intensive loops benefit from `-xarch=v8plus` compilation. For example, compiling the following test program with the Forte Developer 6 Fortran 77 compiler and running it on an Ultra 80 system, we observe approximately 60 percent speedup if `-xarch=v8plus` is set. The performance improvement is caused mainly by the extra floating-point registers that become available for the program with the `-xarch=v8plus` setting.

CODE EXAMPLE 5-1   Test Program That Illustrates `-xarch` Usage

```
c example_xarch.f
c f77 -xO4 -dalign example_xarch.f -xarch=v8plus \
c    -o example_xarch
     program example_xarch
     parameter(idim=400,ntimes=100000)
     real*8 a(4,idim), b(4,idim), r(4,4), d
     real t1,t2,etime,time(2)
```

```
c initialization
      d=1.0d+0
      do i=1,4
          do j=1,4
              r(i,j)=0.25
          end do
          do j=1,idim
              a(i,j)=d*j+0.1
          enddo
      end do
c timing calls around multiplication
      t1=etime(time)
      do n=1,ntimes
          do i=1,idim
c compute b = r'*a
              b(1,i) = r(1,1)*a(1,i) + r(2,1)*a(2,i)
     &          +r(3,1)*a(3,i) + r(4,1)*a(4,i)
              b(2,i) = r(1,2)*a(1,i) + r(2,2)*a(2,i)
     &          +r(3,2)*a(3,i) + r(4,2)*a(4,i)
              b(3,i) = r(1,3)*a(1,i) + r(2,3)*a(2,i)
     &          +r(3,3)*a(3,i) + r(4,3)*a(4,i)
              b(4,i) = r(1,4)*a(1,i) + r(2,4)*a(2,i)
     &          +r(3,4)*a(3,i) + r(4,4)*a(4,i)
          enddo
c copy b to a
          do i=1,4
              do j=1,idim
                  a(i,j)=b(i,j)
              enddo
          enddo
      enddo
      t2=etime(time)
      write(6,*) "  b(2,idim) = ", b(2,idim)
      write(6,'("RUNTIME: ",f6.2," seconds")') t2 - t1
      end
```

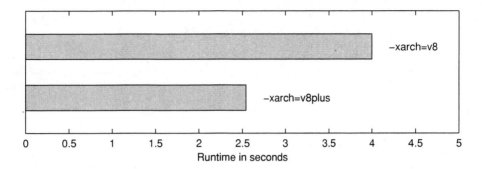

FIGURE 5-2 Performance Benefit of the `-xarch=v8plus` Option—Runs on an Ultra 80 System (Forte Developer 6 Compiler)

Generation of Conditional Move Instructions

The SPARC V9 architecture supports *conditional move* instructions. These instructions conditionally copy a value from a source register to a destination register, depending on the evaluated condition code (integer or floating-point). The use of these instructions improves performance by decreasing the number of branches in code generated from simple program expressions.

The idea behind conditional moves can be explained with the following simple example.

```
int x,y;
double z;
...
z = x > y ? 1.0 : 2.0;
```

This can be rewritten as follows:

```
int x,y,u;
double z;
...
u = (x > y); /* do comparison */
z = 1.0; /* assume that x > y is true */
if (!u) z = 2.0; /* fix if it is not true */
```

The last statement can be implemented in hardware using a conditional move instruction. No branch instructions and prediction are required. In the simple cases of operations, such as max or min, the improvements resulting from the use of conditional moves can be substantial.

Since the conditional move instructions are part of SPARC V9 instruction set, either the -xarch=v8plus[a,b], or -xarch=v9[a,b] setting is required for the compiler to generate these instructions. Consider the following simple program which computes the maximum of an array:

CODE EXAMPLE 5-2   Program That Generated a Conditional Move Instruction When -xarch=v8plus Option is Used for Compilation

```
c example_xarch_move.f
c f77 -xO4 -xarch=v8plus example_xarch_move.f \
   -o example_xarch_move
      program example_xarch_move
      integer len, ntimes
      parameter (len=1*1024*1024, ntimes=500)
      real*4 x(len+16),fmax
      real*4 tarray(2), etime, start, finish
c
c finding max in an array
      fmax=0.0
      start = etime(tarray)
      do n=1,ntimes
         do i=1,len
            x(i) = 0.5*i
            fmax = max(x(i),fmax)
         enddo
      enddo
      finish = etime(tarray)
c
c print the runtime
      write(6,*) 'max= ',fmax
      write(6,'("RUNTIME: ",f6.2," seconds")') finish-start
      end
```

Compiling with the Forte Developer 6 update 1 Fortran 77 compiler we find the
`fmovsule` instruction has been generated by the compiler if the `-xarch=v8plus`
option was used.

```
example% f77 -xO4 -xarch=v8plus example_xarch_move.f -S
```

```
fcmpes          %fcc3,%f0,%f3
fmovsule        %fcc3,%f3,%f0
```

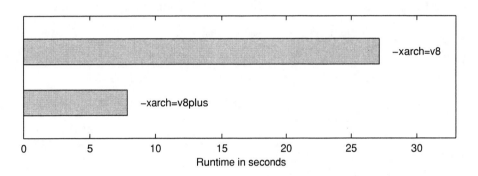

FIGURE 5-3   Performance Improvement Due to the Use of Conditional Move Instruction of
`-xarch=v8plus` on an Ultra 60 (Forte Developer 6 Update 1 Compiler)

We also see a substantial performance difference between the two runs. It should be
noted that use of `-xarch=v8plus` also leads to additional performance
optimizations, so all the gains cannot be attributed to the `fmovsule` instruction
alone.

Creating 64-bit Binaries

Generating 64-bit binaries requires a v9[a,b] setting of -xarch.

Since the addressing mode must be consistent throughout the program, all of the object files that are linked in a 64-bit application must be compiled in 64-bit mode. Otherwise, a linker error occurs.

```
example% f77 -xarch=v8 -c main.f
example% f77 -xarch=v9 -c foo.f
example% f77 main.o foo.o
ld: fatal: file foo.o: wrong machine class
ld: fatal: File processing errors. No output written to a.out
```

While the binaries compiled with -xarch=v8plus[a,b] will run only on UltraSPARC-based systems or higher, the v9[a,b] values impose an additional restriction that the program should run on Solaris 7 (or higher) booted with the 64-bit kernel.

The file(1) command can be used to see what platform is required for a given binary. For example, the following output:

```
example% file a.out
a.out:          ELF 32-bit MSB executable SPARC32PLUS Version 1,
V8+ Required, dynamically linked, not stripped
```

shows that a.out is a 32-bit program and requires an UltraSPARC-based system.

-xchip

This option specifies the target processor. The compiler uses this information for scheduling instructions and handling branches according to the timing and branch prediction characteristics of the target processor. For floating-point applications, it can have a big impact on the performance. For example, this option affects the *load-use separation*, which in turn affects the processor's pipelining efficiency in the execution. The load-use separation is the number of instructions the compiler puts between a load instruction and the first instruction that uses the loaded datum. If the load-use separation is not sufficient for the load to complete by the time the processor needs the data, then the processor pipeline stalls, degrading the performance. The optimal load-use separation is quite different between different chip implementations, as will be illustrated in the following example. Some of the other optimizations affected by the -xchip option are placement of data prefetch instructions (see -xprefetch section later in the chapter), and handling of read-after-write (RAW) dependencies in the generated code (see [Hennessy96] for an explanation of RAW data dependency).

We illustrate the effects of the commonly used -xchip values as follows: -xchip=super2 for optimization for the SuperSPARC II processor, -xchip=ultra2 for optimization for the UltraSPARC II processor, and -xchip=ultra3 for optimization for the UltraSPARC III processor. Note that the value -xchip=ultra3 was introduced in Forte Developer 6 compilers.

The following example computes a dot product.

```
do i = 1,nele
   sum = sum + a(i)*b(i)
enddo
```

We compile this example with different -xchip settings. The full program listing is provided at the end of the section.

```
example% f90 -xO4 -dalign -xchip=super2 -S -o dotsum.s.super2
   example_xchip.f90
example% f90 -xO4 -dalign -xchip=ultra2 -S -o dotsum.s.ultra2
   example_xchip.f90
```

TABLE 5-7 Fragments of Assembly Listings Produced With -xchip=super2 and
-xchip=ultra2 Options—Load-Use Separation is Insufficient for
-xchip=super2 and Sufficient for -xchip=ultra2

super2		ultra2	
. . .		. . .	
cmp	%o4,%g2	add	%g4,32,%g4
ldd	**[%g4-24],%f14 ! <- load**	**ldd**	**[%g4-32],%f14 ! <- load**
fmuld	**%f12,%f14,%f12 ! <- use**	fmuld	%f10,%f4,%f4
ldd	[%o5-16],%f16	faddd	%f30,%f0,%f30
faddd	%f30,%f6,%f6	ldd	[%g3-24],%f0
. . .		ldd	[%g4-24],%f10
		fmuld	%f8,%f2,%f2
		faddd	%f30,%f4,%f30
		ldd	[%g3-16],%f4
		ldd	[%g4-16],%f8
		fmuld	%f6,%f12,%f12
		faddd	%f30,%f2,%f30
		ldd	[%g3-8],%f2
		ldd	[%g4-8],%f6
		fmuld	**%f14,%f0,%f0 ! <- use;**
		ble	.L900000110
		. . .	

The relevant portions of the files dotsum.s.super2 and dotsum.s.ultra2 are
shown in TABLE 5-7. Examining the assembly, we can see that for the code generated
with -xchip=super2, there is no load-use separation for %f14. On an UltraSPARC
II-based system, where the latency for a double-word load is approximately 3 cycles
and 10 cycles to level 1 and level 2 caches respectively, this code will stall the
processor pipeline. Specifically, in the example program, the size of the two arrays is
large enough that they do not fit in the 16 KB level 1 cache, but they do fit in the
large (typically 2MB or larger) level 2 cache. Since the level 1 cache is nonblocking, if
the load-use separation is greater than 10 cycles (or the latency of level 2 cache), the
processor can issue the load and continue executing the subsequent (nondependent)
instructions. After approximately 10 cycles, the datum will return from the level 2
cache and will be available in the floating-point register file for use by the fmuld or
fadd instructions. This happens when the flag -xchip=ultra2 is used.

Compiling the test program with -xchip=super2 and -xchip=ultra2 and
running on an Ultra 80, which uses UltraSPARC II CPU, we obtain the timing results
shown in FIGURE 5-4. The importance of using the correct -xchip value is clearly

highlighted in this figure. Since the bulk of high-performance SPARC systems are UltraSPARC based, we strongly recommend against using -xchip=super2 (or other variants for SuperSPARC and older processors).

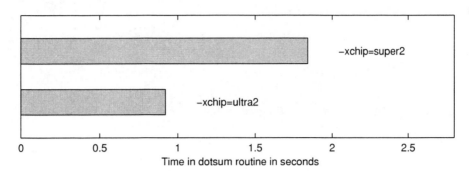

FIGURE 5-4   Time Spent in Subroutine When Compiled With -xchip=super2 and -xchip=ultra2—Runs on an Ultra 80 System (Forte Developer 6 Compiler)

We will now discuss the effect of -xchip=ultra3 setting. On an UltraSPARC III processor there is a 4-way associative, 64 KB level 1 data cache and a 4-way associative 2KB prefetch cache (refer Appendix B). The prefetch cache provides a separate path (in addition to the level 1 cache) to bring data from memory (or level 2 cache) closer to the core processor pipeline. The -xchip=ultra3 option causes the compiler to schedule the instructions such that load-use separation is determined according to latency of level 1 cache. It also leads to adequate separation between dependent store and load instructions that can cause RAW hazards. Under certain circumstances, instead of waiting for completion of a store instruction, the processor can provide the store data to a subsequent load instruction that requests the same data[1]. This is termed as *RAW bypass*. In the case of floating-point data, the separation between the store and dependent load instructions should be at least six cycles for RAW bypass to occur successfully. The option -xchip=ultra3 facilitates this separation in the generated code.

A portion of disassembly of the example_xchip.f90 program is shown below (compiled using Forte Developer 6 update 1 Fortran 95 compiler). On UltraSPARC III, it takes approximately three cycles to load a double-word floating- point datum from level 1 cache. From the following assembly listing, one can see that the code has been generated taking this into account.

```
. . .
prefetch        [%o1+264],0
add       %o1,64,%o1
ldd       [%o2-56],%f4  ! <- load
fmuld     %f0,%f18,%f0
faddd     %f14,%f6,%f6
```

1. Strictly speaking, it is data that fall on the same cache line where the store instruction is storing the data.

```
ldd      [%o1-56],%f18
ldd      [%o2-48],%f14
fmuld    %f8,%f4,%f4 ! <- use
faddd    %f12,%f2,%f2
...
! compiled as f90 -fast -xchip=ultra3 -S example_xchip.f90
```

The listing of the `example_xchip.f90` program follows.

CODE EXAMPLE 5-3   Program to Show Effect of `xchip` Option

```
! example_xchip.f90
! f90 -fast -xchip=<VALUE> example_xchip.f90
!                    -o example_xchip
subroutine dotsum(nele,a,b,sum)
implicit none
integer, parameter :: sgl=SELECTED_REAL_KIND(p=6)
integer, parameter :: dbl=SELECTED_REAL_KIND(p=13)
integer, INTENT(in) :: nele
real (KIND=dbl), INTENT(in), dimension(nele) :: a,b
real (KIND=dbl), INTENT(inout) :: sum
integer :: i
!
sum=0.d0
do i=1,nele
    sum = sum + a(i)*b(i)
enddo
return
end subroutine
!
program dotsumtst
implicit none
integer, parameter :: sgl=SELECTED_REAL_KIND(p=6)       ! single
integer, parameter :: dbl=SELECTED_REAL_KIND(p=13)      ! double
integer, parameter :: numit=1000
integer, parameter :: nele=90381
integer, parameter :: isz=(2*1024*1024)
integer :: i,j,k,n=nele,nloop
real (KIND=dbl) :: dsum,tsum=0.0
real (KIND=dbl), dimension(nele+8) :: a,b
real (KIND=sgl) :: tarray(2),t1=0.0, t2=0.0,time,sum
real (KIND=sgl) :: etime
external etime
!
do nloop=1,numit  ! calling dot product numit times
```

```
    do i=1,nele+8       ! initialization
       a(i) = i*0.001 + nloop
       b(i) = nloop*2.0 + i - 4.6
    enddo
    t1 = etime(tarray)
    call dotsum(n,a,b,dsum)
    t2 = t2 + (etime(tarray) - t1)
    tsum = tsum + 0.000001*dsum
 enddo
 !
 write(6,'("tsum=",e12.5)') tsum/numit
 write(6,'("RUNTIME: ",f6.2," seconds")') t2
 end program
```

-xO Optimization Level

Sun compilers provide five levels of optimization that can be specified with the -xO1 through -xO5 options[1]. The default optimization level can be specified using the -xO option, which is equivalent to -xO2 for C and to -xO3 for Fortran (Forte Developer 6 compilers).

The optimization level does not have to be uniform throughout the application. A typical level for computationally intensive routines is -xO4 or -xO5, which can be specified directly or indirectly with the -fast macro. High levels of optimization result in longer compilation times and an increased size of binaries. To speed up the compilation or to reduce the size of resulting files, parts of the application that are not performance critical can be compiled with low optimization or no optimization at all.

The following is a list of the optimizations the Sun compiler performs at various -xO<n> levels:

- -xO1: Basic local optimization, assembly postpass.

- -xO2: -xO1 plus basic global optimization including algebraic simplification, local and global subexpression elimination, register allocation, elimination of the dead code, constant propagation, and tail-call elimination[2].

- -xO3: -xO2 plus loop unrolling, fusion, and software pipelining.

---

1. Different compiler vendors set various numbers of optimization levels. Generally, the same optimization level has different meanings in different compilers.

2. In Forte Developer 6 compilers, if the code is compiled with -g, then tail-call optimization takes place only at -xO4 and higher optimization levels.

- -x04: -x03 plus function inlining within the module and aggressive global optimization.

- -x05: Highest optimization level, likely to improve performance when used in combination with profile feedback.

Refer to [Dowd98], [Muchnick97], and [Aho85] for an overview of the various techniques.

To illustrate the effect of different optimization levels, we can use a simple example of matrix-matrix multiplication.

CODE EXAMPLE 5-4 Matrix-Matrix Multiplication *(1 of 2)*

```
/* example_optimization.c */
/* cc -xCC -xtarget=ultra -xarch=v8plus -dalign -x04 \
      example_optimization.c -o example_optimization */
#include <sys/time.h>
#define IDIM 32
#define NTIMES 10000
long long int gethrtime(void);
double ddot(int n, double x[], int incx, double y[], int incy);

int main(){
  double a[IDIM][IDIM], b[IDIM][IDIM], c[IDIM][IDIM];
  int i,j,k,iter;
  float time;
  long long int start, end;

  for(i=0;i<IDIM;i++){      // initialization
    for(j=0;j<IDIM;j++){
      a[i][j]=1.0e+0;
      b[i][j]=(double)i/IDIM;
      c[i][j]=(double)j/IDIM;
    }
  }

  start = gethrtime();      // timing
  for(iter=0;iter<NTIMES;iter++){ // performing NTIMES products
    for(j=0;j<IDIM;j++){
      for(i=0;i<IDIM;i++){
        a[i][j] += ddot(IDIM,&(b[i][0]),1,&(c[0][j]),IDIM);
      }
    }
  }
  end = gethrtime();
```

```
  time= (end-start)/(float)1000000000;
  printf("RUNTIME: %6.2f seconds \n",time);
  printf (" a[IDIM-1][IDIM-1] = %f \n", a[IDIM-1][IDIM-1]);
  return 0;
}


double ddot(int n, double x[], int incx, double y[], int incy){
  int k, ix=0, iy=0;
  double dp = 0.0e+0;
  for(k=0;k<n;k++){     // dot product of x and y
    dp += x[ix]*y[iy];
    ix += incx;
    iy += incy;
  }
  return dp;
}
```

This straightforward implementation of matrix multiplication shows benefits from all levels of optimization. We have extracted the innermost operation in a separate routine to illustrate the inlining effect of −xO4 optimization. The performance of the code is improved by more than eight times going from compilation with no optimization to −xO4 level.

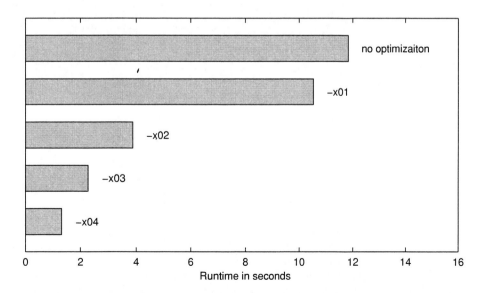

FIGURE 5-5   Matrix-Matrix Multiplication Runtimes on a Sun Blade 1000 System for Different Optimization Levels of Forte Developer 6 Compiler

This example is too small to show a noticeable difference in the compilation time at various optimization levels, but we can see it for a bigger example, the `dblat3` driver for testing BLAS3 routines from NetLib repository (http://www.netlib.org).

As can be seen in the following figure, the compilation time increases considerably when optimization is used (together with `-xtarget=ultra -xarch=v8plus -dalign`).

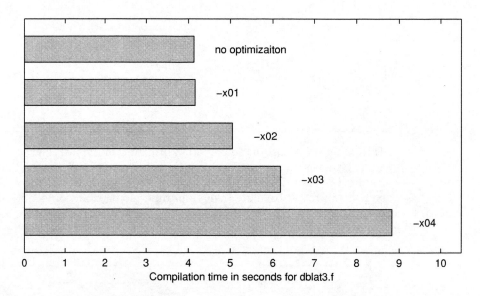

FIGURE 5-6 Forte Developer 6 Compilation Times for the `dblat3.f` Module With Different Optimization Levels on a Sun Blade 1000 System

-xinline,-xcrossfile

The `-xinline` and `-xcrossfile` options allow control of inlining function calls within a single source file, as well as across multiple files.

Inlining can improve the performance of code by eliminating function call overhead, and in some cases, by preventing the register window spills on SPARC architectures when the number of nested function calls is reduced to seven or less (see Chapter 8). Inlining also allows the compiler to optimize the code transparently through the function calls. The downside of inlining is that the resulting binaries become larger and may suffer from higher instruction cache misses.

Option `-xinline=foo1,foo2,foo3` forces the compiler to inline only functions `foo1`, `foo2`, and `foo3` within either the files where they are defined, or in all of the files listed in the command line if the `-xcrossfile` option is also specified.

Automatic inlining of the functions within the same source file occurs when `-xO4` optimization level is used. Therefore, adding the `-inline` flag with `-xO4` can reduce the number of inlined routines and potentially degrade the performance by restricting inlining to only those routines that are in the list.

The `-xinline` option requires `-xO3` optimization or higher. If inlining is performed across multiple files with `-xcrossfile`, the optimization level should be set to `-xO4` or `-xO5`.

The following example shows how inlining improves the performance by eliminating the function call overhead and by allowing the compiler to perform optimizations through the function call boundary.

CODE EXAMPLE 5-5   Program That Makes a Function Call That Will Be Inlined

```
C example_inline_main.f
C f77 -xO4 -dalign example_inline_main.f example_inline_foo.f \
C    -xcrossfile -xinline=foo -o example_inline
      program test
      parameter(nin=1000000, nout=100)
      real t1,t2,etime,time(2)
      integer*8 ii,i
      ii=0
      t1=etime(time)
      do j=1,nout
         do i=1,nin
            call foo(ii)
         enddo
      enddo
      t2=etime(time)
      write(*,*), "ii = ", ii
      write(6,'("RUNTIME: ",f6.2," seconds")') t2-t1
      end
```

CODE EXAMPLE 5-6   Subroutine That Can Be Inlined

```
C example_inline_foo.f
C f77 -xO4 -dalign example_inline_main.f example_inline_foo.f \
C    -xcrossfile -xinline=foo -o example_inline
      subroutine foo(ii)
      integer*8 ii
```

CODE EXAMPLE 5-6   Subroutine That Can Be Inlined *(Continued)*

```
        ii=ii+1
        return
        end
```

Compiling the files without the inlining results in the runtime on an Ultra 80 system of approximately three seconds.

```
example% f77 -xO4 -dalign example_inline_main.f \
        example_inline_foo.f -o example_not_inlined
example% example_not_inlined
RUNTIME:    3.11 seconds
```

By forcing the inlining of foo() we can reduce the runtime by a factor of two.

```
example% f77 -xO4 -dalign example_inline_main.f \
        example_inline_foo.f -xcrossfile -xinline=foo \
        -o example_inlined
example% example_inlined
RUNTIME:    1.56 seconds
```

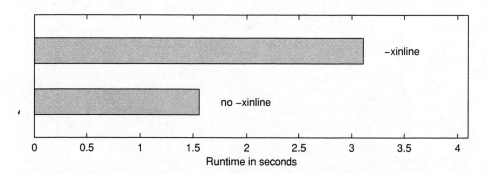

FIGURE 5-7   Effect of Function Inlining—Runtimes on an Ultra-80

To make sure that function foo() is indeed inlined, we can notice that the undefined symbol foo_ is missing in the calling object when it is compiled with -xinline and -xcrossfile options.

```
example% f77 -xO4 -dalign -c example_inline_main.f
example% nm example_inline_main.o | grep foo
[20]    |          0|      0|FUNC |GLOB |0    |UNDEF  |foo_
example% f77 -xO4 -dalign -c example_inline_main.f \
```

```
       example_inline_foo.f -xcrossfile -xinline=foo
example% nm example_inline_main.o | grep foo
example%
```

The benefits or the -xinline option are most clearly seen for the codes that allocate a separate file for each of the routines, in which case the most commonly used small functions can be inlined. If the application does not require cross-file inlining, the -xinline flag should be avoided, and the inlining within single source files should be controlled by the optimization level.

-xdepend

The -xdepend option instructs the compiler to analyze the data dependency within loops and perform loop restructuring. As a result, loops may have a higher degree of unrolling, and other optimizations such as cross-iteration subexpression elimination and scalar replacement take place. When this option is specified, the optimizer also attempts cache blocking[1], as well as loop tiling and fusion. We will further discuss this option in the chapter on automatic and directive-based parallelization as it also instructs the compiler to perform dependency analysis for parallelization of loops.

The -xdepend option requires -O3 optimization level. This flag is a part of the -fast macro Forte Developer 6 Fortran compiler (see -fast section earlier) and can be turned off with -nodepend.

We can reuse the matrix-matrix multiplication example to illustrate the effect of -xdepend.

CODE EXAMPLE 5-7 Matrix-Matrix Multiplication

```
C example_xdepend.f
C f77 -O3 example_xdepend.f -o example_xdepend (-xdepend)
      parameter(idim=320)
      real*8 a(idim,idim), b(idim,idim), c(idim,idim)
      real t1,t2,etime,time(2)

c initialization
      do i=1,idim
         do j=1,idim
            a(i,j)=5.
            b(i,j)=2.
```

1. Cache blocking is the technique where the computation is divided such that data accessed in the divided parts fits in the processor cache. In cases, where same datum is reused many times, this technique gives significant performance improvement. A detailed description of the cache blocking technique is provided in Chapter 8.

```
            c(i,j)=3.
         end do
      end do

c timed multiplication
      t1=etime(time)
         do j=1,idim
            do i=1,idim
               do k=1,idim
                  a(i,j) = a(i,j)+b(i,k)*c(k,j)
               enddo
            enddo
         enddo
      t2=etime(time)

c print the runtime
      print*, a(idim/2,idim/2)
      write(6,'("RUNTIME: ",f6.2," seconds")') t2-t1
      end
```

Compiling with and without -xdepend results in three-fold runtime difference. This dramatic effect is due to cache blocking performed by the optimizer when the -xdepend option is specified. The cache blocking can be performed for loops with regular computations and memory access patterns, such as dense matrix operations, but is rarely possible in more general cases. The general case of programmer implemented cache blocking is discussed in Chapter 8.

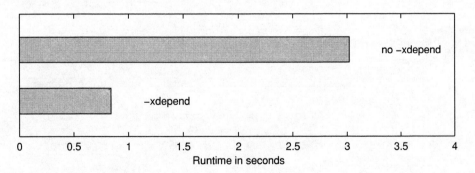

FIGURE 5-8   Performance Impact of -xdepend Option—Runs on Ultra 60 (Sun WorkShop 5.0 Compiler)

-xvector

This option is useful when math library intrinsics, for example `log(3M)`, are being called repeatedly in a loop on an array of arguments. In such cases, the flag will automatically make calls to the optimized vector math library `libmvec`, which can be significantly faster compared to their scalar counterpart routines included in the math library, `libm`. The performance improvements are best observed for large loop-trip counts. Some of the supported functions are `vatan`, `vatan2`, `vcos`, `vsin`, `vsincos`, `vexp`, `vpow`, `vlog`, and `vhypot`.

This option is available in Fortran (`f77` and `f90`/`f95`) Sun WorkShop (5.0 and later version) compilers. It can take one of two arguments: `-xvector=yes` or `-xvector=no`. Specifying `-xvector`, which is equivalent to `-xvector=yes`, also enables the `-xdepend` flag. The flag should be used for both compilation and linking steps as it passes information to linker to load `libmvec` and `libc` libraries.

Consider the following example program, which computes the logarithm of an array.

CODE EXAMPLE 5-8   Program Computing Logarithm of an Array Which Benefits From -xvector Optimization

```
! example_xvector.f90
! f90 -xO4 -dalign example_xvector.f90 -xvector -o example_xvector
program example_xvector
implicit none
integer, parameter :: dbl=SELECTED_REAL_KIND(p=13)      !
integer, parameter :: sgl=SELECTED_REAL_KIND(p=6)       !
integer, parameter :: numit=10000, nele=1000
integer :: i,n=nele,nloop,ni
real (KIND=dbl), dimension(nele+8) :: a,b
real (KIND=sgl) :: tarray(2),t1=0.0,t2=0.0,time,etime
integer nval(9)
data nval /2, 4, 10, 20, 40, 100, 200, 400, 1000/
external etime

do ni=1,9          ! step over nval values
   n=nval(ni)
   do i=1,n+8      ! initialization
      a(i) = i*0.001
      b(i) = 0.0
   enddo
   do nloop=1,numit
      t1 = etime(tarray) ! now time vector kernel
```

CODE EXAMPLE 5-8 Program Computing Logarithm of an Array Which Benefits From
-xvector Optimization *(Continued)*

```
       call veclog(n,a,b)
       t2 = t2 + (etime(tarray) - t1)
    enddo
    write(*,*) 'b(n)= ',b(n)
    write(6,'("Vector length:",i8," RUNTIME:",f6.2," sec.")') n,t2
  enddo
  end program

  subroutine veclog(nele,a,b)
  implicit none
  integer, parameter :: dbl=SELECTED_REAL_KIND(p=13)
  integer, INTENT(in) :: nele
  real (KIND=dbl), INTENT(in), dimension(nele) :: a
  real (KIND=dbl), INTENT(inout), dimension(nele) :: b
  integer :: i
  do i=1,nele
     b(i) = log(a(i))
  enddo
  return
  end subroutine
```

Compiling this program as with f90 -xO4 -dalign -S with and without -xvector
and examining the generated assembly code for subroutine veclog, we find that in
the first case, the compiler inserts a call to the vlog (vector log)

```
call    __vlog_ ! params =  %o1 %o2 %o0 %o3 %o4 ! Result =
```

while in the second case, the standard log function is called.

```
call    __log· ! params =  %o0 %o1     ! Result =  %f0
```

The performance improvements depend on the vector length and the specific
function. The timings for both cases as a function of vector length are plotted in the
following figure. From the runtimes for this case, we can see that vectorization
doesn't provide any benefits for shorter vectors. For longer vectors the plot shows
the substantial speedup as a result of using the vlog function.

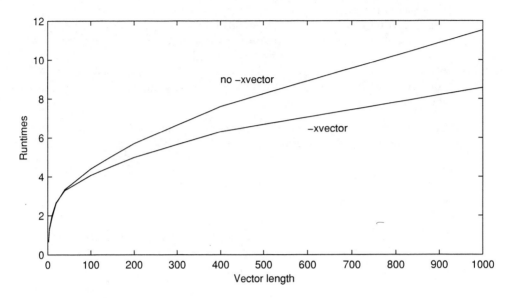

FIGURE 5-9 Effect of `-xvector` for Various Vector Sizes—Runs on Ultra 60 (Forte Developer 6 Update 1 Compiler)

-xsfpconst

A simple, but sometimes overlooked performance problem is that the C compiler treats floating-point constants as doubles unless they are explicitly declared as `float` data types. For example, in the expression `a=1.0/b`, the constant is treated as a double-precision value regardless of the type of `a` and `b`. If `a` and `b` are single-precision variables, then the more efficient operation will be `a=1.0f/b`, which performs a single-precision division and eliminates the need for additional conversion instructions between double-precision and single-precision variables.

The double-precision values can propagate and as the result a large portion of the single-precision application may be effectively computing double-precision values. This may considerably impede the performance for the codes that perform division or square root operations, which require almost twice as many cycles in double-precision compared to their single-precision equivalents. The intrinsic functions, such as `log`, `sin`, and `exp`, are also much slower when called with 64-bit arguments.

For large single-precision applications, where it is often difficult to spot a constant that was not explicitly casted to `float`, one can search the disassembly output (produced with the `dis(1)` command) for double precision instructions to make sure that all of the constants are properly declared, or to get a hint about the location of the double-precision constant. Additionally, one can use the `-xsfpconst` option of Sun C compiler to force the compiler to treat the unsuffixed floating-point constants as single precision quantities. Currently, there is no matching option for the C++ compiler.

The following example shows the performance impact of improper declaration of the constant, and the benefits of `-xsfpconst`.

CODE EXAMPLE 5-9   Floating-Point Constants Treated as Doubles

```c
/* example_xsfpconst.c */
/* cc -xO4 -xCC -o example_xsfpconst \
     example_xsfpconst.c (-xsfpconst) (-DSINGLE) */
#include <stdio.h>

int main()
{
    long long int gethrtime(void), start, end, nano=1000000000;
    float a[10000],b[10000],runtime;
    int i,j,ntimes=10000;

    for(i=0;i<10000;i++){      // initialization
        a[i]=(float)(i+1);
    }

    start = gethrtime();
    for(j=0;j<ntimes;j++){
        for(i=0;i<10000;i++){
#ifdef SINGLE
            b[i] = 1.0f/a[i];  // explicitly declare as float
#else
            b[i] = 1.0/a[i];
#endif
        }
        for(i=0;i<10000;i++){
#ifdef SINGLE
            a[i] = 1.0f/b[i];
#else
            a[i] = 1.0/b[i];
#endif
        }
```

Floating-Point Constants Treated as Doubles *(Continued)*

```
    }
    end = gethrtime();
    runtime= (end-start)/(float)nano;
    (void)printf("b[1]=%f\n",b[1]);
    (void)printf(" RUNTIME: %6.2f seconds \n",runtime);
    return 0;
}
```

If we set -DSINGLE in the command line, the single-precision constant 1.0f will be used in the code. Otherwise, the constant 1.0 will be treated as a double-precision number. Looking at the disassembly of the executables, we can see that depending on the presence or absence of the -DSINGLE switch, we find either double-precision or single-precision division instructions.

```
example% cc -xO4 -xCC -c example_xsfpconst.c -DSINGLE
example% dis example_xsfpconst.o | grep fdiv
    110:   81 a0 89 a4      fdivs       %f2, %f4, %f0
    12c:   89 a0 89 a3      fdivs       %f2, %f3, %f4
    13c:   81 a0 89 a3      fdivs       %f2, %f3, %f0
    154:   81 a0 89 a4      fdivs       %f2, %f4, %f0
    1a4:   81 a0 89 a4      fdivs       %f2, %f4, %f0
    1c0:   89 a0 89 a3      fdivs       %f2, %f3, %f4
    1d0:   81 a0 89 a3      fdivs       %f2, %f3, %f0
    1e8:   81 a0 89 a4      fdivs       %f2, %f4, %f0
    2ec:   81 a1 09 a6      fdivs       %f4, %f6, %f0
```

```
example% cc -xO4 -xCC -c example_xsfpconst.c
example% dis example_xsfpconst.o | grep fdiv
    11c:   81 a0 89 c0      fdivd       %f2, %f0, %f0
    120:   bd a0 89 de      fdivd       %f2, %f30, %f30
    144:   81 a0 89 c4      fdivd       %f2, %f4, %f0
    15c:   bd a0 89 c4      fdivd       %f2, %f4, %f30
    190:   bd a0 89 de      fdivd       %f2, %f30, %f30
    1e4:   81 a0 89 c0      fdivd       %f2, %f0, %f0
    1e8:   bd a0 89 de      fdivd       %f2, %f30, %f30
    20c:   81 a0 89 c4      fdivd       %f2, %f4, %f0
    224:   bd a0 89 c4      fdivd       %f2, %f4, %f30
    258:   bd a0 89 de      fdivd       %f2, %f30, %f30
    354:   81 a1 09 a6      fdivs       %f4, %f6, %f0
```

We can also see the single-to-double and double-to-single conversion instructions fstod and fdtos in the disassembly of program compiled without -DSINGLE.

```
example% cc -xO4 -xCC -c example_xsfpconst.c
example% dis example_xsfpconst.o | grep fstod
       114:   81 a0 19 20          fstod          %f0, %f0
       118:   bd a0 19 24          fstod          %f4, %f30
       138:   89 a0 19 24          fstod          %f4, %f4
       14c:   89 a0 19 24          fstod          %f4, %f4
       180:   bd a0 19 20          fstod          %f0, %f30
       1dc:   81 a0 19 20          fstod          %f0, %f0
       1e0:   bd a0 19 24          fstod          %f4, %f30
       200:   89 a0 19 24          fstod          %f4, %f4
       214:   89 a0 19 24          fstod          %f4, %f4
       248:   bd a0 19 20          fstod          %f0, %f30
       340:   91 a0 19 2a          fstod          %f10, %f8
       374:   89 a0 19 20          fstod          %f0, %f4
example% dis example_xsfpconst.o | grep fdtos
       13c:   81 a0 18 c0          fdtos          %f0, %f0
       150:   8d a0 18 de          fdtos          %f30, %f6
       160:   83 a0 18 c0          fdtos          %f0, %f1
       170:   81 a0 18 de          fdtos          %f30, %f0
       194:   81 a0 18 de          fdtos          %f30, %f0
       204:   81 a0 18 c0          fdtos          %f0, %f0
       218:   8d a0 18 de          fdtos          %f30, %f6
       228:   83 a0 18 c0          fdtos          %f0, %f1
       238:   81 a0 18 de          fdtos          %f30, %f0
       25c:   81 a0 18 de          fdtos          %f30, %f0
       34c:   8d a0 18 c6          fdtos          %f6, %f6
       350:   89 a0 18 c4          fdtos          %f4, %f4
```

Running the program, we can see the performance penalty of using double-precision arithmetic for this example.

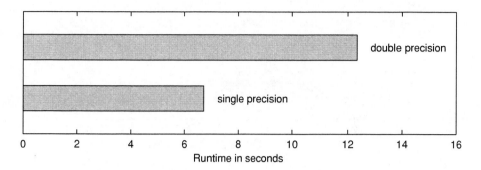

FIGURE 5-10 Different Performance for Single- and Double-Precision Data—Runtimes on an Ultra 60 (Forte Developer 6 Update 1 Compiler)

Alternatively, we could have used the -xsfpconst option to instruct the compiler to treat the constant 1.0 as a single-precision number. In many cases, this approach is more feasible, as it may take considerable effort to change the format of the constants in a large program.

```
example% cc -xO4 -xCC -c example_xsfpconst.c -xsfpconst
example% dis example_xsfpconst.o | grep fdiv
       110:   81 a0 89 a4        fdivs       %f2, %f4, %f0
       12c:   89 a0 89 a3        fdivs       %f2, %f3, %f4
       13c:   81 a0 89 a3        fdivs       %f2, %f3, %f0
       154:   81 a0 89 a4        fdivs       %f2, %f4, %f0
       1a4:   81 a0 89 a4        fdivs       %f2, %f4, %f0
       1c0:   89 a0 89 a3        fdivs       %f2, %f3, %f4
       1d0:   81 a0 89 a3        fdivs       %f2, %f3, %f0
       1e8:   81 a0 89 a4        fdivs       %f2, %f4, %f0
       2ec:   81 a1 09 a6        fdivs       %f4, %f6, %f0
```

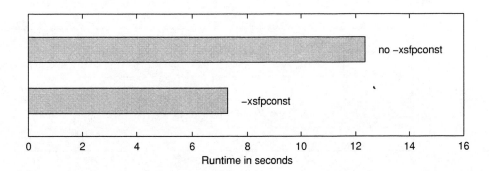

FIGURE 5-11 Effect of -xsfpconst on Single-Precision Program—Runtimes on an Ultra 60 (Forte Devloper 6 Update 1 Compiler)

-xprofile=collect,use

The profile feedback options are used to save runtime execution frequency data of the application, which is subsequently used by the compiler to perform more aggressive optimizations on the portions of the program that are exercised more frequently. The performed optimizations may include register allocation, basic block ordering, code motion and rearrangement, and inlining.

To use profile feedback optimization, the application or its parts should be compiled with the -xprofile=collect:*<name>* option, where *<name>* is the name of the executable. A subsequent run of the application will create a *<name>*.profile directory, which will contain the runtime data. This run (called the *training run*) can take longer than the run of the application compiled without profile feedback. Finally, compilation with -xprofile=use:*<name>* will use the collected data to optimize the program based on information gathered during the training run.

The -xprofile option can be used in combination with other optimizations, but the same set of flags should be used for both -xprofile=collect and for -xprofile=use compilations.

The following small program shows the benefits of the profile feedback optimization.

CODE EXAMPLE 5-10 Profile Feedback Optimization

```
C example_xprofile.f
C f77 -fast example_xprofile.f -o example_xprofile
      real t1, t2, time(2), etime
      integer n, isum
C
      n=100
      isum=0
      t1 = etime(time)
      do i=1,1000000000
         if (i.gt.n) then
             isum=isum+1
         else
             isum=isum-1
         endif
      enddo
      t2 = etime(time)
      print*, 'isum = ', isum
      write(6,'("RUNTIME: ",f6.2," seconds")') t2-t1
      end
```

We compile this program with Sun WorkShop 5.0 compilers both with and without -xprofile optimization on an Ultra 60 system.

```
example% f77 -fast example_xprofile.f -o example_xprofile \
         -xprofile=collect:example_xprofile
example% example_xprofile
 isum =   999999800
RUNTIME:  33.34 seconds
example% f77 -fast example_xprofile.f -o example_xprofile \
         -xprofile=use:example_xprofile
example% example_xprofile
 isum =   999999800
RUNTIME:   5.57 seconds
example% f77 -fast example_xprofile.f -o example_xprofile
example% example_xprofile
 isum =   999999800
RUNTIME:   8.36 seconds
```

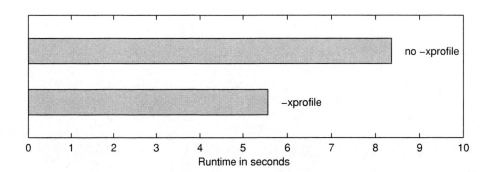

FIGURE 5-12 Speedup Due to Profile Feedback Optimization on an Ultra 60 (Sun WorkShop 5.0 Compiler)

First, we look at a fragment of the assembly code for the program that was compiled without profile feedback information.

```
!      8               !        do i=1,1000000000

/* 0x0014        8 */         sethi    %hi(0x3b9ac800),%g2
/* 0x0018        7 */         st       %f0,[%sp+92]
/* 0x001c        8 */         or       %g0,1,%o2
/* 0x0020          */         add      %g2,512,%o1

!      9               !        if (i.gt.n) then

/* 0x0024        9 */          cmp      %o2,100
                       .L900000113:
/* 0x0028        9 */          ble      .L77000020
/* 0x002c          */          add      %o2,1,%o0

!      10              !            isum=isum+1

/* 0x0030       10 */          add      %i0,1,%i0
/* 0x0034          */          ba       .L900000114
/* 0x0038          */          or       %g0,%o0,%o2
                       .L77000020:

!      11              !        else
!      12              !            isum=isum-1

/* 0x003c       12 */          add      %i0,-1,%i0
/* 0x0040        0 */          or       %g0,%o0,%o2
```

```
                              .L900000114:

!    13            !              endif
!    14            !              enddo

/*  0x0044       14 */           cmp        %o0,%o1
/*  0x0048        */             ble        .L900000113
/*. 0x004c        */             cmp        %o2,100
```

We can see that when the condition (i.gt.n) is true, the isum increment is
performed and then an unconditional branch instruction is used to step over the
else part of the conditional.

Looking at the assembly code generated with -xprofile optimization, we see that
the instruction that decrements isum is placed outside of the main loop with an
unconditional branch instruction following it that guarantees the return to the loop
body. This eliminates the unconditional branch following the increment, and
effectively replaces it with an extra branch following the decrement. This is done
because the runtime information tells the compiler that the then clause of the if
statement is exercised much more frequently than the else clause and therefore, it
is beneficial to optimize the former at the expense of the latter.

```
!    8             !              do i=1,1000000000

/*  0x0014        8 */           sethi      %hi(0x3b9ac800),%g2
/*  0x0018        7 */           st         %f0,[%sp+92]
/*  0x001c        8 */           or         %g0,1,%o0
/*  0x0020         */            add        %g2,512,%o1

!    9             !              if (i.gt.n) then

/*  0x0024        9 */           cmp        %o0,100
                              .L900000114:
/*  0x0028        9 */           ble    .   .L77000019
/*  0x002c         */            add        %o0,1,%o0

!    10            !                 isum=isum+1

/*  0x0030       10 */           add        %i0,1,%i0

!    11            !              else
!    12            !                 isum=isum-1
!    13            !              endif
!    14            !              enddo
```

```
/* 0x0034      14 */        cmp    %o0,%o1
              .L900000113:
/* 0x0038      14 */        ble    .L900000114
/* 0x003c       */          cmp    %o0,100


. . . . .


              .L77000019:
/* 0x00f8      12 */        add    %i0,-1,%i0
/* 0x00fc       */          ba     .L900000113
/* 0x0100       */          cmp    %o0,%o1
```

This example illustrates code rearrangement to optimize the more frequently traveled path in the program execution.

We should point out that compilation with −xprofile=use should be done with caution. Even though it is likely to improve the performance of an application for a particular benchmark or data set, it is also likely to deteriorate the performance for the runs that exercise different branches of the program. This technique can be generally recommended for branch-intensive programs with similar execution patterns for a collection of input data sets. The binary built with profile feedback optimization will usually run faster when exercised on any of these inputs.

The −xprofile option should be used both at compile and link time. Another value for the −xprofile option is tcov, and it can be used to collect the per-line profiling information for a run. This technique was discussed in Chapter 4.

−xprefetch

Prefetching allows overlapping execution with fetching data from memory. It can improve the performance of memory latency bound applications, especially on high latency systems. Prefetching can also considerably improve performance on UltraSPARC III-based systems due to the on-chip prefetch cache, or the P-cache (see Appendix B).

Programs that have repeated memory access patterns, particularly in large loops, typically benefit from prefetching.

The `-xprefetch[={yes|no}]` option was introduced in the Sun WorkShop 5.0 compilers. It instructs the compiler to use the prefetch assembly instruction in the generated code. Forte Developer 6 compilers allow additional prefetching flexibility with a pragma (discussed in Chapter 6) and the corresponding option `-xprefetch=[no%]explicit`. Option `-xprefetch` is synonymous with `-xprefetch=yes`; in Forte Developer 6, `-xprefetch` is synonymous with `-xprefetch=auto`.

The prefetch instruction is a part of the SPARC V9 instruction set [Weaver94] and was implemented in the UltraSPARC II CPU. The UltraSPARC I processor allows the `prefetch` instruction, but treats it as a `nop`. Therefore, the binary that uses the prefetch instruction can run on any UltraSPARC system, but only UltraSPARC II and later systems will benefit from the instruction.

Since the heuristics used for generating the prefetch instructions are closely tied to the core microarchitecture of the target processor, it is best used in combination with `-xchip` and other optimization options.

The following `daxpy(3P)`-type example shows the benefits of `-xprefetch`.

CODE EXAMPLE 5-11 Program That Benefits From `-xprefetch` Optimization

```
C example_xprefetch.f
C f77 -O4 -depend -dalign -xarch=v8plusa example_xprefetch.f \
C    -o example_xprefetch (-xprefetch)
      real t0, t1, time(2), etime
      integer i, j, n, times
      parameter (n=1000000)
      parameter (times=200)
      double precision a(0:n), b(0:n), c(0:n), s(0:times), sum

c initialization
      do i = 0, n
         a(i) = i + 1
         b(i) = 0.3
         c(i) = 0.0
      enddo
      do j = 0, times
         s(j) = j * 0.2
      enddo

c timing the operation
      sum = 0.0
      t0 = etime(time)
      do j = 0, times
         sum = sum + c(0)
```

CODE EXAMPLE 5-11 Program That Benefits From -xprefetch Optimization *(Continued)*

```
       do i = 0, n
          c(i) = a(i) + s(j) * b(i)
       enddo
    enddo
    t1 = etime(time)

c print the runtime
    print *, "sum = ", sum
    write(6,'("RUNTIME: ",f6.2," seconds")') t1-t0
    end
```

We compile this program with and without the -xprefetch option of Forte Developer 6 update 1 Fortran 77 compiler. In the former case, to make sure that the compiler used the prefetch instruction in the generated code, we can look at the disassembled code.

```
example% dis example_xprefetch | grep prefetch
    11298:   c5 6b 60 80        prefetch     [%o5 + 128] , 2
    1129c:   c5 6b 20 80        prefetch     [%o4 + 128] , 2
    11324:   c5 6a e0 40        prefetch     [%o3 + 64] , 2
    1149c:   c5 6a a0 80        prefetch     [%o2 + 128] , 2
    116dc:   c1 6a 60 80        prefetch     [%o1 + 128] , 0
    116e0:   c1 6b e0 80        prefetch     [%o7 + 128] , 0
    11748:   c5 68 60 40        prefetch     [%g1 + 64] , 2
```

The effect of using -xprefetch on runtime of the program on an Ultra 60 system is shown in the following figure.

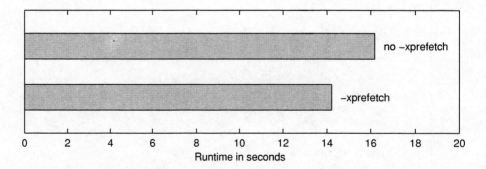

FIGURE 5-13 Performance Effect of -xprefetch Option—Runs on an Ultra 60 (Forte Developer 6 Update 1 Compiler)

The effect of prefetching is more pronounced on a higher latency Enterprise 10000 system as one can see from the next figure. Higher latency also explains the increase in the runtime of this program.

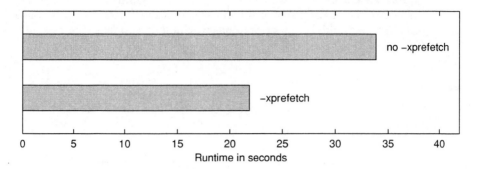

FIGURE 5-14 Performance Effect of `-xprefetch` Option—Runs on an Enterprise 10000 (400 MHzUltraSPARC II Processors With 8 MB Level 2 Cache; Forte Developer 6 Update 1 Compiler)

Because of the P-cache implemented in UltraSPARC III processor, prefetching has even greater effect on UltraSPARC III-based systems. We will discuss some issues relevant to data prefetching on UltraSPARC III in the section on `pragma prefetch` in Chapter 6.

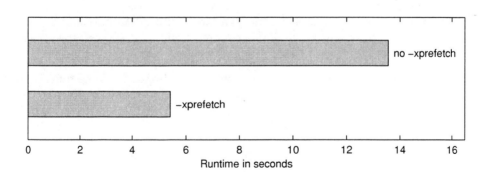

FIGURE 5-15 Performance Effect of `-xprefetch` Option—Runs on a Sun Blade 1000 (Forte Developer 6 Update 1 Compiler)

We recommend using the -xprefetch option selectively for the routines that have large loops and account for large fractions of computational time. Using -xprefetch in compilation of the entire application may result in degraded performance, especially for UltraSPARC I and sometimes for UltraSPARC II-based systems. Greater control over the placement of the prefetch instructions can be accomplished with compiler pragmas (Chapter 6) or by inlining assembly templates (Chapter 8).

Summary

Though importance of proper compiler options for performance optimization cannot be overestimated, the options should be applied selectively. If the size of the binaries or compilation speed is important, only parts of the application identified through profiling need to be compiled with high optimization.

The -fast macro is a collection of the most efficient optimization options. To be effective, the other options that set or disable various optimizations or specify the compilation target (like -xarch) should follow -fast, as the compiler parses the option list once from left to right. The -xtarget macro should generally be avoided as it may introduce unintentional dependency on the compile-time platform.

The choice of target architecture is very important. If an application doesn't target pre-UltraSPARC platforms, -xarch=v8plus[a,b] and -xarch=v9[a,b] should be used for 32-bit and 64-bit programs, respectively. Additionally the -xchip option, which does not limit binary compatibility, can be used to specify code scheduling for a particular processor implementation.

Inlining can improve application performance by reducing the function call overhead, by allowing cross-function optimization, and sometimes by reducing register window spills. Inlining within a single module is invoked with the -xO4 optimization level with no additional flags needed. The -xinline and -xcrossfile options can be used to allow inlining across file boundaries, but can prevent inlining of some functions within a single file that would otherwise be inlined with -xO4.

The -xvector option instructs the compiler to replace the mathematical intrinsic calls with their vectorized counterparts. This can improve the performance of these operations if they are used within large loops.

The -xsfpconst option can give a considerable boost for the performance of the single-precision C applications that don't declare floating-point constants as single-precision quantities. By default, floating-point constants are treated as doubles which can slow down the operations performed on them.

We concluded the chapter discussing optimization with -xprofile and -xprefetch options, both of which should be used selectively and, in general, can degrade performance if misused. The profile-feedback optimization can improve the performance of the programs with consistent execution patterns, while applications with large loops and predictable memory access patterns may benefit from selective use of -xprefetch.

## CHAPTER 6

Advanced Compiler Optimizations

In this chapter, we continue our discussion of compiler optimizations and provide an overview of additional and sometimes more aggressive compiler optimizations. These include optimizations that require certain assumptions on the data dependencies, pointer alias relationships and on memory usage.

We describe optimizations that affect handling of floating-point arithmetic by the compiler. In most cases, the use of these optimizations preserves the correctness of results, but they may not be suitable if Institute of Electrical and Electronics Engineers (IEEE)-compliant behavior is expected in an application. An overview of the IEEE standard for floating-point arithmetic is given at the beginning of the chapter. This is followed by description of compiler options that facilitate data alignment, generation of speculative memory loads, and pointer alias disambiguation in C programs. Some of the options described in this chapter are invoked when the -fast option (see previous chapter) is specified.

Later in the chapter, we describe several compiler pragmas that can be used to provide specific optimization information regarding regions of source code. In particular, we focus on pragma pipeloop, which allows controlling software pipelining of program loops.

IEEE Floating-Point Arithmetic

The IEEE standard 754 (*IEEE Standard for Binary Floating-Point Arithmetic, ANSI/IEEE Standard 754-1985*) was introduced in the 1980s and was designed to standardize the binary representation of, as well as the operations on, floating-point numbers. IEEE also standardizes handling such runtime problems as division by zero, overflow, and invalid operations. This standard is implemented on multiple hardware platforms and ensures similar[1] behavior of floating-point applications on different architectures.

This section gives a brief overview of IEEE arithmetic. Details of the implementation of the IEEE 754 standard in the Solaris Operating Environment can be found in the *Numerical Computation Guide* and in the "Floating-Point Arithmetic" chapter in the *Fortran Programming Guide*. For information on the history of the standard, see [Severance98], [Severance98b].

In some cases, the convenience of standardized floating-point arithmetic comes at a price of degraded performance. In this chapter, we will discuss some of the compiler options that allow the optimizer to violate the IEEE 754 rules in favor of improved performance. A program compiled with Sun compilers with an option that allows non-IEEE-compliant arithmetic prints a warning to `stderr` upon completion.

```
Note: Nonstandard floating-point mode enabled
  See the Numerical Computation Guide, ieee_sun(3M)
```

In some situations, it might be desirable to suppress this warning message (for example, in the case of MPI programs, the warning is printed for each process in the parallel run). The message can be suppressed using the `ieee_retrospective` function defined in the `libsunmath` library and `sunmath.h` header file as illustrated below (see Chapter 7 for a description of the `sunmath` library).

CODE EXAMPLE 6-1   Suppression of IEEE Warning Message

```
/* example to show ieee_retrospective
function to suppress IEEE warning message
cc -fast example_noieeewarn.c -lsunmath -DNOIEEEWARN
 -o example_noieewarn */

#include <stdio.h>
#include <sunmath.h>
#ifdef NOIEEEWARN
```

---

1. Some differences may arise because of different use of guarding bits that are used to prevent precision loss due to cancellation.

CODE EXAMPLE 6-1 Suppression of IEEE Warning Message *(Continued)*

```
void ieee_retrospective(FILE *f);
#endif

int main()
{
    ieee_retrospective(stderr);
    return 0;
}

#ifdef NOIEEEWARN
void ieee_retrospective(FILE *f)
{
 fprintf(f," No IEEE Warning\n");
}
#endif
```

Using the Forte Developer 6 update 1 C compiler, we compile the preceding example with -fast option (later in this chapter we will discuss the components of -fast that affect floating-point arithmetic).

```
example% cc -fast example_noieee.c -lsunmath -o example_ieeewarn
example% cc -fast example_noieee.c -lsunmath -DNOIEEEWARN \
        -o example_noieeewarn
```

Now, running on an Ultra 60, we can see that the message is suppressed in the case of the example_noieeewarn executable.

```
example% example_ieeewarn
  Note: Nonstandard floating-point mode enabled
  See the Numerical Computation Guide, ieee_sun(3M)
example% example_noieewarn
  No IEEE Warning
```

A user defined ieee_retrospective function can be called from Fortran programs in a similar fashion to suppress the nonstandard arithmetic warning message.

Binary Storage Format

The IEEE standard 754 defines the single-precision and double-precision formats of the floating-point numbers. The standard defines the binary representations for these formats that occupy 32 and 64 bits (4 and 8 bytes, respectively). The bits are divided into a sign bit (zero for positive numbers, one for negative numbers), exponent (base two) bits, and the mantissa or the fraction bits. The IEEE standard sets the number of the exponent bits to 8 for single-precision and 11 for double-precision representation. The mantissa occupies the remaining 23 (single-precision) and 52 (double-precision) bits. The bit layout of the binary representations is shown in FIGURE 6-1, where s is the sign bit, e is the exponent, and f is the fractional part or the mantissa.

Single-precision

s	e	f
31	30...23	22...0

Double-precision

s	e	f
63	62...52	51...0

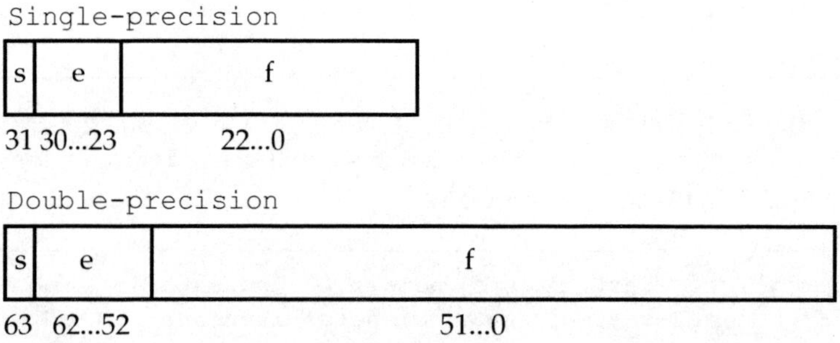

FIGURE 6-1 Bit Layout of Single-Precision and Double-Precision Floating-Point Numbers in IEEE Format

We should point out that the order of bytes in multibyte data storage units is different for big endian and little endian platforms, which complicates porting applications that rely on particular byte order. Refer to [Zucker98] for recommendations on writing endian independent code.

The unsigned value of the exponent is shifted by a bias value which is equal to 127 for single-precision and 1,023 for double-precision, making the ranges of the biased exponent -127 to 128, and -1,023 to 1,024 respectively.

The floating-point numbers are represented as:

$$(-1)^s \times 2^{(e-bias)} \times 1.f$$

where s is the sign bit, e is the exponent, and f is the binary fractional part or the mantissa.

To illustrate the bit representation of floating-point numbers, we can print several double-precision values in hexadecimal and convert them to binary.

CODE EXAMPLE 6-2   Hexadecimal Representation of Floating-Point Numbers

```
/* example_ieee.c */
/* cc -o example_ieee example_ieee.c */
#include<stdio.h>
int main(){
   printf("%11X ;\n", -1.0);
   printf("%11X ;\n", -2.0);
   printf("%11X ;\n", -4.0/3.0);
   return 0;
}
```

This example prints the hexadecimal representations of -1.0, -2.0, and $-4/3$. To convert the output to binary, we can use the bc(1) utility.

```
example% cc -o example_ieee example_ieee.c
example% example_ieee
BFF0000000000000 ;
C000000000000000 ;
BFF5555555555555 ;
example% echo 'ibase=16; obase=2; ' 'example_ieee' | bc
1011111111110000000000000000000000000000000000000000000000000000
1100000000000000000000000000000000000000000000000000000000000000
1011111111110101010101010101010101010101010101010101010101010101
```

The first output line corresponds to the binary representation of $-1.0 = (-1)^1 * 2^{(1023-1023)} * 1.0$. The 52 zeros in the binary string correspond to the zero fractional part in the representation of -1.0. They are preceded by 10 ones that form the value 1,023 of the biased exponent and the sign bit set to 1. The second binary string represents $-2.0 = (-1)^1 * 2^{(1024-1023)} * 1.0$. The only difference here is that the value of the biased exponent is 1,024, which corresponds to 10000000000 in the exponent field of the binary form. The last string represents $-4/3 = (-1)^1 * 2^{(1023-1023)} * 1.010101 \ldots {}_{(2)}$. Note the alternating string of zeros and ones in the binary fractional part of the representation. The precision loss is inevitable for this floating-point number since the binary (and decimal) representation of $4/3$ is an infinite fraction.

The normalized fractional part of this representation always has 1 as a leading digit. This digit is not stored, and is assumed to be 1, which saves an extra bit of storage for the mantissa. A side-effect of this space-saving technique is that zero cannot be represented by the formula above. Additionally, the values of infinity (positive and negative) and NaN, or not a number, defined in the standard require special representation.

To accommodate these values, the IEEE standard reserves the extreme values of the exponent (all zeros and all ones). The infinity is represented by all ones in the exponent and with all zeros in the mantissa. The sign bit determines the sign of the infinity (+Inf, -Inf). NaN, or not a number, is represented by all ones in the exponent and any nonzero combination in the mantissa. All zeros in the exponent are used in the denormalized numbers. In a special case, zero is represented by all zeros in the exponent and in the mantissa. For a description of denormalized numbers, as well as extended precision, refer to the *Numerical Computation Guide*.

Special values reduce the range of the biased exponent available for other numbers by one on each end. Therefore, the ranges of the exponent for nonspecial values are -126 to 127 for single-precision and -1,022 to 1,023 for double-precision. The fractional part can be represented by any bit combination, and can take any values between 1.0 and 1.111...$_{(2)}$ or $2-2^{-23}$ for single-precision and $2-2^{-52}$ for double-precision.

The smallest positive normalized number that can be represented in single-precision is 2^{-126}x1.0, or approximately 1.17×10^{-38}. The largest number is $2^{127} \times (2-2^{-23})$ or 3.40x10^{38}. Similarly the smallest and largest normalized numbers that can be represented in double-precision are $2^{-1022} \times 1.0$ and $2^{1023} \times (2-2^{-52})$, or approximately 2.22×10^{-308} and 1.80×10^{308} in decimal.

The 23 or 52 precision bits in the binary representation of the single- and double-precision numbers translate into approximately 7 and 15 significant decimal digits ($\log_{10}(2^{23}) = 6.92...$ and $\log_{10}(2^{52}) = 15.65...$).

Trap Handling and -ftrap

The IEEE floating-point arithmetic standard identifies five types of floating-point exceptions:

- *Inexact* – The result of the operation cannot be represented without loss of precision.
- *Underflow* – The result of the operation is smaller than the smallest floating-point number that can be represented in given precision.
- *Overflow* – The result of the operation is larger than the largest number that can be represented in given precision.
- *Divide by zero* – The operation performs a division by zero value.
- *Invalid* – The operation is mathematically undefined.

Each of these exceptions is handled by a corresponding trap. Sun compilers allow enabling or disabling the traps with the -ftrap flag. This option can be set to one or more of the following: %all, %none, common, [no%]invalid, [no%]overflow, [no%]underflow, [no%]division, [no%]inexact. To be effective, the -ftrap option should be used for compilation of the main module. It affects the trap-handling behavior of the entire program.

The -ftrap=%none option disables the floating-point traps, -ftrap=common invokes the traps for overflow, division by zero, and invalid operation. Note that Sun Fortran compilers have different default values for -ftrap if no value is specified. The default for Fortran 77 compiler is -ftrap=%none, and for Fortran 90 the default is -ftrap=common.

The following example illustrates all five exceptions. We explicitly include the f77_floatingpoint.h file which defines the exception flags read with the ieee_flags(3M) call.

CODE EXAMPLE 6-3   Five IEEE Floating-Point Exceptions

```
C example_exceptions.F
C f77 -ftrap=%none example_exceptions.F -DINEXACT \
C      -DUNDERFLOW -DOVERFLOW -DDIVIDE_BY_ZERO \
C      -DINVALID_OPERATION -o example_exceptions
#include "f77_floatingpoint.h"
      character*16 out
      double-precision a, d_min_normal, d_max_normal
      integer div, flgs, inv, inx, over, under
C
#ifdef INEXACT
      a=3.0d0
      a=1.0d0 / a                              ! Inxact
      print '("inexact computation: a = ", d15.8)', a
#endif
#ifdef UNDERFLOW
      a = d_min_normal() / 10.0d0             ! Cause underflow
      print '("underflow:        a = ", d15.8)', a
#endif
#ifdef OVERFLOW
      a = d_max_normal() * 10.0d0             ! Cause overflow
      print '("overflow:         a = ", d15.8)', a
#endif
#ifdef DIVIDE_BY_ZERO
      a=0.0d0
      a=1.0 / a                               ! Divide by zero
      print '("divide by zero:   a = ", d15.8)', a
#endif
```

```
#ifdef INVALID_OPERATION
     a=log(-1.0d0)                              ! Invalid operation
     print '("invalid operation:    a = ", d15.8)', a
#endif
C
     flgs=ieee_flags('get','exception','',out)     ! Which are
     inx  = and(rshift(flgs, fp_inexact)  , 1)  ! raised?
     div  = and(rshift(flgs, fp_division) , 1)  !
     under = and(rshift(flgs, fp_underflow), 1)  !
     over = and(rshift(flgs, fp_overflow) , 1)  !
     inv  = and(rshift(flgs, fp_invalid)  , 1)  !
C
     print *, "Highest priority exception is: ", out
     print *, 'Exceptions raised (1 = raised; 0 = it is not):'
     print *, ' invalid   divide   overflow underflow inexact'
     print '(5i9)', inv, div, over, under, inx
     i = ieee_flags('clear', 'exception', 'all', out) ! Clear
     end
```

When all exceptions are invoked and `-ftrap=%none` flag is used, the program is not interrupted and runs through completion.

```
example% f77 -ftrap=%none example_exceptions.F \
   -DINEXACT -DUNDERFLOW -DOVERFLOW -DDIVIDE_BY_ZERO \
   -DINVALID_OPERATION -o example_exceptions
example% example_exceptions
inexact computation: a =  0.33333333D+00
underflow:           a =  0.22250739-308
overflow:            a = Infinity
divide by zero:      a = Infinity
invalid operation:   a = NaN
 Highest priority exception is: invalid
 Exceptions raised (1 = raised; 0 = it is not):
  invalid   divide   overflow underflow inexact
        1         1         1         1         1
```

Setting -ftrap=common results in the program aborting at runtime with the following overflow exception.

```
example% f77 -ftrap=common example_exceptions.F \
   -DINEXACT -DUNDERFLOW -DOVERFLOW -DDIVIDE_BY_ZERO \
   -DINVALID_OPERATION -o example_exceptions
example% example_exceptions
inexact computation: a =  0.33333333D+00
underflow:           a =  0.22250739-308
Floating point exception 4, overflow, occurred at address 11030.
Abort
```

Gradual Underflow and -fns

We already mentioned the denormalized or subnormal numbers that are represented with all zeros in the exponent and nonzero fractional part. The values of subnormal numbers are computed as:

$$(-1)^s \times 2^{(1-bias)} \times 0.f$$

Note that the leading bit in the fractional part is 0, not 1 as in the representation of normalized numbers. This allows the subnormal numbers to approach zero gradually (extending the range of the normalized numbers as the number óf leading zeros increases) keeping the relative errors of the operations bounded. This is known as *gradual underflow*.

In many cases, the numerical benefits of gradual underflow are not needed, and the numbers that are smaller than what fits in the standard representation can be treated as zeros rather than represented as subnormal numbers for improved performance. The option -fns of Sun compilers disables gradual underflow and allows this non-IEEE-compliant handling of floating-point numbers. Similarly to the -ftrap option, -fns affects the behavior of the entire program and should be used for compilation of the main module. The -fns option is part of the -fast macro discussed earlier in Chapter 5.

To see the effect of this flag, we can recompile the previous example with -fns (we can enable just the underflow exception with -DUNDERFLOW).

```
example% f77 -ftrap=common -DUNDERFLOW -fns \
        example_exceptions.F -o example_exceptions
example% example_exceptions
underflow:         a =  0.00000000D+00
 Highest priority exception is: underflow
 Exceptions raised (1 = raised; 0 = it is not):
  invalid   divide   overflow underflow inexact
         0        0        0        1        1
Note: IEEE floating-point exception traps enabled:
    overflow;  division by zero;  invalid operation;
Nonstandard floating-point mode enabled
 See the Numerical Computation Guide, ieee_handler(3M),
ieee_sun(3M)
```

Unlike the example in the previous section, which was compiled without -fns, the value of a is replaced with zero. Note that the inexact exception was also raised.

The following example shows the performance penalty of gradual underflow.

CODE EXAMPLE 6-4 Gradual Underflow Example

```
C example_fns.F
C f77 -ftrap=%none example_fns.F -xO4 -dalign -xarch=v8plus \
C     -o example_fns -fns
#include "f77_floatingpoint.h"
      double-precision small, sum
      integer*8 i
      real t1,t2,etime,time(2)

      small = d_min_normal()
      sum=0.0d0
      t1=etime(time)
      do i=1,100000000
         small=small/1.0000000001d0
         sum=sum+small
      enddo
      t2=etime(time)

      print '("sum = ", d20.10, "  small = ", d15.8)', sum, small
      write(6,'("RUNTIME: ",f6.2," seconds")') t2-t1
      end
```

When compiled with and without -fns, this example shows very different runtimes (FIGURE 6-2). We can also see that the executable compiled with -fns replaces the underflow values with zeros.

```
example% f77 -ftrap=%none example_fns.F -xO4 -dalign \
        -xarch=v8plus -o example_fns
example% example_fns
sum =      0.1462045527D-30     small =   0.14547475D-38
RUNTIME:   4.89 seconds
```

```
example% f77 -ftrap=%none example_fns.F -xO4 -dalign \
        -xarch=v8plus -o example_fns -fns
example% example_fns
sum =      0.0000000000D+00     small =   0.00000000D+00
RUNTIME:   1.78 seconds
```

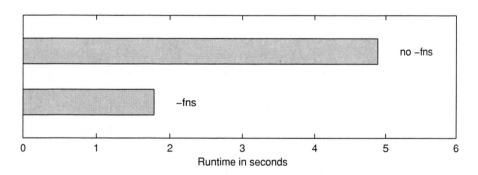

FIGURE 6-2 Performance Impact of Gradual Underflow—Runs on an Ultra 80 (Forte Developer 6 Compiler)

The Sun WorkShop 5.0 (and later) compilers allow passing yes or no values to the -fns flag to override the -fns settings that may come from predefined macros.

-fsimple

One of the options that allow non-IEEE arithmetic is -fsimple. This flag can be used to specify the extent of simplifying assumptions an optimizer can make concerning floating-point operations.

This option can take on three values. The following discussion closely follows the description of this flag as given in the section on compiler options in the *Fortran User's Guide*.

n = 0 No simplifying assumptions are made and the generated code conforms to the IEEE 754 standard.

n = 1 Allow the compiler to make conservative simplification. Resulting code does not strictly conform to IEEE 754, but numeric results of most programs are unchanged. With -fsimple = 1, the optimizer can assume the following:

- IEEE 754 default rounding and trapping modes do not change after process initialization.

- Computations producing no visible result other than potential floating-point exceptions can be deleted.

- Computations with infinities or NaNs as operands need not propagate NaNs to their results; that is, $x*0$ can be replaced by 0.

- Computations do not depend on the sign of zero.

If the -fsimple=1 option is specified, the optimizer is not allowed to optimize completely without regard to roundoff or exceptions. In particular, a floating-point computation cannot be replaced by one that produces different results when rounding modes are held constant at runtime.

n = 2 With -fsimple=2, the optimizer is allowed aggressive optimizations that may lead programs to produce different numeric results due to changes in the order of operations and rounding. For example, -fsimple=2 permits the optimizer to attempt to replace repeated computations of x/y with $x*z$, where $z = 1/y$ is computed once and saved in a temporary, thereby eliminating costly divide operations.

Other optimizations that occur with -fsimple=2 are cycle shrinking, height reduction of the directed acyclic graph representing the dependency chain of the computation, cross-iteration common subexpression elimination, and scalar replacement (see [Muchnick97]). It is best to use -fsimple=2 in conjunction with -xdepend and other high optimization flags. Starting with the Forte Developer 6 release of the compilers, the -fast macro sets -fsimple=2 (see TABLE 5-4 in Chapter 5).

Consider the example program that computes the dot product of two vectors.

CODE EXAMPLE 6-5   Effect of -fsimple Optimizations

```
! example_fsimple.f90
! f90 -fast -fsimple=[0|1|2] -xarch=v8plus example_fsimple.f90 \
!           -o example_fsimple
program dotsumtst
implicit none
integer, parameter :: sgl=SELECTED_REAL_KIND(p=6)
integer, parameter :: dbl=SELECTED_REAL_KIND(p=13)
integer, parameter :: numit=1000, nele=100000
integer :: i,nloop
real (KIND=dbl) :: dsum,dum1=0.0,dum2,sum=0.0
real (KIND=dbl), dimension(nele+9) :: a,b
real (KIND=sgl) :: tsum,tarray(2),t1=0.0, t2=0.0,etime
external etime

! when compiled with -ftrap=%none, this line will produce
! arithmetic exception unless -fsimple=n [n=1 or n=2] is
! also used in compilation
dum2 = 20.0/dum1

do i=1,nele+8    ! initialization of a() and b()
   a(i) = i*0.001 + nloop
   b(i) = nloop*2.0 + i - 4.6
enddo

t1 = etime(tarray)          ! time repeated calls to dotsum kernel
do nloop=1,numit
   call dotsum(nele,a,b,dsum)
enddo
t2 = t2 + (etime(tarray) - t1)
sum = sum + dsum
write(*,'("sum= ",e12.3," RUNTIME:  ",f6.2)') sum/nloop,t2
end program

subroutine dotsum(nele,a,b,sum)
implicit none
integer, parameter :: dbl=SELECTED_REAL_KIND(p=13)
integer, INTENT(in) :: nele
real (KIND=dbl), INTENT(in), dimension(nele) :: a,b
real (KIND=dbl), INTENT(inout) :: sum
integer :: i
```

```
sum=0.d0
do i=1,nele
    sum = sum + a(i)*b(i)
enddo
return
end subroutine
```

If we compile this with -fast -fsimple=0, this program causes an exception to occur as the program has a statement of form

```
dum1 = 0.d0
dum2 = 20.d0/dum1
```

On the other hand, compilation with -fsimple=1 or -fsimple=2 causes the exception to be ignored, because the above two statements are superfluous and have no other program effect, so the optimizer eliminates them.

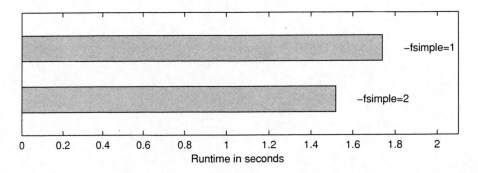

FIGURE 6-3   Performance Effect of -fsimple=1 and -fsimple=2 Options—Runs on a Sun Ultra 60 (Forte Developer 6 Update 1 Compiler)

The dot product requires two double-precision floating-point loads and two floating-point operations (one faddd and one fmuld instruction) at each iteration of the loop. On an UltraSPARC II processor (4-way superscalar), these operations can be performed at best in two processor cycles.

Evaluating the efficiency of the software pipelining of the loops (see section on pragma pipeloop later where we will discuss the concept of software pipelining in more detail), we find that with -fsimple=2, the best possible schedule is generated (assuming hits in level 2 cache). Specifically, the duration of each stage in the generated software pipeline (as modeled in processor cycles, see discussion later) is 3 for -fsimple=1 and 2 for the -fsimple=2 case, respectively. The two floating-point operations (addition and multiplication) are fully overlapped with the two memory operations (loads) in the code compiled with -fsimple=2 option. The additional optimizations performed when −fsimple=2 is set (such as cycle shrinking and height reduction) facilitate the improvement in software pipelining efficiency.

Now, running on an Ultra 60 system, we find that the time in the routine dotsum (in seconds) is approximately 14% slower when compiled with −fsimple=1 than when compiled with −fsimple=2 (see FIGURE 6-3).

We can also illustrate the action of the −fsimple option with an example that illustrates strength reduction. As mentioned above, with the −fsimple=2 setting the compiler may attempt to replace repeated divisions with corresponding multiplications (that is, by the reciprocal of the denominator in the division operation).

CODE EXAMPLE 6-6 Strength Reduction Optimization With −fsimple=2

```
C example_fsimple.f
C f77 -xO4 -dalign example_fsimple.f -fsimple=2 \
C           -o example_fsimple
      parameter (n=10000,iter=10000)
      double-precision a(n)
      real*4 t0,t1,etime,time(2)

c initialization
      do i=1,n
         a(i)=1.0d0 - 1.0d0/i
      enddo

c strength reduction possible for repeated divisions
      t0=etime(time)
      do j=1,iter
         do i=1,n
            a(i)=a(i)/3.0d0
         enddo
         do i=n,2,-1
            a(i)=a(i)*3.0d0
         enddo
      enddo
      t1=etime(time)
      write(6,'("a(n)= ",f10.6," RUNTIME: ",f6.2)') a(n), t1-t0
      end
```

The assembly shows fmuld instructions instead of fdivd and extra unrolling when this example is compiled with −fsimple=2 instead of −fsimple=1. This difference translates into more than fourfold improvement in performance (FIGURE 6-4).

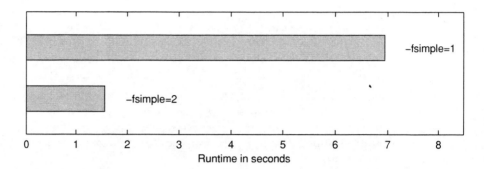

FIGURE 6-4 Strength Reduction Optimization Performed With -fsimple=2 on a Sun Ultra 60 (Forte Developer 6 Update 1 Compiler)

For performance critical modules of an application, we recommend usage of this flag to achieve the best possible floating-point optimizations.

In most cases, changing the order of the operands or performing other algebraic transformations may result in different round off with at most, the few last digits of the result affected. However, in some cases, when the computation is performed with the operands of very different magnitude, the cancellation may cause catastrophic precision loss and the result can be changed dramatically. For example, an expression $-1 + 10^{20} - 10^{20} + 1$ cannot be represented without precision loss even in double-precision. Because of the cancellation, it will be computed as 1 if the operations are performed from left to right as is done in Fortran. If the optimizer changes this expression to an algebraically equivalent one $1+10^{20}-10^{20}-1$, the result of the computation will be -1. Another transformation, $10^{20} - 10^{20} + 1 - 1$, leads to the answer 0.

If the algebraically equivalent transformations allowed by -fsimple considerably change the result of a computation, it may indicate that the algorithm used in the program is numerically unstable. In that case, the IEEE-compliant computation does not necessarily lead to the correct solution, but rather provides a standardized way of selecting an answer from the range of the possible values.

CODE EXAMPLE 6-7 Example of Algebraically Equivalent Operations Producing Different Results

```
c example_order.f
c f77 example_order.f -o example_order
      real*8 a,b,c,d
      a=-1.0d0
      b=1.0d20
      c=-1.0d20
      d=1.0d0
```

CODE EXAMPLE 6-7   Example of Algebraically Equivalent Operations Producing Different Results *(Continued)*

```
c
      print*,"a+b+c+d = ", a+b+c+d
      print*,"d+b+c+a = ", d+b+c+a
      print*,"b+c+a+d = ", b+c+a+d
      end
```

Compiling the above program and running it:

```
example% f77 example_order.f -o example_order
example% example_order
 a+b+c+d =     1.0000000000000
 d+b+c+a =    -1.0000000000000
 b+c+a+d =    0.
```

We should also mention other compiler options that affect the IEEE compliance of floating-point arithmetic. The -fnonstd flag expands to -fns -ftrap=common on SPARC architectures. The -fround option can be set to one of the four IEEE rounding modes: nearest, toward zero, negative, or positive. It takes effect at the start of the program.

-dalign

Most modern microprocessors have preferred alignment restrictions on data types for performance purposes (see section 6.3.1 in [Weaver94] for a discussion about SPARC architecture). Data aligned on its "natural" or "preferred" byte-boundaries can be accessed substantially faster than misaligned data. For example, on the UltraSPARC processor, Fortran double-precision or C/C++ double data that is aligned on 8-byte boundaries can be accessed with a single double-word load/store (ldd/std) instruction, as opposed to two single-word load/store (ld/st) instructions if it were aligned on 4-byte boundaries, or worse with eight byte-sized load/store (ldb/stb) instructions if it were not even aligned on 4-byte boundaries. The performance penalty of misaligned data can be tremendous, therefore, proper data alignment can be a big performance win by helping improve the memory bandwidth of the application.

"Preferred" data alignment rules for different data-types are specified in the standards for different programming languages. For example, the ANSI/ISO rules for data alignment in the C language are listed in the section on "ANSI/ISO C Data Representations" in the *C User's Guide* for Sun C compiler. Similar rules exist for Fortran data types.

However, in general, the compiler cannot assume "preferred" byte-alignment in a user application. In Fortran, the use of COMMON blocks and EQUIVALENCE statements with mixed data types and incompatible lengths is one situation where the compiler makes conservative assumptions on data alignment. By default, it uses an alignment of 4 bytes. The use of the flag -dalign changes the data layout and allows generation of double-word load/store instructions for double-precision data in Fortran and double data in C/C++ programs, respectively. The compiler appropriately inserts padding in Fortran COMMON blocks as necessary; therefore, use of this flag can lead to problems if the program assumes a certain alignment of data for correct functioning. A well-written program should never depend on assumptions that data are aligned in a particular fashion for correct execution.

Consider the following program which copies array b into array a.

CODE EXAMPLE 6-8   Example of -dalign Optimization

```
C example_dalign.f
C £77 -xO4 example_dalign.f -o example_dalign (-dalign)
      program example_dalign
      parameter(numit=1000, n=100000, isz=(2*1024*1024))
      real*4 cc(isz), etime, tarray(2), t1, t2
      real*8 a(n),b(n)
      character argv*10

c read the argument
      call getarg(1,argv )
      if ((argv.ne."L2").and.(argv.ne."memory")) then
        print*,"example_dalign L2 | memory"
        stop
      endif


        sum = 0.0
      do nloop=1,numit
c initalization
        do i=1,n
          a(i) = i*0.001 + nloop
          b(i) = nloop*2.0 + i - 4.6
        enddo

c   clear the cache for runs from memory
        if (argv.eq."memory") then
          do i=1,isz
            cc(i) = nloop + i*0.00001
            sum = sum + cc(i)
          enddo
```

Example of -dalign Optimization *(Continued)*

```
        endif
c timing the call
        t1 = etime(tarray)
        call equal(n,a,b)
        t2 = t2 + (etime(tarray) - t1)
      enddo

      write(*,*) 'b= ',b(n),'  a= ',a(n), '  sum= ', sum
      write(6,'("RUNTIME: ",f6.2," seconds")') t2
      end

      subroutine equal(n,a,b)
      real*8 a(*), b(*)
      do i=1,n
         a(i)=b(i)
      enddo
      return
      end
```

```
example% f77 -xO4 -S example_dalign.f -o equal.s.nodalign
example% f77 -xO4 -dalign -S example_dalign.f -o equal.s.dalign
```

Comparing the two assembly files, one can see that use of -dalign flag causes the compiler to generate ldd/std instructions while, without it, only ld/st (4-byte load/store) instructions are generated. One additionally notices that with -dalign, the inner loop has been unrolled and better instruction scheduling (load-store separation) is used. This is because the use of -dalign implies an 8-byte data alignment and allows the compiler to better carry out other aggressive optimizations. (In this case, software pipelining of the inner loop; we will discuss software pipelining of the loops later in this chapter.)

The example is set up such that the copying operation happens on data that can either reside in memory or in the level 2 cache of the processor. Compiling it as follows, using the Forte Developer 6 Fortran 77 compiler with and without the -dalign option, and running it on an Ultra 80 machine, we obtained timing results in routine equal. These are plotted in FIGURE 6-5.

When this option is used for one module (or routine), it is preferable that all compilation units use it. Specifically, routines in the same call-chain that exchange data (either pass arguments or share global variables) need to be compiled using -dalign.

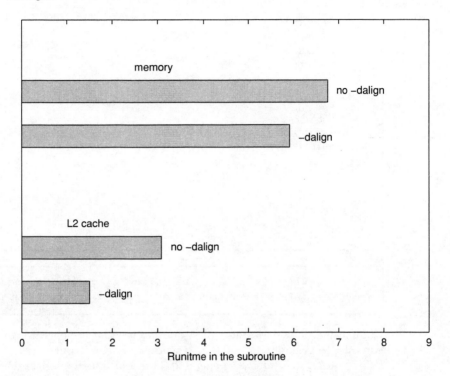

FIGURE 6-5   Effect of -dalign Option on Time Spent in a Subroutine Call—Runs Performed on an Ultra 60 (Forte Developer 6 Update 1 Compiler)

-xsafe=mem

Another option available for compiling binaries for UltraSPARC (V9) platforms is -xsafe=mem. This option allows the compiler to use the speculative load instruction and is only effective if used with -xO5 optimization and when -xarch=v8plus[a,b] or v9[a,b] is specified.

This option allows the compiler to move loads ahead of branches and provides another way for separating the load of datum from its use. This may result in performance benefit for applications that need to use conditionals in large loops.

The -xsafe=mem option can be used if no memory-based traps occur during application execution. Applications that handle exceptional memory-related situations cannot be safely built with this option.

Possible side effects of speculative loads may include extra page faults, cache misses, as well as cache pollution by the data that will not be used.

We illustrate this option with the following example program.

CODE EXAMPLE 6-9   Program That Benefits From -xsafe=mem Optimization

```
/* example_xsafe.c */
/* cc -xarch=v8plus -xO5 example_xsafe.c -o \
   example_xsafe (-xsafe=mem) */
#include<stdio.h>
#include <sys/time.h>
hrtime_t gethrtime(void);
int main()
{
    int a[12000],*p, b_val, b[200], i;
    long long int start, end, nano=1000000000;

    for(i=0;i<200;i++){     /* initalize a[] and b[] */
        b[i]=i;
    }
    for(i=0;i<12000;i++){
        a[i]= (i%10) + 20;
    }

    start = gethrtime();
    for(i=0;i<50000;i++){
        for(p=a+1; p<=a+10000; p+=8){
            b_val = b[(*(p))];
```

```
            if (( (b_val >> *(p+1)) & 1) != 0) break;
            b_val = b[(*(p+1))];
            if (( (b_val >> *(p+2)) & 1) != 0) break;
            b_val = b[(*(p+2))];
            if (( (b_val >> *(p+3)) & 1) != 0) break;
            b_val = b[(*(p+3))];
            if (( (b_val >> *(p+4)) & 1) != 0) break;
            b_val = b[(*(p+4))];
            if (( (b_val >> *(p+5)) & 1) != 0) break;
            b_val = b[(*(p+5))];
            if (( (b_val >> *(p+6)) & 1) != 0) break;
            b_val = b[(*(p+6))];
            if (( (b_val >> *(p+7)) & 1) != 0) break;
            b_val = b[(*(p+7))];
            if (( (b_val >> *(p+8)) & 1) != 0) break;
        }
    }
    end = gethrtime();
    printf("Finish i=%d, *p = %ld \n", i, *p);
    printf("RUNTIME: %6.2f seconds \n",(end-start)/(float)nano);
    return 0;
}
```

The use of -xsafe=mem results in considerable performance benefit as can be seen in FIGURE 6-6.

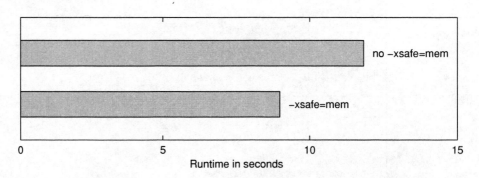

FIGURE 6-6   Performance Impact of -xsafe=mem—Runtimes on Ultra 60 (Sun WorkShop 5.0 Compiler)

We can see the speculative loads in each of the unrolled iterations of the loop when
-xsafe=mem is used.

```
!    19                    !    b_val = b[(*(s+4))];
!    20                    !    if (( (b_val >> *(s+5)) & 1) != 0) break;

/* 0x00f4      20 */              sra       %o3,%o2,%g2
/* 0x00f8         */              lda       [%o0+28]%asi,%o2  ! spec_load
/* 0x00fc         */              and       %g2,1,%g2
/* 0x0100         */              cmp       %g2,0
/* 0x0104         */              bne,pn    %icc,.L77000049
/* 0x0108         */              lda       [%g3+%o4]130,%o3  ! spec_load
/* 0x010c         */              sll       %o1,2,%g3
```

The corresponding part of the disassembly file compiled without -xsafe=mem does
not have speculative loads.

```
!    19                    !    b_val = b[(*(s+4))];
!    20                    !    if (( (b_val >> *(s+5)) & 1) != 0) break;
/* 0x00e0      20 */              ld        [%o0+20],%g2
/* 0x00e4         */              ld        [%o1+%o2],%g3
/* 0x00e8         */              sll       .%g2,2,%o1
/* 0x00ec         */              sra       %g3,%g2,%g2
/* 0x00f0         */              and       %g2,1,%g2
/* 0x00f4         */              cmp       %g2,0
/* 0x00f8         */              bne,a,pn           %icc,.L900000113
/* 0x00fc         */              add       %o7,1,%o7
```

Pointer Alias Analysis Options

In C programs, pointer variables can hide important information about the memory they point to. Specifically, the pointers can point to overlapping regions of memory or, in other words, they can be aliases of one another. This can lead to ambiguous data dependencies in the loops (or other program statements) where these memory locations are accessed. In general, memory alias disambiguation analysis in C programs is very complex (space-time inefficient) for compilers to perform and usually, compilers treat operations through potentially aliased pointers very conservatively. This means that many optimizations occurring as a result of dependency analysis (such as loop unrolling, software pipelining, and redundant load elimination) are not performed, leading to performance degradation.

In this section, we will discuss -xrestrict and -xalias_level options that facilitate pointer alias disambiguation optimizations in the C compiler.

-xrestrict

The -xrestrict flag informs the compiler that the pointers (of same data type) passed as function parameters are restricted or point to distinct regions of storage. This allows the compiler to perform optimization analysis that otherwise risks generating unsafe code. The following example shows single-CPU performance improvement as a result of using this flag. In Chapter 13, we will show its use in the context of compiler parallelization of program loops. Note, the analysis is only performed on function parameters. The -xalias_level option discussed in the next section applies alias disambiguation analysis to all pointers in the program.

The -xrestrict option can take several values: -xrestrict=%none (default) and -xrestrict=%all mean respectively that either none or all of the pointer parameters in a file should be treated as restricted pointers. The -xrestrict=foo option tells a compiler that pointers in a function foo should be treated as restricted.

Consider the following example; specifically we look at the function test.

CODE EXAMPLE 6-10 Benefits of the -xrestrict Option for a C Program

```
/* example_xrestrict.c */
/* cc -xO4 -xtarget=ultra2 -xinline= example_xrestrict.c \
         -o example_xrestrict (-xrestrict)   */
#include <stdio.h>
#include <stdlib.h>
#include <sys/time.h>
```

```c
#define LEN 100000
#define NUMIT 1000
void test(int n, long *a, long *b, long *c, long *d);

int main(int argc, char **argv)
{
   int i,n;
   hrtime_t start, end;
   long *a, *b, *c, *d;
   double ktime=0.0;
   a = (long *) malloc(LEN*sizeof(long));
   b = (long *) malloc(LEN*sizeof(long));
   c = (long *) malloc(LEN*sizeof(long));
   d = (long *) malloc(LEN*sizeof(long));

   for (n=0;n<NUMIT;n++) {
      for (i=0;i<LEN;i++) {
         a[i] = i + n;
         b[i] = 2*n - i;
         c[i] = 0;
         d[i] = 0;
      }
/* now time the kernel */
      start = gethrtime();
      test(LEN-4,a,b,c,d);
      end = gethrtime();
      ktime += (1.e-9)*(end-start);
   }                /* of outermost loop */
   printf(" time in function= %6.2f seconds\n",ktime);
   return 0;
}

void test(int n, long *a, long *b, long *c, long *d)
{
  int i;
  for (i=1;i<n-2;i++) {
     c[i+1] = a[i+2]*b[i];
     d[i+1] = c[i+1]*c[i+1] - a[i-1];
  }
}
```

Using the Sun WorkShop 5.0 C compiler

```
example% cc -xO4 -xtarget=ultra2 -S example_xrestrict.c \
         -o test_norestrict.s
example% cc -xO4 -xtarget=ultra2 -S example_xrestrict.c \
         -xrestrict -o test_restrict.s
```

In the file test_norestrict.s, we can see that no optimization has taken place in the innermost loop. Note specifically, the following statements.

```
st      %o4,[%o2]
ld      [%g1-8],%o3
```

The first statement stores the value c[i+1], and second statement loads a[i-1]. Because alias information is unavailable, a[i-1] has to be reloaded, as it is possible that c[i+2] and a[i] might point to the same location, in which case the previously loaded (at iteration i-3) a[i+2] value cannot be reused. No unrolling or overlapping of computations has taken place.

In file test_restrict.s, the innermost loop has been unrolled five deep, allowing reuse of previously loaded a[i-1] values. Since there are 32 general purpose integer registers in SPARC V8 and V9 architectures, this level of unrolling is close to the maximum that can be done without incurring register spills.

We also note that in test_norestrict.s, the function test is a *leaf routine* (the one that doesn't make further calls) and register windows are not used. On the other hand, in test_restrict.s, the register window model is used (note the use of save, ret, and restore instructions in test_restrict.s, and retl in test_norestrict.s).

The time in function `test` is shown in FIGURE 6-7. Nearly a 15% improvement is observed in the second case. Note that these used the Forte Developer 6 compiler. The reader is encouraged to experiment with Sun WorkShop 5.0 and Forte Developer 6 update 1 compiler versions.

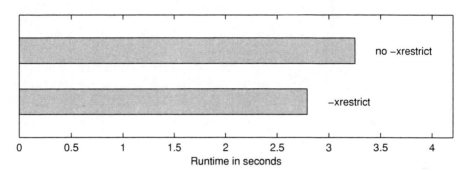

FIGURE 6-7   Runtime for the Program Compiled With and Without `-xrestrict` on a Sun Blade 1000 (Forte Developer 6 Compiler)

For finer control on specification of restricted parameters, the reader is encouraged to look into the use of keyword `_Restrict` supported in the Sun C compiler; it can be inserted along with the argument declaration in the user-code (see the *C User's Guide* for details).

`-xalias_level`

The Forte Developer 6 update 1 C compiler incorporates a new option, `-xalias_level`, which enables programmers to provide compiler type-based information on how pointers are used in a C program. The compiler uses this information along with type-based rules of pointer usage as specified in the ISO 1999 C language standard to perform alias disambiguation optimizations in the program. The type-based alias disambiguation facility performs the alias analysis not only for pointers to basic data types, but also for pointers to user-defined structures and unions. Further, unlike the `-xrestrict` option, the analysis is performed on all (local, as well as global) pointers and data structures in the program.

As we will illustrate with a simple example, providing the compiler with necessary information for determining the *alias relationships* can have a significant performance impact in programs that are load-miss latency bound. There are three possible alias relationships between a pair of memory references: *does alias*, *does not alias*, and *may alias* (see [Boucher99]). As the name suggests, a `does alias` relationship exists between a pair of memory references if during the execution of the program, they access a common portion of memory. In the following example, i and j have a does alias relationship.

```
int *i, j=1;
i = &j
```

The does not alias relationship occurs when the variables cannot access a common portion of memory. For example, none of the following variables can alias each other.

```
double func(double b)
{ double *c;
c = (double *) malloc(sizeof(double));
*c = 10.0;
b = b + *c;
free(c);
return(b);
}
```

Finally, the may alias relationship occurs when the compiler fails to ascertain if either the does alias or does not alias relationship holds. In the following example, even though it may be clear to the programmer that vloc[i] does not change in the inner loop, it is not possible for the compiler to determine this, since sum, vloc, and a may alias each other.

```
int sum, *vloc;
function foo (double *a)
...
for (i=0;i<n;i++) {
for (j=0;j<m;j++) {
   a[vloc[i]+j] = a[vloc[i]+j] + sum;
} }
...
```

In large programs with numerous pointer variables, the may alias relationship occurs most commonly. The compiler errs on the side of caution and the may alias relationship is considered equivalent to the does alias. In most cases, the does alias relationship implies generation of conservative code with extra memory operations[1]. So, in the preceding may alias example, vloc has be to loaded from memory at every iteration of the inner loop. Further, the compiler has to ensure that

---

1. There might be situations, however, where the does alias relationship allows optimizations to occur (see [Boucher99]).

the `vloc` load instruction is placed in the instruction stream after the `a[vloc[i]+j]` store instruction. This is to ensure that load of `vloc[i]` does not occur in the instruction stream prior to `a[vloc[i]+j]` store.

It should be clear to the reader that the larger the number of `does not alias` relationships between pairs of memory references in the program, the more flexibility the compiler has in generating optimized code.

The `-xalias_level` option can be used as:

`-xalias_level=<setting>`

There are seven possible settings: `any`, `basic`, `weak`, `layout`, `strict`, `std`, and `strong`. If `-xalias_level` is specified without any level, the default selected level is `layout`. The `-xalias_level` option must be used in combination with `-x02` or higher optimization.

The levels specify the assumptions that the compiler can make about the alias relationships. As the level is increased, the compiler makes more restrictive assumptions about the pointer usage in the program. If a program satisfies these assumptions, it has a better chance of improved runtime performance. On the other hand, if any of the assumptions are violated, the program will likely generate incorrect results or exhibit undefined behavior. Note that the levels are generally inclusive. That is, the higher levels include the constraints specified at the lower levels.

It is very important that the user fully understands the meaning of different levels of `-xalias_level` option. We strongly recommend reading the *C User's Guide Supplement* in the *Forte Developer 6 update 1 Collection* on `http://docs.sun.com` for a detailed discussion on the `-xalias_level` option. In the following table, a synopsis of various levels is provided. The type can be `typedef` name, `struct` tag, `union` tag, `enum` tag, `void`, or a basic C data type.

TABLE 6-1 Synopsis of Different Levels of the `-xalias_level` Option

Level	Meaning
any	All memory references can alias at this level.
basic	Pointers to different C basic data types do not alias each other. For example, `int *` and `float *` do not alias each other. References using `char *` may alias any other type.
weak	Structure pointers can alias each other but basic C data types are assumed not to alias each other. By making all structure declarations visible (including all relevant header files in compilation unit), offset-based alias disambiguation can be performed. References using `char *` may alias any other type.

TABLE 6-1   Synopsis of Different Levels of the `-xalias_level` Option *(Continued)*

Level	Meaning
`layout`	Structures which have fields with same sequence of basic types (that is, look similar when laid out in memory) may alias each other while types that lay out differently in memory do not alias. Memory accesses through dissimilar `struct` types alias if the initial members of the `struct` lay out similarly in memory. However, a pointer to a `struct` cannot be used to access a field in a dissimilar `struct` that is past the common initial front portion as those are assumed not to alias. Basic C types do not alias. References using `char *` may alias any other type
`strict`	This rule is similar to `layout` with differences related to access of structures with common initial portion. Aliasing is assumed to occur for types such as `struct` or `union` which are same if their tags are removed. If the `struct` or `union` types are dissimilar but their initial members look similar in memory, then they are assumed not to alias. Basic C types do not alias. References using `char *` may alias any other type.
`std`	This level implements the rules of pointer deferencing specified in the 1999 ISO C standard. The types and tags (on `struct` and `union` types) need to be same for aliasing to occur. Since this level implements the ISO C standard, programs conforming to these assumptions are portable and see good performance improvements. References using `char *` may alias any other type.
`strong`	This level is same as `std` but the compiler also assumes that `char *` pointers only access objects of char type. The level also prohibits pointers to members of structures.

Consider the following program, which uses structures similar to those used to represent the undirected graph of a sparse symmetric matrix in graph-partitioning based matrix reordering algorithms.

CODE EXAMPLE 6-11   Example Program for Testing `-xalias_level` Settings   *(1 of 4)*

```
/* example_xalias.c
cc -fast -xalias_level=<VALUE> example_xalias.c
   -o example_xalias (Forte Developer 6 update 1) */
#include <stdio.h>
#include <stdlib.h>
#include <sys/time.h>
#include <sys/types.h>
#include <unistd.h>
#define ITER 50
```

```
typedef struct edst {
   int edge,egwt;
} EdgeType;

typedef struct vtxst {
   int vwgt,nedges,egwtsum;
   EdgeType *edges;
} VertexType;

typedef struct grphst {
   int nvtxs,nedges,tvwgt,label,*vloc;
   double *a,*d;
   VertexType *allvtxs,**vtxs;
} GraphType;

int rows=1000;
GraphType *graph;
EdgeType *edges;

void initgraph(int nrow);
void freegraph();
void setvals();

int main(int argc, char **argv)
{ int i,j;
   hrtime_t start;
   double *b,smax=0.0,t0=0.0;
   if (argc>1) rows = atoi(argv[1]);

   for (j=0;j<ITER;j++) {
      initgraph(rows);
      start = gethrtime();
      setvals();
      t0 += (gethrtime()-start)*1.e-9;
      smax+= graph->tvwgt/graph->nvtxs;
      freegraph();
   }
   printf("smax= %11.2e\n",smax);
   printf("Setval Time= %6.2f seconds\n",t0);
   return 0;
}

void initgraph(int nrow)
```

```
{
    graph = (GraphType *)malloc(sizeof(GraphType));
    graph->nvtxs = graph->nedges = -1;
    graph->tvwgt = graph->label = 0;
    graph->allvtxs = NULL;
    graph->vtxs = NULL;
    graph->nvtxs = nrow;
    graph->nedges = (nrow-1)*nrow;
    graph->vloc = (int *)malloc(graph->nvtxs*sizeof(int));
    edges = (EdgeType *)malloc(graph->nedges*sizeof(EdgeType));
    graph->vtxs = (VertexType **)
                malloc(sizeof(VertexType *)*graph->nvtxs);
    graph->allvtxs = (VertexType *)
                malloc(sizeof(VertexType)*graph->nvtxs);
    graph->a = (double *) malloc(sizeof(double)*graph->nedges);
    graph->d = (double *) malloc(sizeof(double)*graph->nvtxs);
}

void freegraph()
{
    free(graph->d);free(graph->a);
    free(graph->allvtxs);
    free(graph->vtxs);free(graph->vloc);
    free(graph);free(edges);
}

void setvals()
{
    int i,j;
    for (i=0;i<graph->nvtxs;i++) {
        graph->vtxs[i] = graph->allvtxs+i;
        graph->vloc[i] = i*(graph->nvtxs-1);
        graph->vtxs[i]->edges = edges + i*(graph->nvtxs-1);
        graph->vtxs[i]->nedges = graph->nvtxs-1;
        graph->vtxs[i]->vwgt = i;
        graph->tvwgt += graph->vtxs[i]->vwgt;
        graph->d[i] = 1.0;
        for (j=0;j<graph->vtxs[i]->nedges;j++) {
            if (j < i) {
                edges[graph->vloc[i]+j].edge=j;
                edges[graph->vloc[i]+j].egwt=1;
            } else if (j > i) {
                edges[graph->vloc[i]+j].edge=j+1;
```

Example Program for Testing `-xalias_level` Settings *(4 of 4)*

```
            edges[graph->vloc[i]+j].egwt=0;
        }
        graph->a[graph->vloc[i]+j] = 0.1;
        graph->vtxs[i]->egwtsum +=
            edges[graph->vloc[i]+j].egwt;
    }
  }
}
```

Using Forte Developer 6 update 1 C compiler, we compile the program at different levels. The script provided along with the source files of this chapter automatically generates the binaries for all seven levels and runs them for prescribed graph sizes. The results (times measured for function `setvals`) of running the program on a Sun Blade 1000 with a graph with 2,500 vertices is shown in FIGURE 6-8. With the setting of `-xalias_level=strong` a speedup of 70 percent is observed over the case when no alias analysis is performed.

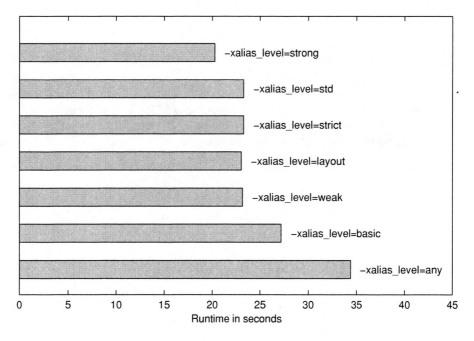

FIGURE 6-8 Results for a Program Compiled With Different Levels of the `-xalias_level` Option on a Sun Blade 1000 (Forte Developer 6 Update 1 Compiler)

We can see from the program source that it is valid to compile the program at all levels (there are no pointers cast to each other). A simple diagnostic one can apply to generated code to assess the effectiveness of alias disambiguation optimization is to count the number of load and store instructions in the generated code. For example, in the function setvals, the number of load instructions (ld instructions) are as follows at different alias levels.

TABLE 6-2 Distribution of ld Instructions as a Function of -xalias_level (Program Compiled on Sun Blade 1000 With -fast -xalias_level=*value*)

-xalias_level	Number of ld Instructions in Function setvals
any	66
basic	36
weak	31
layout	31
strict	21
std	21
strong	14

Here, counts were based on code that was compiled on a Sun Blade 1000 (-xchip=ultra3 value). The number is dependent on other compiler options and target architecture settings. The reader should experiment with -xchip=ultra2 and other settings of various options (-xO<*n*>), and examine how the number of generated ld/st instructions change.

The following analysis pertains to the doubly nested loops in the function setvals (in example_xalias.c).

■ -xalias_level=any: All pointers may alias and the compiler generates very conservative code (as manifested by the high number of loads).

■ -xalias_level=basic: graph->a does not alias with graph->vloc, graph->vtxs, graph->vtxs[i]->edges and other int fields of graph. Similarly for the pointer graph->d.

■ -xalias_level= weak: In addition to the above, the following struct members do not alias. graph->tvwgt does not alias with graph->vtxs[i]->vwgt. edges[].edge does not alias with graph->vloc, graph->vtxs[]->egwtsum, graph->vloc and graph->vtxs[]->egwtsum. graph->vloc does not alias with graph->vtxs[]->egwtsum.

■ -xalias_level=layout: For this example, it is similar to weak. The timing results match, as do the generated codes (the reader is encouraged to verify this by examining the generated assembly listing).

- -xalias_level=strict, std: At these levels, in this program, the struct pointers graph and edges do not alias each other.

- -xalias_level=strong: The compiler assumes that there are no internal pointers to fields of structures pointed to by edges and graph. char * only points to other char pointers.

The type-based alias disambiguation facility in the compiler is quite powerful, but also quite complex. The reader should experiment with -xalias_level settings on their programs with different input sets to ensure that no assumptions are violated and correctness is preserved.

-stackvar

This option instructs the Fortran compilers to treat the variables local to functions as automatic and to allocate them on the stack at runtime. This approach is standard for C programs, but the default behavior of Sun Fortran compilers is to allocate storage for local variables at compilation time in the BSS segment of the executable. We will discuss the use of the stack and the meaning of different segments in executable files in Chapter 7.

The use of automatic variables often leads to fewer relocations required at runtime and allows the local variables to be referenced from the registers instead of memory locations.

We illustrate the action of the -stackvar option with the following basic example. Here, the program repeatedly calls the function foo_stackvar, which contains a dummy loop that only increments an index and compares it against the loop range.

CODE EXAMPLE 6-12 Advantage of Placing Local Function Variables on the Stack With -stackvar

```
c example_stackvar.f
c f77 example_stackvar.f -o example_stackvar (-stackvar)
      program example
      real*4 tarray(2), t1, t2, etime
      integer j
      t1 = etime(tarray)
      do j=1,10000
         call foo_stackvar
      enddo
      t2 = etime(tarray)
      print*, "RUNTIME: ", t2-t1
      end
```

CODE EXAMPLE 6-12 Advantage of Placing Local Function Variables on the Stack With `-stackvar` *(Continued)*

```c
c
        subroutine foo_stackvar()
        integer i
        do i=1,100000
        enddo
        return
        end
```

To see the effect of `-stackvar`, we compile the program with and without this option and compare the results. We don't use any other options as this example is too basic to use any compiler optimization (the optimizer will inline the subroutine and eliminate both loops as dead code).

The loop index `i` is a local variable that is referenced directly from a register when `-stackvar` is used. The disassembly shows that the loop body contains the bare minimum: an increment of the index and a compare instruction.

```
.L29:
        add     %i5,1,%i5
        cmp     %i5,%o1
        ble     .L29
        nop
```

Compilation without `-stackvar` results in the loop body containing extra load and store instructions. In this case, the local variable `i` is referenced from the memory (BSS segment).

```
        sethi   %hi(GPB.foo_stackvar.i),%o2
        or      %o2,%lo(GPB.foo_stackvar.i),%o2
.L29:

        ld      [%o2+0],%o0
        add     %o0,1,%o0
        cmp     %o0,%o1
        ble     .L29
        st      %o0,[%o2+0]
```

The extra instructions result in increased runtime. The following results (FIGURE 6-9) are obtained on an Ultra 60 system.

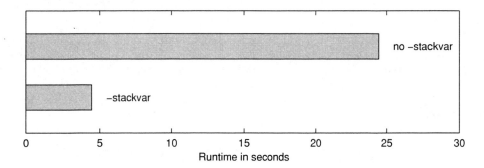

FIGURE 6-9 Improvement Due to `-stackvar` Usage—Runs on an Ultra 60 System (Forte Developer 6 Update 1 Compiler)

As we can see, the optimizer's ability to reference the variables from the registers can make a big difference for scheduling loops. We recommend using the `-stackvar` option for all Fortran programs. But we should also warn that adding `-stackvar` can change the runtime behavior of programs that don't explicitly initialize the variables and rely on zero initial values. In Chapter 3, we described the tools that can detect this and other programming practices that should be avoided. Another point to note is that unlike the variables that have global scope, the variables that are allocated on the stack keep their values only until the function that uses them exits. Care must be taken that the `stacksize` shell limit, which bounds the size of the stack of the entire process, is set to a sufficiently large value to allow allocation of local variables on the stack segment. For example, in a `csh(1)` environment, the following command sets stack size to 512 MB.

```
example% limit stacksize 512m
example% limit
cputime        unlimited
filesize       2048000 kbytes
datasize       262144 kbytes
stacksize      524288 kbytes
coredumpsize   2048000 kbytes
descriptors    1024
memorysize     2048000 kbytes
```

Remember to ensure that the sum of `stacksize` and `datasize` (as shown in `limit` command) is less than or equal to the `memorysize` setting. See the man pages for `limit(1)`, `ulimit`, and `unlimit` for further information on controlling shell limits.

For multithreaded Fortran programs, the use of `-stackvar` is essential as it allows separate threads to have their own private variables in separate stack frames. We will return to this subject later (Chapter 12 and Chapter 13).

Compiler Directives and Pragmas

This section describes several compiler directives and pragmas that can improve program performance. Directives and pragmas are annotations inserted in the source files and are used to provide the compiler with specific instructions regarding parts of the program (usually statements immediately after the directive or pragma). As a matter of terminology, statements inserted in Fortran programs are commonly referred to as *directives*, while those in C programs are referred to as *pragmas*. These statements are such that directives or pragmas specific to a particular compiler are generally ignored by other compilers. Therefore, adding statements still allows the program to be compiled on various platforms. We should point out that even though the use of compiler pragmas requires modifying the source code, its effect is limited to the way the compiler treats parts of the program.

pragma pipeloop

The Sun compiler back-end implements a technique called software pipelining (see [Tirumalai96], [Muchnick97]) to improve the performance of loop-intensive programs by exposing the instruction-level parallelism (ILP) in the loop body. A code compiled such that it has instructions that can be executed independently will better utilize the multiple functional units available on a superscalar RISC processor (such as UltraSPARC processors[1]), compared to code that is not compiled to take advantage of the ILP available on the underlying hardware. The higher utilization of instruction-level parallelism leads to improved program performance since the total runtime of a program is $T = N_{instr} \times Cycle\text{-}time \times CPI$, where N_{instr} is the number of instructions, *Cycle-time* is the inverse of the clock frequency of the processor, and *CPI* is the average cycles per instruction. A higher ILP decreases the average CPI of the program.

---

1. The UltraSPARC I and II processors are 4-way superscalar and feature fully pipelined access to the level 2 cache via a load buffer and a non-blocking level 1 cache (see the *UltraSPARC I and II User's Manual*). The UltraSPARC III processor can issue up to four instructions per cycle and has a large (4-way associative 64 KB) level 1 cache as well as an on-chip prefetch and write caches that provide high memory bandwidth.

The technique of software pipelining works by breaking a loop iteration into multiple parts and overlapping parts from disjoint iterations at the same time. The loop iteration is broken such that the different parts use different functional units of the processor (to the extent possible). While there may be dependence between parts of the same iteration (inhibiting concurrent use of different functional units), by simultaneously executing parts from different iterations (where each part maps onto a different functional unit of the processor), the parallelism in the loop iterations can be efficiently mapped onto the instruction-level parallelism provided by the underlying processor.

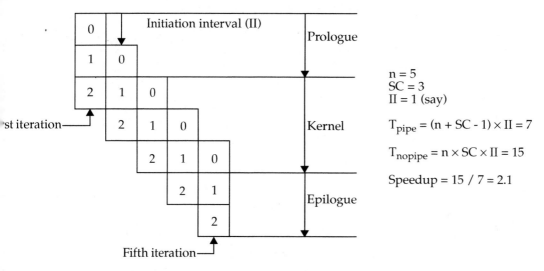

$n = 5$
$SC = 3$
$II = 1$ (say)

$T_{pipe} = (n + SC - 1) \times II = 7$

$T_{nopipe} = n \times SC \times II = 15$

Speedup = 15 / 7 = 2.1

FIGURE 6-10 Modulo Scheduling of a Five Iteration Loop Using a Three-Stage Pipeline— Adapted With Permission From [Tirumalai96]

The variant of software pipelining implemented in Sun compilers is called modulo scheduling [Tirumalai96]. The basic idea is schematically shown in FIGURE 6-10. The modulo scheduler breaks a loop iteration into *stage count* (SC) chunks of equal lengths. New iterations are started after fixed time intervals called *initiation interval* (II). The stages are of length II. As we can see from FIGURE 6-10, after (SC-1) × II cycles (called the *prologue* stage), the loop execution attains a state (called *kernel* stage) where all the stages from different iterations are executing. Towards the end of a loop, a draining of the pipeline occurs. This is called the *epilogue* stage and also requires (SC-1) × II cycles. If the loop trip count is large, the steady state throughput of the loop approaches one iteration per II cycles and modulo scheduling leads to a speedup that approaches SC (compared to the nonpipelined loop execution). Note that this assumes that stages from SC iterations of the loop can be overlapped in the pipeline.

In generating the instruction schedule, the modulo scheduler assumes that the data are available in the level 2 cache on UltraSPARC I and II processors. On UltraSPARC III processor, the schedule is generated assuming that data is present in the level 1 cache. For loops that exhibit a high level 2 cache hit rate (on UltraSPARC I and II processors) or a high level 1 cache hit rate (on UltraSPARC III processors), software pipelining can be applied to extract a higher degree of instruction level parallelism than can be obtained by simple scheduling or loop unrolling type optimizations. In case of loops where data does not reside in processor caches, prefetching (see -xprefetch in Chapter 5 and pragma prefetch later in this chapter) can be applied in conjunction with modulo scheduling to bring data from the memory into level 2 cache (or prefetch cache in case of UltraSPARC III).

Some comments are in order on the interrelationship between loop unrolling and software pipelining optimization approaches. In general, loop unrolling and software pipelining are independent concepts, but they are often combined together as loop unrolling facilitates software pipelining (see [Wadleigh00]). Loop unrolling decreases the overhead in the loop (index calculation, conditional test for loop termination) but does not perform any instruction scheduling to hide instruction latencies. In software pipelining on the other hand, the instructions are scheduled to minimize stalls in processor pipeline. For simple loops, the two techniques are often combined as loop unrolling creates the workload required per loop iteration for the software pipeliner to generate an efficient instruction schedule.

Interested readers should consult [Tirumalai96] for details on the modulo scheduler design and implementation in Sun compilers.

At the optimization level -xO3 (and higher), the modulo scheduling of loops is automatically turned on in Sun C, Fortran 77, and Fortran 95 compilers. However, sometimes it is not safe for the compiler to assume independence in successive iterations of the loop, and it errs on the side of caution by skipping the loops where it detects (or suspects) a loop-carried dependence. For example, consider the following loop.

```
DO I=1,N
A(I)=A(I+K) + D(I)
B(I)=B(I) + A(I)
END DO
```

In this loop, for example, if K = 1, then it is not safe to overlap the calculations of iterations I and I + 1. On the other hand, if K > N, then it is safe to overlap calculations in multiple iterations. But if K and N are not known at compile time, then the compiler skips the pipelining of this loop.

There are other situations under which the software pipelining of loops is turned off in the compiler. These include:

- Fat (computationally dense) loops. Due to higher register pressure, software pipelining could be turned off as the degradation due to register spills can potentially outweigh the benefits of modulo scheduling. Generally, splitting the fat loops into finer loops helps in such situations. We will discuss loop splitting (or fission) in Chapter 8.
- Loops with indirection. The dependence analysis fails in general due to insufficient information at compile time on loop-carried dependences.
- Branches and conditional statements inside the loop-nest inhibit pipelining.
- Loops where the trip count calculation cannot be safely performed do not get pipelined. For example, in C programs, loops with pointer variables or unsigned integers as loop counter variables may not be pipelined. The unsigned counters may overflow and simply wraparound. This can lead to errors in the trip count calculation in the software pipeliner. Currently, the Sun compiler does not modulo schedule such loops (by default). For example, the following loops will not be pipelined (ptr, head and last are pointer variables).

```
for (ptr = head; ptr != last; ptr++)
t0 -= t1*(*ptr++);
. . .
unsigned int i;
for (i=n;i>=0;i--)
t0 -= t1*ptr[i];
. . .
```

In the first two cases, if the semantics of the program allow iteration overlap, then the programmer can make use of the pipeloop pragma to instruct the compiler to software pipeline the loop regardless of the perceived dependence by the compiler back-end phase.

The syntax of the pragma is given in the TABLE 6-3 for Fortran 77, Fortran 90/95, and C programs, respectively. It is not available in the C++ compiler at the time of this writing. The pragma must be placed immediately before a DO loop in Fortran or a for loop construct in C.

TABLE 6-3 Syntax of pragma pipeloop

Language	Syntax
Fortran 77	c$pragma sun pipeloop=n
Fortran 90/95	!$pragma sun pipeloop=n
C	#pragma pipeloop(n)

In TABLE 6-3, values of n such that n >= 0 are allowed. The value (n) asserts the minimum loop-carried dependence distance to the optimizer. A value of n = 0 indicates that there are no dependences and the loop can be freely software pipelined. A positive n value implies that the i - th iteration of the loop has a dependency on the (i - n) - th iteration, and can be pipelined at best for only n iterations at a time.

The user should be careful of the following pitfalls in the usage of this pragma.

- *Loop construct* – The loop should preferably be written as a DO loop in Fortran 77 and Fortran 90/95, and as a for loop in C. Software pipelining may get inhibited if any other construct is used. For example

```
#pragma pipeloop(0)
while (i != N) {
... do stuff ...
} /* LOOP PIPELINING SKIPPED */

#pragma pipeloop(0)
for (i=0;i<N;i++) {
... do stuff ...
/* LOOP PIPELINED */
```

- *Loop-refusion by the compiler* – Even after manual splitting of a fat loop that was not pipelined due to high register pressure, no actual decrease in runtime might be observed. Detailed analysis of the generated code might indicate that the optimizing compiler fused the split loops back (loop fusion is another optimization performed in Sun compilers) and disabled the pipelining. This is an example where two different optimization approaches act in a conflicting manner. In such cases, one has to resort to loop fission with loops rewritten to disable loop fusion by the optimizing compiler. An example follows, where iteration peeling is performed to prevent the compiler from fusing the loops back together (loop peeling is discussed in further detail in Chapter 9). An alternative to loop peeling is to place a call to a dummy function between the split loops. Of course, either of these should be done only if pipelining leads to improved performance over loop-fusion optimization.

Loops Split to Avoid Compiler Fusion

```
do  i = 1,n                          x(1) = y(1)*z(1)
   x(i) = y(i)*z(i)                  do  i = 2,n
   u(i + 1) = v(i + 1) + b(i + 2)       x(i) = y(i)*z(i)
enddo                                enddo
                                     u(n + 1) = b(n + 2)
                                     do  i = 1,n - 1
                                        u(i + 1) = v(i + 1) + b(i + 2)
                                     enddo
                                     u(n + 1) = u(n + 1) + v(n + 1)
```

- *Pointer aliasing in C programs* – In C programs, use of -xrestrict or -xalias_level (wherever applicable) is strongly recommended although even that might not be sufficient. Consider the following code example.

```
extern float **m;
float *v, *vo;
void mpy(int size, int sizem);
void mpy1(int size, int sizem);
void mpy(int size, int sizem)
{
  int i,j;
  for (i=0;i<=size; i++) {
      vo[i] = 0.0;
#pragma pipeloop(0)
    for (j=0;j<=sizem;j++)
        vo[i] += v[j]*m[i][j];
  }
}
void mpy1(int size, int sizem)
{
  int i,j;
  float sum;
  for (i=0;i<=size; i++) {
        sum = 0.0f;
#pragma pipeloop(0)
    for (j=0;j<=sizem;j++) {
        sum += v[j]*m[i][j];
    }
```

```
        vo[i] = sum;
    }
}
```

If we compile (using Forte Developer 6 update 1 C compiler) the above code fragment as -fast -xalias_level=strong, we find that the function mpy1 runs faster than the function mpy. In the case of mpy, even with the use of -xalias_level=strong, it is not guaranteed that m[i][j] and vo[i] do not alias; hence vo[i] cannot be regarded as a loop invariant. Consequently, it has to be loaded/stored at every iteration of the inner loop, thereby increasing the memory traffic and decreasing the performance of function mpy. We will discuss pointer aliasing in further detail in Chapter 8.

We will now give a simple example that shows the performance benefits of pragma pipeloop. Consider the subroutine pipeloop based on a loop extracted from an oil-reservoir simulation code. The inner loop contains indirection which inhibits software pipelining. However, the various arrays assume values in the actual code such.that it is safe to pipeline the loop. Inserting pragma pipeloop allows that to happen.

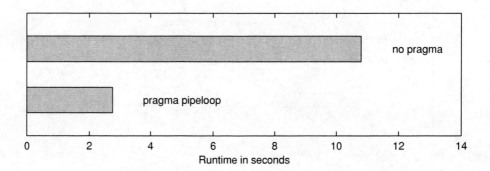

FIGURE 6-11 Impact of pragma pipeloop—Runs on an Ultra 60 (Forte Developer 6 Update 1 Compiler)

Compiling with the Fortran 90 compiler and using the -fast option, the times in the routine pipeloop are shown in FIGURE 6-11. The use of pragma pipeloop results in a dramatic improvement in performance. Note the arrays are loaded in the level 2 cache in the initialization loop and the sizes are selected such that they fit in the 4MB level 2 cache on the machine on which the tests were run. This ensures a high level 2 cache hit rate, which is essential to accrue the full benefits of modulo scheduling on an UltraSPARC II processor.

CODE EXAMPLE 6-13 Program Illustrating the Effect of `pragma pipeloop` *(1 of 2)*

```
! example_pipeloop.f90
! f90 -fast -fsimple=1 example_pipeloop.f90 -o example_pipeloop
program pipelooptst
implicit none
integer, parameter :: sgl=SELECTED_REAL_KIND(p=6)
integer, parameter :: dbl=SELECTED_REAL_KIND(p=13)
integer, parameter :: numit=1000,nele=100000,len1=33,len2=1000
integer :: i,j,k,n,idm1,icf,ksld,nloop,status
integer, dimension(2,1) :: isvs
integer, dimension(3,len2) :: isvr
real (KIND=dbl), dimension(nele+9) :: wrk,a
real (KIND=sgl) :: tarray(2),t1=0.0,t2=0.0,etime
external etime

! set the integer arrays
isvs(1,1) = 1
isvs(2,1) = 2
ksld = 1
icf = 5

do i=1,len2
   isvr(1,i) = 31
   isvr(2,i) = nele - 2*len1
   isvr(3,i) = 7
enddo

do nloop=1,numit
! initialize and load the values in L2-cache
   do i=1,nele+8
      wrk(i) = i*0.001 + nloop
      a(i) = 1.d0
   enddo

! now time pipeloop kernel
   t1 = etime(tarray)
   call pipeloop(ksld, isvs, isvr, icf, idm1, wrk, a)
   t2 = t2 + (etime(tarray) - t1)
enddo
```

```
write(*,'("Total Time: ",f6.2)') t2
end program

subroutine pipeloop(ksld,isvs,isvr,icf,idm1,wrk,a)
implicit none
integer, parameter :: dbl=SELECTED_REAL_KIND(p=13)
integer, INTENT(in) :: ksld,icf,idm1
integer, INTENT(in), dimension(3,*) :: isvr
integer, INTENT(in), dimension(2,*) :: isvs
real (KIND=dbl), INTENT(inout), dimension(idm1) :: wrk
real (KIND=dbl), INTENT(in), dimension(idm1) :: a
integer :: ivr,iv1,iv2,iv,ic,in1,in2

do ivr=isvs(1,ksld),isvs(2,ksld)
   iv1 = isvr(1,ivr)
   iv2 = isvr(2,ivr)
   iv  = isvr(3,ivr)
!$pragma sun pipeloop = 0
   do ic=iv1,iv2
      in1 = ic + iv
      in2 = ic - icf
      wrk(in1) = wrk(in1) - a(in2)*wrk(ic)
   enddo
enddo
return
end subroutine
```

pragma opt

In general, as we increase the optimization level (prescribed by −xO<*n*> flag), the run-time performance of the resulting code improves. However, there are situations where increased optimization may hurt performance. For example, function inlining increases the code size, resulting in larger binary size and larger memory needed to load the program. This may also degrade the instruction-cache hit rate at runtime. There are other situations where higher optimization level might affect the performance negatively. Also, the program compilation time and memory used by a compiler increase as the optimization level used is increased because the optimizer uses more sophisticated algorithms for program transformation and restructuring (see Chapter 5).

Sun Fortran and C compilers incorporate a pragma that provides finer control on the optimization level. The syntax for the pragma is shown in the following table.

TABLE 6-4 Syntax of `pragma opt`

Language	Syntax
Fortran 77	`c$pragma sun opt=n`
Fortran 90/95	`!$pragma sun opt=n`
C	`#pragma opt <n> (funcname[,funcname1])`

Above, n=1, 2, 3, 4, 5 are allowed. For C, the function subprograms must be prototyped before usage of the pragma in the source file. An example (Fortran 77) usage could be:

```
c$pragma sun opt=4
subroutine foo(i,j,a,b)
 . . .
return
end
```

The directive should appear immediately before the subroutine and is only applicable to that routine. For example, if the source file containing the above routine is compiled with -x02, then it will be overridden and routine `foo` will be compiled with -x04.

This pragma should be used in conjunction with the flag -xmaxopt=<n>. This flag specifies the maximum optimization setting used by `pragma opt`. For example, if -xmaxopt=3 is specified, then in the preceding example, the routine `foo` will be compiled with -x03 and not -x04 as the pragma specifies. Also, note that the default value of -xmaxopt is -xmaxopt=off which will disable `pragma opt` in the program. This is a very important point to remember in the proper usage of this pragma in program units.

pragma prefetch

We already discussed the -xprefetch compiler option which allows the compiler to use the prefetch instructions in the generated code. This option works well in most cases, but sometimes, especially for the large routines, it does not provide enough flexibility and may prompt the compiler to generate excessive prefetch instructions.

In addition to the -xprefetch compiler option, directives and APIs that allow specifying which data should be prefetched were introduced in Forte Developer 6 compilers.

The compiler will recognize the following Fortran directives when the -xprefetch[=explicit] option is set.

```
C$PRAGMA SPARC_PREFETCH_READ_ONCE (address)
C$PRAGMA SPARC_PREFETCH_READ_MANY (address)
C$PRAGMA SPARC_PREFETCH_WRITE_ONCE (address)
C$PRAGMA SPARC_PREFETCH_WRITE_MANY (address)
```

They can be used to generate the prefetch instructions in addition to, or instead of, the automatically generated ones with -xprefetch=auto. The prefetch instructions fetch the data into the prefetch cache (UltraSPARC III processor only) or the external cache.

The SPARC_PREFETCH_READ_MANY pragma puts the datum in the external cache and also in the prefetch cache on UltraSPARC III-based systems. On UltraSPARC III systems, the SPARC_PREFETCH_READ_ONCE directive places the datum in the prefetch cache only, bypassing the external cache. On earlier systems, it is equivalent to the SPARC_PREFETCH_READ_MANY directive. Both the SPARC_PREFETCH_WRITE_ONCE and SPARC_PREFETCH_WRITE_MANY directives write datum to the external cache with the distinction that the former one makes the cache line shared.

In C and C++ programs, prefetching can be controlled directly with calls to functions defined in the sun_prefetch.h compiler header file.

```
void sparc_prefetch_read_once(address);
void sparc_prefetch_read_many(address);
void sparc_prefetch_write_once(address);
void sparc_prefetch_write_many(address);
```

In the following example, the pragma suggests the compiler to prefetch the data for the innermost loop. When it is compiled using Forte Developer 6 Fortran 77 compiler with -xprefetch=explicit, the pragma translates into a prefetch instruction.

```
example% f77 -O4 -dalign -fsimple=2 \
        -xarch=v8plus example_pragma_prefetch.f \
        -o example_pragma_prefetch -xprefetch=explicit
example% dis example_pragma_prefetch | grep prefetch
disassembly for example_pragma_prefetch
        114c8:  c3 68 a0 00          prefetch       [%g2 + 0] , 1
```

CODE EXAMPLE 6-14 Example of `pragma prefetch` Usage

```
C example_pragma_prefetch.f
C f77 -O4 -dalign -fsimple=2 \
C    -xarch=v8plus example_pragma_prefetch.f \
C    -o example_pragma_prefetch -xprefetch=explicit
      program example_pragma_prefetch
      parameter(ITER=100,SIZE=100000)
      real*8 d(16,SIZE), a
      real*4 t0,t1,etime,time(2)
      integer noffset(14), n
      data noffset /0,1,2,3,4,5,6,7,8,10,12,16,20,28/
c
c initialization
      do j=1, size
         do k=1, 16
            d(k,j)=1.0
         enddo
      enddo
c
c test run without prefetching
      a=0.0e+0
      t0=etime(time)
      do i=1,iter
         do j=1, size
            do k=1, 16
               a = a + d(k,j)
            enddo
         enddo
      enddo
      t1=etime(time)
      print*,'a= ',a
      write(6,10) t1-t0
 10   format("RUNTIME, no prefetch: ",f6.2," seconds")
c
c prefetching with various parameters
      do ii=1,14
         n=noffset(ii)
         a=0.0e+0
         t0=etime(time)
            do i=1,iter
               do j=1, size
C$PRAGMA SPARC_PREFETCH_READ_ONCE(d(1,j+n))
               do k=1, 16
                  a = a + d(k,j)
```

```
               enddo
            enddo
         enddo
         t1=etime(time)
         print*,'a= ',a
         write(6,11)  n, t1-t0
      enddo
  11    format("RUNTIME, prefetch with offset ",i3,": ",f6.2,"
seconds")
      stop
      end
```

This particular example compares the performance benefit of prefetching with various fetch-ahead latencies. We can see (FIGURE 6-12) that the prefetch pragma provides full control over the prefetch instruction. We will show an equivalent approach in the section on inlining assembly templates in the next chapter.

The following timings are obtained on a Sun Blade 1000 system with 600 Mhz, 8 MB level 2 cache, UltraSPARC III CPU.

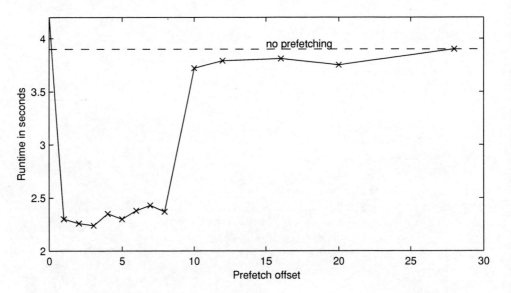

FIGURE 6-12   Enabling Data Prefetching With `pragma prefetch` on Sun Blade 1000 (Forte Developer 6 Update 1 Compiler)

pragma pack

For C and C++ programs that use structures, the layout and alignment of data members can be controlled using the pragma pack directive in source file. The syntax is

```
#pragma pack(n)
```

where n = 1, 2, 4 specifies the strictest alignment desired for members of the structure. Clearly, members that are not on their natural boundaries are affected by this pragma. If n is omitted, then the default alignment rules are used. That is, members on their natural boundaries to the extent permitted. By default, the alignment of the structure is the same as that of the most strictly aligned member (see the *C User's Guide*). Also, the size of structure is chosen such that it is an integral multiple of its alignment in order to ensure correct alignment in cases where an array of this structure is declared.

Consider the following program.

CODE EXAMPLE 6-15 Example of pragma pack Usage

```
/* example_pragma_pack.c */
/* cc example_pragma_pack.c -o example_pragma_pack */
#include <stdio.h>

typedef struct {
   char x;
   double p;
} ttx;

#pragma pack(4)
typedef struct {
   char x;
   double p;
} ttx4;

#pragma pack(2)
typedef struct {
   char x;
   double p;
} ttx2;

#pragma pack(1)
typedef struct {
```

CODE EXAMPLE 6-15 Example of `pragma pack` Usage *(Continued)*

```
      char x;
      double p;
} ttx1;

int main()
{
printf("size of ttx = %d (pragma pack not used)\n", sizeof(ttx));
printf("size of ttx4 = %d (pragma pack(4) used)\n", sizeof(ttx4));
printf("size of ttx2 = %d (pragma pack(2) used)\n", sizeof(ttx2));
printf("size of ttx1 = %d (pragma pack(1) used)\n", sizeof(ttx1));
return 0;
}
```

```
example% cc example_pragma_pack.c -o example_pragma_pack
example% example_pragma_pack
size of ttx = 16 (pragma pack not used)
size of ttx4 = 12 (pragma pack(4) used)
size of ttx2 = 10 (pragma pack(2) used)
size of ttx1 = 9 (pragma pack(1) used)
```

Note, in `struct ttx`, the compiler has put a hole of 7 bytes due to the requirement of aligning the `double` on an 8-byte boundary. When we specify `pragma pack` with different arguments, we can see how the packing of members changes and the size of the structure decreases.

It is important to note that a memory efficient layout may not necessarily be more efficient in performance. For example, forcing a `double` to be aligned on a 4-byte boundary can lead to performance degradation as it is not possible to generate `ldd` and `std` instructions on such data elements. One should use this pragma with caution and, in general, it is better to change the layout of the members of the structure manually so that the largest elements are declared first. For example, in the preceding example, it is better to declare

```
typedef struct {
    double p;
    char x;
} ttx;
```

Now there is no restriction on the compiler to put a hole between the `double` and `char` members.

pragma align

In C and C++ applications, alignment of global and static variables can be controlled by using `pragma align`. Its syntax is as follows.

```
#pragma align <n> (<variable>[, <variable>])
```

where the valid values for n are powers of 2 from 1 to 128. If the specified alignment of a variable is smaller than the system default, then the default alignment is used. The variable declaration should follow the pragma line. Otherwise, the pragma is ignored.

First, we compile and run the following example.

CODE EXAMPLE 6-16 Alignment Control With `pragma align`

```
/* example_pragma_align.c */
/* No alignment: cc example_pragma_align.c -o example_pragma_align
   65536-byte alignment: cc example_pragma_align.c -DALIGNLARGE \
                example_alignlarge.s -o example_pragma_align */
#include <stdio.h>
#ifdef ALIGNLARGE
extern int foo;
extern int bar;
#else
#pragma align 128 (foo)
int foo;
#pragma align 8 (bar)
int bar;
#endif
double x;

int main()
{
  int *x = &foo;
  printf("alignment &foo=%lx,&bar=%lx,&x=%lx\n",&foo,&bar,&x);
  return 0;
}
```

```
example% cc example_pragma_align.c -o example_pragma_align
example% example_pragma_align
alignments &foo=20d00 &bar=20c88 &x=ffbef118
```

For alignments larger than 128 bytes, one can specify it in the assembler. Consider the following, where `foo` is aligned on a 65,536 byte boundary.

CODE EXAMPLE 6-17   Example of Large Alignment in Assembly

```
.section          ".data"

        .global foo
        .align 65536
foo:
        .skip 4
        .size foo, foo-.

        .global bar
bar:
        .skip 4
        .size bar, bar-.
```

Now, we compile and run the program `example_pragma_align.c` as follows:

```
example% cc example_pragma_align.c -DALIGNLARGE \
        example_alignlarge.s -o example_pragma_align
example_pragma_align.c:
example_alignlarge.s:
example% example_pragma_align
alignments &foo=40000 &bar=40004, &x=ffbef118
```

where `foo` is aligned on 65,536-byte boundary. In some cases, one might want to align some data structures on page boundaries (8K by default on `sun4u` architecture in Solaris kernel [Mauro00]) for better memory access usage.

Pointer Alias Analysis Pragmas

Earlier in the chapter, we discussed the `-xalias_level` compiler option introduced in Forte Developer 6 update 1 C compiler for type-based alias analysis in C programs. To provide finer programmer control over compiler alias disambiguation analysis, the `-xalias_level` option is supplemented by several new pragmas. These pragmas (also introduced in Forte Developer 6 update 1 C compiler) enable overriding the alias levels specified in `-xalias_level` option for individual pointer variables in the program module. Pragmas are helpful in large programs with numerous pointer variables that have different alias relationships. In such cases, pragmas allow providing information to the compiler to use different alias levels (as appropriate) in analysis of different pointer types. TABLE 6-5 lists the new pragmas; *level* is one of the seven settings of the `-xalias_level` option. Note that the first pragma takes precedence over the level specified in -xalias_level option and the rest of pragmas override any assumptions applied by the -xalias_level during compilation.

TABLE 6-5   Alias Disambiguation Pragmas Supported in Forte Developer 6 Update 1 C Compiler

Pragma	Meaning
#pragma alias_level	Specifies the alias level applied either to all memory references in the compilation unit or only to those in the list of the pragma. It can be used to apply to pointers of a certain type or to specific pointers as #pragma alias_level *level* (type [, type]) #pragma alias_level *level* (pointer [, pointer])
#pragma alias	Specifies that listed types alias each other in the program. Used as #pragma alias (type [, type]) The other variant prescribes the specific pointer variables that alias each other #pragma alias (pointer [, pointer])
#pragma noalias	Specifies the types of specific pointer variables that do not alias each other #pragma noalias (type [, type]) #pragma noalias (pointer [, pointer])
#pragma may_point_to	Specifies the list of variables that can be pointed to by a pointer variable. #pragma may_point_to (pointer, variable [, variable...])
#pragma may_not_point_to	Specifies the list of variables that are not pointed to by a pointer variable. #pragma may_not_point_to (pointer, variable [, variable]...)

The following are some examples illustrating use of the previous pragmas.

```
long c[LEN+1],d[LEN+1],zz[2*LEN+3];
int *a,b[LEN+1]
double *e;
typedef struct edst {
  int edge,egwt;
} EdgeType;
#pragma alias_level std (EdgeType)
#pragma noalias (int, struct edst)
```

```
#pragma alias (a,e)
#pragma may_point_to (a,zz)
#pragma may_not_point_to (a,c,d)
```

Summary

This chapter gave an overview of advanced optimization compiler options and described several compiler directives and pragmas.

We started with a description of -ftrap, -fns, and -fsimple options that affect the handling of floating-point arithmetic and can speed up computational applications, but may lead to non-IEEE-compliant results.

Data alignment can be controlled with the -dalign option. When this option is specified, a load of an 8-byte data entry will take a single assembly instruction compared with two instructions needed to load data with less strict alignment. Further, on UltraSPARC processor-based systems, the double-word load/store instructions have the same latency as single-word load/store instructions. The data alignment should be consistent throughout the application. Therefore, if -dalign is used, it should appear in all compilation commands used to build a program.

The -xsafe=mem option allows the optimizer to move loads ahead of branches using the speculative load mechanism of the SPARC V9 architecture specification [Weaver94]. This option is effective in combination with -xO5 optimization level and must be used when compiling for UltraSPARC-based platforms only.

C applications can benefit significantly from the alias analysis options -xrestrict and -xalias_level. The -xrestrict option tells the compiler that function arguments specified by pointers do not overlap in memory. This option can bring considerable speedup when used in combination with other optimization options, as it allows the compiler to be more aggressive in the code generation. The -xalias_level option provides a means for passing type-based pointer dereferencing information to the compiler. The option can be used to pass information about usage of all pointers in the program, including structure pointer variables. Well written C programs adhering to the restrictions imposed by ISO 1999 C standard should use -xalias_level=std or -xalias_level=strong settings of this option.

Performance of Fortran programs that do not make assumptions about implicit initialization of variables can be improved by using the -stackvar option, which places all local variables in the program on runtime process stack.

Compiler pragmas allow specifying certain optimizations for loops, subroutines, or data structures. pragma pipeloop gives finer control over software pipelining of loops and can speed up loops with indirection or ambiguous data dependence.

## CHAPTER 7

Linker and Libraries in Performance Optimization

In this chapter, we cover the following topics: using the Solaris linker to develop performance-critical applications, and using optimized mathematical libraries in HPC applications.

We discuss link-editing and the runtime stages of linking, and give a brief overview of different ways to build an executable. We pay special attention to the distinction between static and dynamic linking of various libraries and describe the most commonly used options of the Solaris linker.

We also provide an overview of the mathematical libraries provided with the Solaris Operating Environment, as well as with Forte Developer and the Sun ClusterTools software. The libraries we discuss implement commonly used operations and are highly optimized for Solaris UltraSPARC platforms. Applications linked against these libraries automatically benefit from these performance optimizations.

Later in the chapter, we describe some features of the Solaris linker that can be used for development, debugging, and profiling applications. We also describe how to link programs that take full advantage of the hardware platform that is detected at runtime.

Linking Overview

Linking is an important stage in building and running applications. It has two distinct stages: *link-editing* and *runtime linking*.

The link-editor `ld(1)` concatenates relocatable object files produced by the compiler or assembler to generate relocatable objects, shared libraries, or executables. Relocatable modules are those with an absolute address that is not provided at the assembly stage, but rather is computed at the linking stage. The link-editor also performs symbol resolution to bind external symbols by connecting function references to implementations using the symbol tables in object files and libraries.

The link-editor can handle both 32-bit and 64-bit relocatable objects, but cannot mix them because the two models conform to different ABIs and have incompatibilities in the data type sizes (see Chapter 3). By default, the 64-bit object files start addressing from `0x100000000`, and the entire 64-bit program is placed above the 4 GB mark of the virtual address space. The 32-bit addressing model uses the 4 GB address range from `0` to `0xffffffff`. The link-editor determines if its output should be a 32-bit or 64-bit object by the type of the first object file it encounters.

Once the program is built with the link-editor, it can be executed with the help of the runtime linker.

The runtime, or dynamic, linker `ld.so.1(1)` is a special form of a shared object that loads executable files and shared libraries and generates a runnable process. It does this by mapping the files produced by the link-editor to memory and performing relocations.

Both linking stages can be hidden from the programmer. In many cases, the link-editing is done by the compiler, and the runtime linker is invoked by running the executable. Still, a good understanding of what the linker does and how changing its behavior can result in improved performance of an application is important.

Static and Dynamic Linking

The two approaches to building a program are static and dynamic linking. A static executable contains all of the code it needs for the run, while a dynamic executable may have runtime dependencies on other files. The dependency libraries can be shared by multiple applications and are called *shared libraries*.

Dynamic linking is more common and, in many cases, is preferable for the following reasons:

- Dynamically linked executables are smaller because they don't replicate the code already provided in shared libraries.

- As the name suggests, shared libraries can be shared between several processes running on a system. This improves memory utilization, and reduces paging activity.

- To ensure that an application will run on successive releases of an operating system, one should link the system libraries dynamically. By doing this, the programmer only uses the available interfaces of the system calls without relying on particular implementations that may change between OS releases.

- Dynamic libraries provide much greater flexibility for building and testing an application. They enable a programmer to use extra debugging and profiling features. These features will be the focus of later sections of this chapter.

Static linking of certain libraries has the following advantages:

- A statically built executable contains all of the code it needs to run, making it easier to deploy and test applications.

- A program linked against a static library includes only the code for the functions it uses, while a program linked with a shared library uses the library code in its entirety. If a program uses one call from a very large library available in static and dynamic forms, choosing static linking can be beneficial.

The advantages of static and dynamic linking for specific types of libraries will be discussed in the next section.

Dynamic libraries can be built with position-independent code (PIC), providing an extra level of indirection for access of global data. This defers the symbol lookup until a PIC function is called for the first time, and allows dynamic libraries to be shared by multiple processes as they can be mapped to different addresses. On the other hand, dynamic libraries that don't use PIC, when relocated, are bound to particular addresses in the process space and therefore, cannot be shared.

By default, the object files are not generated as position-independent code because the extra indirection can result in additional work performed by the runtime linker for static executables. In the next section, we will discuss compiler options that lead to the compilation of position-independent code.

Structure of an ELF Binary

Solaris uses the *executable and linking format* (ELF) for its relocatable objects, libraries, and the executable files. ELF object files are comprised of sections that contain the data, instructions for execution, and relocation information. The linker concatenates object file sections into segments that can be mapped by the runtime linker directly to the memory with the mmap(2) call.

The important segments of an executable are the text, which contains the instructions that the program should perform, the data with initialized global and static variables, and the *block started by symbol* (bss) with the space allocated for uninitialized variables. The bss segment doesn't take up any space in an object file. Instead, the required space is allocated at the loading stage by the runtime linker.

Every dynamic dependency of an executable and the executable file itself can have the specialized sections .init and .fini, with instructions that are executed before the program calls its main program entry point and exits respectively. These sections are used to perform initialization and termination tasks for a program. A function can be included in either .init or .fini section with a C pragma.

```
#pragma init (foo1)
#pragma fini (foo2)
```

We will use both the .init and .fini sections in an example demonstrating interposing shared libraries later in this chapter.

In addition to the storage areas allocated when the program is loaded, the dynamic memory allocations are performed at runtime on its *heap* and *stack*. The heap is placed in a process's virtual address space after the bss segment and holds the memory dynamically allocated with malloc(3C) calls. The stack is used to store the automatic variables (C local variables by default, Fortran local variables if compiled with -stackvar, see Chapter 6), temporary variables, and housekeeping information such as the arguments of the function not saved in the register windows (see Chapter 8). Memory dynamically allocated with alloca(3C) is also allocated on the stack and, therefore, is not available after a function allocating the memory exits. The stack starts near the highest virtual address and grows downwards.

The sizes of the `text`, `data`, and `bss` segments of a binary can be viewed with the `size(1)` command. The stack and heap sizes of a running process can be monitored with the `pmap(1)` command. We can use `size` and `pmap` to illustrate the memory layout of a simple program.

CODE EXAMPLE 7-1   Allocation of a Large Array

```
c example_elf.f
c f77 example_elf.f -o example_elf -dn (-stackvar)
      program elf
      integer*8 A(100000)
      A(1)=1
      call sleep(10)
      print*,"Hello"
      call sleep(10)
      end
```

This program declares a large array of integers which we initialize by assigning a value to its first element. If we compile the program without the `-stackvar` option, the memory for the array is allocated in the `bss` segment.

```
example% f77 example_elf.f -o example_elf -dn
example% size example_elf
352290+10697+807381=1170368
```

Here, the size of the `text`, `data`, and `bss` segments and their total is displayed with the `size(1)` command. Once `-stackvar` is used, the allocation moves from `bss` segment to the stack.

```
example% f77 example_elf.f -o example_elf -dn -stackvar
example% size example_elf
352314+10697+7381=370392
```

The memory used by the program can be monitored with the `pmap(1)` command when the program runs in a different shell. The program is linked as a static executable (`-dn`), so the `pmap` output doesn't list any shared libraries.

```
example% ps -ef | grep example_elf | grep -v grep
   ilya 16527  7288  0 18:34:47 pts/9    0:00 example_elf
example% pmap 16527
16527:  example_elf
00010000    352K read/exec        /tmp/example_elf
00076000     16K read/write/exec  /tmp/example_elf
```

```
0007A000      120K read/write/exec      [ heap ]
FFB2A000      792K read/write/exec      [ stack ]
 total       1280K
```

From the size of the segment reported by `pmap` we can see that it contains the storage space for the array. Also, we can see that the segments mapped to the memory have different access permissions. In particular, the `text` segment is mapped for reading and execution only.

Detailed information about linkers and linking formats can be found in [Levine99] and [VanderLinden94].

Solaris Linker Usage

In this section, we will describe static and dynamic library creation in the Solaris environment and the techniques of weak symbol binding and application of linker mapfiles.

Linking Static and Dynamic Libraries

As we already discussed, there are two different approaches to linking libraries into executables. While a static executable has all the definitions of the symbolic references and does not rely on the runtime linker, some of the references of a dynamic executable may be bound at runtime through shared objects.

Depending on the type of a library, we make the following recommendations about using dynamic or static linking:

- **System libraries.** The libraries provided with the Solaris Operating Environment are available in the `/usr/lib` directory and its subdirectories. Solaris 7 and higher provide both 64-bit and 32-bit versions of systems libraries; the latter are available as static archives and dynamic shared objects. For 64-bit system libraries, only dynamic versions are provided. Since the system libraries may use private symbols specific to a particular Solaris release, one should use the dynamic versions of the system libraries to ensure compatibility between the OS versions. Static linking of the system libraries can be detected with the `appcert(1)` tool.

- **Compiler libraries.** There are static and dynamic versions of these libraries shipped with the Forte Developer environment. Since these libraries might not be available on the systems where Forte Developer compilers and tools are not installed, developers can either link them statically, or link the dynamic versions and distribute the libraries with the application. The dynamic versions of the compiler libraries can be redistributed with applications under the terms of the End-User Object Code License. The dynamically linked compiler libraries can be replaced with a later version from a compiler patch, which may improve the performance of the application, though we should warn that replacing a library in a released product raises questions about additional quality assurance tests after the patch version of the library is installed. Static linking of the compiler libraries does not require shipping extra libraries and sometimes can considerably reduce the size of the product if only a small part of a large library (like `libsunperf`) is used.

- **User or application libraries.** These are the libraries used in the development of an application and possibly shipped with a product. An application can use dynamic or static libraries, as well as a mixture of the two. One of the advantages of using dynamic libraries is that the application can be updated without replacing the entire executable. In addition, as we will see in later sections of this chapter, dynamic libraries can be overloaded, which allows one to debug or profile the application without rebuilding it. Also, the Solaris linker provides a mechanism to perform a runtime platform check and use the version of a dynamic library optimized for a particular platform.

The link-editor `ld` can take a number of options that can be used directly, or with C, C++, or Fortran compilers used as linker drivers. The `-G` option tells the linker to produce a shared library rather than an executable. When linking an executable file, the `-dy` option, which is the default option of the linker, allows the use of `-Bstatic` and `-Bdynamic`, which tell the linker to use static archives or shared libraries respectively. These options can act as a toggle and control the linking of the subsequent `-l<library>` arguments until the next `-Bdynamic` or `-Bstatic` option is encountered.

At link time, the path to the location of the libraries can be set with the `-L` option or with the `LD_LIBRARY_PATH` environment variable setting[1]. This variable can be set to a value of the form `path1;path2` where `path1` and `path2` are colon-separated lists of directories that will be searched for the libraries. If another path is set with the `-L` option, it will be searched after `path1`, but before `path2`. The default library locations `/usr/ccs/lib` and `/usr/lib` are searched after the paths set with `-L` and `LD_LIBRARY_PATH`. Similar to the `-L` option, which sets the link-time library path, the `-R` option of the linker sets the runtime search path for dynamic libraries.

The link-editor parses the static libraries from left to right and brings the definitions of previously referenced symbols. Therefore, static libraries should be placed on the link line after the object files that reference their calls. By contrast, all of the dynamic libraries listed in the link command become the dependencies of the executable in the order they are listed. Because of that, the optimized libraries should precede the unoptimized ones in the command.

---

1. Secure applications have a restricted set of directories where the runtime linker can pick the libraries. See the *Linker and Libraries Guide* for details.

By default, the link-editor does not allow multiply defined symbols to be present in an executable. This can be changed with the `-z muldefs` option of `ld`. Similarly, the option `-z nodefs` allows the linker to produce an executable with some symbols undefined. These symbols can be accessed directly with `dlsym(3DL)` calls at runtime to avoid the relocation error that occurs if symbols are not found. The shared libraries can have undefined symbols that can be resolved from other libraries. To change the default behavior and to make the link-editor fail when unresolved symbols are encountered in shared libraries, the `-z defs` linker option can be used.

The single-word options can be passed to the linker directly from compiler drivers. Compound options can be passed with the `-Wl` switch of the C compiler and with `-Qoption ld` for C++ and Fortran. In this case, different parts of compound options are separated by commas, as follows.

```
example% cc -Wl,-z,muldefs ...
example% f77 -Qoption ld -z,muldefs ...
```

As we discussed in the previous section, shared libraries should be built with position-independent code for more efficient relocation. The position independent code is generated when either the `-Kpic` or `-KPIC` compiler option is set. Both of the options result in an extra level of indirection by accessing global data dereferencing pointers in the global offset table. The `-Kpic` option allows the offset sizes in the table to be 13 bits long, effectively setting the table size to 8 KB. This may not be sufficient if a large number of data objects is used. In that case, one should use the `-KPIC` option which allows the global offset table to span up to 32 bits of address range.

We will illustrate the use of the linker options with the following examples. First, we create a static archive `libfoo.a` and a dynamic library `libfoo.so`.

```
example% cat example_libraries_foo.c
/* example_libraries_foo.c */
#include<stdio.h>
void example_libraries_foo(){
    printf("Hello world \n");
}
example% cc -c -Kpic example_libraries_foo.c
example% ar r libfoo.a example_libraries_foo.o
example% cc -G -Kpic example_libraries_foo.o -o libfoo.so
```

Note that different commands are used to created the static and dynamic versions of the library. The static library is created with the `ar(1)` command. The `-r` option adds an object file to the archive creating it, if it does not exist. The dynamic library is built with the compiler which passes the `-G` option to the linker.

First, we link this library dynamically without setting specific options for the link-editor output.

```
example% cat example_libraries.c
/* example_libraries.c */
void example_libraries_foo();

int main(){
  example_libraries_foo();
    return 0;
}


example% cc example_libraries.c -o example_libraries \
        -L. -R. -lfoo
```

The list of library dependencies of a dynamic executable can be generated with the ldd(1) command. We can see that in addition to our user library libfoo.so, which is linked dynamically, the executable also dynamically links the system libraries.

```
example% ldd example_libraries
        libfoo.so =>     ./libfoo.so
        libc.so.1 =>     /usr/lib/libc.so.1
        libdl.so.1 =>    /usr/lib/libdl.so.1
        /usr/platform/SUNW,Ultra-60/lib/libc_psr.so.1
```

By putting the –Bstatic and –Bdynamic options around –lfoo, we force the linker to use the static archive libfoo.a while linking all other libraries dynamically.

```
example% cc example_libraries.c -o example_libraries \
        -L. -R. -Bstatic -lfoo -Bdynamic
example% ldd example_libraries
        libc.so.1 =>     /usr/lib/libc.so.1
        libdl.so.1 =>    /usr/lib/libdl.so.1
        /usr/platform/SUNW,Ultra-60/lib/libc_psr.so.1
```

If we drop the –Bdynamic option, we link libfoo statically together with the system libraries. The resulting binary does not have any dynamic dependencies but is still a dynamic executable because the –dn option was not used. The type of the executable can be displayed with the file(1) command.

```
example% cc example_libraries.c -o example_libraries \
        -L. -R. -Bstatic -lfoo
```

```
example% ldd example_libraries
example% file example_libraries
example_libraries:       ELF 32-bit MSB executable SPARC Version 1,
dynamically linked, not stripped
```

If we use the -dn option we build a static executable.

```
example% cc example_libraries.c -o example_libraries \
        -L. -R. -lfoo -dn
example% ldd example_libraries
ldd: example_libraries: file is not a dynamic executable or shared object
example% file example_libraries
example_libraries:       ELF 32-bit MSB executable SPARC Version 1,
statically linked, not stripped
```

As we already mentioned, only the dynamic versions of the 64-bit system libraries are available. Therefore, an attempt to produce a static 64-bit executable results in the following error.

```
example% cc example_libraries.c -o example_libraries \
        example_libraries_foo.c -xarch=v9 -dn
example_libraries.c:
example_libraries_foo.c:
ld: fatal: library -lc: not found
ld: fatal: File processing errors. No output written to example_libraries
```

Weak Symbol Binding

In some cases, it may be desirable to provide multiple implementations of the same function or to be able to overload an existing standard system function with a customized one. One way of accomplishing this is to create a shared library with a new implementation and use the LD_PRELOAD environment variable (discussed later in this chapter) to preload the library for the execution. This approach is not always applicable. In particular, it does not allow overloading statically linked functions.

The Solaris linker provides another solution by allowing weak binding of the symbols. At link time, the weak symbol will be selected unless the matching strong symbol is found, in which case the strong symbol takes precedence.

The weak symbols can be marked in the source files with `pragma weak`. For example, the following file defines a weak symbol `foo`, which is an alias to `_foo`.

CODE EXAMPLE 7-2   `pragma weak` Marks Symbols for Weak Binding

```
/* example_foo_weak.c */
#pragma weak     foo=_foo

void _foo()
{
        printf("Weak binding \n");
}
```

Once the program is compiled, the bindings of the symbols in the symbol table can be viewed with the `nm(1)` command.

```
example% cc -c example_foo_weak.c
example% nm example_foo_weak.o
example_foo_weak.o:
[Index]    Value       Size     Type  Bind  Other Shndx    Name
[2]     |        0|       0|SECT |LOCL |0    |3      |
[3]     |        0|       0|SECT |LOCL |0    |4      |
[4]     |        0|       0|SECT |LOCL |0    |2      |
[5]     |        0|       0|SECT |LOCL |0    |5      |
[7]     |       16|      36|FUNC |GLOB |0    |2      |_foo
[1]     |        0|       0|FILE |LOCL |0    |ABS    |example_foo_weak.c
[8]     |       16|      36|FUNC |WEAK |0    |2      |foo
[6]     |        0|       0|NOTY |GLOB |0    |UNDEF  |printf
```

If no global (or strong) definition of `foo` is provided at link time, its weak implementation `_foo` is chosen.

```
example% cat example_foo_main.c
/* example_foo_main.c */
int main(){
    foo();
    return 0;
}
example% cc example_foo_main.c -o example_foo example_foo_weak.c
example% example_foo
Weak binding
```

On the other hand, if a global definition of `foo` is found, it is used in the executable.

```
example% cat example_foo_strong.c
/* example_foo_strong.c */
void foo()
{
        printf("Strong binding \n");
}
example% cc example_foo_main.c -o example_foo example_foo_weak.c \
        example_foo_strong.c
example% example_foo
Strong binding
```

Many of the system calls are defined as weak and, therefore, can be overloaded. For example, the following `read(2)` call

```
example% nm /usr/lib/libc.so

. . .
[2731]  |     609052|       40|FUNC  |WEAK  |0     |9         |read
. . .
```

can be redefined by a programmer and used in an application.

We should also note that multiple strong definitions can be present in different libraries linked in a program, in which case the linker picks the first one found. Programmers should keep this in mind and list optimized libraries prior to unoptimized ones.

The following example shows how the difference in the library order affects which definition is chosen.

```
example% cat example_foo_1.c
/* example_foo_1.c */
void foo()
{
        printf("function foo is taken from example_foo_1.c \n");
}
example% cat example_foo_2.c
/* example_foo_2.c */
void foo()
{
        printf("function foo is taken from example_foo_2.c \n");
}
```

These two functions cannot be used directly for linking because the same symbol, `foo`, is multiply defined.

```
example% cc example_foo_main.c -o example_foo example_foo_1.c \
        example_foo_2.c
example_foo_main.c:
example_foo_1.c:
example_foo_2.c:
ld: fatal: symbol 'foo' is multiply defined:
        (file example_foo_1.o and file example_foo_2.o);
ld: fatal: File processing errors. No output written to example_foo
```

But when we put the functions into libraries (static or dynamic), they can both be present in the link command; the first one takes precedence.

```
example% cc -c example_foo_1.c; ar r libfoo_1.a example_foo_1.o
example% cc -c example_foo_2.c; ar r libfoo_2.a example_foo_2.o
example% cc example_foo_main.c -o example_foo -L. -lfoo_1 -lfoo_2
example% example_foo
function foo is taken from example_foo_1.c
example% cc example_foo_main.c -o example_foo -L. -lfoo_2 -lfoo_1
example% example_foo
function foo is taken from example_foo_2.c
```

Linker Mapfiles

Linker mapfiles can be used to tell the linker how to lay out a program in memory. The -M option with an associated mapfile allows changing the default mapping provided by the link-editor.

For large programs, a linker mapfile can improve the time-space locality of the instructions and, as a result, improve the usage of the processor instruction cache. One of the features of the Performance Analyzer tool in Forte Developer 6 is to create a mapfile based on the information collected during the runtime on an application. In Chapter 4 we described how to collect the runtime data. To use this data to create an optimized mapfile, one can use the Create Mapfile option in the Analyzer window. Once the mapfile is created, it can be used with the -M option of the link-editor ld(1).

The following linker mapfile was created by Forte Developer 6 for the `DBLAT` example from Chapter 4.

CODE EXAMPLE 7-3   Linker Mapfile Generated by Forte Developer 6

```
text = LOAD ?RXO;
text: .text%dmmch_: *dblat3.o;
text: .text%dmake_: *dblat3.o;
text: .text%dgemm_: *libgbl3b.a(dgemm.o);
text: .text%dchk1_: *dblat3.o;
text: .text%lderes_: *dblat3.o;
text: .text%dchk5_: *dblat3.o;
text: .text%dchk3_: *dblat3.o;
text: .text%dchk4_: *dblat3.o;
text: .text%dchk2_: *dblat3.o;
text: .text%dsyrk_: *libgbl3b.a(dsyrk.o);
text: .text%dtrsm_: *libgbl3b.a(dtrsm.o);
text: .text%dtrmm_: *libgbl3b.a(dtrmm.o);
text: .text%dsyr2k_: *libgbl3b.a(dsyr2k.o);
text: .text%dsymm_: *libgbl3b.a(dsymm.o);
```

This example is too small to show the benefits of user-provided linker mapfiles, but large applications that frequently call small noninlined functions can benefit from this technique.

In addition to improving the locality of the instructions, linker mapfiles can reduce the symbol scope in a shared library. Changing the binding of a symbol from global to local allows restricting the usage of a function to a single shared library, effectively encapsulating its implementation and prohibiting its direct reference from outside of the library.

The following example shows the change of the scope of a function.

CODE EXAMPLE 7-4   Functions With Global (Default) Symbol Scope

```
/* example_mapfile.c */
/* cc -G -Kpic -o libfoo.so example_mapfile.c -M mapfile
   cc example_mapfile_main.c -L. -R. -lfoo -o example_mapfile */
#include<stdio.h>
void example_mapfile_print();
void example_mapfile_foo();

void example_mapfile_foo(){
    example_mapfile_print();
}
```

Functions With Global (Default) Symbol Scope *(Continued)*

```
void example_mapfile_print(){
   printf("In example_mapfile_print \n");
}
```

The corresponding shared library shows the global scope of both
example_mapfile_foo and example_mapfile_print functions defined here.

```
example% cc -G -Kpic -o libfoo.so example_mapfile.c
example% nm libfoo.so | grep example_mapfile_
[47]    |     1560|     52|FUNC |GLOB |0     |8         |example_mapfile_foo
[42]    |     1632|     56|FUNC |GLOB |0     |8         |example_mapfile_print
```

The preceding function example_mapfile_print can be assigned local scope with
the following mapfile.

```
example% cat mapfile
{
local:  example_mapfile_print;
};
```

Now, compiling with the -M mapfile option reduces the scope of the function.

```
example% cc -G -Kpic -o libfoo.so example_mapfile.c -M mapfile
example% nm libfoo.so | grep example_mapfile_
[47]    |     1504|     52|FUNC |GLOB |0     |8         |example_mapfile_foo
[27]    |     1576|     56|FUNC |LOCL |0     |8         |example_mapfile_print
```

This library allows references to example_mapfile_foo function, but the
implementation of example_mapfile_print is hidden and cannot be accessed
directly or interposed with LD_PRELOAD.

For more information about the linker mapfiles and their usage, refer to the *Linker
and Libraries Guide.*

Linking Optimized Math Libraries

In this section, we discuss the optimized libraries that can be used in computational programs. Using these libraries takes advantage of the highly efficient implementations of standard mathematical functions and can lead to improved performance of applications with relatively little effort on the part of the developer. For each library, we discuss the changes in the source code, compilation, or linking required for its proper use.

The `libm` math library contains the mathematical functions that conform to the various standards that the Solaris operating system adheres to. Providing functionality and standards compliance are the primary design features of this library. It is available in the Solaris environment both as a static library `libm.a` and as a shared object `libm.so`. For Solaris 7 and later versions, support for 64-bit addressing is also available. The supported interfaces are described in the `/usr/include/math.h` header file.

The Sun compilers and Solaris Operating Environment contain many libraries that provide additional functionality and optimized versions of the functions available in `libm`. In this section, we present an overview of these libraries and show the compiler and linker options that enable linking these optimized libraries in user programs. A detailed description is beyond the scope of this book. For more information on this subject, refer to the *Numerical Computation Guide*, *Sun Performance Library User's Guide*, and the man pages `intro(3M)`, `libmvec(3M)`.

- **Sun Math Library**

  The library `libsunmath` is supported on all Sun compilers (Fortran 77, Fortran 90, C, and C++) and extends the `libm` functionality in precision (support for single-, extended-, and quadruple-precision of `libm` functions). It implements elementary transcendental, trigonometric, financial, double-precision trigonometric functions with argument reduction, integral rounding functions, random-number generators (linear congruential and table-driven additive), IEEE classification functions, data conversion, floating-point exception, and user-defined trap-handling functions. To invoke `libsunmath` functions in C and C++, one needs to add the following

  ```
  #include <sunmath.h>
  ```

  and link the library with the `-lsunmath` option. In Fortran programs, it can be simply linked with the `-lsunmath` option. The library is available in both static and dynamic versions, `libsunmath.a` and `libsunmath.so` respectively.

- **Vector Math Library**

  The library `libmvec` contains the following vector versions of elementary mathematical functions: `vatan`, `vatan2`, `vcos`, `vexp`, `vhypot`, `vlog`, `vpow`, `vsin`, and `vsincos` in double and single precision for C, C++, Fortran 77, and Fortran 90 programs. It comes in two flavors; `libmvec` and `libmvec_mt`. The latter contains parallelized (multithreaded) versions of the functions and can be used with automatic parallelization provided by the compiler. Both versions are thread-safe (see Chapter 12). The vector library can be linked in programs with `-lmvec`.

  One can also use the `-xvector` compiler option which automatically replaces calls to the above functions with calls to vectorized counterparts wherever applicable. This approach doesn't require any modifications in the program source code. The `-fast` option of the Fortran 77 and Fortran 95 compilers invokes `-xvector`. The advantage of using the vector library was illustrated in Chapter 5.

- **Optimized `libm` and `libc` libraries**

  The library `libmopt` is a part of the compiler distribution and contains optimized versions of several of the functions in `libm`. The functions contained within this library (`cos(3M)`, `sin(3M)`, `exp(3M)`, `log(3M)`, `log2(3M)`, `tan(3M)`, `pow(3M)`) are noticeably faster than `libm` ones. However, unlike the `libm` versions, which can be configured to provide any of ANSI/POSIX, SVID, X/Open, or IEEE-style treatment of exceptional cases, `libmopt` routines only support IEEE-style handling of these cases.

  The `libcopt` library contains optimized versions of some support routines in `libc`. These are not intended to be called directly by the user and instead replace the support routines in `libc` that are used by the compiler.

  In Fortran 77 and Fortran 90 program, these can be linked using the `-xlibmopt` flag or `-fast`, which includes this option. In C and C++, use `-lmopt` or `-lcopt`.

  Both `libmopt` and `libcopt` are provided in the form of architecture-specific versions. Hence, on UltraSPARC systems, the use of `-xarch=v8plus[a,b]` is recommended in order to link in the appropriate `libmopt` and `libcopt` versions.

- **Optimized Inline Math Templates**

  Certain mathematical operations, such as `floor(3M)`, `ceil(3M)`, `fabs(3M)`, `sqrt(3M)`, as well as the IEEE floating-point functions, such as `iszero(3M)`, `isnan(3C)`, `min_normal(3M)`, can be inlined by the compiler using the `-xlibmil` flag in Fortran (77 and 90), C and C++ compilers. This option is also a part of `-fast`.

The optimized math templates found in `libm.il` are provided in the form of architecture-specific versions and it is recommended that the `-xarch` value be appropriately set as shown here.

```
example% cc ... -xarch=v8plusa -xlibmil ...
```

It is important to use this flag at both compile and link time.

- **Sun Performance Library**

The Sun Performance Library™ is a large collection of functions and routines that perform various operations in computational linear algebra and Fourier transforms. It implements APIs from standard libraries BLAS1, BLAS2, BLAS3, LINPACK, LAPACK 2.0, FFTPACK, and VFFTPACK, as well as other capabilities (such as sparse direct solver, sparse BLAS) that are not included in those collections. Use of the Sun Performance Library, wherever it is applicable, is strongly recommended as the functions are highly optimized for UltraSPARC-based systems, and in some cases (for example, BLAS3 operations like matrix multiplication), the performance attained is close to the theoretical peak machine performance as measured in terms of MFLOPS (see the section on the $PLATFORM token later in the chapter for some performance results for the Performance Library BLAS3 functions).

Many of the routines in the library are multithreaded and can be used to obtain parallel scalability on multiprocessor SMP systems. All functions in the library are additionally thread-safe and come in both 32-bit and 64-bit versions. The library also has versions that support different SPARC architectures and chip implementations. To use the library, one must link the application with the `-xlic_lib=sunperf` option and remove any other libraries or object files that have implementations of the functions provided in the library. We will discuss the Sun Performance Library in detail in Chapter 13.

- **mediaLib Library**

The mediaLib™ library is a collection of C functions (callable from C and C++ applications) designed to provide highly efficient multimedia processing functions based upon the Visual Instruction Set (VIS) available in the UltraSPARC processor (see the *UltraSPARC I and II User's Manual*). To take advantage of these optimized functions, the mediaLib call has to be explicitly put in the applications.

The functions in mediaLib are grouped for applications in imaging, graphics, video, signal, and audio. The VIS instruction set is comprised of several instructions to perform operations such as pixel pack and unpack, partitioned math operations, block load and store, boundary alignments and edge handling. These instructions can process up to eight 8-bit data elements, four 16-bit data elements, or two 32-bit data elements in parallel in a manner similar to a single instruction multiple data (SIMD) architecture. The result of this hardware supported fine-grained parallelism is that operations where the dynamic range of data fits within 8-, 16-, or 32-bit data-representation can be executed very efficiently. Since the current Sun compilers (for UltraSPARC systems) don't automatically generate VIS instructions in user programs, the mediaLib functions were developed to provide easy access to this underlying hardware capability to application developers.

For example, the 64-bit block (noncache polluting) loads and stores provided as part of the VIS have been incorporated in the `memcpy(3C)` and `memset(3C)` functions and implemented in the `/usr/platform/sun4u/lib/libc_psr.so` library. This library is transparently linked in applications on UltraSPARC-based systems using the `$PLATFORM` technique that is discussed later in this chapter.

- **Sun Scalable Scientific Subroutine Library**

  The Sun Scalable Scientific Subroutine Library (also known as S3L) is a collection of functions widely used in scientific and engineering computing. This library is a part of the Sun HPC ClusterTools software. The S3L should be used for programs in C or Fortran that use MPI for message passing between processes. We will discuss S3L in detail in Chapter 14.

Creating Architecture-Specific Libraries

As we already mentioned in earlier sections, binaries built for a particular platform (say, UltraSPARC) lead to better utilization of the architectural features specific to that platform such as the registers, processor pipeline, and the instruction set. However, this improvement often comes at a price. Once platform specific features are used in the binary, it will not run on earlier systems. For example, a 32-bit application compiled with `-xarch=v8plus` can be run on UltraSPARC-based systems, but not on older generation systems.

In some cases, both the optimal performance on the current platforms and the ability to run the code on older systems are important. For that reason, some Solaris applications are distributed in two versions; one for the UltraSPARC systems, and one for all older hardware.

In this section, we will describe several techniques that, used alone or in combination, enable exploiting the performance-enhancing architecture-specific features of a particular platform while still maintaining program portability across different platforms.

$PLATFORM and $ISALIST Linker Tokens

For a dynamic executable, the Solaris linker provides a mechanism to select an appropriate system-specific library at runtime with the $PLATFORM linker token. An application can be compiled for an older SPARC implementation, say V7, but the performance-critical libraries can be provided in two or more versions with the appropriate one chosen at runtime with the help of the $PLATFORM token.

The $PLATFORM token was introduced in Solaris 2.6 and is used "under the hood" for the platform-specific libc_psr.so library.

```
example% dump -Lv /usr/lib/libc.so | grep PLATFORM
[5]      AUXILIARY   /usr/platform/$PLATFORM/lib/libc_psr.so.1
```

At runtime, $PLATFORM expands to the output of the uname -i command. To demonstrate how $PLATFORM works, we create a simple program that makes a call of the function dgemm(3P) implemented in the Sun Performance Library.

CODE EXAMPLE 7-5 Driver for dgemm Calls

```
c example_dgemm.f
c f77 -fast -xarch=v8plus example_dgemm.f -xlic_lib=sunperf \
c    -o example_dgemm
      parameter(m=400,n=500)
      integer m,n,i,j
      double precision a(m,n), b(m,n), c(n,n)
      real*4 t0,t1,etime,time(2)
      external dgemm
c
      do i=1,n
         do j=1,m
            a(j,i)=0.3*i/j
            b(j,i)=a(j,i)+1.2
         enddo
         do j=1,n
            c(i,j)=0.4*i/j
         enddo
      enddo
c
      t0=etime(time)
      do i=1,10
         call dgemm('t', 'n', n, n,
     &              m, 1.0d0, b, m, a, m, 1.0d0, c, n)
      enddo
```

CODE EXAMPLE 7-5 Driver for `dgemm` Calls *(Continued)*

```
        t1=etime(time)
        print*,'          c(n,n) = ', c(n,n)
        print*,'                    DGEMM time: ', t1-t0
c
        stop
        end
```

We create two directories, `sun4u` and `other`, in the current directory and link the `v8plusa` and `v8` versions of `libsunperf.so` from them respectively. The version from the `other` directory will be used for pre-Ultra systems and for systems running Solaris versions earlier than 2.6.

```
example% mkdir sun4u
example% ln -s /opt/SUNWspro/SC5.0/lib/v8plusa/libsunperf.so.2 \
        sun4u/libsunperf.so.2
example% mkdir other
example% ln -s /opt/SUNWspro/SC5.0/lib/v8/libsunperf.so.2 \
        other/libsunperf.so.2
```

Now, we can link various UltraSPARC platforms to the `sun4u` directory.

```
example% foreach platform (SUNW,Ultra-1 SUNW,Ultra-2 \
        SUNW,Ultra-250 SUNW,Ultra-30 SUNW,Ultra-4 \
        SUNW,Ultra-5_10 SUNW,Ultra-60 \
        SUNW,Ultra-Enterprise SUNW,Ultra-Enterprise-10000)
        ln -s sun4u $platform
        end
```

Then, we set the runtime library path and build the program.

```
example% setenv LD_OPTIONS '-R./$PLATFORM:./other'
example% f77 dgemmdemo.f -lsunperf -o dgemmdemo
```

The resulting binary will use the `v8plus` version of the performance library on an Ultra system. For example, on an Ultra 60 system we have

```
example% ldd dgemmdemo | grep libsunperf
        libsunperf.so.2 =>       ./SUNW,Ultra-60/libsunperf.so.2
```

but on a SPARCstation-5, the library is picked from the `other` directory.

```
example% uname -i
SUNW,SPARCstation-5
example% ldd dgemmdemo | grep libsunperf
        libsunperf.so.2 =>        ./other/libsunperf.so.2
```

We can illustrate the advantage of using the libraries optimized for a particular platform with the following example that compares the performance of v8 and v8plus versions of the Sun Performance Library.

CODE EXAMPLE 7-6 Computing Megaflop Rate for `libsunperf` Implementation of dgemm

```
c example_libsunperf.f
c f77 -fast -lsunperf -xarch=v8plus example_libsunperf.f -o
  example_libsunperf
c f77 -fast -lsunperf -xarch=v8 example_libsunperf.f -o
  example_libsunperf
      implicit none
      integer i, j, n, n1, ntimes
      parameter (n=1000, ntimes=10)
      double precision a(n,n), b(n,n), c(n,n)
      real t0,t1,etime,time(2)
      external dgemm
c
      do i=1,N
         do j=1,N
            a(j,i)=0.3*i/j
            b(j,i)=a(j,i)+1.2
            c(i,j)=0.4*i/j
         enddo
      enddo
c
      do n1=400,1000,100
         t0=etime(time)
         do i=1,ntimes
            call dgemm('t', 'n', n1, n1,
     &            n1, 1.0d0, b, n, a, n, 1.0d0, c, n)
         enddo
         t1=etime(time)
         print*,'    c(n1,n1) = ', c(n1,n1)
         print*,'n1 = ', n1, ' dgemm time: ', t1-t0, ' Mflops = ',
     &      ntimes/(t1-t0)/1000000*2*n1*n1*n1
      enddo
```

CODE EXAMPLE 7-6   Computing Megaflop Rate for `libsunperf` Implementation of `dgemm` *(Continued)*

```
c
      stop
      end
```

Compiling this example and linking with `-xarch=v8` and `-xarch=v8plus`, we get different versions of the Sun Performance Library linked in.

```
example% f77 -fast -xlic_lib=sunperf -xarch=v8 example_libsunperf.f \
      -o example_libsunperf
example% ldd example_libsunperf | grep libsunperf
      libsunperf.so.2 =>        /opt/SUNWspro/lib/v8/libsunperf.so.2
example% f77 -fast -xlic_lib=sunperf -xarch=v8plus example_libsunperf.f \
      -o example_libsunperf
example% ldd example_libsunperf | grep libsunperf
      libsunperf.so.2 =>        /opt/SUNWspro/lib/v8plus/libsunperf.so.2
```

These two versions produce very different megaflop rates.

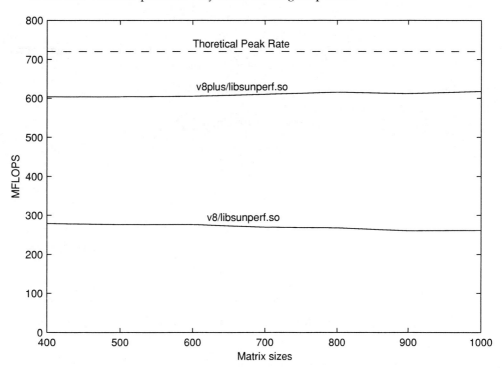

FIGURE 7-1   Megaflop Rates for `v8` and `v8plus` Versions of `libsunperf dgemm` Implementation—Runs on a 360MHz Ultra 60 (Forte Developer 6 Update 1 Compiler)

In addition to $PLATFORM, Solaris 8 introduced new tokens, $OSNAME and $OSREL, which expand to uname -s and uname -r outputs respectively. The Solaris 8 linker also allows one to specify instruction-set-specific shared libraries with the $ISALIST string token. At runtime, this token is replaced by each of the native instruction-sets on the platform shown by the isalist(1) command until the path containing $ISALIST points to an available implementation of the library.

Both instruction-set-specific and system-specific shared objects are often used in combination with filters, the special form of shared objects that provide indirection. A filter is a shared library that at link time provides only a symbol table for some (in the case of auxiliary filters) or all of the symbols whose implementations are taken from another library (filtee) at runtime. This technique, as well as the $PLATFORM and $ISALIST tokens, is described in detail in the *Linker and Libraries Guide*.

$ORIGIN Token

One of the potential problems with executables linked dynamically is that setting the absolute or relative runtime library path with the -R option prescribes either the location of the application itself or its runtime directory relative to the application binaries respectively. One of the solutions to this problem is to run an application from a shell wrapper that appends the LD_LIBRARY_PATH environment variable with the path relative to the location of the application.

A more elegant solution that allows the application to locate its dependencies is to use the runtime linker token $ORIGIN (introduced in Solaris 2.7) that represents the directory in which an object originated.

We can follow the example describing $PLATFORM from the previous section and change the runtime library path setting as follows.

```
example% setenv LD_OPTIONS '-R$ORIGIN/$PLATFORM:./other'
```

Now, after linking the program

```
example% f77 dgemmdemo.f -lsunperf -o dgemmdemo
```

the $ORIGIN expands to the absolute path of the executable ($PLATFORM still points to uname -i output).

```
example% ldd dgemmdemo | grep libsunperf
        libsunperf.so.2 =>
/export/home/examples/ORIGIN/sun4u/libsunperf.so.2
```

Now, the executable and its dependencies can be copied to another location, but the linker still resolves the library path relative to the binary that uses the library regardless of the current directory.

```
example% tar cf tarfile.tar .
example% mkdir /tmp/demo
example% cp tarfile.tar /tmp/demo
example% cd /tmp/demo
example% tar xf tarfile.tar
example% cd /export/home
example% ldd /tmp/demo/dgemmdemo | grep libsunperf
        libsunperf.so.2 =>        /tmp/demo/sun4u/libsunperf.so.2
```

Combining the $PLATFORM and $ORIGIN tokens allows creating relocatable libraries optimized for different hardware platforms. The libraries built using this technique will deliver maximum performance from the hardware transparently to the user.

Runtime Linker in Profiling and Debugging

We will now describe some techniques that are very helpful in profiling and debugging dynamically built binaries. Specifically, shared library interposition is a powerful technique for obtaining information on the runtime behavior of an application without any modifications in the executable.

Interposing Libraries

One of the advantages of using shared libraries is that the dynamically linked libraries of an application can be updated or replaced (for example, with the libraries compiled with -g or -pg) as long as the symbols used in the original version are still defined. The facility of shared library interpostions, through the use of the LD_PRELOAD variable, allows interposing any calls resolved through shared objects without replacing the dynamic libraries. The symbols can be redefined to collect the calling and timing data for the function calls without recompiling or relinking the application. This can be particularly useful when not all of the code necessary for relinking is available.

The following example illustrates this idea. We will be intercepting the calls to the dgemm(3P) function that was used in previous examples in this chapter. We use a function dgemmtest.c for interposing the dgemm calls and collecting its calling data. The function is compiled as a shared library and is interposed with the LD_PRELOAD variable.

CODE EXAMPLE 7-7 Function for Intercepting dgemm Calls From libsunperf

```
/* example_dgemmtest.c */
/* cc -c -KPIC example_dgemmtest.c
   cc -G -o example_dgemmtest.so example_dgemmtest.o */
#include <stdio.h>
#include <dlfcn.h>
#include <sys/time.h>

static dgemm_counter=0;
static hrtime_t t1, t2, timetotal;
static void (*dgemm_handle)(char *, char *, int *, int *, int *, double *,
                        double *, int *, double *, int *,
                        double *, double *, int *) = NULL;
FILE *fdgemm;
int pid;
static char filename[20];

#pragma init (initptrs)
void initptrs()
{
    dgemm_handle=(void(*)(char *, char *, int *, int *, int *, double *,
        double *, int *, double *, int *,double *, double *,
        int *))dlsym(RTLD_NEXT, "dgemm_");
    pid=getpid();
    sprintf(filename,"dgemm.calls_%d",pid);
    fdgemm=fopen(filename, "w");
    fprintf(fdgemm, "\ndgemm calls: \n\n");
    fclose(fdgemm);
}

void dgemm_(char *transa, char *transb, int *m, int *n, int *k, double
        *dalpha, double *da, int *lda, double *db, int *ldb,
        double *dbeta, double *dc, int *ldc)
{
    dgemm_counter++;
    fdgemm=fopen(filename, "a");
    fprintf(fdgemm, "dgemm(%s, %s, %d, %d, %d, %f, A, %d, B, %d, %f,C, %d)\n",
        transa, transb,*m,*n,*k,*dalpha, *lda, *ldb, *dbeta, *ldc);
    t1=gethrtime();
    dgemm_handle(transa,transb,m,n,k,dalpha,da,lda,db,ldb,dbeta,dc,ldc);
    t2=gethrtime();
```

```
    timetotal=timetotal+t2-t1;
    fclose(fdgemm);
    return;
}


#pragma fini (dumpstats)
dumpstats()
{
    fdgemm=fopen(filename, "a");
    fprintf(fdgemm, "\n");
    fprintf(fdgemm, "%d dgemm calls are made: total %f sec.\n",
            dgemm_counter, (float)timetotal/1000000000.0);
    fprintf(fdgemm, "\n");
    fclose(fdgemm);
}
```

```
example% cc -c example_dgemmtest.c
example% cc -G -o example_dgemmtest.so example_dgemmtest.o
example% setenv LD_PRELOAD ./example_dgemmtest.so
```

For each process, this shared object will produce a file with records of all `dgemm` calls (with corresponding arguments) and the time spent in the calls. The `init` and `fini` sections of the code are executed at the beginning and end of each process; therefore, `LD_PRELOAD` should be unset after the run to avoid generating extra files for other processes that are subsequently run from the same shell. Also, note the usage of the `dlsym(3DL)` call that returns the address of the next reference to `dgemm`, which makes the actual computational `dgemm` call.

Now, if we run a test program that calls `dgemm` twice, we get the following output generated by the `LD_PRELOAD`'ed function.

```
example% testprod
example% unsetenv LD_PRELOAD
example% ls | grep dgemm.calls
   2 dgemm.calls_3416
example% cat dgemm.calls_3416

dgemm calls:

dgemm(T, N, 500, 500, 2000, 1.000000, A, 2000, B, 2000, 1.000000, C, 500)
dgemm(T, N, 500, 500, 2000, 1.000000, A, 2000, B, 2000, 1.000000, C, 500)

2 dgemm calls are made: total 5.941649 sec.
```

Using `LD_PROFILE` and `LD_DEBUG`

Starting with Solaris 2.5, the linker supports profiling of shared libraries using the `LD_PROFILE` option. This feature can be used to track multiple processes or commands and has been extensively used to optimize several base operating system libraries such as `libc.so` and `libm.so`. The following example illustrates the use of this environment variable.

```
example% f90 -fast -fsimple=2 -xarch=v8plus dblas3time.f \
        -xlic_lib=sunperf -o dblas3time
example% ldd dblas3time | grep libsunperf
        libsunperf.so.3 => /opt/SUNWspro/lib/v8plus/libsunperf.so.3
example% setenv LD_PROFILE
/opt/SUNWspro/lib/v8plus/libsunperf.so.3
example% setenv LD_PROFILE_OUTPUT /tmp/blas
```

By default, the output is written in `/var/tmp`, but by using the environment variable `LD_PROFILE_OUTPUT`, it can be redirected.

Now, after we run the program as follows

```
example% dblas3time < DBLAT.in
```

a profile file is generated in the `/tmp/blas` directory, as shown here.

```
-rw-------   1 garg     mde    9441928 Apr 11 19:36 libsunperf.so.3.profile
```

This can be analyzed using `gprof(1)` as follows

```
example% gprof /opt/SUNWspro/lib/v8plus/libsunperf.so.3 \
        ./libsunperf.so.3.profile
```

to produce a `gprof`-style output. The top portion of the flat profile is shown here.

% time	cumulative seconds	self seconds	calls	self ms/call	total ms/call	name
18.7	12.96	12.96	800	16.20	16.20	___pl_pp_dgemm_tn_ [4]
18.1	25.53	12.57	1651	7.61	7.61	___pl_pp_dgemm_nt_ [5]
18.1	38.08	12.55	800	15.69	15.69	___pl_pp_dgemm_nn_ [6]
18.0	50.59	12.51	1772	7.06	7.06	___pl_pp_dgemm_tt_ [7]
9.2	56.99	6.40	17528	0.37	0.37	___pl_dram_to_cache_ [8]
5.5	60.78	3.79	2203	1.72	1.72	___pl_pp_dgemm_tt_clean_ [9]

```
    4.7        64.04       3.26       1434       2.27       2.27       ___pl_pp_dgemm_tn_clean_   [10]
    4.2        66.98       2.94       1434       2.05       2.05       ___pl_pp_dgemm_nn_clean_   [11]
    3.4        69.35       2.37       2114       1.12       1.12       ___pl_pp_dgemm_nt_clean_   [12]
```

The preceding information can be used to identify how the time is distributed within library function calls. The utility can also be used to obtain profile of user libraries. See the *Linker and Libraries Guide* for additional details.

The environmental variable LD_DEBUG can be used to obtain information regarding the runtime linker. It causes ld.so.1(1) to print runtime debugging information about the binding and execution of shared library dependencies in a dynamically linked executable.

```
example% setenv LD_DEBUG   help
```

lists the complete list of (comma-separated) tokens allowed to be used as arguments to this variable. By default, the output is sent to stderr, but the environment variable LD_DEBUG_OUPUT may be used to specify a file name (suffixed with the process id of the calling process) to direct the debugging information output.

Two useful settings of LD_DEBUG are files and bindings. The former shows the processing order of the files (binaries and shared objects) when the program is run, and the latter flag shows the bindings of the symbols in shared objects that are used in the program or its dependency files. The following commands collect LD_DEBUG data for date(1) call.

```
example% setenv LD_DEBUG files
example% setenv LD_DEBUG_OUTPUT files_output
example% date
example% setenv LD_DEBUG bindings
example% setenv LD_DEBUG_OUTPUT bindings_output
example% date
example% unsetenv LD_DEBUG
```

The information is collected in the following files.

```
example% ls
total 82                              10 files_output.14302
   72 bindings_output.14304
```

We list the top portions of these files here.

```
example% head -13 files_output.14302
14302:
14302: configuration file=/var/ld/ld.config: unable to process file
14302:
14302:
14302: file=ld.so.1  [ ELF ]
14302:     dynamic:  0x7fbe05b0  base:  0x7fbc0000
14302:     envp:     0xffbef144  auxv:  0xffbef210
14302:
14302: file=/usr/bin/date  [ ELF ]; generating link map
14302:     dynamic:     0x21858 base:     0x10000 size:      0x12420
14302:     entry:       0x10c5c phdr:     0x10034 phnum:          5
14302:     lmid:           0x0
14302:
```

```
example% head -10 bindings_output.14304
14304:
14304: configuration file=/var/ld/ld.config: unable to process file
14304:
14304: binding file=/usr/lib/link_audit/ldprof.so.1 to 0x0 (undefined
weak): symbol '_ex_deregister'
14304: binding file=/usr/lib/link_audit/ldprof.so.1 to 0x0 (undefined
weak): symbol '_ex_register'
14304: binding file=/usr/lib/link_audit/ldprof.so.1 to 0x0 (undefined
weak): symbol '__1cH__CimplKcplus_fini6F_v_'
14304: binding file=/usr/lib/link_audit/ldprof.so.1 to 0x0 (undefined
weak): symbol '__1cH__CimplKcplus_init6F_v_'
14304: binding file=/usr/lib/link_audit/ldprof.so.1 to
file=/usr/lib/link_audit/ldprof.so.1: symbol 'profcookie'
14304: binding file=/usr/lib/link_audit/ldprof.so.1 to
file=/usr/lib/link_audit/ldprof.so.1: symbol '__ldprof_msg'
14304: binding file=/usr/lib/link_audit/ldprof.so.1 to
file=/usr/lib/libc.so.1: symbol '__iob'
```

The `bindings` setting `LD_DEBUG` can be used to verify that a particular symbol has been resolved against the right library. The following example makes a `malloc(3C)` call that can be resolved from `libc(3LIB)` or from `libmtmalloc(3LIB)` if `-lmtmalloc` option is used at link time.

CODE EXAMPLE 7-8   Example of `malloc` Call

```
/* example_bindings.c */
/* cc example_bindings.c -o example_bindings (-lmtmalloc) */
#include <stdio.h>
int main()
{
    int *p=(int*)malloc(4);
    *p=1;
    printf("*p=%ld \n", *p);
    free(p);
}
```

If this program is linked without `-lmtmalloc`, we can see that `malloc` is resolved from `libc`.

```
example% cc example_bindings.c -o example_bindings
example% setenv LD_DEBUG bindings
example% setenv LD_DEBUG_OUTPUT bindings_output
example% example_bindings
*p = 1
example% unsetenv LD_DEBUG
example% grep "malloc'" bindings_output.*
20724: binding file=/usr/lib/libc.so.1 to file=example_bindings:
symbol 'malloc'
20724: binding file=example_bindings to file=/usr/lib/libc.so.1:
symbol 'malloc'
```

When `-lmtmalloc` is set, the symbol is resolved from `libmtmalloc`.

```
example% cc example_bindings.c -o example_bindings -lmtmalloc
example% setenv LD_DEBUG bindings
example% setenv LD_DEBUG_OUTPUT bindings_output
example% example_bindings
*p = 1
example% unsetenv LD_DEBUG
```

```
example% grep "malloc'" bindings_output.*
20733: binding file=/usr/lib/libc.so.1 to file=example_bindings:
symbol 'malloc'
20733: binding file=example_bindings to
file=/usr/lib/libmtmalloc.so.1: symbol 'malloc'
```

Summary

There are two phases of linking: link-editing and runtime relocation. The link-editor ld operates on relocatable object files and generates libraries or executable files. The executables can be linked statically, in which case they contain all of the instructions they need, or dynamically when some of symbol references are resolved at runtime from their dependency libraries. The runtime, or dynamic, linker ld.so.1 loads the executable file and performs the necessary relocations.

In many cases, dynamic linking of the libraries is recommended as it results in smaller binaries and provides greater flexibility for building and running applications. The system libraries need to be linked dynamically to ensure that the application is portable to subsequent OS releases.

Linking application libraries can be controlled with mapfiles which can prescribe or modify the layout of functions in the library and their scope.

Linking with optimized libraries has tremendous potential for the optimization of computational applications. In particular, applications that make heavy use of the Sun Performance Library can achieve performance levels close to theoretical peak on UltraSPARC platforms.

The linker is an important tool in the performance optimization of applications. Dynamically linked libraries allow profiling and debugging an application or its portions without recompilation, as well as collecting the runtime data. The $PLATFORM and $ORIGIN linker tokens can be used to build relocatable dynamically linked executables that are optimized for different platforms with the appropriate version selected at runtime.

## CHAPTER 8

Source Code Optimization

In the previous chapters, we discussed techniques for improving application performance without changing the underlying source code (compiler pragmas were the only exception). Unfortunately, even the best compilers cannot turn a poorly written program into an efficient executable. Therefore, developers should pay close attention to programming the performance-critical parts of the application.

The next two chapters describe some of the programming practices that better utilize the architectural features of UltraSPARC processors (memory hierarchy, CPU pipeline) and assist the compiler to perform optimizations that otherwise are too difficult to perform.

This chapter addresses the optimizations related to improving the program's usage of UltraSPARC data caches, the translation lookaside buffer (TLB), and SPARC architecture-specific features such as register windows. We also illustrate the importance of correct data alignment for UltraSPARC processors, and outline issues relevant to data aliasing in Fortran and C programs. In the next chapter, we will concentrate on relevant techniques for loop nest optimizations. The discussion in these two chapters outlines some common source code modification methods. It is neither our intent, nor is it possible, to enumerate all of the methodologies that performance analysts use in tuning different applications.

Overview of Memory Hierarchy

Many of the compiler optimizations we discussed in the previous two chapters focused on ways to improve the processor utilization. In some cases, the performance of the program is suboptimal because the data needed to perform the operations are not delivered from the memory to the registers by the time the processor is ready to use them. The situation when CPU cycles are wasted because not enough data are supplied to it for full utilization is commonly referred to as *CPU starvation*.

Optimization of memory usage can have a tremendous effect on the performance of some applications. This requires an understanding of the memory organization of the target architecture. Typically, compilers can optimize the use of the registers and on-chip memory, but in many cases, optimizations for other memory levels require source code modifications.

Memory Levels

Historically, memory speed has improved much more slowly than processor clock frequency rates. From TABLE 8-1, which lists several Sun UltraSPARC-based workstation models in the order they were released, we can see that the ratio between the processor and bus frequencies of the UltraSPARC-based workstations increased from two to five.

TABLE 8-1   Improvements in CPU and Bus Frequencies

System	CPU Frequency	System Bus Frequency	Ratio
Ultra 1	167 MHz	83 MHz	2
Ultra 2	300 MHz	100 MHz	3
Ultra 60	360 MHz	120 MHz	3
Ultra 80	450 MHz	113 MHz	4
Sun Blade 1000	750 MHz	150 MHz	5

To bridge the increasing gap between the clock speed of the memory and processor, memory systems are organized in levels that range from very fast and expensive (therefore, small), to large and relatively slow.

The fastest memory available, a *register*, is located directly on the processor. Registers can be accessed in one cycle, but because there are very few of them, they hold a very limited amount of data.

The next level, the on-chip cache or level one (L1) cache, is larger, but is still very limited in size. Even though it is small in size, the level one cache typically uses a significant percentage of the transistors used in the processor.

The level 1 cache is possibly followed in the hierarchy by multiple levels of secondary caches[1], which are slower, but can be made a few orders of magnitude larger than the level 1 caches.

Data and program instructions can be kept in separate caches (this architecture is called the *Harvard cache*) or can be stored in the same *unified cache*.

In many cases, applications access data and instructions sequentially. Instead of bringing in sequential entries one by one, caches operate on *cache lines* comprised of adjacent data entries. A datum replaced in the cache triggers an update for the entire cache line. This considerably reduces the number of cache updates when the data are read sequentially.

Since caches are much smaller than main memory, the address in main memory for a datum needs to be mapped to a much more restricted set of locations in the cache. For *direct mapped* caches, the location of a datum is uniquely determined by its address[2]. *Set-associative* caches allow a memory address to map to a well defined subset of cache locations. For example, a two-way set-associative cache can place a datum in either of the two locations determined by its address. A *fully set-associative* cache can place data items anywhere, regardless of their addresses. The choice between different locations in set-associative caches can be made based on a random or pseudo-random algorithm. A datum can be also placed in a set-associative cache replacing the least-recently used entry in the allowed target locations[3].

The data updated in caches should find their way to the main memory of the system. Depending on how the data are written, caches are classified as *write through* or *write back*. The data block updated in write through caches gets updated in the main memory, as well. The write-back caches update blocks in the main memory only when they are replaced in the cache.

The next level in the hierarchy is the *physical memory* or *random access memory* (RAM) which is a key component of any modern computer. Before the program is executed, it is loaded together with the dependency libraries into the memory by the runtime linker, which also performs necessary relocations and manages the runtime resolution of the symbols.

---

1. The secondary cache(s) could be located either on-chip or off-chip. For example, on an UltraSPARC II processor, the secondary cache is off-chip (also called external cache), while on an UltraSPARC IIe processor, the secondary cache is situated on-chip.

2. Either virtual or physical depending on the type of the cache.

3. Note, there are many other data replacement approaches. Random replacement and least-recently used are the two common ones.

Each process running on the system has its address space in the *virtual memory* (VM) which is backed by the physical memory (and the swap space on the disk). The virtual memory is organized in *pages* of fixed size which correspond to pages in the physical memory. To reduce the virtual-to-physical address translation time, the CPU provides a cache of address translations called the *translation lookaside buffer* (TLB).

Compared to the RAM, magnetic disks offer a much cheaper media for the storage of very large volumes of data. In addition, magnetic disks offer persistent storage that survives the reboots of the system. The obvious disadvantage of disk storage is the very large access time, which is typically several orders of magnitude higher than the access time to the physical memory.

In some cases, it is possible to hide this high latency with asynchronous I/O. This technique is somewhat similar to data prefetching but is performed on the next level of the memory hierarchy.

Another technique that improves the I/O performance is *disk striping* which spreads the file system across multiple disks and allows parallel access to different disks. This is performed with volume management software that can also configure the disks in redundant (RAID) configurations.

Other storage devices, such as tape or CDROM drives, are much slower than magnetic disks and are often used for file transfer and distribution. The data are typically copied from these devices to the disk before they are used by an application.

There are a number of benchmarks designed to measure the performance of various components of the memory hierarchy. The most commonly used ones include lmbench [McVoy96], STREAM [McCalpin95], and HINT [Gustafson95] benchmarks. A detailed description of memory hierarchy used in modern computers systems is provided in [Hennessy96] and [Dowd98].

Memory Organization of UltraSPARC-Based Systems

In this section, we will provide a very brief overview of the UltraSPARC memory hierarchy. A more detailed description of the architecture of UltraSPARC CPUs and interconnects is provided in Appendices B and C.

- **CPU registers.** The UltraSPARC processors implement the SPARC V9 architecture, which has 32 general purpose registers. Of that number, 8 registers are global and the remaining 24 form a *register window* with 8 `local`, 8 `in`, and 8 `out` registers. There are 8 window frames on the CPU which are switched when a program makes or exits a function call ([Weaver94]). For floating-point operations, there are 32 registers which can hold either single-precision or double-precision operands. Registers form the fastest level of memory where the register data can be accessed by the CPU in a single cycle.

- **Level 1 cache.** UltraSPARC processors have separate data and instruction on-chip caches, the D-cache and the I-cache, respectively. Their sizes are 16 KB for both D-cache and I-cache for UltraSPARC I and UltraSPARC II CPUs. The D-cache is direct-mapped, and the I-cache is 2-way set associative, both having 32 byte cache lines. The UltraSPARC III processor has 32 KB I-cache and 64 KB D-cache. Both caches are 4-way set associative and have line sizes of 32 bytes. Level 1 on-chip data cache can be accessed in 3-4 cycles.

- **Prefetch cache and write cache.** In addition to the on-chip instruction and data caches, the UltraSPARC III CPU has two smaller specialized on-chip caches: the prefetch cache, or P-cache, and the write cache, or W-cache. Both caches are 4-way set associative, 2 KB in size, with 64 byte line size.

- **Level 2 cache.** UltraSPARC CPUs have a unified (data and instruction) secondary cache, or external cache (E-cache). Its size varies from 256 KB on low-end workstations to 8 MB on high end systems. The external cache is direct-mapped with the cache line of 64 bytes on UltraSPARC I,II and 512 bytes on UltraSPARC III CPUs[1]. The access time of the data in the E-cache is typically in the range of 7 (UltraSPARC I) to 15 cycles (UltraSPARC III).

- **Virtual memory and translation lookaside buffer.** Currently, the memory pages of the UltraSPARC Solaris systems have a fixed size[2] of 8 KB. The TLB, which is a hardware cache for virtual to physical address translations, is fully associative and is 64 entries in size on UltraSPARC I,II CPUs, and has 512 entries and is 2-way set associative on UltraSPARC III. UltraSPARC III also has a fully associative 16 entry second D-TLB which can hold 64 KB, 512 KB, 4 MB pages, as well as locked pages of any size.

---

1. The external cache is subblocked on UltraSPARC III with block size of 64 bytes. The line size varies with the size of the external cache. It is 64 bytes for 1 MB size external cache and 512 bytes for 8 MB external cache.

2. The exception is the 4 MB pages which can be obtained through the use of Intimate Shared Memory (ISM) mechanism (see [Mauro00]).

- **Physical memory.** The size of the RAM on UltraSPARC systems can vary dramatically, from a minimal configuration of approximately 64 MB on low-end desktop systems, to many tens of Gigabytes for large server systems. UltraSPARC I and UltraSPARC II systems can be configured with up to 1 GB of memory per CPU. In particular, a fully populated Enterprise 10000 system has 64 CPUs and 64 GB of physical memory. The UltraSPARC III-based systems can support up to 8 GB of memory per CPU[1], allowing one to configure high-end systems with very large amounts of memory.

The following table summarizes the memory sizes and access times.

TABLE 8-2   Sizes and Access Times (in CPU Clock Cycles) for Different Memory Levels on UltraSPARC Processors

Memory Level	Size	Access Time
CPU registers	0.5 KB[1]	order of 1 cycle
On-chip cache	2 KB - 64 KB	order of 3-4 cycles
Off-chip cache	256 KB - 8 MB	order of 10 cycles
RAM	64 MB - 64 GB	order of 100 cycles
Magnetic disks	Gigabytes	order of 10^5-10^6 cycles

1. This assumes 32 integer and 32 floating-point registers (8 bytes each). Note, the total space on the processor for integer register file is actually larger in order to support the register window mechanism in the SPARC architecture (see [Weaver94]).

Memory Hierarchy Optimizations

In the previous section, we described the architecture of memory hierarchy and noted that efficient memory utilization is one of the most important considerations in obtaining good application performance. We will now describe some commonly used techniques that improve a program's usage of the underlying memory hierarchy, leading to improved performance.

1. On two-CPU Sun Blade 1000 systems only one processor is equipped with a memory controller, therefore, these systems can have up to 8 GB of physical memory.

Cache Blocking

For cache-based machines, the optimizations that have the greatest potential for significant performance gains are those that improve the program's utilization of cache hierarchy. Cache blocking is perhaps one of the most popular and well-studied of the cache-utilization optimizations.

This technique is a kind of memory reference optimization that attempts to decrease the cache-miss rates of the program by increasing the reuse of data present in the cache. As pointed out in [Hennessy96], blocking improves program performance by enhancing the *temporal locality* and *spatial locality* of data accesses. Temporal and spatial locality are concepts that describe the way memory accesses take place. Temporal locality implies that a data item used now is likely to be used again soon. Spatial locality implies that if a data item is referenced, then data in neighboring locations are also likely to be used in the computation.

A loop computation, such as matrix-matrix multiplication, where different arrays have orthogonal access patterns, requires striding in memory leading to frequent cache misses when the array sizes exceed cache sizes. In cache blocking, loop nests are restructured such that the computation proceeds in contiguous chunks chosen to fit in the cache. If the chunk size or block size is chosen properly, the overall memory traffic (loads from and stores to memory) can be decreased significantly.

The computations that benefit from this technique most are those that have a high operation-count-to-memory-access ratio, such as BLAS3 operations. For example, in a multiplication of $N \times N$ matrices, the operation count scales as $O(N^3)$ while the memory operations scale as $O(N^2)$. The ratio of operation count to memory access is $O(N)$. Hence, for every memory access, one can do $O(N)$ operations; herein lies the potential for data reuse. Not surprisingly, this computation benefits from cache blocking as illustrated in the matrix multiplication example we will discuss in this section (see the schematic shown in FIGURE 8-1).

BLAS2 operations, on the other hand, show less benefits. For a matrix-vector multiplication, the ratio of floating-point operation count to memory accesses is $O(1)$ and cache blocking is not as effective as it is for BLAS3 type operations. It is, therefore, advisable to restructure the programs to promote BLAS2 function calls to BLAS3 function calls as much as possible. The Sun Performance Library provides cache-blocked routines and we encourage users to replace their generic routines for BLAS3 operations with those in the Sun Performance Library. We will discuss the Sun Performance Library in Chapter 13 (also, see Chapter 7).

Cache blocking, specifically as applied to BLAS3 computations, has been the subject of a lot of research and studies. Many variants of blocking have been developed and analysis to obtain optimal blocking parameters has been performed. See [Gallivan90] for a review of the different cache blocking studies and additional references. We should mention that cache blocking is not restricted to loop-based computations; the generic idea of data reuse can be adapted for any algorithm. See [Cockcroft98] for an example related to cache usage in linked list traversal.

The technique is best illustrated by considering the calculation involved in the multiplication of two matrices. Consider the program example_cblock.c, which computes the matrix product $C = AB^T$, where the sizes of matrices A, B, and C are n1 by n2, n3 by n2, and n1 by n3, respectively.

The functions mmul_noblock and mmul_block2 implement the non-blocked and blocked versions, respectively. For the routine mmul_noblock, the access patterns (see FIGURE 8-1) for the matrices A, B, and C are such that each element of C is touched once, A is touched n3 times (once for each column of B^T) and B^T is touched n1 times (once for each row of A). If the matrices are large and do not fit in the cache, there is little reuse between the touches, and the memory traffic is of the same order as the computation: $O(2N^3+N^2)$ memory reads[1] (see [Hennessey96]).

In the case when blocking is applied, a block of C is computed by taking a matrix product of a block of A with a block of B^T. If these subblocks all fit in the cache, then the blocks only need to be loaded from memory once and can be reused several times for computing the entries of C in the subblock. This can significantly reduce the traffic; $O(2N^3/nb + N^2)$ reads from memory ([Hennessy96]). While one would like the block size nb to be larger, it is restricted by the size of cache because the blocked matrices must fit in the cache completely. One will also need to carefully eliminate cache conflicts between blocks. This can be done by suitably padding the leading dimensions of the three arrays that hold the matrices and proper memory alignment.

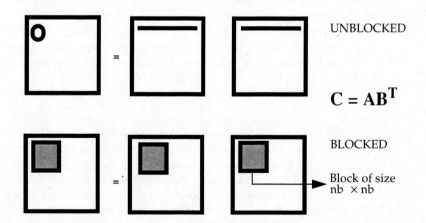

FIGURE 8-1   Blocked and Unblocked Matrix Multiplication

One other factor that determines the size of the blocks is D-TLB. For example, on an UltraSPARC II processor, the D-TLB is fully associative and holds 64 entries. For a page-size of 8 KB, the total amount of memory pages that can be mapped by entries in D-TLB (also referred to as TLB-reach) is 0.5 MB. The largest level 2 cache size on currently available UltraSPARC II-based systems is as large as 8 MB. This implies

1. Assuming n1 = n2 = n3 = N holds.

that blocks that are too large can potentially lead to D-TLB thrashing. Efficient utilization of the D-TLB cache is an important factor that needs to be considered when deciding the size in the blocked submatrices. By contrast, on UltraSPARC III systems, the D-TLB reach is 4 MB.

In order to decrease the D-TLB effect, in the example program we assume that the transpose of B has been computed in an earlier step and the array b holds entries of B^T. This leads to a situation where the accesses over array a (holding matrix A) and array b (holding matrix B^T) occur in a row-wise order (storage order for C programs) thereby decreasing TLB miss penalties. Also, only the outer two loops have been blocked. It should be noted that this example is far from a production quality matrix multiplication code. To obtain the best possible performance in matrix multiplication on UltraSPARC processors, some other issues such as loop tiling (discussed in Chapter 9), balancing the flow of load and store instructions in the CPU pipeline, overhead of modulo scheduling in inner loops, handling of remainder columns, fine-tuning TLB miss penalty, prefetching, and cache conflicts in direct mapped level 2 cache also need to be considered. On UltraSPARC I and II, the blocking should be performed for the level 2 cache because the level 1 cache is small (16 KB) and nonblocking. For the UltraSPARC III processor, blocking should be done for the level 1 cache because it is much larger than the level 1 cache on UltraSPARC II, and accesses to the level 2 cache are blocking. Judicious use of prefetch cache is also needed to keep the processor pipeline supplied with data. Of course, as we saw in Chapter 7 (see FIGURE 7-1), the Sun Performance Library provides optimal performance for matrix multiplies that are implemented simply with BLAS3 library calls.

TABLE 8-3 shows the results of blocked multiplication on an Ultra 60 system. In this table, the level 2 cache hit rate is measured using hardware counters with libcpc APIs used in the code (see Appendix D for a definition of the level 2 cache hit rate).

TABLE 8-3   Comparison of Blocked and Unblocked Matrix Multiplication

Size	Unblocked Level 2 Cache Hit Rate	Unblocked Mflops	Blocking Factor (nb)	Blocked Level 2 Cache Hit Rate	Blocked Mflops
480	0.982	230	32	0.998	311
640	0.932	125	32	0.996	297
800	0.896	92	64	0.996	290
960	0.864	71	80	0.996	286
1120	0.849	63	80	0.996	282

The results illustrate the effect of blocking factor, nb, on the performance. Even a naive blocking, as in this example, leads to a three to fourfold improvement in performance which emphasizes the significance of this technique.

CODE EXAMPLE 8-1 Cache Blocking Example *(1 of 4)*

```
/* example_cblock.c: Example to show cache-blocking
   Multiply C = AB^T; C (n1Xn3), A (n1Xn2), B (n3Xn2)
   cc -fast -xdepend -xrestrict -xarch=v8plusa \
     example_cblock.c -o example_cblock -lcpc */
#include <stdio.h>
#include <stdlib.h>
#include <sys/times.h>
#include <sys/types.h>
#include <inttypes.h>
#include <libcpc.h>
#include <errno.h>
#define CSIZE (1024*512)
#define SIZ 1011
#define IREP 5
#define min(a, b) ((a) <= (b) ? (a) : (b))

void flush_ecache(int n, double *c, double *con1);
void mmul_noblock(int n1, int n2, int n3, double a[][SIZ],
       double b[][SIZ], double c[][SIZ]);
void mmul_block2(int n1, int n2, int n3, double a[][SIZ],
       double b[][SIZ], double c[][SIZ], int nb, int na);
int main(int argc, char **argv)
{
    int i,j,k,kk,len=CSIZE,ITER=10,nrow=160;
    double a[SIZ][SIZ], b[SIZ][SIZ], c[SIZ][SIZ], d[SIZ][SIZ];
    double cc[CSIZE+8],con1=0.0,t1=0.0,t2=0.0,flops=0.0;
    int nb,na,cpuver;
    char *setting = NULL;
    cpc_event_t event, before, after;
    double ecrate_noblk=0.0,ecrate_blk=0.0;

    if ((cpuver = cpc_getcpuver()) == -1) {
       printf("no performance counter hardware \n");
    } else {
       printf("hardware identifier %d\n",cpuver);
    }
    if ((setting = getenv("PERFEVENTS")) == NULL)
       setting = "pic0=EC_ref,pic1=EC_hit";
    if (cpc_strtoevent(cpuver,setting,&event) != 0)
```

```
      printf("Cannot measure %s on this processor\n",setting);
    setting = cpc_eventtostr(&event);
    if (cpc_bind_event(&event, 0) == -1)
    printf("cannot bind lwp %d %s\n",_lwp_self(), strerror(errno));

    for (i=0;i<SIZ;i++) {          /* initialize */
       for (j=0;j<SIZ;j++) {
          a[i][j] = b[i][j] = 1.0;
          c[i][j] = d[i][j] = 0.0;
       }
    }

    for (k=0;k<5;k++) {            /* start timing loop */
       na = nb; t1 = t2 = 0.0;
       flush_ecache(len,cc,&con1);
       ecrate_noblk = 0.0;

       for (i=0;i<IREP;i++) {    /* non-blocked mat-mul */
       if (cpc_take_sample(&before) == -1) break;
       t1 = (1.e-9)*((double)gethrtime());
       mmul_noblock(nrow,nrow,nrow,a,b,c);
       t2 += (1.e-9)*((double)gethrtime()) - t1;
       if (cpc_take_sample(&after) == -1) break;
       ecrate_noblk +=
             ((1.0*(after.ce_pic[1] - before.ce_pic[1]))/
              (after.ce_pic[0] - before.ce_pic[0]));
       }
       flops = ((2.e-6*nrow)*nrow*nrow*IREP)/t2;
       printf("NOBLK: Size: %d E-cache hit-rate: %f\n",
         nrow,ecrate_noblk/IREP);
       printf("NOBLK: Size: %d Time: %f Mflops: %f\n",
         nrow,(t2/IREP),flops);

       nb = 16;
       for (kk=0;kk<ITER;kk++) {
          na = nb; t1 = t2 = 0.0;
          flush_ecache(len,cc,&con1);
          ecrate_blk = 0.0;

          for (i=0;i<IREP;i++) {    /* blocked mat-mul 2-loop */
             if (cpc_take_sample(&before) == -1) break;
             t1 = (1.e-9)*((double)gethrtime());
             mmul_block2(nrow,nrow,nrow,a,b,c,nb,na);
```

```
                t2 += (1.e-9)*((double)gethrtime()) - t1;
                if (cpc_take_sample(&after) == -1) break;
                ecrate_blk +=
                        ((1.0*(after.ce_pic[1] - before.ce_pic[1]))/
                        (after.ce_pic[0] - before.ce_pic[0]));
            }
            flops = ((2.e-6*nrow)*nrow*nrow*IREP)/t2;
            printf("BLK2: Size: %d E-cache hit-rate: %f\n",
              nrow,ecrate_blk/IREP);
            printf("BLK2: nb: %d Size: %d Time: %f Mflops: %f\n",
              nb,nrow,(t2/IREP),flops);
            nb += 16;
        }
        printf("\n");
        nrow += 160;
    }       /* of for (k=0;k<5;k++) loop */
}

void flush_ecache(int n, double *c, double *con1)
{
    int i;
    c[0] = *con1;
    for (i=1;i<n;i++) c[i] = c[i-1]+ i;
    *con1 = c[n];
}
void mmul_noblock(int n1, int n2, int n3, double a[][SIZ],
    double b[][SIZ], double c[][SIZ])
{
    int i,j,k;
    double sum=0.0;
    for (i=0;i<n1;i++) {
        for(j=0;j<n3;j++) {
            sum = 0.0;
#pragma pipeloop(0)
            for (k=0;k<n2;k++) {
                sum = sum + a[i][k]*b[j][k];
            }
            c[i][j] = sum;
        }
    }
}

void mmul_block2(int n1, int n2, int n3, double a[][SIZ],
```

```
            double b[][SIZ], double c[][SIZ], int nb, int na)
{
   int i,j,k,ii,jj;
   double sum=0.0;
   for (ii=0;ii<n1;ii+=na) {
      for (jj=0;jj<n3;jj+=nb) {
         for (i=ii;i<min((ii+na),n1);i++) {
            for (j=jj;j<min((jj+nb),n3);j++) {
               sum = 0.0;
#pragma pipeloop(0)
               for (k=0;k<n2;k++) {
                  sum = sum + a[i][k]*b[j][k];
               }
               c[i][j] = sum;
            }
         }
      }
   }
}
```

Some comments are in order as to the utility of blocking and correlating program performance with the cache hit (or miss) rate. Cache hit or miss rates should always be interpreted in the context of application performance as measured in wall-clock elapsed time, CPI (cycles per instruction), MFLOPS, or another suitable metric. On an Ultra 60 workstation (450MHz UltraSPARC II), it takes approximately 100 CPU cycles[1] to retrieve data from memory to the level 2 cache. Even a 1% level 2 cache miss rate could account for a large proportion of the total runtime of a program (see [Cockcroft98]) and might reflect in the CPI as a dominant component of the data stall rate (see Appendix D). Hence, we caution the reader to relate the cache hit or miss rate measurements carefully with the wall-clock time of the program before and after cache-blocking optimization, and not to interpret a high level 2 cache hit rate, in itself, to indicate better program performance. In the matrix multiplication example, the correlation between a high level 2 cache hit rate, higher MFLOPS, and lower wall-clock time is self-evident. This may not be the case in more complex programs.

---

1. It takes approximately 135 cycles if a D-TLB miss also occurs.

Reducing Cache Conflicts

While direct mapped caches have low cache hit times, they also suffer from higher conflict or collision misses (see [Hennessey96]). Cache conflict misses occur when multiple data items compete for the same specific cache locations in a nonfully associative cache.

Sometimes a single instruction or adjacent instructions operate on data separated in the address space by a distance equal to some integer multiple of the cache size. In direct mapped caches, such data entries will fall on the same cache location, creating a conflict and impeding the performance. Set-associative caches are designed to reduce this problem, but conflicts still may occur if many data items (exceeding the set associativity of the cache) compete for the same location.

Cache conflicts can pose a problem for such recursive computations as Fast Fourier Transforms or the Strassen algorithm for which the data sizes in powers of two are essential.

There are various techniques that reduce cache conflicts. The compiler (Fortran 95 and Fortran 77) option -xpad pads arrays to avoid power of two sizes. Also, Solaris page-coloring algorithms affect the choice of free physical page mapped to the faulted virtual page and reduce the conflicts in the direct mapped level 2 cache of UltraSPARC processors. We will discuss this later in the chapter. In this section, we will present an example program that illustrates the effects of cache conflicts on the program performance.

The example shows the performance penalty of conflicts in the level 1 data cache on UltraSPARC II processor. The main computation in this example is performed in the following line.

```
A(2*N+i)=A(i)+A(N+i)
```

If N is equal to 2,048, the three data entries in this operation are separated by 16 kilobytes, exactly the size of the UltraSPARC II level 1 data cache. The data cache line is 32 bytes and holds four real*8 elements of array A. Therefore, when N is equal to 2,050 or 2,046, there is still overlap in the cache lines that contain the data that cause cache conflicts. When N is either greater than 2,052 or smaller than 2,044, the three data items fall on different cache lines.

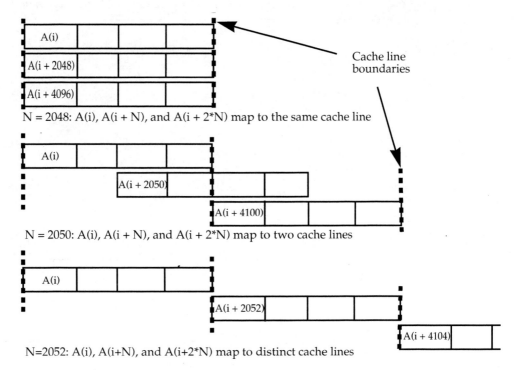

N = 2048: A(i), A(i + N), and A(i + 2*N) map to the same cache line

N = 2050: A(i), A(i + N), and A(i + 2*N) map to two cache lines

N=2052: A(i), A(i+N), and A(i+2*N) map to distinct cache lines

FIGURE 8-2 Cache Line Mappings for Different Stride Values

CODE EXAMPLE 8-2 Performance Impact of Data Cache Conflict

```
c example_dcache.f
c f77 -fast -xarch=v8plus example_dcache.f -xinline= -o
example_dcache
      parameter (k=2048)
      real*8 buffer(k*3+100)
      real t1, t2, time(2), etime
c
      do i=1,3*k
         buffer(i)= 1./i + 1
      enddo
      iter=2000000
c
      do l=-6,6,2
         t1 = etime(time)
         do i=1,iter
            call test(buffer,k+l)
         enddo
```

```
        t2 = etime(time)
        print *, "N = ", k+1, ",    buffer(k) = ", buffer(k)
        write(6,'("RUNTIME: ",f6.2," seconds")') t2-t1
      enddo
c
      stop
      end

      subroutine test(A,N)
      real*8 A(*)
      do i=1,256
        A(2*N+i)=A(i)+A(N+i)
      enddo
      return
      end
```

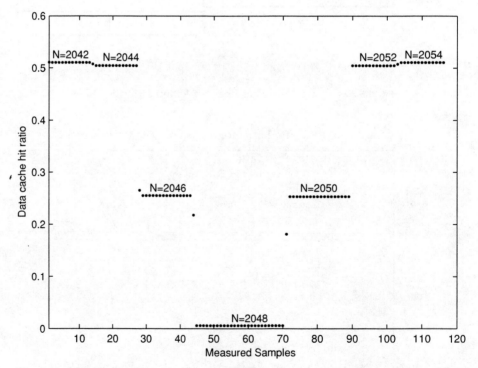

FIGURE 8-3   Data Cache Hits Are Close to Zero for Array Stride N = 2,048—Hit Ratio Improves Once the Stride Doesn't Cause Cache Conflicts

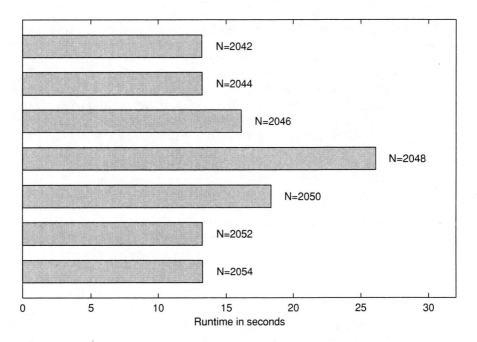

FIGURE 8-4 Stride of 2,048 Results in the Worst Performance—Runs on an Ultra 60 (Forte Developer 6 Compiler)

The figures show the times spent in loops and the data cache hit rates for various values of N. The cache statistics were obtained with the Solaris 8 cputrack(1) command.

```
example% /usr/bin/cputrack -fev -c DC_rd,DC_rd_hit example_dcache
```

We can see that if N equals 2,048, the performance is poor and the data cache hit rate is close to zero. As we expected, changing the stride to 2,046 or 2,050 improves the performance, but still leads to cache conflicts. Stride values further removed from 2048 result in improved performance and a stabilized data cache hit rate. The reader should run the example on a Sun Blade 1000 and observe the behavior on the UltraSPARC III processor.

Reducing TLB Misses

As we discussed earlier in the chapter, the *translation lookaside buffer* or TLB is a hardware (CPU) cache of the *translation software buffer* or TSB used for the translation of virtual to physical addresses of the pages (see the *UltraSPARC I and II User's Manual*, [Mauro00]). Similar to other caches and memories, the TLB greatly speeds up the address translation, if the address that needs to be translated is found in the buffer. If the address is not found, the kernel traps and looks for the entry in the TSB and if it does not find it there, it looks in the software translation table. The last step is the slowest, because it involves going through a linked list (see [Mauro00]).

There is no recipe for writing a program with low TLB misses except for a general suggestion to design the application to operate on localized data for computations. This is likely to improve the utilization of all caches, including the TLB, but can be a challenge to accomplish by a low-level tuning of code. We strongly suggest considering data locality issues during the early stages of designing applications because once the data layouts and computational algorithms have been chosen, it may be quite difficult to restructure the program for improved memory access behavior.

The TLB miss rate is high for parts of program execution that frequently use data from different memory pages, thereby flushing the lookaside buffer. Current versions of the Solaris Operating Environment use memory pages of fixed size (8 KB). We should also note that *intimate shared memory* (ISM) provides the mechanism to use 4 MB pages for an application (see [Mauro00] for discussion on ISM). This technique may reduce the TLB misses and, as a result, improve the performance of applications, but may not be efficient in cases when the memory is fragmented by multiple processes running on the system.

The following example shows the penalties of TLB misses on an UltraSPARC II-based system. The program performs the summation of an array using different strides. The size of the array is chosen to be smaller than the level 2 cache on the machine (4 MB) and the largest stride is approximately equal to the page size (8 KB). We avoided using the exact page size to reduce cache conflicts.

CODE EXAMPLE 8-3 Program Showing TLB Misses Caused by Large Strides

```
c example_tlb.f
c f77 -fast -xarch=v8plus example_tlb.f -o example_tlb
      parameter (L=500000)
      real*8 x(L), sum
      real*4 t0,t1, time(2), ttime
      integer nval(4), stride
      data nval /1, 10, 100, 1000/

      do i=1,L
         x(i)=0.001*i
```

```
         enddo

      do ii=1,4
         call sleep(5)
         ttime=0.0
         ntimes=0
         sum=0.0
         do while (ttime.le.40e0)
            stride=nval(ii)
            t0=etime(time)
            do i=1,stride
               do j=1,L,stride
                  sum=sum+x(j+i)
               enddo
            enddo
            t1=etime(time)
            ttime=ttime+t1-t0
            ntimes=ntimes+1
         enddo
         write(*,10) stride,sum/ntimes,ttime/ntimes*100
      enddo
10    format("stride= ",i5," sum= ",e12.5,";",f11.5,
     &          " sec. per 100 summations")
      end
```

The effect of the TLB miss penalty is most pronounced when the stride is chosen close to 8KB, causing a miss on almost every memory reference. We can see this in FIGURE 8-5 where the runtimes for different strides are plotted. The measured TLB misses per second are plotted for different strides in FIGURE 8-6. As previously mentioned, the size of the array was chosen to fit in the level 2 cache. On the same plot, we show that the level 2 cache utilization is consistently well above 99 percent and can conclude that the D-TLB misses are the primary cause of program slowdown.

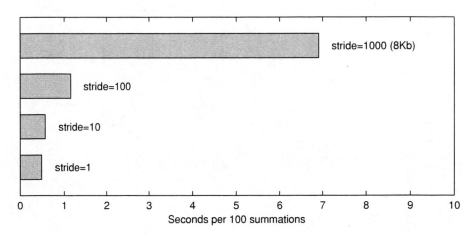

FIGURE 8-5 Runtimes for Array Summation with Various Strides—Runs on Ultra 60 (Forte Developer 6 Compiler)

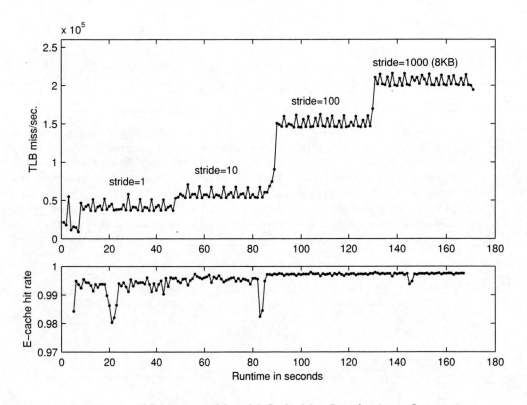

FIGURE 8-6 TLB Misses and Level 2 Cache Miss Rate for Array Summation

Page-Coloring Effects

The level 2 caches on UltraSPARC processors are direct-mapped and physically addressed (physically indexed and physically tagged). Earlier in this chapter, we showed the effects of cache aliasing in the virtually addressed, direct-mapped level 1 data cache on an UltraSPARC II processor. Aliasing occurred due to different (virtual) addresses in the user program mapping to the same cache line. Because the level 2 cache is also direct-mapped, a similar effect can occur if different physical addresses map to the same cache line in the level 2 cache. The placement of physical memory pages in the level 2 cache can, therefore, have an impact on address aliasing and, in turn, on application performance. Further, depending on the virtual to physical mapping, the physical pages acquired by a process may be placed very differently in the level 2 cache between different runs of the same program. This can lead to a run-to-run variation in program performance [Mauro00].

Because the level 2 cache is physically addressed, the address presented by the processor first undergoes a translation (from virtual address to physical address) before access to the level 2 cache is made. To mitigate address aliasing effects in the level 2 cache on UltraSPARC-based systems and to provide consistent performance, the Solaris kernel uses a technique called *page coloring* to map virtual addresses to physical addresses (see [Mauro00]). The kernel supports several different algorithms for computing the physical address given a virtual address. The effects of these algorithms vary from one program to another. One algorithm may provide repeatable run times but exaggerate address aliasing. Another may suppress address aliasing but result in a situation where the performance of a program varies from one run to another. The default algorithm has been selected after extensive experimentation and generally provides consistent performance while placing pages to avoid cache conflicts.

There are three main page-coloring algorithms implemented in the Solaris kernel (versions 2.5.1, 2.6, 7 and 8): *hashed VA*, *P. Addr = V.Addr*, and *bin hopping* [Bugnion96]. The second algorithm, P. Addr = V. Addr, is such that physical addresses map directly to virtual addresses. Not surprisingly, this algorithm results in the most consistent performance (since page placement in the level 2 cache is similar for different runs of a binary). However, it is also most susceptible to pathological cache aliasing. We will demonstrate this with a simple example program. Consult [Mauro00] for details about these various algorithms. The

`/etc/system` parameter, `consistent_coloring`, can be used to change the setting from one algorithm to another. For example, on Solaris 8 systems, the following values can be used to select different algorithms.

```
* hashed VA (default)
set consistent_coloring=0
* P.Addr = V.Addr
set consistent_coloring=1
* Bin hopping
set consistent_coloring=2
```

Note that on Enterprise 10000 systems for the Solaris Operating Environment version 2.6, another algorithm, *Kessler's best bin*, is the default algorithm [Mauro00].

We should point out that changing values in the `/etc/system` file should be done with caution as it may greatly affect the performance and usability of the system.

A technique that is sometimes used to decrease cache conflict misses by increasing the spatial locality is array interleaving or merging [Hennessy96]. Consider the five-point stencil that is commonly used in computational fluid dynamics calculations. It can be represented as follows:

```
y(i,j) = c1(i,j)*x(i - 1,j) + c2(i,j)*x(i,j - 1) + c3(i,j)*x(i,j)
       + c4(i,j)*x (i,j + 1) + c5(i,j)*x(i + 1,j)
```

If the size of the arrays are large enough powers of two, then references to `c1(i,j)`, `c2(i,j)`, `c3(i,j)`, `c4(i,j)`, and `c5(i,j)` [assuming x and y arrays are dimensioned to not cause cache conflicts] map to the same lines in a direct-mapped cache. Since the level 2 cache on an UltraSPARC II has a line size of 64 bytes, a reference (assuming double precision) to `c1(i,j)` will bring eight words, `c1(i,j)` through `c1(i + 7,j)`, into the level 2 cache. Now, since c1, c2, c3, c4, and c5 collide in the cache, the reference to `c2(i,j)` will evict the line holding `c1(i,j)` through `c1(i + 7,j)`. These will later need to be reloaded in the cache and the loop will run at the speed of memory rather than operate out of the cache. We can eliminate this by interleaving the arrays and declaring a compound array as follows

```
real (KIND = 8), dimension(5,nele,nele)::ci
```

and setting `ci(1,:,:)` = c1, `ci(2,:,:)` = c2 and so on. Now, we perform the stencil calculation as follows.

```
y(i,j) = ci(1,i,j)*x (i - 1,j) + ci(2,i,j)*x (i,j - 1)
       + ci(3,i,j)*x (i,j)
       + ci(4,i,j)*x (i,j + 1) + ci(5,i,j)*x (i + 1,j)
```

The references to c1(i,j) and c2(i,j) now do not collide in the level 2 cache. Generally, one should interleave read-only data and not mix write-only data with read-only arrays, as that increases the number of write transactions and degrades performance. Note that we have assumed that the virtual addresses representing these arrays are identical to physical addresses and this leads to aliasing in the level 2 cache on UltraSPARC II and UltraSPARC III processors.

The program is compiled as follows (using a Forte Developer 6 Fortran 90 compiler).

```
example% f90 -xO4 -dalign example_interleave.F90 \
        -o example_interleave
example% f90 -xO4 -dalign -DNOINTLEAVE example_interleave.F90 \
        -o example_nointerleave
```

Now, we run the example on an Ultra 60 for the three different settings of the consistent_coloring parameter. This can be done by changing the /etc/system file and rebooting, or by using adb(1). The measured runtimes[1] are listed in TABLE 8-4.

TABLE 8-4   Comparison Between Interleaved and Noninterleaved 5-Point Stencil Calculations on an Ultra 60 System (Solaris 8) for Different Page-Coloring Algorithms

consistent_coloring Value	Interleaved Time (Seconds)	Noninterleaved Time (Seconds)
0 (hashed VA)	20.5	19.1
1 (P.Addr=V.Addr)	**20.5**	**112.0**
2 (bin hopping)	20.3	19.2

As we can see from the table, the default page coloring in the Solaris kernel is quite effective in alleviating the effects of cache-aliasing. On the other hand, the P.Addr = V.Addr algorithm exhibits the pathological behavior in this example. The preceding result also highlights the use of array interleaving as a technique to reduce cache conflicts. One can also pad arrays, or avoid powers of two, to avoid a severe cache thrashing behaviors (see compiler option -xpad in the *Fortran User's Guide*).

1. The runs were repeated several times and showed negligible run-to-run variation.

In general, the default setting for page coloring works quite well both from the point of view of consistent performance and page placement to decrease cache conflicts. However, if the application exhibits a nonrepeatable timing behavior, then experiments should be run with other algorithms, keeping in mind to accumulate the results over multiple runs of the benchmark.

CODE EXAMPLE 8-4   Program Illustrating Array Interleaving

```
! example to show array interleaving
! f90 -xO4 -dalign example_interleave.F90 \
!   -o example_interleave (-DNOINTLEAVE)
  implicit none
  integer, parameter :: numit=100
  integer, parameter :: nele=1024
  integer :: i,j,k,n=nele,nloop
  real (KIND=8) :: dsum=0.d0
  real (KIND=8), dimension(nele+1,nele+1)::x=0.0,y=0.0
#ifdef NOINTLEAVE
  real (KIND=8), dimension(nele,nele)::c1,c2,c3,c4,c5
#else
  real (KIND=8), dimension(5,nele,nele)::ci
#endif
  real (KIND=4) :: tarray(2),t1=0.0,t2=0.0,etime
  external etime

#ifdef NOINTLEAVE
      c1 = 1.0
      c2 = 0.5
      c3 = 2.0
      c4 = 0.5
      c5 = 1.0
#else
      ci(1,:,:) = 1.0
      ci(2,:,:) = 0.5
      ci(3,:,:) = 2.0
      ci(4,:,:) = 0.5
      ci(5,:,:) = 1.0
#endif

      do nloop=1,numit
         do j=1,nele
           do i=1,nele
              x(i,j) = i*0.001 + nloop + j
              y(i,j) = 0.0
           enddo
```

```
          enddo
! now time 5-pt kernel
          t1 = etime(tarray)
#ifdef NOINTLEAVE
          call fivept_nointlv(n,x,y,c1,c2,c3,c4,c5)
#else
          call fivept_intlv(n,x,y,ci)
#endif
          t2 = t2 + (etime(tarray) - t1)
          dsum = dsum + y(5,5)
      enddo

    write(*,'("dsum ",1pe12.4,2x,"Time= ",f6.2)') dsum,t2
    end program

    subroutine fivept_nointlv(nele,x,y,c1,c2,c3,c4,c5)
    integer :: nele,i,j
    real (KIND=8), dimension(nele,nele) :: x,c1,c2,c3,c4,c5,y

    do j=2,nele-1
      do i=2,nele-1
        y(i,j) = c1(i,j)*x(i-1,j)+c2(i,j)*x(i,j-1)   &
                +c3(i,j)*x(i,j)+c4(i,j)*x(i,j+1)      &
                +c5(i,j)*x(i+1,j)
      enddo
    enddo
    end subroutine

    subroutine fivept_intlv(nele,x,y,ci)
    integer :: nele,i,j
    real (KIND=8), dimension(nele,nele) :: x,y
    real (KIND=8), dimension(5,nele,nele) :: ci

    do j=2,nele-1
      do i=2,nele-1
        y(i,j) = ci(1,i,j)*x(i-1,j)+ci(2,i,j)*x(i,j-1)   &
                +ci(3,i,j)*x(i,j)+ci(4,i,j)*x(i,j+1)      &
                +ci(5,i,j)*x(i+1,j)
      enddo
    enddo
    end subroutine
```

Memory Bank Interleaving

We will close the section on memory hierarchy optimizations with a brief discussion on the effects of memory bank interleaving. On current UltraSPARC-based systems, the main memory is based on dynamic random access memory (DRAM) technology. The faster and more expensive static random access memory (SRAM) technology is used in the on-chip and external cache memories. The DRAM memory is slower than SRAM memory as it requires time for *refreshing*, which restores electrical stability in the memory chip after an access has been made and renews its ability to accept new memory requests again. Refreshing memory chips in DRAM adds to the cost of memory access and increases it compared to the SRAM access time. Consult [Hennessy96] for a description of characteristics of DRAM and SRAM memory technologies.

Traditionally, the memory bandwidth has been increased for systems using DRAM technology for main memory by a variety of techniques. Organizing the memory into multiple independent banks is a common approach ([Hennessy96], [Dowd98]). In banked memory systems, the main memory is organized in such a way that sequential words of memory are stored on different memory banks comprised of multiple DIMM (direct inline memory module) chips. This system is referred to as an *interleaved memory* system. The manner in which addresses are mapped to different banks is called the *interleaving factor*. In an interleaved system, accesses of sequentially stored words are sent to different banks, which can simultaneously provide the data at the requested memory address locations. This hides the refresh time needed to stabilize a recently accessed DRAM chip. Interleaved systems benefit performance of both uniprocessor and multiprocessor systems.

As long as the memory access patterns do not create bank access conflicts, the benefits of an interleaved memory system are observed without any effort on the part of programmer. If the memory access pattern of the program is such that the same memory bank is accessed repeatedly, then a memory hot-spot is created. This situation is referred to as *bank stall*. Earlier in this chapter, we showed how accessing an array with power of two strides (see "Reducing Cache Conflicts" on page 256) or having multiple arrays with power of two dimensions (see "Page-Coloring Effects" on page 263) caused pathological address aliasing. Both of these situations can also lead to memory bank conflicts. Arrays with power of two dimensions must be padded, and accesses that involve power of two strides should be avoided to decrease memory bank stalls.

While the benefits of an interleaved memory system are observed without any special effort on the part of programmer (except the two tips noted above), a careful placement of memory banks is required to configure the system to deliver peak memory bandwidth. UltraSPARC-based systems provide a variety of options for configuring memory. For example, the Sun Blade 1000 system provides options for 1-way, 2-way, and 4-way interleaved configurations. The Enterprise 4500 can have 1-way, 2-way, 4-way, and 8-way interleaving while Enterprise 6500 can have up to 16-way interleaving. On the other hand, Ultra 60 and Ultra 80 desktop systems do not have interleaving and effectively are 1-way interleaved systems. A discussion of all of the various supported configurations is beyond the scope of this book. Consult the hardware product documentation available online under the "Enterprise Servers" and "Ultra Workstations" categories at `http://docs.sun.com` and `http://www.sun.com/products-n-solutions/hardware/index.html` for information on supported memory configurations.

We will illustrate the effect of bank configuration on achieved memory bandwidth with the COPY kernel of the STREAM benchmark [McCalpin95] on three differently configured Enterprise 4500 systems (400 MHz UltraSPARC II, 4 MB level 2 cache, memory interconnect running at 100 MHz). The three configurations are:

- 8-way interleaving with 8 GB memory arranged on four boards with two banks each. Each bank had 1 GB memory.
- 4-way interleaving with 4 GB memory arranged on four boards. Each board had one bank with 1 GB memory.
- 2-way interleaving with 2 GB memory arranged on one board that had two banks. Each bank had 1 GB memory.

The results are shown in FIGURE 8-7. One can clearly see the significant impact of memory interleaving on the measured bandwidth. Memory configuration is not a trivial task and while it is difficult to provide general recommendations, a good guideline to follow is choosing a configuration that yields a high interleave factor.

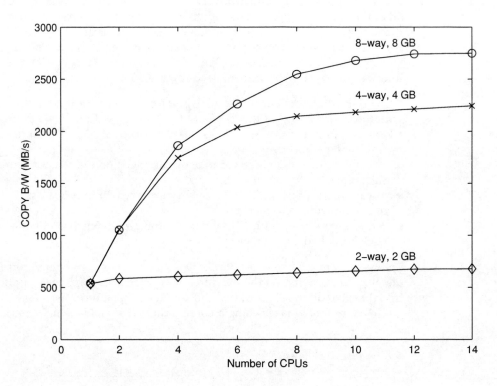

FIGURE 8-7   Effects of Memory Interleaving on STREAM COPY Bandwidth on an Enterprise 4500 System

Inlining Assembly Templates

Even with all the flexibility of high-level languages such as C and Fortran, in some cases, a developer may want to have a direct way to affect the performance-critical parts of the application at the level of assembly language. For example, a developer can explicitly use Visual Instruction Set (VIS) instructions in assembly functions.

One solution is to write the performance-critical routines in assembly language and call them from programs written in high-level languages. Since these routines tend to be small and frequently called, it will be beneficial to inline them to eliminate the function call overhead.

Another mechanism that enables use of assembly language in high-level languages is .il inlining. Assembly functions can be put in the .il file and included in the compilation command. The advantage of this method is that it guarantees that the assembly instructions are inlined at the compilation stage and it does not require any additional actions at linktime.

To illustrate this technique we can rewrite the example from the section on directive-based prefetching (Chapter 6) by replacing the pragma with an inline assembly template.

We create a template that defines the prefetch function.

CODE EXAMPLE 8-5 Assembly Template for Prefetching

```
! inline template
                .inline pr_,1
                prefetch         [%o0+0],0
                .end
```

Then, in the Fortran program, we define this function as an external and call it before the innermost computational loop.

CODE EXAMPLE 8-6 Fortran Program That Makes an Assembly Call From a Template

```
c example_il_prefetch.f
c f77 -O4 -dalign -fsimple=2 -xarch=v8plus example_il_prefetch.f \
c    pf.il -o example_il_prefetch -e
      parameter(ITER=100,SIZE=100000)
      real*8 d(16,SIZE), a
      real*4 t0,t1,etime,time(2)
      integer noffset(14), n
      data noffset /0,1,2,3,4,5,6,7,8,10,12,16,20,28/
c
      do j=1, size
         do k=1, 16
            d(k,j)=1.0
         enddo
      enddo
c
      a=0.0e+0
      t0=etime(time)
      do i=1,iter
         do j=1, size
            do k=1, 16
               a - a + d(k,j)
```

```
            enddo
          enddo
        enddo
        t1=etime(time)
        print*,'a= ',a
        write(6,10) t1-t0
 10     format("RUNTIME, no prefetch: ",f6.2," seconds")
c
        do ii=1,14
          n=noffset(ii)
          a=0.0e+0
          t0=etime(time)
          do i=1,iter
            do j=1, size
c inline funcion call
              call pr(d(1,j+n))
              do k=1, 16
                a = a + d(k,j)
              enddo
            enddo
          enddo
          t1=etime(time)
          print*,'a= ',a
          write(6,11) n, t1-t0
        enddo
 11     format("RUNTIME, prefetch with offset ",i3,
     &       ": ",f6.2," seconds")
        stop
        end
```

To inline the template, we include the `pf.il` file in the compilation command. Then,
we can verify that the prefetch instruction is present in the binary.

```
example% f77 -O4 -dalign -fsimple=2 -xarch=v8plus \
         example_il_prefetch.f pf.il -o example_il_prefetch
example% dis example_il_prefetch | grep prefetch
disassembly for example_il_prefetch
       114c8:   c1 68 a0 00          prefetch      [%g2 + 0] , 0
```

Finally, we run the program and see that the runtimes are similar to those for the
example of prefetching pragma.

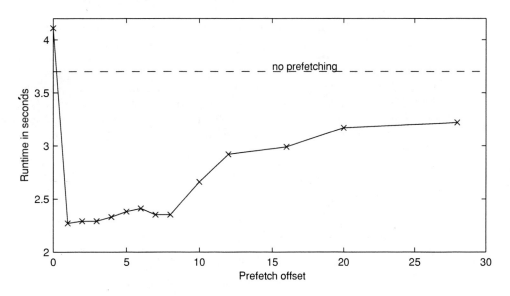

FIGURE 8-8 Effect of Inlining the Prefetch Instruction—Runs on a Sun Blade 1000 (Forte Developer 6 Compiler)

Optimal Data Alignment

In Chapter 5, we discussed the use of the `-dalign` compiler option and in Chapter 6, the use of `pragma align` in C programs to control data alignment assumed by the compiler. We emphasized the importance of maintaining the preferred alignment restrictions for different data types in order to obtain optimal performance. For example, the UltraSPARC double-word load (or store) instructions can be used for Fortran double-precision or C double data which is aligned on 8-byte boundaries. These are, as shown in Chapter 5, significantly faster than the case where single-word, half-word, or byte-by-byte load (or store) instructions are used.

In this section, we will briefly discuss how some simple program restructuring can decrease the possibility of misaligned data, show usage of double-word load (or store) instructions in single-precision programs, and demonstrate subtle performance effects of aligning data on cache-line boundaries.

Restructuring for Better Data Alignment

To handle the different situations that may arise as result of data being aligned differently, Sun compilers provide several options and pragmas (summarized in TABLE 8-5). See the *Fortran User's Guide* and the *C User's Guide* for details about these options and pragmas[1]. We strongly recommend against using the −misalign and −misalign2 options; instead, the program should be modified, wherever possible, to place data aligned on its "natural" boundaries[2]. Generally, for C structures, C global (and static) variables, and Fortran COMMON blocks, the variables should be ordered from the largest data type to the smallest data type. For example, instead of writing the following

```
integer*1 a,zs(10)
real*4 ys(21)
real*8 x(len),y(len),z(len)
common /blk1/a,x,zs,y,ys,z
```

it is preferable to write it as follows.

```
common /blk1/x,y,z,ys,zs,a
```

TABLE 8-5 Data Alignment Compiler Options and Pragmas

Option/pragma	Compiler	Function
−misalign	C	Assume at most 1-byte alignment (−xmemalign=1i)
−misalign2	C	Assume at most 2-byte alignment (−xmemalign=2i)
−dalign	Fortran, C	Assume 8-byte alignment (−xmemalign=8s)
−aligncommon	Fortran	Align data in common blocks
−dbl_align_all	Fortran	Align all data on 8-byte boundary
−f	Fortran	Align common block data on 8-byte boundary
−xmemalign	Fortran, C	New in Forte Developer 6; can be used to prescribe all of above alignment options
pragma align	C	Control alignment of global and static variables in C

1. −dalign, pragma pack, and pragma align were discussed in Chapter 6.

2. For double-precision floating-point data, we recommend using the −dalign option.

In the former case, padding is performed by the compiler, while in the latter declaration, variables are naturally placed on correct boundaries. Similar care should be taken in programs where dynamic memory allocation is used and pointer manipulation is performed. For example

```
char *x; double *y;
x = (char *) malloc(10*sizeof(char));
y = (double *) (x+2);
```

will cause y to be misaligned. In the Solaris 8 Operating Environment, on UltraSPARC systems, the malloc(3C) function returns data that are aligned on 8-byte boundaries for 32-bit programs and 16 bytes for 64-bit programs. Finer control of data alignment can be obtained by using the memalign(3C) or valloc(3C) functions. The latter returns data that are aligned on page-size boundaries.

Double-Word Load and Store Generation

While the use of the -dalign flag leads to ldd (and std) instructions being generated for double-precision data, this optimization is of little use if applied to a single-precision application because each data item is four bytes long and the compiler, in general, has to generate the code under the assumption that these data are aligned on, at most, 4-byte boundaries. However, in some cases, an ldd instruction can be used to load two adjacent elements of a single-precision array, effectively cutting the number of required load instructions in half.

For this optimization to happen, the single-precision array should be aliased to a double-precision array for which the compiler can generate double-word memory instructions. The aliasing can be performed via common pointers, as well as via EQUIVALENCE or COMMON Fortran statements. Proper care should be taken to make sure that the pairs of 4-byte data items are aligned on 8-byte boundaries and therefore can correspond to a properly aligned 8-byte quantity. This can be done with pointer arithmetic in C or by adjusting the offset of an array depending on the alignment of the first element in Fortran. The address of a variable can be determined with the loc(3F) function. It is important to remember that aliasing or use of EQUIVALENCE can cause memory reference ambiguity. Consequently, the optimization we have described in this section should be done carefully. We will discuss aliasing-caused performance problems later in the chapter.

The following example, similar to the one used in the -dalign section of Chapter 5, shows two implementations of copying one single-precision array into another. The copy_real function copies element by element and requires a load instruction for each copy operation. The optimized version copy_double uses a local array of `real*8` elements that can copy with 8-byte load and store instructions. The example also shows how to determine the alignment of the beginning of an array with a `loc` function call.

CODE EXAMPLE 8-7 Taking Advantage of Double-Word Load and Store Instructions

```
c example_alignment.F
c f77 -xO4 -dalign example_alignment.F -o \
c       example_alignment (-DOPTIMIZED)
        parameter(n=29828, numit=100000)
        integer aoff, boff
        real*4 a(n+2),b(n+2)
        real*4 etime, tarray(2), t1, time
        time = 0.

c find the offset to location that is aligned at 8-byte address
        do i=1,2
            if (iand(loc(a(i)),7).eq.0) aoff = i
            if (iand(loc(b(i)),7).eq.0) boff = i
        enddo
        write(*,*) "address of a(1): ", loc(a(1))
        write(*,*) "address of b(1): ", loc(b(1))
        write(*,*) "offsets: aoff= ",aoff," boff= ",boff
        do i=1,n+2
            a(i) = i*0.001
            b(i) = nloop*2.0 + i - 4.6
        enddo

        t1 = etime(tarray)
        do nloop=1,numit
#ifndef OPTIMIZED
            call copy_real(n,a,b)
#else
            call copy_double(n/2,a(aoff),b(boff))
#endif
        enddo
        time = time + (etime(tarray) - t1)

        write(6,10) time
   10   format("RUNTIME : ",f6.2," seconds")
        write(*,*) 'b= ',b(n),'a= ',a(n)
        end

        subroutine copy_real(n,a,b)
```

CODE EXAMPLE 8-7 Taking Advantage of Double-Word Load and Store
Instructions *(Continued)*

```fortran
      dimension a(*),b(*)
      do 100 i=1,n
100      a(i)=b(i)
      return
      end


      subroutine copy_double(N,A,B)
      real*8 a(*),b(*)
      do 200 i=1,n
200      a(i)=b(i)
      return
      end
```

Compiling the example with Forte Developer 6 update 1 Fortran 77 compiler and
running on an Ultra 60 we obtain the following results.

```
example% f77 -xO4 -dalign example_alignment.F -o example_alignment
example% example_alignment
 address of a(1):    157664
 address of b(1):    277008
 offsets: aoff=    1 boff=    1
RUNTIME :   16.82 seconds
 b=     29823.4a=     29823.4
example% f77 -xO4 -dalign example_alignment.F \
         -o example_alignment -DOPTIMIZED
example% example_alignment
 address of a(1):    157464
 address of b(1):    276808
 offsets: aoff=    1 boff=    1
RUNTIME :    8.40 seconds
 b=     29823.4a=     29823.4
```

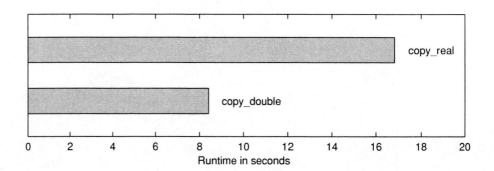

FIGURE 8-9 Performance Benefit of Using a Single-Load (and Store) Instruction for Two 4-Byte Entries

Cache Line Alignment

In some programs, aligning frequently accessed data structures on cache-line boundaries can help improve performance. On UltraSPARC I, II, and III processors, the line size for level 1 D-cache is 32 bytes. For UltraSPARC I and II, the level 1 data cache uses subblocks of 16 bytes which means the data are read from the level 2 cache in 16-byte blocks. UltraSPARC III does not use subblocking in the level 1 D-cache, and on a read-miss, 32 bytes are transferred from the level 2 cache.

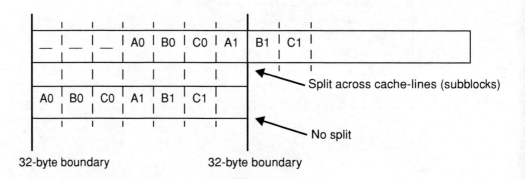

FIGURE 8-10 Data Split Across Level 1 D-Cache Line (Subblocks in Case of UltraSPARC I and II) Boundaries—Aligned Data Exhibits Better Spatial Locality and Results in More Efficient Cache Usage

In the preceding figure, we show how data that are not cache-line aligned might result in "straddling" across different lines. This can lead to less efficient usage of the cache because it can require more transactions between the D-cache and the level 2 cache in case of misses. For example, on a read-miss, in the "split" case, two lines (subblocks) are read from the level 2 cache, while for the aligned case, all the data can reside on the same line.

Consider the following example program; the parameter SIZE is set such that the data structure fully fits in the level 1 D-cache (64KB) on UltraSPARC III. The cache-line alignment is performed using #pragma align.

CODE EXAMPLE 8-8   Cache Line Alignment on UltraSPARC III

```
/* example to show L1 D-cache-line alignment on US-3
cc -fast -xchip=ultra3 example_cachealign.c gettick.il
   -DALIGN32 -o example_cachealign32 */
#define SIZE 64*1024
#define NUM SIZE/32
#define LOOPS 64

#ifdef ALIGN32
#pragma align 32 (ll)
#endif

int dummy;      /* need here else ll aligned on 32-byte bpundary
                   even without "pragma align" as start of
                   data-segment */
struct {
 double x1, y1;
 double x2, y2;  ,
} ll[NUM];

int main (int argc, char ** argv )
{
  int t0, t1, i, j;
  long long tmp_sum, tick_sum[LOOPS];
  double sum=0.0;

  printf("alignment of ll = %lx\n",&ll[0]);
  for (i=0;i<NUM;i++) {
     ll[i].x1=0.0; ll[i].y1 = i;
     ll[i].x2=0.0; ll[i].y2 = 2.0*i;
  }

  for (j=0; j<LOOPS; j++)
```

```
{
    tmp_sum=0;
    for ( i = 0; i < NUM; i++) {
        t0 = get_tick();
        sum += fabs(ll[i].y1 - ll[i].y2);
        t1 = get_tick();
        tmp_sum += t1 - t0;
    }
    tick_sum[j]=tmp_sum;
}

for ( j = 0; j<LOOPS; j++)
{
    printf("average = %f ( total=%lld, iterations=%d)\n",
            ((double)tick_sum[j])/((double)NUM), tick_sum[j], NUM);
}
return sum;
}
```

The inline module `gettick.il` is as follows.

```
.inline get_tick,0
rd    %tick,%o0
.end
```

We compile this program as follows (using Forte Developer 6 C compiler).

```
example% cc -fast -xchip=ultra3 example_cachealign.c \
         gettick.il -DALIGN32 -o example_cachealign32
example% cc -fast -xchip=ultra3 example_cachealign.c \
         gettick.il -o example_cachealign
```

In FIGURE 8-11, the total number of ticks measured at each iteration of the `j`-loop in the preceding program are shown for the two cases. The initial loops in which the cache warm-up takes place have been excluded[1] and only the steady-state measurements are shown. For the nonaligned case, the time is slightly longer and also shows higher iteration-to-iteration variance. Not surprisingly, the difference between aligned and nonaligned cases is quite small. We should also note that the program is very sensitive to data layout and instruction placement in the generated code.

---

1. The number of iterations for cache warm-up (that is, for data to become fully cache-resident) depend on the cache-line replacement policy, amongst other things; on an UltraSPARC III, it is based on a pseudo-random algorithm.

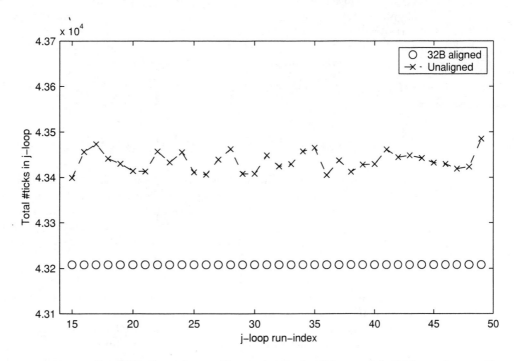

FIGURE 8-11 Total Number of `TICK` Counts (or Cycles) Measured in the Inner Loop with and without Cache-Line Alignment—Measurements Were Performed on Sun Blade 1000 (Forte Developer 6 Compiler)

If dynamic memory allocation is performed, then either `memalign(3C)` or `valloc(3C)` can be used, or pointer offset can be performed to align data on 32-byte boundaries. For example

```
int *a, *b, len; unsigned long temp;
a = (int *) malloc(len*sizeof(int)+32);
temp = ((unsigned long) a + 32) & 0xffffffe0;
b = (int *) temp; /* b is aligned on 32-byte boundary */
```

Cache-line alignment must be used only for fine tuning the program. Forcing 32-byte alignment leads to memory overhead in the form of padding of data structures (as shown above, in case of dynamically allocated data). This should be weighed against the subtle runtime improvements attained with this technique. Aligning data for lines in the level 2 cache can be helpful in parallel programs by helping decrease the problem of false sharing. We will discuss false sharing in Chapter 12.

Finally, we also note that another important byte-alignment boundary is 64-byte alignment for use of UltraSPARC VIS instructions. For example, the VIS block-load and store instructions (which do not allocate in the data caches and directly move data between floating-point registers and memory) require 64-byte data alignment. Refer to the *UltraSPARC II User's Manual* for further details.

Preventing Register Window Overflow

For faster argument interchange between function calls, SPARC architecture uses overlapping register windows [Weaver94]. A 24-register window consists of 16 "general purpose" registers divided into eight "in" and eight "local" registers together with eight "in" registers of the next window. A single instruction can increment or decrement the current window pointer (CWP) register moving the execution up or down the subroutine stack list.

The number of the register windows is not defined in the SPARC standard and is implementation-dependent. UltraSPARC processors have eight windows, one of which is reserved for taking system traps or interrupts. The remaining seven windows can be used by programs for fast switches between subroutines in the call chain. If a program has more than seven nested function calls, it runs out of register windows, causing an overflow trap after which the content of the registers in the active window is saved to memory.

The following simple example shows the performance penalty of register window spill traps. We compile it with no optimization so the penalty is more clearly observed.

CODE EXAMPLE 8-9   Program Making Recursive Calls to Illustrate the Overhead of the Register Window Overflow

```
/* example_register_windows.c
cc -xO1 example_register_windows.c -o example_register_windows */
#include<stdio.h>
#include <sys/time.h>
int iter,n,ntimes=4000000;
long long int gethrtime(void), start, end, nano=1000000000;
float t;
void example_register_recur(int);

int main()
{
    for(n=0;n<12;n++) {
        start = gethrtime();
```

Program Making Recursive Calls to Illustrate the Overhead of the
Register Window Overflow *(Continued)*

```
        for(iter=0;iter<ntimes;iter++){
            example_register_recur(n);
        }
        end = gethrtime();
        t=(end-start)/(float)nano;
        printf("n= %d , RUNTIME: %6.2f seconds \n",n,t);
    }
    return 0;
}

void example_register_recur(int a)
{
    if (a > 0) example_register_recur(a-1);
}
```

We can see that the cost of recursive calls to the function increases linearly with the
depth of the recursion up to the point when n becomes equal to five which
corresponds to six `example_register_recur` calls and a call to `main()`. The next
and consecutive calls to `example_register_recur` are more expensive because of
register window overflow traps. The lower graph shows that the overhead of each
new call stays approximately constant before and after a jump corresponding to the
transition between seven and eight functions in the program stack.

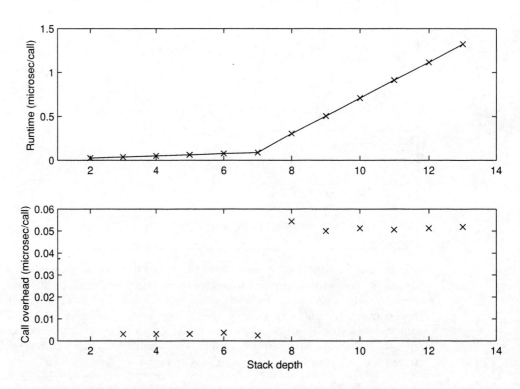

FIGURE 8-12 Function Call Overhead in Microseconds Before and After Register Window Overflow Traps—Runs on an Ultra 60 (Forte Developer 6 Compiler)

To prevent register window spills, one should avoid deeply nested calls and inline frequently called small routines.

Aliasing Optimizations

In this section, we will discuss some issues the programmer should be aware of regarding pointer aliasing and its effect on the correctness and performance of Fortran and C programs.

Aliasing in Fortran Programs

The Fortran language standard does not restrict the compiler with any special conditions on the location of variables in the memory. Because of that, the Fortran compilers can optimize the code under the assumption that all of the variables in the program are independent and stored in nonoverlapping regions of memory. The EQUIVALENCE and COMMON Fortran statements can lead to the violation of this assumption and result in incorrect code generated by the compiler. Similar problems may occur when a programmer passes the same argument to a subroutine more than once, inducing memory aliasing.

The following artificial example prints out the highest powers of two that do not exceed each of the given integers. The function foo takes isum as its first two arguments that are used in the body of the function as isum and i. In the loop body, the statement isum+i effectively doubles isum. The loop increment and the last statement of the function adjust isum to the proper value. Admittedly, it is a rather unconventional method of computing powers of two, and the program abuses argument aliasing rules. The results presented below were obtained using the Forte Developer 6 update 1 Fortran 77 compiler.

CODE EXAMPLE 8-10   Aliasing in Fortran

```
c example_alias.f
c f77 -xO1 example_alias.f -o example_alias
c f77 -xO3 example_alias.f -o example_alias: wrong results
c
      integer n, isum
      do n=1,10
         call foo(isum,isum,n)
         print*,' n = ', n, ' isum = ', isum
      enddo
      end
c
      subroutine foo(i,isum,n)
      integer n, isum, i
```

CODE EXAMPLE 8-10 Aliasing in Fortran *(Continued)*

```
        do i=1,n-1
           isum = isum+i
        enddo
        isum=(isum+1)/2
        return
        end
```

```
example% f77 -xO1 example_alias.f -o example_alias
example% example_alias
  n =    1 isum =   1
  n =    2 isum =   2
  n =    3 isum =   2
  n =    4 isum =   4
  n =    5 isum =   4
  n =    6 isum =   4
  n =    7 isum =   4
  n =    8 isum =   8
  n =    9 isum =   8
  n =   10 isum =   8
```

When we apply the optimization at -xO3 level, the compiler unrolls the loop in the subroutine under the assumptions that all of the variables are distinct in memory. In this example, the assumption does not hold and the unrolling leads to incorrect results.

```
example% f77 -xO3 example_alias.f -o example_alias
example% example_alias
  n =    1 isum =   0
  n =    2 isum =   1
  n =    3 isum =   2
  n =    4 isum =   4
  n =    5 isum =   7
  n =    6 isum =   11
  n =    7 isum =   16
  n =    8 isum =   22
  n =    9 isum =   29
  n =   10 isum =   37
```

In general, relying on aliasing for the correctness of a Fortran program should be avoided as it puts the programmer at the mercy of the optimizing compiler.

Pointer Aliasing in C Programs

The possibility of aliasing in pointer variables causes C and C++ compilers to generate code more conservatively than Fortran compilers. In a general C program, a pointer variable can be an alias of any other pointer reference or a global variable (see [Dowd98] also). A pointer variable can also be an alias for a local variable whose address is referred to using the & operator. This aliasing can occur regardless of the data type of the pointer variables unless the program follows the rules specified in the ANSI/ISO C standard. The ANSI/ISO C standard incorporates rules for stricter type checking and pointer alias disambiguation. According to the ANSI C standard, pointers and variables of different basic data types (such as int, char, double, and float) cannot alias each other. This gives the compiler greater flexibility to perform optimization in programs using pointers to base data types. However, letting the compiler improperly assume ANSI C conformance is dangerous and might cause the generation of incorrect code. For example, consider the following program fragment.

```
#include <stdlib.h>
int *p;
double *q;
void foo();
void foo() {
    int i;
    p = (int *) malloc(sizeof(int)*10);
    q = p; /* not allowed by ANSI C standard */
    for (i=0;i<5;i++)
        q[i] = i;
}
```

This code fragment clearly violates the ANSI C aliasing rules for pointers to basic data types. By default, the Sun C compiler will issue a warning whenever the user attempts to violate this rule (refer to the -Xa, -Xc options in the C compiler). We recommend that ANSI/ISO standard conformance of the program is checked carefully using the lint(1) tool (see Chapter 3) and the -errwarn option in the C compiler.

Recall, in Chapter 6, we discussed the use of the compiler options -xrestrict and -xalias_level in C programs. These options provide the compiler with more information about aliasing restrictions in the program, allowing it to perform more aggressive load (and store) elimination and hoisting loads further away from uses. We showed substantial performance gains as a result of using these options.

While the use of the -xrestrict and -xalias_level options is strongly recommended, there are many applications where it is not possible to assume that pointers are non overlapping to satisfy the restrictions imposed by these options. In such cases, with some simple modifications, the programmer can eliminate aliasing-induced ambiguity and help the compiler generate faster code. Consider the following function that performs a binary search.

CODE EXAMPLE 8-11 Pointer Aliasing Optimizations

```
int key, *array;
void binsearch(int n, int *loc);
void binsearch(int n, int *loc)
{
  int a=0, b=n;
  while (b-a > 8) {
    *loc = (a+b)>>1;
    if (array[*loc] > key)
      b = *loc;
    else
      a = *loc;
  }
  for (*loc=a; *loc<b; (*loc)++) {
    if (array[*loc] == key)
      break;
  }
}
void binsearchmod(int n, int *loc)
{
  int a=0, b=n, c=*loc;
  while (b-a > 8) {
    c = (a+b)>>1;
    if (array[c] > key)
      b = c;
    else
      a = c;
  }
  for (c=a; c<b; c++) {
    if (array[c] == key){
      *loc = c;
      break;
    }
  }
}
```

In the function `binsearch`, the pointer `loc` is a potential alias for both of the global variables: `key` and `array`. As a result, in the `while (b-a > 8)` loop, since `*loc` is updated at each iteration, the variable `key` is also loaded at every iteration and not kept in any of the available integer registers. The second problem is in the `for (*loc=...)` loop. Here also, `*loc` is stored and `key` is loaded at every iteration. The example highlights two situations where minor code changes can improve the generated code. The first is the possibility of aliasing amongst pointers passed to functions, local pointers in functions, and global variables. The second situation is the usage of pointer variables as loop-index variables. In the function `binsearchmod`, the use of `*loc` has been replaced with a local variable `c`, which no longer can be an alias for the global variables `key` or `array`. In the `while(...)` loop, the variable `key` is now kept in a global register. In the `for` loop, the extra store (and load) instruction(s) are not generated any longer. The reader is encouraged to verify these observations by compiling (using Forte Developer 6 update 1 C compiler) the example as follows

```
example% cc -fast -xalias_level=any -S example_bsearch.c
```

and by examining the generated assembly listing. Note, that while `key` and `array` are potential aliases, in `binsearch`, they are not used as *lvalues* (that is, they are only read from but not written to). This is recognized by the compiler.

Compiler-based alias disambiguation in programs using structure pointers is significantly more difficult than aliasing analysis in pointers to basic data types. Applications that make extensive use of structure pointers (such as database, graphics rendering, verilog simulation) may suffer from lack of sufficient load hoisting due to possible aliasing in structure definitions. As we demonstrated in Chapter 6, the correct use of `-xalias_level` in programs using structure pointers can lead to substantial performance improvements. We will now give an example of how source code modifications that simplify or eliminate the use of structure pointers lead to performance improvements.

Let us revisit the `example_xalias.c` program used in the `-xalias_level` section in Chapter 6. In CODE EXAMPLE 8-12, we list a rewrite of the function `setvals()`. Note how local variables are used to eliminate use of structure pointers from the computation. This helps eliminate redundant load instructions in the generated code.

CODE EXAMPLE 8-12 Modifications That Lead to Performance Improvement by Decreasing Pointer Aliasing

```
void setvalsmod()
{
   int i,j,loc,nvtxs=graph->nvtxs,sum1=0,sum2=0;
   int vwgt,jlen,edge,egwt;
   for (i=0;i<nvtxs;i++) {
```

CODE EXAMPLE 8-12   Modifications That Lead to Performance Improvement by Decreasing Pointer Aliasing *(Continued)*

```
      graph->vtxs[i] = graph->allvtxs+i;
      graph->vloc[i] = loc = i*(nvtxs-1);
      graph->vtxs[i]->edges = edges + i*(nvtxs-1);
      graph->vtxs[i]->nedges = jlen = nvtxs-1;
      vwgt = i; graph->vtxs[i]->vwgt = vwgt;
      sum1 += vwgt; sum2 = 0;
      graph->d[i] = 1.0;
   for (j=0;j<jlen;j++) {
      if (j < i) {
         edge=j;egwt=1;
      } else if (j > i) {
         edge=j+1;egwt=0;
      }
      edges[loc+j].edge=edge;
      edges[loc+j].egwt=egwt;
      sum2 += egwt;
      graph->a[loc+j] = 0.1;
   }
      graph->vtxs[i]->egwtsum = sum2;
   }
      graph->tvwgt = sum1;              .
}
```

Now, we compare the performance of the functions setvals() and setvalsmod(), compiled as −fast −xalias_level=any and as −fast −xalias_level=strong. The results for a graph with 2,500 vertices are shown in FIGURE 8-13 for an Ultra 60 workstation. Note that the runtime improvements between the setvals:any and setvalsmod:any cases. The comparable performance for setvalsmod() compiled as −xalias_level=any and setvals() compiled as −xalias_level=strong should give the reader an idea of the type of transformations performed by the compiler when the −xalias_level=strong setting is used in a program.

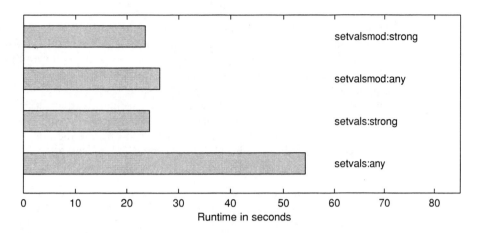

FIGURE 8-13 Runtime Improvements With Source Modification to Eliminate Structure Pointer Aliasing—Times on an Ultra 60 for Functions `setvals` and `setvalsmod` Compiled With the `-xalias_level=any` and `-xalias_level=strong` Settings (Forte Developer 6 Update 1 Compiler)

Summary

In this chapter, we discussed several programming techniques that should be used in combination with compiler optimizations to achieve the best performance in the application.

As we mentioned before, the proper choice of algorithms and data structures can have a huge impact on the efficiency of an application. The algorithm selection is beyond the scope of this book, but we strongly advocate using computational methods that have high data locality and a regular memory access pattern. These types of computations are likely to have better cache and TLB utilization than those with less regular data access.

Data should be organized according to cache sizes (and latencies) of the target platform. Since it takes approximately an order of magnitude longer to retrieve data from the main memory than from the level 2 cache, blocking the data to fit in the external cache can give a substantial boost to program performance. On UltraSPARC III, additional blocking for level 1 D-cache should be attempted as the size of D-cache is four times bigger than UltraSPARC II's D-cache. Further, while UltraSPARC II's D-cache is nonblocking, on UltraSPARC III, the D-cache blocks on a cache miss. Hence, blocking for D-cache is more important on an UltraSPARC III processor than it is on an UltraSPARC II processor.

Array strides that match a multiple of large power of two should be avoided as these can cause data items to compete for particular cache lines.

Data locality will improve not just memory cache utilization, but also the utilization of the translation lookaside buffer (TLB), which caches the table for virtual to physical address translation. We also showed how page coloring in the Solaris kernel helps alleviate conflicts in the second level direct mapped caches on UltraSPARC processors. Memory bank conflicts can also be decreased by avoiding large power-of- two array strides. While it is not in the direct control of programmer, the interleave factor of main memory in the system has a substantial impact on delivered memory bandwidth. For fully exploiting the memory bandwidth that the interconnect architecture is capable of providing, special attention should be paid to memory configuration, particularly in server systems.

Misaligned data can have a significant performance penalty. Hence, program variables should be laid out to facilitate the compiler to best utilize the alignment characteristics of the UltraSPARC processors.

Finally, we discussed data aliasing in C and Fortran programs and showed how it can affect both the correctness and performance of a program. Some ideas were presented on source code modifications that decrease pointer ambiguity in C applications and lead to generation of more efficient compiled code.

## CHAPTER 9

Loop Optimization

Loops are one of the most commonly used constructs in scientific and HPC applications. Since loops encompass repetitive computations, they often account for a large percentage of the runtime for computational programs. This chapter focuses on methods that can be used to optimize the performance of large computational loops. These techniques include loop nest unrolling and tiling, loop fusion and fission, and loop peeling. Many of these optimizations are performed by the compiler, but in general, the problem of getting the best performance from loops can be very complex and may require changes at the source code level. This is particularly true in cases where there are interiteration data dependencies or a loop is structured such that the compiler has to make conservative assumptions on account of potential data dependencies in the computations performed inside the loop. Some optimizations discussed in this chapter, such as restructuring a loop with a conditional, are not likely to be performed by the compiler and should be done by the programmer based on knowledge of program behavior.

As the sophistication of compiler optimization algorithms improves, it is possible that the transformations discussed here will be automatically performed by the compiler. Hence, it is recommended that modifications performed based on suggestions presented in this chapter be reevaluated with the availability of newer compilers to ascertain whether or not they are required. Sometimes, these optimizations (for example, manually unrolled loops) can hurt an optimizing compiler's transformations.

In this chapter we also discuss general optimization techniques, such as strength reduction (as applied in uncommon cases), that are most effective when applied within the body of a loop with large iteration count. Since each source line within a loop can be executed a large number of times, loops tend to magnify the performance effects (positive or negative) of different programming practices.

The techniques presented in this chapter by no means cover all of the possible loop transformation approaches that have been applied by performance analysts for improving program runtime. Our objective is to present a representative sample and illustrate how simple source code changes can lead to significant runtime reductions.

Loop Unrolling and Tiling

Similar to the technique of cache blocking, where the size of the data structures is chosen to fit in the cache, data can be further partitioned to fit in the registers available on the processor. Computations involving temporary variables that are used repeatedly can benefit immensely from a *register blocking* approach. This technique, when applied to loop nests, is commonly referred to as *loop tiling* ([Wolf92] and [Muchnick97]). It involves simultaneous unrolling with respect to the different loop indices in the loop nest. A schematic of untiled and 2 by 2 tiled loop nest follows. Note how the memory operation count decreases in the tiled loop nest and how the ratio of floating-point operation count to memory operation count increases compared to the untiled loop nest. The memory operation count assumes that there are mn loads (and stores) of array c in the untiled loop nest.

Untiled Loop Nest	2X2 Tiled Loop Nest (Assume m, n Divisible by 2)

<pre>do j=1,m
  do i=1,n
    do k=1,p
      c(i,j)=c(i,j) + a(k,i)*b(k,j)
    enddo
  enddo
enddo</pre>
	<pre>do j=1,m,2
	  do i=1,n,2
	    f11=c(i,j)
	    f21=c(i+1,j)
	    f12=c(i,j+1)
	    f22=c(i+1,j+1)
	    do k=1,p
	      f11=f11 + a(k,i) * b(k,j)
	      f21=f21 + a(k,i+1) * b(k,j)
	      f12=f12 + a(k,i) * b(k,j+1)
	      f22=f22 + a(k,i+1) * b(k,j+1)
	    enddo
	    c(i,j) =f11
	    c(i+1,j) =f21
	    c(i,j+1) =f12
	    c(i+1,j+1)=f22
	  enddo
	enddo</pre>

<pre>Floating Pt. Ops ~ 2mnp
Memory Ops ~ 2mnp + 2mn</pre>
	<pre>Floating Pt. Ops ~ 2mnp
	Memory Ops ~ mnp + 2mn</pre>

To unroll a loop, one needs to repeat several iterations in the loop body, adjust the loop index increment accordingly, and take proper care of the remainder of the unrolled loop. This enables the compiler to perform better instruction scheduling as the loop body becomes larger, and also reduces the overhead of the index increment as the computation and related conditional check is performed less frequently.

The compiler is very efficient in performing loop unrolling optimization, and in general, manual unrolling of singly nested loops is discouraged as it interferes with the compiler's loop unrolling analysis. However, in the case of complex multiply-nested loops with unknown bounds for different loops, often the user (with a knowledge of runtime loop bounds) can better control unrolling amounts for different loops in the nest.

As a rule of thumb, in loop tiling, the innermost loop should not be unrolled (it will usually be unrolled and modulo scheduled by the compiler). The tiling should be applied only on the outer loops. By unrolling the outermost loops, we essentially increase both the spatial and temporal locality in the computation. To obtain better results, loops may need to be interchanged before tiling is applied (see the next section). For nested loops with floating-point computations, the size of the tile (combined unroll factors for the outer loops) depends on the latency to cache[1], the latency of floating-point operations (flops), the ratio of number of flops in the loop to the number of memory operations (load and stores), and the number of available registers on the processor. The tile should be selected to be large enough to maximize the ratio of flops to memory operations, but should not use more registers than are available, causing the compiler to generate *register spills*. Register spills are stores to (and corresponding loads from) the runtime program stack of temporary values that occur as a result of the compiler running out of available free registers.

Determination of the optimal tile size for arbitrarily sized loop nests is a difficult theoretical problem. Many heuristic approaches have been developed and applied to loop tiling in different applications. (See [Lam91], [Wolf92], and [Panda99] for techniques of loop nest tiling optimization in compilers; see [Whaley98] and [Dayde99] for examples of loop tiling applied to BLAS3 algorithms.) In fact, the problem of matching tile shapes with loop nest dimensions can be considered to be a variant of a well known NP-complete problem known as "'two-dimensional bin packing." A heuristic approach applied to sparse symmetric matrix factorization is presented in [Garg99].

Loop tiling can, and should, be used in combination with cache blocking to ensure that data items needed for software pipelining of the tiled loop nest are in the cache. The option `-xarch=v8plus[a,b]` should be used in a 32-bit application that uses this technique to make all 32 floating-point registers of the UltraSPARC processor available to the binary. We should also point out that this type of optimization should be used only for loops with sufficiently large iteration counts. Shorter loops are not likely to benefit from unrolling (or software pipelining, for that matter) because the initialization and the shutdown stages of the pipeline will dominate the computation. We will illustrate the benefits of tiling with an example program that performs multiplications of square 24 by 24 matrices with different tilings. This small size is chosen so that all of the matrices fit in the D-cache (both on UltraSPARC II and III processors). We can see that the best runtime corresponds to the 4 by 4

---

1. UltraSPARC I and II have pipelined access to the level 2 cache and the compiler schedules loads (and stores) to level 2 cache to take advantage of this feature. On UltraSPARC III, the loads are scheduled to level 1 D-cache. On UltraSPARC II, double floating-point loads that hit in D-cache complete in two clock cycles, while on UltraSPARC III, they complete in three clock cycles.

tiling (see FIGURE 9-1). This tiling has 16 additions, 16 multiplications, and eight loads. The ratio of floating-point operations to memory load is two, and it is higher than either 4 by 3 or 3 by 4 tilings. Both of these have 12 floating-point operations (12 additions, 12 multiplications) and seven loads. A careful look at the assembly code shows that in all the three cases, the innermost loop is unrolled two deep and software pipelined. For example, in 4 by 4 tiling, computations in the innermost loop are scheduled such that one iteration can complete in 16 processor cycles (assuming all data are available). The 4 by 4 and 3 by 4 tilings use 28 floating-point registers while the 4 by 3 tiling uses 26 registers. The version that is not tiled (`subroutine mmul`) results in the worst runtime.

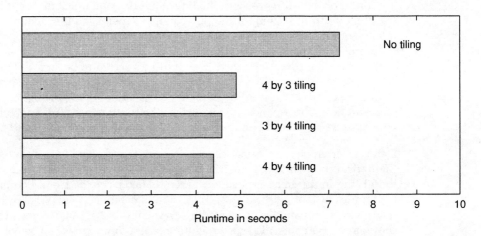

FIGURE 9-1   Performance Effect of Different Loop Tilings—Runs on Sun Blade 1000 (Forte Developer 6 Update 1 Compiler)

The software-pipelining algorithm is implemented differently in the compiler for different `-xarch` and `-xchip` compilation targets. The implementation may also change between releases of the compilers. One should carefully check if a particular choice of tiling parameters is still optimal when an application is recompiled with a new compiler version or for a new hardware platform.

CODE EXAMPLE 9-1   Different Tiling Strategies *(1 of 3)*

```
c example_tiling.f
c f77 -xO4 -dalign -native -xarch=v8plus -stackvar \
c    example_tiling.f example_tiling_mmul.f -o example_tiling
      real*8  a(24,24), b(24,24), c(24,24)
      real t1, t2, time(2), etime
c
      call intabc(a,b,c)
      t1 = etime(time)
```

```
      do i=1,200000
         call mmul_4x3(a, b, c)
      enddo
      print*,'4 by 3 tiling: c(1,1) = ', c(1,1)
      t2 = etime(time)
      write(6,10) t2-t1
c
      call intabc(a,b,c)
      t1 = etime(time)
      do i=1,200000
         call mmul_3x4(a, b, c)
      enddo
      print*,'3 by 4 tiling: c(1,1) = ', c(1,1)
      t2 = etime(time)
      write(6,10) t2-t1
c
      call intabc(a,b,c)
      t1 = etime(time)
      do i=1,200000
         call mmul_4x4(a, b, c)
      enddo
      print*,'4 by 4 tiling: c(1,1) = ', c(1,1)
      t2 = etime(time)
      write(6,10) t2-t1
c
      call intabc(a,b,c)
      t1 = etime(time)
      do i=1,200000
         call mmul(a, b, c)
      enddo
      print*,'no tiling: c(1,1) = ', c(1,1)
      t2 = etime(time)
      write(6,10) t2-t1
c
  10  format("runtime: ",f6.2," seconds")
      stop
      end

      subroutine intabc(a,b,c)
      double precision  a(24,24), b(24,24), c(24,24)
      do i=1,24
         do j=1,24
            a(j,i)=0.3 + .5/j
```

```
         b(j,i)=0.2 + .5/i
         c(i,j)=0.0
      enddo
   enddo
   return
   end
```

The implementations for different tilings are included in the file
`example_tiling_mmul.f`; the 4 by 3 tiling and no tiling subroutines are as
follows.

CODE EXAMPLE 9-2   Subroutines With No Tiling and With 4 by 3 Tiling

```
c example_tiling_mmul.f
c f77 -xO4 -dalign -native -xarch=v8plus -stackvar \
c .  example_tiling.f example_tiling_mmul.f -o example_tiling
      subroutine mmul(a, b, c)
      double precision   a( 24, 24 ), b( 24, 24 ), c( 24, 24 )
      integer            i, j, l
      do j = 1, 24
         do i = 1, 24
            do l = 1, 24
               c(i,j) = c(i,j) + a( l, i )*b( l, j )
            enddo
         enddo
      enddo
      return
      end


      subroutine mmul_4x3 (a, b, c)
      double precision   a( 24, 24 ), b( 24, 24 ), c( 24, 24 )
      integer            i, j, l
      double precision   f11, f12, f21, f22, f31, f32, f41, f42
      double precision   f13, f23, f33, f43
      do j = 1, 24, 3
         do i = 1, 24, 4
            f11 = c( i,j )
            f21 = c( i+1,j )
            f12 = c( i,j+1 )
            f22 = c( i+1,j+1 )
            f13 = c( i,j+2 )
            f23 = c( i+1,j+2 )
            f31 = c( i+2,j )
```

```
                f41 = c( i+3,j )
                f32 = c( i+2,j+1 )
                f42 = c( i+3,j+1 )
                f33 = c( i+2,j+2 )
                f43 = c( i+3,j+2 )
                do l = 1, 24
                    f11 = f11 + a( l, i )*b( l, j )
                    f21 = f21 + a( l, i+1 )*b( l, j )
                    f12 = f12 + a( l, i )*b( l, j+1 )
                    f22 = f22 + a( l, i+1 )*b( l, j+1 )
                    f13 = f13 + a( l, i )*b( l, j+2 )
                    f23 = f23 + a( l, i+1 )*b( l, j+2 )
                    f31 = f31 + a( l, i+2 )*b( l, j )
                    f41 = f41 + a( l, i+3 )*b( l, j )
                    f32 = f32 + a( l, i+2 )*b( l, j+1 )
                    f42 = f42 + a( l, i+3 )*b( l, j+1 )
                    f33 = f33 + a( l, i+2 )*b( l, j+2 )
                    f43 = f43 + a( l, i+3 )*b( l, j+2 )
                enddo
                c( i,j ) = f11
                c( i+1, j ) = f21
                c( i, j+1 ) = f12
                c( i+1, j+1 ) = f22
                c( i, j+2 ) = f13
                c( i+1, j+2 ) = f23
                c( i+2, j ) = f31
                c( i+3, j ) = f41
                c( i+2, j+1 ) = f32
                c( i+3, j+1 ) = f42
                c( i+2, j+2 ) = f33
                c( i+3, j+2 ) = f43
            enddo
        enddo
        return
        end
```

Loop Interchange

Another loop-based optimization one can apply to improve spatial locality and maximize usage of data brought into the cache is *loop interchange* or reordering. In this technique, loops are reordered to minimize the stride and align the access pattern in the loop with the pattern of data storage in memory. For example, in Fortran, two-dimensional arrays are stored column-wise, while in C, the storage order is row-wise. A Fortran loop which accesses arrays row-wise would stride in memory and discard elements already present in the cache without using them. In such cases, a simple interchange of loops may be all that is needed to improve the runtime performance.

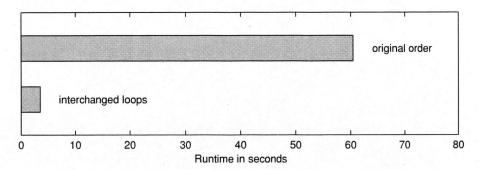

FIGURE 9-2   Benefit of Interchanging the Loop Order—Runs on a Sun Blade 1000 (Forte Developer 6 Update 1 Compiler)

Consider the example program and examine the routines nochange and change. This example demonstrates the performance improvement one can obtain by decreasing array strides in memory and aligning accesses, as much as possible, to the natural memory storage layout of data structures.

CODE EXAMPLE 9-3   Loop Interchange *(1 of 3)*

```
! example_loop_interchange.F90
! f90 -xO4 -dalign example_loop_interchange.F90 -o \
!          example_loop_interchange (-DNOCHANGE)
program changetst
   implicit none
   integer, parameter :: numit=100, nele=1024
   integer :: i,j,k,n=nele,nloop
   real (KIND=8) :: dsum=0.d0
   real (KIND=8), dimension(nele,nele)::x,y
   real (KIND=4) :: tsum,tarray(2),t1=0.0, t2=0.0,time,sum,etime
```

```fortran
   external etime
   tsum = 4.5e2
   do nloop=1,numit
! initialize the vectors
     do j=1,nele
       do i=1,nele
         x(i,j) = i*0.001 + nloop + j
         y(i,j) = 0.0
       enddo
     enddo
     t1 = etime(tarray)
#ifdef NOCHANGE
     call nochange(n,x,y)
#else
     call change(n,x,y)
#endif
     t2 = t2 + (etime(tarray) - t1)
     dsum = dsum + y(5,5)
   enddo
   write(*,*) 'dsum= ',dsum
   write(6,1000) t2
1000     format(" RUNTIME: ",f6.2," seconds")
end program
subroutine nochange(nele,x,y)
   implicit none
   integer, INTENT(in) :: nele
   real (KIND=8), INTENT(in), dimension(nele,nele) :: x
   real (KIND=8), INTENT(inout), dimension(nele,nele) :: y
   integer :: i,j
   do i=1,nele
     do j=1,nele
       y(i,j) = 2.0*x(i,j)
     enddo
   enddo
   return
end subroutine
subroutine change(nele,x,y)
   implicit none
   integer, INTENT(in) :: nele
   real (KIND=8), INTENT(in), dimension(nele,nele) :: x
   real (KIND=8), INTENT(inout), dimension(nele,nele) :: y
   integer :: i,j
   do j=1,nele
```

```
      do i=1,nele
         y(i,j) = 2.0*x(i,j)
      enddo
   enddo
   return
end subroutine
```

Loop Fusion

Loop fusion is another technique that can yield substantial performance improvement in loop intensive programs. As the name suggests, adjacent or closely located loops are fused into one single loop. The benefits of this technique include decreased loop index calculation overhead, increased computational density, and improved cache-locality of data structures. This provides the compiler with better opportunities for exploiting instruction-level parallelism. The latter improvement is particularly important when the same arrays or other data structures are accessed in different loops that perform calculations on common data.

The compiler automatically attempts loop fusion when the -xdepend[1] flag is used for compilation. However, there are cases when it may not be able to identify candidates for fusion and, in such cases, it may be necessary to fuse the loops manually to obtain the benefits described here.

Consider the example program and the routines nofusion and fusion. If we compile the following program

```
example% cc -fast -fsimple=2 -xrestrict \
        -xdepend example_loop_fusion.c -o example_loop_fusion \
        -DNOFUSION
example% cc -fast -fsimple=2 -xrestrict \
        -xdepend example_loop_fusion.c -o example_loop_fusion
```

and examine the assembly files, then we note that in routine nofusion, the two loops are separate, which means that the compiler fails to recognize that the common portions of the two loops can be fused together. It software-pipelines the two loops, but c[i] and a[i] are loaded again; therefore, if the arrays are large

---

1. Recall from Chapter 5 that for Fortran 77 and 90 compilers (Forte Developer 6 update 1), -fast macro includes -xdepend.

enough not to fit in the level 2 cache, we incur cache misses on `c[i]` and `a[i]` twice in the two loops. On the other hand, the fused loop takes advantage of the temporal locality in the calculation and reuses the cache accesses already made.

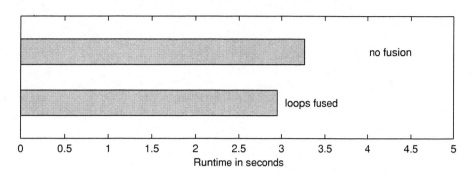

FIGURE 9-3   Loop Fusion Technique—Runs on a Sun Blade 1000 (Forte Developer 6 Update 1 Compiler)

In this example, we see around 10% improvement gained by loop fusion. As with other optimizations, one has to be careful not to apply it indiscriminately. If the fused loop becomes computationally "very fat" (that is, the loop has a very large number of memory and floating-point operations[1]), the resulting performance might degrade instead of showing improvements. Specifically, the modulo-scheduling efficiency of the unfused and fused loops should be carefully monitored.

CODE EXAMPLE 9-4   Loop Fusion *(1 of 3)*

```
/* example_loop_fusion.c */
/* cc -xO4 -dalign -xarch=v8plus -xrestrict \
   example_loop_fusion.c -o example_loop_fusion (-DNOFUSION) */
#include <stdio.h>
#include <sys/times.h>
#include <sys/types.h>
#define len 98991   /* makes the run cache resident */
#define ITER 1000

void nofusion(double *a, double *b, int nodes, double *c,
              double *d, double small, double relaxn);
void fusion(double *a, double *b, int nodes, double *c,
              double *d, double small, double relaxn);

int main(int argc, char **argv)
```

1. Whether or not a loop can be considered "very fat" is subjective and dependent on the target machine characteristics, such as the number of CPU registers, the sizes of level 1 and level 2 caches, the latencies of memory loads and stores to caches, and the memory access patterns in the program.

```
{  int i,j,k;
   double *a, *b, *c, *d, relaxn, small;
   hrtime_t start, time=0;
   a = (double *) malloc(len*sizeof(double));
   b = (double *) malloc(len*sizeof(double));
   c = (double *) malloc(len*sizeof(double));
   d = (double *) malloc(len*sizeof(double));
   relaxn = 1.0; small = 0.5;

   for (k=0;k<ITER;k++) {
      for (i=0;i<len;i++) {
         a[i] = 0.01*i + ITER;
         b[i] = 0.1 + i - ITER;
         c[i] = 0.0; d[i] = 0.5 - i;
      }
      start = gethrtime();
#ifdef NOFUSION
      nofusion(a,b,len,c,d,small,relaxn);
#else
      fusion(a,b,len,c,d,small,relaxn);
#endif
      time = time + gethrtime() -start;
   }
   printf("RUNTIME: %6.2f seconds \n",time*(1.e-9));
   return 0;
}

void nofusion(double *a, double *b, int nodes, double *c,
              double *d, double small, double relaxn)
{  int i,dummy;
   for (i=0;i<nodes;i++) {
      a[i] = a[i]*small;
      c[i] = (a[i] + b[i])*relaxn;
   }
   for (i=1;i<nodes-1;i++) {
      d[i] = c[i] - a[i];
   }
   dummy=0;
}

void fusion(double *a, double *b, int nodes, double *c,
            double *d, double small, double relaxn)
{  int i,dummy;
```

```
   a[0] = a[0]*small;
   c[0] = (a[0]+b[0])*relaxn;
   a[nodes-1] = a[nodes-1]*small;
   c[nodes-1] = c[nodes-1]*relaxn;
   for (i=1;i<nodes-1;i++) {
      a[i] = a[i]*small;
      c[i] = (a[i] + b[i])*relaxn;
      d[i] = c[i] - a[i];
   }
   dummy=0;
}
```

Loop Fission

Often in programs, there are loops that have conditionals embedded along with arithmetic computation. Software pipelining of such loops is inhibited due to the *flow-control dependency* introduced by the conditional statements. In such cases, if the loop trip count is reasonably large and there is sufficient amount of arithmetic computation, a technique called *loop fission* can be applied to improve the performance. The original loop is split into two loops; one with the conditional and one without the conditional (assuming the semantics of the loop allow the conditional calculation to be placed in a separate loop). By placing the conditional separately, the compiler is free to perform optimizations, such as unrolling or modulo scheduling, on the conditional-free loop. Overall, the split loops may run faster than the original unsplit loop.

Another situation where one can apply loop fission is in the case of "fat loops" or loops with excessive computations. Such loops could overwhelm the compiler's capacity for register management during software pipelining and may lead to register spills causing degraded performance. In such cases, loop splitting can be applied to alleviate register pressure and generally, if the loop trip counts are large, this leads to faster execution.

Consider the following example program (adapted from a computational fluid dynamics application) and examine the functions `nofission` and `fission`. In `fission`, we have put the conditional statement that transfers control in a different loop and also used `#pragma pipeloop`. If we compile this program as follows

```
example% cc -fast -fsimple=2 -xrestrict \
        -xdepend example_loop_fission.c -o example_loop_fission
example% cc -fast -fsimple=2 -xrestrict \
        -xdepend example_loop_fission.c \
        -o example_loop_fission -DNOFISSION
```

and examine the generated assembly code for the two functions, we see substantial differences between the two cases. In the `nofission` case, there is virtually no optimization done; there is no unrolling, load-use separation, or register allocation (as can be seen by no separation between dependent `faddd`, `fmuld`, and `fabsd` instructions). In the `fission` case, the loop is pipelined and all the associated optimizations take place.

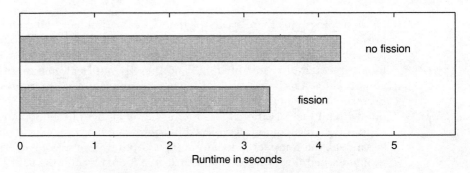

FIGURE 9-4 Loop Fission Technique—Runs on a Sun Blade 1000 (Forte Developer 6 Update 1 Compiler)

As a caveat, we note that sometimes the compiler may fuse the manually split loops back; therefore, it is always recommended to check the assembly file (that can be generated using the -S flag) to see if the optimizing compiler has re-fused the loops. In such cases one can *peel* (see the next section) either the first or the last iteration of the loop to force the compiler to turn off loop fusion. Another technique is to insert a call to a dummy function between the split loops. The overhead of the call must be monitored, and care must be taken to ensure that the compiler does not eliminate the dummy function call as dead code.

CODE EXAMPLE 9-5   Loop Fission

```
/* example_loop_fission.c */
/* cc -fast -fsimple=2 -xrestrict -xdepend example_loop_fission.c
      -o example_loop_fission -DNOFISSION */
#include <stdio.h>
#include <math.h>
#include <sys/times.h>
#include <sys/types.h>
#define len 98991  /* makes the run cache resident */
#define ITER 1000

int main(int argc, char **argv)
{
    int i,j,k,ierror=0;
    double *a, *b, *c, small, hgreat, ratinpmt, relaxn;
    hrtime_t start, time=0;
    a = (double *) malloc(len*sizeof(double));
    b = (double *) malloc(len*sizeof(double));
    c = (double *) malloc(len*sizeof(double));
    small = 0.5; ratinpmt = 0.5; relaxn = 1.0;
    hgreat = 1.0e50;

    for (k=0;k<ITER;k++) {
        for (i=0;i<len;i++) {
            a[i] = 0.01*i + ITER;
            b[i] = 0.1 + i - ITER;
            c[i] = 0.0;
        }
        start = gethrtime();
#ifdef NOFISSION
        nofission(a,b,len,c,small,hgreat,ratinpmt,relaxn,&ierror);
#else
        fission(a,b,len,c,small,hgreat,ratinpmt,relaxn,&ierror);
#endif
        time = time + gethrtime() -start;
    }
    printf("RUNTIME: %6.2f seconds \n",time*(1.e-9));
    return 0;
}
```

```
int nofission(double *a,double *b,int nodes,double *temp1,
    double small,double hgreat,double ratinpmt,double relaxn,
    int *ierror)
{   int i,dummy;
    double dtime=0;
    for (i=0;i<nodes;i++) {
        a[i] = a[i]*small;
        dtime = a[i] + b[i];
        dtime = fabs(dtime*ratinpmt);
        temp1[i] = dtime*relaxn;
        if(temp1[i] > hgreat) {
            *ierror = 4;
            break;
        }
    }
    dummy=0;
    return 0;
}

int fission(double *a,double *b,int nodes,double *temp1,
    double small,double hgreat,double ratinpmt,double relaxn,
    int *ierror)
{   int i,dummy;
    double dtime=0;
#pragma pipeloop(0)
    for (i=0;i<nodes;i++) {
        a[i] = a[i]*small;
        dtime = a[i] + b[i];
        dtime = fabs(dtime*ratinpmt);
        temp1[i] = dtime*relaxn;
    }
    for (i=0;i<nodes;i++) {
        if(temp1[i] > hgreat) {
            *ierror = 4;
            break;
        }
    }
    dummy=0;
    return 0;
}
```

Loop Peeling

Another optimization that can be applied to loops is called *loop peeling*. Peeling k iterations of the loop from the beginning or end of the loop body means removing these from the loop body and appropriately placing them ahead of or after the loop. Typically, loop peeling is an optimization that will be applied by the compiler as part of its loop-nest optimization-related transformations (see [Muchnick97]), but for some complex loops, the compiler may fail to deduce the dependencies (or lack of) and bypass this transformation in favor of generating conservative, but correct, code.

The transformation is best explained with an example. Consider the loop in routine foo (in program example_loop_peel.f listed at end of this section) extracted from the SPECfp92 program tomcatv. In this loop, y(1,n) is loaded and updated in the first iteration, and thereafter, later iterations only load its value. Similarly, iterations 1 through n-1 read y(n,n) and it is updated at the n-th iteration. If the first and last iterations are peeled out, then only x(i,1) needs to be loaded and y(i,n) needs to be stored. In routine foo1, we manually perform this transformation. In the transformed loop, there is only one load and store operation and it runs considerably faster than the loop in routine foo, as shown in the following figure.

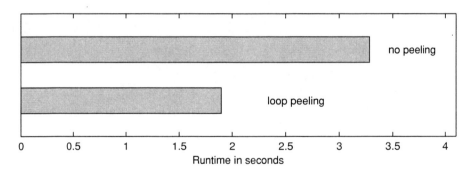

FIGURE 9-5   Loop Peeling Technique—Runs on a Sun Blade 1000 (Forte Developer 6 Update 1 Compiler)

As we can see, with loop peeling, a substantial speedup is observed.

CODE EXAMPLE 9-6   Loop Peeling *(1 of 3)*

```
c example_loop_peel.f
c f77 -fast example_loop_peel.f -o example_loop_peel
      parameter (idim=2011, itimes=100000)
      real*8 x(idim,idim), y1(idim,idim)
      real*8 y2(idim,idim), sum1, sum2
```

```
      real t1,t2,tdif1,tdif2,etime,time(2)
      tdif1 = 0.0
      tdif2 = 0.0
      sum1 = 0.0
      sum2 = 0.0
      len = idim - 1
      do n=1,itimes
         do i=1,len
            x(i,1) = 1.0
            y1(i,len) = n + i - 200.0
         enddo
         t1 = etime(time)
         call foo(len,x,y1)
         t2 = etime(time)
         tdif1 = tdif1 + t2 - t1
         sum1 = sum1 + y1(len,len)
         do i=1,len
            x(i,1) = 1.0
            y2(i,len) = n + i - 200.0
         enddo
         t1 = etime(time)
         call foo1(len,x,y2)
         t2 = etime(time)
         tdif2 = tdif2 + t2 - t1
         sum2 = sum2 + y2(len,len)
      enddo
      write(*,*) 'sum1 = ',sum1,' sum2= ',sum2
      write(6,'("RUNTIME (no peel): ",f6.2," sec.")') tdif1
      write(6,'("RUNTIME (peel): ",f6.2," sec.")') tdif2
      end

      subroutine foo(n,x,y)
      real*8 x(n,*),y(n,*)
      integer n
      do i=1,n
         y(i,n) = (1.0-x(i,1))*y(1,n)+x(i,1)*y(n,n)
      enddo
      return
      end

      subroutine foo1(n,x,y)
      real*8 x(n,*),y(n,*)
      real*8 t1,t2
```

```
integer n
t2 = y(n,n)
y(1,n) = (1.0-x(1,1))*y(1,n)+x(1,1)*t2
t1 = y(1,n)
do i=2,n-1
    y(i,n) = (1.0-x(i,1))*t1 + x(i,1)*t2
enddo
y(n,n) = (1.0-x(n,1))*t1 + x(n,1)*t2
return
end
```

Loops With Conditionals

Somewhat similar to vector processors, modern RISC or CISC microprocessors have deep pipelines to exploit instruction-level parallelism and achieve higher performance. For example, UltraSPARC II has a ten-stage-deep pipeline, while UltraSPARC III has a fourteen-stage-deep pipeline, allowing it to be scaled to substantially higher clock-cycle frequencies [Horel99]. Branches are a significant problem on pipelined architectures despite sophisticated techniques used to alleviate branch misprediction penalty in the hardware (for example, UltraSPARC II and UltraSPARC III use a dynamic branch prediction scheme). The branch misprediction penalty is high because the processor pipeline gets stalled. "In-flight" instructions have to be discarded, and the pipeline has to be started fresh with the instructions at the branch target address. All this leads to high overhead.

Manual restructuring of the code is often needed to decrease the impact of branches. Specifically, eliminating or restructuring the loops with branches can have a significant impact on loop execution time. In the presence of if statements, the loop is almost certain not to be modulo scheduled except in very simple cases where a static compile-time prediction is possible. The basic approach to improving the performance of loops with if statements is to try, as much as possible, to move them out of the loop body. This may not always be possible, in which case restructuring the loop might help. A detailed discussion of branches within loops and their optimization is presented in [Dowd98]. Following [Dowd98], we note that conditional statements in loops fall within several categories: loop invariant conditionals, loop index-dependent conditionals, independent loop conditionals, dependent loop conditionals, reductions, and conditionals that transfer control.

Some of the optimizations, such as loop invariant conditionals and reductions, may be applied by the compiler, though generally, hand-modification is recommended when possible. We discussed optimization of conditionals that transfer control in the section on loop fission, and will discuss reductions in the chapter on parallelization of programs (Chapter 13).

Consider the following example program. The conditional in the routine noconditional is an example of a loop-index-dependent if statement. By splitting the inner loop into two loops with varying lengths, one can completely eliminate the if statement as is done in the routine conditional. Now, the two inner loops get modulo scheduled by the compiler.

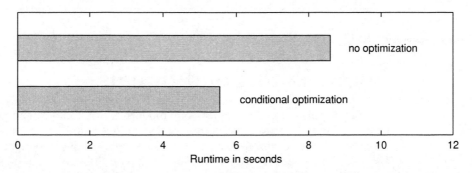

FIGURE 9-6   Loops With Conditionals—Runs on a Sun Blade 1000 (Forte Developer 6 Update 1 Compiler)

Optimization of conditionals is a difficult task, and there are no general recipes. The various approaches outlined in [Dowd98] are very specific and have to be applied on a case-by-case basis.

CODE EXAMPLE 9-7   Optimizing a Loop With a Conditional Statement *(1 of 3)*

```
! example_loops_cond.F90
! f90 -xO4 -dalign -xtarget=ultra3 -xarch=v8plusa
!    example_loops_cond.F90 -o example_loops_cond (-DCONDITIONOPT)
program branchtst
    implicit none
    integer, parameter :: numit=7000, len2=255
    integer :: i,j,n2=len2,nloop
    real (KIND=8) :: con1=1.d0
    real (KIND=8), dimension(len2+8,len2+8) :: a2d,b2d
    real (KIND=4) :: t3=0.0

    do nloop=1,numit
! initialize the vectors
        do i=1,len2
```

```
          do j=1,len2
             a2d(j,i) = i*0.001 + nloop - j
             b2d(j,i) = 1.d0
          enddo
       enddo

#ifdef CONDITIONOPT
call nocondition(con1,n2,a2d,b2d,t3)
#else
call condition(con1,n2,a2d,b2d,t3)
#endif

   enddo
   write(6,'(" RUNTIME: ",f6.2," seconds")') t3
end program

subroutine condition(con1,len2,a2d,b2d,t3)
   implicit none
   integer, INTENT(in) :: len2
   real (KIND=4), INTENT(inout) :: t3
   real (KIND=8), INTENT(in) :: con1
   real (KIND=8), INTENT(inout), dimension(len2,len2) :: a2d
   real (KIND=8), INTENT(in), dimension(len2,len2) :: b2d
   integer :: i,j
   real (KIND=4) :: tdum1=0.,tdum2=0., etime,tarray(2)

   tdum1 = etime(tarray)
   do i=1,len2
      do j=1,len2
         if(j < i) then
            a2d(j,i) = a2d(j,i) + b2d(j,i)*con1
         else
            a2d(j,i) = 1.0
         endif
      enddo
   enddo
   tdum2 = etime(tarray)
   t3 = t3 + tdum2 - tdum1
   tdum1 = tdum2
   return
end subroutine

subroutine nocondition(con1,len2,a2d,b2d,t3)
```

```
    implicit none
    integer, INTENT(in) :: len2
    real (KIND=4), INTENT(inout) :: t3
    real (KIND=8), INTENT(in) :: con1
    real (KIND=8), INTENT(inout), dimension(len2,len2) :: a2d
    real (KIND=8), INTENT(in), dimension(len2,len2) :: b2d
    integer :: i,j
    real (KIND=4) :: tdum1=0.,tdum2=0., etime,tarray(2)

    tdum1 = etime(tarray)
    do i=1,len2
        do j=1,i-1
            a2d(j,i) = a2d(j,i) + b2d(j,i)*con1
        enddo
        do j=i,len2
            a2d(j,i) = 1.0
        enddo
    enddo
    tdum2 = etime(tarray)
    t3 = t3 + tdum2 - tdum1
    tdum1 = tdum2
    return
end subroutine
```

Strength Reduction in Loops

Strength reduction usually refers to the optimization of arithmetic expressions by replacing computationally expensive operations with more efficient ones. This technique can lead to considerable performance improvements if applied to operations in loops with large iteration count. Some strength-reduction optimizations (for example, replacing multiplication by two with additions, replacing integer powers with floating-point multiplication, and replacing integer multiplication or division by powers of two with left or right bit shifts) are usually performed by the compiler ([Muchnick97] and [Wadleigh00]). However, there are more cases where the user has to perform this transformation manually. In this section, we will give two examples of manual strength-reduction transformations as applied to loop operations.

Division Replacement

On UltraSPARC processors, as well as most other modern RISC processors, the cost of floating-point division is substantially higher than that of floating-point multiplication operation. For example, on an UltraSPARC III microprocessor, the cost of double-precision floating-point division is around 20 clock cycles, whereas that of multiplication is around four clock cycles. Additionally, the multiplication operation can be pipelined (with resulting throughput of 1 multiplication per clock cycle) while the division cannot be pipelined, adding to the overall penalty. Thus, replacing divisions with multiplications, especially within loops, can result in performance improvement.

In Chapter 6, we presented an example of replacement of the calculation x/y with $x*z$, where $z = 1.0/y$ by use of the flag -fsimple=2. Here, we will present an example when multiple divisors are being used, and, using the trick outlined below, one can replace a floating-point division with a multiplication leading to significant gains (see the program listed at the end of the section). The program replaces the computation on the left with the one on the right as follows.

Unoptimized	Optimized
z(i) = x(i)/y(i)	tmp = 1.0/(y(i)*v(i))
w(i) = u(i)/v(i)	z(i) = x(i)*v(i)*tmp
	w(i) = u(i)*y(i)*tmp

We can check the generated assembly and see that in the routine plaindiv, there are no fmuld (multiplication) instructions. Not only is the divide replaced by multiply, but there is a reuse of the temporary variable tmp in tunediv, and an additional opportunity for the compiler to perform instruction overlap with the single division in the loop. The results (see FIGURE 9-7) show a considerable speedup in the tunediv case. As with the single-division replacement, this modification should be performed only after checking that the floating-point accuracy of the results is acceptable and the stability of the calculation remains unaffected.

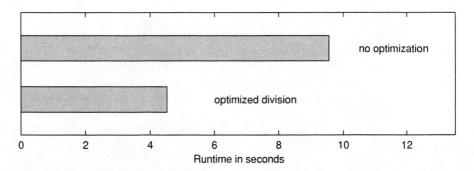

FIGURE 9-7 Strength Reduction Example—Runs on a Sun Blade 1000 (Forte Developer 6 Update 1 Compiler)

The following is a listing of the program.

CODE EXAMPLE 9-8 Strength Reduction in Loops

```
! example_twodiv.f90
! f90 -fast example_twodiv.f90 -o example_twodiv
program example_twodiv
   parameter (numit=2000,len=99829)
   integer :: i,j,n
   real(KIND=8) :: u(len),v(len),w(len),x(len),y(len),z(len)
   real(KIND=8) :: sum1=0.d0,sum2=0.d0
   real(KIND=4) :: tarray(2), t1=0.0,time1=0.0,time2=0.0, etime
   z = 0.d0
   w = 0.d0
   do i=1,len
      x(i) = i
      y(i) = 2.d0*i
      u(i) = 5.d0*i
      v(i) = 10.d0*i
   enddo
   do n=1,numit
      t1 = etime(tarray)
      call plaindiv(len,x,y,z,u,v,w)
      time1 = time1 + etime(tarray) - t1
      sum1 = sum1 + z(len) + w(1)
      t1 = etime(tarray)
      call tunediv(len,x,y,z,u,v,w)
      time2 = time2 + etime(tarray) - t1
      sum2 = sum2 + z(len) + w(1)
```

```
      enddo
      write(6,'(2p2e11.4)') sum1,sum2
      write(6,'("RUNTIME (unoptimized): ",f6.2)') time1
      write(6,'("RUNTIME (optimized):   ",f6.2)') time2
   end program

   subroutine plaindiv(n,x,y,z,u,v,w)
      integer i,n
      real(KIND=8) u(n),v(n),w(n),x(n),y(n),z(n)
      do i=1,n
         z(i) = x(i)/y(i)
         w(i) = u(i)/v(i)
      enddo
      return
   end

   subroutine tunediv(n,x,y,z,u,v,w)
      integer i,n
      real(KIND=8) u(n),v(n),w(n),x(n),y(n),z(n),tmp
      do i=1,n
         tmp = 1.d0/(y(i)*v(i))
         z(i) = x(i)*v(i)*tmp
         w(i) = u(i)*y(i)*tmp
      enddo
      return
   end
```

Operations on Complex and Real Operands

Complex multiplication and division are defined as floating-point operations on the real and imaginary parts of the operands.

```
Re(a*b) = Re(a)*Re(b) - Im(a)*Im(b)
Im(a*b) = Im(a)*Re(b) + Re(a)*Im(b)

Re(a/b) = (Re(a)*Re(b) + Im(a)*Im(b))/(Re(b)*Re(b) + Im(b)*Im(b))
Im(a/b) = (Im(a)*Re(b) - Re(a)*Im(b))/(Re(b)*Re(b) + Im(b)*Im(b))
```

These operations can be numerically unstable and lead to precision loss due to cancellation. Because of that, the compiler uses an implementation that may give extra precision in cases when the standard computation is imprecise. This extra precision for corner cases comes at a price of lower performance for these operations.

Applications that are not likely to suffer from precision loss in complex operations can be written with real data types with direct implementation of complex arithmetic. This optimization is similar to strength reduction and is most effective when used in loops. The following example performs complex multiplication and division both with complex operands and with equivalent operations on real numbers. We can see a nearly fourfold difference in performance (see FIGURE 9-8) in the case of division operation. Note, the performance of multiplication is approximately similar for the two cases.

CODE EXAMPLE 9-9 Operations on Complex and Real Operands

```
c example_complex.f
c f77 -fast -xarch=v8plus example_complex.f -o example_complex
      parameter(ITER=1000)
      complex*8 a(100000), b(100000), c(100000), icompl
      real*4 ar(100000), br(100000), cr(100000),
     &         ai(100000), bi(100000), ci(100000), tmp
      real*4 t0,t1,etime,time(2)
      integer icount
      icompl=(0.0d0,1.0d0)
      icount=0
c
      do i=1,100000
         ar(i)=i
         ai(i)=-i
         br(i)=2.0d0*i
         bi(i)=i
         a(i)=i-icompl*i
         b(i)=2.0d0*i+icompl*i
      enddo
c
      t0=etime(time)
      do ii=1,ITER
         icount=icount+1
         do i=1,100000
            c(i)=a(i)*b(i)
         enddo
      enddo
      t1=etime(time)
```

```
       print*,'c(8) = ', c(8), ' icount = ', icount
       write(6,10) t1-t0
 10    format("RUNTIME: ",f6.2," seconds - complex multiplication")
c
       t0=etime(time)
       do ii=1,ITER
          icount=icount+1
          do i=1,100000
             cr(i)=ar(i)*br(i)-ai(i)*bi(i)
             ci(i)=ai(i)*br(i)+ar(i)*bi(i)
          enddo
       enddo
       t1=etime(time)
       print*,'(cr(8),ci(8))=(',cr(8),ci(8), '), icount = ',icount
       write(6,11) t1-t0
 11    format("RUNTIME: ",f6.2," seconds - real multiplication")
c
       t0=etime(time)
       do ii=1,ITER
          icount=icount+1
          do i=1,100000
             c(i)=a(i)/b(i)
          enddo
       enddo
       t1=etime(time)
       print*,'c(8) = ', c(8), ' icount = ', icount
       write(6,12) t1-t0
 12    format("RUNTIME: ",f6.2," seconds - complex division")
c
       t0=etime(time)
       do ii=1,ITER
          icount=icount+1
          do i=1,100000
             tmp=1.0/(br(i)*br(i)+bi(i)*bi(i))
             cr(i)=(ar(i)*br(i)+ai(i)*bi(i))*tmp
             ci(i)=(ai(i)*br(i)-ar(i)*bi(i))*tmp
          enddo
       enddo
       t1=etime(time)
       print*,'(cr(8),ci(8))=(', cr(8),ci(8),'), icount = ', icount
       write(6,13) t1-t0
 13    format("RUNTIME: ",f6.2," seconds - real division")
       end
```

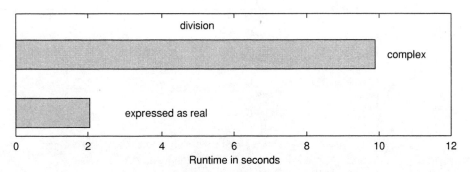

FIGURE 9-8 Performance of Operations With Complex Operands—Runs on a Sun Blade 1000 (Forte Developer 6 Update 1 Compiler)

Summary

This chapter described several of the commonly used techniques for loop optimization. Some of them can be performed by the compiler, but it is recommended to monitor the compiler optimization of the important loops in the application and, if necessary, perform hand-tuning at the source-code level. The most heavily used loops can be identified with profiling tools such as prof and tcov, or with Performance Analyzer (see Chapter 4).

Loop unrolling and tiling can be used for improved register reuse, better software pipelining, and reduced index increment overhead. Loop fusion and fission are complementary techniques. Loop fusion ensures that the loop body has a sufficient amount of computations that can be efficiently optimized. Loop fission can prevent excessive amount of computation within the loop body or can help extract a difficult-to-optimize computation in a separate loop. Additionally, we provided examples of loop peeling and loop restructuring with a conditional statement.

This chapter also discussed strength reduction techniques as applied to expressions within a loop body. We provided an example of eliminating a division operation, and discussed the efficiency of complex operations and their direct implementations via real and imaginary parts.

As is the case with other source-code-level tuning techniques, the performance of loop optimization approaches discussed in this chapter should always be reevaluated when new compilers and hardware platforms become available.

PART **III** Optimizing Parallel Applications

## CHAPTER 10

Parallel Processing Models on Solaris

In previous chapters we have covered topics related to optimizing the serial performance of an application. We now turn our attention to application performance enhancement by the use of parallel processing. In the next several chapters, we will give an overview of the techniques, tools, and software that are available on Solaris UltraSPARC platforms to enable efficient program parallelization.

The subject of designing and tuning parallel scientific computing programs is vast with extensive literature published and multiple paradigms available to parallelize an algorithm. There are also a wide variety of architectural approaches to building parallel computers. To name a few, there are: nonuniform memory access architectures (NUMA), cache-coherent nonuniform memory access architectures (ccNUMA), and symmetric multiprocessor (SMP). Similarly, at the software level, there are many programming models that can be used for parallelizing a program, such as data-parallel, control-parallel, single-program multiple data (SPMD) or multiple-program multiple data (MPMD). It is beyond the scope of this book to cover the conceptual and implementation details of all the various approaches. Instead, we will limit the discussion to the more commonly used approaches in HPC applications and on the practical details of optimizing parallel programs on the Solaris UltraSPARC platforms. We refer the interested reader to any of the following numerous publications on parallel programming and architectures: [Culler99], [Dowd98], [Pfister98], [Foster95], [Kumar94], and [Hockney88].

We begin this chapter with a brief review of some of the important concepts in parallel processing, namely, scalability metrics and programming models. The purpose of this discussion is to present the context in which the topics in the next several chapters will be presented. An overview of implementing the five most commonly used approaches to parallelize a program (compiler automatic, OpenMP directives, POSIX threads, UNIX `fork/exec`, and MPI) on Sun UltraSPARC platforms will be illustrated with simple examples and appropriate comparisons between the various models will be presented. Finally, the hybrid MPI-OpenMP approach will also be outlined.

Parallelization Overview

This section provides a brief overview of concepts relevant to quantifying parallel performance, and describes various parallel architectural and programming models.

Parallel Scalability Concepts

In most instances, the objective of implementing an application on parallel computers is to obtain a decrease in its execution runtime. It is then of primary interest to measure this decrease as a function of the number of processors used to execute the program on a given parallel architecture. The parallel runtime for an application is dependent on many factors: problem size, number of processors used to solve the problem, mapping of the algorithm on the machine architecture, characteristics of the parallel machine (processor speed, interconnection architecture, system software, libraries), and others. As a result, the performance of a parallel algorithm cannot be measured in isolation of the underlying machine architecture on which it is implemented. Collectively, the parallel program and the architecture is referred to as the *parallel system* [Kumar94]. The *speedup* of a parallel system is defined as:

$$S_p = \frac{T_1}{T_p}$$

where T_1 and T_p are the runtimes for serial (time taken by algorithm to execute on single processor of the parallel system) and parallel executions respectively. P is the number of processors used in the parallel execution. The problem size is assumed to remain constant and hence this is also referred to as *constant problem size speedup*. The system exhibits *linear speedup* (usually considered to be ideal speedup) if:

$$S_p = P$$

The speedup, as defined here, is also called the *relative speedup*. *Absolute speedup* is measured as:

$$S_p^{abs} = \frac{T_1^{best}}{T_p}$$

that is, it is measured relative to the "best" serial performance [Foster95].

The *parallel efficiency* is defined with respect to linear speedup:

$$E = \frac{S_p}{P}$$

The efficiency is usually less than one due to imperfections in the parallel implementation (nonparallelized portions in the program or parallel overheads such as synchronization costs, communication costs, and load imbalance). There are, however, cases where $E > 1$ is observed. This is referred to as *superlinear speedup*.

In some cases, hierarchical memory effects can lead to superlinear speedup. It can happen that for cache-based multiprocessors, a larger and larger portion of the working set of the program fits in the increasing cumulative cache of the system as the number of processors is increased. This leads to a decrease in the memory access time of the program (owing to increased residence of program data in faster structures of the memory hierarchy) and associated improvements in performance (see [Gustafson90]).

Superlinear speedup can also be caused by subtle algorithmic changes that are introduced with the parallelization. Algorithms where the runtime execution path is nondeterministic can show a solution behavior that varies with the number of processors used in the solution. For example, such effects are seen in iterative solvers or tree-search schemes, such as the branch-and-bound algorithm used in integer programming applications (see [Kumar94], [Winston94]). Since multiple paths in the tree are concurrently searched in the parallel case, one often discovers the optimal solution superlinearly faster than performing a serial search in a depth-first manner.

Nearly every parallel system has a sequential component that does not scale as the number of processors used to solve the problem is increased. Eventually, the serial component limits the attained speedup. This concept is expressed as the well known Amdahl's law [Amdahl67]:

$$S_p = \frac{1}{t_1^{ser} + \dfrac{t_1^{par}}{P}}$$

where t_1^{par} and t_1^{ser} are the fractions of the total time taken in the parallel and the serial components of the system, respectively, when the program is run on a single CPU. It is also assumed that the parallel component scales linearly.

The serial bottleneck manifests itself in the form of speedup curves showing a tendency to saturate as the number of processors is increased (FIGURE 10-1).

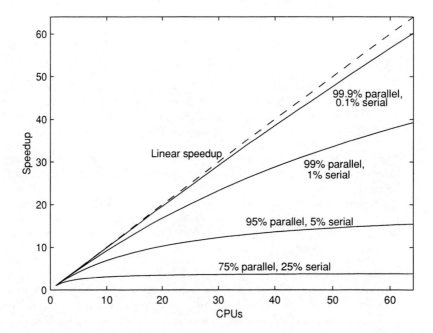

FIGURE 10-1 Illustration of Amdahl's Law

A related observation is that for the same number of processors, it is common that a larger instance of the same problem exhibits a higher speedup. Since increasing the number of processors decreases the parallel efficiency, and increasing the problem size increases the efficiency, it is possible to keep the efficiency constant by simultaneously increasing both the problem size and the number of processors used to solve it. These ideas have been exploited by researchers to develop the concepts of *scaled problem size speedup* ([Gustafson88], [Gustafson90]) and *parallel isoefficiency* [Grama93].

In the scaled problem size speedup, it is assumed that the problem size is scaled linearly with the number of processors. If t^{ser} and t^{par} represent the fractions of the total time taken in serial and parallel components for the scaled parallel system, then the serial time would be:

$$T = T_p(t^{ser} + P \cdot t^{par})$$

The scaled speedup is given as:

$$S_p^{scaled} = t^{ser} + P \cdot t^{par} = P + (1 - P) \cdot t^{ser}$$

Now, as the size of the problem grows and the serial component of the computation decreases, the attained speedup approaches linear. This idea has been used to implement highly scalable algorithms on large-scale massively parallel processors [Gustafson88]. The motivation to scale the problem size often can be found in the need to solve a larger problem or to produce a more accurate solution of the problem being simulated.

The scaled speedup approach assumes that the problem size (in terms of processor work) is scaled linearly with the number of processors. In many cases, it is observed that this is not sufficient and the problem size may need to be scaled faster than linearly. The metric that enables determination of the problem size as a function of number of processors in order to keep the parallel efficiency constant is called the *isoefficiency function* of the system. This concept provides valuable insights into the behavior of a parallel algorithm. A parallel system that has an isoefficiency function of $\sim O(P)$ is considered highly scalable while one that shows $\sim O(P^2)$ is considered poorly scalable ([Grama93], [Kumar94]).

There are other metrics of scalability that have been explored by researchers. They include the *memory constrained scaling*, where the problem size increase is limited by the amount of available memory [Sun90], or *time-constrained scaling* where the problem size is scaled to keep the runtime constant ([Worley90], [Gustafson92]).

Sometimes it is not feasible to obtain the solution of the parallel algorithm on a single processor. This might be due to insufficient memory on one processor (as in the case of distributed memory computers or clusters) or due to the fact that the runtime for the solution of the complete problem is prohibitively large. In such cases, one might use a *relative scaling* as:

$$S_p = \frac{T_{min}}{T_p} \cdot \frac{P_{min}}{P}$$

where P_{min} is the minimum number of processors on which it is practical to solve the problem, and T_{min} is the time to solution using P_{min} processors. While not as powerful as measuring the speedup with respect to serial execution, this value provides an estimate of the performance of the parallel system.

Finally, it is worth mentioning that with the recent development of parallel architectures, such as ccNUMA and cache-only memory architecture (COMA) systems [Dahlgren99], the traditional metrics as discussed above might not be most suitable in understanding parallel system performance. In such cases, metrics that provide dynamic information about the behavior of a system's memory migration and replication mechanisms are more suitable for performance evaluation. See [Noordergraaf99] for a discussion about alternate measures for performance evaluation on a Sun ccNUMA prototype system.

Parallel Architectural Models

The Von Neumann computer model elegantly encapsulated computer architecture in a simple machine model that allowed development of algorithms, programming languages, and software applications to proceed largely independent of the low-level details of the underlying computer architecture [Foster95]. Motivated by its success, a similar effort was devoted to developing simple and realistic parallel machine models. The classification known as *Flynn's taxonomy* [Flynn72] is one such approach and continues to be widely applicable to the machines today. It divides all computers into four categories:

- *Single Instruction Single Data (SISD)* – Single-processor system with one instruction stream and one data stream. All PCs and single-processor workstations fall into this category.

- *Multiple Instruction Single Data (MISD)* – Same data is processed by multiple processors running multiple instruction streams. There do not appear to be any commercial systems built using this model.

- *Single Instruction Multiple Data (SIMD)* – Multiple processors execute the same instruction stream, but operate on different data. Numerous such computers have been built. This concept is also exploited in the Visual Instruction Set (VIS) implemented in the UltraSPARC processors.

- *Multiple Instruction Multiple Data (MIMD)* – Different processors execute independent instruction streams on different data. These are the most flexible and commonly available parallel computers. The Sun multiprocessor (MP) desktops, workgroup, midrange and high-end server products (discussed in Chapter 2) all fall into this category.

These classes of computers can be further divided ([Dowd98], [Culler99]) based on memory architecture into shared-memory parallel and distributed-memory parallel systems. The shared-memory parallel systems can have a uniform memory access (UMA) architecture or nonuniform memory access (NUMA) architecture. NUMA systems, in turn, can be cache-coherent (ccNUMA) or non-cache-coherent systems. The ccNUMA systems are also referred to as distributed shared-memory (DSM) systems [Chandra00] while the shared-memory parallel, cache-coherent, UMA systems are known as Symmetric Multiprocessors (SMPs).

The currently (Fall 2000) shipping Sun MP desktops, workgroup, midrange and high-end UltraSPARC servers fall in MIMD, shared-memory, cache-coherent, UMA category (or SMP systems), while clusters of these systems and the Technical Compute Farm product can be classified as MIMD, distributed-memory parallel computers.

Parallel Programming Models

The models mentioned above are geared towards categorizing the parallel computers from a hardware architecture point of view. We will now give an overview of some of the popular parallel software models.

In developing parallel programs on any of the different hardware architectures discussed above, the issues to be considered include mapping the software model on the hardware model, portability, and partitioning the problem to expose parallelism. Partitioning the problem is the first step in designing parallel algorithms and, not surprisingly, performance and scalability are closely linked to how the problem decomposition scheme is chosen. The two main approaches are data decomposition and functional decomposition [Foster95]. In data decomposition, partitioning is performed based on the data associated with the computational problem. This approach is more often used in applications involving a solution of partial differential equations on a physical domain of interest (hence, it is also referred to as domain decomposition). The functional partitioning approach seeks to expose the inherent parallelism in the tasks associated with the problem. This approach is also referred to as task-level parallelism.

The programming models that encapsulate many of the parallel programs for HPC applications (irrespective of the partitioning technique or the underlying hardware model on which they are implemented) are:

- *Single Program Multiple Data (SPMD) abstraction* – As the name suggests, the different processors execute the same program, but operate on different data. Typically, data on which different tasks execute are controlled with the use of conditional statements in the program. In case of most SPMD programs, a fixed number of tasks are created at program startup. Usually, the tasks are neither created nor destroyed during program execution. The SPMD model is the most commonly used programming approach for HPC applications.

- *Multiple Program Multiple Data (MPMD) abstraction* – This is the most general model in that the problem is solved using different programs each operating on completely independent data or on data that have been decomposed among different processors. This model also includes the case where tasks are dynamically created and destroyed.

A third model (which might be considered a special case of SPMD model) is the *data-parallel* model. This model, which maps naturally to the SIMD-based machines exploits the parallelism in the problem by applying the same operation on the different elements of a data structure. High Performance Fortran (HPF) is a data-parallel language that provides features for the programmer to specify the data distribution and task division in the problem. The compilers for data-parallel languages typically translate the data-parallel program in an SPMD formulation and generate the necessary code for achieving the communication, synchronization, and data sharing required between parallel tasks. Another example of a data-parallel model is loop-level parallelism using compiler directives (for example, OpenMP directives).

On distributed memory machines, the coordination between the different parallel tasks is accomplished by *message passing*. Tasks send and receive messages to and from each other in order to exchange the information required to perform the calculation. This is needed as each task has access only to data residing in its address space. Message passing is more commonly used in conjunction with the domain decomposition approach in the form of an SPMD program. The SPMD message-passing program can be implemented either as a *node-only* program [Darema88] or as a *master-slave* program. In the node-only program, all of the tasks in the program participate in the computation equally. In the master-slave model, a "master" task performs the problem allocation amongst "slave" tasks and orchestrates the task scheduling for the problem. The most popular message-passing facility used in parallel HPC programs is that implemented as the Message Passing Interface (MPI) specification (see [Gropp99]). Parallel Virtual Machine (PVM) is another message-passing specification (see [Geist95]), but it has largely been superseded by MPI.

In the case of shared-memory machines, tasks share a common address space. While this simplifies programming because explicit knowledge of data "ownership" and communication is not needed, tasks need to be synchronized when modifying shared data. The functional decomposition approach and algorithms where tasks are dynamically created (and destroyed) are better suited to shared-memory machines as compared to message-passing programming. Shared-memory parallel programs are often implemented as multithreaded programs. Two common interfaces for multithreaded programs are POSIX threads [Kleinman96] and compiler directives such as OpenMP directives (see [Chandra00]). It should be noted that message-passing programs can also be implemented on shared-memory machines in a straightforward fashion. In fact, on such machines, the message-passing library can take advantage of the shared memory to improve communication performance.

The implementation of the parallel tasks from an operating system perspective is achieved mainly by two means (see [Wadleigh00] also):

■ Multiple Processes or Heavyweight Process model – This model relies on the traditional process model used by the UNIX OS to execute a program on the computer. The parallel program is run as a set of multiple UNIX processes. The communication between the processes can be accomplished by any of several techniques for interprocess communication supported in the OS (shared memory, sockets, file input/output, memory map [Mauro00]). Message passing programs are usually based on a multiple process model.

■ Multiple Threads or Lightweight Process (LWP) model – This model is based on the concept of a thread, which is defined as an independent flow of control within the program with its own context: stack and a set of registers [Kleinman96]. The different threads in the program share its address space but execute a different sequence of instructions. This approach is, thus, restricted to the shared address space abstraction.

Both approaches have their advantages and disadvantages. The multithreaded model conserves system resources as the threads share process data and opened files. It also has lower overhead since thread creation and destruction can be substantially faster than process creation. With an increasing number of threads, however, the overhead due to contention for access to shared resources (protected by locks) can dramatically increase, thereby limiting the attained speedup of the parallel system. Multithreaded programs can also be limited by the global address space limitation for the process (4 GB for a 32-bit process). The multiprocess model has higher overhead associated with process creation and destruction but is not limited by process memory size because each process can grow up to 4 GB in 32-bit addressing. By requiring the user to explicitly partition the data and prescribe interactions between the processors, the multiprocess paradigm can lead to more efficient parallel programs [Kumar97]. More on comparisons between multithreaded and multiprocess models can be found in Chapter 14.

Finally, one can combine the two approaches to create a hybrid parallelism model. This has recently become particularly attractive with the emergence of SMP clusters and the popularity of MPI and OpenMP interfaces. In such a model, MPI (or multiple processes) is used for the parallelism between the cluster nodes, and OpenMP (or multithreading) is used to expose the concurrency within the SMP node. We will further discuss the hybrid MPI-OpenMP models and their applicability on Solaris in Chapter 14.

Multithreading Models

In the preceding section, we gave an overview of some of the numerous hardware and software parallel programming models. As can be concluded from the section, there are many possible approaches for program parallelization. In this section, we will illustrate the orchestration of different multithreading models on a Solaris system with a simple example program. Later in the chapter, we will use the same example to illustrate the implementation of different multiprocess and hybrid models.

The example problem computes the value of pi using the trigonometric identity:

$$\pi = 4\operatorname{atan}(1)$$

and the relation:

$$\pi = 4\int_{0}^{1}\frac{1}{1+x^2}dx$$

The serial program implementing the previous computation follows.

CODE EXAMPLE 10-1 Serial Program for Pi Computation

```
! example_pi.f90
! f90 -fast -stackvar example_pi.f90 -o example_pi ! serial
! f90 -fast -xautopar -xreduction -stackvar
!    example_pi.f90 -o example_pi_autopar  ! auto parallelization
  implicit real*8(a-h,o-z)
  integer ndiv
  parameter (ndiv=10000000)

  real*8 h,sum,tmp,pical,piex,x
  real*4 tarray(2), t1, t2, etime
  piex = 4.0*datan(1.d0)

  h = 1.d0/ndiv
  sum=0.0d0

  t1 = etime(tarray)
  do i=1,ndiv        ! add points x=(i-0.5)*h
     x = (i-0.5d0)*h
     sum = sum + 1.0d0/(1.0+x*x)
  enddo
  t2 = etime(tarray)
  pical = 4.0d0*sum*h

  write(*,10) t2-t1
10 format(' RUNTIME:  ',f6.4, ' seconds')
  write(*,100) piex
  write(*,200) pical
100 format(1x,'Reference Pi  ',f18.16)
200 format(1x,'Computed Pi   ',f18.16)

  stop
  end
```

Compiling with the Forte Developer 6 Fortran 95 compiler and running the program on an Enterprise 4500 system produces the following output.

```
example% f90 -fast -stackvar example_pi.f90 -o example_pi
example% example_pi
 RUNTIME:  0.5500 seconds
 Reference Pi  3.1415926535897931
 Computed Pi   3.1415926535897309
```

Before describing the different approaches, we should point out that this example is tiny and can hardly be used to predict the relative performance of real applications with different parallelization implementations. The reader is encouraged to verify that in the range of 1–10 processors, all models show near-linear scaling. This is not surprising because the program has almost perfect parallelism with very little communication or synchronization requirement.

We will show the use of three approaches for multithreading that are particularly applicable for HPC applications. These are:

- Compiler auto-parallelization.
- OpenMP compiler directives.
- Explicit multithreading using P-threads (POSIX threads for C language).

Compiler Auto-Parallelization

In order to use compiler auto-parallelization for the preceding program, one needs only to recompile and relink with the flags -xautopar and -xreduction. These flags instruct the compiler to auto-parallelize program loops and perform reductions wherever applicable. These and other automatic parallelization features in the SPARC compilers will be discussed in detail in Chapter 13.

```
example% f90 -fast -xautopar -xreduction -stackvar \
         example_pi.f90 -o example_pi_autopar
```

To run the auto-parallelized program, one needs to set the environment variable PARALLEL to the number of threads desired for the run. For example:

```
example% example_pi_autopar
 RUNTIME:   0.5500 seconds
 Reference Pi   3.1415926535897931
 Computed Pi    3.1415926535897309
example% setenv PARALLEL 2
example% example_pi_autopar
 RUNTIME:   0.2758 seconds
 Reference Pi   3.1415926535897931
 Computed Pi    3.1415926535899228
example% setenv PARALLEL 4
example% example_pi_autopar
 RUNTIME:   0.1386 seconds
 Reference Pi   3.1415926535897931
 Computed Pi    3.1415926535896697
```

Note that even though the program runtime is small, compiler parallelization on this simple program is quite effective in terms of the speedup observed in the parallel runs. Unfortunately, large applications rarely benefit from auto-parallelization due to the conservative assumptions the compiler needs to make about data dependencies in large programs. We can also see from the above outputs that in this case, parallelization introduces subtle differences in results due to different round-off errors. The user should always carefully evaluate the impact of parallelization caused round-off differences in program results and ascertain whether or not the solution quality is acceptable.

OpenMP Compiler Directives

For more efficient compiler parallelization, pragmas can be used to instruct the compiler which parts of the program should be parallelized. The OpenMP version of the same program appears as follows.

CODE EXAMPLE 10-2 OpenMP Version of Pi Computation

```
! example_pi_omp.f90
! f90 -fast -openmp example_pi_omp.f90 -o example_pi_omp
  implicit real*8(a-h,o-z)
  integer ndiv,n
  parameter (ndiv=10000000)

  real*8 h,sum,tmp,pical,piex,x
  integer*8 gethrtime, time1, time2
  external gethrtime
  piex = 4.0*datan(1.d0)
  h = 1.d0/ndiv
  n = ndiv
  sum=0.0d0
  time1 = gethrtime()

!$omp parallel &
!$omp private(i,x), firstprivate(h,n), shared(sum)
!$omp do reduction(+:sum)
  do i=1,n       ! add points  x=(i-0.5)*h
     x = (i-0.5d0)*h
     sum = sum + 1.0d0/(1.0+x*x)
  enddo
!$omp end do
!$omp end parallel
```

OpenMP Version of Pi Computation *(Continued)*

```
   time2 = gethrtime()
   pical = 4.0d0*sum*h
   write(*,10) (time2-time1)*1.e-9
10 format(' RUNTIME:  ',f6.4, ' seconds')
   write(*,100) piex
   write(*,200) pical
100 format(1x,'Reference Pi  ',f18.16)
200 format(1x,'Computed Pi   ',f18.16)
   stop
   end
```

As one can see, the insertion of directives to multithread the program is fairly straightforward. This is by design because OpenMP is targeted towards incremental parallelization of loop-oriented scientific programs (see [Dagum98]). Note, the use of the `gethrtime` timer in the program as opposed to the `etime` timer. We will discuss timing issues relevant to OpenMP programs in the next chapter.

The program is compiled as

```
example% f90 -fast -openmp example_pi_omp.f90 -o example_pi_omp
```

where `-openmp` is a macro for use in Fortran programs with OpenMP directives (for Forte Developer 6 and Forte Developer 6 update 1 Fortran 95 compiler). It expands to `-stackvar -mp=openmp -explicitpar -D_OPENMP`.

In order to run the program, we only need to set the environment variable `OMP_NUM_THREADS`. It is recommended that the environment variable `PARALLEL` be unset for OpenMP programs.

```
example% setenv OMP_NUM_THREADS 1
example% example_pi_omp
 RUNTIME:  0.5508 seconds
 Reference Pi  3.1415926535897931
 Computed Pi   3.1415926535897309
example% setenv OMP_NUM_THREADS 2
example% example_pi_omp
 RUNTIME:  0.2760 seconds
 Reference Pi  3.1415926535897931
 Computed Pi   3.1415926535899228
example% setenv OMP_NUM_THREADS 4
example% example_pi_omp
 RUNTIME:  0.1386 seconds
 Reference Pi  3.1415926535897931
 Computed Pi   3.1415926535896697
```

We see that the scaling is comparable to that of the automatically parallelized version of the program. In general, OpenMP programs show better performance than auto-parallelized versions. This example is simple enough for the automatically generated code to be as efficient as the user-directed version.

Explicit Multithreading Using P-threads

The final example of this section illustrates the use of the POSIX thread (or P-thread) interfaces for C programs. The programming complexity compared to the OpenMP version is obvious. This is the case in general, as well. Although difficult to program, P-thread APIs can be used to implement irregular, dynamic applications efficiently and allow finer user control on performance of the program.

CODE EXAMPLE 10-3 P-thread Version of Pi Computation *(1 of 3)*

```
/* example_pi_thread.c
cc -fast example_pi_thread.c -lm -lpthread -o example_pi_thread */
#define _REENTRANT
#include <unistd.h>
#include <limits.h>
#include <stdio.h>
#include <stdlib.h>
#include <math.h>
#include <pthread.h>
#include <sys/types.h>
#include <sys/time.h>
#include <inttypes.h>

#define NDIV 10000000
typedef struct {
    double h, sumloc;
    int mynum, ist, ien;
} thr_args;

void *thr_sub(void *);

int main(int argc, char **argv)
{
    int i, j, n=NDIV, chnk, rem, thr_count = 1;
    double h, piex, picomp, sum;
    hrtime_t st, et, tt;
    float secs;
    pthread_attr_t *pt_attr;
```

```
pthread_t *id_vec;
thr_args *param_arr;
if (argc == 2) {
   thr_count = atoi(argv[1]);
}
else {
   printf("Running with Default value %d\n",thr_count);
}
piex = 4.0*atan(1.0);
h = 1.0/NDIV;
chnk = NDIV/thr_count;
rem = NDIV%thr_count;
sum = 0.0;

id_vec = (pthread_t *)malloc(sizeof(pthread_t)*thr_count);
pt_attr = (pthread_attr_t *)
          malloc(sizeof(pthread_attr_t)*thr_count);
param_arr = (thr_args *) malloc(thr_count*sizeof(thr_args));

for (i=0;i<thr_count;i++) {
   pthread_attr_init(&pt_attr[i]);
   pthread_attr_setscope(&pt_attr[i], PTHREAD_SCOPE_SYSTEM);
   param_arr[i].mynum = i;
   param_arr[i].h = h;
   param_arr[i].sumloc = 0.0;
   param_arr[i].ist = i*chnk;
   param_arr[i].ien = i*chnk + chnk - 1;
   if (i==(thr_count-1))
      param_arr[i].ien = param_arr[i].ien + rem;
}

st= gethrtime();
/* create threads */
for (i=0;i<thr_count;i++) {
   pthread_create(&id_vec[i], &pt_attr[i], thr_sub,
                  (void *)&param_arr[i]);
}
/* parent waits for joining */
for (i=0;i<thr_count;i++) pthread_join(id_vec[i], NULL);

for (i=0;i<thr_count;i++) sum += param_arr[i].sumloc;
picomp = 4.0*sum*h;
```

```
    et= gethrtime();
    tt = et - st;
    secs = (( float) tt / (float) 1000000000);
    printf(" RUNTIME: %6.4f Seconds \n", secs);
    printf(" Reference Pi %18.16f \n",piex);
    printf(" Computed Pi  %18.16f \n",picomp);

    for (i=0;i<thr_count;i++) pthread_attr_destroy(&pt_attr[i]);
    return 0;
}

void *thr_sub(void *arg)
{
    thr_args *thr_args_ptr = (thr_args *) arg;
    int mynum = thr_args_ptr->mynum;
    int ist = thr_args_ptr->ist;
    int ien = thr_args_ptr->ien;
    double h = thr_args_ptr->h;
    int i;
    double x, sum = 0.0;
    for (i=ist;i<=ien;i++) {
        x = ((double)i+0.5)*h;
        sum += 1.0/(1.0+x*x);
    }
    thr_args_ptr->sumloc = sum;
    return((void *)0);
}
```

Note, the use of the #define _REENTRANT statement in the program. This could either be explicitly defined in the program, or the -mt option in the compiler could be used both at the compiling and linking steps (additional details are provided in Chapter 12).

```
example% cc -fast example_pi_thread.c  -lm -lpthread -o \
          example_pi_thread
example% example_pi_thread 1
 RUNTIME: 0.5504 Seconds
 Reference Pi 3.1415926535897931
 Computed Pi  3.1415926535897309
example% example_pi_thread 2
 RUNTIME: 0.2756 Seconds
 Reference Pi 3.1415926535897931
 Computed Pi  3.1415926535899228
example% example_pi_thread 4
```

```
RUNTIME: 0.1383 Seconds
Reference Pi 3.1415926535897931
Computed Pi  3.1415926535896697
```

The results for this model also show a near perfect scaling for this particular calculation. More on comparisons between the OpenMP and P-threads approaches can be found in Chapter 13.

Multiprocessing Models

We will now illustrate the parallelization of the pi example from the last section, using the UNIX fork(2) call and using the MPI message-passing models. These methods show how to use the multiprocess model for parallelization on Solaris systems. As mentioned in the previous section, we caution the reader not to use the results of this example to compare the performance of various models. Our aim is primarily to illustrate the orchestration of different approaches on Solaris systems.

UNIX fork/exec Model

The fork/exec method can be used in cases when the computation can be naturally partitioned into several tasks that are almost disjointed and, therefore, require minimal interprocess communication. This restriction limits the applicability of this parallelization model, but when it is applicable, it is often fairly straightforward (albeit tedious) to implement or port between different UNIX platforms. The communication between processes can be accomplished by placing the data in shared-memory regions, by writing the data in the same file, or by using sockets. The following example provides the listing of a program that spreads the computation of pi across forked child processes. They access the process counter and the intermediate pi value stored in the shared-memory segment. The access is protected by a semaphore.

CODE EXAMPLE 10-4 UNIX fork/exec Version of Pi Computation *(1 of 4)*

```
/* Computation of pi using fork/exec and
   interprocess communication facilities
cc -fast example_pi_ipc.c -lm -o example_pi_ipc */
#include <stdio.h>
#include <sys/types.h>
#include <sys/ipc.h>
#include <sys/shm.h>
```

```
#include <sys/sem.h>
#include <unistd.h>
#include <wait.h>
#include <math.h>
#define SEM_ID    250

void sem_lock(int sem_set_id)
{
    struct sembuf sem_op;
    sem_op.sem_num = 0;
    sem_op.sem_op = -1;
    sem_op.sem_flg = 0;
    semop(sem_set_id, &sem_op, 1);
}

void sem_unlock(int sem_set_id)
{
    struct sembuf sem_op;
    sem_op.sem_num = 0;
    sem_op.sem_op = 1;
    sem_op.sem_flg = 0;
    semop(sem_set_id, &sem_op, 1);
}

int main(int argc, char* argv[])
{
    int sem_set_id;        /* ID of the semaphore set.*/
    union semun {
            int           val;
            struct semid_ds *buf;
            ushort_t      *array;
    } sem_val;
    int shm_id;            /* ID of the shared memory segment.*/
    char* shm_addr;        /* address of shared memory segment.*/
    int* cpu_num;          /* cpu counter in shared mem. */
    double* pical;
    struct shmid_ds shm_desc;
    int rc;                /* return value of system calls.*/
    pid_t pid;             /* PID of child process.*/
    int ndiv=10000000,myid,numprocs=1,i,chnk,rem,ist,ien;
    int child_status;
    double piex = 4.0*atan(1.0);
    double sumloc, h, sum, x;
```

```
   hrtime_t st, et, tt;

   if (argc == 2) {
      numprocs = atoi(argv[1]);
   }
   else {
      printf("Running with Default value %d\n",numprocs);
   }
   chnk = ndiv/numprocs; rem = ndiv%numprocs;

   sem_set_id = semget(SEM_ID, 1, IPC_CREAT | 0600);
   if (sem_set_id == -1) { perror("main: semget"); exit(1); }
   sem_val.val = 1;

   rc = semctl(sem_set_id, 0, SETVAL, sem_val);
   if (rc == -1) { perror("main: semctl"); exit(1); }

   shm_id = shmget(100, 1048, IPC_CREAT | IPC_EXCL | 0600);
   if (shm_id == -1) { perror("main: shmget: "); exit(1); }

   shm_addr = shmat(shm_id, NULL, 0);
   if (!shm_addr) { perror("main: shmat: "); exit(1); }

   cpu_num = (int*) shm_addr;
   *cpu_num = 0;
   pical = (double*) cpu_num + sizeof(int);
   *pical=0.0;

   st= gethrtime();
   for (i=0;i<numprocs;i++){
      pid = fork();
      switch (pid) {
         case -1:  /* error */
            perror("fork: ");
            exit(1);
            break;
         case 0:    /* child */
            sem_lock(sem_set_id);
            myid = *cpu_num;
            (*cpu_num)++;
            sem_unlock(sem_set_id);
            h    = 1.0 / (double) ndiv;
            ist = myid*chnk;
```

CODE EXAMPLE 10-4 UNIX `fork`/`exec` Version of Pi Computation *(4 of 4)*

```
            ien = myid*chnk + chnk - 1;
            sum = 0.0;
            for (i=ist; i<=ien; i++) {
                x = h*((double)i+0.5);
                sum += (1.0 / (1.0 + x*x));
            }
            sumloc = 4.0*h*sum;
            sem_lock(sem_set_id);
            *pical = *pical + sumloc;
            sem_unlock(sem_set_id);
            exit(0);
            break;
        }
    }
    for (i=0;i<numprocs;i++){
        wait(&child_status);
    }
    et= gethrtime();
    tt = et - st;
    printf(" RUNTIME: %6.4f Seconds \n",
            (float)tt/(float)1000000000);
    printf(" Reference Pi %18.16f \n",piex);
    printf(" Computed Pi  %18.16f \n",*pical);

    if (shmdt(shm_addr) == -1) {perror("main: shmdt: ");}
    if (shmctl(shm_id, IPC_RMID, &shm_desc) == -1)
        {perror("main: shmctl:");}
    return 0;
}
```

The complexity of the program is self evident. Compiling and linking the program and running it on an Enterprise 4500 system, we obtain the following results.

```
example% cc -fast example_pi_ipc.c -lm -o example_pi_ipc
example% example_pi_ipc 1
 RUNTIME: 0.5519 Seconds
 Reference Pi 3.1415926535897931
 Computed Pi  3.1415926535897309
example% example_pi_ipc 2
 RUNTIME: 0.2775 Seconds
 Reference Pi 3.1415926535897931
 Computed Pi  3.1415926535899228
example% example_pi_ipc 4
```

```
RUNTIME: 0.1407 Seconds
Reference Pi 3.1415926535897931
Computed Pi  3.1415926535896697
```

MPI Message-Passing Model

Next, we will illustrate the use of MPI programming on Solaris. MPI programs are usually more difficult to write than directive-based ones, and it is often difficult to increase the parallelism of MPI programs incrementally (something that makes the multithreading model attractive). The advantage of the MPI approach, and message passing in general, is that it allows one to run applications not only on a single SMP system, but also to distribute parallel runs across different systems within a cluster. This requires MPI software to be installed on all systems in the cluster.

The following Fortran 90 program shows how to use MPI to parallelize the example used in this chapter. Note that we have used the `mpi_send` and `mpi_receive` calls to accumulate the local sums instead of the `mpi_reduce` function call to show how explicit communication can be performed in an MPI program.

CODE EXAMPLE 10-5 MPI Version of Pi Computation *(1 of 3)*

```
! example_pi_mpi.f90
! mpf90 -fast example_pi_mpi.f90 -lmpi -o example_pi_mpi
!

  implicit real*8(a-h,o-z)
  include 'mpif.h'
  integer ndiv
  parameter (ndiv=10000000)

  integer ierr,myid,numproc,istatus,itag
  integer ichnk,irem,ist,ien
  real*8 h,sum,sumloc,sumtmp,pical,piex,x
  real*8 t1, t2

  call MPI_Init(ierr)
  call MPI_Comm_rank(MPI_COMM_WORLD, myid, ierr)
  call MPI_Comm_size(MPI_COMM_WORLD, numproc, ierr)

  piex = 4.0*datan(1.d0)
  h = 1.d0/ndiv
  sumloc = 0.d0
  sumtmp = 0.d0
  ichnk = ndiv/numproc
  irem = ndiv - ichnk*numproc
```

```
ist = myid*ichnk
ien = ist + ichnk - 1
if (myid.eq.(numproc-1)) ien = ien + irem
call MPI_Barrier(MPI_COMM_WORLD,ierr)
if (myid.eq.0) then
   t1 = MPI_Wtime()
   sum = 0.0d0
endif

do i=ist,ien
   x = (i+0.5d0)*h
   sumloc = sumloc + 1.d0/(1.0+x*x)
enddo
if (numproc.eq.1) then
   sum = sum + sumloc
else
  if (myid.eq.0) then
     sum = sum + sumloc
     do i=1,numproc-1
        itag = i
        call MPI_Recv(sumtmp,1,MPI_DOUBLE_PRECISION,        &
                   i,itag,MPI_COMM_WORLD,istatus,ierr)
        if (ierr.ne.MPI_SUCCESS) then
           write(*,*) 'fatal error while receiving'
           call MPI_Abort(MPI_COMM_WORLD,1,ierr)
        endif
        sum = sum + sumtmp
     enddo
  else
     itag = myid
     call MPI_Send(sumloc,1,MPI_DOUBLE_PRECISION,0,    &
                itag,MPI_COMM_WORLD,ierr)
  endif
endif
call MPI_Barrier(MPI_COMM_WORLD,ierr)
if (myid.eq.0) then
   pical = 4.d0*sum*h
   t2 = MPI_Wtime()
   write(*,10) t2-t1
10 format(' RUNTIME:  ',f6.4, ' seconds')
   write(*,100) piex
   write(*,200) pical
100 format(1x,'Reference Pi  ',f18.16)
```

CODE EXAMPLE 10-5 MPI Version of Pi Computation *(3 of 3)*

```
200   format(1x,'Computed Pi    ',f18.16)
   endif

   call MPI_Finalize(ierr)
   stop
   end
```

The program is compiled and linked as

```
example% mpf90 -fast example_pi_mpi.f90 -lmpi -o example_pi_mpi
```

The script `mpf90` is a wrapper provided with the Sun HPC ClusterTools software to enable easier compiling and linking of Fortran 90 and Fortran 95 MPI programs. The binary is executed using the `mprun` utility as follows.

```
example% mprun -np 1 example_pi_mpi
 RUNTIME:  0.5502 seconds
 Reference Pi  3.1415926535897931
 Computed Pi   3.1415926535897309
example% mprun -np 2 example_pi_mpi
 RUNTIME:  0.2752 seconds
 Reference Pi  3.1415926535897931
 Computed Pi   3.1415926535899228
example% mprun -np 4 example_pi_mpi
 RUNTIME:  0.1377 seconds
 Reference Pi  3.1415926535897931
 Computed Pi   3.1415926535896697
```

The preceding assumes that the Cluster Runtime Environment (CRE) has been enabled on the system. In Chapter 14, we will take a careful look at building MPI programs and at the performance issues related to MPI programming in the Sun HPC ClusterTools environment. Even though a number of other MPI implementations are available for Solaris systems, we strongly recommend using the version that comes with Sun HPC ClusterTools because of its good performance characteristics and the extensive tool and library set that comes with this product. The public domain MPI implementations include MPICH developed at Argonne National Laboratory and Mississippi State University (see http://www-unix. mcs.anl.gov/mpi/mpich) and the LAM implementation from the Ohio Supercomputer Center currently maintained at Notre Dame University (see http://www.mpi.nd.edu/lam).

Hybrid Models

In this section, we will revisit the pi computation example from the previous sections and show how to implement a hybrid MPI-OpenMP model on a Solaris platform. The implementation of OpenMP directives in an SPMD-style MPI program is straightforward (the pi MPI example in the previous section uses the SPMD style). Here, we simply insert OpenMP directives in the pi MPI example to execute the computational loop in a multithreaded manner.

CODE EXAMPLE 10-6   Hybrid MPI-OpenMP Version of Pi Computation *(1 of 3)*

```
! example_pi_hyb.f90
! mpf90  -fast -openmp example_pi_hyb.f90 \
!     -lmpi -o example_pi_hyb
  implicit real*8(a-h,o-z)
  include 'mpif.h'
  integer ndiv
  parameter (ndiv=10000000)
  integer ierr,myid,numproc,istatus,itag
  integer ichnk,irem,ist,ien
  real*8 h,sum,sumloc,sumtmp,pical,piex,x
  real*8 t1, t2

  call MPI_Init(ierr)
  call MPI_Comm_rank(MPI_COMM_WORLD, myid, ierr)
  call MPI_Comm_size(MPI_COMM_WORLD, numproc, ierr)
  piex = 4.0*datan(1.d0)
  h = 1.d0/ndiv
  sumloc = 0.d0
  sumtmp = 0.d0
  ichnk = ndiv/numproc
  irem = ndiv - ichnk*numproc
  ist = myid*ichnk
  ien = ist + ichnk - 1
  if (myid.eq.(numproc-1)) ien = ien + irem
  call MPI_Barrier(MPI_COMM_WORLD,ierr)
  if (myid.eq.0) then
     t1 = MPI_Wtime()
     sum = 0.0d0
  endif

!$omp parallel  &
```

```
!$omp private(i,x), firstprivate(h,ist,ien), shared(sumloc)
!$omp do reduction(+:sumloc)
  do i=ist,ien
      x = (i+0.5d0)*h
      sumloc = sumloc + 1.d0/(1.0+x*x)
  enddo
!$omp end do
!$omp end parallel

  if (numproc.eq.1) then
      sum = sum + sumloc
  else
    if (myid.eq.0) then
        sum = sum + sumloc
        do i=1,numproc-1
            itag = i
            call MPI_Recv(sumtmp,1,MPI_DOUBLE_PRECISION,      &
                        i,itag,MPI_COMM_WORLD,istatus,ierr)
            if (ierr.ne.MPI_SUCCESS) then
                write(*,*) 'fatal error while receiving'
                call MPI_Abort(MPI_COMM_WORLD,1,ierr)
            endif
            sum = sum + sumtmp
        enddo
    else
        itag = myid
        call MPI_Send(sumloc,1,MPI_DOUBLE_PRECISION,0,     &
                        itag,MPI_COMM_WORLD,ierr)
    endif
  endif
  call MPI_Barrier(MPI_COMM_WORLD,ierr)
  if (myid.eq.0) then
      pical = 4.d0*sum*h
      t2 = MPI_Wtime()
      write(*,10) t2-t1
10    format(' RUNTIME:  ',f6.4, ' seconds')
      write(*,100) piex
      write(*,200) pical
100   format(1x,'Reference Pi  ',f18.16)
200   format(1x,'Computed Pi   ',f18.16)
  endif
```

Hybrid MPI-OpenMP Version of Pi Computation *(3 of 3)*

```
call MPI_Finalize(ierr)
stop
end
```

The compilation and linking of the program is done as follows.

```
example% mpf90 -fast -openmp example_pi_hyb.f90 -lmpi -o
        example_pi_hyb
```

We run it as follows (note the setting of environment variable OMP_NUM_THREADS).

```
example% setenv OMP_NUM_THREADS 1
example% mprun -np 1 example_pi_hyb
 RUNTIME:  0.5508 seconds
 Reference Pi  3.1415926535897931
 Computed Pi   3.1415926535897309
example% setenv OMP_NUM_THREADS 2
example% mprun -np 1 example_pi_hyb
 RUNTIME:  0.2760 seconds
 Reference Pi  3.1415926535897931
 Computed Pi   3.1415926535899228
example% setenv OMP_NUM_THREADS 1
example% mprun -np 2 example_pi_hyb
 RUNTIME:  0.2759 seconds
 Reference Pi  3.1415926535897931
 Computed Pi   3.1415926535899228
example% setenv OMP_NUM_THREADS 2
example% mprun -np 2 example_pi_hyb
 RUNTIME:  0.1386 seconds
 Reference Pi  3.1415926535897931
 Computed Pi   3.1415926535896697
example% setenv OMP_NUM_THREADS 1
example% mprun -np 4 example_pi_hyb
 RUNTIME:  0.1389 seconds
 Reference Pi  3.1415926535897931
 Computed Pi   3.1415926535896697
```

Other model combinations (for example, MPI with auto-parallelization, MPI with P-threads) are possible, but for the sake of brevity, only one was presented. We close this section with the caveat that mixing different multithreading models (for example, using both P-threads and OpenMP directives in the same program) is not recommended, and in as much as possible, should be avoided. We will revisit this in the context of nested parallelism and thread-safety issues in Chapters 12 and 13.

Summary

In this chapter, we presented a review of important concepts in parallel programming including scalability metrics, and hardware and software parallel models. We illustrated models with the implementations of six different approaches to parallelize a simple problem in the Solaris environment and discussed specific details of compilation and linking for different models. The models described in the chapter were: compiler auto-parallelization, OpenMP directives in Fortran, P-threads for C programs, the UNIX `fork/exec` model, the MPI message-passing library, and, finally, a combined MPI-OpenMP approach.

The examples presented here point to the rich parallelization support available on Solaris platforms. The applicability of each of these approaches is problem-dependent and, while it is difficult to recommend one over the other, for HPC programs, three of the popular techniques are P-threads, OpenMP, and MPI-based parallelization. In the next several chapters, we will examine these in further detail and discuss optimization issues specific to each model.

## CHAPTER 11

Parallel Performance Measurement Tools

In this chapter, we will give an overview of the various tools available on UltraSPARC-based systems for performance measurement in parallel programs. In Chapter 4, we discussed tools and methodologies for measuring serial programs. As we will see, some of the same tools can also be applied in the case of parallel applications. However, as described in the previous chapter, the two main models for developing parallel programs are multithreading and multiprocessing. There are sufficient differences between these models that tools with significantly different features are required to study performance of programs employing the two models. In the previous chapter, we also saw that these models can be implemented using many different approaches. For example, a program can be multithreaded either using compiler directives or explicitly using P-threads. The differences between the two approaches require parallel tools to account for these differences and report data in the context of the approach used in the program. The programming model differences, as well as the inherent complexity in behavior of parallel programs, lead to parallel performance evaluation tools usually being more complex than their serial counterparts. The development of parallel tools is an active area of research, and new tools are continually being introduced.

Many tools for parallel performance evaluation are available on Solaris systems, and it is important that their scope of applicability be understood prior to their usage. In this chapter, the description of various tools is presented from the point of view of their suitability to different flavors of parallel applications.

The topics covered in the chapter are: techniques for timing both whole and portions of parallel (both multithreaded and MPI) programs, usage of the Forte Developer 6 Performance Analyzer tool for multithreaded programs (OpenMP, P-threads), the Prism environment for tracing MPI programs, and various system-level monitoring tools available as part of the Solaris Operating Environment. The trace normal format facility (TNF), which allows high-resolution tracing in the Solaris operating system, is also described with an example program.

Measurement Methodology

The fundamental principle in measuring the performance of parallel programs is the same as it is for serial programs: benchmarking must be performed to ensure repeatable and consistent results while minimizing *probe effects* and tool overheads. All of the steps outlined in the section about measurement methodology in Chapter 4 are applicable to parallel performance studies, and the reader is encouraged to read it prior to reading this section.

There are, however, many additional issues that must be taken into account while studying parallel applications. Since the approaches to parallelize an application, as well as to parallel computer architectures, are so diverse, it is difficult to describe a measurement procedure that is uniformly applicable to all parallel programs. Each combination of the programming and architectural model requires creating a specific set of tools and methodology for performance measurement. In what follows, we will attempt to outline some "best practices" to keep in mind when designing parallel performance measurement experiments (see [Foster95] and *Sun HPC ClusterTools 3.1 Performance Guide* also):

- *Parallelism vs. Concurrency* – It is important to remember the distinction between exploiting parallelism and concurrency in applications using either multiple threads or processes. Our discussion is focused on computationally intensive applications parallelized for runtime performance improvements using multiple threads or processes running simultaneously on multiple processors. These applications, if run with multiple threads (or processes), will experience significant performance degradation when run on a single processor. There is a class of applications where multiple threads (or processes) can be used to expose concurrency in the program: when a task (and the thread executing it) blocks (say for I/O or network access), some other thread (or process) can be activated, and the program continues to execute. These programs will benefit from multithreading even on a single processor. Measurement issues for such programs are not discussed in this chapter, but the reader is advised to keep this distinction in mind when measuring parallel applications.

- *Dedicated mode of benchmarking* – In Chapter 4, we stressed running serial programs in dedicated mode to decrease interference from other user programs. This is even more applicable in the case of parallel jobs. If the job is being run in shared mode (possibly due to resource constraints), then it is important to use the right timer for measuring user and wall-clock times (see next section).

- *Number of processors* – Because this discussion is focused on decreasing program runtime, the machine on which measurements are performed should have at least as many physical processors as the number of threads[1] (in the multithreaded model) or number of processes (in the multiprocess model) that perform

---

1. We are assuming bound threads. See the discussion in the next section and in Chapter 12 about bound threads in Solaris.

computational tasks in the application. In fact, it is recommended to have at least one extra processor available to handle system activity while the user program is running, as parallel jobs can be more sensitive to system activity than serial programs. For example, on a 20-processor machine, if a 20-process MPI job is being run, the system activity (on one of the processors) may cause a large load imbalance. Additional threads or processes may be needed if I/O and computation are being overlapped.

- *Choice of timer and time criterion* – For serial programs that are compute-bound (that is, perform little system and I/O activity), the difference between wall-clock and user time is small. We have seen this in the examples presented in earlier chapters on serial program optimization. For parallel programs, this is not the case. Depending on whether the program is being run in dedicated or shared mode and what timing tool is being used, the wall-clock and user times could be very different. Choosing the correct timing tool is, therefore, crucial (see the next section). Additionally, one could measure the time for each thread or each MPI process. We recommend that both the maximum and minimum times that are measured in the program be monitored as the program is tuned and the number of processors changed in the run.

- *Processor-set configuration* – In many cases, parallel speedup results are measured by varying the number of processors in powers of two. That may have originated from the idea of measuring speedup due to processor doubling and also due to early parallel machines that were only available in power-of-two processor configurations. In Chapter 13, we will show an example of *stair-stepping* speedup in loop parallelization that occurs due to the imbalance caused by loop iterations not being evenly divisible by the processor sizes chosen in the measurement. It is recommended that the number of processors used in speedup measurements be carefully selected based on benchmark characteristics to avoid artificially generated overheads.

- *Processor allocation in clusters* – The method used for the allocation of processors by the operating system and resource scheduling software (for example CRE software in HPC ClusterTools product) in a cluster of SMPs can have a significant impact on performance. For example, in a cluster of four Enterprise 4500 (say with 12 processors each) nodes, an eight-process MPI job can be run on a single SMP node or it can be distributed amongst the nodes. Clearly, the performance in the two cases could be vastly different.

Timing a Parallel Program and Its Portions

Tools available in the Solaris Operating Environment for measuring the entire program and program portion times for serial programs were presented in Chapter 4. In this section, we will extend that discussion to include tools for measuring computationally intensive parallel programs.

In Chapter 4, the `ptime` tool was recommended for serial programs. We also recommend its usage for whole program timing in the case of multithreaded programs.

Consider the `example_pi_thread.c` program in Chapter 10. Compiling and running this program on a 12-CPU Enterprise 4500 we obtain the following.

```
example% ptime example_pi_thread 1
Running with Default value 1
RUNTIME: 0.5504 Seconds
 Reference Pi 3.1415926535897931
 Computed Pi  3.1415926535897309
real         0.585
user         0.553
sys          0.006
example% ptime example_pi_thread 2
 RUNTIME: 0.2756 Seconds
 Reference Pi 3.1415926535897931
 Computed Pi  3.1415926535899228
real         0.310
user         0.553
sys          0.006
example% ptime example_pi_thread 4
 RUNTIME: 0.1383 Seconds
 Reference Pi 3.1415926535897931
 Computed Pi  3.1415926535896697
real         0.179
user         0.553
sys          0.007
```

The `real` time as measured by `ptime` is decreasing, indicative of speedup with an increasing number of threads. The `user` time, however, stays constant and greater than the `real` time when more than one thread is used. This happens because the `user` time is the combined CPU usage time for all the user threads in the process.

This is the case regardless of whether the threads are bound or unbound (see Chapter 12) and whether they run on independently available processors on the machine or timeshare the available processors. In this example, the different threads are well load-balanced, no synchronization takes place, and no system calls are made from the program. As a result, the `user` time is constant between the runs with different thread numbers. In general, the `user` time for multithreaded runs is likely to be larger than `real` time (assuming negligible I/O, network, system time) and not as correlated with single-thread `user` time as in this simplistic example.

MPI applications spawn multiple UNIX processes. Currently under the ClusterTools CRE environment, there are no standard timers similar to `ptime`, `timex`, and `time` that can provide the time for execution of the MPI job. For single binary MPI programs (which do not require to be run using shell scripts), under the CRE environment one can use `timex` or `ptime` along with the `mprun` command to indirectly obtain times for different processes of the MPI job. For example, for the Pi-calculation program from Chapter 10

```
example% mprun -np 2 ptime example_pi_mpi
RUNTIME:   0.2761 seconds
 Reference Pi   3.1415926535897931
 Computed Pi    3.1415926535899228


real        0.374
user        0.326
sys         0.039


real        0.391
user        0.331
sys         0.033
```

Note that outputs of `ptime` from different processes may become interwoven.

We will now describe techniques that can be used for measuring time in portions of a multithreaded program on a per-thread basis. The discussion pertains to the case when bound threads are created in the user application. In the Solaris environment, either bound or unbound threads can be created both for POSIX and Solaris thread API libraries. Further discussion on bound and unbound threads is deferred until the next chapter. Here, we merely mention it is recommended to use bound threads in a computationally intensive application for achieving best parallel scaling. Bound user threads do not migrate between LWPs and are scheduled by the kernel. Unbound threads are scheduled by the thread library. Thus, if sufficient number of physical processors are available, the bound threads each will be scheduled on different processors. When the number of processors available is less than the number of threads, the different threads will compete for available CPUs in a manner similar to processes competing for CPU time in a multitasking operating system on a single-processor machine. The compiler generates bound threads in programs with OpenMP directives to realize maximum parallelism in the application.

In Chapter 4, we discussed the high-resolution timer `gethrtime(3C)`. Since it is MT-safe (Chapter 12), it can be used to measure accurately the elapsed time on a per-thread basis in a multithreaded program. In Chapter 10, the use of `gethrtime` was demonstrated in the pi-calculation examples for P-threads (C program) and OpenMP directives (Fortran 90) respectively.

While the `gethrtime` function can be used to obtain the elapsed `real` time on a per-thread basis, it cannot provide the CPU or `user` time[1]. To obtain `user` time on a per-thread basis, assuming that the threads are bound, the function `gethrvtime(3C)` can be used. This function (also MT-safe) returns the CPU time on a per-LWP basis. Since, in the case of bound threads, there is a one-to-one mapping between user level threads and LWPs (see Solaris thread scheduling model discussion in next chapter and [Mauro00], [Kleinman96]), this function will provide meaningful results for user-level threads. It requires that microstate accounting be enabled in the program. The following examples will highlight some of the differences between `gethrtime` and `gethrvtime` functions.

CODE EXAMPLE 11-1 Difference Between the Time Reported by `gethrtime` and `gethrvtime` Timers

```
/* example_gethrvtime.c */
/* cc example_gethrvtime.c -o example_gethrvtime (-DSLEEP) */
#include <sys/time.h>
#include <stdio.h>
int main ()
{
   hrtime_t time0, timev0;
   double time,timev,s=0.0;
   int i;
   time0  = gethrtime();
   timev0 = gethrvtime();
#ifdef SLEEP
   sleep(2);
#endif
   for (i=0; i<5000000; i++) s=s+(double)i;
   time  = 1.0e-9*(gethrtime() - time0);
   timev = 1.0e-9*(gethrvtime()- timev0);
   printf("time = %18.9e\n",time);
```

---

1. If a computationally intensive application using bound threads is run on a machine with more processors than number of bound threads and not making any system calls (or I/O calls), the difference between the elapsed and CPU time (on a per-thread basis) will be negligible.

```
    printf("timev= %18.9e\n",timev);
    return 0;
}
```

Compiling and running the above program on an Enterprise 4500 system produces

```
example% cc example_gethrvtime.c -o example_gethrvtime -DSLEEP
example% ptime example_gethrvtime
time =    2.372225277e+00
timev=    3.751369060e-01

real      2.391
user      0.376
sys       0.003
```

Note the use of ptime to enable the microstate accounting in the Solaris kernel. As expected, gethrtime returns the real time (printed as time in the preceding output) which includes time spent in the call sleep(2). The gethrvtime call, on the other hand, returns the user time (printed as timev in the output above). Next, we compile the program without -DSLEEP, essentially removing the line sleep(2).

```
example% cc example_gethrvtime.c -o example_gethrvtime
example% ptime example_gethrvtime
time =    3.750650380e-01
timev=    3.750277490e-01

real      0.394
user      0.376
sys       0.003
```

We can see that the times reported by the two timers match closely to one another and to the real and user times reported by ptime.

Now, consider a slightly modified P-thread version of the Pi example from the previous chapter.

CODE EXAMPLE 11-2 Difference Between gethrtime and gethrvtime Timers in Multithreaded Programs *(1 of 4)*

```
/* example2_pi_thread.c
 cc -fast example2_pi_thread.c  -lm
    -lpthread -o example2_pi_thread */
```

```
#define _REENTRANT
#include <unistd.h>
#include <limits.h>
#include <stdio.h>
#include <stdlib.h>
#include <math.h>
#include <pthread.h>
#include <sys/types.h>
#include <sys/time.h>
#include <inttypes.h>

#define NDIV 10000000
#define MAXTHREADS 64

typedef struct {
    double h,sumloc;
    int mynum,ist,ien;
} thr_args;
double timew[MAXTHREADS],timev[MAXTHREADS];

void *thr_sub(void *);

int main(int argc, char **argv)
{
    int i,j,n=NDIV,chnk,rem,thr_count = 1;
    double h,piex,picomp,sum;
    pthread_attr_t *pt_attr;
    pthread_t *id_vec;
    thr_args *param_arr;

    if (argc == 2) {
        thr_count = atoi(argv[1]);
    }
    else {
        printf("Running with Default value %d\n",thr_count);
    }
    for (i=0;i<MAXTHREADS;i++) timew[i] = timev[i] = 0.0;

    piex = 4.0*atan(1.0);
    h = 1.0/NDIV;
    chnk = NDIV/thr_count;
```

```
   rem = NDIV%thr_count;
   sum = 0.0;

   id_vec = (pthread_t *)malloc(sizeof(pthread_t)*thr_count);
   pt_attr = (pthread_attr_t *)
           malloc(sizeof(pthread_attr_t)*thr_count);
   param_arr = (thr_args *) malloc(thr_count*sizeof(thr_args));

   for (i=0;i<thr_count;i++) {
    pthread_attr_init(&pt_attr[i]);
    pthread_attr_setscope(&pt_attr[i], PTHREAD_SCOPE_SYSTEM);
    param_arr[i].mynum = i;
    param_arr[i].h = h;
    param_arr[i].sumloc = 0.0;
    param_arr[i].ist = i*chnk;
    param_arr[i].ien = i*chnk + chnk - 1;
    if (i==(thr_count-1)) param_arr[i].ien=param_arr[i].ien+rem;
   }

   /* create threads */
   for (i=0;i<thr_count;i++) {
    pthread_create(&id_vec[i], &pt_attr[i], thr_sub,
                  (void *)&param_arr[i]);
   }
   /* parent waits for joining */
   for (i=0;i<thr_count;i++) pthread_join(id_vec[i], NULL);

   for (i=0;i<thr_count;i++) sum += param_arr[i].sumloc;
   picomp = 4.0*sum*h;

   printf(" Reference Pi %18.16f \n",piex);
   printf(" Computed Pi  %18.16f \n",picomp);

   printf("    Thread   Timew       Timev\n");
   for (i=0;i<thr_count;i++) {
     pthread_attr_destroy(&pt_attr[i]);
     printf(" ID%5d   %11.4e %11.4e\n",i,timew[i],timev[i]);
   }

   return 0;
}
```

```
void *thr_sub(void *arg)
{
    thr_args *thr_args_ptr = (thr_args *) arg;
    int mynum = thr_args_ptr->mynum;
    int ist = thr_args_ptr->ist;
    int ien = thr_args_ptr->ien;
    double h = thr_args_ptr->h;
    int i;
    hrtime_t time0,timev0;
    double sum = 0.0;

    time0  = gethrtime();
    timev0 = gethrvtime();
    sleep(2*mynum);

    for (i=ist;i<=ien;i++)  sum+=1.0/(1.0+((i+0.5)*h*(i+0.5)*h));
    thr_args_ptr->sumloc = sum;

    timew[mynum]  = 1.0e-9*(gethrtime() - time0);
    timev[mynum] = 1.0e-9*(gethrvtime()- timev0);
    return((void *)0);
}
```

In the program we inserted the `sleep(2*mynum)` call inside the function called by each thread (that is, the function `void *thr_sub`) and measure the time using both `gethrtime` and `gethrvtime` for each thread.

We compile the program and run it using one thread (on a 12-CPU Enterprise 4500 system).

```
example% cc -fast example2_pi_thread.c -lm -lpthread -o
         example2_pi_thread
example% ptime example2_pi_thread
Running with Default value 1
 Reference Pi 3.1415926535897931
 Computed Pi  3.1415926535897309
    Thread Timew        Timev
 ID    0    5.5011e-01  5.5005e-01

real         0.575
user         0.553
sys          0.007
```

The values printed under the column Timew are times measured using the gethrtime call while under the Timev column, measurements obtained using gethrvtime are printed. As expected, for the single-thread run there is no difference in times reported by the two timers. Next, we run the program using two and four threads, respectively.

```
example% ptime example2_pi_thread 2
 Reference Pi 3.1415926535897931
 Computed Pi   3.1415926535899228
     Thread  Timew       Timev
 ID    0     2.7509e-01  2.7505e-01
 ID    1     2.2778e+00  2.7509e-01

real          2.303
user          0.553
sys           0.007
example% ptime example2_pi_thread 4
 Reference Pi 3.1415926535897931
 Computed Pi   3.1415926535896697
     Thread  Timew       Timev
 ID    0     1.3756e-01  1.3753e-01
 ID    1     2.1404e+00  1.3757e-01
 ID    2     4.1402e+00  1.3752e-01
 ID    3     6.1401e+00  1.3752e-01

real          6.164
user          0.553
sys           0.007
```

The different behavior of the two timers is apparent from the resulting outputs shown above. We can see that the values reported by gethrtime include the time spent in the sleep call, whereas those reported by gethrvtime only include the CPU usage time.

For Fortran multithreaded programs, the etime function should not be used as it is not MT-safe. Instead, the gethrtime and gethrvtime functions (either directly, as supported in Forte Developer 6 Fortran 95 compiler, or using a wrapper, as shown in Chapter 4) are recommended.

For measuring the elapsed time in portions of an MPI program, one can use the MPI_Wtime function available in Fortran, C, and C++ bindings. The use of MPI_Wtime in a Fortran 90 program was illustrated in the previous chapter (example_pi_mpi.f90 program); it can be used in a similar fashion in C and C++ programs. In Sun MPI implementation, MPI_Wtime uses the gethrtime timer and is thus, highly accurate. However, since MPI processes may not be synchronized, care might be needed to synchronize the processes (by inserting calls to `MPI_BARRIER`, for example) at the start and stop of the portion of the program to eliminate any skew in measured timings. Further, ensure that only the time differences (between stop and start values obtained by `MPI_Wtime` for each MPI process) are compared between the different MPI processes. See Chapter 7 of *Sun HPC ClusterTools 3.1 Performance Guide* for additional discussion. Since times are measured separately on each MPI process, statistics such as minimum, maximum, median, mean, and standard deviation can provide useful insights in program execution and load balance.

Parallel Performance Monitoring With Forte Developer 6 Tools

In Chapter 4, we discussed how to use the Sampling Collector and Performance Analyzer tools of Forte Developer 6 (and Forte Developer 6 update 1) to collect profiling data for serial applications. In this section, we focus on the features of these tools that allow measurements specific to parallel applications.

As a first example, we reuse the OpenMP version of the program discussed in the previous chapter. Since parallelization of this program is trivial, and the computation is well-balanced between the different threads, we modify the code to include an artificial imbalance. The easiest way to do that is just to include a `sleep(3F)` call within the parallel region.

CODE EXAMPLE 11-3 Modified OpenMP Example

```
! example_pi_omp.f90
! f90 -fast -openmp example_pi_omp.f90 -o example_pi_omp
  implicit real*8(a-h,o-z)
  integer ndiv,n
  parameter (ndiv=10000000)
  real*8 h,sum,tmp,pical,piex
  integer OMP_GET_THREAD_NUM
  integer*8 gethrtime, time1, time2
  external gethrtime
  piex = 4.0*datan(1.d0)
  h = 1.d0/ndiv
  sum = 0.0d0      ! add f(0)

  time1 = gethrtime()
!$omp parallel
```

Modified OpenMP Example *(Continued)*

```
!$omp& private(i), firstprivate(h,ndiv), shared(sum)
!$omp do reduction(+:sum)
  do i=1,ndiv      ! add points  x=(i-1)*h
    sum = sum + 1.0d0/(1.d0+((i-0.5d0)*h*(i-0.5d0)*h))
  enddo
!$omp end do
  call sleep(3*OMP_GET_THREAD_NUM())
!$omp end parallel
  pical = 4.0d0*sum*h
  time2 = gethrtime()

  write(*,'(" RUNTIME: ",f6.4," seconds")') (time2-time1)*1.e-9
  write(*,'(1x,"Reference Pi  ",f18.16)') piex
  write(*,'(1x,"Computed Pi  ",f18.16)') pical
  end
```

When we run this example with the OMP_NUM_THREADS environment variable set to 2, one of the threads (thread 1) will wait three seconds after the computation.

```
example% setenv OMP_NUM_THREADS 2
example% ptime example_pi_omp_sleep
 RUNTIME:  3.2784 seconds
 Reference Pi  3.1415926535897931
 Computed Pi  3.1415926535899228
real        3.330
user        3.562
sys         0.013
```

We can see that adding three seconds of artificial delay to one of the threads increased the runtime by three seconds. We can also see that the user time, or the time the CPUs spent in user mode, increased by three seconds, as well. This increase is caused by the thread that continues to spin and use CPU cycles waiting for the sleeping[1] thread.

To observe this imbalance with the Sampling Collector and Performance Analyzer tools, we load the example_pi_openmp_sleep program in workshop debugger, set OMP_NUM_THREADS environment variable to 2, and run it though the Sampling Collector (as described in Chapter 4) with only the Clock-based Profiling check box selected. After the run completes, we load the collected data in Performance Analyzer and display the profile information (FIGURE 11-1).

---

1. Note, when a thread calls sleep system call, the Solaris dispatcher causes it to yield the CPU and the LWP is not charged any CPU usage time while it is in sleep state.

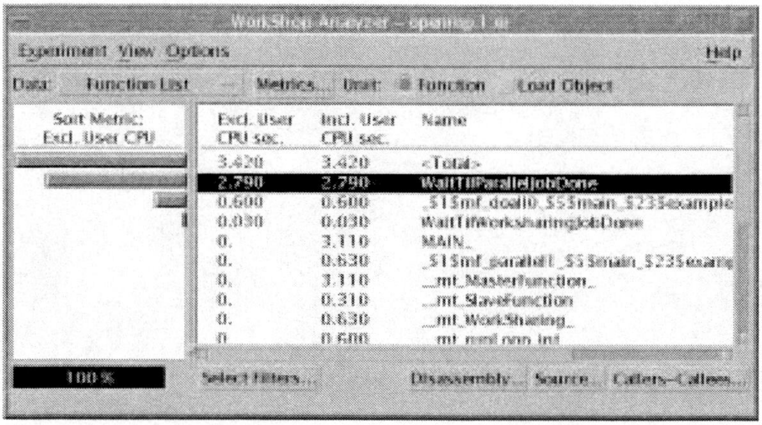

FIGURE 11-1 Analyzing an OpenMP Program With Forte Developer 6

The most time consuming function is `WaitTillParallelJobDone` called by the master thread to synchronize the slave threads at the end of the parallel region (see Chapter 13 for further discussion on the master-slave model used by the OpenMP compiler). In this example, one of the threads waits for the other thread to come out of the `sleep` function. To get more specific information about this function, we can highlight it and choose the Show Summary Metrics option from the View menu.

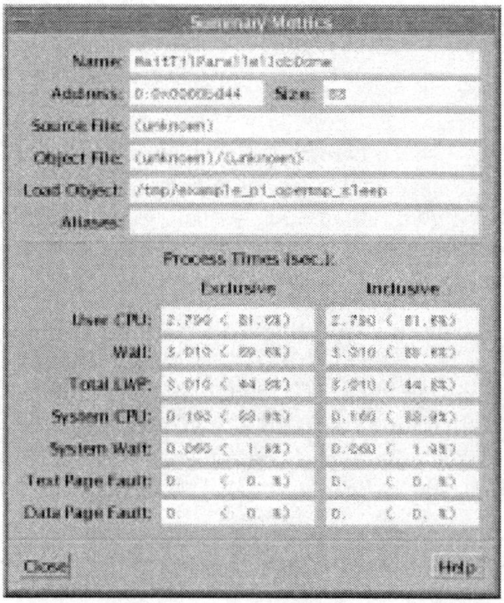

FIGURE 11-2 Performance Analyzer Information for a Particular Function

This summary displays the elapsed time for this function and breaks it down into user, system, and system wait times (see FIGURE 11-2). It also shows the percentage of the runtime spent in `WaitTillParallelJobDone` and the percentage of the per-lightweight process (LWP) which, in this case, is exactly half of the full run percentage. The granularity of the measurement was set in the Sampling Collector window. For this measurement, we used the default value of 10 milliseconds.

The previous example was very similar to the one discussed in Chapter 4. Because in this example threads consume CPU cycles, we can see the poor load balancing from the profile of the run. If the application is parallelized such that the threads do not continue to spin while waiting for additional work and instead yield the CPU (this will be discussed further in Chapter 13), the profiling data does not reveal the time spent in synchronizing the threads or the load balance problems. In such cases, the Sampling Collector tool can be used to identify the functions that spend time waiting for synchronization.

Similar to adding the artificial load imbalance in the OpenMP example, we can modify the POSIX thread example from the previous chapter by adding a `sleep` call to the `thr_sub` routine.

CODE EXAMPLE 11-4 Modified Threaded Example

```
void *thr_sub(void *arg)
{
    thr_args *thr_args_ptr = (thr_args *) arg;
    int mynum = thr_args_ptr->mynum;
    int ist = thr_args_ptr->ist;
    int ien = thr_args_ptr->ien;
    double h = thr_args_ptr->h;
    int i;
    double sum = 0.0;

    for (i=ist;i<=ien;i++) sum += 1.0/(1.0+((i+0.5)*h*(i+0.5)*h));
    sleep(3*mynum);

    thr_args_ptr->sumloc = sum;
    return((void *)0);
}
```

If we compile this modified example and run it using two threads, we can see that the real time increased by three seconds, but the user time did not.

```
example% ptime example_pi_thread_sleep 2
 RUNTIME: 3.2795 Seconds
 Reference Pi 3.1415926535897931
 Computed Pi  3.1415926535899228
```

real	3.319
user	0.553
sys	0.007

In this case, the faster slave thread joins with the parent thread, the
pthread_join(3THR) call, and does not wait for the other one to exit from the
sleep call. The parent thread also does not consume the CPU cycles while waiting
for slaves to join the pthread_join(3THR) call.

We can analyze the wait time with the Sampling Collector and Performance
Analyzer tools. To collect the runtime data, we load the program
example_pi_thread_sleep in the debugger, select the Clock-based Profiling and
Synchronization Wait Tracing options in the Sampling Collector, and start the run.
Note that Forte Developer 6 update 1 has a stand-alone tool collect(1) which
allows one to collect data without invoking workshop or the debugger. After
loading the collected data in the Performance Analyzer tool, we can view the
inclusive synchronization time spent in each function (shown in FIGURE 11-3).

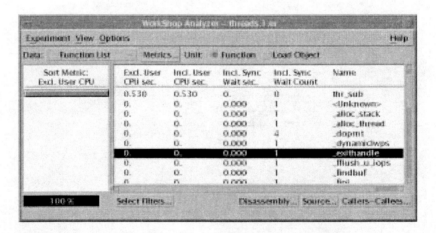

FIGURE 11-3 Analyzing a Threaded Application With Forte Developer 6

By default, functions are sorted by the Excl. User CPU sec. metric, and in FIGURE 11-3,
we see thr_sub at the top of the sorted list. We can choose to sort the functions by
their exclusive time spent in synchronization wait. To do that, we select appropriate
boxes from the Performance Analyzer Metrics menu. The new view (FIGURE 11-4)
shows the synchronization wait time spent in pthread_join call.

The above examples illustrate the capabilities of the Performance Analyzer tool to
monitor parallel applications that are either explicitly multithreaded or use compiler
parallelization (for example, OpenMP directives). For more information, see
Analyzing Program Performance With Sun WorkShop.

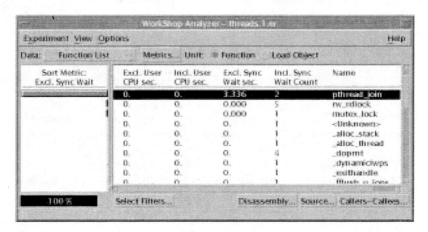

FIGURE 11-4 Functions Sorted by Exclusive Time Spent in Synchronization

Trace Normal Form Utilities

The *trace normal form* (TNF) facility is a collection of utilities and APIs that can be used to trace the execution of an application and Solaris kernel activity. The TNF suite comprises utilities and libraries bundled as part of the Solaris operating system, as well as utilities that can be freely downloaded from the Sun web site. The TNF facility operates by inserting tracepoints or event-logging points in the user application or in the system libraries executed on behalf of the user program. When a trace point (or the trace probe) is triggered, a trace record is written to a trace file. This record typically consists of a high-resolution timestamp, process-id, cpu-id, thread-id, and record of any user-prescribed variables. When kernel tracing is activated, which can be done only with superuser privileges, the event record of kernel probes is archived in the trace file. Subsequently, the trace file can be analyzed by a number of tools and utilities that have been developed for this purpose and are described in this section.

The TNF facility can be used both for debugging and performance tuning programs. It is especially useful in multithreaded applications as the probes automatically record thread-specific (thread ID) information which later can be used to construct execution timelines on a per-thread basis. The TNF facility is also useful in multiprocess programs, and the HPC ClusterTools suite includes a version of the Sun MPI library instrumented with TNF probes. The information generated can be analyzed with the Prism tool to profile MPI programs (see the next section).

Compared to profiling tools, tracing tools provide a much finer picture of application execution. While profiling provides an overall summary of how the time is spent in the program over the entire run and cannot distinguish between individual events, tracing generates information on runtime distributions and exact event histories. This additional information, however, comes at the cost of an increase of *probe-effect* on program execution and a substantial increase in the amount of data collected, making data analysis difficult [Kleinman96].

The TNF probes are designed to be lightweight and have negligible overhead when tracing is deactivated. Trace information can be obtained for an application or library that has been built with the probes inserted into it. The Solaris kernel comes with a number of "built-in" probes that provide data collection on kernel activity. These probes trace events such as system calls, page faults, swapping, I/O calls, and thread state transitions (see the *Programming Utilities Guide*).

The TNF components that are provided with the Solaris Operating Environment (release 2.5.1 and later) are as follows:

- The prex(1) utility enables or disables probes for user or kernel tracing. It can be used to trace an application directly or attach to a running process. By default, probes built into an application are disabled and can be enabled using the prex utility. There are numerous features that allow controlling the size of trace file, libraries that are preloaded in the application being traced and selectively enable or disable probes.

- The tnfdump(1) utility converts the trace file into an ASCII file that can be used in the performance diagnosis of collected data.

- The tnfxtract(1) utility extracts the kernel trace output from an in-core buffer in the Solaris kernel and generates a binary file in a format similar to that generated by the prex utility. Subsequently, this file can be converted into ASCII format using the tnfdump tool. Note, kernel tracing can only be performed with superuser privileges.

- A set of APIs for use in C and C++ programs for inserting probes. These are predefined macros named TNF_PROBE_0(), TNF_PROBE_1(), ... , TNF_PROBE_5() described in the TNF_PROBE(3X) man pages. These various probe functions record up to five arguments in a trace, and the data recorded by a probe are written to a circular buffer as a TNF event. In cases where a large amount of data are expected to be generated, the default size of the trace file (4 MB) should be overridden with prex.

- A set of libraries to support TNF facilities: libtnf, libtnfprobe, and libtnfctl.

Several unsupported tools are available for free download on the Solaris Developer Connection web site at `http://soldc.sun.com/developer/support/driver/tools/tools.html`. They are:

- The `tnfview` Motif-based graphical tool provides a graphical display of timeline and thread-based event records in an event trace file.

- The `tnfmerge` tool merges several trace files into a single file with events ordered by the trace timestamp.

- The `tnftrace` tool is a wrapper script for easy invocation of a target application with tracing enabled. It automatically sets up the environment and invokes `prex` for trace collection.

- The interposition libraries with pre-inserted probes for `libthread` (`libthread_probe`), `libpthread` (`libpthread_probe`), and selected functions in `libc` (`libc_probe`) work using the `LD_PRELOAD` feature of the Solaris linker, discussed in Chapter 7. These libraries are very useful for collecting execution traces on function calls to `libc`, `libthread`, and `libpthread` even for applications that have not been instrumented with TNF probes.

Now, we will show the use of some of these utilities with the following example P-thread program.

CODE EXAMPLE 11-5 Program to Show TNF Utilities

```
/* cc example_tnf.c -lpthread -o example_tnf    */
#define _REENTRANT
#include <stdio.h>
#include <stdlib.h>
#include <pthread.h>
#include <tnf/probe.h>

#define ARRSIZE   (256*512)
void *thr_sub(void *);
pthread_mutex_t lock;
double glbsum1=0.0,glbsum2=0.0;

main(int argc, char **argv)
{   int i, j, thr_count = 1;
    pthread_attr_t *pt_attr;
    pthread_t *id_vec;
    if (argc == 2) thr_count = atoi(argv[1]);
    pthread_mutex_init(&lock, NULL);
    id_vec = (pthread_t *)malloc(sizeof(pthread_t)*thr_count);
    pt_attr = (pthread_attr_t *)
              malloc(sizeof(pthread_attr_t)*thr_count);
    for (i=0;i<thr_count;i++) {
```

CODE EXAMPLE 11-5 Program to Show TNF Utilities *(Continued)*

```
        pthread_attr_init(&pt_attr[i]);
        pthread_attr_setscope(&pt_attr[i], PTHREAD_SCOPE_SYSTEM);
    }
    for (j=0;j<25;j++) {
        glbsum1=glbsum2=0.0;
        for (i=0;i<thr_count;i++)
          pthread_create(&id_vec[i], &pt_attr[i], thr_sub,
                          (void *)0);
        for (i=0;i<thr_count;i++) pthread_join(id_vec[i], NULL);
#ifdef SLOW
        printf(" glbsum1= %11.4e, glbsum2= %11.4e\n",glbsum1,
               glbsum2);
#else
        printf(" glbsum2= %11.4e\n",glbsum2);
#endif
    }
    for (i=0;i<thr_count;i++) pthread_attr_destroy(&pt_attr[i]);
    pthread_mutex_destroy(&lock);
    return;
}


void *thr_sub(void *arg)
{   int arr[ARRSIZE], i;
    double sum = 0.0;
    TNF_PROBE_0(thr_sub_start, "thrsub_module thr_sub",
                "start thr_sub");
    for (i=0; i<ARRSIZE; i++)  arr[i] = i;
    for (i=0; i<ARRSIZE; i++) {
        sum += (double) arr[i];
#ifdef SLOW
        pthread_mutex_lock(&lock);
        glbsum1 += (double) arr[i];
        pthread_mutex_unlock(&lock);
#endif
    }
    pthread_mutex_lock(&lock);
    glbsum2 += sum;
    pthread_mutex_unlock(&lock);
    TNF_PROBE_0(thr_sub_end, "thrsub_module thr_sub",
                "end thr_sub");
}
```

Note the use of `TNF_PROBE_0()` in this example. It defines two probes
`thr_sub_start` and `thr_sub_end`; these can be combined to obtain the start and
end times for each invocation of `thr_sub` routine. The program is compiled as

```
example% cc example_tnf.c -lpthread -o example_tnf
```

and tracing (on a 2-CPU Ultra 60) is performed as (2 is the argument to
`example_tnf` program to indicate that two threads should be used)

```
example% prex example_tnf 2
Target process stopped
Type "continue" to resume the target, "help" for help ...
/usr/bin/sparcv7/prex> list probes $all
name=thr_sub_start enable=off trace=on file=example_tnf.c line=54 funcs=<no value>
name=thr_sub_end enable=off trace=on file=example_tnf.c line=67 funcs=<no value>
/usr/bin/sparcv7/prex> enable $all
/usr/bin/sparcv7/prex> list probes $all
name=thr_sub_start enable=on trace=on file=example_tnf.c line=54 funcs=<no value>
name=thr_sub_end enable=on trace=on file=example_tnf.c line=67 funcs=<no value>
/usr/bin/sparcv7/prex> continue
 glbsum2=  1.7180e+10
 glbsum2=  1.7180e+10
 glbsum2=  1.7180e+10
 glbsum2=  1.7180e+10
 glbsum2=  1.7180e+10
 glbsum2=  1.7180e+10
 glbsum2=  1.7180e+10
...
/usr/bin/sparcv7/prex: target process exited
```

The probes are enabled with the `enable probes $all` macro and the list of enabled
probes can be checked with `list probes $all`.

The `prex` utility automatically preloads the `libtnf` and `libtnfprobe` libraries
needed by the inserted TNF probes. Alternately, one could have also linked these
libraries directly in the application as   .

```
example% cc example_tnf.c -lpthread -o example_tnf -ltnf
-ltnfprobe
```

This is needed when `prex` is attached to a running process.

The generated TNF trace file can be examined by using `tnfdump` utility.

```
example% tnfdump trace.dat
probe   tnf_name: "thr_sub_start" tnf-string: "keys thrsub_module thr_sub;file
example_tnf.c;line 54;start thr_sub"
probe   tnf_name: "thr_sub_end" tnf_string: "keys thrsub_module thr_sub;file
example_tnf.c;line 67;end thr_sub"
---------------- ---------------- ----- ----- ---------- ---
------------------------ ----------------------
   Elapsed (ms)     Delta (ms)   PID LWPID    TID  CPU Probe Name           Data
/ Description . . .
---------------- ---------------- ----- ----- ---------- ---
------------------------ ----------------------
        0.000000         0.000000 13633     5           5   - thr_sub_start
        0.651521         0.651521 13633     4           4   - thr_sub_start
       37.456888        36.805367 13633     5           5   - thr_sub_end
       37.761176         0.304288 13633     4           4   - thr_sub_end
       39.178743         1.417567 13633     7           6   - thr_sub_start
       39.269413         0.090670 13633     8         · 7   - thr_sub_start
       71.573315        32.303902 13633     8           7   - thr_sub_end
       71.635560         0.062245 13633     7           6   - thr_sub_end
       72.147807         0.512247 13633     9           8   - thr_sub_start
       72.250815         0.103008 13633    10           9   - thr_sub_start
...
```

The entire output is not listed in the interest of preserving space, but we can see that `tnfdump` outputs the probe records on a per-thread (and LWP) basis. In this program, since PTHREAD_SCOPE_SYSTEM is used (that is bound threads), the number of threads is equal to the number of LWPs and there is a one-to-one mapping. Generally, the `tnfdump` output could be quite large and difficult to process in the ASCII format that it generates. A more useful form of data presentation is provided by the `tnfview` tool. To use it, we first run `tnftrace`.

```
example% tnftrace -m test.tnf -i libpthread -s 5000 \
         -c example_tnf 2
==================== prex and/or target program output =========================
prex(13660), target(13661): Target process stopped
Type "continue" to resume the target, "help" for help ...
 glbsum2=  1.7180e+10
 glbsum2=  1.7180e+10
 glbsum2=  1.7180e+10
 glbsum2=  1.7180e+10
 glbsum2=  1.7180e+10
....
....
....
glbsum2=  1.7180e+10
/usr/bin/sparcv7/prex: target process exited
==================== prex and/or target program are done =========================
tnfmerge -o test.tnf /tmp/utrace.tnf
Counting events records...Found 506 events.
Creating internal tables... Done.
```

```
Sorting event table... Done.
Processing events... Done.
Writing events to output file... Done.
```

In the preceding example, the -m option specifies the trace file, -i indicates the library that should be interposed (in this case libpthread), -s specifies the size of trace file (5 MB), and -c is the command to be traced. To trace both libc and libpthread, one can use

```
example% tnftrace -m test.tnf -i libpthread -i libc -s 5000 \
         -c example_tnf 2
```

The trace file viewer is started as

```
example% tnfview -f test.tnf
```

The tnfview utility offers many features. Some of the notable ones are:

- Event timeline on a per-thread basis. The viewer combines data from both user inserted probes, as well as probes in system libraries to generate a unified execution timeline of the program.

- Analysis on pairs and patterns of events (user-defined, as well as automatically selected pairs by the tool).

- Event latencies. The latency of a pair of events is defined as the elapsed time between the two events. The tool can be used to generate a latency histogram, statistics (mean, standard deviation, total), and real-latency scatter plot (a plot of latency on the Y-axis and event occurrence on the X-axis). This can be used to study the cost of event pairs as the program execution takes place and detect trends and anomalies. For example, one might observe that a few events cost substantially more than the majority of events. With the latency scatter plot, the occurrence of such events can be readily identified.

- Activity analysis allows the user to define a sequence of events and count the occurrences of these sequences. This can be used to identify critical paths in program execution.

FIGURE 11-5 shows the timeline for the test.tnf trace file. The Y-axis is the vid (virtual id), and corresponds to the distinct threads in the process. In the program, threads are created and joined in a loop. We can see that clearly in the timeline as the vid increases with time. The symbols (in different color) represent different events and the event on which the crossbar is focused is listed below in the table (pthread_mutex_lock_start in the figure). The table lists the tid, lwpid, pid, address of mutex lock, and the time (in program execution) when the event occurs.

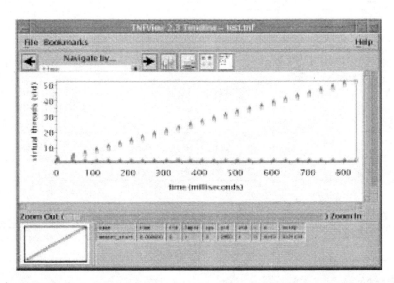

FIGURE 11-5 Timeline Display on a Per-Thread Basis in the `tnfview` Tool

FIGURE 11-6 and FIGURE 11-7 show some of the event latency analysis capabilities in the `tnfview` tool. First, the latency histogram of the event `pthread_mutex_lock` (measured from probes in `libpthread_probe`) is shown. The filter attribute is used to show only data within five standard deviations of the mean value. A detailed distribution in tabular format can be seen by clicking the Table button. The table shows that the initial events take longer and the cost per event settles down as program execution continues. FIGURE 11-7 shows the table form of distribution for the event `pthread_mutex_unlock`. Information on interval count on a per-thread basis is presented. We recommend that the reader runs this program and obtains the mean latencies for the `pthread_mutex_lock` and `pthread_mutex_unlock` events. They should verify that the mean latency for `pthread_mutex_unlock` is lower than it is for the `pthread_mutex_lock` event (in our runs, we measured the mean latencies to be approximately 0.0049 and 0.0029 milliseconds for the `pthread_mutex_.lock` and `pthread_mutex_unlock` events, respectively).

Additional information on TNF tools and utilities can be obtained from the *Programming Utilities Guide* and [Kleinman96].

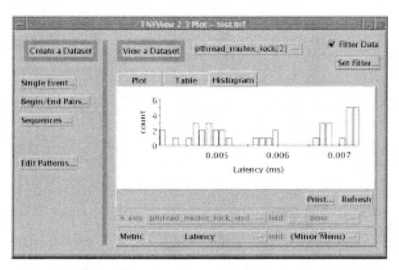

FIGURE 11-6 Latency Histogram Generated by the `tnfview` Tool for Pairs of Events That Measure Time in the `pthread_mutex_lock` Function

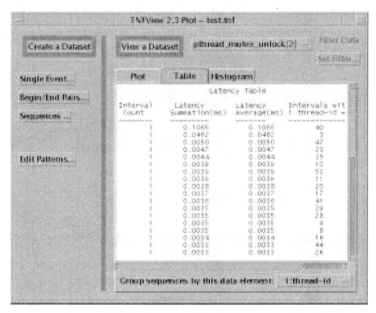

FIGURE 11-7 Latency Table Generated by the `tnfview` Tool for Pairs of Events That Measure Time in the `pthread_mutex_unlock` Function

Analyzing and Profiling MPI Programs With the Prism Environment

The Prism environment is a GUI-based tool packaged with the Sun HPC ClusterTools software. It provides an environment for debugging and getting the runtime performance information for MPI applications, as well as for threaded and nonthreaded serial applications.

The Prism environment supports applications compiled with C, C++, Fortran 77, and Fortran 95 Sun compilers. To enable Prism debugging capabilities, an application should be compiled with -g, which can be used in combination with most optimization options.

Like conventional debuggers, the Prism tool allows one to step through the source code of the program, as well as analyze the core files created by a program. A program can be loaded into the Prism environment either from the command line or with the Load option from the File menu. A running process can also be attached to a Prism session for debugging.

To illustrate debugging and profiling an MPI application in the Prism environment, we can reuse the MPI example of computing pi from the previous chapter, adding a sleep(3F) call after the computational loop.

```
call sleep(myid*3)
```

To debug the program, we compile the preprocessed file with the -g option and load the executable with the following command.

```
example% prism -n 4 example_pi_mpi
```

The -n 4 option is similar to the argument taken by the mprun script and tells the Prism debugger to run the program on four CPUs.

The main Prism window appears and displays the source code of the program.

FIGURE 11-8 Debugging an MPI Application With Prism

The breakpoints can be set by clicking the appropriate line of the source file or through the Stop option on the Events menu. The commands can also be typed directly to the lower panel of the Prism window. Once the breakpoints are set, the execution can be started with the Run command. The execution can be controlled by the Next and Step commands which have the same effect as they have in the dbx environment.

What distinguishes the Prism debugger from the standard debuggers, such as dbx, is its ability to debug multiprocess message-passing programs. The Prism debugging command can be applied to all running MPI processes or to a particular subset of processes. To make a particular choice, the Current Pset (current processor set) field should be set to All or to a process number by clicking the arrow buttons next to the Current Pset field. This feature of the Prism environment is very handy for debugging MPI applications distributed across a large number of processors when a large part of the program executes identically on all processors.

The Prism environment can also be used for collecting performance data for MPI programs. The performance analysis is based on the TNF probes described in the previous section.

One can collect and view the TNF performance data of an MPI application by selecting the Collection option from the Performance menu, clicking Run, and selecting Display TNF Data from the Performance menu. Alternatively, these commands can be typed directly in Prism input panel as

```
(prism all) tnfcollection on
(prism all) run
(prism all) tnfview
```

The first command loads the MPI library instrumented with TNF probes from the tnf library subdirectory in HPC ClusterTools installation directory. In addition, TNF probes can be added directly to the programs written in C or C++.

The sleep command, mentioned above, introduces an imbalance in the MPI program computing pi. Viewing the TNF data, we see that there are three MPI_Recv calls with latencies close to 3,000 milliseconds. The high MPI_Recv latencies, which, in this case are introduced artificially, would indicate poor load balance in real applications.

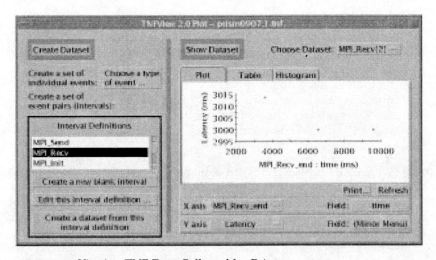

FIGURE 11-9 Viewing TNF Data Collected by Prism

In this section, we covered only the basic capabilities of the Prism environment. Refer to the *Prism User's Guide* for a full description of Prism features. The *Sun HPC 3.1 ClusterTools Performance Guide* and [Sistare99] include examples of its application to performance analysis of large-scale MPI programs including two case studies.

Parallel System Monitoring Tools

In this section, we will discuss some of the tools available in the Solaris Operating Environment that gather system activity statistics in multiprocessor systems. We have already discussed similar tools for uniprocessor systems in Chapter 4. We start the section with a discussion on how to control which CPUs (available on the system) are utilized in a parallel run.

Binding a Program to a Set of Processors

The Solaris Operating Environment provides mechanisms to control the distribution and migration of processes on a multiprocessor system. This can be accomplished with the pbind(1M) and psrset(1M) commands.

The pbind command can be used to bind all of the LWPs of a process to a particular CPU. In some cases, this can improve the performance of serial applications that may suffer from the overhead of refreshing the data in caches once the process migrates from one CPU to another. We should point out that the improved scheduling in recent Solaris releases made this effect almost negligible, but the pbind command may still be useful when increased CPU resource control is required. It can be particularly useful when a serial program, run on a system with a large number of CPUs, is monitored with a tool that collects the information on a per-CPU basis, for example, mpstat and cpustat.

One should note that process binding is not exclusive and other processes can be scheduled by the kernel on the selected CPU.

The following command binds a process or processes to a CPU.

```
example% pbind -b <processor_id> <pid(s)>
```

The option -u can be used to remove the bindings. For example, we can bind and unbind a process to CPU 0.

```
example% pbind -b 0 4606
process id 4606: was not bound, now 0
example% pbind -u 4606
process id 4606: was 0, now not bound
```

The IDs of the available CPUs can be viewed in the first column of the mpstat output or with the psrinfo(1M) command.

The `psrset(1M)` command provides additional control over CPU resources and is more appropriate for work with parallel applications. With this command, one can bind a program to a set of CPUs. Superuser privileges are needed to use this command for the creation and management of the processor sets. Option `-c` can be used to create a processor set, for example

```
# psrset -c 4
created processor set 1
processor 4: was not assigned, now 1
# psrset
user processor set 1: processor 4
```

The processors can be added to an already created set with `psrset -a`.

```
# psrset -a 1 5 8
processor 5: was not assigned, now 1
processor 8: was not assigned, now 1
```

The option `-e` of `psrset` allows one to submit a command bound to a particular processor set. Since bindings are inherited, creating a shell bound to a processor set will force all the processes originating from this shell to be bound to the same set. The bindings can be removed with the `psrset -u` command.

```
# psrset -e 1 /bin/csh
```

```
example% perfbar &
[1] 1428
example% psrset -u 1428
process id 1428: was 1, now not bound
```

Finally, we should mention the `psrset` options `-f` and `-n` that respectively disable and enable the interrupts for all the processors within a specified set.

For Sun MPI-based applications, the MPI processes comprising the job can be bound to processors using the `MPI_PROCBIND` environment variable. Further discussion about this can be found in Chapter 14.

Measuring Performance on a Per-CPU Basis

On multiprocessor systems, the vmstat (1M) utility presents data that are an average of all processors in the system. A utility that provides similar data on a per-CPU basis is mpstat (1M). We will use the example_tnf.c program (from "Trace Normal Form Utilities" on page 367) to illustrate the use of the mpstat tool. The program is first compiled as

```
example% cc -DSLOW example_tnf.c -lpthread -o example_tnf
```

and then run (on a 12-CPU Enterprise 4500 system) by creating 24 threads as

```
example% ptime example_tnf 24
```

Now, in a separate window, we run mpstat[1]. A snapshot of the generated output appears as follows.

```
example% mpstat 3
. . .
CPU minf mjf xcal  intr ithr  csw icsw migr smtx  srw syscl usr sys wt idl
  0    8   0    0   559  145 4382  199  250 6819    0  4862   5  87  0   8
  1   12   0   14   444    0 5414  341  339 11202   0  9152  11  81  0   8
  4   12   0    0   370    0 4451  213  255 7159    0  5255   7  82  0  11
  5    0   0    0   572    1 5609  420  367 10839   0  8795  10  76  0  14
  8    0   0    0   416    0 4399  252  250 7298    0  5241   7  80  0  13
  9    0   0    0   502    3 4851  367  315 9352    0  7565   8  77  0  15
 10    9   0    0   435    0 4472  283  228 7165    0  5203   6  81  0  13
 11    5   0    0   594    0 5706  476  374 11194   0  9159  17  67  0  16
 12    8   0    0   418   24 4417  237  230 6958    0  5107   7  79  0  14
 13   13   0 2068   603    0 5233  449  346 10032   0  8181   9  73  0  18
 14    6   0    0   399    0 4503  240  237 7422    0  5366   6  84  0  10
 15    0   0    0   489    0 5413  366  371 10421   0  8466   5  75  0  20
```

Note that as with vmstat, the first sample in the mpstat output is a summary since system boot, and should be ignored.

We will now discuss the above output in more detail and explain what the various quantities reported by mpstat mean. The xcal column lists processor cross-calls. Cross-calls are interrupts delivered on behalf of the Solaris kernel to another processor on the system and operations performed by the kernel for virtual address space unmapping to implement cache consistency (see [Mauro00]). The columns intr and ithr indicate the interrupts-per-second sent to each processor and the interrupts handled on an interrupt thread. Interrupts at level 10 and below

---

1. Using the commands discussed in the previous section, one may bind the process to specific processors on the system. This can facilitate the interpretation of mpstat output.

(low-level interrupts) are handled by Solaris threads [Mauro00]. The columns `csw` and `icsw` list number of context switches and involuntary context switches. Involuntary context switches occur when a thread is preempted or its time quantum is completed. Voluntary context switches (occurring as a result of a thread being blocked on a system call) can be computed as the difference of the `csw` and `icsw` fields. `migr` is the number of thread migrations, `smtx` is number of times a mutex lock is not obtained, `srw` is the number of spins on reader/writer locks, `syscl` is number of system calls. The remaining four columns give the distribution of time amongst user, system, I/O wait, and idle components, respectively.

Compiling the program `example_tnf.c` with `-DSLOW` and running as described above creates a pathological program in which, at every outer loop iteration, 24 bound threads (on a 12-processor system) are created. The threads repeatedly contend for the same mutex lock. Several of these contending threads block and yield the processor both voluntarily and involuntarily (as there are more threads than available processors) as controlled by the operating system scheduler. These threads periodically wake up to check for availability of the lock and create a situation in which multiple threads wake up simultaneously to acquire the same lock, referred to as the "thundering herds" problem in thread programming parlance.

If we run the same program as

```
example% ptime example_tnf 12
```

then a snapshot of the `mpstat` output appears as follows.

```
example% mpstat 3
...
CPU minf mjf xcal  intr ithr  csw icsw migr  smtx  srw syscl  usr sys  wt idl
  0    0   0    0   246  144 7857    8    5 10449    0  7955   11  78   0  11
  1    0   0    0    12    1 5113    8   10  9130    0  7836    5  55   0  40
  4    0   0    0    14    0 7419    8    6 10064    0  7757   10  74   0  16
  5    0   0    0    12    0 6973    9   11 12679    0 11039   15  65   0  21
  8    0   0    0    10    0 5610    7    6  7556    0  5824    6  69   0  25
  9    0   0    0    16    3 6722   11    6 12099    0 10451   18  57   0  25
 10    0   0    0    12    0 7294    7    4  9985    0  7852    7  74   0  19
 11    0   0    0    20    0 5864   15    9 10979    0  9473   13  56   0  31
 12    0   0    0    29   16 7296   10   10  9703    0  7441    8  75   0  17
 13    0   0    0    10    0 6740    9    6 11840    0 10054   12  63   0  25
 14    0   0    0    17    0 7833   10   10 10943    0  8461    9  76   0  15
 15    0   0    0     8    0 4685    6   13  9078    0  7772    8  57   0  35
```

Comparing the two cases, one can see, as expected, that very low rates of involuntary context switches and thread migrations occur in the 12-thread run. The `csw` numbers in both cases are high due to contention on the same lock. The number of interrupts in the 24-thread case are higher due to higher involuntary context switching and thread migration activity. Both cases show pathological behavior in that system activity (smtx, syscls) is high and threads are idle for a large percentage of time owing to blocking for mutex locks. The high interrupts on CPU 0 in the second case is possibly due to its being the CPU designated by the operating system for servicing regular system interrupts (such as clock interrupts generated by default 100 times in a second). Running mpstat on the above system when it is idle yields the following output, supporting the above.

```
example% mpstat 3
. . .
CPU minf mjf xcal  intr ithr  csw icsw migr smtx  srw syscl  usr sys  wt idl
  0    0   0    0   211  111   19    0    0    4    0   265    0   0    0 100
  1    0   0    0     0    0    7    0    0    0    0     0    0   0    0 100
  4    0   0    0     0    0   16    0    0    9    0   232    0   0    0 100
  5    0   0    0     0    0    9    0    0    1    0    32    0   0    0 100
  8    0   0    0     0    0    5    0    0    0    0    13    0   0    0 100
  9    0   0    0     3    3   12    0    0    0    0    23    0   0    0 100
 10    0   0    0     0    0   17    0    0    0    0    33    0   0    0 100
 11    0   0    0     0    0    1    0    0    0    0     0    0   0    0 100
 12    0   0    0    23   23   12    0    0    0    0    18    0   0    0 100
 13    0   0   73     0    0   15    0    0    0    0    40    0   0    0 100
 14    0   0    0     1    1   12    0    0    0    0     0    0   0    0 100
 15    0   0    0     0    0   10    0    0    0    0     4    0   0    0 100
```

As the preceding example shows, mpstat is a useful tool and can be used for looking at the machine balance in terms of the number of interrupts and system calls being serviced by various CPUs on an MP machine.

Monitoring Kernel Lock Statistics

Another utility that performs measurements that can be useful for the performance analysis of parallel programs is lockstat(1M). This tool, introduced in Solaris 2.6, monitors kernel lock statistics and provides information about kernel mutex and reader/writer locks. The use of this tool requires superuser privileges.

The lockstat command used with no arguments displays the list of events that can be monitored with the tool. The events for which data can be collected are selected with the -e option. For example, we can illustrate the use of the tool on the same example_tnf program that we used earlier in this section. We can collect data about the frequency of the adaptive mutex spin locks in the kernel when the program is run with lockstat -e 0.

```
# lockstat -n 50000 -e 0 example_tnf 24 | grep events
Adaptive mutex spin: 13095423 events in 130.906 seconds (100037 events/sec)
```

As previously mentioned, when `example_tnf` is run with 24 threads, the program spends most of its time in the kernel mode because of the thread contention. We can see that in this case `lockstat` measured more than 100,000 adaptive mutex spin locks per second. The preceding -n option is used to set the maximum number of records in the output.

If we submit the same program with one thread, most of the runtime is spent in user mode, and kernel mutex lock count is very small.

```
# lockstat -n 50000 -e 0 example_tnf 1 | grep events
Adaptive mutex spin: 7 events in 1.487 seconds (5 events/sec)
```

The `lockstat` utility is often used for profiling kernel activity triggered by the application. The `gprof`-like output can be generated when `lockstat` is used with -IWk options. When used with the -I option, `lockstat` generates periodic interrupt for profiling. Options -W and -k combine the output for each function regardless of the particular interrupt or where it was sampled.

Profiling the `example_tnf` program run with 24 threads generates the following output.

```
# lockstat -IWk example_tnf 24
. . .
Profiling interrupt: 151649 events in 130.282 seconds (1164 events/sec)
Count indv cuml rcnt     nsec Hottest CPU+PIL        Caller
-------------------------------------------------------------------------------
85698  57%  57% 1.00      188 cpu[12]                mutex_vector_enter
14247   9%  66% 1.00      160 cpu[9]+10              disp_getwork
12792   8%  74% 1.00      746 cpu[14]                mutex_tryenter
10359   7%  81% 1.00      280 cpu[5]                 (usermode)
 1951   1%  82% 1.00       59 cpu[1]                 splx
 1648   1%  84% 1.00      365 cpu[5]+10              _resume_from_idle
 1510   1%  85% 1.00      490 cpu[9]+10              disp
 1259   1%  85% 1.00      255 cpu[15]+10             setfrontdq
 1247   1%  86% 1.00      442 cpu[15]                mutex_enter
 1170   1%  87% 1.00      230 cpu[15]                lwp_mutex_lock
 1043   1%  88% 1.00      535 cpu[11]                mutex_exit
 1006   1%  88% 1.00       72 cpu[1]                 idle
  944   1%  89% 1.00      348 cpu[13]+10             fp_fksave
  876   1%  90% 1.00      522 cpu[5]                 utl0
  873   1%  90% 1.00      453 cpu[9]+10              lwp_release
  872   1%  91% 1.00      439 cpu[9]                 fuword8_noerr
  864   1%  91% 1.00      396 cpu[5]+10              disp_lock_enter
  838   1%  92% 1.00       44 cpu[13]                spl6
  770   1%  92% 1.00      269 cpu[13]+10             sleepq_insert
  707   0%  93% 1.00      560 cpu[13]+10             disp_ratify
-------------------------------------------------------------------------------
```

Hardware Counter Tools for Parallel Performance Monitoring

In this section, we will demonstrate the use of hardware counter measurement tools that are part of the Solaris 8 Operating Environment (namely `cpustat(1M)`, `cputrack(1M)`, and `busstat(1M)`) in parallel program performance analysis.

cpustat and cputrack Tools

To illustrate the use of the CPU counter-based tools, we consider the following C program.

CODE EXAMPLE 11-6 Program for `cpustat` Measurements

```
/* example_hwtools.c */
/* cc -fast -xO4 -xdepend -xarch=v9 -xexplicitpar \
   -xvpara example_hwtools.c (-DFAST) */
#include <stdio.h>
#include <stdlib.h>
#include <sys/types.h>
#include <sys/time.h>
int main(int argc, char * argv[])
{  void **mem_array, **mem_array_2;
   int i,size,shift,index;
   hrtime_t t0,t1,t2,ttot;
   unsigned int seed=1;
   if (argc > 1) sscanf(argv[1], "%d", &size);
   printf("using size %d\n", size);
   mem_array = (void **)malloc(size * sizeof(void *));
   mem_array_2 = (void **)malloc(size * sizeof(void *));
   t0 = gethrtime();
#pragma MP taskloop private(i,index) readonly(seed)
#pragma MP taskloop shared(size,mem_array)
   for (i = 0; i < size; i++) {
#ifdef FAST
      index = i;
#else
      index = ((rand_r(&seed) % size) + i) % size;
#endif
      mem_array[i] = (void *)(mem_array + index);
```

```
    }
    t1 = gethrtime();
#pragma MP taskloop private(i,index) readonly(seed)
#pragma MP taskloop shared(size,mem_array,mem_array_2)
    for (i = 0; i < size; i++) {
#ifdef FAST
        index = i;
#else
        index = ((rand_r(&seed) % size) + i) % size;
#endif
        mem_array_2[i] = *((void **)mem_array[index]);
    }
    t2 = gethrtime();
    ttot = (t1 - t0) + (t2 - t1);
    printf("Array Init and access time in secs %12.5e\n",
        1.e-9*ttot);
}
```

This program accesses two arrays in linear (when -DFAST is used in compilation) and random sequences, respectively. In the case of random accesses, there is significantly higher data sharing (both true, as well as false sharing), therefore, a larger number of cache-line invalidations take place, leading to lower performance and scalability. We compile the program as

```
example% cc -fast -xO4 -xdepend -xarch=v9 -xexplicitpar -xvpara \
           example_hwtools.c.c -o a.slow
example% cc -fast -xO4 -xdepend -xarch=v9 -xexplicitpar -xvpara \
           example_hwtools.c -DFAST -o a.fast
```

Now, we run the program on a 12-CPU Enterprise 4500 system with different numbers of threads and array sizes. We encourage the reader to perform the various possible experiments. Here, we will present the comparison for the case of 6 threads and an array size of 150 million. The program memory requirements in this case are approximately 2.5 GB. As described previously, to monitor the performance with the cpustat tool, we first create a processor set (as a superuser)

```
# psrset -c 0 1 4 5 8 9
```

The processor IDs are obtained using the psrinfo command. We also turn off all interrupts on these CPUs (to decrease system interference) as

```
# psrset -f 1
```

Now, the `a.slow` binary is run as

```
# setenv PARALLEL 6
# psrset -e 1 ptime a.slow 150000000
```

and in a separate window, we run the `cpustat` tool as a superuser

```
# psrset -e 1 cpustat -c pic0=EC_snoop_inv,pic1=EC_snoop_cb 2 > &
  cpu.slow.6p
```

Then, after the run is completed, we run `a.fast` in a similar fashion

```
# setenv PARALLEL 6
# psrset -e 1 ptime a.fast 150000000
```

and measure its data in another window, running `cpustat` simultaneously

```
# psrset -e 1 cpustat -c pic0=EC_snoop_inv,pic1=EC_snoop_cb 2 > &
  cpu.fast.6p
```

The above counters measure the E-cache snoop invalidations and snoop copybacks for each CPU in the processor set.

The measurements could also have been taken with the `cputrack` tool. However, `cpustat` (which gives system-wide statistics on a per-processor basis) has lower overhead than `cputrack` which gives statistics for every LWP in a process. For runs using a large number of threads, this overhead can become noticeable. We recommend that the reader experiment between the two tools and compare the overheads on their specific benchmarks.

A snapshot of the file `cpu.slow.6p` appears as follows.

```
example% more cpu.slow.6p
time cpu event      pic0        pic1
....
20.009   0  tick     79748       87186
20.009   1  tick     76082       83105
20.009   8  tick    101898      116318
20.009   9  tick    101375      112206
20.009   4  tick     67147       79261
20.009   5  tick     63825       65554
```

A similar snapshot for `cpu.fast.6p` appears here.

```
example% more cpu.fast.6p
time cpu event      pic0      pic1
....
20.002   5  tick    39334     39523
20.002   4  tick    70112     67325
20.002   1  tick    87988     83740
20.012   0  tick    67371     63149
20.012   8  tick    59737     58092
20.012   9  tick    62314     59618
```

It is clear from the snapshots how the `a.slow` binary shows larger cache-line invalidations compared to the `a.fast` binary. We will use similar measurements in the following chapter to demonstrate the effect of the false sharing.

busstat Tool

Next, we will show measurements of address packets and cache-line invalidations on the memory interconnect (called Gigaplane) in an Enterprise 4500 system. These can be measured using the `busstat` tool. On this system, the following devices were available.

```
# busstat -l
Busstat Device(s):
sbus0 sbus1 sbus2 sbus3 ac0 ac1 ac2 ac3 ac4 ac5 ac6 ac7
```

As we can see, it has four SYSIO S-bus interfaces and seven Address Controllers. The events that can be measured on these devices can be shown with the `-e` option of `busstat`, for example

```
# busstat -e ac
```

Now, we rerun the random memory access benchmark (`a.slow`) for different values of the `PARALLEL` environment variable. The runtimes for PARALLEL=1,4,10 are as follows.

```
example% setenv PARALLEL 1
example% a.slow 150000000
using size 150000000
Array Init and access time in secs  1.35278e+02
example% setenv PARALLEL 4
```

```
example% a.slow 150000000
using size 150000000
Array Init and access time in secs   3.54444e+01
example% setenv PARALLEL 10
example% a.slow 150000000
using size 150000000
Array Init and access time in secs   1.94015e+01
```

During each of the runs, we also measure the following counters using the busstat tool (superuser privilege is needed to run it with these options).

```
# busstat -w ac,pic0=addr_pkts,pic1=upa_a_inv_to >&
  bus.slow.64.10p
```

The counter addr_pkts measures total address packets on the system bus while upa_a_inv_to provides a measure of cache-line invalidation transactions on the interconnect (see Appendix D).

A snapshot of bus.slow.64.10p appears as follows.

```
. . .
10   ac0   addr_pkts        9323457   upa_a_inv_to      43601
10   ac1   addr_pkts        9322911   upa_a_inv_to      38327
10   ac2   addr_pkts        9322567   upa_a_inv_to      38099
10   ac3   addr_pkts        9322261   upa_a_inv_to       3069
10   ac4   addr_pkts        9322117   upa_a_inv_to      37877
10   ac5   addr_pkts        9321914   upa_a_inv_to      38234
. . .
```

A similar snapshot for the bus.slow.64.4p case is

```
. . .
10   ac0   addr_pkts        4628142   upa_a_inv_to       4101
10   ac1   addr_pkts        4628157   upa_a_inv_to       1880
10   ac2   addr_pkts        4628133   upa_a_inv_to       1820
10   ac3   addr_pkts        4628118   upa_a_inv_to      29809
10   ac4   addr_pkts        4628163   upa_a_inv_to      28501
. . .
```

As expected, we can see that a higher number of address packets and cache-line invalidations are generated in the ten processor run compared to the four-processor run. While not shown here, the numbers for a one-processor case are still lower.

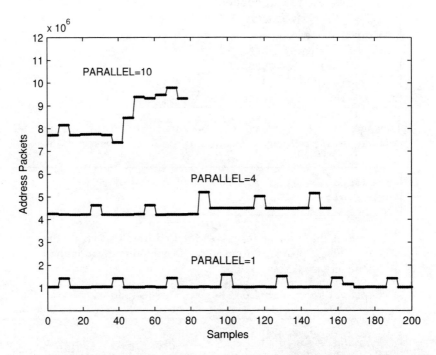

FIGURE 11-10 Measurements of `addr_pkts` Counter Values Measured Using the `busstat` Tool on an Enterprise 4500 System

The measurements of the `addr_pkts` counter for the three different cases are plotted in the preceding figure. Not all of the sample for `PARALLEL=1` is shown[1]. We can clearly see how the number of address packets (and, therefore, the address bus utilization, see Appendix D) increases with the number of processors used in the run.

---

1. The Enterprise 4500 system on which the runs were performed had seven address controllers. The `busstat` tool reports values for each controller every second. The measured data for each address controller are plotted.

Summary

Measuring the performance of a parallel application is a more difficult task than monitoring a serial program. In addition to the standard measurements, like the elapsed time or the distribution between user and system time modes, a parallel environment has more factors that are relevant to the application performance, such as the number of processors available for the application, their distribution over the nodes in a clustered environment, and others. In addition, since there are a variety of approaches to the parallelization of a program, measurement tools need to be chosen carefully to allow measurements applicable for a particular parallelization model.

Measuring the elapsed time for a multithreaded parallel application is similar to measuring a serial program. We recommend using the `ptime` utility as it invokes the Solaris microstate accounting facility. The recommended functions for performing fine-grained timing of the parts of a multithreaded program are `gethrtime` and `gethrvtime` which measure the elapsed and user times, respectively. These C functions can be called directly in Fortran 90 and Fortran 95 or via wrappers in Fortran 77.

Forte Developer 6 provides an extensive environment for performance analysis that can be applied to parallel applications. The Sampling Collector and Performance Analyzer tools can be used to generate performance analysis and profile data of threaded applications (both threaded explicitly and via compiler directives). Analysis of distributed message-passing applications can be performed with the tools included in Sun HPC ClusterTools package. The Prism environment provides for the development, debugging, and profiling of the MPI programs. The Prism performance analysis capabilities are based on the trace normal form (TNF) facility of Solaris Operating Environment. In this chapter, we also provided an overview of the tools and utilities of the TNF suite that can be used to analyze system activity.

We concluded the chapter with two sections that describe Solaris tools available for monitoring the system activity that can be particularly useful for analyzing parallel applications. We discussed the Solaris commands `pbind` and `psrset` which provide control over CPU resources and allow setting the runtime bindings between applications and processor sets. The output of the `mpstat` command provides a detailed account of the system usage on a per-CPU basis. The kernel lock statistics and the profile of the kernel usage can be generated with the `lockstat` command. Finally, we discussed the hardware counter-based tools `cpustat`, `cputrack`, and `busstat`, and provided examples of their use in a multiprocessor environment.

## CHAPTER 12

Optimization of Explicitly Threaded Programs

During the past decade, multithreading has emerged as an increasingly popular programming paradigm. Threads provide a mechanism to distribute the execution of a process between several concurrent paths. Although this chapter focuses on issues specific to computationally intensive parallel applications, we should point out that the multithreaded approach is applicable for a much more general class of programs. Today, a thread-based approach is standard for many programming areas, such as client-server applications, graphical user interfaces, or signal handlers. In fact, the threading paradigm is so important that it heavily influenced the design of modern languages such as the Java language.

The Solaris Operating Environment is multithreaded and supports multitasking. In this chapter, we discuss the threading implementations available in the Solaris Operating Environment and provide recommendations on building threaded C and Fortran applications. We describe the issues specific to optimizing multithreaded programs and focus on improving the performance of parallel applications by reducing synchronization times. In particular, we discuss synchronization methods based on the *compare and swap* (cas) instruction. We also discuss the effect of data sharing between threads, as well as false sharing, which may impede the performance of parallel applications because of cache thrashing effects. We conclude the chapter by considering other performance-related issues such as topics related to thread stack size and thread creation.

Many of the optimization considerations raised in this chapter also apply to compiler-driven parallelization which uses threads as an underlying technology. Parallelization with compiler directives and related performance topics are the subject of the next chapter.

Programming Models for Multithreading

In this section, we will give a brief overview of programming models and performance issues related to the design and implementation of multithreaded programs. Models and issues are described from a point of view of parallel performance, even though many of the same issues are also applicable to multithreading for program concurrency. Refer to the books [Kleinman96] and [Norton96] for comprehensive information about thread programming models including detailed algorithmic discussion and complete example programs.

When multithreading a program for parallel performance, the primary performance issues to consider are: breaking a problem into parallel tasks, balancing the amount of computations amongst tasks, synchronization between threads, and data sharing between different threads. The models that we will discuss differ in how these issues are handled and are, therefore, suitable to different types of programs. The granularity of the computation should also be considered when choosing a particular model for multithreading. In some cases, no approach gives good performance and one may need to use a combination of these paradigms or devise an entirely new scheme to multithread an application.

In order to maximize parallelism, it is recommended that the program is running in a dedicated mode on the parallel system and that the number of threads performing the computations is equal to or less than the number of processors on the system (additional threads can handle I/O and other noncomputational tasks). It is difficult to prescribe exactly how many threads should be created in an application, and users are required to experiment to determine an appropriate number of threads.

The three paradigms discussed are the *master-slave* model, the *work-crew* model and the *pipeline* model.

Master-Slave Model

In the *master-slave* model, one of the threads (often the thread running the main program) divides the work into several tasks that are processed by the slave threads (generated by the master thread). While the slave threads work on their tasks, the master performs other processing (for example, generating additional tasks for slave threads) or waits at a synchronization point for slaves to complete their processing. This process may be repeated if additional tasks need to be computed. In the most general form of this model, slaves may perform different tasks with an unequal amount of computation which might involve the execution of different functions in the program. Once all tasks are completed, the master processes the final results (if required). Following [Kleinman96], a schematic of this model is given here.

Master Thread	Slave Thread

initialization;
create N slave threads;
while (work to do) {
  create work for slaves;
  call barrier function;
  slaves running, master
  performs its processing, if any;
  call barrier and wait for all
  slaves to arrive;
  process results and check if
  more work to do;
}
join slave threads;
finalize and perform any
other calculation;
	while (work to do) {
	  call barrier function and
	  wait for master to create
	  work;
	  process its portion of
	  work;
	  put results into global
	  memory or passed parameters;
	  call barrier and wait till
	  all slaves finish;
	}
	call thread exit;

This model requires two barrier synchronization calls. If the time it takes for the master thread to set up the work for slaves and to process the results is quite small compared to the amount of time taken by slaves to compute the tasks, then efficiency can be improved using spin barriers. These cause slaves not to block and decrease context switch and scheduling overhead [Norton96]. The best load balance in this model is obtained if the tasks require an equal amount of computation. Hence, this model is suitable for cases where the amount of work is known in advance and can be equally divided amongst slave threads.

In the simplest form of this model, only one set of tasks with an equal amount of work is distributed amongst the slave threads, and each slave's work is independent of other slaves (that is, the slave threads do not need any synchronization). This situation requires no barrier synchronization resulting in a very efficient parallel implementation.

Worker-Crew Model

The master-slave model is not very suitable to the case where tasks are created dynamically or vary in the amount of work. A model suitable to programs with load-imbalance and dynamic work creation is the *worker-crew* model (also referred to as the *workpile* model). In this model, threads obtain work from a central task queue, perform the task, and then request more work. Threads can also add tasks to the queue (dynamic workpile). The process continues until all tasks are exhausted in the workpile. The algorithm for this model appears as follows.

Main
Initialize task-queue and create worker threads;
wait for threads to exit;

Worker
for (;;) {
  t = get task from queue;
  if global-->done flag set then break;
  check if max task queue length reached or work finished;
  if true then set global->done flag (under protection of mutex lock)
  add new tasks to workpile if any (put task);
  check if t is valid task and perform the task;
}

In a variant of this model, one or more of the threads create and add tasks to the queue. The other threads perform these tasks. This is referred to as the *boss-worker* model (see [Norton96]) and is ideal for a client-server type application.

The worker-crew model is applicable to a wide variety of programs. Some examples are: search algorithms, divide-and-conquer algorithms, sparse matrix factorization, ray tracing, and loop parallelization. Consider a loop with an unequal amount of work in different iterations. In this situation, a *static* work queue (with known length) can be used in a worker-crew model. Because the worker threads pick different iterations of the loop dynamically, the load is balanced across the computation. Right-looking Cholesky factorization of a sparse symmetric matrix is an example of dynamic work queue as the worker threads also add tasks dynamically to the queue during the calculation (see [Gallivan90]).

The synchronization overhead in the *worker-crew* model is typically higher than it is in the *master-slave* model as the access to the central workpile needs to be protected[1]. The contention for queue access can become a bottleneck as the number of threads in the computation increases. In the case of a static workpile, only the update to the pointer at the head of the queue needs to be protected (as tasks are only dequeued) whereas in the dynamic workpile, the lock overhead is higher as tasks are also

---

1. The locking needed to protect the workpile is inherent in the model and is required even if no synchronization is needed between the worker threads in order to perform their tasks.

enqueued. The performance also depends on how the tasks are enqueued in the workpile: whether using LIFO (depth-first) or FIFO (breadth-first) schemes (see [Kleinman96]).

Since data structures are accessed by various threads dynamically, the data-sharing or false-sharing overhead in the worker-crew model could be higher than in other models[1] (see the section on false sharing later in the chapter).

Pipeline Model

The final model we will discuss is the *pipeline* model which encapsulates the computation in a producer-consumer programming idiom. In the simplest form, the producer thread creates work and puts it on a shared queue. The consumer thread, which is waiting until work is put on the queue, dequeues the work and starts the task computation. In the meantime, the producer thread could be working to create additional tasks to add to the shared queue.

For the case of a multistage pipeline, the data are passed along different stages with a thread corresponding to each stage working on its own independent portion of the data. There is an input and output queue associated with each stage of the pipeline. The output queue for the i-th stage is the input queue for the $i+1$-th stage. Synchronization is required when work is added or removed from one of these queues. It is easy to see that only two threads are involved in the synchronization of a queue at the i-th stage. Thus, one way to decrease locking overhead is to maintain separate locks for each of the queues in the model. A simple schematic of this model follows. There are two types of pipeline models [Kleinman96]: inhomogeneous pipelines and homogeneous pipelines. In an inhomogneous pipeline, threads at different stages perform tasks with different functionality. Parallelism is limited to

---

1. Unless a static workpile with sequentially ordered tasks is being used.

the number of independent tasks in the problem, and load balancing these could be tricky. In a homogenous pipeline, each stage performs an identical task (though on different data).

```
Pipeline
if stage = 0 { put work in queue 0; /* 0 <= stage <= NSTAGES */
for (;;) {
  if (stage > 0) { get work from queue (stage-1); /* wait if no work */
    if (task = EXIT or DONE) {
      if (stage < NSTAGES) put EXIT or DONE in queue (stage+1);
      break and then terminate;
    } /* end of if (task = EXIT or DONE) */
  } /* end of if (stage > 0) */
  Perform the work and update shared data;
  if (stage = 0) {
    check if all work done;
    if all work done {put DONE in queue 0; break and terminate;}
    if an error {put EXIT in queue 0; break and terminate;}
    put work in queue 0;
  } else if (stage > 0 and stage < NSTAGES) {
    put work in queue (stage + 1); /* wait if queue being accessed */
  } /* end of if (stage = 0) */
}
```

The synchronization costs in the pipeline model are lower than in the other models, but load balancing is harder compared to the worker-crew model. The model also exhibits a good data locality compared to the worker-crew model. Some examples of pipeline model usage are graphics rendering, tridiagonal matrix solution, and iterative solvers.

Multithreading in the Solaris Operating Environment

In this section we will discuss the multithreading implementation on Solaris platforms, as well as topics specific to building multithreaded applications.

Thread Models

Solaris thread support was introduced in release 2.4 of the operating environment. At that time, there was no industry-wide standard for threading implementation. The standard appeared as POSIX (Portable Operating System Interface) P1003.1c and the POSIX-compliant threading implementation was first integrated in Solaris 2.6, in addition to the original Solaris thread (also known as *Unix International* or *UI* threads) support. Both POSIX and Solaris thread models are very similar and provide virtually the same functionality. There are some subtle differences, though. For example, `fork(2)` calls from POSIX threads duplicate just the calling thread. When using Solaris threads, `fork` duplicates all the threads of the process. The `fork1(2)` system call was introduced to provide POSIX-like functionality of `fork` for Solaris threads.

For developing new applications, we generally recommend using POSIX threads as this implementation provides greater portability and is more likely to be the subject of future development. We provide the details for building threaded applications in the next section of this chapter.

Threads within a multithreaded program reside within the address space of the program process and share its attributes, such as user ID, working directory, open files and their descriptors, and others. Each thread within a process has its unique thread ID, stack, register state, priority, and thread-private storage. Since they don't independently have all of the attributes (and associated data structures) of processes, creating new threads can be relatively inexpensive. Further, common address space makes it very simple to share data between threads. Also, developing applications, and especially debugging, is often not as difficult when dealing with multiple threads rather than with multiple processes.

We already mentioned that the Solaris environment is multithreaded. At runtime, user application threads get bound to kernel threads as *lightweight processes* (LWPs), which are dispatched to CPUs by the operating system.

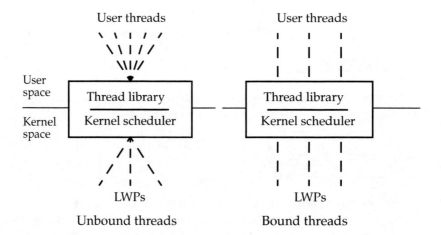

User threads   User threads

User space

Kernel space

Thread library   Thread library

Kernel scheduler   Kernel scheduler

LWPs   LWPs

Unbound threads   Bound threads

FIGURE 12-1 Bound and Unbound Thread Mapping to LWPs

There are two scheduling options for threads that can be set at thread creation (see the schematic in FIGURE 12-1). Unbound threads (or threads with process scope) can migrate within the pool of LWPs in the process. This model can be advantageous for applications with a large number of user threads, such as client-server programs. The other option is to create bound threads (or threads with system scope) that stick to a particular LWP for their lifetime. This model is recommended for parallel computational programs where the number of threads performing computational tasks does not exceed the number of available CPUs.

Starting with release 8, the Solaris Operating Environment includes an alternative implementation of the thread library. This implementation provides a one-to-one binding between user and kernel threads, effectively enforcing the system scope of the threads. The associated shared libraries are located in the /usr/lib/lwp and /usr/lib/lwp/64 directories and are fully interchangeable with their counterparts from /usr/lib. The alternative thread libraries can be used with existent binaries if the environment variable LD_LIBRARY_PATH is properly set.

Concurrent execution of different threads within the same process address space poses a number of problems that are not encountered when dealing with single-threaded applications. In particular, global and static data can be changed by one thread when another thread's correct execution may rely on the original values. To avoid this problem, programmers should pay special attention to protecting shared data and to synchronization between threads. Synchronization mechanisms include: *mutual exclusion locks*, or *mutex locks*, *read/write locks*, *semaphores*, and *condition variables*. We will discuss synchronization and related performance issues later in this chapter.

Solaris system calls and libraries are divided into the following categories with respect to their safety level for multithreading:

- *Unsafe* – No support for concurrent calls from different threads. Unsafe functions can be used in multithreaded programs, but only in cases when just one thread makes the call at a time.

- *Safe* – Safe calls protect their global and static data and, therefore, can be used by multiple threads. No special precautions are needed for correct execution of these functions in multithreaded applications. However, safe functions might not provide any concurrency between the calls made from different threads.

- *MT safe* – These functions are fully ready for use in multithreaded applications. They are thread safe and, in addition, provide some degree of concurrency.

- *Async signal safe* – This group describes the functions that can be safely used in signal-handler threads and are guaranteed not to cause deadlocks when interrupted by a signal.

More details for thread safety levels are provided in the `attributes(5)` man pages. In some literature, MT safe functions that provide a high degree of concurrency are called *MT hot*. We should point out, however, that this terminology is not standard in Solaris documentation. The implementation of the `malloc(3C)` call in the Solaris (release 7 and higher) `libmtmalloc(3LIB)` library can be very efficient when called simultaneously from a large number of threads. This version of `malloc` is sometimes called MT hot.

For further information about multithreading and related programming issues, refer to the books on multithreaded programing by Lewis and Berg [Lewis97], Kleinman, Shah and Smaalders [Kleinman96], and Norton and Dipasquale [Norton96]. They provide an excellent overview of the POSIX standard and its implementations, as well as numerous suggestions about programming with threads. The specifics of Solaris thread implementation are provided in the *Multithreaded Programming Guide*.

Compiling Threaded Applications

As we described in the previous section, a multithreaded application can use either POSIX or UI threads in the Solaris environment (or it can mix both models, though it is not recommended). The POSIX function names typically have a `pthread_` prefix and are implemented in the `libpthread(3THR)` library; the corresponding prototypes are provided in the file `pthread.h`. With few exceptions, the Solaris thread implementation gives the same functionality through the `libthread(3THR)` library with the `libthread.h` header file. The differences between the POSIX and Solaris threads are listed in the `threads(3THR)` man page.

The thread library APIs are C interfaces that can be called directly from C or C++ programs. For example, the following program creates a POSIX thread that has a particular set of attributes (we will look at the attributes later in this section) and calls a user-defined function.

CODE EXAMPLE 12-1 Creating a Thread With a Set of Attributes

```
/* example_thread.c */
/* cc -D_POSIX_C_SOURCE=199506L example_thread.c \
   -o example_thread -lpthread */
#include <stdio.h>
#include <pthread.h>
void *thr_foo(void *);

int main(int argc, char **argv)
{
   pthread_attr_t t_attr;
   pthread_t id;
   int param=1;

   pthread_attr_init(&t_attr);
   pthread_attr_setscope(&t_attr, PTHREAD_SCOPE_SYSTEM);
   pthread_attr_setstacksize(&t_attr, 1000);

   pthread_attr_setdetachstate(&t_attr, PTHREAD_CREATE_JOINABLE);
   printf("In main thread BEFORE creating a joinable thread \n");
   pthread_create(&id, &t_attr, thr_foo, (void *)&param);
   pthread_join(id, NULL);
   printf("In main thread AFTER creating a joinable thread \n\n");
   sleep(2);

   pthread_attr_setdetachstate(&t_attr, PTHREAD_CREATE_DETACHED);
   printf("In main thread BEFORE creating a detached thread \n");
   pthread_create(&id, &t_attr, thr_foo, (void *)&param);
   printf("In main thread AFTER creating a detached thread \n");
   sleep(2);
   pthread_attr_destroy(&t_attr);

   printf("\nIn main thread before exit \n\n");
   return 0;
}

void *thr_foo(void *arg)
{
   int *ip = (int*) arg;
```

```
    int param = *ip;
    sleep(param);
    printf("    In the created thread \n");
    return((void *)0);
}
```

An application that uses POSIX threads should be compiled with
-D_POSIX_C_SOURCE set to a number 199506L or higher or with -D_REENTRANT
and linked with -lpthread.

```
example% cc -D_POSIX_C_SOURCE=199506L example_thread.c -lpthread \
          -o example_thread
example% example_thread
In main thread BEFORE creating a joinable thread
    In the created thread
In main thread AFTER creating a joinable thread

In main thread BEFORE creating a detached thread
In main thread AFTER creating a detached thread
    In the created thread

In main thread before exit
```

Similarly, applications that use the Solaris thread model have to be compiled with
-D_REENTRANT and linked with -lthread. We should mention that while the
POSIX thread library (libpthread) implements only POSIX thread APIs, the
Solaris thread library (libthread) implements both POSIX and UI APIs and,
therefore, can be used instead of libpthread. In fact, the Solaris thread library is
invoked underneath libpthread in POSIX threaded applications. The previous
example can be built as follows.

```
example% cc -D_REENTRANT example_thread.c -lthread \
          -o example_thread
```

We should also mention the -mt option of C and C++ compilers that expands to
-D_REENTRANT -lthread. An equivalent way to compile the preceding example
appears as follows.

```
example% cc -mt example_thread.c -o example_thread
```

Parallel computational programs that use bound threads often set the required number of LWPs for a particular run (not exceeding the number of available processors). This can be done with the `thr_setconcurrency(3THR)` call in `libthread`. Note, that the `thr_setconcurrency` call provides a hint to the thread library and the actual number of allocated LWPs can be different from the requested one.

The semaphore routines for the POSIX thread model are defined in the `libposix4(3LIB)` library. Therefore, an application that uses them should be linked with `-lposix4`, and the file `posix4.h` should be included in the source. No special precautions are needed for Solaris threads as their semaphore calls are in `libthread`.

The Solaris C library `libc(3LIB)` provides stubs for some `libpthread` and `libthread` calls. This allows one to link the MT safe functions, which use synchronization calls, into single-threaded programs that don't use the thread library. The `libc` stubs are null functions and usually don't create extra runtime overhead.

As we have mentioned, the Solaris 8 Operating Environment provides an alternative single-level implementation of the thread library. The alternative library can be used at runtime if `LD_LIBRARY_PATH` is set to point to `/usr/lib/lwp`. The runtime path can be also set at link time with `-R` option.

```
example% cc ... -R/usr/lib/lwp -lthread ...
```

Let us take a closer look at the attributes of the threads created in the preceding example. The `pthread_attr_t` data type is provided to store the attribute information for a POSIX thread. The thread attributes are initialized and destroyed with the `pthread_attr_init(3THR)` and `pthread_attr_destroy(3THR)` calls. The scope of the threads can be set with `pthread_attr_setscope(3THR)`, which takes values `PTHREAD_SCOPE_SYSTEM` for bound threads and `PTHREAD_SCOPE_PROCESS` for unbound threads (the default). The preceding example sets the size of the stack for the created threads with `pthread_attr_setstacksize(3THR)`. The default thread stack size values are 1 MB for 32-bit applications and 2 MB for 64-bit applications. In many cases, explicit stack sizes have to be set. We will discuss this further later in this chapter.

Another attribute makes a thread detached or joinable. A *detached* thread exits and releases its resources without an explicit `pthread_join(3THR)` call from the thread that created it. This attribute is set with `pthread_attr_setdetachstate(3THR)`, which takes `PTHREAD_CREATE_JOINABLE` and `PTHREAD_CREATE_DETACHED` values. The joinable state is the default for POSIX threads. The output of the example program shows that in the first case, the main thread waits until the created thread finishes its execution at the `pthread_join` call. In the second case, the main thread does not wait for the created thread that exits and does not affect the main thread.

We conclude the section by providing an example of creating user threads directly from a Fortran program. To do that, we can use calls to external _thr_create. The attribute flags are passed by their numeric values from thread.h in the fifth argument of _thr_create. This particular example creates a detached thread.

CODE EXAMPLE 12-2   Creating Threads in a Fortran Program

```
c example_thread.f
c f77 example_thread.f -lthread -stackvar -o example_thread
      program main
      integer    args(2), istat
      integer    _thr_create
      external   _thr_create    !$pragma c(_thr_create)
      external   thr_sub
      args(1)=1
      args(2)=22
      print*,"main thread: before _thr_create call"
      istat = _thr_create (%val(0), %val(0), thr_sub,
     &          args(1), %val(64), %val(0))
      print*,"main thread: after _thr_create call"
      call sleep(2)
      print*,"main thread: before exit"
      end

      subroutine thr_sub(argv)
      integer    argv(2)
      call sleep(1)
      print*,"created thread: argv(1)=",argv(1),", argv(2)=" ,argv(2)
      end
```

```
example% example_thread.f -lthread -stackvar -o example_thread
example% example_thread
 main thread: before _thr_create call
 main thread: after _thr_create call
 created thread: argv(1)=  1, argv(2)=  22
 main thread: before exit
```

Similarly, synchronization calls can be made directly from Fortran programs.

Finally, we should make a special remark for assembly programmers. The Solaris kernel reserves global registers %g6 and %g7 of SPARC platforms for special use in multithreaded programs. Register %g6 is used internally by libthread and libpthread, and register %g7 contains the pointer to the thread structure of the running thread. If a procedure written in assembly is intended for use in a multithreaded program (even if it is not called from multiple threads at the same time), these two registers should not be used.

True and False Data Sharing

An ideal program for parallelization is one that can be divided into separate subproblems of equal size that require no (or a negligible) amount of communication between the subproblems. Problems of this type are commonly called *embarrassingly parallel*. Unfortunately, most of the problems are not so easily parallelizable and often require substantial communication or data sharing between threads of execution.

Extra data shared between the threads lead to extra locks or synchronization that, in turn, make parallel performance less efficient. We can illustrate the point with a simple program that performs summation of a 4 by 100,000 array.

```
for(i=0;i<4;i++){
    for(j=0;j<100000;j++){
        sum=sum+array[j][i];
    }
}
```

Since the leading dimension of the array is four, we can try to use four threads to perform this calculation with each thread operating on a vector of 100,000 elements. For this example, making the variable `sum` shared between the threads is a recipe for a disaster, as it will require protecting access to it. The parallel performance will suffer not just because the execution becomes serial, but also because of the overhead of repeated synchronization.

What appears to be a solution is to create a vector of local variables to hold the summation values for each thread. If the computation is arranged that way, the problem becomes embarrassingly parallel, requiring no communication or synchronization between threads. However, that does not solve the problem. The following example performs both serial and parallel summation of the array and we can see that parallel runtime is higher than serial. We compile this program with the lowest optimization to highlight the problem.

CODE EXAMPLE 12-3 Example of False Data Sharing *(1 of 3)*

```
/* example_false_sharing.c */
/* cc -mt example_false_sharing.c -xO1 -o example_false_sharing */
#include <stdio.h>
#include <pthread.h>
#include <sys/time.h>
#define MAXITER 100
#define SIZE 100000
void array_init(double array[][]);
```

CODE EXAMPLE 12-3 Example of False Data Sharing *(2 of 3)*

```
void *thr_sub(void *);

double array[SIZE][4], sum, s[4];
int i,j,iter;
typedef struct {
    int mynum;
} thr_args;

int main(){
    float secs;
    hrtime_t st, et;
    pthread_attr_t *pt_attr;
    pthread_t *id_vec;
    thr_args *param_arr;

    array_init(array);
    sum = 0.0;
    st= gethrtime(); /* single threaded summation */
    for(iter=0;iter<MAXITER;iter++){
        for(i=0;i<4;i++){
            for(j=0;j<SIZE;j++){
                sum=sum+array[j][i];
            }
        }
    }
    et= gethrtime();
    secs = (( float) (et-st) / (float) 1000000000);
    printf("sum = %f \n", sum);
    printf(" RUNTIME (One thread) : %6.4f Seconds \n", secs);

    id_vec = (pthread_t *)malloc(sizeof(pthread_t)*4);
    pt_attr = (pthread_attr_t *) malloc(sizeof(pthread_attr_t)*4);
    param_arr = (thr_args *) malloc(4*sizeof(thr_args));
    for (j=0;j<4;j++) {
        pthread_attr_init(&pt_attr[j]);
        pthread_attr_setscope(&pt_attr[j], PTHREAD_SCOPE_SYSTEM);
        param_arr[j].mynum = j;
    }

    st= gethrtime(); /* four threaded summation */
    for (j=0;j<4;j++) {
    i = pthread_create(&id_vec[j], &pt_attr[j], thr_sub,
            (void *)&param_arr[j]);
```

```
        }
        /* parent waits for joining */
        for (j=0;j<4;j++) pthread_join(id_vec[j], NULL);
        sum = 0.0;
        for (j=0;j<4;j++) sum+=s[j];
        et= gethrtime();
        secs = (( float) (et-st) / (float) 1000000000);
        printf("sum = %f \n", sum);
        printf(" RUNTIME (Four threads) : %6.4f Seconds \n", secs);
        return 0;
}

void array_init(double array[SIZE][4]){
    for(i=0;i<4;i++){ /* array initilization */
        for(j=0;j<SIZE;j++){
            array[j][i]=1./(double)(i+1) + 1./(double)(j+1);
        }
    }
    sum = 0.0;
    return;
}

void *thr_sub(void *arg)
{
    thr_args *thr_args_ptr = (thr_args *) arg;
    int mynum = thr_args_ptr->mynum, j1, iter1;
    double mysum = 0.0;
    s[mynum] = 0.0;
    for(iter1=0;iter1<MAXITER;iter1++){
        for (j1=0;j1<SIZE;j1++){
            s[mynum] += array[j1][mynum];
        }
    }
    return((void *)0);
}
```

Running on the Enterprise 4500 system we get the following.

```
example% cc -mt example_false_sharing.c -o example_false_sharing
example% example_false_sharing
sum = 20838169.391802
 RUNTIME (One thread) : 3.2394 Seconds
sum = 20838169.391788
 RUNTIME (Four threads) : 8.8611 Seconds
```

What happens here? The thread private sums are stored in a vector of four sequential 8-byte values. This 32-byte sequence either fits in a single cache line (both for level 1 and level 2 caches) or it is split between two adjacent cache lines. In a parallel run, different threads are trying to update the same cache line. Because cache coherence is maintained at a cache-line level, this leads to the cache line containing the array s being repeatedly invalidated, causing a substantial increase in the traffic on the memory bus.

Looking at the EC_snoop_inv and EC_snoop_cb events with the cputrack tool, we can see that cache snooping stays at a low level when the computation is performed serially, but skyrockets once the run enters its multithreaded phase.

```
. . .
   1.073    4326    1       tick       462        506
   1.014    4326    2       tick        14          9
   0.045    4326    3       tick        18         16
   2.093    4326    1       tick       100        107
   2.014    4326    2       tick         0          0
   0.045    4326    3       tick         0          0
. . .
   3.474    4326    8       tick         0          0
   3.457    4326    1       tick         0          0
   6.014    4326    2       tick         0          0
   3.474    4326    3       tick         0          0
   6.093    4326    4       tick   1023090    1019874
   6.093    4326    5       tick   1023104    1019008
   6.094    4326    6       tick   1023361    1020391
   6.094    4326    7       tick   1023328    1019657
   3.474    4326    8       tick         0          0
   3.457    4326    1       tick         0          0
   7.014    4326    2       tick         0          0
   3.474    4326    3       tick         0          0
   7.104    4326    4       tick   1024083    1021300
   7.104    4326    5       tick   1023743    1019784
```

```
7.104    4326    6       tick    1024498    1021366
7.103    4326    7       tick    1024398    1020483
. . .
```

This phenomenon of shared cache lines between threads when there is no actual data sharing is called *false sharing*. False sharing has two degrading effects on performance. First, the performance is degraded due to an increase in the number of cache misses. The second impact is due to an increase in the miss penalty because of the cache-line ownership becoming a serial bottleneck as different processors can be simultaneously waiting for ownership of the shared line. From a processor architecture design point of view, false sharing may lead to a behavior in which increasing cache line size leads to an increase in the number of cache misses even though the program has high spatial locality (see [Eggers89]).

Once the problem of false sharing is identified, there are many ways to eliminate it. The following list identifies some of the techniques that have been proposed for decreasing or eliminating false sharing in multithreaded programs (see [Torellas90], [Culler99]):

- *Restructuring program loops and constructs* – This involves modifying the program structure, for example blocking, aligning, or peeling loops such that data structures accessed in different iterations in a parallel loop fall on distinct cache lines.

- *Changing data structures* – The layout of the data structures that are causing false sharing are modified, for example, by padding or aligning arrays. In array padding, extra elements are inserted in the arrays such that the elements that cause false sharing fall on different cache lines. In array alignment, either dummy variables are inserted or arrays are repositioned (in common blocks) such that the starting addresses of the offending data structures get changed, changing its mapping in the processor cache. Cache-line alignment of data structures also helps single-CPU performance of a program (recall the discussion in Chapter 8).

- *Data duplication* – In this approach, a temporary data structure is used to copy the portion of an array (or other structure) that is used in the loop such that the temporary is better suited to the access pattern in the loop and does not exhibit false sharing. After the completion of the loop, the temporary is copied back into the original structure. The two drawbacks of this approach are that there is extra memory overhead, and the copying in and out may exhibit false sharing. If the amount of computation and the number of memory accesses that occur in the loop are much larger than a single copy in and out, this approach may be beneficial.

- *Changing loop scheduling parameters* – This technique is strictly applicable to false sharing elimination in computational loops and involves scheduling different iterations of the loop onto different processors in a manner such that these iterations involve access to data elements falling on disjoint cache lines. In the next chapter, we will discuss different loop scheduling options in the Sun parallelizing compilers and revisit the issue of how loop scheduling scheme impacts data sharing (both true and false) in a parallelized loop.

Coming back to the program shown in CODE EXAMPLE 12-3, eliminating the false sharing in the four elements of the array s involves separating them enough to fall on different cache lines. If we transform the vector of local thread sums into a two-dimensional array, we essentially pad the variables with unused space to ensure sufficient separation. In our case, variables are 8 bytes long so we can use 8 as the second dimension of the array to make the thread local parameters 64 bytes apart (recall, the level 1 and level 2 cache lines of the UltraSPARC-II CPU are 32 bytes and 64 bytes, respectively). The changes are shown here.

```
example% diff example_false_sharing.c example_false_sharing_fixed.c
1,2c1,2
< /* example_false_sharing.c */
< /* cc -mt example_false_sharing.c -xO1 -o example_false_sharing */
---
> /* example_false_sharing_fixed.c */
> /* cc -mt example_false_sharing_fixed.c -xO1 -o example_false_sharing */
11c11
< double array[SIZE][4], sum, s[4];
---
> double array[SIZE][4], sum, s[4][8];
55c55
<     for (j=0;j<4;j++) sum+=s[j];
---
>     for (j=0;j<4;j++) sum+=s[j][1];
78c78
>     s[mynum] = 0.0;
---
>     s[mynum][1] = 0.0;
81c81
<         s[mynum] += array[j1][mynum];
---
>         s[mynum][1] += array[j1][mynum];
```

Now, compiling the modified program and running it

```
example% cc -mt example_false_sharing_fixed.c -xO1 -o \
        example_false_sharing
example% example_false_sharing
sum = 20838169.391802
 RUNTIME (One thread) : 3.2215 Seconds
sum = 20838169.391788
 RUNTIME (Four threads) : 0.7301 Seconds
```

we can see that separating the thread-private variables results in large speedup (see FIGURE 12-2). We can also see the corresponding drop in the bus traffic compared to the previous run.

```
...
  1.071    4380    1        tick       320       339
  1.011    4380    2        tick         4         3
  0.048    4380    3        tick        19        15
  2.091    4380    1        tick       194       206
  2.011    4380    2        tick         0         0
  0.048    4380    3        tick         0         0
...
  3.483    4380    1        tick        22       187
  4.001    4380    2        tick         0         0
  3.501    4380    3        tick        18       250
  4.091    4380    4        tick       260     19788
  4.091    4380    5        tick       381      2167
  4.091    4380    6        tick       275       295
  4.091    4380    7        tick       112       162
  3.501    4380    8        tick        12         2
...
```

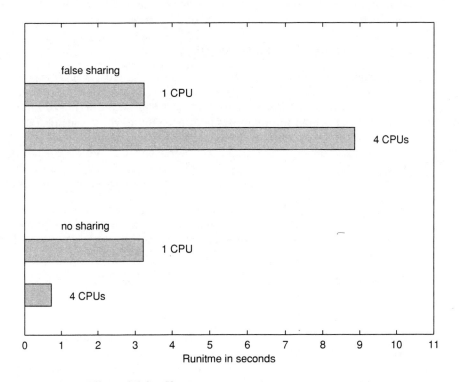

FIGURE 12-2 Effect of False Sharing

Synchronization and Locking

In a multithreaded program, different threads communicate with each other using shared data (global, static variables). Because the threads share the address space, this is an extremely efficient communication mechanism. However, in general, for programs to execute correctly, it requires a developer to synchronize the access to shared data structures. The thread libraries (both Solaris UI and POSIX) implement several synchronization functions that allow different threads in a program to manage shared resources exclusively. The functions supported in UI and POSIX threads are:

- UI library – Mutual exclusion locks (mutexes), counting semaphores, reader/writer locks, condition variables, and thread join.

- P-thread library – Mutual exclusion locks (mutexes), counting semaphores, and thread join.

Another important form of synchronization, namely barrier synchronization, is not supported directly in these libraries, but can be constructed using the above supported primitives (for example, see [Kleiman96], [Culler99] for discussion on barrier synchronization implementation).

Synchronization introduces overhead in multithreaded programs. Time is spent in executing synchronization functions (latency of synchronization) and, importantly, in waits induced by those synchronizations. The waits are caused by the serialization as a result of contention by multiple threads for access to the shared resources being protected by the synchronization functions. Thus, decreasing the synchronization overhead is crucial in obtaining good performance in multithreaded programs. To efficiently use locking functions, it is important to understand how they are implemented and how they interact with the underlying multiprocessor hardware.

In this section, we will give a brief overview of hardware and operating system kernel support in UltraSPARC-based platforms for locking functions and discuss some practical guidelines for the use of locking primitives in UI and P-thread libraries.

The two basic implementation issues for synchronization primitives are (1) *atomic memory operations* and (2) *global data visibility* of the state of the synchronization lock to all the processors on the machine.

An atomic operation is one that is indivisible. Once started, it is guaranteed to complete without any interruptions. The atomic operation is performed at the level of a machine instruction (for example, the `ldstub` instruction on SPARC architectures described later in this section), but it can correspond to atomic execution of a statement in a high-level language. The programmer usually only needs to worry about protecting simultaneous accesses to a line or portion of code and not about atomicity at the instruction level. On the other hand, atomic instructions are crucial to the implementor of synchronization functions in thread libraries. The performance of atomic instructions is closely tied to the cache coherence protocols used in the multiprocessor system.

Global data visibility relates to the effects of instruction reordering and load (store) buffers in the processor as specified by the memory consistency model implemented in the processor architecture. For programs to work correctly, the mutex primitive must flush all of the store buffers to keep the memory coherent between the processors after an unlock operation.

The memory model is a set of rules that constrains the order of completion of memory references. While the cache coherence mechanism keeps multi-level caches consistent, load and store buffers may not be included in the coherence protocol. Their impact on program correctness is then tied to the memory consistency model and the availability of memory barrier instructions in the architecture. Cache coherence applies to the consistency of the same memory location in different caches, while the memory model is related to maintaining a consistent ordering of memory operations to different locations. A detailed discussion of memory consistency models is beyond the scope of this text. See [Weaver94], [Hennessy96], and [Culler99] for further information.

We briefly describe both of these issues as they relate to UltraSPARC-based systems running the Solaris Operating Environment.

The SPARC V9 architecture and UltraSPARC processors provide the following atomic instructions that can be used to build various mutual exclusion functions:

- *Atomic test and set* – The ldstub instruction provides the functionality of reading a byte from memory and storing all ones (0xFF) in it atomically. It is used extensively in Solaris thread libraries and the kernel to build locking code. Below, we provide a pseudo code for a simple mutex that is at the heart of numerous synchronization functions. This implementation uses ldstub and has a delay to cause contending threads to yield the CPU. The first thread that locks the mutex executes ldstub and loads all ones into the address. Subsequent threads, on the other hand, receive a one from the address of the lock and spin with retries to acquire the lock. A thread releasing the lock simply sets the byte to zero again. Note, this pseudo code assumes a Total Store Order (see below) memory model.

CODE EXAMPLE 12-4 Pseudo-Code for a Simplified Mutex Lock Using an ldstub Instruction

```
Lock_function
        membar #StoreLoad ! assume TSO model


                         ! load 1 byte from location 'address'
                         ! and store 1's into it.
retry:  ldstub address, register
        cmp register, 0  ! check if loaded value is 0
        beq gotit        ! if value is 0, we got the lock
        call delay       ! if value is 1, then lock is held
                         ! by someone else. Go to sleep before
                         ! retrying
        jmp retry        ! Wake up and rety to acquire lock
gotit:  return


Unlock_function
        stub 0, address     ! Store 0 in 'address' byte
```

- *Atomic exchange* – The swap instruction atomically exchanges the value of a register with the contents of a memory location. We will show its usage with an example later in the chapter.

- *Compare-and-swap* – The cas instruction atomically exchanges the value in a memory address with that in a register if the contents of the memory location match the value in another register (also specified as part of cas instruction). The `cas` instruction is more powerful than `ldstub` or `swap` instructions and can be used for mutual exclusion locks, wait-free synchronization (*fetch_and_add*), linked list insertion, and other primitives. We will give an example of its usage in atomic *fetch_and_add* later in this section.

The SPARC V9 architecture [Weaver94] supports three memory models: *total store order* (TSO), *partial store order* (PSO), and *relaxed memory order* (RMO). Currently, all UltraSPARC and Solaris Operating Environment systems only support the TSO model [Mauro00]. To provide a means of preserving the ordering between the reads and writes for the supported memory models, memory barrier (or fence) instructions are provided in the architecture. The two supported instructions are:

- *Store barrier* – The `stbar` instruction orders store instructions. Stores that are issued by the processor before `stbar` will complete before the stores that are issued after the `stbar` instruction.

- *Memory barrier* – The `membar` instruction provides the means of ordering the loads and stores issued by the processor with respect to each other. This is called the ordering variant of `membar`. Another variant, called the sequencing `membar`, allows both ordering and completion of load and store memory operations [Weaver94]. For example, in the TSO model, the following `membar` instruction is needed in the synchronization functions as loads issued after stores (to different locations) may complete prior to completion of store instructions.

```
membar #StoreLoad
```

We remind the reader that the issues related to use of memory fence instructions and memory consistency models in mutual exclusion functions is something that the reader will normally not have to be concerned about. The thread library incorporates all necessary functionality for the code to work correctly on multiprocessor systems.

We will now give an example of the use of a `cas` instruction in atomically incrementing a shared counter, that is an operation of the type

```
counter = counter + 1; /* fetch_and_add primitive */
```

The `fetch_and_add` function (see the `example_fadtest.c` program listed later for its prototype) can be implemented using `cas` as follows.

CODE EXAMPLE 12-5 `fetch_and_add` Function Implemented Using `cas` Instruction

```
! void fetch_and_add(int *count, int incr);
! %o0: count, %o1: incr
! atomically performs: *count = *count + incr;

        .section        ".text"
        .align  1

        .global fetch_and_add
fetch_and_add:
        membar #StoreLoad ! assume TSO model
retry:
        ld [%o0],%l0       ! %l0 = *count
        add %l0,%o1,%l1    ! %l1 = *count + incr
        cas [%o0],%l0,%l1  ! compare *count with %l0;
                           ! if equal, swap contents of
                           ! count with %l1
        cmp %l0,%l1        ! compare %l0 & %l1
        bne retry          ! continue looping if unequal
        nop
        retl
        nop

        .type   fetch_and_add,2
        .size   fetch_and_add,(.-fetch_and_add)
```

The listing for the C program that compares the preceding `cas`-based implementation with an approach that uses the `pthread_mutex_lock` and `pthread_mutex_unlock` functions as follows.

CODE EXAMPLE 12-6 Example Program to Compare `cas` With the `pthread_mutex_lock` Function *(1 of 4)*

```
/* void fetch_and_add(int *count, int incr);
   atomically implements the operation
   *count = *count + incr;   (count points to a shared variable)
   cc -xarch=v8plus example_fadtest.c fetch_and_add.s \
      -lpthread -lc -o example_fadtest (-DCAS) */
#define _REENTRANT
#include <stdio.h>
#include <stdlib.h>
```

```c
#include <sys/time.h>
#include <sys/types.h>
#include <pthread.h>

#define MINITER 32
#define MAXTHREAD 64
#define NUMTIMER 5
#define max(a, b) ((a) >= (b) ? (a) : (b))
#define min(a, b) ((a) <= (b) ? (a) : (b))

double timer[MAXTHREAD][NUMTIMER];
pthread_mutex_t sync_mutex;
int countT, countB;

typedef struct {
  int mynum,myiter;
} thr_args;

void fetch_and_add(int *count, int incr);

void *thread_func(void *arg) {
   thr_args *thr_args_ptr = (thr_args *) arg;
   int mynum = thr_args_ptr->mynum;
   int myiter = thr_args_ptr->myiter;
   int i;
   hrtime_t start, end;

   for (i = 0; i < myiter; i++){
      start = gethrtime();
#ifdef CAS    /* fetch-and-add implementation  */
      fetch_and_add(&countB,1);
#else         /* standard mutex */
      pthread_mutex_lock(&sync_mutex);
      countB++;
      pthread_mutex_unlock(&sync_mutex);
#endif
      end = gethrtime();
      timer[mynum][0] += (end-start)*(1.e-9);
   }
   return(0);
}
```

```
int main(int argc, char **argv){
    int numiter=MINITER, nothreads, i, j, k;
    thr_args *param_arr;
    pthread_t *id_vec;
    pthread_attr_t *pt_attr;
    double tmax=0.0,tmin=1.e40;

    if (argc == 3) {    /* start up the threads */
        nothreads = atoi(argv[1]);
        numiter = atoi(argv[2]);
    } else if (argc == 2)  nothreads = atoi(argv[1]);
    else  nothreads = 5;
    countT = nothreads; countB = 0;
    printf("Numiter %d NumThreads %d\n",numiter,nothreads);

    id_vec = (pthread_t *)malloc(sizeof(pthread_t)*nothreads);
    pt_attr =
        (pthread_attr_t *) malloc(sizeof(pthread_attr_t)*nothreads);
    param_arr = (thr_args *) malloc(nothreads*sizeof(thr_args));

    pthread_mutex_init(&sync_mutex, 0);
    for (i=0; i<nothreads; i++) {
        pthread_attr_init(&pt_attr[i]);
        pthread_attr_setscope(&pt_attr[i], PTHREAD_SCOPE_SYSTEM);
        param_arr[i].mynum = i;
        param_arr[i].myiter = numiter/nothreads;
    }
    for (i=0;i<MAXTHREAD;i++)
    for (j=0;j<NUMTIMER;j++) timer[i][j] = 0.0;

    for (i=0;i<nothreads; i++) {
        j = pthread_create(&id_vec[i], &pt_attr[i],
                thread_func, (void *)&param_arr[i]);
    }
    for (i=0; i<nothreads; i++) pthread_join(id_vec[i], NULL);

    printf ("countB %d\n",countB);
    for (i=0; i<nothreads; i++) {
        tmax = max(tmax,timer[i][0]); tmin = min(tmin,timer[i][0]);
    }
    printf("%11.4e %11.4e\n",tmax,tmin);

    for (i=0;i<nothreads;i++) pthread_attr_destroy(&pt_attr[i]);
```

CODE EXAMPLE 12-6 Example Program to Compare `cas` With the `pthread_mutex_lock` Function *(4 of 4)*

```
        pthread_mutex_destroy(&sync_mutex);
        free(id_vec); free(pt_attr); free(param_arr);
        return(0);
}
```

We performed two different compilations of the program and ran them on a 64-CPU Enterprise 10000 system.

```
example% cc -DCAS -xarch=v8plus example_fadtest.c \
         fetch_and_add.s -lpthread -lc -o example_fadtest
example% cc -xarch=v8plus example_fadtest.c \
         fetch_and_add.s -lpthread -lc -o example_fadtest
```

The value of `numiter` in the program was set to 25 million. The time per thread was measured using `gethrtime` and the maximum over all of the threads was computed for different values of number of threads. FIGURE 12-3 compares the maximum values as a function of number of threads for the `cas` and mutex cases.

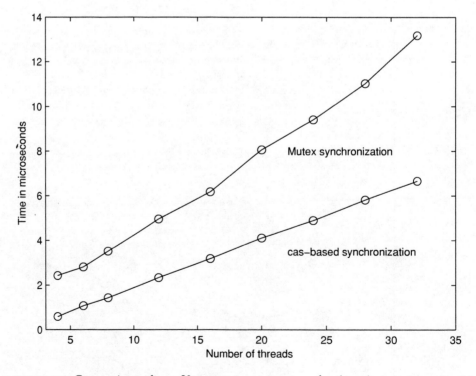

FIGURE 12-3 Comparison of `cas` Versus `pthread_mutex` for Atomic `fetch_and_add` Operation on Enterprise 10000 System

The preceding results might seem counterintuitive in that the runtime increases as more threads are added, but that's because this example measures the synchronization overhead in the counter update. From the figure, we can see that the cas-based version is substantially faster than the mutex version. This is not surprising; mutex locks implemented in the Solaris threads library are general purpose and designed to provide good throughput in the presence of multiple user jobs sharing the CPUs on the system. Mutex locks are also designed to work in both parallel and concurrent applications. Threads contending for the mutex lock are placed on a turnstile, which is an array of sleep queues [Mauro00]. When the lock is released, a thread waiting in the queue is granted access to the lock (or any other synchronization object). This adds overhead (or latency) in the mutex calls, but makes the mutex locks applicable to synchronization in arbitrarily complex programs. The adaptive nature of mutex locks, where locks quietly wait their turn in the scheduler queue (turnstile) without consuming shared resources, makes the overall system scalable and the kernel can handle many thousands of mutex locks (or other synchronization objects) being used in same or different programs.

By contrast, the cas-based implementation is nonblocking but continues to use up interconnect transactions. This is characteristic of cas implementations; the latency of the operation is small, but it is forced to perform a high-overhead bus-consuming atomic operation on every retry. In this example, however, we see that the bandwidth available on the Enterprise 10000 interconnect handles the contention generated in the cas retry loop well, and the overall performance is better than using the pthread_mutex function. Note that simple spin locks protect the interconnect by spinning on a word in the private cache of the processor (see the swap-based spin lock in the section about thread pools).

The preceding example highlights how contention for a shared lock scales with the number of threads (in this example, for both cases, the scaling is $O(p)$). As a general guideline, very small and frequently occurring critical sections, such as above, should be restructured, to the extent possible, and merged to create larger critical regions. It is difficult to prescribe a recipe for an optimum size of a critical region, for example, in terms of lines of code or number of instructions. A large region increases the serialized parts of the program and also hurts scalability. Experimentation performed on the specific application running on the target platform is needed to fine tune the size of critical regions.

Some words are also in order on the use of volatile qualifier (in C and C++ languages) and "self-synchronization" without the explicit use of synchronization primitives. For example:

```
/* THE FOLLOWING SHOULD NEVER BE DONE */
volatile int mylock = 0;
while (mylock != 0) ;
mylock = 1;
......execute critical region code.......
mylock = 0;
```

It may appear that the `volatile` qualifier will cause an optimizing compiler to cause `mylock` to be reloaded every time in the `while` loop and the synchronization will work. The fact is that it will not work and the program might hang intermittently in the `while` loop. This will happen because in this type of "locking code" there is no consideration to the restrictions imposed by the requirement of atomicity at instruction level and memory consistency model implementation in the underlying architecture[1]. These type of errors are often difficult to detect since the application can successfully pass initial testing but under certain conditions can deadlock. Additional complexity can arise if the locking conditions are difficult to reproduce.

Thread Stack Size

The thread stacks created by the user in a multithreaded program are automatically managed by the thread library with virtually no user intervention. When a thread is created, its stack is memory-mapped (using `mmap`) from anonymous, zeroed memory (`/dev/zero`). The anonymous memory is mapped using the `MAP_NORESERVE` flag in `mmap` such that actual virtual memory swap space is not reserved until the pages are actually used in the program. This makes the library very efficient and also allows supporting a large number of threads in a process without substantially decreasing the available virtual address space.

To prevent stack overflow, the Solaris thread library also allocates a guard page (also called the *red zone*) between the stacks of different threads. When a thread overflows its stack and enters the guard page, a segmentation violation (`SIGSEGV`) occurs, causing the program to abort [Kleinman96].

Both POSIX and UI thread libraries create threads that, by default, have a size of 1 MB for 32-bit programs and 2 MB for 64-bit ones. This size has been determined after extensive experimentation and optimized across the program address space, system resource usage and the number of threads supported in the application. For most applications, the default stack size is sufficient and need not be changed.

However, in cases where an application requires a large amount of space for automatic variables, or creates a large number of threads, or the program makes many deeply nested function calls, control over thread stacks might be required. POSIX provides APIs for changing the size of created stacks using the function `pthread_attr_setstacksize`. POSIX also provides APIs for managing thread stack addresses (`pthread_attr_setstackaddr`), but users are strongly discouraged from trying to manage stack addresses explicitly in their programs.

---

1. The behavior is likely to be even more unpredictable on the out-of-order instruction issue microprocessors.

When numerous threads (greater than 100) are created and destroyed in the program, specifying a size smaller than the default might make sense. For example, if 2000 threads are created in the program, a 1 MB default implies that 2 GB of virtual memory will be reserved for stack usage. Clearly, for such an application a smaller stack size makes sense, or the application may need to be compiled as a 64-bit program to support such a large thread stack.

It is important for users to estimate carefully the minimum size of stack needed; two considerations are system calls (most system libraries require at least an 8 KB stack size) and the maximum function call depth in the program.

When the stack size needs to be specified larger than the default, the user must consider its impact on the total virtual memory usage in the program, as well as the impact on the overhead in the system for managing threads with large stack sizes. Consider the following C program, which generates threads of different stack sizes and compares the overheads in the different cases.

CODE EXAMPLE 12-7 Example Program to Show Effect of Different Thread Stack Sizes

```
/* example_thrstack.c */
/* cc example_thrstack.c -o thrstack -lpthread */
#define _REENTRANT
#include <stdio.h>
#include <stdlib.h>
#include <pthread.h>
#include <limits.h>
#include <unistd.h>
void* foo(void *arg);

void* foo(void *arg)
{
    return 0;
}

int main(int argc, char **argv)
{
    pthread_attr_t attr;
    pthread_t       threadIds[100];
    size_t          j, i = 0;
    int             errNo, stksize;
    void *result;
    if (argc == 2) stksize = atoi(argv[1]);
    else  {
     printf("An argument needed, exiting\n");
     exit(-1);
```

Example Program to Show Effect of Different Thread
Stack Sizes *(Continued)*

```
    }
    stksize = stksize*1000000;
    pthread_attr_init(&attr);
    pthread_attr_setscope(&attr, PTHREAD_SCOPE_SYSTEM);
    pthread_attr_setstacksize(&attr, stksize);
    for (j = 0; j < 250; ++j) {
        for (i = 0; i < 30; ++i) {
            errNo = pthread_create(&threadIds[i], &attr, foo, 0);
            if (errNo != 0) {
                printf("Error: %s\n", strerror(errNo));
                break;
            }
        }
        for (i = 0; i < 30; ++i) {
            pthread_join(threadIds[i], &result);
        }
    }
}
```

We compile the program as follows.

```
example% cc example_thrstack.c -o thrstack -lpthread
```

Subsequently, we run it (for example, with 16 MB thread stacks).

```
example% ptime thrstack 16
```

The elapsed time (`real` field of `ptime` output) is shown as a function of the stack size in FIGURE 12-4 on an Enterprise 4500 system.

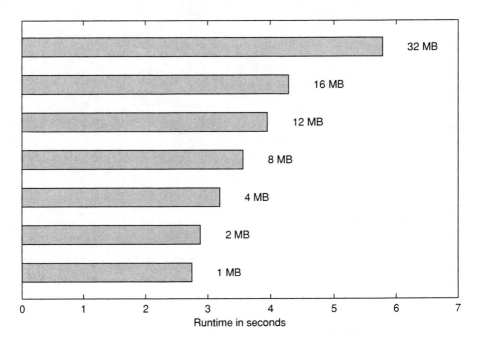

FIGURE 12-4 Effect of Different Thread Stack Sizes

The plot shows that the cost increases with increasing thread stack sizes. To understand why, we compare the `truss` outputs for 1 MB and the 16 MB runs, respectively.

```
example% truss -c thrstack 1
syscall           seconds   calls   errors
_exit               .00       1
open                .00       6       1
close               .00       8
time                .00       1
brk                 .00       3
stat                .00       1
getpid              .00       1
fstat               .00       5
execve              .00       1
sigprocmask         .19     7502
sigaction           .00       5
sigpending          .00       1
mmap                .98     7518
mprotect            .90     7510
```

```
munmap                    1.73      7504
sysconfig                  .00         3
lwp_create                1.58     15006
lwp_exit                  1.15      7500
lwp_continue               .82      7502
lwp_self                   .00      7503
lwp_mutex_wakeup           .00        12
lwp_mutex_lock             .00        77
llseek                     .00         1
door                       .00         5
lwp_schedctl               .01      7505
                       -------   -------   ----
sys totals:               7.36     75181       1
usr time:                  .46
elapsed:                 11.20
```

```
example% truss -c thrstack 16
syscall               seconds    calls   errors
_exit                      .00        1
open                       .00        6        1
close                      .01        8
time                       .00        1
brk                        .00        3
stat                       .00        1
getpid                     .00        1
fstat                      .00        5
execve                     .00        1
sigprocmask                .38     7502
sigaction                  .00        5
sigpending                 .00        1
mmap                      1.13     7518
mprotect                  1.32     7510
munmap                    2.83     7504
sysconfig                  .00        3
lwp_create                1.44    15006
lwp_exit                  1.13     7500
lwp_continue              1.16     7502
lwp_self                   .00     7503
lwp_mutex_wakeup           .00        5
lwp_mutex_lock             .00       18
llseek                     .00        1
door                       .00        5
lwp_schedctl               .00     7505
                       -------   -------   ----
```

```
sys totals:              9.40    75115         1
usr time:                 .38
elapsed:                12.79
```

We can see the difference in the cost of `mmap` related operations (`mmap`, `mprotect`, and `munmap`). Even with the `MAP_NORESERVE` option, in the case of larger thread stacks, too many large stacks may cause a slowdown in multilevel page tables when large distant segments are allocated. The kernel incurs additional overhead in tracking the page tables and other data structures for larger thread stacks.

From the above results, we can see that while there is an overhead, it is quite small (the order of milliseconds in the 16 MB case). The preceding example is contrived, and in real life applications, so many calls to bound thread creations with large stacks are unlikely to occur. However, the reader is still advised to carefully select thread stack size to conserve both virtual memory address space and kernel resources.

Thread Creation Issues

The following questions about thread creation and thread management in multithreaded programs are commonly asked:

- How many threads should be created?
- Should bound or unbound threads be used?
- Should threads be created statically or dynamically?
- Should a pool of threads be used?

We have already provided the answer to the first two questions. To reiterate, for computationally intensive applications (to be run in a dedicated mode), bound threads should be used and the number of threads performing the computations must be less than or equal to the number of physical processors on the system. In this section, we will discuss the last two questions.

In applications where the amount of work is known in advance and does not change as the program runs (for example, a loop-based computation such as matrix multiplication), static thread creation is preferable because it is simpler to implement and has less synchronization overhead. Dynamic thread creation, or changing the number of threads from one program segment to another, is suitable when the workload is not known or changes. Examples of this include tree-based algorithms, such as hierarchical N-body calculation, or client-server programs. In such applications, additional threads might be created to handle extra work and then terminated when the threads are idle for long durations.

Pool of Threads

While unbound thread creation and destruction is very efficient, for bound threads, the cost is comparable to the cost of creating a heavyweight process with a `fork` call. If threads perform many small calculations, the overhead of creating and joining threads repeatedly might be quite high. In this case, creating a pool of threads that processes the work as it is generated might be more efficient than repeated thread creation and termination. The Sun parallelizing compilers use a pool of threads that processes a parallel loop and then waits until the next parallel worksharing construct or the next parallel region is encountered. We will discuss this in the next chapter.

We will use a simple example program adapted from a multithreaded discrete event simulation application that compares the pool of threads approach with thread creation and destruction. The program performs a very small amount of work in the function do_evnts, which is called repeatedly in an outer loop in main().

In the thread-create-and-join version, the main thread creates NUM_CPU-1-bound threads, all of which execute do_evnts (the main also executes it) and then are joined. This is repeated in the for (k=0; k < itr...) loop in main(). The listing of the program example_create.c appears as follows.

CODE EXAMPLE 12-8 Overhead of the Repeated Thread Create-Join *(1 of 3)*

```
/* example_create.c: thread create-join in a loop
   cc example_create.c -x04 -mt -lpthread -o example_create
   run as  example_create <numiter> */
#include <sys/time.h>
#include <sys/types.h>
#include <stdio.h>
#include <stdlib.h>
#include <pthread.h>
#include <signal.h>
#define NUM_CPU   8    /* master + 7 slave threads */

typedef struct {
   pthread_t    tid[2];
   int          idx;
   double       num_itr,sum;
} THREAD_INFO_T;

pthread_attr_t pt_attr;
double  timer[NUM_CPU], globsum=0.0;
int status;
THREAD_INFO_T thr_list[NUM_CPU];
```

```
static void doit(int mynum, int *dumb) {*dumb = 5*(mynum+1);}

static void* do_evnts(void* argp)
{
   register THREAD_INFO_T* ct = (THREAD_INFO_T*)argp;
   int id = ct->idx - 1, dumb;
   ct->num_itr++;
   doit(ct->idx,&dumb);
   ct->sum += dumb;
   if (ct->idx > 0) pthread_exit((void *)&status);
}

void initthreads()
{
   int i;
   register THREAD_INFO_T *x = thr_list;
   pthread_attr_init(&pt_attr);
   pthread_attr_setscope(&pt_attr, PTHREAD_SCOPE_SYSTEM);
   for (i=0; i < NUM_CPU; ++i, ++x) {
      x->idx = i; x->num_itr = 0;
      x->sum = 0.0; timer[i] = 0.0;
   }
}

int main(int argc, char* argv[] )
{
   int i,k, itr = argc > 1 ? atoi(argv[1]) : 200;
   register THREAD_INFO_T *x;
   hrtime_t start, end;
   initthreads();
   start = gethrtime();
   for (k=0; k < itr; ++k ) {
      x = thr_list+1;
      for (i=1; i < NUM_CPU; ++i, ++x) /* create threads */
         if (pthread_create(&x->tid[0],&pt_attr,do_evnts,x))
         perror("thr_create");
      x=thr_list; do_evnts((void *)x); x++;
      for (i=1; i < NUM_CPU; ++i, ++x) /* join the threads */
         pthread_join(x->tid[0],NULL);
   }
   end = gethrtime();
   timer[0] += (end-start);
   for (i=0; i < NUM_CPU; ++i) globsum += thr_list[i].sum;
```

```
    printf("globsum= %e\n",globsum);
    printf("time %e\n",timer[0]);
    return 0;
}
```

Compiling (using Forte Developer 6 C compiler) and running on a 12-CPU
Enterprise 4500, we obtain the following.

```
example% cc example_create.c -xO4 -mt -lpthread -o example_create
example% ptime example_create 100000
globsum= 1.800000e+07
time 6.654879e+10
real      1:06.560
user        47.560
sys       1:13.837
```

The pool of threads version uses the master-slave programming model with POSIX
counting semaphores for synchronization between master and slave threads. The
master thread creates the slaves that run in an infinite loop waiting for work to do.
The master then runs the for (k=0; k < itr...) loop in the main. The slaves all
synchronize with the master at the beginning of each outer iteration, then go on to
do their work and then synchronize again with the master when they complete their
work in the do_evnts function. As we can see, the slaves do not perform any
synchronization with each other (as is the case in many master-slave-based
programs). The listing for the program example_sempool.c appears as follows.
The reader should examine how semaphores are used in the program.

CODE EXAMPLE 12-9 Pool of Threads Approach *(1 of 4)*

```
/* example_sempool.c: master-slave model with a pool of threads
   cc example_sempool.c -xO4 -mt -lposix4 -lpthread \
   -o example_sempool
   run as   example_sempool <numiter>
*/
#include <sys/time.h>
#include <sys/types.h>
#include <stdio.h>
#include <stdlib.h>
#include <signal.h>
#include <unistd.h>
#include <semaphore.h>
#include <pthread.h>
#define NUM_CPU   8      /* master + 7 slave threads */
```

```
typedef struct {
   pthread_t    tid[2];
   int          idx;
   double       num_itr,sum;
} THREAD_INFO_T;

sem_t    sema_list[NUM_CPU];
sem_t    sem_lis1[NUM_CPU];
double   timer[NUM_CPU], globsum=0.0;
THREAD_INFO_T    thr_list[NUM_CPU];

static void doit(int mynum, int *dumb) {*dumb = 5*(mynum+1);}

static void* do_evnts( void* argp )
{
   register THREAD_INFO_T* ct = (THREAD_INFO_T*)argp;
   int id = ct->idx - 1, dumb;
   for (;;) {
      sem_wait( &sem_lis1[ct->idx] ); /* slave waits */
      ct->num_itr++;
      doit(ct->idx,&dumb);
      ct->sum += dumb;
      sem_post( &sema_list[ct->idx] ); /* release */
   }
}

static void* do_evntsmaster( void* argp )
{
   register THREAD_INFO_T* ct = (THREAD_INFO_T*)argp;
   int id = ct->idx - 1, dumb;
   ct->num_itr++;
   doit(ct->idx,&dumb);
   ct->sum += dumb;
}

void initthreads()
{                        /* create the pool of threads */
   int i;
   pthread_attr_t pt_attr;
   register THREAD_INFO_T *x = thr_list;
   pthread_attr_init(&pt_attr);
   pthread_attr_setscope(&pt_attr, PTHREAD_SCOPE_SYSTEM);
   for (i=0; i < NUM_CPU; ++i) {
```

```
        if (sem_init(&sema_list[i],  0, 0 )) perror("sema_init");
        if (sem_init(&sem_lis1[i],  0, 0 )) perror("sema_init2");
    }

    for (i=0; i < NUM_CPU; ++i, ++x) {
        x->idx        = i;
        x->num_itr = 0; x->sum = 0.0;
        timer[i] = 0.0;
        if (i==0) continue;
        if (pthread_create(&x->tid[0],&pt_attr,do_evnts,x))
        perror("thr_create");
    }
}


void terminate()
{
    int i;
    register THREAD_INFO_T *x = thr_list;
    for (i=0; i < NUM_CPU; ++i, ++x) {
        if (i>0) (void)pthread_kill( x->tid[0], SIGTERM );
        (void)sem_destroy( &sema_list[i] );
        (void)sem_destroy( &sem_lis1[i] );
    }
}


int main(int argc, char* argv[] )
{
    int i,k, itr = argc > 1 ? atoi(argv[1]) : 200;
    register THREAD_INFO_T *x;
    hrtime_t start, end;

    initthreads();
    start = gethrtime();
    for (k=0; k < itr; ++k ) {
    /* master signals slaves to start processing */
        for (i= 1; i < NUM_CPU; ++i )
         if (sem_post(&sem_lis1[i])) perror("sema_post");
        x = thr_list; do_evntsmaster((void *)x);
                /* master waits for slaves to finish */
         for (i= 1; i < NUM_CPU; ++i )
         if (sem_wait(&sema_list[i])) perror("sema_wait");
    }
    end = gethrtime();
```

```
    timer[0] += (end-start);
    for (i=0; i < NUM_CPU; ++i) globsum += thr_list[i].sum;
    printf("globsum= %e\n",globsum);
    printf("time %e\n",timer[0]);
    terminate();
    return 0;
}
```

Compiling the program and running on the same 12-CPU Enterprise 4500 as the program example_create.c, we obtain the following.

```
example% cc example_sempool.c -xO4 -mt -lposix4 -lpthread \
         -o example_sempool
example% ptime example_sempool 100000
globsum= 1.800000e+07
time 4.445679e+10
real       44.471
user       31.086
sys      1:30.778
```

We can see that the pool of threads approach is nearly 50% faster than the thread create-join approach.

Pool of Threads With Spin Locks

In the pool of threads approach, the main cost is in the synchronization between master and slave threads using semaphores. The semaphores can be replaced with swap-based spin locks where a value of one indicates that the lock is being held by a thread and a value of zero releases it. The listing of the program example_spinpool.c follows. The spin locks are implemented using SWAPINITLOCK(lp), SWAPLOCK(lp), and SWAPUNLOCK(lp) macros, respectively. Note that SWAPLOCK takes advantage of the cache coherency in the system by spinning on a private variable, which substantially reduces expensive bus transactions.

CODE EXAMPLE 12-10 Pool of Threads Using Spin Lock Function *(1 of 4)*

```
/* example_spinpool.c: master-slave model with a pool of threads
   cc example_spinpool.c swap.il -xO4 -mt -lpthread \
   -o example_spinpool
   run as  a.spinpool <numiter> */
#include <sys/time.h>
```

```
#include <sys/types.h>
#include <stdio.h>
#include <stdlib.h>
#include <pthread.h>
#include <signal.h>
#define NUM_CPU    8      /* master + 7 slave threads */
#define SWAPINITLOCK(lp)   (*(lp) = 1)
#define SWAPLOCK(lp)       {do { while ((volatile int)(*lp)==1); \
                              } while(swapval(lp,1)); }
#define SWAPUNLOCK(lp)     {swapval(lp,0); }

typedef struct {
   pthread_t    tid[2];
   int          idx;
   double       num_itr,sum;
} THREAD_INFO_T;

int enter[NUM_CPU-1], leave[NUM_CPU-1];
double  timer[NUM_CPU], globsum=0.0;
THREAD_INFO_T    thr_list[NUM_CPU];

int swapval(int *lp, int num);

static void doit(int mynum, int *dumb) {*dumb = 5*(mynum+1); }

static void* do_evnts( void* argp )
{
   register THREAD_INFO_T* ct = (THREAD_INFO_T*)argp;
   int id = ct->idx - 1, dumb;
   int *ent = &(enter[id]);
   int *lev = &(leave[id]);
   for (;;) {
     SWAPLOCK(ent);  /* slave waits (spins) for master's signal */
     ct->num_itr++;
     doit(ct->idx,&dumb);
     ct->sum += dumb;
     SWAPUNLOCK(lev);  /* release waiting (spinning) master */
   }
}

static void* do_evntsmaster( void* argp )
{
   register THREAD_INFO_T* ct = (THREAD_INFO_T*)argp;
```

```
      int id = ct->idx - 1, dumb;
   ct->num_itr++;
   doit(ct->idx,&dumb);
   ct->sum += dumb;
}


void initthreads()
{                  /* create the pool of threads */
   int i;
   pthread_attr_t pt_attr;
   register THREAD_INFO_T *x = thr_list;
   pthread_attr_init(&pt_attr);
   pthread_attr_setscope(&pt_attr, PTHREAD_SCOPE_SYSTEM);
   for (i=0; i < NUM_CPU; ++i, ++x) {
      x->idx          = i;
      x->num_itr = 0; x->sum = 0.0;
      timer[i] = 0.0;
      if (i==0) continue;
      if (pthread_create(&x->tid[0],&pt_attr,do_evnts,x))
         perror("thr_create");
   }
}


void terminate()
{
   int i;
   register THREAD_INFO_T *x = thr_list;
   for ( i=1; i < NUM_CPU; ++i, ++x)
        (void)pthread_kill( x->tid[0], SIGTERM );
}


int main(int argc, char* argv[] )
{
   int i,k, itr = argc > 1 ? atoi(argv[1]) : 200;
   int *lp1, *lp2;
   register THREAD_INFO_T *x;
   hrtime_t start, end;

   for (i= 1; i < NUM_CPU; ++i ){
      lp1 = &enter[i-1];
      lp2 = &leave[i-1];
      SWAPINITLOCK(lp1);
      SWAPINITLOCK(lp2);
```

```
    }
    initthreads();
    start = gethrtime();
    for (k=0; k < itr; ++k ) {
        for (i= 1; i < NUM_CPU; ++i ){ /* master signals slaves */
                SWAPUNLOCK(&enter[i-1]);
    }
    x = thr_list;
    do_evntsmaster((void *)x);
    for (i= 1; i < NUM_CPU; ++i ) /* master waits for slaves */
                SWAPLOCK(&leave[i-1]);
    }
    end = gethrtime();
    timer[0] += (end-start);
    for (i=0; i < NUM_CPU; ++i) globsum += thr_list[i].sum;
    printf("globsum= %e\n",globsum);
    printf("time %e\n",timer[0]);
    terminate();
    return 0;
}
```

The listing of the swap.il file appears as follows.

CODE EXAMPLE 12-11 swap.il inline template.

```
! int swapval(int *lp, int num)
! %o0 = lp; %o1 = num
! atomically swap  *lp with num
! and return num
        .inline swapval,8
        swap [%o0], %o1
        mov %o1, %o0
        .end
```

Compiling the preceding program and running on the same Enterprise 4500, we obtain the following.

```
example% cc example_spinpool.c swap.il -xO4 -mt -lpthread \
        -o example_spinpool
example% ptime example_spinpool 100000
globsum= 1.800000e+07
time 7.614244e+08
```

```
real        0.774
user        6.108
sys         0.009
```

We see a dramatic improvement (almost two orders of magnitude) in performance. This is not at all surprising, because spin locks based on the swap instruction are highly efficient for such calculations, but are limited in applicability when compared to semaphores, which are more general purpose and robust synchronization primitives.

We should point out that in this example we didn't pay attention to possible false sharing effects. Interested readers are encouraged to experiment with enter and leave arrays and change the code in such a way that their entries are placed on different cache lines.

Summary

Multithreading a program for exploiting parallelism or concurrency has become a popular approach for increased performance. We gave a brief overview of the three approaches to multithread programs, namely master-slave model, worker-crew model and the pipeline model. Each of these models is applicable to a different class of applications and the user should carefully select one at the initial stages, as it may not be easy to change from one model to the other in later stages of program development.

The Solaris Operating Environment provides extensive features to enable the development of high-performance, robust multithreaded programs. There is full support for both POSIX and UI thread APIs, and the two libraries have been implemented in a fashion that a program can mix the two APIs transparently (though this is not recommended for portability and program maintenance reasons). The Solaris standard threads library implements a two-level thread scheduling model where user threads are scheduled onto LWPs which, in turn, are scheduled by the kernel on the physical processors in the machine. When parallel scaling is important, bound threads should be used, in which case there is a one-to-one mapping between user threads and LWPs.

In the Solaris 8 Operating Environment, an alternate thread library implementing a single-level scheduling model is also available. For obtaining maximum performance in computationally intensive applications, users should experiment with both the standard and alternate libraries.

True data sharing is inevitable in multithreaded programs. The programmer can restructure a program or change the algorithm to decrease it, but complete elimination is usually not possible. Another form of sharing, called false sharing, is a consequence of coherence being maintained on a cache line granularity by cache-coherent shared-memory multiprocessor systems. We discussed various techniques to eliminate false sharing and showed usage of the array padding approach with an example program.

Since data sharing is inevitable in multithreaded programs, some form of synchronization is also inevitable in order to protect access to shared data for correct program execution. We discussed the concepts of atomic instructions and global data visibility support in hardware and how it relates to efficient implementation of synchronization primitives in thread library. Two important performance issues that the programmer should keep in mind when synchronizing critical regions are the latency of synchronization primitive being used and the impact of contention for the synchronization primitive amongst different threads. When the programmer needs to create very small critical regions, the use of fast spin locks should be considered over the use of thread library mutexes that are designed for general purpose usage. We showed how a swap-based spin lock performed significantly faster than a semaphore-based implementation of a pool of threads example program. The comparison between cas instruction and mutex lock-based *fetch_and_add* primitive was also shown. While spin locks may be used for very small critical regions, these also cause heavy contention as the number of threads increase. There is no easy solution for this situation except that as a rule of thumb, the programmer should avoid having many small critical sections[1] in the program.

The general recommendation on thread stack size is not to change the default selected by the thread library. If, however, the user needs to decrease it, then care must be taken to ensure it is sufficient for system library calls and also sufficient for the call-stack depth of the program. On the other hand, if it is to be increased, its effect on the cost of thread creation and usage of program virtual memory should be considered.

Finally, we discussed the issues related to thread creation and showed how caching bound threads (creating a pool of threads) can be more efficient than repeated thread creation and destruction. This is the approach taken in the parallelizing Sun Fortran and C compilers, the subject of the next chapter.

---

1. The same is true for large critical sections that lead to increased serialization of the program and an associated decrease in parallel scaling.

## CHAPTER 13

Optimization of Programs Using Compiler Parallelization

Parallelizing compilers enable multithreading of applications with relatively little effort. They provide directives that mark regions of the program that should or should not run in parallel and allow automatic parallelization based on the compiler's analysis of the program. In recent years, compiler-based parallelization has gained popularity among programmers of scientific applications. These programs typically use large loops that can be parallelized efficiently by compilers.

The format and the functionality of parallelization directives vary from one compiler to another, which limits portability of programs that use a particular set of directives. The industry-wide parallelization standard OpenMP (http://www.openmp.org) was created to bridge incompatibilities between different implementations and was adopted by many hardware manufacturers and compiler vendors. The Forte Developer 6 and Forte Developer 6 update 1 Fortran 95 compiler provides full support for the OpenMP 1.1 standard.

The implementation of automatic and directive-based parallelization in Sun compilers is based on Solaris threads, and, therefore, the resulting multithreaded programs share many of the features of explicitly threaded applications. The compiler transforms portions of the program selected for parallelization into subroutines that are passed to the threads by driver functions defined in the microtasking library, libmtsk. This library also contains the standard runtime parallelization functions required by the OpenMP standard.

In this chapter we describe parallelization capabilities of Sun Fortran and C compilers and related performance issues. We discuss the Sun and Cray style directives in Fortran 77 and Fortran 95, parallelization pragmas for C, and OpenMP support in Fortran 95. An overview of different OpenMP programming styles and performance considerations, such as data scoping, memory bandwidth requirements, and synchronization overhead, is included. We also compare the P-threads approach with OpenMP directives-based parallelization. An overview of the parallel Sun Performance Library is also provided.

For information on the theoretical aspects of parallelizing compilers, such as data dependence analysis techniques (which are not covered here), refer to [Wolfe89], [Muchnick97], [Dowd98], and [Chandra00].

Parallelization Support in Sun Compilers

In this section, we describe the parallelization model in the Sun compilers, as well as the support for automatic and explicit directive-based parallelization. The model described here is contained within the overall architecture and structure of Sun compilers described in Chapter 5. We recommend reading Chapters 5 and 6 before reading the following section.

Parallelization Model

The Sun Fortran and C compilers (for SPARC platforms) support automatic and directive-based parallelization of programs. At the time of this writing, the parallelization support in Sun compilers can be summarized as:

- Auto-parallelization – Supported in Fortran 77, Fortran 95, and C compilers.
- Sun-style directive-based parallelization – Supported in Fortran 77, Fortran 95, and C compilers.
- Cray-style directive-based parallelization – Supported in Fortran 77 and Fortran 95 compilers.
- OpenMP-style directive-based parallelization – Supported in Fortran 95 compiler (OpenMP 1.1 standard).

A summary of compiler options available to support these parallelization modes is in TABLE 13-1. Details of these options are provided in later sections of this chapter. The information in the table is based upon the Forte Developer 6 update 1 version of the compilers. In Fortran, some of the flags are also available without the leading x (for example -xautopar and -autopar). For further information, see documentation at http://docs.sun.com.

TABLE 13-1 Parallelization Compiler Options and Environment Variables in Sun Fortran and C Compilers

Fortran 77, Fortran 95	C	Comments
-xautopar, -xparallel, -xreduction	-xautopar, -xparallel, -xreduction	Options to be used both for automatic and directive parallelization
-xexplicitpar, -openmp, -mp={sun,cray,openmp}	-xexplicitpar	Options to be used (only) for directive-based parallelization
-stackvar		Option needed in Fortran
-xdepend, -xO<n> (n=3 or higher), -fast	-xdepend, -xO<n> (n=3 or higher), -xrestrict, -fast, -xalias_level	Options recommended or required for use with parallelizing options listed above (especially -xdepend flag)
-xloopinfo, -vpara	-xloopinfo, -xvpara	Options to generate parallelization information and warnings
STACKSIZE, PARALLEL, SUNW_MP_THR_IDLE, Various OpenMP environment variables	STACKSIZE, PARALLEL, SUNW_MP_THR_IDLE	Supported environment variables

The high-level structure and architecture of Sun compilers is covered in Chapter 5. The tasks performed by different components involved in generation of parallelized executable are as follows (see [Aoki96] also):

- *Front Ends* – The language-specific compiler front ends perform the role of recognizing the directives, checking syntax and grammar, and generating a common intermediate representation (IR) known as SunIR, which it passes to the IR optimizer called the iropt stage.

- *SunIR Optimizer* – iropt performs optimization on the incoming SunIR and generates optimized IR, which is passed to the code generator (cg) on the way to generation of the final executable. In the iropt stage, data dependence analysis, loop transformations (interchange, fission, fusion and others), interprocedural optimization, traditional local, and global optimizations take place. Parallel code generation and insertion of calls to microtasking library functions also occur in this stage. For auto-parallelization, the profitability analysis and generation of both serial and parallel loop copies is performed.

- *Microtasking library* – The microtasking library (`libmtsk`) is composed of functions that at runtime generate threads used in execution of parallelized loops and regions of the program. It supports loop scheduling strategies and runtime environment variables (see TABLE 13-1) and manages threads running in parallel. The library uses the master-slave model (see Chapter 12) wherein the master thread executes the serial portions of the program, during which the slave threads busy-wait or sleep. When a parallel region is encountered, the master thread engages the slave threads in the execution of the parallel construct. The master also participates in the processing of the parallel work. A pool of threads approach (refer to Chapter 12) is employed; the slave threads are created once, when the first parallel region is encountered, then used in all parallel regions of the program. A schematic is shown in FIGURE 13-1.

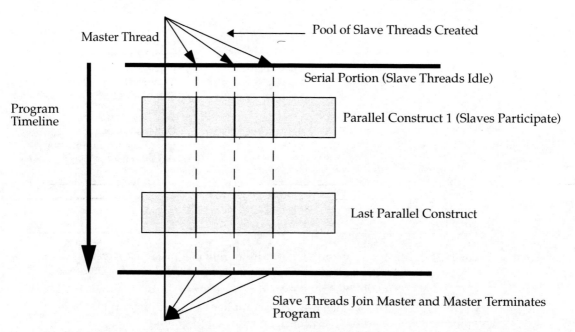

FIGURE 13-1 Master-Slave Model and Thread-Pool Approach in Microtasking Library

Parallel directives undergo a series of transformations in the front-end and `iropt` stages of the compiler. The optimizer first analyzes the parallel region to determine its composition (whether it consists of parallel sections, worksharing constructs, synchronization primitives, and other functions) and performs data scoping analysis (to identify shared, private, reduction, and other scoping qualifiers). The body of the parallel construct is then extracted and placed in a separate subroutine called an *outlined function*. The private variables are declared as local variables in the outlined function (hence separate copies can be allocated on individual thread stacks) and code is generated to handle copy-in for OpenMP `firstprivate` variables (readonly variables in Sun style), and copy-out for OpenMP `lastprivate` variables, reduction, and synchronization operations. The shared variables are passed as arguments to the outlined function.

The compiler then inserts a call to a driver routine executed by the master thread in place of the original parallel region, and the address of the outlined function along with other information relevant to parallel execution (such as loop scheduling parameters) is passed to this function. When the first call to the driver function is encountered by the master thread, a team of slave threads is created and the outlined function (which now represents the parallel region) is executed by multiple threads. On subsequent calls to the driver function, the outlined functions representing the other parallel regions of the program are executed. After the slave threads complete the task assigned by the master, they synchronize with each other as necessary by a call to a barrier function and wait for the assignment of the next task.

Consider the following code fragment.

```
subroutine foo(m,x,y,a,b)
integer m,i
real x(m),y(m),a,b
do i=2,m
    x(i) = a*x(i)+b*y(i-1)
enddo
return
end
```

We compile it using a Forte Developer 6 Fortran 95 compiler

```
example% f95 -fast -xparallel -loopinfo -vpara -S foo.f
f90: Warning: -xarch=v8plusa is not portable
"foo.f", line 4: PARALLELIZED, and serial version generated
```

On examining the generated assembly listing we find the master function call

```
call      __mt_MasterFunction_    ! params =  %o1 %o2 %o3 %o4 %o0
%o5          ! Result =
```

and the outlined function representing the parallelized loop

```
. . .
!
! SUBROUTINE _$1$mf_doall0_$4$foo_$5$foo$_
```

```
. . .

            _$1$mf_doall0_$4$foo_$5$foo$_ :

. . .
```

Runtime Settings

Both C and Fortran programs that use compiler parallelization read the environment variable PARALLEL at run time to select the number of threads for the run. If this variable is not set, by default the programs run serially. The number of OpenMP threads can be also set with the OMP_NUM_THREADS environment variable. If both PARALLEL and OMP_NUM_THREADS variables are set, they must be set to the same value. For maximum efficiency, the number of threads should be equal to or less than the number of available CPUs on the system.

The size of the slave thread stacks is set with the STACKSIZE variable, which takes its argument in kilobytes. The default thread stack size is 1 MB for 32-bit applications and 2 MB for 64-bit applications. The following sets the thread stacksize to 8 MB.

```
example% setenv STACKSIZE 8192
```

We should remind the reader of the difference between the STACKSIZE environment variable and the stacksize shell limit, which bounds the size of the stack of the entire process originated in the shell. The stacks of the threads generated by the compiler are not taken from the stack space controlled by the stacksize limit, but are directly mapped to memory.

Another important point is that parallelized programs have to put all local variables on the stack. This is done automatically by the C compiler (per the C language standard), but Fortran compilers need to be instructed to do so either with the AUTOMATIC qualifier or with the -stackvar option.

The worker threads in parallelized programs continue to spin-wait when the master thread enters a serial port. This results in optimal performance in a dedicated mode, but it also results in wasting resources if a program shares the system with other computational processes. The spin-wait can be disabled with the SUNW_MP_THR_IDLE variable. This variable sets the time interval (in seconds or milliseconds) after which the threads go to sleep. For example, the setting

```
example% setenv SUNW_MP_THR_IDLE 10ms
```

causes threads to spin for ten milliseconds, then go to sleep, allowing other tasks to use CPU resources.

The setting

```
example% setenv SUNW_MP_THR_IDLE sleep
```

specifies that the worker threads go to sleep immediately after finishing their work in a parallel region. Note, it does not affect the threads waiting for a synchronization primitive (barrier, critical section, or locks); these never go to sleep but continue to spin-wait until the synchronization operation finishes.

Automatic Parallelization

Sun C and Fortran compilers automatically parallelize programs when the -xautopar or -xparallel option is specified. The latter option also instructs the compiler to follow parallelization directives explicitly put in programs. We discuss explicit parallelization in the later sections of this chapter. Automatic and explicit compiler parallelization requires the optimization level set to -xO3 or higher.

When automatic parallelization is invoked, the compiler attempts to parallelize only DO loops in Fortran and for loops in C. For both Fortran and C, only loops with integer indexes and whose iteration count is known at runtime are targets for automatic parallelization. Further, the compiler usually parallelizes only the loops whose order of iterations does not affect the result of the computation. It is recommended to use the -xdepend option to increase the level of dependency analysis for parallelized programs. Also, C compiler options -xrestrict and -xalias_level (see Chapter 6) and _Restrict keyword should be used when applicable, as these may result in significant optimization and parallelization improvements.

For a loop nest, the compiler attempts to parallelize only the outermost loop. Any loop that is contained within a parallel loop is not parallelized.

Parallelization is not applied when loop iterations change a variable aliased through a pointer or an EQUIVALENCE statement. Also, automatic parallelization does not apply to the loops that allow the flow control to jump from the loop body. That situation includes loops with function calls (including I/O statements). For example, the following loop is not parallelized by the compiler.

```
do i=1,n
  a(i) = ...
...
  if (a(i).lt.s) goto 100
...
enddo
```

Generally, loops whose iterations update the same scalar variable do not get parallelized. An exception to this rule is *reduction*, a computation that transforms a vector into a scalar. The types of reductions recognized by Sun compilers include sums and products of vector elements, dot products of two vectors, and operations of finding a maximum or a minimum of a vector of values. Loops that perform reductions may get parallelized if the option -xreduction is specified in addition to -xautopar or -xparallel.

The compiler option -xloopinfo displays which loops get parallelized. For example, in the following subroutine, the first loop can be safely parallelized, the parallelization of the second loop is unsafe as there is an interiteration dependency, and the last loop performs a reduction operation, which gets parallelized only if we use the -xreduction option.

CODE EXAMPLE 13-1 Automatic Parallelization of Program Loops

```
c example_autopar.f
c f77 -c -xO3 -autopar -xloopinfo example_autopar.f (-reduction)
      subroutine test(a,b,c,n,sum)
      integer n, i
      double precision a(n), b(n), c(n), sum
c
      do i=1,n
         a(i)=b(i)+c(i)
      enddo
c
      do i=1,n-1
         a(i+1)=a(i)+b(i)
      enddo
c
      sum=0.0
      do i=1,n
         sum= sum+a(i)
      enddo
c
      end
```

```
example% f77 -c -xO3 -autopar -xloopinfo example_autopar.f
example_autopar.f:
        test:
"example_autopar.f", line 7: PARALLELIZED, and serial version
generated
"example_autopar.f", line 11: not parallelized, unsafe dependence
"example_autopar.f", line 16: not parallelized, unsafe dependence
example% f77 -c -xO3 -autopar -xloopinfo example_autopar.f \
        -xreduction
```

```
example_autopar.f:
       test:
"example_autopar.f", line 7: PARALLELIZED, and serial version
generated
"example_autopar.f", line 11: not parallelized, unsafe dependence
"example_autopar.f", line 16: PARALLELIZED, reduction, and serial
version generated
```

We can see that adding -xreduction leads to the parallelization of the last loop. Also, note that because the number of loop iterations is not known at compilation time, both parallelized and serial versions of loops are generated. The selection between the versions is performed at runtime depending on the number of iterations. If this number is high enough, the parallel version is selected. Otherwise, the overhead of the parallelized version may degrade the performance and the serial version is chosen.

When performing parallelization, the compiler can transform loops to make multithreading more efficient. Increased granularity of parallelization can be accomplished by parallelizing the outermost loop in a loop nest or by loop interchange or fusion. Also, if a loop cannot be safely parallelized, the compiler can split it and parallelize some of the resulting parts.

Reduction operations performed with automatic parallelization may lead to answers different from the ones obtained with serial execution of the same problem due to different round-off error accumulation. In most practical cases, these discrepancies are small and acceptable.

Parallelization of the loops by the compiler adds some overhead to the program. The loops are transformed to subroutines that are used in calls to the thread library. In addition, for correct execution, each thread may need a private copy of a variable or an array. Extra memory requirements and loop rearrangements lead to changes in the cache utilization, which in some cases might degrade performance.

In conclusion of this section, we should say that automatic parallelization has its limitations and often does not lead to good parallel performance, particularly in large applications. The compiler often has to make conservative assumptions and might not parallelize important computationally intensive loops. In addition, for parallel loops the compiler attempts to assign equal number of iterations to each thread (*static loop scheduling*) and in some cases this leads to unbalanced computational load between different threads.

Explicit Parallelization

A more efficient way to use multithreading capabilities of compilers is to specify which loops or regions of a program should or should not be parallelized along with the required parallelization parameters. This can be accomplished by using explicit parallelization directives supported in Sun Fortran and C compilers. This type of parallelization requires the knowledge of what parts of program consume most of the computational time and, therefore, might benefit from multithreading. Even though this approach requires analysis of the program and some modifications to the source code, it is still much simpler than explicit multithreading.

In this section we describe two formats of parallelization directives for Sun Fortran compilers, Sun style and Cray style, as well as C parallelization pragmas. In the next section we discuss OpenMP directives supported in Forte Developer 6 and Forte Developer 6 update 1 Fortran 95 compilers.

Explicit parallelization is invoked when either the -xexplicitpar or -xparallel option of the C or Fortran compiler is set. Otherwise the directives are treated as comments and do not affect the compilation. As in the case of automatic parallelization, only DO loops in Fortran and for loops in C with integer indices and iteration count known at run time can be parallelized with explicit directives.

The Sun style directive that marks a loop for parallelization is DOALL. Other Sun style directives are TASKCOMMON, DOSERIAL*, and DOSERIAL. The last two directives mark loop nests and loops that should not be parallelized automatically if the -xparallel compiler option is used. The TASKCOMMON directive declares the variables in a COMMON block to be thread private. The Sun style Fortran parallelization directives[1] begin with C$PAR, !$PAR, and *$PAR.

```
C$PAR DOALL
      do i=1,N
...
```

In loops marked for parallelization, variables and arrays can be declared as thread private or can be shared between threads (data scoping is discussed in detail later in this chapter). This can be done using the scoping qualifiers PRIVATE and SHARED of the DOALL directive. For example, in the following, variables A,B,C are declared as shared and D,E,F have private scope.

```
C$PAR DOALL SHARED(A,B,C) PRIVATE(D,E,F)
      do i=1,N
...
```

---

1. In Fortran 90, only !$PAR is allowed.

Qualifiers can also be used to declare that a variable is not changed in the loop body (READONLY) and that the loop performs a reduction operation (REDUCTION), as well as to set the maximum number of threads that execute a particular loop (MAXCPUS).

An important qualifier for a DOALL directive is SCHEDTYPE, which affects how the loop iterations are distributed between available threads. Different scheduling types can be used to improve load balancing between threads, depending on the amount of computational work in the iterations. The Sun style directives allow the following values for the SCHEDTYPE qualifier:

- STATIC - Uniform distribution of the iterations between threads. This is the default scheduling type.

- SELF (*chunksize*) - The threads take chunksize of iterations at a time rather than taking their entire fair share at once. If the chunksize value is not set, it gets selected by the compiler.

- FACTORING (*m*) - The first half of the iterations get equally divided between threads, then half of the remaining iterations are distributed, and so on. The parameter m sets the minimum for the size of the chunk of the iterations assigned to each thread. If this number is not specified, the compiler selects a value.

- GSS (*m*) - The number of iterations is divided by the number of threads and one chunk is assigned to a thread. The remaining iterations are again divided by the same number and the corresponding chunk goes to another thread. The scheduling proceeds until all the iterations are assigned to threads that become available. Again, m specifies the minimum number of iterations assigned for each thread in a single chunk. Note, GSS stands for *guided self scheduling*. In the next section, we give an example where GSS is beneficial (see CODE EXAMPLE 13-4).

The following table illustrates all four scheduling types for distributing 16 iterations between four threads. Iterations grouped in brackets represent chunks assigned at one time.

TABLE 13-2 Distributing 16 Iterations Between Four Threads Using Different Scheduling Types of Sun Style Directives

	Thread 1	Thread 2	Thread 3	Thread 4
STATIC	[1, 2, 3, 4]	[5, 6, 7, 8]	[9, 10, 11, 12]	[13, 14, 15, 16]
SELF (2)	[1, 2] [9, 10]	[3, 4] [11, 12]	[5, 6] [13, 14]	[7, 8] [15, 16]
FACTORING (1)	[1, 2] [9] [13]	[3, 4] [10] [14]	[5, 6] [11] [15]	[7, 8] [12] [16]
GSS (2)	[1, 2, 3, 4]	[5, 6, 7] [16]	[8, 9] [12, 13]	[10, 11] [14, 15]

Sun style directives have default scoping rules for variables. Unless they are explicitly declared with qualifiers, scalars are treated as private and arrays are treated as shared.

Multiple qualifiers for a single `DOALL` directive can span several lines. In this case, the continuation symbol has to be put in the sixth position of the line.

```
C$PAR DOALL SHARED(A,B,C) PRIVATE(D,E,F)
C$PAR& SCHEDTYPE(SELF(10))
      do i=1,N
...
```

If the number of iterations in a parallelized loop is low compared to the number of threads, then the parallel speedup can be limited regardless of the chosen scheduling strategy. We illustrate this situation with the following example where the parallelized loop performs 32 iterations. We put a `sleep` call in the loop body to simulate a ten-second computation.

CODE EXAMPLE 13-2 Stair-Stepping Effect

```
c example_stair.f
c f90 -xO3 example_stair.f -o example_stair -xdepend \
c    -explicitpar -stackvar
      integer*8 gethrtime, time1, time2, s
      s=0
      time1 = gethrtime()
c$par doall private(j) reduction(s)
      do j=1,32
         call sleep(10)
         s=s+1
      enddo
      time2 = gethrtime()
      print*,"s =", s
      write(6,10) (time2-time1)*1.e-9
 10   format("RUNTIME: ",f6.2," seconds")
      stop
      end
```

When we compile this program and run it on an Enterprise 10000 system using various numbers of processors, we get scaling results illustrated in FIGURE 13-2. We can see that the scaling plot is not a continuous function, but rather is formed by distinct plateaus. This is not surprising. First, we can note that the best possible speedup for this problem is 32 when each of the iterations is run on a separate thread. That explains the final plateau corresponding to the speedup of 32 for 32 and larger numbers of threads. Then, we can note that if the number of threads is between 16 and 31, the corresponding number of iterations are executed simultaneously followed by the remaining ones executed in the second round. This results in the speedup of 16 for the entire range of numbers of threads. Similarly we can explain the other plateaus.

This effect is known as *stair stepping* (see FIGURE 13-2) and can be observed for applications that are dominated by loops that have a relatively small iteration count. Programs dominated by loops with small but different iteration counts don't show such crisp scaling plateaus, but still suffer from similar effects and show degraded scaling results. In sum, the best parallel speedup does not exceed the iteration count of typical parallelized loops in the application, regardless of the number of CPUs used for the run.

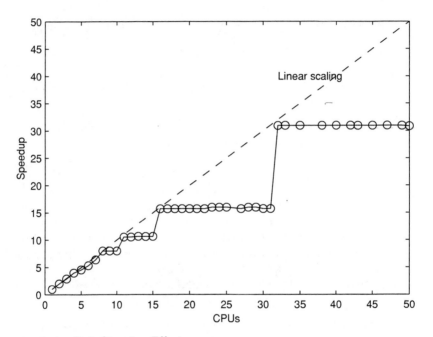

FIGURE 13-2 Stair-Stepping Effect

Sun style parallelization is enabled by default or when -mp=sun option is used. The Cray style is enabled with -mp=cray option. The Cray directives recognized by Sun compilers begin with CMIC$, *MIC$, or !MIC$. Only the !MIC form can be used in the free form of Fortran 90.

The four basic directives are the same for Cray style parallelization: DOALL, TASKCOMMON, DOSERIAL*, and DOSERIAL. There are, though, some differences in qualifiers of the DOALL directive. There are no default scoping rules for Cray style parallelization; all variables have to be declared as either PRIVATE or SHARED. Also, the Cray style scheduling type is different.

- CHUNKSIZE(n) - Same as Sun style SELF(n).

- SINGLE - Repeatedly distributes one iteration per thread. Same as CHUNKSIZE(1).

- NUMCHUNKS (*m*) - Distributes n/m iterations to each thread at a time, where n is the total number of iterations.

- GUIDED (*m*) - Distribute iterations by use of guided self scheduling. Same as GSS (*m*) Sun style scheduling.

Different scheduling types for distributing 16 iterations between four threads are illustrated in the following table. Again the iterations grouped in brackets represent chunks assigned at a time.

TABLE 13-3 Distributing 16 Iterations Between Four Threads Using Different Scheduling Types of Cray Style Directives

	Thread 1	Thread 2	Thread 3	Thread 4
SINGLE or CHUNKSIZE(1) or NUMCHUNK(16)	[1] [5] [9] [13]	[2] [6] [10] [14]	[3] [7] [11] [15]	[4] [8] [12] [16]
CHUNKSIZE(2)	[1, 2] [9, 10]	[3, 4] [11, 12]	[5, 6] [13, 14]	[7, 8] [15, 16]
GUIDED(2)	[1, 2, 3, 4]	[5, 6, 7] [16]	[8, 9] [12, 13]	[10, 11] [14, 15]

As in the case of automatic parallelization, the use of AUTOMATIC qualifier in the source code or the -stackvar compiler option is required for explicit parallelization of Fortran programs that make function calls from parallelized loops. It is needed to ensure that local variables are placed on the local thread stacks. We should point out that Fortran programs that rely on zeroing uninitialized data generate the wrong results if compiled with -stackvar, as the following illustrates. It is always recommended to initialize the variables used in the program.

CODE EXAMPLE 13-3 Fortran Program That Relies on Uninitialized Variable

```
c f77 -xO3 example_stackvar.f -o example_stackvar (-stackvar)
      integer*8 j,s
c     s=0
      do j=1,32
        s=s+1
      enddo
      print*,"s =", s
      end
```

```
example% f77 -xO3 example_stackvar.f -o example_stackvar
example% example_stackvar
 s =   32
example% f77 -xO3 example_stackvar.f -o example_stackvar -stackvar
example% example_stackvar
 s =   4290703728
```

For C programs, the pragma `MP taskloop` marks the `for` loop that follows the pragma as a candidate for parallelization. The pragmas `serial_loop` and `serial_loop_nested` can be used to prevent automatic parallelization of a loop or a loop nest if the `-xparallel` compiler option is set.

The `private` and `shared` scope of the variables and other qualifiers, such as `readonly` and `reduction`, can be specified as qualifiers to the pragma. Multiple options for pragma `MP taskloop` should occupy different lines, for example:

```
#pragma MP taskloop shared(a,b)
#pragma MP taskloop private(c)
#pragma MP taskloop readonly(d)
```

The scheduling of the loop is controlled with the `schedtype` qualifier. The types of scheduling are the same as Fortran Sun style scheduling types, namely `static`, `self`, `gss`, and `factoring`. For example, the following pragma parallelizes the loop with guided self scheduling using chunks of at least ten iterations assigned for each thread.

```
#pragma MP taskloop schedtype(gss(10))
```

The compiler option `-xloopinfo`, available in both C and Fortran compilers, shows which loops are parallelized and which are not. Warnings about potential parallelization problems are displayed with the `-xvpara` option.

The C compiler (Forte Developer 6 and Forte Developer 6 update 1 releases) include pragmas for providing additional information to the compiler about the use of global variables. These are as follows.

```
#pragma does_not_read_global_data (funcname [, funcname])
#pragma does_not_write_global_data (funcname [, funcname])
```

As the names indicate, the former asserts that the functions in the argument list of the pragma do not read global data directly or indirectly, while the latter pragma asserts that these functions do not write global variables. The reader is encouraged to try these pragmas in their parallel programs.

For a more detailed description of parallelization capabilities of Sun compilers, refer to the *Fortran Programming Guide* and the *C User's Guide*.

OpenMP Support in Fortran 95 Compiler

Forte Developer 6 and Forte Developer 6 update 1 Fortran 95 compilers provide full support for OpenMP 1.1 standard (http:/www.openmp.org). OpenMP programs should be compiled with the -explicitpar and -mp=openmp options. The OpenMP directives can be combined with either Sun style or Cray style parallelization, as long as the directives of different types are not nested within each other. In that case, both parallelization styles should be listed as arguments of the -mp option, for example -mp=openmp, sun. OpenMP programs can be also built with the -openmp option, which is a macro for -mp=openmp -explicitpar -stackvar -D_OPENMP. At runtime the number of OpenMP threads is determined based on the value of the OMP_NUM_THREADS environment variable.

The Fortran OpenMP directives are accepted in the forms C$OMP, *$OMP, and !$OMP. Only the last format can be used in the free form of Fortran 95. For example, the following pair of directives mark the beginning and the end of a region of the code that should be executed using multiple threads.

```
!$omp parallel
...
!$omp end parallel
```

The !$omp do directive specifies the loops whose iterations should be executed in parallel (also called a work-sharing construct in OpenMP programming parlance). For example:

```
!$omp do
do i=1,n
  x(i) = x(i)*y(i)
enddo
```

The corresponding scheduling type is set with the SCHEDULE clause, which can be set to either STATIC (which is the default), DYNAMIC, or GUIDED. A useful feature of !$omp do scheduling is that the choice can be deferred until runtime when the value of SCHEDULE is set to RUNTIME. In that case, the scheduling is selected based on the value of the OMP_SCHEDULE environment variable. This allows tuning the schedule type for the cases when the optimal selection is not obvious.

In the following example, we multiply the triangular part of matrix b by the square matrix c. Equal distribution of the iterations between the threads is unbalanced because the initial iterations have much less computational work to perform than the subsequent ones. This situation is not well suited to STATIC scheduling but is perfectly handled with GUIDED scheduling. We set the value of SCHEDULE to RUNTIME and test both scheduling types for the resulting binary.

CODE EXAMPLE 13-4 Runtime Scheduling for OpenMP

```
! example_sched.f90
! f90 -xO3 example_sched.f90 -o example_sched -xdepend -openmp
      parameter(idim=500)
      real*8 a(idim,idim), b(idim,idim), c(idim,idim), atmp2
      integer*8 gethrtime, time1, time2
      do i=1,idim
         do j=1,idim
            a(i,j)=5.
            b(i,j)=2.
            c(i,j)=3.
         end do
      end do
      time1 = gethrtime()
!$omp parallel &
!$omp private(i,j,k), shared(a,b,c)
!$omp do schedule(runtime)
         do j=1,idim
            do i=1,idim
               atmp=a(i,j)
               do k=1,j
                  atmp = atmp+b(i,k)*c(k,j)
               enddo
               a(i,j)=atmp
            enddo
         enddo
!$omp end do
!$omp end parallel
      time2 = gethrtime()
      atmp2=a(idim/2,idim/2)
      ops=2*float(idim)**3
      print*,atmp2
      write(6,10) (time2-time1)*1.e-9
 10   format("RUNTIME: ",f6.2," seconds")
      stop
      end
```

As expected, we see (FIGURE 13-3) fairly poor performance for STATIC scheduling but near linear scaling when OMP_SCHEDULE is set to GUIDED.

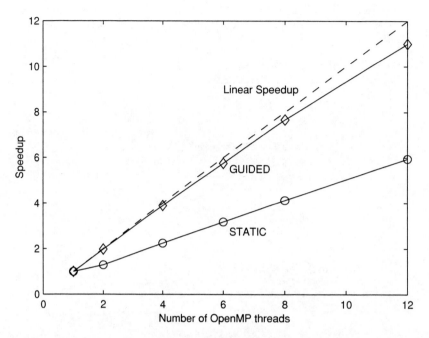

FIGURE 13-3 Performance Effect of Different OpenMP Schedule Types

In Forte Developer 6 and Forte Developer 6 update 1 Fortran 95 compilers, the default setting for the `OMP_DYNAMIC` environment variable is `TRUE`. Specifically, if user sets `OMP_NUM_THREADS` to a value greater than the number of online processors, the library resets the number of threads to the number of online processors. To disable dynamic thread adjustment, one should set `OMP_DYNAMIC` to `FALSE`.

The OpenMP standard provides a rich functionality that includes directives to specify parallel sections, critical sections, barriers, atomic operations, nested directives and other features. In addition to directives, the OpenMP specification describes a number of environment variables and functions calls, which perform such operations as to set the number of threads to be used in the parallel region, or to set or release a lock.

In the next few sections we look at some important programming and performance issues to consider when using OpenMP for program parallelization. Details on OpenMP features can be obtained from [Chandra00] and from the standard, available from the `http://www.openmp.org` website.

OpenMP Programming Styles

OpenMP provides functionality to parallelize a program not just at the granularity-of-loop level but over arbitrary regions by using *parallel region* directives. OpenMP supports incremental parallelization of a large application in a range of programming styles. It also provides flexibility to mix these approaches in the same application if desired. We have already illustrated fine-grained or loop-level parallelization in the previous section. In this section, we discuss task parallelism support and SPMD style programming using OpenMP directives.

Section Parallel Style

When sections of code can be executed independently with little or no synchronization, the `!omp parallel sections` directive can be used to create parallel sections. This can be used to obtain functional or task-level parallelism for cases where there are limited fixed tasks to be performed in separate blocks of a program. Consider the following program that solves the second-order differential equation arising in a damped mass-spring oscillator problem using explicit Euler and second-order Runge-Kutta time integration schemes. The intent of the program is to compare two schemes for this problem. The solution is first computed with explicit Euler followed by the Runge-Kutta scheme; the relative error in the two schemes (compared to the known exact solution) is printed at the end of the program. The two calculations are independent, and in this case the `!omp parallel sections` directive can be used to run the two tasks concurrently.

CODE EXAMPLE 13-5 `!omp Parallel Sections` Directive *(1 of 3)*

```
        program example_dampvib
c    f90 -openmp example_dampvib.f -o example_dampvib
        implicit real(a-h,o-z)
        real yex,yex1,yeul,yrk2
        fac = 45./atan(1.)   ! 180.0/pi
        dt=0.0001
        iter=100000
        omg=4.
        cd=4.
        yex=0.0
        yeul=0.0
        yrk2=0.0
c$omp parallel sections shared(yeul,yrk2,yex)
c$omp& private(yex1), firstprivate(dt,iter,omg,cd)
```

```
c$omp section              ! solve using Explicit Euler
        call exp_eul(dt,iter,omg,cd,yex,yeul)
c$omp section              ! solve using RK2
        call adv_rk2(dt,iter,omg,cd,yex1,yrk2)
c$omp end parallel sections
        erreul = abs(yeul-yex)/abs(yex)
        errrk2 = abs(yrk2-yex)/abs(yex)
        write(*,'(2(2x,e14.6))') erreul*100.0,errrk2*100.0
        stop
        end


        subroutine exp_eul(dt,iter,omg,cd,yex,yeul)
c solve using explicit Euler; first parallel section task
        implicit real(a-h,o-z)
        real y1,y1old,y2old,dt,omg,cd,rt
        pi = 4.0*atan(1.0)
c assign initial vals
        yt0=10.0*pi/180.0
        y2old=yt0
        y1old=0.0
        rt=0.0
        alp=(4.*omg*omg-cd*cd)**(0.5)/2.
c do time-advancement (Explicit Euler)
        do 10 i=1,iter
          y1=y1old-dt*(cd*y1old+omg*omg*y2old)
          yeul=y2old+dt*y1old
          rt=rt+dt
        yex=exp(-cd*rt/2.)*yt0*(cos(alp*rt)+(2./alp)*sin(alp*rt))
          ydex=-exp(-cd*rt/2.)*yt0*(alp*alp+4.)*sin(alp*rt)/alp
          y1old=y1
          y2old=yeul
10      continue
        return
        end


        subroutine adv_rk2(dt,iter,omg,cd,yex,yrk2)
c solve using RK2; second parallel section task
        implicit real(a-h,o-z)
        real  y1,y1old,y2old,y1i,y2i,dt,omg,rt,cd
        pi = 4.0*atan(1.0)
c assign initial vals
        yt0=10.0*pi/180.0
        y2old=yt0
```

```
        y1old=0.0
        rt=0.0
        alp=(4.*omg*omg-cd*cd)**(0.5)/2.
c do time advancement (Runge Kutta 2nd order)
        do 10 i=1,iter
c step 1
         y1i=y1old -(dt/2.)*(cd*y1old+omg*omg*y2old)
         y2i=y2old +(dt/2.)*y1old
c step 2
         y1=y1old -dt*(cd*y1i+omg*omg*y2i)
         yrk2=y2old +dt*y1i
         rt=rt+dt
        yex=exp(-cd*rt/2.)*yt0*(cos(alp*rt)+(2./alp)*sin(alp*rt))
         ydex=-exp(-cd*rt/2.)*yt0*(alp*alp+4.)*sin(alp*rt)/alp
         y1old=y1
         y2old=yrk2
10       continue
         return
         end
```

If OpenMP directives are removed from this example, the program becomes serial. As can be seen from this example, parallelization using the section directives can be quite straightforward to implement. The main issues to be cautious of when using parallel sections directive are variable scoping and data sharing between threads (discussed in next section), need for synchronization, and size of thread stacks running sections (see earlier discussion on STACKSIZE environment variable).

Compiling and running the program on a two-processor Ultra-60 (300MHz UltraSPARCII) workstation, one can see the speedup resulting from using the section parallelism in this program

```
example% f90 -openmp example_dampvib.f -o example_dampvib
example% setenv OMP_NUM_THREADS 1
example% ptime example_dampvib
0.990624E+00    0.261609E+00
real         0.389
user         0.364
sys          0.018
example% setenv OMP_NUM_THREADS 2
example% ptime example_dampvib
0.990624E+00    0.261609E+00
real         0.220
user         0.371
sys          0.019
```

We can see that scaling is not perfect in this example because the amounts of computational work required by the explicit Euler and Runge-Kutta methods are different. Coarse-grained parallelism based on parallel sections with unequal amounts of computational work can lead to suboptimal load balancing between different threads.

The !omp parallel sections directive is useful in cases where n-way (assuming n section directives follow the sections directive) parallelism exists in the problem, which sets a limit on the parallel scalability. The sections directive can also be used for nested parallelism, wherein loop-based parallelization can be performed for each of the tasks that is being run in the independent section directives. Nested parallelism of this form is currently not supported in Sun parallelizing compilers.

Single Program Multiple Data (SPMD) Style

The SPMD style of programming in OpenMP can be accomplished by starting N threads in the main program in a manner similar to MPI programs. The created threads execute the same set of modules in the program but operate on different parts of data structures as dictated by control flow statements inserted in the program in a manner analogous to an SPMD program using the MPI facility ([Wallcraft99] and [Hisley99]). No loop-based worksharing OpenMP construct is used, as the work division is performed explicitly by the programmer. The SPMD style relies on the "region-parallelism" accomplished using parallel region directives.

We illustrate the SPMD style with an example. Consider a calculation that is representative of forward and backward column sweeps in an Alternating Direction Implicit (ADI) iterative method (see [Golub98]) applied on a 2D cartesian grid. In an ADI method, the computation alternates between the row and column sweeps, but in the example, we only look at the sweeps in the column direction. The calculation performs the column sweeps as shown in the following code fragment:

```
      integer m,n,i,j
      real x(m,n),a,b
c Forward column sweep
      do j=1,n-1
        do i=2,m
          x(i,j) = a*x(i,j)+b*x(i-1,j)
        enddo
      enddo

c Backward column sweep
      do j=n,2,-1
        do i=m-1,1,-1
```

```
            x(i,j) = a*x(i,j)+b*x(i+1,j)
         enddo
      enddo
```

Consider both the SPMD[1] and OpenMP-loop based parallelization of this computation. These are schematically shown in FIGURE 13-1. The left shows the SPMD style in which case a process (or thread) operates on the same data slice while in the OpenMP-loop-based parallelization on the right, the thread may operate on a different slice in the backward sweep than it did in the forward sweep. A 1D decomposition of the computational grid is assumed in the SPMD version.

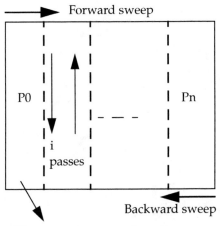

PO operates on same data slice
in both sweeps

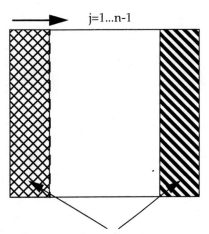

PO may operate on different slices in
forward and backward sweeps

FIGURE 13-4 Schematic for the ADI Column Sweeps Example Program

The complete listing of the SPMD MPI version of the program (example_adimpi.f) is as follows:

CODE EXAMPLE 13-6 MPI Version of ADI Column Sweep *(1 of 3)*

```
      program example_adimpi
c mpf90 -fast example_adimpi.f -lmpi
      implicit real(a-h,o-z)
      include 'mpif.h'
      integer imax,jmax,niter,np,jp,iroot
      parameter(np=1) !change to desired num. MPI procs.
```

1. The SPMD versions were implemented in both MPI and OpenMP.

```
      parameter(imax=4099,jmax=4201,jp=(jmax-1)/np)
      real x(imax,jp+1),a,b
      integer ierr,istatus,itag,nproc
      integer i,j,im,jm,n,iam,myst,myen
      real*8 time1,time2,tmax

      call mpi_init(ierr)
      call mpi_comm_rank(MPI_COMM_WORLD, iam, ierr)
      call mpi_comm_size(MPI_COMM_WORLD, nproc, ierr)
      if (np.ne.nproc) then
         write(*,*) 'nproc and np do not match, stopping'
         stop
      endif
      a = 0.75
      b = 0.25
      im = imax
      jm = jp
      niter=100
      iroot=0
      do j=1,jp
       do i=1,imax
         x(i,j) = 1.0
       enddo
      enddo
          time1 = MPI_Wtime()
          myst = 1
          myen = jp
          do 60 i=1,niter
           call adisweep(im,jm,x,a,b,iam,myst,myen,nproc)
           call mpi_barrier(MPI_COMM_WORLD,ierr)
 60        continue
          time2 = MPI_Wtime()
          time2 = time2 - time1
          call mpi_reduce(time2,tmax,1,MPI_DOUBLE_PRECISION,
     &        MPI_MAX,iroot,MPI_COMM_WORLD,ierr)

      if (iam.eq.0) then
         write(*,*) ' ***** COLUMN SWEEP ***** '
         write(*,'(1x," LENGTH ",1x," MIN TIME ")')
         write(*,'(1x,i5,3x,1pe12.4)') imax,tmax
      endif
      stop
      end
```

```
        subroutine adisweep(m,n,x,a,b,iam,myst,myen,np)
        implicit none
        integer m,n,i,j,iam,myst,myen,np
        real x(m,n),a,b
        if (iam.eq.(np-1)) myen = myen-1
        do j=myst,myen
          do i=2,m
            x(i,j) = a*x(i,j)+b*x(i-1,j)
          enddo
        enddo
        if (iam.eq.0) myst = myst+1
        do j=myen,myst,-1
          do i=m-1,1,-1
            x(i,j) = a*x(i,j)+b*x(i+1,j)
          enddo
        enddo

        return
        end
```

The program starts `np` MPI processes, each of which then performs the sweep calculation (in the subroutine `adisweep`). Note that for each MPI process, the loops run from `j=myst,myen` and `j=myen,myst,-1` for the forward and backward sweeps, respectively. In this simple example, the calculation for each sweep is independent of other sweeps. No communication or synchronization is required between MPI processes.

The program `example_adiopenmp.f` is the same program rewritten using both OpenMP loop-parallelization and SPMD styles, respectively. In the interest of preserving space, we do not present the complete listing but only show relevant portions. The program is available in its entirety with other examples of this chapter, and the reader is encouraged to examine it. The SPMD portion of the driver program is listed as:

```
        if (iprog.eq.0) then    ! SPMD Style Path in Driver
            time1 = gethrtime()
c$omp parallel private(i,iam,myst,myen,np)
c$omp& firstprivate(niter,im,jm,a,b),shared(x)
            iam = omp_get_thread_num()
            np = omp_get_num_threads()
            myst = iam*(jm/np)+1
            myen = myst + (jm/np) - 1
```

```
              do 60 i=1,niter
                call adispmd(im,jm,x,a,b,iam,myst,myen,np)
c$omp barrier
60            continue
c$omp end parallel
              time2 = gethrtime()
              timin = (time2-time1)

           elseif (iprog.eq.1) then      ! Loop Style Path
```

The corresponding routine `adispmd` is as follows.

```
         subroutine adispmd(m,n,x,a,b,iam,myst,myen,np)
c spmd style version of adi column sweep
         implicit none
         integer m,n,i,j,iam,myst,myen,np
         real x(m,n),a,b
         if (iam.eq.(np-1)) myen = myen-1
         do j=myst,myen
           do i=2,m
             x(i,j) = a*x(i,j)+b*x(i-1,j)
           enddo
         enddo
         if (iam.eq.0) myst = myst+1
         do j=myen,myst,-1
           do i=m-1,1,-1
             x(i,j) = a*x(i,j)+b*x(i+1,j)
           enddo
         enddo

         return
         end
```

Comparing `adispmd` with the `example_adimpi.f` program, we see how SPMD styles are similar for both MPI and OpenMP implementations. In fact, the routine `adisweep` and `adispmd` are identical in the two programs.

The portion of the driver program for loop-based parallelization is as follows.

```
         elseif (iprog.eq.1) then      ! Loop Style Path
           time1 = gethrtime()
```

```
c$omp parallel private(i)
c$omp& firstprivate(niter,im,jm,a,b),shared(x)
          do 70 i=1,niter
            call adiloop(im,jm,x,a,b)
70          continue
c$omp end parallel
          time2 = gethrtime()
          timin = (time2-time1)


        endif
```

The corresponding routine `adiloop` implementing column sweeps is listed next. As we can see, the insertion of OpenMP directives is straightforward.

```
        subroutine adiloop(m,n,x,a,b)
c loop style version of adi column sweep
        implicit none
        integer m,n,i,j
        real x(m,n),a,b
c$omp do private(j,i)
        do j=1,n-1
          do i=2,m
            x(i,j) = a*x(i,j)+b*x(i-1,j)
          enddo
        enddo
c$omp enddo

c$omp do private(j,i)
        do j=n,2,-1
          do i=m-1,1,-1
            x(i,j) = a*x(i,j)+b*x(i+1,j)
          enddo
        enddo
c$omp enddo
        return
        end
```

Note how loop-based and SPMD OpenMP styles differ. In the SPMD style, a barrier synchronization is required only after the complete sweep, while in the loop-based approach, a synchronization may be needed after every work-sharing construct. This is the case in this example because an implicit barrier is needed after both the do loops in the subroutine `adiloop`. In the loops-based approach, there is flexibility to use different loop scheduling schemes on a per-loop basis, whereas in the SPMD style, the partitioning (static in this case) has to be implemented explicitly by a programmer.

For this simple program, the variable scoping required in the SPMD OpenMP version is trivial. For efficiency purposes, we made the variables `niter`, `im`, `jm`, `a`, and `b` of scope `firstprivate`. In more complex programs, to create the `private` variable space implicit in MPI programs, one may need to privatize explicitly global (or shared) data either by using `private`, `firstprivate`, and `lastprivate` clauses or `threadprivate` for common blocks in Fortran programs. Care is required in creating a `private` variable space due to default scoping rules of OpenMP constructs and the language used in the program. For example, variables declared in `DATA` statements or saved using a `SAVE` statement in Fortran programs automatically become shared and must be handled differently if private copies are required (see [Wallcraft99]). We discuss variable scoping in more detail in the next section.

We ran the MPI, OpenMP loops, and OpenMP SPMD versions (compiled using Forte Developer 6 Fortran 95 compiler and HPC 3.1 `mpf90` wrapper) on a 12-CPU Enterprise 4500 system (400MHz UltraSPARCII processors with 8 MB level 2 cache, Solaris 8). The times for 100 ADI iterations are listed in TABLE 13-4.

TABLE 13-4   Comparison Between SPMD (MPI, OpenMP) and Loop-Parallelization Styles for the Column ADI Sweep Example on a 4099x4201 Grid

# Processors	OpenMP-Loops (sec.)	OpenMP-SPMD (sec.)	MPI-SPMD (sec.)
1	106.83	104.16	104.15
2	66.58	51.78	51.64
4	40.13	24.58	24.58
8	25.03	8.49	8.46
12	18.97	5.72	5.68

Times are listed for 100 iterations. For the grid used in this example, the total memory for array x in the program is 4,099 x 4,201 x 4 bytes (approximately 66 MB). Because the benchmark machine used processors with an 8-MB level 2 cache, as expected, we see superlinear speedups in both the SPMD versions. In the SPMD style, the data locality is preserved in the program. In the loop-parallelization-based approach, there is no guarantee of data reuse between the forward and backward sweeps as the compiler (in general) may assign data slices to threads in any order for the two loops. So even though the working set-size of the program fits in the cumulative level 2 cache for eight or more processors, the loop approach does not take advantage of it and the scaling is inferior compared to the SPMD approach.

Even though there are many possible modifications to the example provided in this section (such as improving performance, making loop and SPMD codes look more similar, and simplifying code), it illustrates what actually tends to happen in some applications.

While the former example demonstrates how performance of the SPMD style is superior to the loop-parallelization style, this may not be the case for an arbitrary program and one cannot make a general statement in favor of one style over another. Each style is suited to a different class of programs, and experimentation with different styles might be required to determine the optimal approach for an application.

OpenMP Performance Considerations

We now examine some important performance considerations for OpenMP programs. The topics covered in this section are synchronization issues, data scoping, and memory bandwidth requirements.

Synchronization Issues

We included a detailed section on synchronization and locking issues for multithreaded programs in the previous chapter. Because the compiler-generated threads use Solaris threads library underneath, all of those issues are equally applicable to OpenMP programs. In this section, some tips specific to synchronization when using OpenMP directives are included.

The OpenMP specification includes `critical`, `atomic`, `flush`, and `barrier` directives for synchronization purposes. Additionally, there are functions for user-inserted locks, in a manner similar to mutex locks in P-threads library.

When using `critical` directive, it is recommended to associate it with a name because all unnamed critical sections map to the same name. Separately named critical sections (assuming program logic allows it) can provide more information to the runtime library to associate a separate lock with the name as compared to unnamed critical sections where the same lock might be shared for many critical regions in the program.

```
!$omp critical (lock1)
. . . . .
!$omp end critical (lock1) ! this is preferable to unnamed critical
!$omp critical
. . . .
!$omp end critical
```

Similarly, in C OpenMP applications, the use of lock functions might result in better performance (though at the cost of requiring more code changes in a serial program).

For updates, such as

```
!$omp critical (lock1)
x(i) = max(x(i), sqrt((y(i)*z(i)**0.35)/v(i)))
!$omp end critical (lock1)
```

use the `atomic` directive

```
!$omp atomic
x(i) = max(x(i), sqrt((y(i)*z(i)**0.35)/v(i)))
```

The `atomic` directive guarantees atomicity on load of `x(i)`, update of `x(i)`, and store of `x(i)`; the intermediate operation of calculating the operations in `sqrt(....)` can be performed concurrently by the different threads executing the `atomic` directive. If this is the intent of the program, then `atomic` directive should be used, because in the case of `critical` directive the entire statement is executed serially.

In the previous chapter, we strongly warned against using a "self-synchronization" type operation for mutual exclusion. Such a primitive can be constructed in OpenMP using the `flush` directive, which provides the atomicity and memory consistency needed for it to work correctly. So, for example, the point-to-point synchronization needed in the pipeline parallel algorithm used in the NAS Parallel Benchmark LU [Jin99] is implemented as follows.

```
      iam = omp_get_thread_num()
      if (iam .gt. 0 .and. iam .le. mthreadnum) then
         neigh = iam - 1
         do while (isync(neigh) .eq. 0)
!$omp flush(isync)
         end do
         isync(neigh) = 0
!$omp flush(isync)
      endif /* loop and wait till isync set to 1 by neighbor */
...
...
      isync(neigh) = 0
      if (iam .lt. mthreadnum) then
         do while (isync(iam) .eq. 1)
!$omp flush(isync)
         end do
         isync(iam) = 1 /* release the neighbor */
!$omp flush(isync)
      endif
```

To avoid false sharing, variables that are flushed should preferably be placed on different cache lines by padding or not declaring them contiguously.

We should also mention ordered regions in parallel programs. An ordered region is essentially a critical region with the additional constraint of preserving the order in which the loop iterations are executed. An ordered region might be created explicitly by using the !$omp ordered directive or implicitly by the loop structure. Similarly, the !$omp ordered directive might be useful in a routine where threads perform I/O or other library calls that require sequential order. However, its use in a parallelizable do loop should be avoided as much as possible.

Wherever the logic of the program allows, the nowait qualifier should be used to eliminate the implicit barrier at the end of the parallel do loop that is required by the standard

```
!$omp do
......
!$omp enddo nowait !.eliminates barrier synch. at end of loop
```

In particular, this qualifier should be used for the last do loop in a parallel region because there is already an implicit barrier at the end of the parallel region. For example:

```
!$omp parallel
.....initialize and other statements....
!$omp do
.....
!$omp enddo
.....other statements and !$omp do loops in the parallel region..
!$omp do ! this is the last do loop
....
!$omp enddo nowait ! use nowait here to eliminate extra barrier
!$omp end parallel
```

The reader should put nowait in between the do loops in the subroutine adiloop in the example_adiopenmp.f program from the previous section and observe the performance behavior[1] of the program. One should avoid using the nowait qualifier in a loop with reduction clause, because the value of reduction variable(s) stays undefined until all threads have completed their portions of the reduction operation. Hence, the barrier at the end of the do loop ensures an update to the reduction variables by all the participating threads.

---

1. Strictly speaking, the data dependency in the ADI sweeps does not allow placement of the nowait qualifier in between the forward and backward sweeps.

Data Scoping

When parallelizing programs using compiler directives, one of the most important (and complicated) issues from a correctness and performance point of view is scoping of variables in a parallel construct. Variable scoping attempts to address the questions of where a particular variable should be allocated prior to execution of the parallel construct (in most cases parallel `DO` or `for` loops) and how it should be accessed by the different threads during the execution of the construct.

OpenMP provides several clauses, such as `shared`, `private`, `firstprivate`, `lastprivate`, and `threadprivate`, for user controlled variable scoping (see TABLE 13-5) and `default` clause for default scoping. In this section, we provide some guidelines to follow in using `shared`, `private`, and `firstprivate` clauses when parallelizing programs.

TABLE 13-5 Synopsis of OpenMP 1.1 Fortran Data Scoping Constructs

OpenMP Scoping Clause	Synopsis
shared	All threads share the same variable.
private	A separate copy of the variable is created for each thread in the parallel construct.
firstprivate	Same as private. Additionally, the private copies are initialized with the original value of the variable before the parallel construct.
lastprivate	Same as private. Additionally, the value of the variable after the parallel construct is the same as it would be in sequential execution. For example in `!$omp do` construct, the thread that executes sequentially the last iteration updates the value of the variable.
threadprivate	Private copies of Fortran common blocks are created on a per thread basis.

Refer to the OpenMP specification for additional details. The variables accessed in a parallel construct can be primarily classified by the programmer as either shared or private[1]. As the name suggests, a shared variable is one that can be accessed by all the threads whereas a private variable is allocated in the "private stack memory" of each thread and accessible only by that thread. The concept of shared and private variables is related to the notion of global and local variables in the Fortran (or C) language. As a general rule, shared variables can be thought of as global variables and private variables roughly correspond to local variables. There are exceptions to this and we discuss those later. For Fortran programs, the correspondence is closer

---

1. Strictly speaking, because the OpenMP threads share a common address space of the parent process, all variables are allocated in this common address space and are accessible to all threads in the program.

when the `-stackvar` compiler flag is used, in which case all the local variables are allocated on the stack segment of virtual memory. The shared or private variables can be further sub-typed as type scalars or arrays.

Another important concept for data scoping is whether the variable is read-only (that is the variable is only used in the parallel loop) or is written into the loop (that is, its value is set).

Using these concepts, we now list some of the guidelines to follow for scoping variables in parallel regions and loops of the program. Only the important points are listed.

- If a scalar is used (read-only) in a parallel loop, then it should be scoped `shared`. For example, `bb` should be scoped `shared` in:

```
do i=1,N
    x(i) = bb*y(i)
enddo
```

- An array variable is by default shared if its index variable is a function of the parallel loop index. For example, in the previous loop both x and y are shared arrays. If it is only used (read-only) and its index is independent of the parallel loop index, then it can be considered a constant array. In the loop nest below, y should be a constant shared array.

```
do i=1,N
    do j=1,M
        x(i) = x(i) + bb*y(j)
    enddo
enddo
```

- A scalar variable that is first used, then set[1] should be a shared variable. For example, `sum` should be a shared scalar[2] in the loop:

```
sum = 0.0
do i=1,N
    sum = sum + x(i)
enddo
```

1. Setting a variable may require protection with a critical section.

2. This is a special case in which sum is a reduction variable.

- A private scalar is one that is first set, then used in the loop. For example, the index of the parallel loop and `temp` are both private scalars in the loop:

```
do i=1,N
   temp = sqrt(x(i)/y(i))
   u(i) = temp + u(i)
enddo
```

- An array should be a private variable if all of its elements are set in the loop before being used. It can also be considered to be private if its index expression is independent of the loop index. The array `y` should be declared private in the following example.

```
do i=1,N
   do j=1,M
      y(j) = j+1
      x(i) = x(i) + bb*y(j)
   enddo
enddo
```

While these guidelines work for the variable scoping analysis of a variety of loops, there are many exceptional situations.

An important situation occurring commonly in large applications is that of a subroutine being called from inside the parallel loop. For example:

```
do i=1,N
   call abc(x,y,...)
enddo
```

In such situations, variable scoping can be quite difficult. The variables in COMMON blocks and SAVE statements are of global scope and might need to be declared privately for each thread.

```
subroutine foo(u,v)
common /com1/c,d
!$omp parallel do
do i=1,m
   call bar(u)
enddo
...
subroutine bar(u)
common /com1/c,d
common /com2/e(100)
```

```
save xsave
... c,d and e used/modified in bar ...
...
```

In the previous example, the common blocks com1 and com2 must be declared threadprivate (or taskcommon for Sun or Cray style directives) for threads to not clobber the global copy. Similarly, the save statement on xsave can cause problems depending on how it is used. If it is a read-only variable, then it may be left unchanged. Otherwise, the save qualifier should be removed. In general, save variables should be changed when a routine is called in a parallel construct. The previous is an example of global variables requiring private scoping in the OpenMP construct.

The readonly clause in Sun-style directives creates private copies for the specified variables and initializes them with original values (that is, the values of the variables before beginning the parallel region or parallel loop). In OpenMP, this can be achieved using the firstprivate clause. We used this in the example_adiopenmp.f program in the previous section

```
...
c$omp& firstprivate(niter,im,jm,a,b),shared(x)
          do 70 i=1,niter
            call adiloop(im,jm,x,a,b)
...
```

The variables a and b are read-only and, therefore, declared firstprivate. One thing to be cautious of in declaring firstprivate (or readonly) is the implicit overhead incurred by the compiler: storage overhead in declaring private copies and runtime overhead of copying-in from the original variable into temporary copies.

As an example of a local variable scoped as shared in an OpenMP construct, consider the following code fragment.

```
subroutine foo(x0,y0,x,y,n)
integer i,n
real*8 x0,y0,x(n),y(n),distmax
distmax = 0.0
!$omp parallel do private(i), firstprivate(x0,y0,n)
!$omp& shared(x,y), reduction(max:distmax)
do i=1,n
   distmax = max(distmax,((x(i)-x0)**2 + (y(i)-y0)**2))
enddo
!$omp end parallel do
.....
return
end
```

In this example, the local variable distmax is of the scope shared for the parallel do loop.

The default scoping of variables in OpenMP is shared; as a good programming practice we suggest using the default(none) directive and explicitly declaring all the variables as either shared or private. In large loops, it can be quite difficult to trace scalars not declared as private. In such cases, using default(none) can be quite helpful as illustrated in the following simple example.

```
        subroutine loop(m,n,x,a,b)
c example to illustrate default(none) scoping
c compile as f90 -openmp -c example_scope.f
        implicit none
        integer m,n,i,j
        real x(m,n),a,b
c$omp parallel do default(none)
c$omp& private(j,i), shared(x), firstprivate(a,m,n)
        do j=1,n-1
          do i=2,m
            x(i,j) = a*x(i,j)+b*x(i-1,j)
          enddo
        enddo
c$omp end parallel do
        return
        end
```

Compiling it as

```
example% f90 -x03 -openmp -c loop.f
            x(i,j) = a*x(i,j)+b*x(i-1,j)
                        ^
"loop.f", Line = 10, Column = 31: ERROR: Variable "B" must have
its data scope explicitly declared because DEFAULT(NONE) was
specified.
...
```

The compiler catches that the data scope for variable b was not specified and this can help identify subtle bugs in the program caused by incorrect data scoping.

Only a brief discussion of data scoping rules was presented. More information on this topic can be found in the book [Chandra00].

Memory Bandwidth Requirement

In the previous chapter and earlier sections of this chapter, we discussed the effects of data sharing, synchronization overhead, and load balance for parallel scaling of multithreaded applications. Another important issue is the memory bandwidth requirement of the application being parallelized and how it relates to the bandwidth available on the SMP system. Understanding the memory bandwidth requirement is quite important in parallelization of an application, regardless of the programming model (multiple threads or multiple processes) utilized.

As more threads are added in the parallel program, additional simultaneous requests for memory access (reads or writes) are generated, increasing the traffic on the system interconnect. Overall speedup depends on the system being able to satisfy independent memory requests generated by different processors. Eventually, a parallel application's bandwidth requirement might exceed what the hardware can deliver, and the application no longer scales, even if more processors run it. To illustrate how the memory bandwidth required in the application increases and eventually begins to saturate the memory bus, we consider the COPY kernel from the well-known STREAM benchmark [McCalpin95]. The test program is listed as follows.

CODE EXAMPLE 13-7 STREAM COPY Kernel

```
        program example_copy
! f90 -fast -openmp example_copy.f -o example_copy
        parameter (nmax=32*1024*1024, ntimes=20)
        real*8 a(nmax+8), b(nmax+8)
        integer*8 gethrtime
        external gethrtime
        integer*8 tstart, tend
        real*8 titer,bandw
        integer iter,i
        do i=1,nmax
           a(i) = i
           b(i) = 0.0
        enddo
        iter = nmax
        tstart = gethrtime()
        do i = 1,ntimes
           call vcopy(a,b,iter)
        enddo
        tend = gethrtime()
        titer = dble(tend - tstart) * 1.d-9
        bandw = (iter*ntimes)*16.0/titer
        print 1,iter,(titer*1d9)/(ntimes*iter),bandw/1.d9
```

CODE EXAMPLE 13-7 STREAM COPY Kernel *(Continued)*

```
1         format (i9,1x,1p2e14.6)
          end

          subroutine vcopy(a,b,iter)
          real*8 a(*), b(*)
          integer iter

c$omp parallel do shared(a,b) private(j)
          do 30 j = 1,iter
              b(j) = a(j)
   30     continue

          end
```

This kernel performs a copy of one array (with a total of 32 million entries) into another vector and involves only memory operations. The bandwidth is calculated based on an 8-byte load and an 8-byte store per element copy.

Because UltraSPARCII's external cache uses a write-allocate policy, a store miss causes the entire cache line (64 bytes) to be loaded first from the memory in the external cache. This means an extra load occurs per iteration (because the store array has to be first loaded in before it is written into). Therefore, the bandwidth[1] based on the actual interconnect traffic that occurs on the system in the case of COPY kernel can be calculated as:

Total Bandwidth = 1.5 × STREAM Bandwidth

Compiling the program as

```
example% f90 -fast -openmp example_copy.f -o a.copy
```

---

1. Non-allocating block load and store instructions can be used to eliminate this overhead (refer to VIS extension to SPARC instruction set).

We ran it on a 14-CPU Enterprise 4500 (running 400 MHz UltraSPARC II, 8 MB level 2-cache, and 100MHz gigaplane bus with 14 GB memory) for different values of OMP_NUM_THREADS and measured the bandwidth. It is listed in TABLE 13-6.

TABLE 13-6 Measured Bandwidth for STREAM COPY Kernel on 14-CPU Enterprise 4500

Number of CPUs	Measured STREAM COPY Bandwidth (in GB/sec)	Total STREAM COPY Bandwidth (in GB/sec)
1	0.29	0.44
2	0.57	0.85
4	0.99	1.49
6	1.25	1.88
8	1.44	2.16
10	1.53	2.30
12	1.53	2.30

From the table, we see how the bandwidth in this benchmark increases and eventually begins to saturate with the number of processors. While the Sun Enterprise server systems are designed to provide high memory bandwidth, it may vary with the amount of memory, number of CPUs, memory boards, and bank interleaving on the system (see Chapter 8). As such, our objective is not to report the best achievable numbers for this benchmark on this machine but to highlight the effect of system bandwidth on the application's performance.

Although for a large application it might be quite difficult to ascertain how its bandwidth requirements increase as a function of the number of processors, it is nevertheless quite important to understand this issue. We recommend creating kernel benchmarks that are representative of an application's memory access patterns, and using these to study application bandwidth requirements. That helps determine the suitability of a particular system to running the benchmark and help find the "sweet spot" for a configuration, maximizing the delivered bandwidth on the system under the desired workload.

OpenMP and P-threads

The OpenMP and P-threads APIs for shared memory parallelization of programs present developers with two powerful approaches. It is natural for the question to arise as to how to choose between the two when multithreading an application. A definitive answer to this question is quite difficult to provide and here we highlight some differences between the two approaches to help the reader choose the approach suitable to their problem (see also [Dagum98], [Kuhn99] and [Shah99]).

- *Parallelization of an existing program* – OpenMP provides a flexible approach to parallelize the program in an incremental fashion at loop level quite easily. By contrast in P-threads approach, the effort required is often considerably higher. For example, the function outlining automatically is done by the OpenMP compiler, whereas in P-threads approach, an equivalent operation has to be explicitly performed by the programmer.

- *Thread-safety and data scoping* – In OpenMP, because variables can be scoped as shared and private by using directives, making functions thread-safe is much easier compared to explicit threading. In P-threads, private variables need to be assembled in a separate data structure and one needs to pass a pointer to each thread's private copy to all the routines in the call chain. Similarly, pointers to shared variables might also be required to be passed to each thread. These may require substantial modifications to the serial program.

- *Performance* – The OpenMP specification is targeted towards parallelization of compute-bound applications. Many performance-enhancing features are provided. For example, there is support for atomic, barrier, and flush synchronization primitives (in addition to critical sections) which are not directly supported in P-thread APIs. Similarly, different loop scheduling schemes are supported.

- *Irregular applications* – Currently, there is no support (in OpenMP 1.1 specification) for handling programs where irregular tasks are dynamically spawned and destroyed. For example, this situation can occur in problems that use recursive or tree structure algorithms. The P-threads APIs are more suitable for such applications. OpenMP is also not suited for programs where exploiting concurrency (and not parallelism) is the objective.

- *Exception and signal handling* – The P-thread libraries and APIs have support for exception and signal handling capability in user programs, though it is tricky to implement (see [Kleinman96]). OpenMP does not provide for unstructured control flow to cross a parallel construct boundary, and exception handling is not supported directly in the standard. See [Kuhn99] for an example of exception handling based upon using a polling mechanism in the interrupt handler in an OpenMP program.

It should be clear to the reader that OpenMP and P-threads approaches are suited to different classes of programs. For example, loop-oriented programs such as these arising in computational fluid dynamics, structural analysis, seismic analysis, and others are quite well suited to the OpenMP approach. Applications such as discrete event simulation, branch and bound methods, client-server programs, adaptive mesh partitioning, and tree-based methods are more efficiently implemented using a P-threads approach.

Parallel Sun Performance Library

The Sun Performance Library, `libsunperf`, is a part of Forte for High Performance Computing and Sun Performance WorkShop products. It implements a variety of mathematical functions highly optimized for different SPARC architectures (see also Chapter 7). The functions provided in this library include the *Basic Linear Algebraic Subroutines* (BLAS), the LAPACK and LINPACK functions, as well as the fast Fourier transform calls from FFTPACK and VFFTPACK. Starting with Forte Developer 6 release, the Performance Library implements functions that operate on sparse matrices including support for sparse BLAS operations and sparse direct matrix factorization.

The versions of the library shipped with Forte for High Performance Computing are optimized for `v8`, `v8plus`, `v8plusa`, `v8plusb`, `v9a`, and `v9` architectures. All the functions in the library are thread safe and have interfaces for calls from Fortran 77, Fortran 95, and C.

We included the description of the Sun Performance Library in this chapter because some of the functions it implements are efficiently parallelized and can contribute to the parallel speedup of an application.

Linking the Library

To link a serial program with the Sun Performance Library, we need to use a special format.

```
example% f77 example.f ... -xlic_lib=sunperf
```

In Forte Developer 6 release, the library was built with Fortran 95 compiler and it uses the functions from the Fortran 95 libraries. Linking with `-xlic_lib` option ensures that all required libraries are included.

The library is provided in different versions optimized for various architectures located in corresponding subdirectories of the compiler installation location. It is important to use the -xarch setting at the linking stage, because it determines the version of the library used in the resulting executable. For example, to link the version optimized for v8plusb architecture, one can use:

```
example% cc example.c -xarch=v8plusb ... -xlic_lib=sunperf
```

The Sun Performance Library requires that all its arguments are aligned on the double-word boundaries, therefore applications that use the library should be compiled with the -dalign compiler option.

The Sun Performance Library provides parallelized implementations of many of its functions. Parallelization is implemented in two different ways suitable for programs that use either compiler parallelization or are explicitly multithreaded. The implementation is chosen based on the way the Sun Performance Library is linked in the application.

Programs built with compiler parallelization should link the Sun Performance Library with the -explicitpar, -autopar, or -parallel options. For example:

```
example% f95 -dalign -xarch=v8plusa -xparallel ... example.f90 \
        -xlic_lib=sunperf
```

Multithreaded programs should be linked with -mt option (discussed in Chapter 12.)

```
example% f77 -dalign -xarch=v8plusa -mt ... example.f \
        -xlic_lib=sunperf
```

Runtime Issues

The number of parallel threads used in Sun Performance Library calls is controlled by the PARALLEL environment variable. This setting can be overridden by specifying explicitly the number of threads with `libsunperf` routine USE_THREADS() in the source code of the program.

Sun Performance Library calls in the programs built with compiler parallelization use the same pool of threads used in other parallelized constructs and require the STACKSIZE environment variable to be set to at least 4 MB.

```
example% setenv STACKSIZE 4000
```

This setting is not required for multithreaded programs that use the Sun Performance Library. In this case, `libsunperf` creates its own threads with sufficiently large stacksizes.

The `libsunperf` calls do not get parallelized when they are contained within regions parallelized by the compiler. For example, in the following code fragment

```
C$PAR DOALL
      DO I=1,N
          CALL DGEMM(...)
      ENDDO
```

multiple serial DGEMM implementations are executed in parallel. Conversely, if the PARALLEL environment variable is set, then in the following loop (assuming that there are no parallel directives that encapsulate it), the parallel implementation of DGEMM executes.

```
      DO I=1,N
          CALL DGEMM(...)
      ENDDO
```

Two different synchronization mechanisms are implemented in the Sun Performance Library. When `libsunperf` is linked in an explicitly threaded application, it uses `libthread` synchronization primitives, which are relatively heavyweight, but they free the processor when the thread is idle, providing good throughput and resource usage in a shared environment. By contrast, when `libsunperf` is linked with the compiler parallelization options, it uses spin locks. The use of spin locks leads to more efficient synchronization, but also results in aggressive consumption of CPU cycles. The Sun Performance Library should be linked in this mode only in a dedicated execution environment.

As we mentioned earlier in this chapter, the environment variable SUNW_MP_THR_IDLE can be used to control the spin-wait characteristics at run time. For example, the following settings

```
example% setenv SUNW_MP_THR_IDLE spin
example% setenv SUNW_MP_THR_IDLE 100ms
example% setenv SUNW_MP_THR_IDLE sleep
```

causes thread to spin-wait (which is the default behavior), spin for 100 milliseconds before sleeping, or go to sleep immediately after completing the task.

64-bit Integer Arguments

Sun Performance Library supports 64-bit floating-point data types. The double precision and double complex arguments are used in functions whose names start with D and Z, respectively, for example, the DAXPY(3P) or ZAXPY(3P) functions. The v9, v9a, and v9b versions of the library also support 64-bit addressing. These versions provide additional interfaces for 64-bit integer arguments.

The 64-bit integer interfaces can be called by appending the suffix _64 to the standard library name. For example, using daxpy_64 in place of daxpy allows passing 64-bit integers to the daxpy function.

C programs should use long instead of int arguments in _64 versions of libsunperf calls. For example,

```
#include <sunperf.h>
long n, incx, incy;
double alpha, *x, *y;
daxpy_64(n, alpha, x, incx, y, incy);
```

instead of

```
#include <sunperf.h>
int  n, incx, incy;
double alpha, *x, *y;
daxpy   (n, alpha, x, incx, y, incy);
```

In Fortran, the corresponding arguments should be declared explicitly as INTEGER*8 instead of INTEGER*4, or with -xtypemap=integer:64... compiler option.

Fortran SUNPERF Module

The Sun Performance Library also provides a Fortran module for additional ease-of-use features with Fortran 90 or Fortran 95 programs. To use this module, the following line should be included in the source code of a program.

```
USE SUNPERF
```

This module allows simplifications in the calling sequences of libsunperf calls, based on data types of arguments. In particular, when a libsunperf function is called with 64-bit integer arguments, the appropriate implementation is used. Similarly, the type of the floating-point arguments determines the type of function called (prefixed with S, D, C, or Z for single-precision, double-precision, complex, and double-complex data types respectively).

In the following example, the function gemm is replaced with dgemm if the arguments are of type double, but it can also get replaced by sgemm if we compile it with -DSINGLE and pass single-precision arguments to the function.

CODE EXAMPLE 13-8 Type-Independent gemm Call

```
! example_gemm.F90
! f90 -xO4 -dalign -xarch=v8plus example_gemm.F90 -o example_gemm
! -stackvar (-explicitpar) -xlic_lib=sunperf (-DSINGLE) (-mt)
   use sunperf
   parameter (m=600,n=2000)
   integer (kind=8) gethrtime, time1, time2, timediff
#ifndef SINGLE
   real (kind=8) :: a(m,n),b(m,n),c(n,n),alpha=1.0d0,beta=1.0d0
#else
   real (kind=4) :: a(m,n),b(m,n),c(n,n),alpha=1.0e0,beta=1.0e0
#endif
!   initialization
   do i=1,n
      do j=1,m
         a(j,i)=0.3*i/j
         b(j,i)=a(j,i)+1.2
      enddo
      do j=1,n
         c(i,j)=0.4*i/j
      enddo
   enddo
   time1 = gethrtime()
   call gemm ('t', 'n', n, n, m, alpha, b, m, a, m, beta, c, n)
```

```
time2 = gethrtime()
print*,' c(1,1) = ', c(1,1)
print*,' Mflops = ', 2.0d0/(time2-time1)/(1.e-3)*m*n*n
print*, (time2-time1)/(1.0d9)," seconds"
end
```

If we compile this program and subsequently run it on a multiprocessor system, it benefits from parallelism of dgemm or sgemm calls without any parallelization effort at the application level. FIGURE 13-5 shows the scaling for this program on an Enterprise 6500 system (336 MHz UltraSPARCII processors with 4 MB level 2 cache, Solaris 2.6 operating system). A speedup of 16.4 on 20 processors is achieved.

```
example%  f90 -xO4 -dalign -xarch=v8plus -stackvar \
          -xlic_lib=sunperf -mt example_dgemm.F90 -o example_dgemm
```

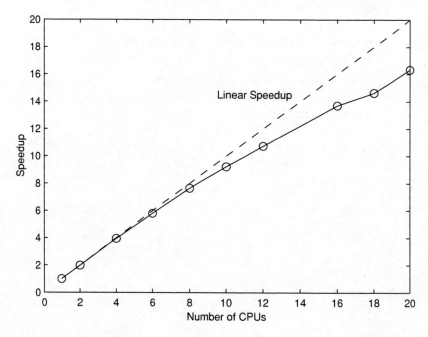

FIGURE 13-5 Scaling of dgemm Call in Sun Performance Library (Forte Developer 6 Update 1 Version)

Summary

Compiler-directed parallelization is a popular approach to exploit parallelism in a variety of applications, particularly loop-intensive programs. Sun compilers provide extensive support for both automatic parallelization as well as compiler-directive-based parallelization of Fortran and C programs.

For best performance, compiler options for automatic parallelization (-xautopar, -xparallel, -xreduction) should be used with dependency analysis option -xdepend and other aggressive serial optimization options (refer to Chapters 5 and 6). For Fortran programs, the -stackvar option is required.

In C programs, the -xrestrict option should be considered if pointer data types point to distinct memory locations. Similarly, the compiler's alias disambiguation analysis can be improved using the -xalias_level option. The environment variable SUNW_MP_THR_IDLE can be used to fine-tune performance for either throughput in a multiuser environment or turnaround in a dedicated environment. Also, special attention should be paid to the thread stack size, which can be controlled by the STACKSIZE environment variable.

For loop-based parallelization of programs, the choice of loop scheduling can have a significant impact on performance. While static scheduling is better from the point of view of data locality and lower synchronization overhead, guided and dynamic schemes are better suited for load-balancing. We showed with an example of triangular matrix multiply how a guided scheme demonstrated better speedup compared to static loop scheduling.

OpenMP provides flexibility for using different programming styles when multithreading a program. We illustrated section parallelism and SPMD programming styles with examples. Specifically, the SPMD style programming example was chosen to illustrate how the different programming styles can lead to different data access patterns, data affinities and scaling performance.

The importance of data scoping in OpenMP programs from correctness and performance point of view was discussed in detail. As a guideline, shared scoping should be associated with global variables and private scoping with local variables, keeping in mind the situations where exceptions to this rule occur. We also recommend the reader not rely on default scoping rules. Instead, it is better to use the default(none) scoping qualifier and explicitly declare all variables in a parallel construct with either shared or private scope.

Some tips on usage of synchronization functions, critical sections, atomics, flush, and the nowait qualifier were also outlined. The importance of estimating the memory bandwidth requirements of an application and how these relate to the hardware interconnect bandwidth was shown with the STREAM copy kernel example program. We also presented some pros and cons of the OpenMP and P-threads approaches for multithreading application programs.

Finally, we discussed the different features of the Sun Performance Library and illustrated its scalability on shared-memory parallel systems with an example.

CHAPTER **14**

Optimization of Message-Passing Programs

In previous chapters, we discussed parallelization of programs using explicit multithreading or compiler directives. The chapters described how to build threaded programs and presented performance aspects of parallel programming with threads.

Despite the advantages of the multithreading model, its applicability is limited to cache-coherent shared address space systems. Parallel programming for clusters of SMP systems (distributed address space) requires a multiprocess approach. Communication between processes can be accomplished by different means, such as remote shared memory or socket connections. In recent years, an industry-wide message-passing standard, the *Message Passing Interface* (MPI), has become common for programming in a distributed memory environment. The first version of the MPI standard, MPI-1, was released in 1993-1994. The current version of the standard, MPI-2, was released in 1997. The official standard documents for various MPI releases are available on the internet at `http://www.mpi-forum.org`.

In this chapter, we give an overview of MPI programming models and describe features of the Sun MPI implementation. We outline how to build and run MPI programs with Sun ClusterTools software. The effects of Sun MPI environment variable settings on the performance of MPI applications are also discussed. The focus is on the issues specific to the performance of MPI programs, such as communication between processes and synchronization overhead. Another component of the ClusterTools package, the Sun Scalable Scientific Subroutine Library (S3L), which is a collection of message-passing implementations of standard computational subroutines, including ScaLAPACK calls, is also discussed. (The use of the Prism environment for debugging and profiling MPI programs is described in Chapter 11). This chapter closes with a discussion of comparative advantages and disadvantages of MPI and OpenMP programming for parallelization.

Programming Models and Performance Considerations

The MPI standard facilitates implementation of the explicit message-passing model. In this model, groups of computational tasks perform part of a program's work and cooperate with each other by explicitly sending and receiving messages. The distribution of the work can be performed by using data, functional, or hybrid decomposition (see Chapter 10). The computational task is process-based, that is, parallelization is based on multiple processes with independent address spaces, rather than on multiple threads sharing a single address space. The two important concepts in designing message-passing programs are *organization of the computing tasks* and *distribution of workload* (see [Geist95] and [Gropp99]). The performance of a message-passing program is closely tied to these concepts as they affect the programming and implementation complexity, communication and synchronization requirements, ratio of computation to communication, and load balancing among computing tasks in a parallel program.

The communication requirements in a message-passing parallel application can be characterized by ([Singh94] and [Sivasubramaniam95]):

- *Volume*: The size and number of messages exchanged in a program.
- *Frequency*: The frequency with which message exchange requests are generated by a parallel task, that is, the time interval between successive network accesses by each task. It also includes the interleaving in time of accesses from different tasks and essentially pertains to the temporal nature of communication in the application. The frequency of communication has a significant impact on contention for network resources.
- *Communication Pattern*: The structure of source-destination pairs for message passing. The pattern determines how well the application exploits the network topology. For example, the NEWS (north, east, west, south) nearest neighbor exchange communication pattern on a 2D mesh (such as arising in many finite-difference applications) maps perfectly on a 2D Torus network topology (see [Hennessy96]).
- *Tolerance*: The ability of an application to overlap communication with computation and hide network overheads.

The volume and communication pattern can be collectively thought of as related to the spatial nature of the communication in the application. As we discuss in this section, the organization of computing tasks and workload distribution can have a significant impact on the attributes of application communication.

The organization of the computing tasks can be done in several ways. The most common approach is the *crowd* ([Geist95]) or *SPMD* model (see Chapter 10), in which different processes (asynchronously) run separate copies of the same program, performing computations on different portions of program data. The processes exchange information and intermediate results as necessary during the course of the computation. The SPMD model can be implemented as either a *master-slave* (or *host-node*) model or a *node-only* model. The master-slave SPMD message-passing model is conceptually similar to the master-slave model that we discussed in Chapter 12 for explicit multithreading. A master process controls the initialization, work distribution, collection of results, and I/O, while the slave processes perform the computation. In the node-only model, all processes participate in the execution of the program workload using either static or dynamic work distribution.

The second approach for organizing computational tasks is the *MPMD* model. It is also referred to as the *tree* computing model ([Geist95]). In this model, the different tasks could be executing different programs and cooperate with each other by exchanging messages. The processes could be created once in the beginning or dynamically spawned during the course of the computation. They could also be preexisting (started independently) and connect at some point during their execution to exchange intermediate results needed for further progress in their execution. The support for dynamic process management in the MPI-2 standard[1] makes it convenient to implement the MPMD model using MPI. The dynamic process spawn capability in Sun MPI implementation is illustrated later in this chapter.

One can also combine these two models to create a hybrid structure of computing tasks, where groups of processes structured in SPMD style could be dynamically spawned (or connected in case of preexisting groups) in MPMD style.

Workload Distribution

Two approaches to workload distribution are commonly used: functional decomposition and data decomposition [Foster95]. Functional decomposition entails division of work based on performing different operations or functions in parallel tasks. In contrast, in data decomposition, the parallel tasks perform similar computational operations but operate on different portions of a program's data structures.

The functional decomposition approach can be implemented either as separate programs representing different stages of an application being executed by different parallel tasks, or as parallel tasks executing different modules or subalgorithms within the same program. It may also involve spawning new tasks dynamically. The

---

1. See [Gropp00] for an overview of MPI-2 standard.

pipeline model discussed in Chapter 12 can be considered as an example of the functional decomposition approach. The dynamic process management features in MPI-2 facilitate implementation of functional decomposition in MPI programs.

The data decomposition approach has been the more popular between the two in message-passing scientific HPC applications.

Data decomposition can be either performed statically or dynamically. As the name implies, the case where each parallel task's share of the workload is fixed during the duration of the computation is called *static data decomposition*. In the case of *dynamic data decomposition*, the workload distribution is performed at runtime and the portion of data that each task works on may change as the program executes. For example, in the master-slave model, the master process might allocate work portions to different slave processes at runtime; this allocation might depend on the inputs to the program and vary from one run to next. The static and dynamic data partitioning can also be thought of as being related to the concepts of static and dynamic scheduling of parallel tasks. Due to inherent complexity in its implementation, dynamic scheduling is less commonly used in message-passing programs and more commonly in explicitly multithreaded programs (the worker-crew model that we discussed in Chapter 12 is well suited to dynamic task scheduling).

In the remainder of this section, some common techniques for static data partitioning in scientific applications are described.

Scientific applications such as those arising in fluid dynamics, elasticity, seismic, electromagnetics, and other areas usually involve solution of partial differential equations on a prescribed problem domain. Typically, the equations are solved by discretizing them on numerical meshes (also referred to as computational grids). In such applications, the data structures representing the known and unknown quantities of the physical simulation correspond to values defined on the grid points, and data decomposition is equivalent to decomposition of the computational domain (see [Chan94] for a survey of iterative methods based on domain decomposition). Be aware of the distinction between data decomposition and domain decomposition, as there are other classes of applications such as those arising in molecular dynamics, robotics, pattern recognition, linear programming, and N-body methods which are not solved on a computational grid or a prescribed domain.

The mesh-based applications can be further divided based on mesh structure, computational kernels, and spatial and temporal discretization techniques ([Sarukkai95]). The mesh structure could be structured grids or unstructured. The spatial discretization could be based on a local method (finite difference, finite volume, and finite element) or a global method (spectral representation, a panel method, and others). Similarly, temporal discretization could be either based on explicit time-advancement schemes (such as Adams-Bashforth, Runge-Kutta) or implicit schemes (for example implicit Euler or Crank-Nicolson).

A direct or iterative matrix system solution technique might be used to solve the discretized matrix system. The choice of the technique is also influenced by whether a steady-state or transient solution is desired. Further, different computational kernels (for example FFTs) might arise depending on the spatial and temporal discretization algorithms. All of these lead to different data dependencies and grid connectivities in the numerical scheme and, accordingly, different domain decomposition schemes are suitable for the parallel implementation.

In what follows, we discuss some commonly used approaches for partitioning structured and unstructured grids (methods for domain decomposition in spatial directions). In iterative solutions of certain problems, partitioning can be applied such that it exploits parallelism in the time (or iteration index) direction and the computation for several successive iterations is performed in parallel. These techniques are not covered in this book. See [Ferziger99] for a discussion on application of time-parallel techniques in computational fluid dynamics.

For structured grid-based applications, a classification of data dependencies arising in different algorithms based on their parallelization potential is very helpful in analyzing the parallel efficiency of different domain decomposition schemes. [Naik93] presented one such classification:

- *Parallel by point*: In these algorithms, the computations at each grid point can be performed independently of the computation at other grid points. These are also called "data-parallel" calculations. Examples are explicit time advancement schemes (for example multistage Runge-Kutta methods) and point-iterative methods such as the Jacobi scheme.

- *Parallel by line*: In these algorithms the computations at a grid point are coupled to other grid points in a fixed direction but are independent of the computations at grid points on other lines in that direction. Examples are algorithms such as line relaxation iterative schemes, multicolor (for example red-black) iterative schemes, ADI schemes, and others.

- *Parallel by plane*: These data dependencies are hardest to parallelize. In this case, the computation involves data dependencies that span two or more dimensions. Examples are LU factorization and Line Gauss-Seidel iterative methods.

The two main approaches for partitioning the domain of structured grid computations are *unipartition* schemes and *multipartition* schemes. These are schematically shown in FIGURE 14-1, where the transpose partitioning approach is also shown. The figure also shows 1D and 2D variants of the unipartitioning scheme.

In the unipartitioning scheme, the computational domain is subdivided into P partitions (P is total number of processors) and each partition assigned to one processor. The domain could be evenly partitioned along one direction, along two directions, or all three directions, which lead to 1D, 2D, and 3D variants of unipartitioning. Since each processor is assigned one chunk of the domain, the scheduling of computations within a processor is relatively straightforward. While it reduces communication and memory overhead, unipartitioning is not suitable for computations with data dependency along the direction of partitioning (parallel by line and parallel by plane dependencies). Further, because domain is so coarsely divided, achieving balanced load across subpartitions is difficult.

The spatial nature of communication between 1D, 2D, and 3D unipartitions is quite different. In the 2D case (as opposed to 1D case), the number of messages exchanged and the number of neighbors of a given processor are higher, but the message size (proportional to subpartition interface area) is smaller.

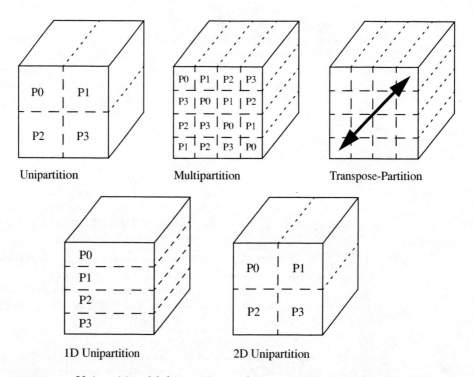

FIGURE 14-1 Unipartition, Multipartition, and Transpose-Partition Schemes for Domain Decomposition of Structured Grid Computations

In the multipartition scheme, the domain is split into subpartitions such that there are more partitions than processors, and each processor is assigned more than one subpartition (see FIGURE 14-1). An advantage of multipartitioning is that it reduces the data dependency delays characteristic of parallel-by-line methods. It also allows better load balancing by more finely distributing the work, because each subpartition covers a smaller extent of the computational domain, compared to subpartitions in unipartitioning schemes. An interesting effect of the 2D multipartition scheme[1] is that each processor has the same two neighbors. This can

---

1. One can have a 3D variant of multipartition schemes also (see [Naik93]).

be exploited by the communication network to decrease contention. Compared to unipartitioning schemes, multipartition schemes entail more message exchanges and are conceptually harder to implement.

Another variation of partitioning is the case where processors are initially partitioned in only one direction as in 1D unipartitioning. The partition direction is chosen in a way that in the first stage of computation no interprocessor communication takes place. Thereafter, the data are transposed such that in the next phase of calculations no communication is required. There is, however, a massive global exchange communication required in the transposition stage. The advantages of this method are implementation ease as communication and computation stages are completely separated. It is often an effective technique to parallelize a legacy application without substantial changes in the program source. The global transpose can be accomplished with $O(P^2)$ messages (P is the number of processors), which might not be large compared to the frequency and number of messages required in uni- and multipartition techniques. However, the size of messages in transpose is large because it is often used with 1D unipartitioning. In the 1D unipartitioning case, fewer transposes are required compared to 2D unipartitioning, and it is therefore the preferred approach for transpose method. One common application of transpose method is multidimensional FFTs (as used in NAS Parallel Benchmark FT, [Bailey94]).

We now briefly mention some approaches for domain decomposition in unstructured grid computations. Unstructured grid computations arise in applications such as structural analysis based on finite element methods or fluid dynamic analysis using finite volume methods. The partitioning methods used for unstructured meshes are based on a graph theoretical approach. Given a domain and number of processors, P, the domain decomposition algorithm's goal is to partition the domain in P parts so as to minimize load imbalance and communication. Minimizing communication is dependent on the boundary length of subdomains and also the number of neighboring subdomains. In the graph theoretical context, the domain decomposition problem becomes equivalent to partitioning the vertices of an undirected graph in P roughly equal parts, such that the number of edges connecting the vertices in different parts is minimized. It is well-known that this problem is NP-complete and researchers have developed many heuristic approaches, such as *recursive coordinate bisection (RCB)*, *recursive graph bisection (RGB)*, *recursive spectral bisection (RSB)*, and *multilevel nested dissection partitioning* (see [Pothen90], [Karypis99]). For all these algorithms, the domain is first subdivided into two optimal partitions, then the same algorithm is repeated recursively (divide-and-conquer) on each subpartition until a total of P partitions is obtained.

In the RCB technique, the vertices are sorted by the coordinate (x, y, or z) in the direction in which the domain is longest, then half of the vertices are assigned in one subdomain. This approach is repeated recursively on each subdomain. RCB is good for computations with local communication, yet is not suitable in cases where global or longer distance communication occurs. It has been shown to produce disconnected and long, skinny domains leading to increased communication. The weakness of the RCB algorithm is that it does not take advantage of the connectivity information given by the graph.

In the RGB approach, the Euclidean distance between two connected vertices in the graph is used to sort vertices, thereby incorporating the connectivity information. Half of sorted vertices are assigned to one partition and the other half to the other partition. This is then repeated recursively to obtain P partitions.

The RSB algorithm is quite different from these two approaches. It is derived from a graph bisection strategy developed in [Pothen90], which is based on the computation of a specific eigenvector of the Laplacian matrix of the graph. The second eigenvector of the Laplacian matrix of the graph is computed and vertices sorted according to size of entries in this vector. Again, half the vertices are assigned to one subdomain and the method is recursively repeated. RSB and its derivative approach, *spectral nested dissection* ([Pothen92]), have become quite popular and shown to be considerably superior to the RCB and RGB algorithms ([Simon91] and [Chan97]).

Recently, the *multilevel nested dissection* approach has become popular and has been shown to produce better quality partitions than RSB in significantly lower runtime. In multilevel graph partitioning, the size of graph is reduced (that is, the graph is coarsened) by collapsing the vertices and edges, partitioning is applied at the coarsest level, then it is uncoarsened to construct a partition for the original graph. See [Karypis99] and references therein for further information. A similar approach that applies the multilevel subspace correction method to the eigenvalue problem arising in spectral bisection is discussed in [Sharapov97].

Pipeline Method

For algorithms that exhibit parallel-by-line data dependencies, another commonly used approach for parallelization is pipelining. When a number of independent tasks, each of which is sequential in nature (that is, has data dependence in one or more directions) is executed, then pipelining can be quite effective at extracting parallelism out of these tasks. A well-known example is solution of large numbers of banded matrix equations such as those arising in approximate factorization algorithms for solution of partial differential equations (see [VanderWijngaart93]) or hybrid spectral finite difference algorithms in computational fluid dynamics (see [Garg95] and [Garg97]). Pipelining is straightforward to implement and requires small message sizes due to small interface areas. Its disadvantages are a large number of small messages (which leads to high message-passing overhead), pipeline fill-up and drain-down delays, boundary effects, and processor interrupt skews ([VanderWijngaart96]).

We illustrate the pipeline method with a simple example involving solution of a large number of tridiagonal systems of equations. Recall that solving a tridiagonal system of equations involves a serializing data dependency (see [Press92]), which inhibits parallelization. The pipeline technique is schematically represented in FIGURE 14-2. Only the fill-up stage is shown in the figure; there is a similar drain-down stage at the end of the pipeline calculation. Once the pipeline fills up, all the processors become busy and parallelization is achieved. The load imbalance in the computation occurs mainly in the fill-up and drain-down stages.

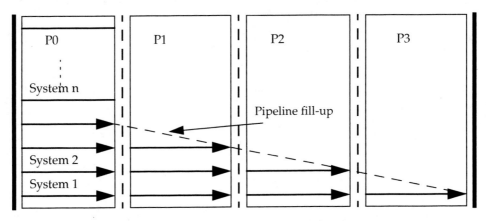

FIGURE 14-2 Pipeline Method to Parallelize Methods With Data Dependencies

The program `example_thpip.f` implements a pipelined tridiagonal solver. In the interest of conserving space, the complete listing of the program is not given here. It is included in the collection of example programs. The reader is encouraged to download the program and examine it. We list routines `tridvsf` and `tridvss`, which are the forward elimination and back-substitution stages in the solver, respectively. Note how the pipeline is established. In this example, we used `mpi_send()` and `mpi_recv()` functions. The reader is encouraged to modify the program and try the nonblocking calls `mpi_isend()`, `mpi_irecv()`, and `mpi_sendrecv()`.

CODE EXAMPLE 14-1 Forward Elimination and Backward Substitution Routines in Pipelined Tridiagonal Solver Program *(1 of 3)*

```
...
          subroutine tridvsf(a,b,c,f,np,pznum,nmodp,k_st,len,me)
c factorization stage of parallel Thomas algo.
c a,b,c,f are the portions of the vectors stored on each node
c np:  Nz/pznum (Nz: no. of unknowns, pznum: no of Proc. in z)
c nmodp: Nz modulo pznum; len: num. of independent systems
c k_st: starting index for forward elimination
```

```
c smsg: message packet send, contains (b,c,f)_np
c rmsg: message packet recd, contains (b,c,p)_np (from node p+1)
c me: my MPI process-id

      implicit double precision(a-h,o-z)
      include 'mpif.h'
      integer pznum,np,nmodp,itag,ireq
      integer istatus(MPI_STATUS_SIZE)
      dimension a(np+nmodp,len),b(np+nmodp,len)
      dimension c(np+nmodp,len),f(np+nmodp,len)
      dimension smsg(3),rmsg(3)

      if(pznum.eq.1)then       ! do serial fwd. elim.
         do 5 i=1,len
            call fwdloop(i,a,b,c,f,smsg,np,nmodp,
     &            k_st,np)
5        continue
      else                     ! do parallel fwd. elim.
       k1=2
       k2=np
       if (me.eq.(pznum-1)) k1=k_st
       if (me.eq.0) k2=np+nmodp
       do i=1,len
        if(me.lt.(pznum-1)) then
            call mpi_recv(rmsg,3,MPI_DOUBLE_PRECISION,
     &          me+1,me+1,MPI_COMM_WORLD,istatus,ierr)
          b(1,i)=b(1,i)-a(1,i)*rmsg(2)/rmsg(1)
          f(1,i)=f(1,i)-a(1,i)*rmsg(3)/rmsg(1)
        endif
         call fwdloop(i,a,b,c,f,smsg,np,nmodp,k1,k2)
        if (me.gt.0) then
          call mpi_send(smsg,3,MPI_DOUBLE_PRECISION,
     &          me-1,me,MPI_COMM_WORLD,ierr)
        endif
       enddo
       call mpi_barrier(MPI_COMM_WORLD,ierr)
      endif   ! of if (pznum.eq.1) statement

      return
      end

      subroutine tridvss(b,c,f,x,np,pznum,nmodp,len,me)
c solution stage of parallel Thomas algo.
```

```
c b,c,f,x are the portions of the vectors stored on each node
c me: my MPI process-id

        implicit double precision(a-h,o-z)
        include 'mpif.h'
        integer pznum,np,nmodp,itag,ireq
        integer istatus(MPI_STATUS_SIZE)
        dimension x(np+nmodp,len),b(np+nmodp,len)
        dimension c(np+nmodp,len),f(np+nmodp,len)

        n1=np+nmodp
        k1=np-1
        if(pznum.eq.1)then     ! do serial back substitution
          do i=1,len
            x(np,i)=f(np,i)/b(np,i)
            call bckloop(i,b,c,f,x,n1,k1)
          enddo
        else                   ! do parallel back-subs
         do i=1,len
          if(me.eq.0)then
            x(np+nmodp,i)=f(np+nmodp,i)/b(np+nmodp,i)
            k1=np+nmodp-1
          else
            call mpi_recv(x(np,i),1,MPI_DOUBLE_PRECISION,
     &             me-1,me-1,MPI_COMM_WORLD,istatus,ierr)

            x(np,i)=(f(np,i)-c(np,i)*x(np,i))/b(np,i)
          endif
            call bckloop(i,b,c,f,x,n1,k1)
          if(me.lt.(pznum-1))then
            call mpi_send(x(1,i),1,MPI_DOUBLE_PRECISION,
     &           me+1,me,MPI_COMM_WORLD,ierr)
          endif
         enddo
         call mpi_barrier(MPI_COMM_WORLD,ierr)
        endif     ! of if (pznum.eq.1) statement

        return
        end
...
```

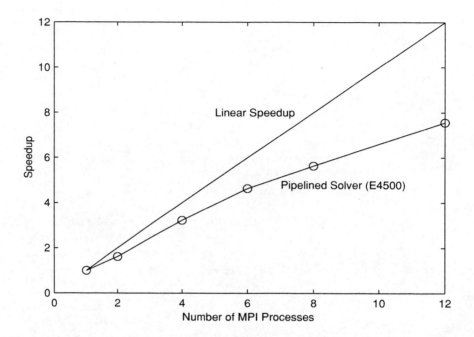

FIGURE 14-3 Speedup of Pipelined Tridiagonal Solver on a 12-Processor Enterprise 4500 System

The program is compiled with Forte Developer 6 compilers and HPC 3.1 ClusterTools release as (we discuss details of building MPI programs in the next section):

```
example% mpf90 -fast example_thpip.f -lmpi -o a.out
```

The reader can use the script `thpip.csh` (available with the program) to compile and run automatically for a different number of processors. FIGURE 14-3 shows the speedup from running the program (with parameters `kmax=4096, len=8193` in `example_thpip.f` program) on a 12-processor Enterprise 4500 system. As we can see, the speedup efficiency is around 63% with 12 processors and shows a sublinear trend. While these results show the viability of the pipelining approach, the example program should not be used in production code. For the purposes of illustration simplicity the program is written so that a separate message is exchanged for every line solve, which leads to the program suffering from worst possible message-passing latency for this algorithm. In production code, the message-passing latency effects can be considerably reduced by packing several solves together in a single message (see [Naik93] and [Garg97]). The optimal packing parameter can be determined based on the consideration of balancing the increased pipeline overheads (time spent in fill-up and drain-down stages) with the decrease in number of messages that are exchanged. A common optimization for decreasing pipeline overhead is two-way pipelining, that is, starting the solves from both ends of the computational system [Walshaw93].

Loop Parallelization Methods

The discussion of domain decomposition presented so far is targeted in general towards a coarse-grained parallelization of the algorithm using MPI. There are also programs where fine-grained parallelization in a manner similar to compiler directive-based loop-level parallelization (Chapter 13) might be required. Parallelization at the loop granularity level in MPI can also be performed in a straightforward manner, and one can schedule iterations of the loop using various schemes such as block, cyclic, guided, and others, as we discussed for compiler directives in Chapter 13. We illustrate the implementation of block and cyclic loop scheduling using MPI with a simple program that is representative of particle force calculation in molecular dynamics. The listing of the program example_force.F90 is shown in CODE EXAMPLE 14-2. The bulk of computation occurs in the doubly nested loops of the form:

```
do i=1,idim-1
do j=i+1,idim
.....
```

This range of (i,j) iterations represents accessing the upper triangle of an idim × idim array and the loops are not suitable for block distribution of iterations due to load imbalance. The cyclic distribution, where the loop iterations are interleaved across different processors, performs much better in terms of load balancing. The program is written such that arrays are not split across processors and all communication occurs in a single call to the mpi_allreduce() function.

CODE EXAMPLE 14-2 Loop Parallelization Methods in MPI *(1 of 3)*

```
program force
! mpf90 -fast -DBLOCKD example_force.F90 -o a.block -lmpi
! mpf90 -fast example_force.F90 -o a.cyclic -lmpi
    implicit double precision(a-h,o-z)
    include 'mpif.h'
    parameter (idim=50000,nrep=1)
    real*8 x(idim),f(idim),tmp(idim)
    integer me,nproc,ierr

    call MPI_INIT(ierr)
```

```
      call MPI_COMM_RANK(MPI_COMM_WORLD, me, ierr)
      call MPI_COMM_SIZE(MPI_COMM_WORLD, nproc, ierr)

      do i=1,idim
         x(i) = i*(100.0/(idim-1))
      enddo
#ifdef BLOCKD
      nmod = (idim-1) - ((idim-1)/nproc)*nproc
      ist = 1 + me*((idim-1)/nproc)
      ien = ist + ((idim-1)/nproc) -1
      if (me.eq.(nproc-1)) ien = ien + nmod
#endif

      call mpi_barrier(MPI_COMM_WORLD,ierr)
      time_i = mpi_wtime()

      do n=1,nrep
        do i=1,idim
           f(i) = 0.0
           tmp(i) = 0.0
        enddo
#ifdef BLOCKD
        do i=ist,ien
#else
        do i=1+me,idim-1,nproc
#endif
          do j=i+1,idim
             dum = 1.0/(x(j)-x(i))
             f(i) = f(i) + dum
             f(j) = f(j) - dum
          enddo
        enddo
        call mpi_allreduce(f,tmp,idim,MPI_DOUBLE_PRECISION, &
            MPI_SUM,MPI_COMM_WORLD,ierr)
        do i=1,idim
           x(i) = x(i) + tmp(i)
enddo
        enddo

      time_f = mpi_wtime() - time_i
      call mpi_reduce(time_f,timem,1,MPI_DOUBLE_PRECISION,  &
          MPI_MAX,0,MPI_COMM_WORLD,ierr)
```

```
      if(me.eq.0) write(10,100) nproc,timem
 100      format('P= ',i4,' Time= ',f12.4)

      call mpi_finalize(ierr)
      stop
      end
```

We compiled this program using HPC 3.1 ClusterTools release and Forte Developer 6 compilers as

```
example% mpf90 -fast example_force.F90 -lmpi -o a.cyclic
example% mpf90 -fast -DBLOCKD example_force.F90 -lmpi -o a.block
```

and ran it on a 12-processor Enterprise 4500 system and on a Sun Technical Compute Farm (TCF), comprised of 50 Enterprise 420R clustered systems. Each 420R system is a 4-processor SMP system (450MHz UltraSPARC-II, 4MB level 2 cache, Solaris 8). See Chapter 2 for additional description of Sun TCF systems.

Note that on the TCF system, the jobs were run such that only one MPI process was allocated on each Enterprise 420R system. Thus, all MPI communication occurred over the TCP/IP-based network connection in the compute farm. This was done using the -Ns option of the mprun command (the mprun command is discussed later in the chapter). For example, in the following command each of the four MPI processes are scheduled on a different node of the TCF system.

```
example% mprun -Ns -np 4 a.cyclic
```

The scripts used for running the program are available with the program source.

The scaling results are shown in FIGURE 14-4 for both the block and cyclic loop distributions. As expected, the speedups with cyclic distribution are significantly better than the block distribution on both systems. The total runtime is dominated by the computational time for the range of processors used in the runs (that is, communication time is a small fraction of the computation time). The speedups are therefore comparable on both the Enterprise 4500 and TCF systems. The slight differences occur due to the computational differences (TCF used a 450MHz UltraSPARC-II processor with 4 MB level 2 cache, while Enterprise 4500 used a 400 MHz UltraSPARC-II processor with 8 MB level 2 cache) and the communication differences (nodes in TCF communicated over TCP network, while in 4500 the communication occurred over the Gigaplane interconnect) between the two systems.

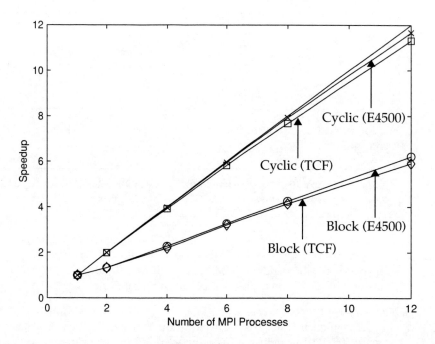

FIGURE 14-4 Scaling for Different Loop Parallelization Methods With MPI

Communication Metrics

Point-to-point communication is the core of most communication libraries and most commonly used MPI functions in message-passing programs are point-to-point communication functions. The simplest performance model for point-to-point communication is based upon a linear dependence of transfer time on the message size:

transfer time = (start-up time) + (message-size / bandwidth-rate)

Here, *start-up time* is the time required to send a null-length message, also referred to as *latency* in message-passing literature (for example, see [Hockney93]). To avoid confusion with the more conventional definition of *latency* (for example, as defined in [Hennessy96]), we refer to the transfer time for null-length message as *start-up time* in this text. In the equation, *bandwidth-rate* is the asymptotic rate for sending very long messages. In the limit of infinitely long messages, it is equal to *Total Bandwidth* defined as

Total Bandwidth = message-size/transfer time

Two other useful concepts are *overhead* and *bisection bandwidth*. Overhead is the amount of communication time that cannot be hidden by asynchronous communication[1]. Bisection bandwidth is the sum of bandwidths of connections generated when the interconnection network is divided in two. It measures the aggregate bandwidth a system can deliver.

There are many ways to measure these metrics. Some commonly used techniques are token ring benchmark [Saphir94], ping-pong benchmark [Hockney93], and saturation benchmark. We present ping-pong benchmark results later in this chapter using the Sun MPI library.

Sun MPI Implementation

The Sun HPC ClusterTools package includes a highly optimized implementation of the MPI standard which provides support for C, C++, Fortran 77, and Fortran 90. The Sun MPI library implements all routines defined in MPI 1.1 standard (available at http://www.mpi-forum.org/) and a subset of MPI 2 routines. The applications built with Sun MPI run on a single SMP system as well as on a cluster of SMP machines.

Some of the salient features of the Sun MPI implementation are as follows:

- Thread-safety.
- Support for Cluster Runtime Environment (CRE), Load Sharing Facility (LSF) and other job-scheduling software tools.
- Support for Prism performance monitoring and debugging environment.
- Optimized collective communication for SMP and clusters of SMPs.
- Numerous environment variables for fine-tuning communication performance.
- Support for MPI-2 features (MPI I/O, dynamic process spawn, and limited support of one-sided communication).
- Process yielding and coscheduling to decrease performance degradation in oversubscribed runs.

Sun MPI has the ability to select different communication protocols. For example, on an SMP node, the Sun MPI library takes advantage of the hardware and operating system to use shared memory support for message passing between MPI processes. In a clustered environment, for message passing between processes on different nodes, the library can either use Remote Shared Memory (RSM) for Scalable Coherent Interface (SCI) based clusters or the standard TCP protocol for any other commonly used interconnects, such as Ethernet, ATM, or FDDI.

1. Overlap of communication and computation is not possible for the current generation of Sun multiprocessor systems and the Sun MPI implementation.

The Sun MPI library also has support for process yielding and coscheduling to decrease the effects of busy-waiting and to improve system throughput. In yielding mode, the MPI process yields the usage of the processor, whereas in coscheduling, a group of related processes are scheduled (or descheduled) approximately simultaneously (via the `spind` daemon in ClusterTools software). Coscheduling has a higher overhead compared to yielding, but results in better resource usage in oversubscribed systems. Sun MPI also implements a progress engine to support better nonblocking point-to-point message passing. Finally, a variety of algorithms are used for message exchanges between MPI processes. For example, in the shared memory environment, different algorithms are used depending on the sizes of the messages and environment variables are available to tune this behavior.

There is also support for both eager and rendezvous message exchange protocols (see [Gropp99]). The collectives have also been highly optimized and use different algorithms depending on whether the operation is being performed between processes on an SMP node or between processes on different nodes of a cluster (see [Sistare99b]). The algorithms have been designed to take advantage of any groupings of processes on the nodes of a cluster.

Additional information on Sun MPI implementation can be found in *Sun MPI 4.1 Programming and Reference Guide*.

The cost of interprocess synchronization resulting from explicit synchronization, computational load imbalance, or from implicit synchronization (in point-to-point message passing) is a large component of the overhead in MPI programs. For obtaining high performance in MPI programs with the Sun MPI implementation, one should look at issues related to synchronization overhead, buffering, polling, data packing, and use of optimized collectives. Restructuring the program such that frequency and volume of communication are decreased is an obvious way to improve communication performance. Some general good practices to follow when using MPI communication APIs are listed as follows. Consult *Sun HPC ClusterTools 3.1 Performance Guide* for additional details.

- Decrease the amount of explicit synchronization in the program. This requires reducing number of `MPI_Barrier()` calls and collective operations such as `MPI_Allreduce()` and `MPI_Bcast()`.

- Use of `MPI_Ssend()` and `MPI_Rsend()` should be avoided. These may require additional synchronization overhead and cause performance degradation.

- Communication calls requiring explicit buffering should be avoided as they lead to additional cost of local memory copies. However, if buffering is required, consider using `MPI_Bsend()`. A well-written program should not rely on standard sends (that is `MPI_Send()` calls) to provide needed buffering when large messages are being exchanged.

- Use of nonblocking message passing calls should be considered. The sends should be posted ahead of receives to the extent possible. For example, one way to use nonblocking calls is

```
m1 = MPI_Isend(buffer1, dest1)   ! send buffer1 to dest 1
...perform computation...
m2 = MPI_Irecv(buffer2, src1)    ! receive buffer2 from src 1
...perform computation...
call MPI_Wait(m2)   ! wait for completion of recv
call MPI_Wait(m1)   ! wait for completion of send
```

Note, MPI_Wait() calls can be replaced by any of its variants: MPI_Waitall(), MPI_Waitany(), or MPI_Waitsome().

- The program should avoid MPI_ANY_SOURCE and post only specific receives. Further, calls such as MPI_Probe() and MPI_Iprobe() should be used as little as possible. The receives should be posted in the same order as the corresponding sends.

- Sun MPI environment variables should be tuned to provide sufficient system buffering, suppress message polling, and turn off synchronizing message exchange protocols. A detailed discussion on tuning of Sun MPI environment variables is presented later in the chapter.

In the remainder of this section, we describe steps involved in building and running MPI programs in the HPC ClusterTools environment. We also illustrate usage of two important features of MPI-2 standard, namely, dynamic process management and MPI I/O in the Sun MPI implementation.

Building and Running MPI Programs

We recommend the reader follow instructions in the *Sun HPC ClusterTools 3.1 Installation Guide* and the *Sun HPC ClusterTools 3.1 Administrator's Guide* for installation of the software, settings of the /etc/system file, starting the node daemons, and configuring the Sun HPC cluster with /opt/SUNWhpc/conf/hpc.conf file. Once this procedure is complete, the status of the nodes in the cluster can be monitored with mpinfo -N command.

The default location for the Sun HPC ClusterTools software is /opt/SUNWhpc and the ClusterTools commands are located in the /opt/SUNWhpc/bin subdirectory. The MPI library, libmpi, can be found in the /opt/SUNWhpc/lib directory with the 64-bit version in the sparcv9 subdirectory. For both 32-bit and 64-bit implementations of the MPI library, two additional versions are available, the thread safe-version libmpi_mt and the version built with TNF probes (see Chapter 11) provided in the tnf subdirectory.

The include files for the MPI programs are located in the /opt/SUNWhpc/include directory. The mpi.h file should be included in all C and C++ programs that make MPI calls. Fortran programs use the mpif.h include file.

Sun HPC ClusterTools software provides scripts that facilitate compilation and linking of MPI programs. Fortran 77, Fortran 90, C, and C++ programs can be compiled with mpf77, mpf90, mpcc, and mpCC drivers respectively. These commands pass their options to the compiler, provide the paths for the include and library directories, and add the dependency libraries of libmpi. For example, the following two commands are equivalent.

```
example% mpcc -fast example.c -lmpi
example% cc -I/opt/SUNWhpc/include -R/opt/SUNWhpc/lib \
        -L/opt/SUNWhpc/lib -fast example.c -lmpi \
        -lrte -ldl -lposix4
```

The scripts point the linker to the v9 subdirectories if -xarch=v9[a,b] is set. All other options don't affect the behavior of scripts and are passed to the compiler. The -v option prints the string of compiler options used.

```
example% mpcc -fast example.c -xarch=v9 -lmpi -v

--------------------
cc   -I/opt/SUNWhpc/include/v9 -R/opt/SUNWhpc/lib/sparcv9
-L/opt/SUNWhpc/lib/sparcv9  -fast example.c -xarch=v9 -lmpi -v
-lrte -ldl -lposix4
--------------------
...
```

In addition, the option -dryrun displays the verbose output of the compiler commands without running them (similar to the -dryrun option in Fortran compiler and -### option in C compiler).

As we already mentioned, the MPI trace libraries are provided in tnf subdirectory of /opt/SUNWhpc/lib. These libraries can be linked in using -L option with matching -R for runtime library path setting.

```
example% cc -I/opt/SUNWhpc/include/v9 \
        -R/opt/SUNWhpc/HPC3.1/lib/tnf/sparcv9 \
        -L/opt/SUNWhpc/HPC3.1/lib/tnf/sparcv9 \
        -fast example.c -xarch=v9 -lmpi -v -lrte -ldl -lposix4
```

Alternatively, the trace libraries can be used if the runtime library path is set appropriately with LD_LIBRARY_PATH environment variable.

```
example% setenv LD_LIBRARY_PATH
        /opt/SUNWhpc/HPC3.1/lib/tnf/sparcv9
```

This method does not require any special compilation and can be used to generate performance data for an existing MPI application.

Multithreaded programs should use the libmpi_mt version of the MPI library. This can be done by using -lmpi_mt option rather than -lmpi:

```
example% mpcc -fast example.c -lmpi_mt
```

Calls to the thread library libthread are resolved if either libmpi or libmpi_mt are linked. Using ldd command, one can see that libthread is a dependency of libmpi and is not required to be explicitly linked.

```
example% ldd libmpi.so
        libc.so.1 =>      /usr/lib/libc.so.1
        libsocket.so.1 =>        /usr/lib/libsocket.so.1
        libnsl.so.1 =>    /usr/lib/libnsl.so.1
        libthread.so.1 =>        /usr/lib/libthread.so.1
        libdl.so.1 =>     /usr/lib/libdl.so.1
        librte.so.1 =>    /opt/SUNWhpc/lib/librte.so.1
        libhpcshm.so.1 =>        /opt/SUNWhpc/lib/libhpcshm.so.1
        libpfs.so.1 =>    /opt/SUNWhpc/lib/libpfs.so.1
        libmp.so.2 =>     /usr/lib/libmp.so.2
        libposix4.so.1 =>        /usr/lib/libposix4.so.1
        libaio.so.1 =>    /usr/lib/libaio.so.1
        /usr/platform/SUNW,Ultra-Enterprise/lib/libc_psr.so.1
```

Once an MPI program is built, it can be submitted to run on a Sun HPC cluster with mprun(1) command. We describe a few of the most commonly used options of mprun. A complete list can be found in the *Sun HPC ClusterTools 3.1 User's Guide.*

The number of processes for an MPI run is set with the -np option. For example the following command submits a four-process run.

```
example% mprun -np 4 sample_mpi_job
```

Option -Ns can be used to disable spawning of multiple processes from a job on any one node of a cluster. This option was used in the previous section to distribute MPI processes over different nodes of the Sun Technical Compute Farm.

More complex node resource allocation requirements can be set with the -R and -Mf options. For example, the following command submits a four-process MPI run with two processes submitted on system hpc-node0 and the other two on hpc-node1.

```
example% mprun -np 4 -R "[2a2b]:a.name=hpc-node0 &
         b.name=hpc-node1" sample_mpi_job
```

With the -Mf option, the user can specify a file that includes information on how the processes should be distributed. For example, if the file rankmapfile contains the following

```
hpc-node0 2
hpc-node1 2
```

then the following command submits two processes each on hpc-node0 and hpc-node1.

```
example% mprun -np 4 -Mf rankmapfile sample_mpi_job
```

The mprun command can be used if the Sun HPC Cluster is configured with the Cluster Runtime Environment (CRE). If the cluster is configured with the Platform Computing Corporation's Load Sharing Facility (LSF), the MPI jobs must be submitted with the bsub command. For example, the following command submits an MPI job with four processes in the LSF environment.

```
example% bsub -n 4 sample_mpi_job
```

Dynamic Process Management

The ability of an MPI process to start new processes and to establish communication with separately started MPI processes is a new feature in MPI-2. In MPI parlance, the creation of new sets of processes is called *spawning* and establishing communication with preexisting MPI processes is termed as *connecting*. Both these features add significant flexibility to MPI applications. In particular, spawning is motivated by similar facilities in Parallel Virtual Machine (PVM) APIs (see [Geist95]) and is useful in irregular applications. In these applications, better load balancing is obtained by being able to vary the number of MPI processes in the computation dynamically rather than being fixed in the beginning of the execution (MPI-1 model). Applications based on the master-slave model in particular benefit from spawning.

Establishing connection between existing MPI processes is useful in MPMD models, where two or more programs (for example a multiphysics simulation application) are used in the overall application run. In this case, by being able to connect, the two programs can communicate relevant information, while still being separate jobs (and being maintained in form of separate source codes also). Connection also facilitates implementation of parallel client-server or peer-to-peer model-based programs using MPI (see [Gropp00]).

We illustrate dynamic process spawning in Sun MPI with an example. The program example_parent.c uses the MPI_Comm_spawn function to spawn nspawn child MPI processes. The program is set up such that each child process and the parent form a different intercommunicator. The parent and child processes exchange some messages and thereafter the child processes terminate. The parent creates additional children upon user input.

The program example_parent.c is listed as follows:

CODE EXAMPLE 14-3 Dynamic Process Spawning in MPI (Parent Process)

```
/* example_parent.c program to show dynamic process mgt.
in Sun MPI. spawns several child programs and exchanges
messages with them;
mpcc example_parent.c -o parent -lmpi */
#include <stdio.h>
#include <stdlib.h>
#include <time.h>
#include <signal.h>
#include "mpi.h"

void sighand(int sig);
main(int argc, char **argv)
{ char      msg[8],logn[256];
```

```c
int        nspawn, mypid,i,world_size,rmypid;
MPI_Comm logtid[100];   /* intercommunicators */
MPI_Comm everyone;
MPI_Request request;
MPI_Status mystatus;

if ( argc < 3 )
 printf("Usage: %s number_to_spawn char_to_break\n",
        argv[0] ),exit(1);
nspawn = atoi ( argv[1]);
msg[0] = *(argv[2]);
strcpy(logn, "child");
printf(" program to be spawned is %s\n", logn );
printf(" %s started\n", argv[0] );
MPI_Init(&argc, &argv);
MPI_Comm_size(MPI_COMM_WORLD, &world_size);
MPI_Comm_rank(MPI_COMM_WORLD,&mypid);
printf(" %s: mytid %x\n\n", argv[0], mypid );

while ( 1 ) {
    for ( i=0; i<nspawn; i++ ) {
      MPI_Comm_spawn(logn,MPI_ARGV_NULL, 1, MPI_INFO_NULL,
        0,MPI_COMM_SELF,&(logtid[i]),MPI_ERRCODES_IGNORE );
      MPI_Isend((void *)(&mypid),1,MPI_INT,0,5,
                logtid[i],&request);
      MPI_Wait(&request, &mystatus);
      MPI_Irecv((void *)(&rmypid),1,MPI_INT,MPI_ANY_SOURCE,
        6,logtid[i],&request);
      MPI_Wait(&request, &mystatus);
    }
    sleep(10);
    for ( i=0.; i<nspawn; i++ ) {
     MPI_Isend((void *)(&mypid),1,MPI_INT,0,7,logtid[i],
               &request);
     MPI_Wait(&request, &mystatus);
    }
    for ( i=0; i<nspawn; i++ )
     MPI_Comm_disconnect(&(logtid[i]));
    printf("All spawned children have been killed\n");
    if ( msg[0] == 'y' || msg[0] == 'Y' ) {
      printf("Stopping\n"); break; }
}
    MPI_Finalize();
}
```

The `example_child.c` program is listed as follows:

CODE EXAMPLE 14-4 Dynamic Process Spawning (Child Process)

```
/* example_child.c program; it is started dynamically
by parent program;
mpcc example_child.c -o child -lmpi */
#include <stdio.h>
#include <time.h>
#include <signal.h>
#include "mpi.h"

void sighand(int sig);

main(int argc, char **argv)
{ int   mypid, rmypid, world_size;
  MPI_Comm parent;
  MPI_Request request;
  MPI_Status mystatus;

  MPI_Init(&argc, &argv);
  MPI_Comm_size(MPI_COMM_WORLD, &world_size);
  MPI_Comm_rank(MPI_COMM_WORLD,&mypid);
  MPI_Comm_get_parent(&parent);
  printf(" %s: mytid %x\n\n", argv[0], mypid );
  MPI_Irecv((void *)(&rmypid),1,MPI_INT,MPI_ANY_SOURCE,
            5,parent,&request);
  MPI_Wait(&request, &mystatus);
  MPI_Isend((void *)(&rmypid),1,MPI_INT,0,6,parent,&request);
  MPI_Wait(&request, &mystatus);
  MPI_Recv((void *)(&rmypid),1,MPI_INT,MPI_ANY_SOURCE,
            7,parent,&mystatus);
  MPI_Comm_disconnect(&parent);
  MPI_Finalize();
}
```

The two programs are compiled as

```
example% mpcc example_parent.c -lmpi -o parent
example% mpcc example_child.c -lmpi -o child
```

and run as

```
example% mprun -np 1 parent 8 y
program to be spawned is child
 parent started
 parent: mytid 0
 child: mytid 0
 child: mytid 0
 child: mytid 0
 child: mytid 0
 child: mytid 0
 child: mytid 0
 child: mytid 0
 child: mytid 0
All spawned children have been killed
Stopping
```

Note that the argument to np is 1, which is the number of parent processes. The first command line argument to parent executable is 8; this is the number of child processes spawned by the parent process.

MPI I/O

The MPI-2 specification defines a file I/O interface for efficient access to shared files by multiple processes on multiple nodes. This interface, called MPI I/O, allows MPI programmers to take advantage of the high performance file systems available on many contemporary high performance computers, while retaining the convenience of a single file shared transparently between different MPI processes (see [Gropp00] for a detailed discussion on parallel I/O features in the MPI-2 standard). MPI I/O was partially implemented in Sun HPC ClusterTools 2.0. Starting with the 3.0 release, the Sun HPC ClusterTools package provides full implementation of the specification.

The Sun MPI I/O functions are implemented in libmpi and can be called from Fortran 77, Fortran 95, C, and C++ programs. In addition to standard file systems, such as UFS or NFS, the Sun MPI I/O implementation can use the Sun Parallel File System (PFS), a cost-effective high performance I/O solution that can span a large number of disks. Sun PFS is a part of HPC ClusterTools software. A performance comparison of PFS, UFS, and NFS can be found in [Wisniewski99].

Sun MPI I/O allows different processes to access a file with three types of file offsets. With an explicit offset, the programmer explicitly specifies the pointer within a file. The individual offsets are file pointers that can be used only by a process that opened a file. Shared file pointers allow a group of processes (that collectively opened a file) to access it with a single file pointer.

The MPI I/O calls have functionality similar to the standard I/O functions. For example `MPI_File_open(3SunMPI)`, `MPI_File_seek(3SunMPI)`, `MPI_File_read(3SunMPI)`, and `MPI_File_close(3SunMPI)` are analogous in functionality to the `open(2)`, `seek(2)`, `read(3)`, and `close(2)` functions.

The following program illustrates the use of MPI I/O calls. It creates a file and each MPI process writes data into it. Subsequently, each process reads the file and the correctness of the data are verified.

CODE EXAMPLE 14-5 Program Illustrating MPI I/O Calls

```
/* example_mpiio.c
   mpcc example_mpiio.c -lmpi -o example_mpiio */
#include <stdio.h>
#include <string.h>
#include <stdlib.h>
#include <mpi.h>
#define NUM 100000
#define FILENAME "test_file"

int main(int argc, char **argv)
{int *buf, *buf1, i, ier, myid, np;
 MPI_File fh;
 MPI_Status status;

 MPI_Init(&argc, &argv);
 MPI_Comm_rank(MPI_COMM_WORLD, &myid);
 MPI_Comm_size(MPI_COMM_WORLD, &np);

 buf = (int*)malloc(NUM*sizeof(int));
 for (i=0; i<NUM; i++) buf[i] = myid*NUM + i;/* fill buffer */

 MPI_File_open(MPI_COMM_WORLD, FILENAME, MPI_MODE_CREATE |
         MPI_MODE_RDWR, MPI_INFO_NULL, &fh);
 MPI_File_set_view(fh, (MPI_Offset)(myid*NUM*sizeof(int)),
                   MPI_INT, MPI_INT, "native",
                   MPI_INFO_NULL);
 MPI_File_write(fh, buf, NUM, MPI_INT, &status);/* write file */
 MPI_File_close(&fh);

 MPI_File_open(MPI_COMM_WORLD, FILENAME, MPI_MODE_CREATE |
         MPI_MODE_RDWR, MPI_INFO_NULL, &fh);/* reopen */
 buf1 = (int *)malloc(NUM*sizeof(int));
 MPI_File_set_view(fh, (MPI_Offset)(myid*NUM*sizeof(int)),
                   MPI_INT, MPI_INT, "native",
```

CODE EXAMPLE 14-5 Program Illustrating MPI I/O Calls *(Continued)*

```
                        MPI_INFO_NULL);
MPI_File_read(fh, buf1, NUM, MPI_INT, &status); /*reread */
MPI_File_close(&fh);

for (i=0; i<NUM; i++)                /* verify the data */
   if (buf1[i] != buf[i]) {
        printf("Process %d: wrong entry in the file",myid);
        MPI_Abort(MPI_COMM_WORLD, ier); }
printf("Process %d: correct data \n", myid);

if (myid == 0)
  MPI_File_delete(FILENAME, MPI_INFO_NULL);

free(buf);free(buf1);
MPI_Finalize();
return 0;
}
```

Compiling and running the program:

```
example% mpcc example_mpiio.c -lmpi -o example_mpiio
example% mprun -np 2 example_mpiio        .
Process 0: correct data
Process 1: correct data
```

The multithreaded MPI library `libmpi_mt` provides nonblocking asynchronous implementations of MPI I/O calls. These routines have the letter i before read or write in the routine name, for example, `MPI_File_iwrite()`. The nonblocking calls allow overlap between the I/O operations and computation (or communication between processes).

Sun MPI Environment Variables

The Sun MPI implementation provides many environment variables that can be used to manually tune message-passing performance in an application. While the default values of these variables have been set to deliver near-optimal performance on a wide range of programs, there are situations where significant improvements can be observed by experimenting with other settings. The environment variables can be broadly categorized into six areas: informational, general performance tuning, tuning memory for point-to-point performance, numerics, tuning rendezvous, and miscellaneous. A complete description of all environment variables is beyond the scope of this book. We discuss some important ones, and the performance effect of varying them is shown with simple example programs.

Consult *Sun HPC ClusterTools 3.1 Performance Guide* and *Sun MPI 4.1 Programming and Reference Guide* for complete details on Sun MPI environment variables.

Diagnostic Information

The environment variables MPI_PRINTENV, MPI_SHOW_ERRORS and MPI_SHOW_INTERFACES can be used to obtain runtime diagnostic information that is useful in debugging and performance tuning. The first one set to 1 causes MPI environment variables and hpc.conf settings to be printed while error messages are printed to standard error when MPI_SHOW_ERRORS is set to 1. MPI_SHOW_INTERFACES shows information on the interfaces being used by MPI library.

Some suggested settings of these variables are as follows:

```
example% setenv MPI_PRINTENV 1
example% setenv MPI_SHOW_INTERFACES 3
example% setenv MPI_SHOW_ERRORS 1
```

For example, running the force calculation example (CODE EXAMPLE 14-2) with the previous environment variables set generates the following output on an Enterprise 4500 system (running HPC 3.1 ClusterTools release)

```
example% mprun -np 4 a.cyclic
rank 0: MPI_PROCBIND=0
rank 0: MPI_SHM_CYCLESIZE=8192
rank 0: MPI_SHM_CYCLESTART=24576
rank 0: MPI_SHM_PIPESIZE=8192
```

```
rank 0: MPI_SHM_PIPESTART=2048
rank 0: MPI_SHM_SBPOOLSIZE=73728
rank 0: MPI_SHM_CPOOLSIZE=24576
rank 0: MPI_SHM_SHORTMSGSIZE=256
rank 0: MPI_SHM_NUMPOSTBOX=16
rank 0: MPI_SHM_GBPOOLSIZE=20971520
rank 0: MPI_SHM_RENDVSIZE=24576
rank 0: MPI_SHM_REDUCESIZE=256
rank 0: MPI_SHM_BCASTSIZE=32768
rank 0: MPI_SHM_WARMUP=0
MPI_CANONREDUCE=0
MPI_COSCHED=2
MPI_EAGERONLY=1
MPI_FLOWCONTROL=0
MPI_FULLCONNINIT=0
MPI_OPTCOLL=1
MPI_POLLALL=1
MPI_PRINTENV=1
MPI_QUIET=0
MPI_SHOW_ERRORS=0
MPI_SHOW_INTERFACES=3
MPI_SPIN=0
MPI_SPINDTIMEOUT=1000
MPI_WARMUP=0
MPI_TCP_SAFEGATHER=1
hpc.conf: coscheduling=2
hpc.conf: pbind=2
hpc.conf: progressadjust=1
hpc.conf: spindtimeout=1000
```

Dedicated and Timeshared System Execution

The Sun MPI library is by default optimized for execution in a timeshare
environment, where the total number of MPI processes might be greater than the
number of processors on the system. In this section, we discuss environment
variables that provide finer control depending on whether the job is being run in a
dedicated or timeshared environment.

On dedicated systems for fastest possible program turnaround execution, the
environment variable MPI_SPIN can be used. The setting

```
example% setenv MPI_SPIN 1
```

causes MPI processes to spin aggressively when waiting for MPI function calls to complete (for example waiting for a message to arrive or a collective operation to finish). The default is for MPI processes to yield the processor after some period of unsuccessful spinning. It is very important to use this variable on an undersubscribed, dedicated system. On such a system, the setting usually leads to an improvement in performance of the MPI job. However, when used on a shared, oversubscribed system, the above setting of MPI_SPIN can lead to degraded performance. We illustrate this effect using the force calculation example in CODE EXAMPLE 14-2. We perform two separate but simultaneous 12-process runs of the executable a.block for different settings of MPI_SPIN for each of the runs on a 12-processor Enterprise 4500 system (denoted as Run A and Run B, respectively in TABLE 14-1). For example, in one window the following commands are typed

```
example% setenv MPI_SPIN 1
example% mprun -np 12 a.block
```

and similarly another job is run in a different shell at the same time. The results are listed in TABLE 14-1 (times are in seconds); case 1 is when only one job is run.

TABLE 14-1 Effect of MPI_SPIN Environment Variable on Job Throughput

Case	MPI_SPIN (Run A)	Time in sec. (Run A)	MPI_SPIN (Run B)	Time in sec.(Run B)
Case 1	0 (or 1)	11.1	-	-
Case 2	0	19.9	0	23.1
Case 3	1	28.7	0	31.1
Case 4	1	120.5	1	122.5

As expected, case 4 results in significant degradation of performance, whereas for cases 2 and 3, the degradation (compared to case 1) is more graceful. For the setting of MPI_SPIN=0, the stacktrace of an MPI process in the job is as:

```
example% pstack 25965
25965:  a.block
----------------- lwp# 1 / thread# 1 -------------------
 fdc1a2d0 yield      (fdc7250c, fdc72d70, 0, 3, 0, d67c0080) + 8
 fdc5fb48 mpip_shm_reduce (1, 1, d67c0000, 8, 800, feb43158) + 30c
 feaa686c MPIP_Allreduce (83630, e50b0, feb44478, feb44478, feb43158, feb45900) + 168
 feaa6aac pmpi_allreduce_ (83630, e50b0, 117e0, 117e4, 117e8, 117d0) + cc
 00011534 MAIN_      (1, ffbef7bc, fdea4940, 0, 21a18, 30d2) + 3f4
 0001110c main       (1, ffbef7bc, ffbef7c4, 21800, 0, 0) + 3c
 000110a8 _start     (0, 0, 0, 0, 0, 0) + f8
----------------- lwp# 2 / thread# 2 -------------------
 fdc19634 signotifywait ()
 fe1cea04 _dynamiclwps (fe1ee000, 5c, 0, 0, 0, 0) + 1c
 fdc14b4c thr_errnop (0, 0, 0, 0, 0, 0) + 20
```

```
---------------- lwp# 3 -------------------------------
fdc19c18 lwp_cond_wait (fe1f55b0, fe1f55c0, fe755bf0)
fdc11968 _lwp_cond_timedwait (0, 39ff7cc8, fe755c58, fe1f55b0, fe1f55c0, 0) + 98
fe1c8e28 _age     (fe1eedc8, fe1eedcc, fe1ee000, 0, 0, 4) + 94
fdc17254 _door_return (fe1ef6b8, 3, fe1ee000, 1, fe755cb8, fe1ca450) + 68
---------------- lwp# 4 -------------------------------
fdc171f8 door     (0, 0, 0, 0, fe4d5d18, 4)
fe1ca450 _lwp_start (0, 0, 0, 0, 0, 0) + 18
------------------------- thread# 3 --------------------
fe1cd9bc _reap_wait (fe1f2a18, 20920, 0, fe1ee000, 0, 0) + 38
fe1cd714 _reaper   (fe1eee40, fe1f4780, fe1f2a18, fe1eee18, 1, fe400000) + 38
fe1dbc08 _thread_start (0, 0, 0, 0, 0, 0) + 40
```

We see that the MPI process calls `yield` function in the `MPI_ALLREDUCE` call, while waiting for other processes to complete.

Similarly, the coscheduling behavior of MPI library can be controlled with `MPI_COSCHED` environment variable. The default value of `MPI_COSCHED` is 0, which specifies that the MPI processes should not be descheduled. When coscheduling is enabled (`MPI_COSCHED=1`), the amount of time a message waits for `spind` daemon (coscheduling daemon) to return is controlled with `MPI_SPINDTIMEOUT` variable.

The environment variable `MPI_PROCBIND` can be used to bind the MPI processes on the processor. This may be helpful when using analysis tools that monitor specific processors on the system rather than processes (for example `mpstat` tool discussed in Chapter 11)

```
example% setenv MPI_PROCBIND 1
```

The setting causes the MPI library to bind MPI processes to different processors using a particular mapping. The setting should not be used in a timeshared system or when there are multiple MPI jobs on a node, as these jobs could compete for the same processors. Further, it should not be used if the MPI job uses multiple threads, as all of the threads are forced by the operating system to share the processor on which the MPI process is bound.

Optimized Collectives

Sun MPI implements collectives that are highly optimized for SMPs and clusters of SMPs. On an SMP system, the collectives read from and write to shared memory collectively rather than use point-to-point message-passing operations. In a cluster (where each node is an SMP), the library organizes processes to minimize traffic between nodes while also applying the SMP algorithms to minimize traffic on any one node (see [Sistare99b]). These methods take advantage of the high bandwidth and low latency of the SMP interconnect and provide highly efficient collective operations.

The environment variable MPI_OPTCOLL has a default setting of 1, which enables optimized collectives. To illustrate the effect of optimized collectives, we compare the effect of the setting setenv MPI_OPTCOLL 0 with setenv MPI_OPTCOLL 1 for the synchronization benchmark SYNCH1 in the PARKBENCH application suite. The PARKBENCH suite is available on the internet at http://www.netlib.org/parkbench/html/. The SYNCH1 benchmark measures the time to execute a barrier synchronization statement as a function of the number of processes taking part in the barrier. We extracted the SYNCH1 benchmark from PARKBENCH suite, and made it available with the other programs for this chapter. The reader can either use the version we included with the programs in this book or directly download it from the internet site referenced.

FIGURE 14-5 shows the results of the comparison on a 12-CPU Enterprise 4500 system. We can see almost an order of magnitude performance degradation when using MPI_OPTCOLL=0 setting. Although the usage of optimized collectives is the default, under certain circumstances, the library reverts to using slower collectives. This is discussed next, along with guidelines on how a developer can ensure that the library does not select slower algorithms.

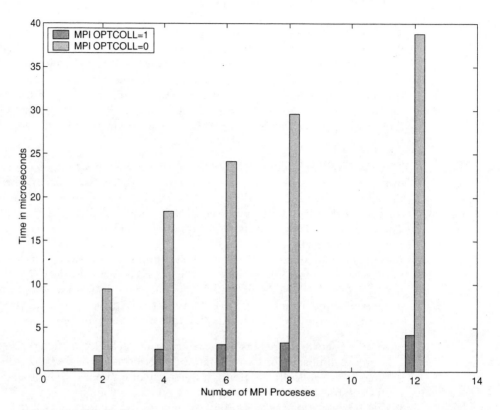

FIGURE 14-5 Effect of `MPI_OPTCOLL` Environment Variable on `MPI_BARRIER()` Performance in the SYNCH1 Benchmark on a 12-CPU Enterprise 4500 System

On shared-memory systems, the performance of collective operations can be fine-tuned using the `MPI_SHM_GBPOOLSIZE`, `MPI_SHM_BCASTSIZE`, and `MPI_SHM_REDUCESIZE` environment variables. The `MPI_SHM_GBPOOLSIZE` variable has a default setting of 20,971,520 (that is 20 MB) and is the size (in bytes) of the shared memory global buffer pool used by MPI processes participating in the collective operation on the SMP node. For broadcast and reduction operations on large message sizes, the library breaks them into smaller chunks and pipelines the operations. `MPI_SHM_BCASTSIZE` and `MPI_SHM_REDUCESIZE` represent the chunk sizes used in the pipelined broadcast and reduction operations. For broadcast operations:

$$(P/4) \times 2 \times \texttt{MPI\_SHM\_BCASTSIZE}$$

bytes of memory are allocated from the shared-memory global buffer pool. Here P is the number of MPI processes on the SMP node. For the reduction operation:

$$P^2 \times \texttt{MPI\_SHM\_REDUCESIZE}$$

bytes are allocated from the global buffer pool. When modifying these environment variables, care must be taken to ensure sufficient buffer pool size is available, otherwise slower collective algorithms are used, resulting in significant performance degradation (see the previous discussion on MPI_OPTCOLL). For example, the following condition must be met so that optimized reduction algorithms are used:

$$P^2 \times \text{MPI\_SHM\_REDUCESIZE} < \text{MPI\_SHM\_GBPOOLSIZE}.$$

The effects of varying the value of MPI_SHM_REDUCESIZE are shown with an example program:

CODE EXAMPLE 14-6 Effect of MPI_SHM_REDUCESIZE Environment Variable

```
      program reduce
! mpf90 -fast example_reduce.f90 -lmpi -o reduce
      implicit double precision(a-h,o-z)
      include 'mpif.h'
      parameter (idim=100000,nrep=500)
      real*8 f(idim),tmp(idim)
      integer me,nproc,ierr
      call MPI_INIT(ierr)
      call MPI_COMM_RANK(MPI_COMM_WORLD, me, ierr)
      call MPI_COMM_SIZE(MPI_COMM_WORLD, nproc, ierr)
      call mpi_barrier(MPI_COMM_WORLD,ierr)
      time_i = mpi_wtime()
      do n=1,nrep
        do i=1,idim
          tmp(i) = 0.0
        enddo
        do i=1+me,idim-1,nproc
            f(i) = me + i
        enddo
        call mpi_allreduce(f,tmp,idim,MPI_DOUBLE_PRECISION, &
            MPI_SUM,MPI_COMM_WORLD,ierr)
      enddo
      time_f = mpi_wtime() - time_i
      call mpi_reduce(time_f,timem,1,MPI_DOUBLE_PRECISION,  &
          MPI_MAX,0,MPI_COMM_WORLD,ierr)
      if(me.eq.0) write(10,100) nproc,timem
100     format('P= ',i4,' Time= ',f12.4)
      call mpi_finalize(ierr)
      stop
      end
```

We compile the program as (Forte Developer 6 Fortran 95 compiler and HPC 3.1 ClusterTools)

```
example% mpf90 -fast example_reduce.f90 -lmpi -o reduce
```

and run it on a 12-processor Enterprise 4500 system, varying the MPI_SHM_REDUCESIZE environment variable (its default value is 256 bytes):

```
example% setenv MPI_SHM_REDUCESIZE 512
```

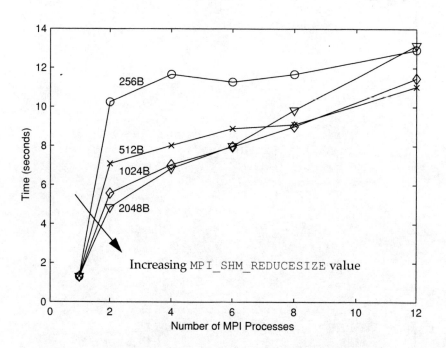

FIGURE 14-6 Effect of MPI_SHM_REDUCESIZE Environment Variable

The results (maximum of measured time over all MPI processes; printed in the file fort.10 in the example_reduce.f90 program) are shown in FIGURE 14-6. As MPI_SHM_REDUCESIZE is increased, the efficiency of the MPI_ALLREDUCE() operation improves but the overhead of the pipeline (amount of time to fill it and drain it) also increases. As a result, one can see that there are crossover points between different curves. For example, with 12 processors, the default setting (256 bytes) is better than a value of 2,048 bytes.

Point-to-Point Communication

The point-to-point communication facilities are the most commonly used functions in MPI applications and Sun MPI provides several environment variables to fine tune point-to-point communication performance. Different algorithms are used in Sun MPI library for optimizing point-to-point communication between MPI processes on the same shared-memory SMP node, RSM (for SCI clusters), or TCP-based cluster systems[1]. In this section, we briefly discuss environment variables applicable to point-to-point message passing between two processes on the same shared-memory SMP node. FIGURE 14-7 illustrates the approach used in Sun MPI library to select the suitable message-passing algorithm based on the size of the message (denoted as B in FIGURE 14-7). The size of message is compared against various limits, which are provided as environment variables and can be changed by the user at runtime. The different algorithms have been implemented with the objective of providing sufficiently large message buffers to avoid congestion, while minimizing the memory overhead associated with maintaining them.

As mentioned earlier, Sun MPI implements both eager and rendezvous message exchange protocols [Gropp99]. The environment variable MPI_EAGERONLY allows one to choose between rendezvous and eager message exchange protocols. In the eager protocol, the sender is eager and initiates sending the message without any explicit acknowledgement from the receiver. In the rendenzvous protocol, the sender waits to receive an acknowledgement on the readiness of the receiver before initiating the message transfer. The rendezvous protocol eliminates potential extra receiver-side copying, but incurs higher synchronization overhead.

The environment variables for tuning point-to-point message passing over shared memory are MPI_SHM_NUMPOSTBOX, MPI_SHM_SHORTMSGSIZE, MPI_SHM_PIPESIZE, MPI_SHM_PIPESTART, MPI_SHM_CYCLESIZE, MPI_SHM_CYCLESTART, MPI_SHM_CPOOLSIZE, and MPI_SHM_SBPOOLSIZE. Similarly, there are variables for tuning message passing over RSM and TCP connections.

---

1 The library can automatically determine at runtime whether to send the messages over shared memory, RSM, or TCP connection.

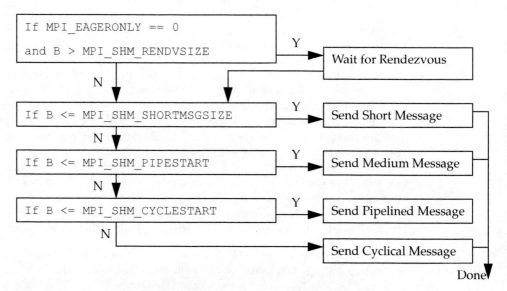

FIGURE 14-7 Point-to-Point Message Passing Over Shared Memory in Sun MPI Implementation (Reproduced with permission from *Sun HPC ClusterTools 3.1 Performance Guide*)

In the Sun MPI implementation of point-to-point message exchanges, the sender writes a portion of the message into shared buffers and the receiver reads the message from these buffers. The pointers to these buffers are kept in shared-memory postboxes. When the sender finishes writing into a postbox, the receiver can read the postbox and buffers pointed to by the postbox. The message-passing operation is pipelined: the sender can be writing into one buffer while the receiver could be reading from a previously available buffer. The size of each shared-memory buffer is fixed at 1 KB (in HPC 3.1 Clustertools Sun MPI library). The number of postboxes used by the library can be controlled by the MPI_SHM_NUMPOSTBOX environment variable. The messages are exchanged using either connection pools or send-buffer pools. In connection pools, separate buffers are allocated for each sender-receiver pair (denoted as a connection). For P processes on a node, there are thus P × (P-1) connection pools. Each connection has shared memory buffering associated with it, which is of size determined by the MPI_SHM_CPOOLSIZE environment variable. In send-buffer pools, a common buffer is maintained per sender, with buffers shared among the sender's P-1 connections. Thus, there are a total of P send-buffer pools for P processes. The size of send-buffer pools can be controlled by the variable MPI_SHM_SBPOOLSIZE. The memory implications of using connection pools or send-buffer pools are quite different. In the case of connection pools, the size of shared-memory area (bytes) used by the library for point-to-point message passing is as follows:

$P \times (P-1) \times (\texttt{MPI\_SHM\_NUMPOSTBOX} \times (64+\texttt{MPI\_SHM\_SHORTMSGSIZE})+$
$\texttt{MPI\_SHM\_CPOOLSIZE})$

whereas for send-buffer pools, the shared area (bytes) is as follows:

$P \times (P-1) \times \texttt{MPI\_SHM\_NUMPOSTBOX} \times (64+\texttt{MPI\_SHM\_SHORTMSGSIZE}) + P \times$
$\texttt{MPI\_SHM\_SBPOOLSIZE}.$

The default values of all of these variables, allowed range of legal values, and memory constraints are discussed in *Sun HPC ClusterTools 3.1 Performance Guide* and *Sun MPI 4.1 Programming and Reference Guide*. The reader is strongly advised not to arbitrarily change these variables without first understanding their interrelationships and restrictions. In general, the default values should be used. The defaults are, however, targeted towards low memory consumption by the library and performance oriented readers may want to experiment with these settings (see *Sun HPC ClusterTools 3.1 Performance Guide*). These settings might improve performance over default settings and lead to a decrease in the cost of implicit process synchronization overheads associated with the point-to-point message passing.

- *Avoid cyclic message passing*: For very large messages, the Sun MPI library employs cyclic message passing, which is implemented to prevent the message from overflowing the shared-memory buffer used by the library to exchange messages between MPI processes. Added synchronization is performed and the entire message is cycled between two fixed sets of buffers. Due to added synchronization, cyclic message passing can be more expensive than the other algorithms used for message exchange. Cyclic message passing can be suppressed with the following setting for 32-bit applications:

```
example% setenv MPI_SHM_CYCLESTART 0x7fffffff
```

and for 64-bit applications:

```
example% setenv MPI_SHM_CYCLESTART 0x7fffffffffffffff
```

- *Suppress polling for system buffers*: To help drain system buffers, Sun MPI can poll all incoming connections for messages, to check whether a corresponding receive has been posted or not. This polling is turned on by default to prevent deadlock in MPI applications that rely on unlimited buffering for standard send (example, MPI_Send) even though such reliance is explicitly forbidden by the MPI standard. To decrease the overhead of general polling, turn off the environment variable MPI_POLLALL with

```
example% setenv MPI_POLLALL 0
```

- *Provide large shared-memory buffer space*: In order to decrease sender stalls due to insufficient buffer sizes, the shared-memory buffer area used by Sun MPI library can be modified using the `MPI_SHM_CPOOLSIZE`, `MPI_SHM_SBPOOLSIZE`, and `MPI_SHM_NUMPOSTBOX` environment variables. The following sets `MPI_SHM_SBPOOLSIZE` to 20 MB and `MPI_SHM_NUMPOSTBOX` to 256.

```
example% setenv MPI_SHM_SBPOOLSIZE 20000000
example% setenv MPI_SHM_NUMPOSTBOX 256
```

When modifying `MPI_SHM_NUMPOSTBOX`, it is recommended that there is at least one postbox available for every 8,192 bytes of data per connection. For example, if messages up to a size of 524,288 bytes are exchanged, then at least 524,288/8,192 (= 64) postboxes must be made available to MPI library. Refer to *Sun HPC ClusterTools 3.1 Performance Guide* for additional examples and tips on setting shared-memory buffer sizes for efficient message passing.

To illustrate the effect on performance of some of the variables, we use the COMMS1 ([Hockney93]) and COMMS3 benchmarks. These are available as part of the PARKBENCH application suite. The benchmarks were extracted from the suite and provided with other programs included in this book. Alternately, the reader can download the PARKBENCH suite on the internet from `http://www.netlib.org/parkbench/html/`.

In the COMMS1, or ping-pong benchmark, a message of variable length, N, is sent from a master node to a slave node. The slave node receives the message into a Fortran data array, and immediately returns it to the master. The bandwidth is computed as N/T, where T is half of the recorded time for the message ping-pong. In the COMMS3 benchmark, each processor (in a P-processor system) sends a message of length N to the other (P-1) processors, then waits to receive the (P-1) messages directed at it. The time for this generalized ping-pong operation is the time to send P(P-1) messages. The generalized ping-pong operation is considered complete when all messages are received by all processors. COMMS3 has been referred to by its authors as the communication saturation bandwidth benchmark and measures how well the communication system scales with number of processors.

We ran the COMMS3 benchmark on a 12-CPU Enterprise 4500 system for message sizes up to 1 MB. A message of this size requires up to 1,048,576/8,192 (= 128) postboxes. For six MPI processes, a total of 6*5*1 = 30 MB buffer space is required. The following settings were used to provide ample buffering in the case when sender buffer pools are used

```
example% setenv MPI_SHM_SBPOOLSIZE 64000000
example% setenv MPI_SHM_NUMPOSTBOX 192
```

The maximum saturation bandwidth reported in the benchmark for two, four, and six MPI processes is listed in TABLE 14-2. We can see that the saturation bandwidth is increasing as a function of number of MPI processes.

TABLE 14-2 COMMS3 Saturation Bandwidth on 12-CPU Enterprise 4500 System

Number of MPI Processes	Maximum Total Saturation Bandwidth (MB/sec)
2	227.5
4	307.5
6	391.9

Alternately, if connection pools are used for message passing, then the variable MPI_SHM_CPOOLSIZE needs to be set to an adequate value, for example

```
example% setenv MPI_SHM_CPOOLSIZE 1500000
example% setenv MPI_SHM_NUMPOSTBOX 192
```

The reader is encouraged to run COMMS3 with different settings of environment variables and examine the effects on the benchmark's results.

As discussed earlier, for very large message exchanges, Sun MPI uses cyclic message-passing protocol. The variable MPI_SHM_CYCLESIZE represents the cycle-size used for cycling the large messages, and MPI_SHM_CYCLESTART represents the message size above which cyclic message passing is used (see FIGURE 14-7). The value should be set such that the following condition holds:

MPI_SHM_CYCLESTART$\geq 2 \times$ MPI_SHM_CYCLESIZE

If these conditions are not met[1], the MPI library emits a warning and attempts to automatically adjust the variables such that the necessary constraints are satisfied.

The COMMS1 ping-pong benchmark was run for varying values of MPI_SHM_CYCLESIZE and MPI_SHM_CYCLESTART.

The results of the run are shown in FIGURE 14-8. The figure shows that the asymptotic ping-pong bandwidth on this system is approximately 250 MB/second. We see the impact of cyclesize on cyclic message passing for MPI_SHM_CYCLESIZE=1024 in the figure. The MPI_SHM_CYCLESTART=24576 curve only attains an asymptotic bandwidth of approximately 170 MB/second, which is well below what is attained when cyclic message passing is turned off. The default cycle size in the MPI library (MPI_SHM_CYCLESIZE=8192) was chosen to minimize additional synchronization in cyclic message passing. This is observable in the middle and lower plots, where

1. Except in the case when cyclic message passing is turned off by setting
   MPI_SHM_CYCLESTART=0x7fffffff.

curves for `MPI_SHM_CYCLESIZE=8192` and `MPI_SHM_CYCLESIZE=16384` show approximately equivalent bandwidths. Generally, cyclic message passing should be altogether suppressed with the setting `MPI_SHM_CYCLESTART=0x7fffffff`.

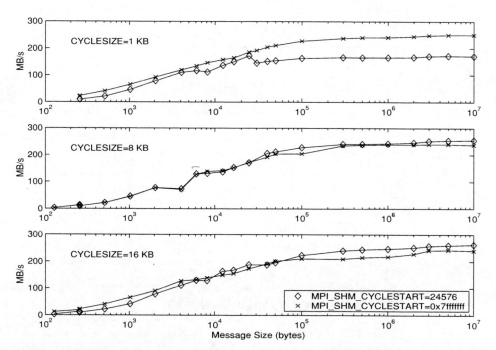

FIGURE 14-8 COMMS1 Ping-pong Bandwidth Measured as a Function of `MPI_SHM_CYCLESIZE` and `MPI_SHM_CYCLESTART` Environment Variables on an Enterprise 4500 System

In the figure, note that for `MPI_SHM_CYCLESIZE=16384`, the curve with diamonds corresponds to `MPI_SHM_CYCLESTART=32768`.

General Performance

A brief discussion of miscellaneous performance-related MPI environment variables is presented in this section.

Sun MPI has the option of establishing connections between senders and receivers when they are needed (lazy connection mode) or all the connections at once when `MPI_INIT()` is called (full connection mode). The former decreases the initialization cost but increases the cost when the first connection is established, while the latter makes the initialization more expensive. `MPI_FULLCONNINIT` can be used to choose between lazy and full connection modes. For full connection startup, the following setting is required

```
example% setenv MPI_FULLCONNINIT 1
```

An advantage of establishing all the connections upfront is that performance analysis is easier than establishing connections later in the execution of the job.

If rendezvous message passing is used (`MPI_EAGERONLY=0`), the size of the message above which the rendezvous-exchange protocol is used can be varied with the `MPI_SHM_RENDVSIZE`, `MPI_TCP_RENDVSIZE`, and `MPI_RSM_RENDVSIZE` variables for shared memory, TCP, and RSM connections, respectively. The following example sets the limit to 524,288 bytes for rendezvous message passing over the TCP connection.

```
example% setenv MPI_TCP_RENDVSIZE 524288
```

The TCP protocol guarantees data reliability by retransmitting messages as needed. If the interconnection network is unreliable (loses data packets), the data retransmission rates can skyrocket, causing significant degradation in message-passing performance. In such situations, it might be useful to throttle TCP transmissions with increased synchronization between the sender and receiver. This can be done by setting `MPI_EAGERONLY` environment variable as

```
example% setenv MPI_EAGERONLY 0
```

(that is, selecting the rendezvous message exchange protocol) and lowering the TCP rendezvous threshold setting by lowering the value of `MPI_TCP_RENDVSIZE` environment variable. For reliable TCP networks, performance can be improved with the following setting

```
example% setenv MPI_TCP_SAFEGATHER 0
```

This example enables use of optimized algorithms for MPI_Gather() and MPI_Gatherv() functions over the TCP interconnection networks.

Sun Scalable Scientific Subroutine Library

The Sun Scalable Scientific Subroutine Library, also known as S3L, is a part of the Sun ClusterTools software suite. It provides parallel implementations of basic functions commonly used in scientific applications. Similar to MPI applications, programs built with S3L library calls can run on SMP systems as well as on clusters of such systems.

S3L implements linear algebra functions, fast Fourier transforms, and other standard procedures. In addition, the library provides functions for data and process management called toolkit functions.

The S3L core functions include ScaLAPACK calls and linear algebra procedures such as sparse system solve, sparse matrix-vector multiplication, least squares solve, iterative eigensolve, and the singular value decomposition. It also implements parallel sorts and parallel random number generation.

The S3L toolkit routines allow one to set up and exit the S3L environment, perform processor grid management, set up parallel arrays, and perform operations on their elements. They also allow conversion between S3L and ScaLAPACK array descriptors.

S3L functions are callable from C, C++, Fortran 77, and Fortran 90 programs. The C or C++ programs that use S3L calls must include the s3l/s3l-c.h and s3l/s3l_errno-c.h files. The corresponding files for use in Fortran programs are s3l/s3l-f.h and s3l/s3l_errno-f.h, respectively.

Because the S3L library is compiled with the -dalign compiler option (see Chapter 6), a program that uses S3L must also be compiled and linked with -dalign option for consistent data alignment. As with MPI programs, it is recommended to use the mp* drivers (described earlier in this chapter) for building programs that use S3L. The use of drivers ensures that the library and include paths are set properly. The program itself should be linked with -ls3l. This links the MPI library libmpi as well, because it is a dependency of libs3l.

For computations within a single node, the S3L library calls the equivalent functions from the Sun Performance Library (see Chapter 13). This guarantees high performance of computations within the SMP nodes. Because the functions in the performance library are highly optimized for different architectures, it is very important to specify the target architecture with the −xarch option to make sure that the correct version of libsunperf is linked in. A warning is printed if a suboptimal version of libsunperf is used with S3L.

The following example performs a matrix-matrix multiplication using the S3L_mat_mult(3) function. This example is derived from the matmult.f program provided with numerous other examples in the HPC ClusterTools 3.1 software. We recommend the reader browse the /opt/SUNWhpc/examples directory to obtain more information on using Sun HPC ClusterTools components.

CODE EXAMPLE 14-7 Distributed Matrix-Matrix Multiplication With S3L

```
! example_matmult.f90
! mpf90 -xO4 -xdepend -stackvar -dalign example_matmult.f90 \
!    -ls3l (-xarch=v8plusa)
include 's3l/s3l-f.h'
include 'mpif.h'

integer*4 m, n
parameter(m = 600, n = 2000)
integer*8 gethrtime, time1, time2, timediff

! global array descriptors
double precision a, b, c
integer*4 ext(2), axis_is_local(2)
integer*4 mypid, np
integer*4 ier

call s3l_init(ier)
call mpi_comm_rank(MPI_COMM_WORLD, mypid, ier)
call mpi_comm_size(MPI_COMM_WORLD, np, ier)

!  create distributed arrays
axis_is_local(1) = 0
axis_is_local(2) = 0

! declare arrays a, b, c
ext(1) = n
ext(2) = m
call s3l_declare(a, 2, ext, S3L_float, axis_is_local, &
                 S3L_USE_MALLOC, ier)
ext(1) = m
ext(2) = n
call s3l_declare(b, 2, ext, S3L_float, axis_is_local, &
                 S3L_USE_MALLOC, ier)
```

CODE EXAMPLE 14-7 Distributed Matrix-Matrix Multiplication With S3L *(Continued)*

```
ext(1) = n
ext(2) = n
call s3l_declare(c, 2, ext, S3L_float, axis_is_local, &
                S3L_USE_MALLOC, ier)

! fill the distributed arrays with random numbers
call s3l_rand_lcg(a, 1, ier)
call s3l_rand_lcg(b, 2, ier)
call s3l_rand_lcg(c, 3, ier)

! perform multiplication c = c + ab
time1 = gethrtime()
call s3l_mat_mult(c, a, b, 1, 2, ier)
time2 = gethrtime()
print*, "Mflops = ", 2.0d0/(time2-time1)/(1.e-3)*m*n*n
print*, (time2-time1)/(1.0d9)," seconds"

call s3l_free(a, ier)
call s3l_free(b, ier)
call s3l_free(c, ier)
call s3l_exit(ier)
end
```

If we compile this program without the -xarch specification, and subsequently run it on two CPUs of an Enterprise 4500 system, a warning states that a suboptimal version of libsunperf was used.

```
example% mpf90 -xO4 -xdepend -stackvar -dalign \
        example_matmult.f90 -ls3l
example% mprun -np 2 a.out
S3L warning: Using libsunperf not optimized for UltraSPARC.
 For better performance, link using -xarch=v8plusa .
·Mflops =   714.6588630935953
 6.71649093  seconds
 Mflops =   713.303020531157
 6.7292576  seconds
```

The warning disappears if -xarch option is set properly (also note almost twofold decrease in the runtime).

```
example% mpf90 -xO4 -xdepend -stackvar -dalign \
        example_matmult.f90 -ls3l -xarch=v8plusa
example% mprun -np 2 a.out
 Mflops =  1372.8491619814403
```

```
3.49637812   seconds
Mflops =   1371.0912256825017
3.50086098   seconds
```

The functions in the S3L library are thread safe and are optimized for concurrent use by multiple threads that can perform tasks on different portions of arrays. Multithreaded applications that use S3L should invoke `S3L_thread_comm_setup(3)` from each thread that makes S3L calls.

The S3L library allows using arrays with up to 32 dimensions. The routines `S3L_from_ScaLAPACK_desc(3)` and `S3L_to_ScaLAPACK_desc(3)` allow conversion between S3L and ScaLAPACK array descriptors. The S3L library supports three types of distribution of elements of array axes between the nodes. The *local* distribution stores all elements on a single node. The *block* distribution divides the elements among the nodes with at most one sequential block per node. Finally, the *cyclic* distribution divides the elements into smaller sequential blocks that are distributed between nodes in a round-robin fashion.

The S3L library provides an extensive runtime error checking mechanism. There are three S3L safety levels: 2, 5, and 9, in addition to level 0 which disables runtime checking and can be used for a well-tested application.

The safety level can be set with the environment variable `S3L_SAFETY`, for example

```
example% setenv S3L_SAFETY 9
```

or it can be set and read programmatically with `S3L_set_safety(3)` and `S3L_get_safety(3)` calls, respectively.

At level 2, an S3L program reports warnings when more than one function attempts to use the same parallel array, thus detecting potential race conditions. At level 5 the program performs explicit synchronization before and after each S3L call, making it easy to pinpoint an error in a multiprocessor run. Finally, the highest safety level 9 additionally forces the S3L program to perform explicit synchronization for lower-level calls performed from within S3L.

The S3L safety mechanism can be used in the development cycle to enable warnings when an S3L function exits with a nonzero status or to locate an error that occurs during a parallel run. The error checking leads to additional overhead; therefore, it should not be used for performance-critical runs after the program has been successfully tested.

This section provided a brief overview of S3L. Refer to *Sun S3L 3.1 Programming and Reference Guide* and the *Sun HPC ClusterTools 3.1 Performance Guide* for detailed descriptions of S3L functionality and features.

MPI, OpenMP, and Hybrid Approaches

In this final section, we outline some differences between the MPI and OpenMP approaches for program parallelization, and we present some issues revealed by recent studies in literature that pertain to hybrid MPI-OpenMP implementations.

MPI and OpenMP Approaches

As mentioned before, both MPI and OpenMP models have advantages and disadvantages, and as such, it is not possible to make a general conclusion as to which approach is superior. Some differences between the two are as follows:

- *Parallel Implementation and Programming Ease:* In the message-passing model, each process needs to communicate explicitly with other processes through send-receive pairs, whereas in an OpenMP program all data are accessible through loads and stores. The hardware cache coherence mechanism causes a load/store miss to be serviced in the form of replication of a cache line in the local processor's cache. This transparent naming of program data leads to considerable programming simplicity at the conceptual level. At implementation level also, the OpenMP based parallelization has been observed to be easier compared to the use of MPI. This is especially true for incremental parallelization of an existing application. Loop-level parallelization using OpenMP, in particular, is quite straightforward and quick to implement. SPMD style parallelism in OpenMP is more involved but usually simpler than MPI implementation (see the comparison in Chapter 13). OpenMP based parallelization tends to increase the size of the program (measured as lines of code) typically by 2-25% [Chandra00], whereas code size increase in MPI programs could be much larger. This is due to the need to parallelize the entire program all at once and explicitly partition program data structures. Generally, this also leads to reduced readability of the program. The ease of OpenMP programming is a big factor in its growing popularity.

- *Functionality and Portability:* The MPI based applications are portable to a wider class of computers. OpenMP programs are limited to shared-address-space systems (SMP, ccNUMA) only. MPI programs can run on shared-address space as well as distributed-address-space systems (cluster of SMPs, or any other distributed memory systems). In terms of functionality and programming models, conceptually, MPI supports more models than can be supported in OpenMP programs. For example, implementation of the MPMD model in OpenMP programs is not possible. Also, because MPI is a library-based approach, there is enhanced support for exception and signal handling.

- *Development Environment:* OpenMP programs require compiler support whereas MPI is a library-based approach. Debugging and performance tools for OpenMP programs are extensions of tools for serial programs because the uniprocess model is used. On the other hand, debuggers and performance tools for MPI programs are relatively harder to implement because the MPI program executes as different processes on the underlying computing system.

- *Performance Considerations:* The performance implication of using either OpenMP or MPI are quite different and dependent on the application. An MPI program requires coarse-grained parallelization of the algorithm while with OpenMP, fine-grained (loop-level) parallelism can be relatively easily implemented. Loop-level parallelism usually incurs additional thread management and synchronization overhead as compared to a coarser grained parallelization and may lead to lower parallel scaling. Further, blocking communication (in MPI) leads to implicit synchronization and can be used to decrease (or eliminate) explicit synchronization between computing tasks. However, for irregular and adaptive algorithms, load balancing with MPI is usually more difficult compared to OpenMP (or multithreading) implementation. Dynamic load balancing is particularly difficult for the message-passing model, and any approach based on dynamic migration of data across MPI processes for load balancing entails significant communication cost and programming complexity (see [Shan00]). Conversely, data locality could be difficult to control at the program level in OpenMP programs as compared to MPI implementation, where explicit data partitioning leads to better data locality and affinity [Shan99]. While true data sharing and dependencies in the program have to be dealt with in both approaches[1], MPI programmers do not need to be explicitly concerned with false cache-line sharing in program data structures.

Many recent studies (see [Bova99], [Shan99], [Smith99], [Armstrong00], [Garg00], [Henty00], [Shan00] and references therein) present comparisons between MPI and OpenMP approaches. Not surprisingly, the results are dependent on the architecture and application, with neither approach being a clear winner when various issues are taken into consideration.

Hybrid Approach

The increasing popularity of clusters of SMPs (also referred to as Clusters of Multiprocessors or CLUMPs) is motivating development of applications using a hybrid message-passing and shared address space (that is MPI+OpenMP) programming model[2]. The message passing is used for communication between the SMP nodes, and OpenMP is used to exploit parallelism within the node. In Chapter 10, we demonstrated how the hybrid model (MPI+OpenMP) can be

---

1. In MPI, the requirement of sharing data between two or more processes has to be explicitly implemented by a programmer via message passing. In OpenMP, access to shared data has to be explicitly protected by the programmer via use of synchronization and locking primitives.

2. The shared address space portion of the hybrid model could be implemented using any multithreading approach, such as P-threads or Solaris threads. The use of OpenMP has gained more popularity due to portability and simplicity in implementation.

implemented in the Solaris environment with the Pi-calculation example. Based on the methodology outlined there, large applications can be built for execution in a hybrid environment in a similar fashion.

While pure MPI-based programs port easily to clusters, in some cases, better performance can be obtained using the hybrid approach (see [Bova00], [Cappello00]). The choice between pure MPI, pure OpenMP, and a hybrid model depends on performance considerations and ease of implementation and, in general, may vary from application to application. We describe some issues to keep in mind when developing a hybrid model. The reader should note that mixed MPI+OpenMP programming model is an area of active research. As new mixed-model-based applications are developed, new issues and implementation techniques emerge.

The hybrid approach can be beneficial in several situations over a pure MPI or pure OpenMP model. Examples include the following:

- Increasing functionality and scaling over a pure OpenMP implementation.
- Improving performance in situations where an MPI library is not fully optimized for communication within an SMP system.
- Programs where portions can be more efficiently and easily parallelized using shared memory than using MPI.
- Better memory efficiency by having only one copy of a data structure per SMP as opposed to one copy per MPI process.

Typically, the hybrid approach is applied in a way that MPI is used for coarse-grained parallelism and OpenMP is used for fine-grained parallelism. What this means is that the outermost loop in the program is parallelized using MPI, and each MPI process then executes inner loops parallelized using OpenMP directives. Included here is the case where a single outer loop has enough iterations that it can be split into two nested loops. This approach has been implemented in several applications (see [Bova99], [SDSC99], [Cappello00] and [Henty00]).

In general, it is recommended that MPI calls should be avoided within OpenMP parallel regions. Usually, the OpenMP parallelism is implemented in the computational part of the MPI process and the MPI communication is kept separate from OpenMP parallel regions. This ensures that the program works even if the underlying MPI implementation is not thread safe. The Sun MPI library is MT safe. The thread-safe version can be linked as `-lmpi_mt`.

A schematic of the two-level approach (MPI at process level and OpenMP at loop level) is shown in FIGURE 14-9.

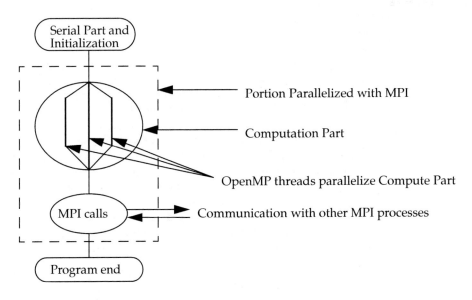

FIGURE 14-9 Schematic of Parallelization Using MPI at Process Level and OpenMP at Loop Level

The other approach of hybrid parallelization is to use SPMD style (coarse-grained) OpenMP implementation (see Chapter 13) where OpenMP threads are created in the main program just after the initialization of MPI processes. The OpenMP parallelization is also applied to the outermost loop level of the program. It is the programmer's responsibility to distribute work among threads and synchronize shared data accesses as necessary.

MPI calls may be issued from within OpenMP parallel regions, which means that MPI calls and OpenMP constructs are intermingled in the source. While in the two-level model (MPI at process level and OpenMP at loop level), a thread-unsafe MPI library might work (because MPI calls are made in the portion of program where only the main thread is active), in the coarse-grained approach, a thread-safe MPI library is almost a necessity. A suggested practice is to use one thread to perform all MPI communications [Bova99]. For some applications, the coarse-grained approach might be preferable as the SPMD-style OpenMP model can lead to better data locality (see Chapter 13) and load balancing [Hisley99].

Whichever approach is chosen, an effort should be made to implement the parallel constructs in a way so that a single set of source files can be used to generate serial, OpenMP-only, MPI-only, and hybrid binaries of the program (for example, see [Henty00]). The serial and OpenMP-only versions might either require conditional compilation or dummy stub libraries with MPI and OpenMP interfaces.

Summary

Explicit message passing is a dominant programming model for parallelization of programs. In particular, the use of the MPI standard to implement message passing has gained widespread popularity. Conceptually, the message-passing model is more general than explicit multithreading and compiler directive-based parallelization because it is applicable to distributed as well as shared address space systems. The SPMD model and MPMD model are the two main styles for organizing various computing tasks in an MPI program. Many techniques for workload distribution by data decompositions have been developed for parallelization of scientific programs. These were briefly described. Specifically, static data partitioning techniques for structured and unstructured grid-based computations were discussed from the point of view of load balance and communication requirements. We also defined communication metrics, such as startup time, bandwidth, and bisection bandwidth.

The Sun HPC ClusterTools software includes a highly optimized implementation of MPI-1.1 and portions of MPI-2 standard that is referred to as the Sun MPI implementation. Compilation and linking of MPI programs should be done using the mpcc, mpf90, and other mp* wrappers (in /opt/SUNWhpc/bin) in order to include and link all relevant MPI files and libraries. ClusterTools software supports CRE and LSF job scheduling tools packages for managing and running MPI programs on cluster systems. Some examples of common usage of mprun and bsub commands for job submission and control were provided in this chapter.

The Sun MPI implementation has many features to support high performance MPI applications on Sun platforms. Some of the important features of Sun MPI library are as follows:

- Transparent support for shared memory, RSM (for SCI-based clusters), and TCP protocols for communication
- Support for process yielding and coscheduling
- Support for CRE and LSF software
- Support for the Prism development tool
- Support for MPI-1.1 and MPI-2 features

Two features of the MPI-2 standard, namely, dynamic process management and MPI I/O, were illustrated with example programs.

A detailed description of Sun MPI environment variables for performance tuning and diagnostic information was presented. These variables can be used for fine-tuning dedicated execution control, collective communication, and point-to-point communication performance. Their effects on performance were shown with example programs. In general, the recommendation is not to change default values unless the interrelationships between the variables and their memory implications are well understood by developers. Arbitrarily changing values of the Sun MPI environment variables can lead to unpredictable results. If, however, a developer understands memory implications, then changing default values (such as for the variables `MPI_SHM_SBPOOLSIZE`, `MPI_SHM_NUMPOSTBOX`, and `MPI_SHM_REDUCESIZE`) can lead to considerable performance improvements depending on the program characteristics.

We also discussed the Sun Scalable Scientific Subroutine Library (S3L), which implements linear algebra calls, fast Fourier transforms, and other standard mathematical procedures for use in MPI programs, and illustrated its features such as runtime error checking mechanisms, called safety levels.

Finally, the MPI and OpenMP approaches were contrasted from the point of view of implementation, portability, development environment, and performance. Implementation issues relevant to hybrid models (mixed MPI+OpenMP approach) were also briefly discussed.

PART **IV** Appendices

Commands That Identify System Configuration Parameters

For efficient application development and tuning, it is very important to be able to determine parameters of a hardware platform and the software installed on the system. Knowing the version of the compiler can tell the developer what options and features are available. The version of the operating system may shed some light on available commands and libraries. To draw meaningful conclusions from benchmarking or from application performance measurements, it is essential to be able to determine hardware parameters such as CPU type and clock rate, or the sizes of available physical memory and caches. An application may determine some of these parameters at runtime and use this information for selecting optimal values for parameters used in computational algorithms.

In this appendix, we provide a partial list of commands available in the Solaris operating environment that can be used to determine system parameters and versions of commonly used software packages. We also give examples of obtaining system information from programs.

Hardware Parameters

The most basic system information can be generated with the uname(1) command. This command takes options to display one or more system characteristics. For example, with -i option it prints the name of the hardware platform. The option -a provides a combined listing of system characteristics.

```
example% uname -i
SUNW,Ultra-60
example% uname -a
SunOS example 5.8 Generic sun4u sparc SUNW,Ultra-60
```

The basic hardware parameters of an UltraSPARC-based system can be displayed with the prtdiag(1M) utility[1] located in the *<platform>*/sbin subdirectory of /usr/platform, where *<platform>* is the output of the uname -i command.

This utility lists the speed of the memory bus, the size of the physical memory (RAM), as well as the types, clock rates, sizes of level 2 caches, and other information for all the CPUs on the system. On server systems, it also shows the layout of physical memory.

Following is the output of the prtdiag command on an Enterprise 4500 system.

```
example% /usr/platform/`uname -i`/sbin/prtdiag
System Configuration:   Sun Microsystems   sun4u 8-slot Sun
Enterprise E4500/E5500
System clock frequency: 100 MHz
Memory size: 12288Mb


========================== CPUs ==========================


                      Run    Ecache   CPU     CPU
Brd   CPU   Module    MHz     MB      Impl.   Mask
---   ---   -------   -----   ------   ------   ----
 0     0      0       400     8.0     US-II    10.0
 0     1      1       400     8.0     US-II    10.0
 2     4      0       400     8.0     US-II    10.0
 2     5      1       400     8.0     US-II    10.0
 4     8      0       400     8.0     US-II    10.0
 4     9      1       400     8.0     US-II    10.0
 5    10      0       400     8.0     US-II    10.0
 5    11      1       400     8.0     US-II    10.0
```

1. On the Enterprise 10000 systems diagnostic, information can be found in the messages file in /var/opt/SUNWssp/adm directory.

```
  6    12    0     400    8.0    US-II    10.0
  6    13    1     400    8.0    US-II    10.0
  7    14    0     400    8.0    US-II    10.0
  7    15    1     400    8.0    US-II    10.0


========================= Memory =========================


                                               Intrlv.  Intrlv.
Brd    Bank   MB    Status   Condition  Speed   Factor   With
---    -----  ----  -------  ---------- -----   -------  -------
 0      0     1024  Active   OK         60ns    8-way    A
 0      1     1024  Active   OK         60ns    8-way    A
 2      0     1024  Active   OK         60ns    8-way    A
 2      1     1024  Active   OK         60ns    8-way    A
 4      0     1024  Active   OK         60ns    8-way    A
 4      1     1024  Active   OK         60ns    4-way    B
 5      0     1024  Active   OK         60ns    8-way    A
 5      1     1024  Active   OK         60ns    4-way    B
 6      0     1024  Active   OK         60ns    8-way    A
 6      1     1024  Active   OK         60ns    4-way    B
 7      0     1024  Active   OK         60ns    8-way    A
 7      1     1024  Active   OK         60ns    4-way    B


========================= IO Cards =========================


       Bus   Freq
Brd    Type  MHz   Slot  Name                                Model
---    ----  ----  ----  --------------------------------
                         ---------------------
 1     SBus  25     2    SUNW,qfe                     SUNW,sbus-qfe
 1     SBus  25     2    SUNW,qfe                     SUNW,sbus-qfe
 1     SBus  25     2    SUNW,qfe                     SUNW,sbus-qfe
 1     SBus  25     2    SUNW,qfe                     SUNW,sbus-qfe
 1     SBus  25     3    SUNW,hme
 1     SBus  25     3    SUNW,fas/sd (block)
 1     SBus  25    13    SUNW,socal/sf (scsi-3)          501-3060
 3     SBus  25     1    QLGC,isp/sd (block)          QLGC,ISP1000U
 3     SBus  25     3    SUNW,hme
 3     SBus  25     3    SUNW,fas/sd (block)
 3     SBus  25    13    SUNW,socal/sf (scsi-3)          501-3060


No failures found in System
===========================
```

```
No System Faults found
========================
```

The output shows that this system has 12 UltraSPARC-II CPUs running at 400 MHz rate with 8 MB level 2 caches. It also shows that the system has 12 GB of physical memory.

The CPU type, approximate clock rate, floating point unit (FPU) type, and clock rate can be shown with the fpversion(1) command, which is a part of the compiler distribution. This option also suggests the optimal values for -xtarget and -xcache compiler options for a particular platform.

```
example% fpversion
  A SPARC-based CPU is available.
  CPU's clock rate appears to be approximately 356.2 MHz.
  Kernel says CPU's clock rate is 360.0 MHz.
  Kernel says main memory's clock rate is 120.0 MHz.
  Sun-4 floating-point controller version 0 found.
  An UltraSPARC chip is available.
  FPU's frequency appears to be approximately 369.5 MHz.
  cpu_arch=0x8 cpu_mach=0x0 psr_impl=0xf psr_vers=0xe fsr_vers=0x0 which=5
  Use "-xtarget=ultra2 -xcache=16/32/1:4096/64/1" code-generation option.
  Hostid = 0x80AAE9F3.
```

Another important command that prints system information is prtconf(1M). Its output includes the name of the hardware implementation, the amount of physical memory available on the system, and the configuration of system peripherals. This command also displays parameters of the memory caches, including the associativity and line sizes.

```
example% prtconf -pv | grep cache | sort -u
        dcache-associativity:  00000001
        dcache-line-size:  00000020
        dcache-size:  00004000
        ecache-associativity:  00000001
        ecache-line-size:  00000040
        ecache-size:  00400000
        icache-associativity:  00000002
        icache-line-size:  00000020
        icache-size:  00004000
```

The sizes of caches, in particular the size of a level 2 cache, can be used by applications for determining parameters for optimizing cache usage. The following code example shows how the `prtconf` call can be made from a program.

CODE EXAMPLE A-1   Example of `prtconf` Call Made From a Program

```
/* example_prtconf.c
   cc example_prtconf.c -o example_prtconf */
#include <stdio.h>
#include <stdlib.h>
#include <string.h>
#include <unistd.h>
#include <sys/types.h>

int main(int argc, char *argv[])
{
   char buf[BUFSIZ];
   FILE *f = popen("/usr/sbin/prtconf -pv | "
                   "/usr/bin/grep cache | "
                   "/usr/bin/sed 's/^[ ]*//' | "
                   "/usr/bin/sort -u ", "r");
   long cachelines=0, cachelinesize=0, val;
   if (f == NULL) perror("popen"), exit(-1);

   while (fgets(buf, BUFSIZ, f) != NULL) {
      char *p = strchr(buf, ':');
      if (p != NULL) {
         *p = '\0';
         val = strtol(p+1, NULL, 16);
         if (strcmp(buf, "ecache-size") == 0)
             printf("Level two cache size == %ld bytes\n", val);
         if (strcmp(buf, "dcache-size") == 0)
           printf("Level one data cache size == %ld bytes\n", val);
      }
   }
   pclose(f);
   return 0;
}
```

```
example% cc example_prtconf.c -o example_prtconf
example% example_prtconf
Level one data cache size == 16384 bytes
Level two cache size == 4194304 bytes
```

A command that displays information about processors is psrinfo(1M). The status of a processor can be changed with psradm(1M) command. It is possible to check on which CPU a running process is scheduled, by looking into the psinfo file in the /proc file system. The following example prints out the ID of the CPU on which it is scheduled. It can also give the same information for another serial process whose ID is passed to it as an argument.

CODE EXAMPLE A-2 Checking processor_ID

```
/* example_processor_ID.c
   cc example_processor_ID.c -o example_processor_ID */
#include <procfs.h>
#include <fcntl.h>
int main(int argc, char *argv[]){
   psinfo_t psinfo;
   int fd;
   char pname[20]="/proc/self/psinfo";
   if(argc-1) sprintf(pname,"/proc/%s/psinfo",argv[1]);
   fd=open(pname,O_RDONLY);
   read(fd,&psinfo,sizeof(psinfo_t));
   printf("Processor ID: %d\n",psinfo.pr_lwp.pr_onpro);
   return 0;
}
```

```
example% cc example_processor_ID.c -o example_processor_ID
example% example_processor_ID
Processor ID: 2
example% example_processor_ID
Processor ID: 0
example% example_processor_ID 2431
Processor ID: 2
```

System Configuration

The host name of the system can be displayed with uname -n. The host ID, a unique numeric identifier for the system, can be printed with the hostid(1) command. The IP address and other network interface parameters can be configured with the ifconfig(1M) utility.

The -r option of uname shows the release level of the operating system. Full information about the version of the Solaris operating environment is stored in the /etc/release file.

Solaris 7 and 8 environments can be booted in either 32-bit or 64-bit mode. The isainfo(1) command can display whether the booted kernel can run 64-bit applications.

```
example% isainfo -v
64-bit sparcv9 applications
32-bit sparc applications
```

For successful compilation of the programs, it is essential to have the Solaris environment that provides developer system support. The choice between the developer and end-user versions of Solaris environment is performed at the installation stage. An easy way to tell which version is installed on a system is to check if the packages with the header files and development utilities are installed on the system. This can be done with the pkginfo(1) command.

```
example% pkginfo SUNWhea SUNWxcu4t
system      SUNWhea        SunOS Header Files
system      SUNWxcu4t      XCU4 make and sccs utilities
```

It is always recommended to install the latest patches for the operating system kernel and for Sun software products. The patches can be downloaded from http://sunsolve.sun.com web site. The Solaris command showrev(1M) with option -p displays the revision information about the patches installed on the system.

The system definition information and the value of some kernel tunables, including the parameters for inter process communication, can be obtained with the sysdef(1M) command.

```
example% sysdef
...
20897792         maximum memory allowed in buffer cache (bufhwm)
```

```
    15946        maximum number of processes (v.v_proc)
       99        maximum global priority in sys class (MAXCLSYSPRI)
    15941        maximum processes per user id (v.v_maxup)
       30        auto update time limit in seconds (NAUTOUP)
       25        page stealing low water mark (GPGSLO)
        5        fsflush run rate (FSFLUSHR)
       25      minimum resident memory for avoiding deadlock (MINARMEM)
       25      minimum swapable memory for avoiding deadlock (MINASMEM)
...
* IPC Messages
*
  2048  max message size (MSGMAX)
  4096  max bytes on queue (MSGMNB)
    50  message queue identifiers (MSGMNI)
    40  system message headers (MSGTQL)
*
* IPC Semaphores
*
    10  semaphore identifiers (SEMMNI)
    60  semaphores in system (SEMMNS)
    30  undo structures in system (SEMMNU)
    25  max semaphores per id (SEMMSL)
    10  max operations per semop call (SEMOPM)
    10  max undo entries per process (SEMUME)
 32767  semaphore maximum value (SEMVMX)
 16384  adjust on exit max value (SEMAEM)
*
* IPC Shared Memory
*
2120000000      max shared memory segment size (SHMMAX)
     1  min shared memory segment size (SHMMIN)
   200  shared memory identifiers (SHMMNI)
   200  max attached shm segments per process (SHMSEG)
...
```

The configurable system parameters can be determined programmatically with the
sysconf(3C) call. The following example determines the number of processors on
the system and their status.

CODE EXAMPLE A-3 Usage of sysconf to Determine Number and Status of CPUs

```
/* example_sysconf.c
   cc example_sysconf.c -o example_sysconf */
#include <stdio.h>
#include <unistd.h>
#include <sys/processor.h>


int main(int argc, char *argv[])
{
```

CODE EXAMPLE A-3 Usage of `sysconf` to Determine Number and Status of CPUs

```
processorid_t prid;
processor_info_t info;
int pcount, ncpu = sysconf(_SC_NPROCESSORS_CONF);
for (prid=0, pcount=0; pcount < ncpu; prid++) {
    if (processor_info(prid, &info) != -1) {
        pcount++;
        printf("CPU[%d] (%s) type=%-6s clock=%dMHz\n",
        prid, info.pi_state==P_ONLINE ? "online":"offline",
        info.pi_processor_type, info.pi_clock);
    }
}
return 0;
}
```

```
example% cc example_sysconf.c -o example_sysconf
example% example_sysconf
CPU[0] (online) type=sparcv9 clock=360MHz
CPU[2] (online) type=sparcv9 clock=360MHz
```

Additional system information can be read with the `sysinfo(2)` call. The type and status of a processor can be also determined from a program with a `processor_info(2)` call.

The amount of the disk space available on all local and mounted file systems can be viewed with the `df(1M)` command. By default it shows the disk space in blocks. The same information is written in kilobytes if the `-k` option is set. The output of `df` lists both the amount of used and available space for the file systems. If the `-l` option is specified, the `df` command lists only local file systems.

The `du(1M)` command provides a more detailed report of disk usage within a file system. It displays the space occupied by a directory with all its subdirectories either in blocks or in kilobytes if the `-k` option is set.

The amount of disk space dedicated to `swap` can be shown and managed with `swap(1M)` command. The sizes of swap partitions or files is displayed with the `swap -a`. A user with superuser privileges can add or delete selected swap areas with the `swap -a` and `swap -d` commands, respectively.

Parameters of Installed Software and Hardware

We discussed the compilers and development tools for Solaris in Chapter 3. Here we repeat that the default location for Sun compilers is /opt/SUNWspro and that the version of the compilers can be shown with the -V option.

```
example% /opt/SUNWspro/bin/cc -V
cc: Sun WorkShop 6 2000/04/07 C 5.1
usage: cc [ options] files.  Use 'cc -flags' for details
```

The utility dumpstabs(1) that comes with compilers prints the debug information present in object files and executables. It can be used to find out which version of a compiler and which options were used for creating a binary.

```
example% dumpstabs a.out | grep SUNWspro
   2:   .stabs "/tmp; /opt/SUNWspro/bin/../WS6/bin/cc -fast
-xarch=v8plusa -xrestrict -c  example_test.c
-W0,-xp",N_CMDLINE,0x0,0x0,0x0
```

The output shows that the executable a.out was built from the file example_test.c, which was compiled with -fast -xarch=v8plusa -xrestrict options. Also, the WS6 directory in the path of cc command indicates that Forte Developer 6 compiler was used for compilation. The same information can also be obtained using the /usr/ccs/bin/dump utility:

```
example% dump -c a.out | grep SUNWspro
   <67>          /tmp; /opt/SUNWspro/bin/../WS6/bin/cc -fast
-xarch=v8plusa -xrestrict -c  example_test.c -W0,-xp
```

The symbol table and the debugging information can be removed with the strip(1) command.

The information on the version of the HPC ClusterTools software can be obtained using the mpadmin(8) command

```
example% mpadmin -V
mpadmin: HPC 3.1 17 Feb 2000 RTE 1.1_64
```

There are several types of graphics boards, or frame buffers, available for Sun systems. They include PGX, Creator3D, Elite3D, and Expert3D. The configuration of the corresponding graphics accelerators can be inspected or modified with `m64config`(1M), `ffbconfig`(1M), `afbconfig`(1M), and `ifbconfig`(1M). The generic command `fbconfig`(1M) can be used on Solaris 8 if the type of frame buffer is not known.

Many graphics and visualization applications use OpenGL libraries. The OpenGL software is distributed with the Solaris Operating Environment. It can be also freely downloaded from `http://www.sun.com/software/graphics/OpenGL/` together with documentation and recommended patches. The installed OpenGL software can be tested with the installation demo program `ogl_install_check` placed in the `/usr/openwin/demo/GL` directory. This program opens a window and displays a spinning wheel. It also prints such information as the version of OpenGL and the version of the graphics board to the standard output.

```
example% ogl_install_check


=================================================================
Sun Microsystems:          ogl_install_check        64-bit
-----------------------------------------------------------------
  OpenGL Vendor:                 Sun Microsystems, Inc.
  OpenGL Version:                1.2 Sun OpenGL 1.2 for Solaris
  OpenGL Renderer:               Elite-3D, VIS
  OpenGL Extension Support:      GL_ARB_imaging
                                 GL_EXT_abgr
...
```

The version of the *Java Development Kit* (JDK) installed on the system can be displayed with `java -version` or `java -fullversion` commands.

```
example% java -version
java version "1.2.1"
Solaris VM (build Solaris_JDK_1.2.1_04c, native threads, sunwjit)
example% java -fullversion
java full version "Solaris_JDK_1.2.1_04c"
```

Summary of Commands

We summarize some commands in TABLE A-1 for quick reference.

TABLE A-1   Selected Solaris Commands to Determine System Parameters

Command	Output
uname	Basic information about the system including hardware implementation, system name, and operating system version.
cat /etc/release	Full information about the release of the operating system. Solaris 2.6 and later.
hostname	Name of the system.
hostid	Unique numeric identifier of the system.
showrev -p	Revision information about installed patches.
prtdiag	System configuration and diagnostic information, including the size of the physical memory, CPU type, clock rate, and level 2 cache size.
fpversion	Information about the CPU and FPU. This utility is a part of compiler distribution. It measures the approximate clock rates by executing and timing a test loop.
prtconf	System configuration information including memory size and cache parameters.
sysdef	System definitions including kernel tunables and parameters for interprocess communication.
ifconfig	Network interface parameters.
isainfo -v	Which applications (32-bit or 64-bit) can run on the system. Solaris 7 or 8.
psrinfo	IDs and status information for all CPUs on the system.
df	Amount of used and available disk space on mounted file systems.
du	Disk usage within a file system.
swap -l	Information about swap areas on the system.
fbconfig	Frame buffer configuration.

Architecture of UltraSPARC Microprocessor Family

The salient architectural features of UltraSPARC microprocessors, which are used in Sun workstations and server product lines, are described in this appendix. At the time of this writing, the UltraSPARC microprocessor family comprises the S-series (UltraSPARC I, II, and III), I-series (UltraSPARC IIi), and E-series (UltraSPARC IIe).

For detailed information, refer to the following publications: *UltraSPARC I and II User's Manual*, *UltraSPARC IIi User's Manual*, *UltraSPARC IIe User's Manual*, and *UltraSPARC III Programmer's Reference Manual*.

UltraSPARC I and II Processors

UltraSPARC I, the first member of the UltraSPARC family, was introduced in 1995. It was designed with simplicity and high performance in mind and with a view to scale it to high clock frequencies. UltraSPARC I implementations ranged from 143Mhz to 200Mhz in processor clock frequency. It is a full implementation of the 64-bit architecture with support for a 44-bit virtual address space and a 41-bit physical address space.

UltraSPARC I is a four-way superscalar in-order issue, out-of-order completion processor. The design uses up to 3.8 million transistors to implement two on-chip caches, a memory management unit, an external cache controller, a large register file, dual instruction and data Translation Lookaside Buffers (TLBs), load and store buffers that decouple data accesses from the pipeline, and a central pipelined compute core with nine separate execution stages.

The processor core consists of two integer Arithmetic Logic Units (ALUs), two floating-point/graphics units, a load/store unit, and a branch prediction unit. Most integer instructions (except multiply and divide) complete in a single processor clock while floating-point multiply and add have latencies of three cycles and can be fully pipelined. Floating-point divide and square root have latencies of 12 and 22 cycles, respectively for single and double operands. A total of up to four instructions can be issued in each cycle (a combination of two integer instructions, two floating-point instructions, a load/store instruction, and a branch instruction). The pipeline consists of nine stages: the integer portion is six and three stages are devoted to floating-point and graphics operations. The instruction prefetch and dispatch unit prefetches instructions before they are actually needed in the pipeline. It has a buffer to store up to 12 instructions before sending them to the rest of the pipeline.

UltraSPARC I's level 1 D-cache is a 16-KB direct-mapped, virtually indexed, physically tagged cache. It is write-through, nonallocating on write-miss with 32-byte line size and 16-byte subblocks in each of the lines. The processor implements nonblocking loads. That is, loads that miss the D-cache do not necessarily stall the processor pipeline. The loads are instead directed to the load buffer where they wait for data to return from level 2 cache (which returns 16-bytes of data to level 1 D-cache). The pipeline stalls only when the instruction that uses the data returned by the load is executed and the data are not available. Similarly, the store buffer allows the processor pipeline to continue executing even if the data that are needed in the store instruction(s) are not ready. The address of the store instruction is buffered until the data are eventually available.

The Instruction cache is 16-KB pseudo-two way set associative, physically indexed, physically tagged with 32-byte line size. The level 2 external cache is a unified instruction and data direct-mapped, physically indexed, physically tagged, write-back, allocating on write-miss cache with 64-byte line size (with no subblocking). The size of level 2 cache is variable and UltraSPARC I supported from 512 KB to 4 MB. Both level 2 cache data and tags are located off-chip as SRAM memory.

The level 1 data and instruction caches are fully contained in the level 2 cache. The memory management unit (MMU) is comprised of a 64-entry fully associative Instruction and data TLBs. The data TLB supports page sizes of 8 KB, 64 KB, 512 KB, and 4 MB.

The second member of the UltraSPARC S-series is the UltraSPARC II microprocessor. It uses the same microarchitecture as UltraSPARC I, but uses a newer process technology, higher clock frequency, larger external cache sizes, multiple SRAM modes, multiple system to processor clock frequency ratios, and support for the SPARC V9 prefetch instruction. The processor debuted at 250 MHz and has been continuously scaled, with the fastest shipping systems (as of year 2000) at 480 MHz frequency. The size of supported external cache has been increased up to 8 MB and runs at one-half of processor clock frequency. For example, on a 400 MHz UltraSPARC II, the external cache frequency is 200 MHz.

UltraSPARC III Processor

UltraSPARC III is the third and latest member of the S series of UltraSPARC processors. It is designed to scale up to high clock frequencies (in excess of 1 GHz) and uses a microarchitecture completely different from UltraSPARC I. The first implementations of the processor are available in 600 MHz, 750 MHz, and 900 MHz clock frequencies. The processor has up to 16 million transistors and uses a 6-metal-layer 0.18-micron CMOS technology operating at 1.7 volts. It provides full binary compatibility with previous generation SPARC processors while incorporating new instructions for interval arithmetic support and enhancement of the VIS instruction set.

UltraSPARC III is architected as a 6-way superscalar, in-order instruction issue, out-of-order completion RISC processor. It can issue up to four instructions per cycle. A combination of up to two integer, one conditional, one load (or store), and two floating-point instructions can be executed in a clock cycle. It has a 14-stage pipeline, deeper than its predecessors (UltraSPARC II has a 9-stage pipeline) in order to meet the clock rate and performance goals of the processor. The pipeline is essentially composed of several separate pipelines, each executing different types of instructions. These are as follows: A0 (integer ALU pipe 0), A1 (integer ALU pipe 1), BR (branch prediction pipe), MS (memory/special pipe), FM (floating-point , graphics multiple pipe), and FA (floating-point , graphics addition pipe), respectively. The fourteen stages of the pipeline are summarized in TABLE B-1:

TABLE B-1 Pipeline Stages in UltraSPARC III Processor

Pipeline Stage	Function
A	Generate instruction fetch address
P	Start of instruction cache access
F	Second cycle of instruction cache access
B	Branch target address calculation
I	Decode second cycle of instructions
J	Steering of decoded instructions to execution units
R	Read integer register file, steer FP instructions to FPU
E	Execute integer instructions, access FP register file, D-cache access
C	Second cycle of D-cache access; execute first cycle of FP instructions
M	D-cache miss detection
W	Execute third cycle of FP instructions

TABLE B-1 Pipeline Stages in UltraSPARC III Processor *(Continued)*

Pipeline Stage	Function
X	Last cycle for FP instructions
T	Trap signaling
D	Write results to register files

The processor has six main functional units: Instruction Issue Unit (IIU), Integer Execution Unit (IEU), Floating-point Execution Unit (FPU), Data Cache Unit (DCU), External Memory Unit (EMU), and System Interface Unit (SIU).

The instruction issue unit (IIU) fetches instructions and feeds them to execution pipelines in a processor. The IIU is comprised of an instruction cache, a 16K entry branch prediction table, an instruction TLB, a 20-entry instruction queue, and logic for predecoding and steering instructions into different execution pipelines.

The integer execution unit (IEU) executes all the integer data type instructions, which include arithmetics, logicals, shifts, branches and memory (loads and stores). The A0, A1, MS, and BR pipes can be used to execute a combination of two integer (arithmetic, logical, and shift), one memory (load and store) and one branch instructions every clock cycle. The MS pipe also executes floating-point data type memory instructions. So, it can be used either for integer or floating-point data type memory operations in a given cycle.

The floating-point execution unit (FPU) executes all the floating-point and partitioned fixed-point data type instructions. The unit is shared for execution of both floating-point and VIS instructions. It allows fully pipelined execution of floating-point and fixed-point add, subtract, compare, and multiply instructions. Additionally, a third data path allows a nonpipelined division to proceed concurrently with the multiply and add pipes (FM and FA).

The data cache unit (DCU) consists of all the level 1 on-chip data caches and data TLB. The DCU unit was designed for both low latency and high bandwidth as it is crucial for the overall performance delivered by the processor. In UltraSPARC III, the latencies of level 1 cache accesses were decreased by use of sum addressed cache memory, and bandwidths were scaled through the use of wave-pipelined SRAM design [Horel99]. The DCU comprises of a D-cache, a prefetch cache, a write cache, and data TLB. More details on these caches are provided later.

The external memory unit (EMU) controls the off-chip level 2 cache (built using SRAM and up to 8 MB) and the main memory (up to 8 GB per processor and implemented using SDRAM memory). The EMU also contains a 90-KB on-chip cache tag RAM (to support 8-MB cache), which allows early detection of level 2 cache misses and improves snoop bandwidth for cache coherency in multiprocessor systems. The data path to level 2 cache is 256 bits wide and can deliver the entire level 1 cache line (32-bytes) in a single SRAM cycle. With the level 2 cache clock frequency at 200 MHz, this results in a L2 cache bandwidth of 6.4 GB/sec.

The on-chip integration of the memory controller in UltraSPARC III substantially improves memory bandwidth and latency compared to UltraSPARC I and II processors. The memory bandwidth per processor is 2.4 GB/sec.

The system interface unit (SIU) controls the interaction of the processor with peripheral devices (I/O) and other processor and memory subsystems in multiprocessor systems. The unit is designed to handle up to 15 outstanding transactions to external devices with support for out-of-order data delivery on completion of a transaction. This is particularly helpful on multiprocessor systems in enabling faster servicing of memory requests. UltraSPARC III also provides extensive error correction facilities in the external cache and memory system. There is ECC on the level 2 cache data SRAM memory and on the system data bus to detect errors as soon as possible. Error correction is performed on every external chip-to-chip transaction to isolate correctly any fault to its source. Parity check is performed on the system address bus, and an independent 8-bit-wide "back-door" bus is implemented. In the event of error detection on main system bus, the "back-door" bus can be used to diagnose the problem.

UltraSPARC III uses a sophisticated hierarchy of caches (on-chip and off-chip) and translation lookaside buffers to decrease the effect of memory latency and provide data at a high enough bandwidth to keep the processor's different execution units busy.

The instruction cache is a four-way associative, 32-KB, physically indexed, physically tagged cache. It is not included in the level 2 (external) cache and has a 32-byte line-size with no subblocking. The instruction TLB is two-way associative and has 128 entries for 8 KB pages (16 entry fully associative for 64 KB, 512 KB, and 4 MB page sizes).

The level 1 D-cache is four-way associative, 64 KB with 32-byte line size. It is virtually indexed, physically tagged, write-through, has a no write-allocate, and it is not included in the external cache. The prefetch cache is four-way associative, 2 KB physically indexed, physically tagged, and is also not included in the external cache. It has a 64-byte line size with 32-byte subblocks. The prefetch cache is globally invalidated on context changes and memory management unit updates. Individual lines are invalidated on store hits.

The processor also contains a four-way associative, 2 KB, 64-byte line (32-byte subblocks) write cache. The write cache is physically indexed, physically tagged, and is included in the external cache. This cache enhances the store bandwidth of the processor. The D-TLB is 512-entry, two-way associative for 8-KB page-sizes. There is also a 16-entry fully-associative TLB for other supported page sizes (64 KB, 512 KB, and 4 MB). The level 2 external cache is a 1-8 MB, direct-mapped, physically indexed, and physically tagged cache. It uses write-allocate, write-back policy. The line size is 64-bytes for 1 MB, 256-bytes for 4 MB, and 512-bytes for 8 MB; the lines are subblocked in sizes of 64-bytes.

The prefetch capability implemented in the UltraSPARC III processor represents a significant improvement over the UltraSPARC II processor. In UltraSPARC III, up to 8 prefetch instructions can be in progress (that is, outstanding) at the same time. The integer data can be brought up to level 2 cache while floating-point data can be brought all the way into the prefetch cache (from memory). Prefetch cache allows the ability to issue two floating-point loads every processor cycle.

TABLE B-2 provides average latencies in clock cycles for some simple operations for both UltraSPARC II and III processors. Note that though the latency as measured in processor clock cycles is generally higher for UltraSPARC III, the absolute latency (as measured in nanoseconds) is lower due to higher clock rate.

TABLE B-2 Latencies (in Clock Cycles) of Selected Instructions and Operations on UltraSPARC II and III Processors

Operation	UltraSPARC II (450 MHz)	UltraSPARC III (900 MHz)
Load latency to D-cache	2-3 cycles	2-3 cycles
Load latency to Level 2 cache	9-10 cycles	14-16 cycles
Simple floating-point (add/mul) and VIS	3 cycles	4 cycles
Floating-point divide/sqrt	13-22 cycles	17-29 cycles
Simple integer operations (add, shift)	1 cycle	1 cycle
Integer multiply (upper bound)	20 cycles	8 cycles
Branch misprediction penalty	4 cycles	4-8 cycles
Integer divide (upper bound)	36 cycles	39 cycles

UltraSPARC IIi Processor

The UltraSPARC IIi processor is derived from the UltraSPARC II processor and provides full support for SPARC V9 architecture and VIS extensions, while maintaining compatibility with SPARC V8 specification. The processor is designed to support low-cost uniprocessor systems and is designed for running networked applications that need compute power, multimedia capabilities, and optimized data throughput. To achieve these goals, the processor integrates an on-chip PCI bus controller to interface directly with a 32-bit PCI bus, an on-chip I/O memory management unit, an on-chip external cache controller, an on-chip memory controller, and an on-chip UPA64S graphics control unit.

The processor core is essentially identical to UltraSPARC II and consists of a Prefetch and Dispatch Unit (PDU), an Integer Execution Unit (IEU), a Floating Point Unit (FPU), a Load and Store Unit, and instruction and data Caches. The PDU prefetches instructions from all levels of memory hierarchy and issues them to different execution units. It consists of a 12-entry instruction buffer, a two-way associative 16 KB physically indexed, physically tagged instruction cache, branch prediction, and instruction grouping logic. The processor can issue up to four instructions per cycle to a nine-stage-deep pipeline, which has two integer ALUs and two floating-point / graphics execution units.

As in the case of UltraSPARC I and II processors, the memory management unit supports a 44-bit virtual address space and a 41-bit physical address space. To accelerate address translation, there are instruction and data TLBs on-chip. These are 64-entry, fully associative buffers of page descriptors.

The UltraSPARC IIi data cache is a 16-KB direct mapped, write-through, nonallocating cache that is used on load or store accesses from the CPU to cacheable pages of main memory. It is a virtually indexed and physically tagged cache. The D-cache is organized as 512 lines, with two 16-byte subblocks of data per line. Each line has a cache tag associated with it. On a data cache miss to a cacheable location, 16-bytes of data are written into the cache. The external cache is direct mapped, physically indexed, physically tagged, write back, and allocating on write miss. Its size can be 256 KB, 512 KB, 1 MB, or 2 MB with a line size of 64-bytes and no subblocking. The external cache is nonblocking and provides overlapped processing during load and store misses. For instance, stores that hit the E-cache can proceed while a load miss is being processed.

UltraSPARC IIe Processor

The UltraSPARC IIe processor is designed for embedded applications in network service provider and telecommunications markets. It is available in 400-500 MHz processor clock frequencies. Its design borrows many features from the UltraSPARC IIi processor and as such it is fully application software binary compatible with the entire UltraSPARC processor family[1]. The chip consumes the least amount of power among UltraSPARC processors: 8 watts (maximum) when operating at 400 MHz clock frequency with a 1.5-volt supply and 13 watts (maximum) at 500 MHz clock frequency with a 1.7-volt supply. It also features a power management mechanism to slow down processor clock speed and decrease power consumption.

UltraSPARC IIe implements SPARC V9 architecture and full support for 64-bit addressing. It consists of a four-way superscalar pipeline with two integer units, two floating-point/graphics units, one load/store unit, a branch prediction unit, and SDRAM memory controller that supports up to 2 GB memory. It has an integrated unified instruction and data level 2 cache, which is four-way set associative and can be programmed to be direct mapped. This internal cache eliminates the external cache and external cache controller featured in other UltraSPARC processors. Similar to UltraSPARC IIi, the UltraSPARC IIe processor does not include a UPA bus interface; instead the external controllers (PCI and memory) are integrated in the processor.

---

1. New instructions (byte shuffle and SIAM instruction) introduced in UltraSPARC III are not supported on other currently shipping UltraSPARC processors.

Architecture of UltraSPARC Interconnect Family

The UltraSPARC microprocessor family (described in Chapter 2 and Appendix B) is used in a varied line of desktop and server products targeted for high performance computing applications. An overview of the architecture of interconnects used in UltraSPARC-based products is given in this appendix, with references for further information.

As discussed in Chapter 2 and Appendix B, systems based on I and E series UltraSPARC processors do not require any external interconnect technology. UltraSPARC I and II processors (S series) use the Ultra Port Architecture (UPA), Gigaplane and Gigaplane XB interconnect technologies, depending on the product line (see Chapter 2). The first UltraSPARC III based systems use the Sun Fireplane Interconnect architecture.

Ultra Port Architecture Interconnect

The UPA is the interconnect definition for processors implementing SPARC V9 architecture, such as UltraSPARC processors. It describes the specification of the various interface ports to the processor and requirements imposed on the system interconnect by different devices such as the memory controller and I/O controller device.

The UPA interconnect is designed for S-series UltraSPARC I and II processors to support their high bandwidth requirements and to configure multiple devices requiring different bandwidths in an efficient cost-effective fashion. UPA is a flexible architecture designed to meet the cost/performance needs of desktop as well as multiprocessor server systems. Although it is used in systems of different configurations, the design has been optimized for one to four processor systems.

UPA supports a wide range of ports (processor port, memory port, I/O port to SBus or PCI device, and UPA graphics port) of different widths. For example, the I/O port is 72 bits (64 bits + 8 bits for error-checking) while the processor port is 144 bits (128 bits + 16 bits for error-checking). As data flows through the UPA switch, the data rate could change depending on what part of the system is being accessed. The support for ports of different sizes decreases cost (as low-cost devices can use a smaller UPA port) without sacrificing performance (as each device has dedicated access to its port).

The UPA uses a packet switched bus protocol with separate address and data lines and provides a point-to-point write-invalidate MOESI (Modified, Own, Exclusive, Shared and Invalid) coherency on 64-byte wide cache lines. The bus clock frequencies are in the range of 83 to 120 Mhz with all ports operating at the same frequency. The address bus is 64 bits wide to implement the 64-bit SPARC V9 architecture while the data bus is 144-bits wide. Since the data and address busses are separate, no dead cycles are created as would be in the case of a bus that is shared for both address and data transfers. The data transfer rate is 16 bytes in each UPA cycle (a peak data bandwidth of 16x100 = 1.6 GB/second for 100 MHz bus). The address transfer rate is once every 4 data cycles (or UPA cycles). For example at 100 MHz, the UPA switch can handle 25 million address transfers per second.

The point-to-point messages required for the coherency are implemented by a centralized controller for desktop systems (1 to 4 processors) and by means of a distributed controller for larger systems. UPA can maintain a duplicate set of all cache tags in the system allowing memory operations to be initiated in parallel with lookups of duplicate tags. Some ports are considered *master* ports (such as processor or I/O port); these can issue read/write transactions to the interconnect using a distributed arbitration protocol for driving the address bus. The *slave* interfaces (such as a graphics device) can only receive read/write transactions from master interfaces. A UPA port can also become an *interrupter interface* or an *interrupt handler interface*.

There are many benefits of the multiple point-to-point buses in the UPA switch; it minimizes the number of arbitration cycles, and the system controller can process multiple simultaneous requests. This reduces latency and possibility of contention under heavy system load.

Additional information on UPA can be obtained from the whitepaper *The Ultra Port Architecture*, available from `http://www.sun.com/microelectronics/whitepapers/index.html`.

Gigaplane Interconnect

The Enterprise series (comprising of EXX00 and EX000 series[1]) is a family of uniform memory access (UMA) symmetric multiprocessor (SMP) systems designed for significantly higher performance and scalability than their UltraSPARC-based desktop counterparts. These systems are designed around a passive backplane system bus called the Gigaplane interconnect. The Gigaplane is designed to provide high bandwidth and low latency while supporting up to 30 processors and multiple high performance I/O devices (SBus or PCI based).

The Gigaplane bus is implemented as a centerplane with connections for 8 board slots in front and 8 in back. The EXX00 and EX000 systems support three types of boards: a CPU/memory board that can have two processors and up to 2 GB of memory, a dual SBus or PCI bus[2] I/O board, and a graphics fast-frame buffer board. A system is required to have at least one I/O board, implying that up to 15 CPU/memory boards, or a total of 30 processors, can be configured in a Gigaplane system. The on-board connections are built using the UPA bus. For example, the two processors and memory banks on a CPU/memory board are interfaced to the Gigaplane via the UPA switch. In this regard, the Ultra Enterprise series systems use a two-level bus scheme architecture. Each board also consists of an address controller and a data controller interfaced to the Gigaplane.

The Gigaplane is a packet-switched bus running in the range of approximately 83 MHz to 100 MHz frequency. It consists of an address bus (an address packet consists of a 41-bit physical address and 7-bit source id) and a 288-bit-wide data bus (256-bit data plus 32-bit ECC). The packet-switched design with separate busses leads to no dead cycles on the bus, because it provides the ability to complete transactions in any order (as opposed to completion in the order in which transactions were issued). The bus also has 16 dedicated lines to implement a distributed two-cycle arbitration scheme for data and address transfers.

The data packets also carry data id tags as they may be sent in an order that is different from the address packets. The data bus carries 64-byte data in two cycles; this is the same amount of time required by the address bus to carry an address transaction (an address is broadcast in one cycle and snoop results returned on the second cycle). At 100 MHz, this provides a coherency bandwidth of 50 million addresses per second and a data bandwidth of $32 \times 100 = 3.2$ GB/second. The measured lmbench ([McVoy96]) latency for an Enterprise 6500 running Gigaplane at 83.5 MHz is approximately 306 nanoseconds (see [Singhal96]).

---

1. The EXX00 family comprises Enterprise 3500, Enterprise 4500, Enterprise 5500, and Enterprise 6500 systems; the EX000 family comprises Enterprise 3000, Enterprise 4000, Enterprise 5000, and Enterprise 5000 systems.

2. Only EXX00 systems support the PCI bus I/O boards.

Gigaplane uses an invalidation-based snooping MOESI cache coherence protocol. The address controller on each board has duplicate tags for snooping of each device. The split transaction protocol in Gigaplane uses no transient states, making it simpler to pipeline multiple transactions on a bus. It allows up to 112 system wide (7 from each board) outstanding transactions with out-of-order responses. This decreases the effects of contention and long latency operations on system performance. The design increases reliability and uptime of systems by allowing hot-plug and hot-unplug of boards.

Further information on Gigaplane design can be obtained from [Singhal96] and [Cockcroft98].

Gigaplane XB Crossbar Interconnect

The Sun Enterprise 10000 system is the largest UltraSPARC-processor-based SMP system. It uses an active centerplane interconnect called Gigaplane XB. The Enterprise 10000 uses a single board type where each board can have 4 processors, 4 memory banks (4 GB of memory), and two I/O buses. A fully configured system can have up to 16 boards for a total of 64 processors and 64 GB of memory. The Gigaplane XB interconnect is designed to provide the bandwidth required by a system using up to 64 processors, provide flexibility in the system in form of dynamic system domains, and provide a very high level of reliability, availability, and serviceability.

Like EXX00 and EX000 systems, Enterprise 10000 also has a two-level interconnect system. UPA is used to connect the on-board components (CPUs, memory, I/O buses) to Gigaplane XB, which transfers addresses and data between the boards. The Enterprise 10000 uses a uniform memory access architecture, and memory accesses always go on the centerplane even if the requested memory location is physically located on the board originating the memory transaction. Additionally, the memory latency is independent of locations of boards where memory transactions originate and memory is located.

The Gigaplane XB uses separate address and data interconnects with different topologies. It operates at frequencies in the range of approximately 83 MHz to 100 MHz (see [Cockcroft98]). There are four interleaved address busses, each covering a quarter of the physical memory on the system. Address transactions take two cycles (busses snoop every other cycle and update the duplicate tags in alternate cycles). Because there are four busses, at 100 MHz frequency the coherency bandwidth is $4 \times 100/2 = 200$ Million addresses per second. Because data bandwidth is coherency bandwidth multiplied by snoop block size (64 bytes for UPA), the data rate required to match coherency bandwidth is $200 \times 64 = 12.8$ GB/second at 100 MHz.

The data interconnect is a 16-by-16 interboard crossbar with a data path width of 144 bits (128 data + 16 ECC). A data packet transfer occurs in 4 cycles. The capacity of the data crossbar increases as boards are added, with maximum capacity achieved when all 16 boards are configured. In this case, the peak data bandwidth of 12.8 GB/second (for 100 MHz interconnect frequency) is attained. The latency for a load-miss as measured by the lmbench benchmark is around 470 nanoseconds [Charlesworth98]. Also, for information on data bandwidth variation with the number of configured boards in an Enterprise 10000 system, see [Charlesworth98] or [Cockcroft98].

The Gigaplane XB interconnect provides point-to-point wires, which leads to less electrical load, faster clock, higher reliability (failure in one board has lesser effect on other boards), and allows partitioning into independent multiboard domains. All the router circuitry in the centerplane is physically and electrically in the middle of the system. There is also support for hot-swap and dynamic reconfiguration. With dynamic reconfiguration, boards can be moved in and out of domains as well as between different domains in a running system [Charlesworth98]. Dynamic reconfiguration also allows moving boards in and out or between active and inactive domains.

A comparison of the UPA-based interconnects with Sun's prior interconnect busses is shown in TABLE C-1:

TABLE C-1 Characteristics of UPA Compared to Prior Generation Interconnects Used in Sun Systems

Feature	Mbus Based	XDBus Based	UPA Based
Clock (Mhz)	40	40-55	83-120
Address and Data Paths	Multiplexed	Multiplexed	Separate
Path Switching	Circuit	Packet	Packet
Data Port Width (bytes)	8	8	16
Physical Connections	Busses	Busses	Busses and Routers
Snooping Control On	Separate Chip	Separate Chip	Separate Chip
Clocks Per Snoop	16	11	2
Number of Snoopy Busses	1	1,2,4	1,4
Small System Size (# CPUs)	4	2	4
Medium System Size (# CPUs)	Not Applicable	20	30
Large System Size (# CPUs)	Not Applicable	64	64

TABLE C-1 Characteristics of UPA Compared to Prior Generation Interconnects Used in Sun Systems *(Continued)*

Feature	Mbus Based	XDBus Based	UPA Based
Small System Bandwidth (MB/sec.)	80	232	1,600 (100 MHz)
Medium System Bandwidth (MB/sec.)	Not Applicable	464	3,200 (100 MHz)
Large System Bandwidth (MB/sec.)	Not Applicable	1,200	12,800 (100 MHz)

Fireplane Interconnect

The Sun Fireplane interconnect is the new coherent shared-memory protocol interconnect between the processor, memory, I/O, and other devices in UltraSPARC III based systems. It improves upon the previous generation UPA interconnect in both performance and functionality. At the time of writing, this interconnect is being used in the UltraSPARC III-based Sun Blade 1000 and the Sun Fire 280R systems. One of the novel features of the Fireplane interconnect is that it does not define a data path topology but defines only the interface protocols for devices attached to the interconnect. Thus, the Fireplane does not define a strict interconnection topology and could be used to build a range of interconnections. This makes it applicable to a range of present and future generation UltraSPARC III-based systems.

In addition to supporting separate address and data paths, the Fireplane interconnect allows multiple outstanding transactions on the interconnect at the same time. The requests can complete out-of-order, permitting interleaving of different requests and decreasing contention when accessing the devices attached to the interconnect. For example, in the Sun Blade 1000, up to 15 outstanding 64-byte data transfer requests can be supported on the interconnect.

In the Sun Blade 1000, the interconnect takes a packet-switched (split transaction) bus topology for both data and address paths. The data path is a 288-bit (256 data + 32 ECC) on-chip bus implemented as a set of six identical ASICs (Application Specific Integrated Circuits). The ASICs cumulatively are called the combined processor memory switch (CPMS). There is point-to-point connectivity between the data path and the devices attached to the data path. The bus-based topology eliminates the need for a central system controller and simplifies the arbitration logic.

The memory controller is integrated on the UltraSPARC III processor, which leads to a reduction in memory latency and improved memory bandwidth. In the two-processor Sun Blade 1000 system, the memory controller on only one of the UltraSPARC III processors is enabled. One of the processors can directly access the memory through its port, while the other processor accesses memory over the Fireplane interconnect. Note that all address requests go over the interconnect to allow snooping for the purpose of ensuring coherency between the processor caches. The cache consistency protocol is based on invalidations and utilizes the MOESI cache state-transition algorithm.

The UltraSPARC III processor that has the memory attached to it interfaces to the interconnect through a data-switch ASIC, which provides a 144-bit-wide data path. The other processor interfaces directly to the Fireplane interconnect. The data-switch ASIC is connected to the memory via a 576-bit (512 data + 64 ECC) wide path. The data bandwidth for a single processor system is $16 \times 150 = 2.4$ GB/seconds. For a two-processor system, the Fireplane interconnect can deliver up to $32 \times 150 = 4.8$ GB/seconds bandwidth.

In the UPA interconnect, the ports are designated as either master or slave. The data are "pushed" onto the interconnect when a write transaction is issued by a master device. By contrast, in the Fireplane interconnect, the target device "pulls" the data from the source when it needs it rather than data being "pushed" by the source device. This simplifies implementation and provides more balanced usage of system bandwidth.

For further information on Fireplane interconnect, refer to the whitepaper, *The Sun Blade 1000 Workstation Architecture*, available from `http://www.sun.com/desktop/sunblade1000`.

APPENDIX **D**

Hardware Counter Performance Metrics

UltraSPARC processors and the various application-specific integrated circuits (ASICs) on UltraSPARC-based systems have built-in hardware counters that provide a facility for low overhead measurement of a variety of events such as clock cycles, cache hits, load stalls, memory bank reads, and others. These measurements can be used to obtain directly and indirectly (based on derived quantities) useful information on the performance of a system as a whole under a workload or for an application.

In most of these devices, there is a single Performance Control Register (PCR), which is used to control a pair of 32-bit Performance Instrumentation Counters (PIC). The PICs count events independently of each other and can accumulate up to 4 billion events before wrapping around silently. Prior to the Solaris 8 operating environment release, access to these counters was privileged, and they could only be accessed via a special driver.

The support required in the kernel and tools to measure hardware counters depends on how these counters are used for data collection. The data can be collected in the following three ways:

- *Fine-grained*: The counters are used to measure short enough instruction or code sequences such that less than 4 billion events take place during the measurement interval. In this mode, only the ability to read the counter values is required

- *Medium-grained*: In this case, the measurement interval is long enough that more than 4 billion PIC events take place, and the counters overflow during the data collection experiment. For this type of measurement, the kernel and tool are required to provide support for accumulating counter values in 64-bit virtualized counters kept on a system-wide or a per-process basis.

- *Coarse-grained*: This type of measurement is one in which more than 4 billion counter events take place and also different types of events are recorded during the run. In this case, the ability to multiplex measurement of many different events simultaneously is needed in the kernel and the tool.

Beginning with the Solaris 8 operating environment, there is support in the kernel to virtualize the 32-bit hardware counters as 64-bit counters. Two tools (`cpustat` and `busstat`) are provided that can be configured to collect data in three ways (fine-, medium-, or coarse-grained). In the case of CPU counters, there is also support for collecting data on a per-process basis using the `cputrack` tool. When a context switch occurs, the kernel saves current values with the other state for a process and these values are updated with samples obtained from hardware counters. As long as the sampling of hardware counters is done at a granularity small enough that they do not wrap around between the samples, accurate counts for a long-running process can be obtained.

We discussed `cputrack`, `cpustat`, and `busstat` tools in Chapters 4 and 11. There we showed how these tools can be used to measure events and data used to analyze program performance. This appendix extends that discussion and gives a brief overview of some useful performance metrics that can be derived from data collected using these tools.

CPU Counters

UltraSPARC I and II microprocessors provide counters that measure events related to instruction execution rates (such as clock cycles and instruction count), pipeline stalls, load-use stalls, and cache access statistics.

In UltraSPARC III processor, the number and type of events that can be measured with counters have been significantly increased upon the UltraSPARC I and II processors. UltraSPARC III (with support in Solaris kernel) provides a feature whereby a trap is generated when a counter overflows. This can be used in dynamic profiling of an application based on conditional sampling of a specified event, because a given counter could be preloaded such that the processor traps when a given number of the events take place. We discussed this feature of Forte Developer 6 update 1 Performance Analyzer tool in Chapter 4.

The types of events supported on UltraSPARC III are as follows: instruction execution rates, branch prediction statistics, pipeline stalls, recirculate counts, cache access statistics, floating-point operation counts, system interface statistics, and memory controller statistics. On UltraSPARC III, because the memory controller is integrated with the processor, the relevant events can be measured using on-chip counters.

Refer to *UltraSPARC I and II User's Manual* and *UltraSPARC III Programmer's Reference Manual* for complete descriptions of the various events these processors measure.

Using raw data obtained from hardware counters, many useful measures of program performance can be obtained. The formulas for some of these are listed in TABLE D-1.

TABLE D-1 Derived Performance Metrics From UltraSPARC CPU Counters

Useful Measure	UltraSPARC I and II	UltraSPARC III
CPI	cycle_cnt/instr_cnt	cycle_cnt/instr_cnt
MIPS	cpu_clock/CPI	cpu_clock/CPI
Address bus utilization	(ec_ref-ec_hit+ec_wb) × 2/ (cycle_cnt × bus_clock/cpu_clock)	(ec_misses + ec_wb)/ (cycle_cnt × bus_clock/cpu_clock)
D-cache miss rate	1 - ((dc_rd_hit + dc_wr_hit)/ (dc_rd + dc_wr))	(dc_rd_miss + dc_wr_miss)/ (dc_rd+dc_wr)
I-cache miss rate	1 -ic_hit/ic_ref	(ic_miss-ic_miss_canceled)/ic_ref
L2 miss rate	1 - ec_hit/ec_ref	ec_misses/ec_ref
I-TLB miss rate		itlb_misses/ic_ref
D-TLB miss rate		dtlb_miss/(dc_rd + dc_wr)
Branch rate		(iu_stat_br_count_taken + iu_stat_br_count_untaken) / instr_cnt
Branch miss rate		(iu_stat_br_miss_taken + ' iu_stat_br_miss_taken) / (iu_stat_br_count_taken + iu_stat_br_count_untaken)
Data stall rate	(load_use + load_use_raw + dispatch0_storebuf)/cycle_cnt	((re_dc_miss+rstall_storeq + re_raw_miss) + 12 x (re_pc_miss + re_fpu_bypass + re_endian_miss)) / cycle_cnt
Instruction stall rate	dispatch0_ic_miss/cycle_cnt	dispatch0_ic_miss/cycle_cnt
FP stall rate	dispatch0_fp_use/cycle_cnt	rstall_fp_use/cycle_cnt
IU stall rate		rstall_iu_use/cycle_cnt
Branch stall rate	dspatch0_mispred/cycle_cnt	(dispatch0_mispred + dispatch0_2nd_br + dispatch0_br_target + dispatch_rs_mispred)/cycle_cnt
FLOPS		(fa_pipe_completion + fm_pipe_completion) / (cycle_cnt x cpu_clock)

In TABLE D-1, the letter I (in caps) refers to instruction, while D refers to data, and L2 refers to level 2. FP refers to floating-point, IU refers to integer unit, `cpu_clock` refers to CPU clock frequency, and `bus_clock` refers to frequency of memory interconnect. The factor of 2 in the formula for address utilization (UltraSPARC I and II column) comes from the fact that an address request takes two bus cycles to complete on the Gigaplane interconnect (see Appendix C and [Singhal96]). The metric FLOPS is based on counting only floating-point addition and multiplication events. Clearly, if in a program these are not the dominant floating-point operations (for example if floating-point division occurs frequently), then the formula in TABLE D-1 should not be used, or it must be interpreted appropriately.

An explanation and definition of the metrics listed in TABLE D-1 follows:

- Cycles Per Instruction (CPI): An important metric used by CPU designers to evaluate performance of the processor architecture ([Hennessy96]). The total runtime of a program is related to CPI as

RunTime = (Num. of Instructions) × (CPI) × (CPU Clock Rate)

The CPI can be broken down into components representing the fraction of time spent performing various operations. For example, on an UltraSPARC II based system, the CPI can be broken into:
- Pipeline: Cycles spent actually executing instructions in the CPU pipeline.
- Instruction stall: Cycles spent waiting for next instruction to be available on a miss in the level 1 Instruction Cache (IC) or the level 2 cache.
- Branch Predict: Cycles spent waiting due to incorrect branch prediction.
- Load Use: Cycles spent waiting for load instruction to return data on a level 1 D-cache or level 2 cache miss.
- Store Buffer: Cycles spent waiting for store buffer to be flushed.
- Load Use RAW: Cycles spent waiting for results of a load instruction on hold due to a Read After Write (RAW) hazard situation.
- Floating Point: Cycles spent waiting for results of an earlier floating-point instruction to become available.

Component distribution of the CPI is a very useful way to analyze program performance and identify usage of various parts of the processor system.

- Million Instructions Per Second (MIPS): This measure includes the impact of both processor architecture design (CPI) and process technology used in processor fabrication (CPU Clock Rate).

- Floating Point Operations Per Second (FLOPS): A measure of how fast the floating-point operations are performed on the processor. Usually, the two most common operations are additions and multiplications.

- Cache Miss Rates: Miss rates of the various caches (level 1 and 2) are a measure of how well the program utilizes memory hierarchy.

- Stall rates: The various stall rates can be used to compute the component breakdown of CPI. We mentioned in Chapter 8 that sometimes even if level 2 (or level 1) cache miss rates are small, the program performance could be significantly off from the possible peak performance. The stall metrics could be used to identify why that is happening. For example, the data stall rate is a measure of the fraction of a CPU cycle wasted in waiting for data, either waiting to arrive or depart from the processor core. This could be due to cache misses, TLB misses, or how instructions are grouped and scheduled in a processor pipeline. For example, even if all data fits in the level 1 (or level 2) cache, if pairs of stores and loads that can cause RAW hazards are not sufficiently separated in the instruction stream, then stalls would occur and CPU cycles would be wasted. In this case, it would be misleading to try to correlate CPI with cache miss rates.

System ASIC Counters

On systems based on the UltraSPARC I and II processors, the following ASICs have hardware counter support:

- Address Controller: This ASIC is only on the Enterprise 3500, Enterprise 4500, Enterprise 5500, and Enterprise 6500 systems. There is one address controller on every board in these systems. There are a pair of 32-bit counters that measure various events.

- SBus Interface: This is a UPA-based SBus interface chip. There is one SBus chip in the SBus based desktop systems Ultra-1 and Ultra-2 and one or two SBus chips on each SBus I/O board on the Enterprise 3500, Enterprise 4500, Enterprise 5500, and Enterprise 6500. Two 32-bit PICs and a PCR register are available on the chip.

- PCI Interface: This chip is the connection between UPA system bus and a PCI based I/O subsystem. There is one PCI chip in the PCI based desktop and workgroup server systems Enterprise 250, Enterprise 450, Ultra 30, Ultra 60, and Ultra 80 and one PCI chip on each PCI I/O board on the PCI based Enterprise 3500, Enterprise 4500, Enterprise 5500, and Enterprise 6500 systems. This chip has a pair of 32-bit counters.

Refer to hardware manuals on Ultra Workstations and Enterprise Servers linked from http://docs.sun.com for further information on the system architecture and functionality of the various ASICs on these computers.

Hardware counters on these devices can be accessed using the busstat tool. Options -l and -e can be used to list the events supported by various devices. For example, some of events supported in the address controller are as follows

```
example% busstat -l
Busstat Device(s):
sbus0 ac0 ac1 ac2 ac3 ac4 ac5 ac6 ac7
example% busstat -e ac0
pic0
mem_bank0_rds
```

```
mem_bank0_wrs
mem_bank0_stall
mem_bank1_rds
mem_bank1_wrs
mem_bank1_stall
clock_cycles
addr_pkts
data_pkts
...
...

pic1
...
rts_pkts
rtsa_pkts
rto_pkts

upa_a_cpb_to
upa_a_inv_to
...
....
```

A detailed explanation of what the different events (on these ASICs) measure is beyond the scope of this book. In TABLE D-2, we list some that are most useful in performance studies:

TABLE D-2 Events Supported on Address Controller, SBus, and PCI on UltraSPARC II Based Systems

ASIC	EVENT	What It Measures
ac	mem_band0_rds	Number of reads to memory bank 0
ac	mem_band0_wrs	Number of writes to memory bank 0
ac	mem_band0_stall	Stalls of memory bank 0
ac	mem_bank1_rds	Number of reads to memory bank 1 (assuming valid bank 1 on the CPU/memory board)
ac	mem_bank1_wrs	Number of writes to memory bank 1 (assuming valid bank 1 on the CPU/memory board)
ac	mem_bank1_stall	Stalls on memory bank 1
ac	clock_cycles	System clock cycles
ac	addr_pkts	Total address packets on the bus (address packets take 2 cycles on the address bus)

TABLE D-2   Events Supported on Address Controller, SBus, and PCI on UltraSPARC II
Based Systems *(Continued)*

ASIC	EVENT	What It Measures
ac	data_pkts	Total data packets on the bus (data packets take 2 cycles on the data bus).
ac	rts_pkts	Total RTS (Read-To-Share) transactions. These are issued for data reads that miss in the L2 cache.
ac	rtsa_pkts	Total RTSA (Read-To-Share-Always) transactions. These count instruction reads that miss in the L2 cache.
ac	upa_a_cpb_to	Counts copyback requests to UPA on a board. A copyback occurs when a read request from another device is in E/M/O state (of MOESI protocol) and the read request is to be satisfied from the cache and not memory.
ac	upa_a_inv_to	Total invalidates to UPA. An invalidate occurs when another address controller device wants to write a line that is valid in the cache of processor attached to this UPA port.
sbus	dvma_stream_rd	Number of separate streaming mode DVMA read transfers from memory to this SBus device.
sbus	dvma_stream_wr	Number of separate streaming mode DVMA write transfers from memory to this SBus device.
sbus	dvma_cycles	Number of SBus cycles used for DVMA.
sbus	dvma_bytes_xfr	Number of bytes transferred in DVMA (read or write).
sbus	interrupts	Number of interrupts sent by this SBus device.
pci	dvma_stream_rd_a	Number of streaming DVMA read transfers for PCI bus A.
pci	dvma_stream_wr_a	Number of streaming DVMA write transfers for PCI bus A.
pci	interrupts	Number of interrupts sent by this PCI device.

Using raw data obtained from counting the events (using `busstat` tool), one can compute several useful quantities. Some of these are listed in TABLE D-3. Note that in TABLE D-3, EXX00 refers to Enterprise 3500, Enterprise 4500, Enterprise 5500, and Enterprise 6500 series systems.

TABLE D-3   Derived Performance Metrics From System ASIC Counters on UltraSPARC II Based Systems

Useful Measure	Formula	Description
ABUtil	(addr_pkts x2)/clock_cycle	Utilization of the address bus on the EXX00 systems. Useful to evaluate scalability of the system.
DBUtil	(data_pkts x2)/clock_cycles	Utilization of the data bus on the EXX00 systems. Metric similar to ABUtil to evaluate whether adding more CPUs will help scalability.
Bank0Util	((mem_bank0_rds+mem_bank0_wrs) × 10)/clock_cycles	Utilization of memory bank 0 in EXX00 systems. Formula assumes that a memory bank is busy for 10 cycles per memory transaction. Similarly, utilization of Bank1 can be calculated.
BrdUtil	((mem_bank0_rds + mem_bank0_wrs + mem_bank1_rds + mem_bank1_wrs) x 7)/ clock_cycles	Utilization of memory board in EXX00 systems. Formula assumes that the memory controller on the board is busy for seven cycles per memory transaction.
InstrMix	(rtsa_pkts/addr_pkts)	Instruction traffic on the Gigaplane in EXX00 systems, based on the fact that instruction misses in L2 cache use RTSA transactions.
DataMix	(addr_pkts-rtsa_pkts)/ addr_pkts	Data traffic on the Gigaplane in EXX00 systems.
MrdN/sec	mem_bankN_rds/seconds	Rate of reads for memory bank N on EXX00 systems.
MWrN/sec	mem_bankN_wrs/seconds	Rate of writes for memory bank N on EXX00 systems.

Note that in the above table, `clock_cycles` refer to the bus clock cycles and not the CPU clock cycles.

Interval Arithmetic Support in Forte Developer 6 Fortran 95 Compiler

In this appendix we give a brief overview of interval arithmetic ([Moore66] and [Walster88]) and give examples of its usage.

Interval arithmetic computations provide guaranteed bounds on errors, which can detect numerical instability of the computation or loss of precision due to cancellation. In addition, algorithms based on the interval approach can provide new ways of solving nonlinear systems of equations and optimization problems. The interval paradigm naturally applies to computations that operate on ranges of numbers, for example, when the input parameters are known to be imprecise.

Forte Developer 6 and Forte Developer 6 update 1 provide intrinsic support for interval arithmetic for the Fortran 95 compiler. It implements the INTERVAL data type with support of the standard intrinsic functions and operations, relational operations, and format edit descriptors. For a detailed description of the implementation, refer to the *Interval Arithmetic Programming Reference*. Also, interval support was introduced in Forte Developer 6 update 1 C++ compiler. Additional information can be found at
`http://www.sun.com/forte/info/features/intervals.html`.

Interval Arithmetic Basics

An *interval* is a continuum of real numbers bounded by its endpoints:

$$[a, b] = \{x | a \leq x \leq b\}$$

The standard arithmetic operations can be defined for interval operands:

$$[a, b] \lozenge [c, d] = \{x \lozenge y | x \subseteq [a, b], y \subseteq [c, d]\}$$

where the operation is addition, subtraction, multiplication, or division.

When the exact representation of the interval endpoints is not possible, the rounding must be performed in the outward direction to ensure that all possible values are included in the resulting interval.

In the following example, x is declared as INTERVAL*8, which is the interval data type based on the REAL*4 floating-point type. Note the use of the -xia option allows the compiler to accept interval code.

CODE EXAMPLE E-1   Directed Rounding for Interval Data Type

```
! example_interval_1.f90
! f90 -xia -o example_interval_1 example_interval_1.f90
interval*8 :: x = [1.2, 3.8]
print*, "[1.2, 3.8] -> ", x
end
```

```
example% f90 -xia -o example_interval_1 example_interval_1.f90
example% example_interval_1
 [1.2, 3.8] ->  [1.1999999,3.8000002]
```

Because endpoints of the interval [1.2, 3.8] cannot be represented without precision loss (see Chapter 6 for a discussion of binary representation of floating-point numbers) and outward rounding is performed: the left endpoint is rounded down, while the right endpoint is rounded up.

In addition to basic arithmetic operations on intervals, the compiler recognizes intrinsic functions that are provided to access the endpoints (infimum and supremum) of an interval, as well as its width and midpoint.

CODE EXAMPLE E-2   Interval-specific Functions

```
! example_interval_2.f90
! f90 -xia -o example_interval_2 example_interval_2.f90
interval*8 :: x = [1.2, 3.8]
print*, "wid([1.2, 3.8]) = ", wid(x)
print*, "sup([1.2, 3.8]) = ", sup(x)
print*, "inf([1.2, 3.8]) = ", inf(x)
print*, "mid([1.2, 3.8]) = ", mid(x)
end
```

```
example% f90 -xia -o example_interval_2 example_interval_2.f90
example% example_interval_2
 wid([1.2, 3.8]) =   2.6000003
 sup([1.2, 3.8]) =   3.8000001
 inf([1.2, 3.8]) =   1.1999999
 mid([1.2, 3.8]) =   2.5
```

The compiler also provides interval versions of standard mathematical functions such as `sin()`, `cos()`, `sqrt()`, `exp()`, and `log()`.

CODE EXAMPLE E-3   `sqrt` Function Operating on an Interval

```
! example_interval_3.f90
! f90 -xia -o example_interval_3 example_interval_3.f90
interval*16 :: x = [4.0, 9.0]
print*, "sqrt([4.0, 9.0]) = ", sqrt([4.0, 9.0])
end
```

```
example% f90 -xia -o example_interval_3 example_interval_3.f90
example% example_interval_3
 sqrt([4.0, 9.0]) =   [2.0,3.0]
```

Because intervals represent ranges of numbers, interval comparisons such as `.GT.` and `.LE.`, have different meanings from their floating-point counterparts. The comparison operations on the intervals can apply to entire intervals, their parts, or can be interpreted in the set-theoretical sense.

The compiler recognizes the standard Fortran order operations prefixed with C, P, or S, which stand for *certainly, possibly,* and *set,* respectively. The certainly operators hold for all the points in the interval. For example, X1.CLT.X2 statement is true if every point in X1 is smaller than every point in X2. The possibly operators are less restrictive and hold true for certain points in the intervals. The X1.PLT.X2 statement is true if there exists a point selected from X1 and another point selected from X2 such that the former is smaller than the latter. If true, the certainly operator implies the corresponding possibly operator. Finally, the set operators apply to the endpoints of the intervals. For example, X1.SLT.X2 means that the endpoints of X1 are pair-wise smaller than the corresponding endpoints of X2.

The following program gives examples of true and false order relations performed in the certainly, possibly, and set sense.

CODE EXAMPLE E-4   Order Relations for Intervals

```
! example_interval_4.f90
! f90 -xia -o example_interval_4 example_interval_4.f90
interval*8 :: x = [0, 3], y=[2, 7], z=[5, 6]
print*, "[0, 3].clt.[2, 7] : ", x.clt.y
print*, "[0, 3].clt.[5, 6] : ", x.clt.z
print*, "[5, 6].plt.[0, 3] : ", z.plt.x
print*, "[2, 7].plt.[0, 3] : ", y.plt.x
print*, "[5, 6].slt.[2, 7] : ", z.slt.y
print*, "[0, 3].slt.[2, 7] : ", x.slt.y
end
```

```
example% f90 -xia -o example_interval_4 example_interval_4.f90
example% example_interval_4
 [0, 3].clt.[2, 7] :    F
 [0, 3].clt.[5, 6] :    T
 [5, 6].plt.[0, 3] :    F
 [2, 7].plt.[0, 3] :    T
 [5, 6].slt.[2, 7] :    F
 [0, 3].slt.[2, 7] :    T
```

Solution of Nonlinear Problems

In some cases, the numerical method based on interval analysis can be better suited for solution of nonlinear problems than floating-point algorithms.

For example, the problem of finding roots of a nonlinear function can be solved with the traditional (floating-point) Newton method. This procedure defines each successive iteration as the root of the linear approximation[1] to the function.

$$l(x) = f'(x_0) \times (x - x_0) + f(x_0)$$

$$x_1 = x_0 - \frac{f(x_0)}{f'(x_0)}$$

Graphically shown in FIGURE E-1, the next iteration corresponds to the intersection of the tangent line to $f(x)$ at x_0 and the x-axis.

The convergence of the method can be very sensitive to the choice of the initial approximation. When the method converges, it finds only one root of the function, while the problem can have multiple solutions.

---

1. We assume that the function is continuously differentiable

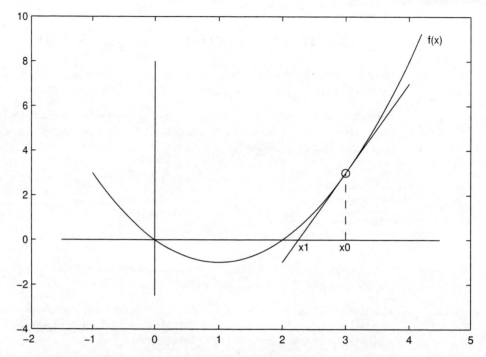

FIGURE E-1 Iteration of a Floating-point Newton Method

To overcome these limitations, the standard Newton method was extended ([Moore66]) using interval analysis. Instead of floating-point iterations, the modified method uses intervals to bound the solution. The function is evaluated at the midpoint of the interval, but the derivative is taken over the entire interval. The linearized approximation to $f(x)$ becomes

$$L(X_0, x) = f'(X_0) \times (x - mid(X_0)) + f(mid(X_0))$$

This function takes zero value in the interval

$$N(X_0, x) = mid(X_0) - \frac{f(mid(X_0))}{f'(X_0)}$$

In the algorithm, it is critical that $mid(X_0)$ is evaluated as an interval to bound the rounding errors.

The intersection $N(X_0,x)$ and X_0 forms the next interval approximation X_1. FIGURE E-2 illustrates the modified method. Instead of a single tangent line, we have a region formed by lines with the various slopes corresponding to different values of the derivative of $f(x)$ over the interval X_0. This region intersects the x-axis over the interval $N(X_0,x)$.

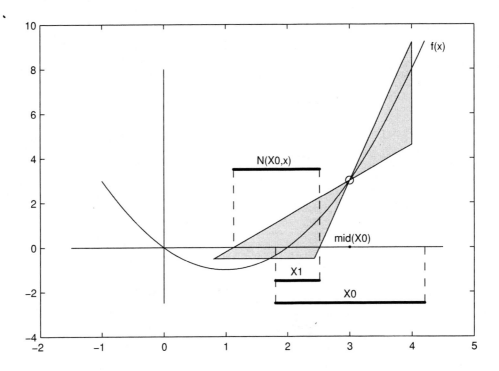

FIGURE E-2 Iteration of an Interval-based Newton Method

It can be shown that if the intersection of $N(X_0,x)$ and X_0 is empty, then the interval X_0 contains no roots of the function (see FIGURE E-3). A remarkable result is that if $N(X_0,x)$ is a proper subset of X_0, then it proves that there is a simple root in $N(X_0,x)$.

If the derivative takes values of different sign over the interval X_0, then $N(X_0,x)$ takes value zero in two open-ended intervals (see FIGURE E-4). Their intersection with X_0 forms two disjoint intervals each of which may contain the roots of $f(x)$ (in this case both do).

CODE EXAMPLE E-5 gives a very basic implementation of the interval Newton method for finding the root of $log(x)=1$.

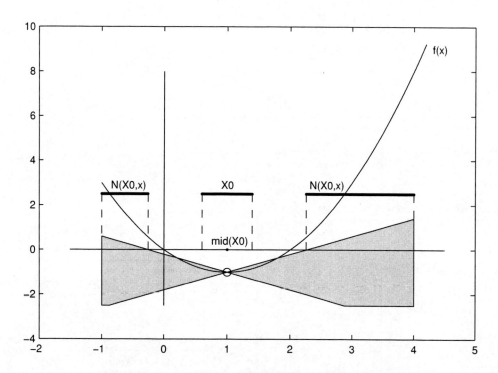

FIGURE E-3 Empty Intersection Indicates No Roots in Interval X_0

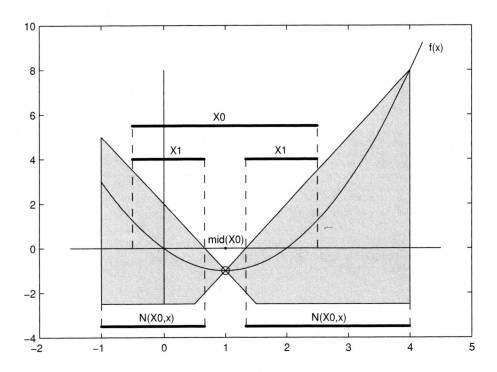

FIGURE E-4 Two Disjointed Intervals in the Intersection May Contain Roots--No Roots are Located in the Removed Interval

CODE EXAMPLE E-5 Interval Newton Solution of a Nonlinear Equation

```
! example_newton.f90
! f90 -xia -o example_newton example_newton.f90
! Interval-based Newton solution of log(x)=1
interval*8 :: X, fderiv, N, f, xmid
logical :: root_exists = .false.
!
! initial guess
X = [ 0.1 , 500. ]
!
! iterations
do i = 1, 12
    xmid = mid(X)
    f = log(xmid) - 1
    fderiv = 1 / X
    N = xmid - f / fderiv
    write(6,'("i=", I2," X=", VF25.6," N=", VF27.6)') i,X,N
```

```
!
! test if N became a proper subset of X
   if (.not.(root_exists).and.(N.PSB.X)) then
      write(6,10)
      root_exists = .true.
   endif
   X = N .ix. X
enddo
10 format(7x,"N proper subset of X -> at least one simple root")
end
```

```
example% f90 -xia -o example_newton example_newton.f90
example% example_newton
i= 1  X=[    0.099999, 500.000000]  N=[-2010.781000,   249.597900]
i= 2  X=[    0.099999, 249.597900]  N=[ -830.388400,   124.466300]
i= 3  X=[    0.099999, 124.466300]  N=[ -327.506600,    61.969950]
i= 4  X=[    0.099999,  61.969950]  N=[ -119.869000,    30.791460]
i= 5  X-[    0.099999,  30.791460]  N=[  -38.049290,    15.272000]
i= 6  X=[    0.099999,  15.272000]  N=[   -8.187722,     7.582059]
i= 7  X=[    0.099999,   7.582059]  N=[    1.219605,     3.806456]
         N proper subset of X -> at least one simple root
i= 8  X=[    1.219605,   3.806456]  N=[  · 2.608782,     2.811878]
i= 9  X=[    2.608782,   2.811878]  N=[    2.717972,     2.718568]
i=10  X=[    2.717972,   2.718568]  N=[    2.718281,     2.718282]
i=11  X=[    2.718281,   2.718282]  N=[    2.718281,     2.718282]
i=12  X=[    2.718281,   2.718282]  N=[    2.718281,     2.718282]
```

Note that in this code example, we used formatted output for intervals.

For more information about interval arithmetic support in Forte Developer 6, refer to the *Interval Arithmetic Programming Reference*.

APPENDIX **F**

Differences in I/O Performance

Throughout this guide we described various ways of improving the performance of CPU-bound applications, purposefully avoiding any discussion of I/O related issues. Undoubtedly, the I/O performance can be a very important factor for an application, but a thorough discussion of this subject should include not just optimization at the application level but also system configuration, volume management software, and specific hardware considerations that are beyond the scope of this book. We refer the reader to [Cockcroft98] and [Wong97], and [McDougall99] for a detailed discussion of these subjects.

To highlight the importance of I/O optimization at the application level, in this appendix, we give an example of how changes at the application level can greatly affect the I/O performance. In this example we create a file and write an integer array into it. Then we use different ways to read the array from the file and compare the performance. The file is cached at the time it is created and reading is done from the memory. That way we don't measure the disk access time, but rather the overhead of different reading strategies. We ran the examples on an Ultra 60 system under the Solaris 8 Operating Environment.

Reading a File with `read/lseek`

We start with reading the file with the `read(2)` call. First we read the entire array with a single read operation. Then we perform the read operations for each element of the array. With each call the file pointer is moved to the next element of the array and no `lseek(2)` calls are needed to change the pointer. Finally we read the array backwards starting with the last element. That way we need to decrease the pointer by the size of two elements to ensure that it points to the right element.

CODE EXAMPLE F-1   Reading File With `read` System Call

```
/* example_read.c
   cc example_read.c -o example_read */
#include <stdio.h>
#include <sys/time.h>
#define N 1000000
FILE *example_file;
int x[N], i;
hrtime_t st, et;
float secs;

int main() {
   create_file();
   read_file_read();
   return 0;
}

int create_file(){
   int i, numwritten;
   for ( i = 0; i < N; x[i++]=i);
   if( (example_file = fopen( "ex_file", "w+t" )) == NULL ){
      printf( "Problem opening the file\n" ); return -1; }
   st= gethrtime();
   numwritten = fwrite( x, sizeof( int ), N, example_file );
   et= gethrtime();
   secs = (( float) (et-st) / (float) 1000000000);
   printf( "Wrote %d items\n", numwritten );
   printf(" RUNTIME (writing file): %6.4f Seconds \n", secs);
   fclose(example_file);
   return 0;
}
```

```
#include <unistd.h>
int read_file_read(){
   if( (example_file = fopen( "ex_file", "r" )) == NULL ){
      printf( "Problem opening the file\n" ); return -1; }
   st= gethrtime();
   read(fileno(example_file), x, sizeof(int)*N);
   et= gethrtime();
   secs = (( float) (et-st) / (float) 1000000000);
   printf( "x[11111] = %ld \n", x[11111] );
   printf(" RUNTIME (single read): %6.4f Seconds \n", secs);
   fclose(example_file);

   if( (example_file = fopen( "ex_file", "r" )) == NULL ){
      printf( "Problem opening the file\n" ); return -1; }
   st= gethrtime();
   for ( i = 0; i < N; i++){
      read(fileno(example_file), x+i, sizeof( int ));
   }
   et= gethrtime();
   secs = (( float) (et-st) / (float) 1000000000);
   printf( "x[11111] = %ld \n", x[11111] );
   printf(" RUNTIME (Multiple read): %6.4f Seconds \n", secs);
   fclose(example_file);

   if( (example_file = fopen( "ex_file", "r" )) == NULL ){
      printf( "Problem opening the file\n" ); return -1; }
   fseek(example_file, ((N-1)*sizeof(int)), SEEK_CUR);
   st= gethrtime();
   for ( i = N-1; i >= 0; i--){
      read(fileno(example_file), x+i, sizeof( int ));
      lseek(fileno(example_file), -2*sizeof(int), SEEK_CUR);
   }
   et= gethrtime();
   secs = (( float) (et-st) / (float) 1000000000);
   printf( "x[11111] = %ld \n", x[11111] );
  printf(" RUNTIME (Multiple read/lseek): %6.4f Seconds\n", secs);
   fclose(example_file);

   return 0;
}
```

```
example% cc example_read.c -o example_read
example% ptime example_read
Wrote 1000000 items
 RUNTIME (writing file): 0.3049 Seconds
x[11111] = 11111
 RUNTIME (single read): 0.0166 Seconds
x[11111] = 11111
 RUNTIME (Multiple read): 11.8831 Seconds
x[11111] = 11111
 RUNTIME (Multiple read/lseek): 15.6432 Seconds


real         28.172
user          6.892
sys          19.911
```

We can see that repeated calls to read result in a very large overhead compared to reading the file as a whole and the lseek calls in the last measurements result in additional slowdown.

Reading a File with fread/fseek

For the second example we replace the read and lseek operations with fread(3C) and fseek(3C) calls respectively. In this case the single fread command is slower than read but the sequential reading from the first element to the last with repeated calls is much faster than in the first example. We can also see that repeated fseek calls are more expensive than analogous lseek calls.

CODE EXAMPLE F-2   Reading File With fread System Call

```
/* example_fread.c
   cc example_fread.c -o example_fread */
#include <stdio.h>
#include <sys/time.h>
#define N 1000000
FILE *example_file;
int x[N], i;
hrtime_t st, et;
float secs;

int main() {
   create_file();
   read_file_fread();
```

```
   return 0;
}

int read_file_fread(){
   if( (example_file = fopen( "ex_file", "r" )) == NULL ){
      printf( "Problem opening the file\n" ); return -1; }
   st= gethrtime();
   fread( x, sizeof( int ), N, example_file);
   et= gethrtime();
   secs = (( float) (et-st) / (float) 1000000000);
   printf( "x[11111] = %ld \n", x[11111] );
   printf(" RUNTIME (single fread): %6.4f Seconds \n", secs);
   fclose(example_file);

   if( (example_file = fopen( "ex_file", "r" )) == NULL ){
      printf( "Problem opening the file\n" ); return -1; }
   st= gethrtime();
   for ( i = 0; i < N; i++){
      fread( x+i, sizeof( int ), 1, example_file);
   }
   et= gethrtime();
   secs = (( float) (et-st) / (float) 1000000000);
   printf( "x[11111] = %ld \n", x[11111] );
   printf(" RUNTIME (Multiple fread): %6.4f Seconds \n", secs);
   fclose(example_file);

   if( (example_file = fopen( "ex_file", "r" )) == NULL ){
      printf( "Problem opening the file\n" ); return -1; }
   fseek(example_file, ((N-1)*sizeof(int)), SEEK_CUR);
   st= gethrtime();
   for ( i = N-1; i >= 0; i--){
      fread( x+i, sizeof( int ), 1, example_file);
      fseek(example_file, -2*sizeof(int), SEEK_CUR);
   }
   et= gethrtime();
   secs = (( float) (et-st) / (float) 1000000000);
   printf( "x[11111] = %ld \n", x[11111] );
   printf("RUNTIME (Multiple fread/fseek): %6.4f Seconds\n",secs);
   fclose(example_file);
}
```

```
example% cc example_fread.c -o example_fread
example% ptime example_fread
Wrote 1000000 items
 RUNTIME (writing file): 0.2960 Seconds
x[11111] = 11111
 RUNTIME (single fread): 0.0389 Seconds
x[11111] = 11111
 RUNTIME (Multiple fread): 0.3061 Seconds
x[11111] = 11111
 RUNTIME (Multiple fread/fseek): 43.4280 Seconds
real        44.232
user         6.279
sys         36.467
```

Mapping a File to Memory

Finally, we use the mmap(2) call to map the file to the memory area and then read the elements of the array directly from the memory, bypassing the I/O calls. We can see that this approach is orders of magnitude more efficient for both forward and backward sequential reading of the file. Replacing the I/O operations with mmap calls should always be considered for applications that perform frequent I/O operations.

CODE EXAMPLE F-3   Reading File After mmap System Call

```
/* example_mmap.c
   cc example_mmap.c -o example_mmap */
#include <stdio.h>
#include <sys/time.h>
#define N 1000000
FILE *example_file;
int x[N], i;
hrtime_t st, et;
float secs;

int main() {
   create_file();
   read_file_mmap();
   return 0;
}
```

```
#include<sys/mman.h>

int read_file_mmap(){
   char *example_map;
   int offset;
   if( (example_file = fopen( "ex_file", "r" )) == NULL ){
      printf( "Problem opening the file\n" ); return -1; }
   st= gethrtime();
   example_map=mmap(NULL,N*sizeof(int),PROT_READ,
               MAP_SHARED,fileno(example_file),0);
   offset = 0;
   for ( i = 0; i < N; i++){
      x[i] = *(int*)(&example_map[offset]);
      offset = offset + sizeof(int);
   }
   et= gethrtime();
   secs = (( float) (et-st) / (float) 1000000000);
   printf( "x[11111] = %ld \n", x[11111] );
   printf(" RUNTIME (mmap): %6.4f Seconds \n", secs);
   fclose(example_file);

   if( (example_file = fopen( "ex_file", "r" )) == NULL ){
      printf( "Problem opening the file\n" ); return -1; }
   st= gethrtime();
   example_map=mmap(NULL,N*sizeof(int),PROT_READ,
               MAP_SHARED,fileno(example_file),0);
   offset = (N-1)*sizeof(int);
   for ( i = N-1; i >= 0; i--){
      x[i] = *(int*)(&example_map[offset]);
      offset = offset - sizeof(int);
   }
   et= gethrtime();
   secs = (( float) (et-st) / (float) 1000000000);
   printf( "x[11111] = %ld \n", x[11111] );
   printf(" RUNTIME (mmap): %6.4f Seconds \n", secs);
   fclose(example_file);

   return 0;
}
```

```
example% cc example_mmap.c -o example_mmap
example% ptime example_mmap
Wrote 1000000 items
```

```
 RUNTIME (writing file): 0.2961 Seconds
x[11111] = 11111
 RUNTIME (mmap): 0.0972 Seconds
x[11111] = 11111
 RUNTIME (mmap): 0.0982 Seconds
real       0.607
user       0.244
sys        0.105
```

As we mentioned, in these examples the reading was performed from a file that was already cached in the memory. Many I/O-intensive programs tend to use large files with irregular access patterns and caching or buffering can provide limited help. Some applications may even benefit from direct I/O, which bypasses the memory buffer.

We should also mention that on systems with a large amount of memory, I/O-intensive applications will benefit from reading from or writing to the /tmp file system, effectively using the memory instead of the disk. That way the application hides the latency of I/O operations but requires more memory.

Another way to decrease I/O overhead without using extra memory is to use *asynchronous I/O* or *async I/O*, which allows overlap of the read or write operations with the tasks performed by the CPU. The ansynchronous I/O functions aioread(3AIO) and aiowrite(3AIO) implemented in libaio(3LIB) initiate read and write calls asynchronously and then return control to the program prior to completion of the operations. Programming with these APIs is difficult, especially for applications with irregular data access patterns such as sparse linear solvers. On the other hand, asynchronous I/O can be very effectively used for programs with regular, predictable reads or writes, such as dense matrix algebra problems, in particular for dense linear solvers.

References

[Aho85] Aho, A.V., Sethi, R. & Ullman, J. D. *Compilers : Principles, Techniques, and Tools*. Addison-Wesley Pub Company, 1985.

[Amdahl67] Amdahl, G. *Validity of the Single Processor Approach to Achieving Large-Scale Computer Capabilities*. In AFIPS Conference Proceedings, vol. 30 (Atlantic City, NJ), AFIPS Press, Reston, VA. 1967.

[Aoki96] Aoki, C., Damson, P., Goebel, K., Kong, X., Lai, M., Subramaniam, K., Tirumalai, P. & Wang, J.Z. *A Parallelizing Compiler for UltraSPARC*. In Proceedings of Hot Chips 8, Stanford, CA, August 1996. Available on the internet at http://www.hotchips.org.

[Armstrong00] Armstrong, A., Kim, S.W. & Eigenmann, R. *Quantifying Differences between OpenMP and MPI Using a Large-Scale Application Suite*. In Proceedings of International Workshop on OpenMP: Experiences and Implementations, Tokyo, Japan, October 2000.

[Bailey94] Bailey, D. H., Barszcz, E., Barton, J., Browning, D., Carter, R., Dagum, L., Fatoohi, R., Fineberg, S., Frederickson, P., Lasinski, T., Schreiber, R., Simon, H., Venkatakrishnan, V. & Weeratunga, S. *The NAS Parallel Benchmarks*. Technical Report RNR-94-007, NASA Ames Research Center, March, 1994.

[Barber92] Barber, M. *The Trouble with Benchmarks, Revisited*. In Microprocessor Report, vol. 6, no. 10, July, 1992.

[Bennett90] Bennett, J.P. *Introduction to Compiling Techniques*. McGraw-Hill, Berkshire, England, 1990.

[Boucher99] Boucher, M. *Optimization Techniques for HPC Languages*. In Proceedings of Sun Users Performance Group, Spring Meeting, Washington DC, May, 1999.

[Bova99] Bova, S.W., Breshears, C.P., Gabb, H., Eigenmann, R., Gaertner, G., Kuhn, R., Magro, W. & Salvini, S. *Parallel Programming with Message Passing and Directives*. Purdue Univ. School of ECE, High-Performance Computing Lab. ECE-HPCLab-99201, November 1999.

[Bova00] Bova, S.W., Breshears, C.P., Cuicchi, C., Demirbilek, Z. & Gabb, H. *Dual-level Parallel Analysis of Harbor Wave Response Using MPI and OpenMP*. In Intl. Journal of High Performance Computing Applications, vol. 11, # 1, Spring 2000.

[Bugnion96] Bugnion, E., Anderson, J.M., Mowry, T.C., Rosenblum, M. & Lam, M. S. *Compiler Directed Page Coloring for MultiProcessors*. In Proceedings of Seventh Intl. Symp. on Arch. Support for Prog. Languages and Operating Systems. Cambridge, MA, October, 1996.

[Cappello00] Cappello, F. & Etiemble, D. *MPI versus MPI+OpenMP on the IBM SP for the NAS Benchmarks*. In Proceedings of Supercomputing'00, Dallas, TX, November, 2000.

[Chan94] Chan, T.F. & Mathew, T.P. *Domain Decomposition Algorithms*. In *Acta Numerica*, Cambridge University Press, 1994. Available on the Internet at http://www.math.ucla.edu/applied/cam/index.html.

[Chan97] Chan, T.F. & Szeto, W.K. *On the Optimality of the Median Cut Spectral Bisection Graph Partitioning Method*. In SIAM J. Sci. Comput. 18(3), 1997. Available on the Internet at http://www.math.ucla.edu/applied/cam/index.html.

[Chandra00] Chandra, R., Dagum, L., Kohr, D., Maydan, D., McDonald, J. & Menon, R. *Parallel Programming in OpenMP*. Morgan Kaufmann Publishing, 2000

[Charlesworth98] Charlesworth, A., *Starfire: Extending the SMP Envelope*. In IEEE Micro, January/February 1998.

[Cockcroft98] Cockcroft, A. & Pettit, R. *Sun Performance and Tuning : Java and the Internet*. Second Edition, Prentice Hall, 1998.

[Cockcroft98b] Cockcroft, A. *CPU Time Measurement Errors*. Paper 2038 at The Computer Measurements Group 1998 International Conference, Anaheim, CA, 1998. On the internet at http://www.cmg.org/cmg98/index.html.

[Culler99], Culler, D.E., Singh, J.P. & Gupta, A. *Parallel Computer Architecture: A Hardware Software Approach*, Morgan Kaufmann Publishing, 1999.

[Dagum98] Dagum, L. & Menon, R. *OpenMP: An Industry-Standard API for Shared Memory Programming*. In IEEE Computational Science and Engineering, vol. 5, no. 1, 1998.

[Dahlgren99] Dahlgren, F. & Torrellas, J. *Cache-Only Memory Architectures*. In IEEE Computer, June, 1999.

[Darema88] Darema, F., George, D.A., Norton, V.A. & Pfister, G.F. *A Single-Program Multiple-Data Computational Model for EPEX/FORTRAN*. In Parallel Computing, vol. 7, 1988.

[Darwin88] Darwin,L. *Checking C Programs with Lint*. O'Reilly & Associates, 1988.

[Dayde99] Dayde, M.J. & Duff, I.S. *The RISC BLAS: A Blocked Implementation of Level 3 BLAS for RISC Processors.* In ACM Transactions on Mathematical Software, Vol. 25, 1999.

[Dowd98] Dowd, K. & Severance, C., *High Performance Computing.* Second Edition, O'Reilly & Associates, 1998.

[Eggers89] Eggers, S.J. & Katz, R.H. *The Effect of Sharing on the Cache and Bus Performance of Parallel Programs.* In ACM Intl. Conf. on Architectural Support for Programming Languages and Operating Systems, 1989.

[Ferziger99] Ferziger, J.H. & Peric, M. *Computational Methods for Fluid Dynamics.* Springer Verlag, Second Edition, April, 1999.

[Flynn72] Flynn, M.J. *Some Computer Organizations and Their Effectiveness.* In IEEE Transactions on Computing, C-21, September, 1972.

[Foster95] Foster, I. T. *Designing and Building Parallel Programs: Concepts and Tools for Parallel Software Engineering.* Addison-Wesley Publishing Co., 1995.

[Gallivan90] Gallivan, K.A., Heath, M.T., Ng, E., Ortega, J.M., Peyton, B.W., Plemmons, R.J., Romine, C.H., Sameh, A.H. & Voigt, R.G. *Parallel Algorithms for Matrix Computations.* Society for Industrial & Applied Mathematics, 1990.

[Garg95] Garg, R.P., Ferziger, J.H. & Monismith, S.G. *Implementation of a Spectral Finite-Difference Method for Simulation of Stratified Turbulent Flows on Distributed Memory Multiprocessors.* In Proc. of Seventh SIAM Conf. on Parallel Processing for Scientific Computing. San Francisco, CA, February, 1995.

[Garg97] Garg, R.P., Ferziger, J.H. & Monismith, S.G. *Hybrid Spectral Finite-Difference Simulations of Stratified Turbulent Flows on Distributed Memory Architectures.* In Intl. Journal for Numerical Methods in Fluids, Vol. 24, 1997.

[Garg99] Garg, R.P. & Tirumalai, P. P. *Using Tiling to Improve Performance in a Sparse Symmetric Direct Matrix Solver.* US Patent Pending (filed in May, 1999).

[Garg00] Garg, R.P., Nadgir, N., Singh, S.P. & Mayergoyz, I. *Parallelization of a Semiconductor Device Modeling Application Using OpenMP and MPI.* Ist SIAM Conf. on Computational Science and Engineering, Washington DC, September, 2000.

[Geist95] Geist, A., Geguelin, A., Dongarra, J., Jiang, W., Manchek, R. & Sunderam, V. *PVM: Parallel Virtual Machine* MIT Press, Cambridge (1995).

[Golub98] Golub, G. & Van Loan, C. *Matrix Computations.* Second Edition, Johns Hopkins University Press, 1998.

[Graham82] Graham, S.L., Kessler, P.B. & McKusick, M.K. *gprof: A Call Graph Execution Profiler.* In Proceedings of the SIGPLAN '82 Symposium on Compiler Construction, SIGPLAN Notices, Vol. 17, No. 6, June 1982.

[Grama93] Grama, A., Gupta, A. & Kumar, V. *Isoefficiency Function: A Scalability Metric for Parallel Algorithms and Architectures*. In IEEE Parallel and Distributed Technology, Special Issue on Parallel and Distributed Systems: From Theory to Practice, vol. 1, no. 3, August 1993.

[Gropp99] Gropp, W., Lusk, E. & Skjellum, A. *Using MPI: Portable Parallel Programming with the Message-Passing Interface*. MIT Press, Cambridge (1999).

[Gropp00] Gropp, W., Lusk, E. & Thakur, R. *Using MPI-2: Advanced Features of the Message Passing Interface*. MIT Press, Cambridge (2000).

[Gustafson88] Gustafson, J.L., Montry, G.R. & Benner, R.E. *Development Of Parallel Methods For A 1,024-Processor Hypercube*. In SIAM Journal of Scientific and Statictical Computing, vol. 9, no. 4, 1988.

[Gustafson90] Gustafson, J.L. *Fixed Time, Tiered Memory, and Superlinear Speedup*. In Proceedings of the Fifth Distributed Memory Computing Conference (DMCC5), October, 1990.

[Gustafson92] Gustafson, J.L. *The Consequences of Fixed Time Performance Measurement*. In Proc. of the 25th Hawaii Intl. Conference on System Science: Vol III, 1992.

[Gustafson95] Gustafson, J. L. and Snell Q.O., *HINT - A New Way To Measure Computer Performance*, Proceedings of the HICSS-28 Conference, Wailela, Maui, Hawaii, January 3-6, 1995.

[Hennessy96] Hennessy, J., Patterson, D. & Goldberg, D. *Computer Architecture : A Quantitative Approach*. Second Edition, Morgan Kaufmann Publishing, 1996.

[Henty00] Henty, D.S. *Performance of Hybrid Message-Passing and Shared-Memory Parallelism for Discrete Element Modeling*. In Proceedings of Supercomputing'00, Dallas, TX, November, 2000.

[Hisley99] Hisley, D., Agrawal, G., Satya-narayana, P. & Pollock, L. *Porting and Performance Evaluation of Irregular Codes Using OpenMP*. In Proceedings of First European Workshop on OpenMP - EWOMP'99, Lund, Sweden, September, 1999. Available on internet at `http://www.it.lth.se/ewomp99/`.

[Hockney88] Hockney, R.W. & Jesshope, C.R. *Parallel Computers 2: Architecture, Programming and Algorithms*. Published under Adam Hilger imprint by IOP Publishing Ltd., 1988.

[Hockney93] Hockney, R.W., *The Communication Challenge for MPP: Intel Paragon and Meiko CS-2*. In Parallel Computing, vol. 20, 1994.

[Horel99] Horel, T. & Lauterbach, G. *UltraSPARC-III: Designing the Third Generation 64-bit Performance*. In IEEE Micro, May/June, 1999.

[Jin99] Jin, H., Frumpkin, M. & Yan, J. *The OpenMP Implementation of NAS Parallel Benchmarks and Its Performance*. NAS Tech. Report NAS-99-011, NASA Ames Research Center, Mountain View, CA. Available on internet at http://www.nas.nasa.gov/~hjin/PBN.html.

[Karypis99] Karypis, G. & Kumar, V. *A Fast and High Quality Multilevel Scheme for Partitioning Irregular Graphs*. In SIAM Journal on Scientific Computing, Vol. 20, No. 1, 1999.

[Kleinman96] Kleinman, S., Shah, D. & Smaalders, B. *Programming With Threads*. SunSoft Press (A Prentice Hall Title), 1996.

[Kuhn99] Kuhn, R., Peterson, P. & O'Toole, E. *OpenMP vs. Threading in C/C++*. In Proceedings of First European Workshop on OpenMP - EWOMP'99, Lund, Sweden, September, 1999. Available on internet at http://www.it.lth.se/ewomp99/.

[Kumar94] Kumar, V., Grama, A., Gupta, A. & Karypis, G. *Introduction to Parallel Computing: Design and Analysis of Algorithms*. The Benjamin/Cummings Publishing Company, Inc., 1994.

[Kumar97] Kumar, V., Karypis, G. & Grama, A. *Role of Message-Passing in Performance Oriented Parallel Programming*. In Proceedings of the Eighth SIAM Conference Conference on Parallel Processing for Scientific Computing, March 1997.

[Lam91] Lam, M.E., Rothberg, E. & Wolf, M. *The Cache Performance and Optimizations of Blocked Algorithms*. In 4th International Conference on Architectural Support for Programming Languages and Operating Systems, Santa Clara, CA, April 1991.

[Levine99] Levine, J. *Linkers and Loaders*. Morgan Kaufmann Publishers, 1999.

[Lewis97] Lewis, B, & Berg, D. *Multithreaded Programming with P-threads*. Prentice Hall, 1997.

[Mauro00] Mauro, J. & McDougall, R., *Solaris Internals : Core Kernel Architecture*. Prentice Hall, 2000.

[McCalpin95] McCalpin, J.D. *A Survey of Memory Bandwidth and Machine Balance in Current High Performance Computers*. In Newsletter of IEEE Tech. Committee on Computer Architecture, December, 1995. Available on internet at http://www.cs.virginia.edu/stream/ref.html.

[McDougall99] McDougall, R., Cockcroft, A., Hoogendoorn, E., Vargas, E. & Bialaski, T. *Resource Management*. Prentice Hall, 1999.

[McVoy96] McVoy L. & Staelin, C. *lmbench: Portable Tools for Performance Analysis*. In Proceedings of the 1996 USENIX Conference, 1996.

[Moore66] Moore, R.E. *Interval Analysis*. Prentice-Hall, Englewood Cliffs, NJ, 1966.

[Muchnick97] Muchnick, S. *Advanced Compiler Design and Implementation*. Morgan Kaufmann Publishers, 1997.

[Naik93] Naik, N.H., Naik, V.K. & Nicoules, M. *Parallelization of a Class of Implicit Finite Difference Schemes in Computational Fluid Dynamics*. In International Journal of High Speed Computing, Vol. 5, No. 1, 1993.

[Noordergraaf99] Noordergraaf, L. & Pas, R. van der. *Performance Experiences on Sun's Wildfire Prototype*. In Proceedings of Supercomputing'99, Portland, OR, November, 1999.

[Norton96] Norton, S.J. & Dipasquale, M.D. *Thread Time: Multithreaded Programming Guide*. Published by Prentice Hall, 1996.

[Panda99] Panda, P., Nakamura, H. Nicolau, A. *Augmenting Loop Tiling with Data Alignment for Improved Cache Performance*. In IEEE Transactions on Computers, vol. 48(2), February 1999.

[Pfister98] Pfister, G. *In Search of Clusters*. Prentice Hall, Second Edition, 1998.

[Pothen90] Pothen, A., Simon, H. & Liou, K.P. *Partitioning Sparse Matrices with Eigenvectors of Graphs*. In SIAM Journal of Matrix Analysis & Applications, Vol. 11, No. 3, 1990.

[Pothen92] Pothen, A., Simon, H. & Bernard, S.T. *Towards a Fast Implementation of Spectral Nested Dissection*. In Proceedings of Supercomputing'92, Minneapolis, MN, November, 1992.

[Press92] Press, W.H., Flannery, B.P., Teukolsky, S.A. & Vetterling, W.T. *Numerical Recipes in FORTRAN : The Art of Scientific Computing*. Second Edition, Cambridge University Press, 1992.

[Press93] Press, W.H., Flannery, B.P., Teukolsky, S.A. & Vetterling, W.T. *Numerical Recipes in C: The Art of Scientific Computing*. Second Edition, Cambridge University Press, 1993.

[Saphir94] Saphir, W. *Sorting Out Communication Libraries: A Comparison of NX, CMMD, PVM and MPI*. Tutorial presented at Supercomputing'94, Washington DC, November, 1994.

[Sarukkai95] Sarukkai, S. & Van der Wijngaart, R. *Techniques and Tools for Performance Tuning of Parallel and Distributed Scientific Applications*. Tutorial presented at Intl. Parallel Processing Symposium, Santa Barbara, CA, 1995.

[SDSC00] *Hybrid MPI/OpenMP Programming for the SDSC Teraflop System*. Online Volume III, Issue 14, July 1999. Available on the internet at `http://www.npaci.edu/online/v3.14/SCAN.html`.

[Severance98] Severance, C. *An Interview with the Old Man of Floating-Point*. February 1998. Available online at `http://www.cs.berkeley.edu/~wkahan/ieee754status/754story.html`.

[Severance98b] Severance, C. *IEEE 754: An Interview with William Kahan*. In IEEE Computer, vol. 31, no. 3, March 1998. Avaliable online at `http://computer.org/computer/co1998/r3toc.htm`.

[Shah99] Shah, S., Haab, G., Peterson, P. & Throop, J. *Flexible Control Structures for Parallel C/C++*. In Proc. of First European Workshop on OpenMP- EWOPM'99, Lund, Sweden, September 1999. Available on internet at `http://www.it.lth.se/ewomp99/`.

[Shan99] Shan, H. & Singh, J.P. *A Comparison of MPI, SHMEM and Cache-Coherent Shared Address Space Programming Models on the SGI Origin 2000*. In Proceedings of 13th Intl. Conference on Supercomputing, 1999.

[Shan00] Shan, H., Singh, J.P., Oliker, L. & Biswas, R. *A Comparison of Three Programming Models for Adaptive Applications on the Origin 2000*. In Proceedings of Supercomputing'00, Dallas, TX, November, 2000.

[Sharapov97] Sharapov, I. *Multilevel Subspace Correction for Large-Scale Optimization Problems* (Ph.D. Thesis), CAM Report 97-31, Department of Mathematics, University of California, Los Angeles, 1997. Available on the Internet at `http://www.math.ucla.edu/applied/cam/index.html`.

[Simon91] Simon, H. *Partitioning Unstructured Problems for Parallel Processing*. NAS Technical Report RNR-91-008, NASA Ames Research Center, 1991.

[Singh94] Singh, J.P., Rothberg, E. & Gupta, A. *Modelling Communication in Parallel Algorithms: A Fruitful Interaction between Theory and Systems*. In Proceedings of Sixth Annual ACM Symposium on Parallel Algorithms and Architectures, 1994.

[Singhal96] Singhal, A., Broniarczyk, D., Cerauskis, F., Price, J., Yuan, L., Cheng, C., Doblar, D., Fosth, S., Agarwal, N., Harvey, K., Hagersten, E. & Liencres, B. *Gigaplane: A High Performance Bus for Large SMPs*. In Proceedings of Hot Interconnects IV, IEEE, 1996.

[Sistare99] Sistare, S., Dorenkamp, E., Nevin, N. & Loh, E. *MPI Support in the Prism Programming Environment*. In Proceedings of Supercomputing'99, Portland, OR, November, 1999.

[Sistare99b] Sistare, S., VandeVaart, R. & Loh, E. *Optimization of MPI Collectives on Clusters of Large Scale SMP's*. In Proceedings of Supercomputing'99, Portland, OR, November, 1999.

[Sivasubramaniam95] Sivasubramaniam, A., Singla, A., Ramachandran, U. & Venkateswaran, H. *On Characterizing Bandwidth Requirements of Parallel Applications*. In Proceedings of ACM SIGMETRICS Conference, 1995.

[Smith99] Smith, L.A. & Kent, P. *Development and Performance of a Mixed OpenMP/MPI Quantum Monte Carlo Code*. In Proceedings of First European Workshop on OpenMP, Lund, Sweden, September, 1999.

[Sun90] Sun, Xian-He & Ni, L.M. *Another View of Parallel Speedup*. In Proceedings of Supercomputing'90, 1990.

[Tirumalai96] Tirumalai, P. P., Beylin, B. & Subramanian, K. *The Design of a Modulo Scheduler for a Superscalar RISC Processor*. In 1996 Conference on Parallel Architectures and Compilation Techniques (PACT '96). Available on internet at http://www.computer.org/cspress/CATALOG/pr07632.htm.

[Torrellas90] Torrellas, J., Lam, M.S. & Hennessy, J.L. *Shared Data Placement Optimizations to Reduce Multiprocessor Cache Miss Rates*. In Intl. Conference on Parallel Processing, 1990.

[VanderLinden94] Van der Linden, P. *Expert C Programming*. Prentice Hall, 1994.

[VanderWijngaart93] Van der Wijngaart, R. *Efficient Implementation of a 3-Dimensional ADI method on the iPSC/860*. In Proceedings of Supercomputing'93, Portland, OR, November, 1993.

[VanderWijngaart96] Van der Wijngaart, R., Sarukkai, S.R. & Mehar, P. *Analysis and Optimization of Software Pipeline Performance on MIMD Parallel Computers*. In Journal of Parallel and Distributed Computing, Vol. 38, 1996.

[Wadleigh00] Wadleigh, K.R. & Crawford, I.L. *Software Optimization for High Performance Computing*. Prentice Hall, 2000.

[Wallcraft99] Wallcraft, A.J. *SPMD OpenMP vs MPI for Ocean Models*. In Proc. of First European Workshop on OpenMP -EWOPM'99, Lund, Sweden, September 1999. Available on internet at http://www.it.lth.se/ewomp99/.

[Walshaw93] Walshaw, C. & Farr, S.J. *A Two-way Parallel Partition Method for Solving Tridiagonal Systems*. Univ. of Leeds, School of Computer Studies Research Report Series, Report No. 93.25, 1993.

[Walster88] Walster, G.W. *Philosophy and Practicalities of Interval Arithmetic*. In *Reliability in Computing* (Edited by R.E. Moore), Academic Press, Inc., San Diego, 1988.

[Weaver94] Weaver, D. & Germond, T., *The SPARC Architecture Manual*. Prentice Hall, 1994.

[Whaley98] Whaley, R.C. & Dongarra, J.J. *Automatically Tuned Linear Algebra Software (ATLAS)*. Technical Report, Univ. of Tennessee, 1998. Available on internet at http://netlib.org/atlas.

[Winsor99] Winsor, J. *Solaris 7 Reference*. Prentice Hall, 1999

[Winston94] Winston, W.L. *Operations Research: Applications and Algorithms*. Duxbury Press, 1994.

[Wisniewski99] Wisniewski, L., Smisloff, B. & Nieuwejaar, N. *Sun MPI I/O: Efficient I/O for Parallel Applications*. In Proceedings of Supercomputing'99, Portland, OR, November, 1999.

[Wolfe89] Wolfe, M. *Optimizing Supercompilers for Supercomputers*. MIT Press, Cambridge, MA, 1989.

[Wolf92] Wolf, M.E. *Locality and Parallelism in Nested Loops*. Ph.D. Dissertation, Tech. Report CSL-TR-92-538, Dept. of Computer Science, Stanford Univ., Stanford, CA, 1992.

[Wong97] Wong, B. *Configuration and Capacity Planning for Solaris Servers*. Prentice Hall, 1997.

[Worley90] Worley, P.H. *The Effect of Time Constraints on Scaled Speedup*. In SIAM Jour. of Scientific and Statistical Computing, 11(5), 1990.

[Zagha96] Zagha, M., Larson, B., Turner, S. & Itzkowitz, M. *Performance Analysis Using the MIPS R10000 Counters*. In Proceedings of Supercomputing'96, Pittsburgh, PA, November, 1996.

[Zucker98] Zucker, S. *Endianness in Solaris*, SunSoft white paper, 1998. Available on the Internet at `http://www.sun.com/realitycheck/endian.pdf` .

Index

SYMBOLS

`/etc/release` file, 17, 61
`/etc/system` file, 80, 264
`_REENTRANT`, 338, 403
`_Restrict`, 181, 445

NUMERICS

64-bit development and porting, 38 to 45, 115, 124

A

ABI
   See application binary interface
absolute speedup, 324
Adams-Bashforth method, 490
`adb`, 265
address controller, 575
`afbconfig`, 553
`aioread`, 596
`aiowrite`, 596
algebraic simplifications, 129
alias disambiguation analysis, 109, 178 to 189, 208 to 209, 287, 289
`alloca`, 214
alternating direction implicit (ADI) method, 460
Amdahl's law, 325
Analyzer
   See Performance Analyzer

annotated source code, 82, 98
`appcert`, 18, 29, 216
application binary interface (ABI), 29, 73
application specific integrated circuit (ASIC), 94, 575
`apptrace`, 31, 88
`ar`, 218
arithmetic logic unit (ALU), 555
array padding, 265, 275, 410
ASIC counters
   See hardware counters
assembly template inlining, 110, 270 to 272
asynchronous calls, 246, 514, 596
atomic operations, 414, 415, 416, 456, 467, 468
automatic parallelization, 333 to 334, 440, 445 to 447, 453
automatic variables, 189, 422, 444

B

bank stall, 268
barrier synchronization, 414, 456
basic block, 77
benchmarks, 60
   HINT, 246
   lmbench, 246, 565, 567
   NAS Parallel Benchmark, 468, 493
   ping-pong, 503, 526
   SPECfp, 309
   STREAM, 269, 475

big-endian platforms, 158
binary compatibility, 29 to 31
binary search, 288
BLAS, 228, 249, 295, 479
boss-worker model, 396
branch misprediction, 92, 311
bss segment, 214
bsub, 508
bus frequencies, 244
bus traffic, 412, 475
busstat, 63, 94, 388 to 390, 572, 575

C

C
    ANSI standard, 287
    automatic parallelization, 445 to 447
    explicit parallelization, 448 to 453
    interoperability with Fortran, 50
    memory layout of multidimensional arrays, 51,
       300
    parallelization directives, 440, 453
cache blocking, 135, 249 to 255, 295
cache coherence, 414, 433, 534, 558, 564
cache only memory architecture (COMA), 327
cache-coherent non-uniform memory access
    architecture (ccNUMA), 323, 327, 328
caches, 244 to 248
    access times, 248
    associativity, 546, 562
    D-cache, 247, 256, 279, 291, 295, 556, 559, 561,
       573
    direct mapped, 245, 256
    E-cache, 92, 194, 202, 247, 561
    Harvard, 245
    I-cache, 110, 247, 559, 573
    level 1, 245, 247, 256, 558
    level 2, 194, 247, 279, 556, 558
    line alignment, 279, 410
    lines, 245, 256, 410, 411, 546
    miss rate, 92, 410, 573, 574
    P-cache, 148, 194, 202, 247, 559
    set associative, 245, 256
    unified, 245
    W-cache, 247, 559
    write back, 245

    write through, 245
cas, 417
cb, 37
cflow, 37
cg, 109, 441
Cholesky factorization, 396, 479
Cluster Runtime Environment (CRE), 22, 345, 508
code generation, 107, 441
code motion and rearrangement, 144, 148
collect, 366
Collector
    See Sampling Collector
common subexpression elimination, 109, 129, 135
communication overhead, 503
compare-and-swap, 415
compilation time, 117
compiler, 106 to 109
    code generator (cg), 109, 441
    documentation, 27
    front ends, 108, 441
    microtasking library, 442
    patches, 21
    SunIR optimizer (iropt), 109, 441
compiler libraries, 27, 109, 216, 226 to 229
    which can be redistributed, 27, 217
compiler options
    -#, 26
    -###, 506
    -aligncommon, 274
    -C, 36
    -dalign, 111, 113, 171 to 174, 274, 480, 530
    -dbl, 47
    -dbl_align_all, 274
    -dryrun, 506
    -e, 49
    -errwarn, 33, 287
    -explicitpar, 454
    -f, 274
    -fast, 111, 112 to 114, 129, 135
    -flags, 26
    -fnonstd, 171
    -fns, 113, 163 to 165
    -fround, 171
    -fsimple, 113, 117, 166 to 171
    -ftrap, 47, 113, 160 to 163
    -g, 82, 376

-KPIC, 218
-Kpic, 218
-loopinfo, 441
-misalign, 274
-misalign2, 274
-mp, 335, 451, 454
-mt, 338, 403, 480
-native, 113, 114
-openmp, 335, 454
-p, 74
-pg, 74
-Qoption ld, 218
-r8, 47
-S, 306
-stackvar, 36, 47, 117, 189 to 192, 215, 335, 441, 444, 452, 471
-u, 36
-V, 26, 552
-v, 26, 32
-vpara, 441
-Wl, 218
-Xa, 287
-xalias_level, 113, 117, 181 to 189, 287, 445
-xarch, 29, 41, 73, 111, 114, 118 to 124, 175, 227, 295, 480, 532
-xautopar, 333, 441, 445, 480
-Xc, 287
-xcache, 114, 546
-xchip, 111, 114, 125 to 127
-xcrossfile, 132 to 135
-xdepend, 113, 135 to 136, 137, 166, 302, 441, 445
-xexplicitpar, 441, 448
-xia, 580
-xinline, 132 to 135
-xlang, 49, 53
-xlibmil, 113, 227
-xlibmopt, 113, 227
-xlic_lib, 228
-xlic_lib, 479
-Xlist, 34
-xloopinfo, 446, 453
-xmemalign, 274
-xO, 129 to 132
-xO1, 129
-xO2, 129, 183
-xO3, 129, 133, 135, 194, 286, 441, 445
-xO4, 130, 133
-xO5, 113, 130, 133, 175

-xpad, 113, 265
-xparallel, 441, 445, 448, 453
-xpp, 38
-xprefetch, 111, 113, 118, 148 to 152, 201
-xprofile, 78, 144 to 148
-xreduction, 333, 441, 446
-xrestrict, 111, 117, 178 to 181, 287, 445
-xsafe=mem, 175 to 177
-xsfpconst, 139 to 143
-xtarget, 111, 114, 116, 546
-xtime, 117
-xtypemap, 43, 45
-xvector, 113, 137 to 138, 227
-xvpara, 453
compiler options order, 114
compiler parallelization
    See explicit prallelization and automatic parallelization
compiler pragmas
    pragma alias, 209
    pragma alias_level, 209
    pragma align, 207 to 208, 274, 279
    pragma fini, 214
    pragma init, 214
    pragma may_not_point_to, 209
    pragma may_point_to, 209
    pragma MP serial_loop, 453
    pragma MP serial_loop_nested, 453
    pragma MP taskloop, 453
    pragma noalias, 209
    pragma opt, 200 to 201
    pragma pack, 205 to 206
    pragma pipeloop, 192 to 199
    pragma prefetch, 194, 201 to 204
    pragma weak, 221
complementary optimizations, 111
complex and real operations, 317
concurrency and parallelism, 352, 478
condition variables, 400, 413
conditional move, 121
conditional sampling, 92
consistent_coloring, 264
constant folding and propagation, 109
context switch, 395
control-parallel model, 323
core files, 85
cpp, 38

CPU counters
    See hardware counters
CPU starvation, 244
cpustat, 63, 93, 385 to 388, 572
cputrack, 572
cputrack, 63, 93, 259, 385 to 388, 409, 572
Crank-Nicolson method, 490
CRE
    See Cluster Runtime Environment
critical region, 421
critical section, 467
cross compilation, 116
cscope, 37
csplit, 38
current window pointer (CWP), 282
cycle shrinking, 166
cycles per instruction (CPI), 192, 574

D

data alignment, 171 to 174, 205, 207, 410
data cache
    See caches, D-cache
data cache unit (DCU), 558
data decomposition, 329, 490
data parallel model, 323, 329
data prefetching, 148 to 152, 201 to 204, 560
data sharing, 397, 406 to 412
dbx, 87, 377
dead code elimination, 109, 129
dependency analysis, 135, 445
df, 551
direct I/O, 596
direct inline memory module (DIMM), 268
dis, 140, 150, 272
disk striping, 246
distributed make, 27
distributed shared memory (DSM), 328
division operation, 315, 317
division replacement, 315
dlopen, 85
dlsym, 218, 237
dmake, 27

DOALL directive, 451
domain decomposition, 329, 490
DOSERIAL directive, 451
double-to-single conversion, 142
double-word alignment
    See compiler options, -dalign
dtime, 63, 71
du, 551
dump, 552
dumpstabs, 552
dynamic data decomposition, 490
dynamic linking, 213, 216 to 220
dynamic random acceess memory (DRAM), 268

E

ELF
    See executable and linking format
embarrassingly parallel problems, 406
End User Object Code License
    See compiler libraries which can be redistributed
endian independent code, 158
environment variables
    LD_DEBUG, 238, 239
    LD_LIBRARY_PATH, 217, 234, 400, 507
    LD_OPTIONS, 231
    LD_PRELOAD, 220, 225, 235, 369
    LD_PROFILE, 238
    LD_PROFILE_OUTPUT, 238
    MPI_EAGERONLY, 523
    MPI_FULLCONNINIT, 529
    MPI_POLLALL, 525
    MPI_PRINTENV, 515
    MPI_PROCBIND, 518
    MPI_SHM_BCASTSIZE, 520
    MPI_SHM_CPOOLSIZE, 527
    MPI_SHM_CYCLESIZE, 527
    MPI_SHM_CYCLESTART, 523, 527
    MPI_SHM_NUMPOSTBOX, 526
    MPI_SHM_REDUCESIZE, 520
    MPI_SHM_SBPOOLSIZE, 526
    MPI_SHOW_ERRORS, 515
    MPI_SHOW_INTERFACES, 515
    MPI_SPIN, 516
    MPI_TCP_RENDVSIZE, 529
    OMP_DYNAMIC, 456

`OMP_NUM_THREADS`, 335, 454, 456
`OMP_SCHEDULE`, 454
`PARALLEL`, 333, 335, 441, 444
`STACKSIZE`, 441, 444, 481
`SUNW_MP_THR_IDLE`, 441, 444, 482
`etime`, 63, 70
Euler method, 457, 490
exception handling, 478
executable and linking format (ELF), 214
explicit parallelization, 440 to 456
   data scoping, 442, 448, 453
extended precision, 160
external cache
   See caches, E-cache, 202
external memory unit (EMU), 558

F

`fabsd`, 306
`faddd`, 306
false sharing, 397, 406 to 412, 469
fast code generator, 108
`fbconfig`, 553
`ffbconfig`, 553
FFT, 493
FFTPACK, 228, 479
`file`, 124, 219
file descriptors, 399
filters, 234
`fini` section, 214, 237
FirePlane interconnect, 12, 568 to 569
floating point operations per second (FLOPS), 574
floating-point arithmetic
   See IEEE floating-point arithmetic
floating-point unit (FPU), 546, 558, 561
flow-control dependency, 305
Flynn's taxonomy, 328
`fmuld`, 306, 315
`fork`, 399, 428
`fork/exec` multiprocessing model, 339 to 342
`fork1`, 399
Forte Developer tools, 19 to 21, 79 to 83, 362 to 366
Fortran
   automatic parallelization, 445 to 447

compatibility library, 50
continuation lines, 49
creating threads, 405
explicit parallelization, 448 to 453
extensions to the standard, 48
Fortran 77/95 compatibility, 48
free and fixed source form, 48, 451, 454
interoperability with C, 50
linking with C++, 53
memory layout of multidimensional arrays, 51, 300
support for interval arithmetic, 579 to 588
Fortran directives
   Cray-style, 48, 440, 451
   OpenMP, 48, 440
   Sun-style, 48, 440, 448
`fpp`, 38
`fpversion`, 116, 546
`fread`, 592
`fseek`, 592
`fsplit`, 38
functional decomposition, 329

G

Gauss-Seidel method, 491
`gethrtime`, 63, 65, 356
`gethrvtime`, 63, 356
Gigaplane interconnect, 12, 565
Gigaplane XB interconnect, 12, 566 to 567
global data visibility, 414
global offset table, 218
global symbol scope, 225
`gmon.out` file, 74
`gprof`, 63, 74, 238, 384
gradual underflow, 163 to 165
graph partitioning, 493
guard page, 422
guided self scheduling, 449

H

hardware counters, 73, 79, 92 to 102, 251, 385 to 390, 572 to 575, 575 to 578

heap, 214
High Performance Fortran (HPF), 22, 329
HINT benchmark, 246
hostid, 549
HPC ClusterTools
    See Sun HPC ClutsterTools
hpc.conf file, 505
hybrid parallelization models, 346 to 348, 535

I

I/O performance, 61, 589 to 596
IEEE floating-point arithmetic, 114, 156 to 165, 166
    to 171
    binary representation, 158
    exceptions, 47, 160
    gradual underflow, 163 to 165
    Inf, 160
    NaN, 160
    trap handling, 91, 160 to 163
ifbconfig, 553
ifconfig, 549
ILP32 model, 39
indent, 37
init section, 214, 237
inlining, 80, 109, 130, 132, 144
instruction cache
    See caches, I-cache
instruction issue unit (IIU), 558
instruction level parallelism (ILP), 192, 311
instruction set architecture (ISA), 29, 118
integer execution unit (IEU), 558, 561
inter-iteration dependency, 446
interleaved memory, 268
interleaving factor, 268
intermediate representation (IR), 106, 441
inter-procedural analysis, 109
inter-process communication (IPC), 339, 549
interval arithmetic, 557, 579 to 588
    directed rounding, 580
    intrinsic functions, 581
    Newton method, 583
    order operations, 582
intimate shared memory (ISM), 85

iostat, 91
IP address, 549
iropt, 109, 441
ISA
    See instruction set architecture
isaexec, 44
isainfo, 38, 549
isalist, 29, 38, 234
isoefficiency function, 327

J

Jacobi method, 491
Java Development Kit (JDK), 553

K

kernel
    monitoring, 90
    tracing, 367
    tunable parameters, 549
kstat, 63, 90

L

LAPACK, 228, 479
large file support, 40
latencies of instructions and operations, 560
ld
    See link-editor
ld.so.1
    See runtime linker
LD_DEBUG, 238, 239
LD_LIBRARY_PATH, 217, 234, 400, 507
LD_OPTIONS, 231
LD_PRELOAD, 220, 225, 235, 369
LD_PROFILE, 238
LD_PROFILE_OUTPUT, 238
ldd, 219
ldstub, 414
leaf routine, 180
libraries
    libaio, 596

`libc`, 369, 404
`libc_probe`, 369
`libc_psr`, 229, 230
`libcopt`, 227
`libcpc`, 63, 92, 100, 251
`libf77compat`, 50
`libm`, 137, 226
`libm.il`, 228
`libmopt`, 227
`libmpi`, 367, 505
`libmtmalloc`, 401
`libmtsk`, 442
`libmvec`, 137, 227
`libmvec_mt`, 227
`libpctx`, 92
`libpthread`, 369, 401, 413
`libpthread_probe`, 369
`libs31`, 229, 530, 533
`libsunmath`, 226
`libsunperf`, 228, 249, 479 to 484, 530
`libthread`, 369, 401, 413, 507
`libthread_probe`, 369
`libtnf`, 368
`libtnfctl`, 368
`libtnfprobe`, 368
`mediaLib`, 228
light-weight process (LWP), 330, 365, 379, 399
linear speedup, 324
link-editor, 106, 212
link-editor options
  `-Bdynamic`, 217
  `-Bstatic`, 217
  `-dy`, 217
  `-G`, 217
  `-L`, 217
  `-M`, 223
  `-R`, 217, 234
  `-z defs`, 218
  `-z muldefs`, 218
  `-z nodefs`, 218
link-editor options passed by compiler, 218
linker mapfiles, 223 to 225
linker tokens
  `$ISALIST`, 230, 234
  `$ORIGIN`, 234, 242
  `$OSNAME`, 234
  `$OSREL`, 234
  `$PLATFORM`, 229, 230, 242

LINPACK, 228, 479
`lint`, 32, 42, 287
little-endian platforms, 158
lmbench benchmark, 246, 565, 567
load and store elimination, 287
load balancing, 362, 395, 396, 398, 454, 493
load instruction, 171
load latency, 126
Load Sharing Facility (LSF), 22, 508
load-use separation, 125
`loc`, 275
local symbol scope, 225
locking
  See synchronization
`lockstat`, 63, 91, 383 to 384
loop carried dependence, 196
loop optimizations, 293 to 320, 441
  fission, 109, 195, 196, 305 to 306
  fusion, 109, 129, 196, 302 to 303
  interchange, 109, 300
  peeling, 109, 306, 309
  tiling, 109, 294
  unrolling, 109, 129, 180, 286, 294 to 298
loop scheduling, 410, 447, 453
  using Cray-style directives, 452
  using MPI, 499
  using OpenMP, 454
  using Sun-style directives, 449
loops with conditionals, 311 to 312
LoopTool, 83
LP64 model, 39
`lseek`, 590
LSF
  See Load Sharing Facility
LU factorization, 491
lvalue, 289

M

`m64config`, 553
`malloc`, 214, 275, 401
master-slave model, 330, 364, 395, 442, 489
matrix reordering, 184
`MAXCPUS` qualifier, 449

memalign, 275, 281
membar, 416
memcpy, 229
memory
    bandwidth, 475 to 477
    bank interleaving, 268
    barrier, 416
    consistency models, 415
    hierarchy, 244 to 248
    interleaving, 268
    pages, 246, 250
    refresh, 268
memory constrained scaling, 327
memory management unit (MMU), 556
memset, 229
message passing, 330
Message Passing Interface
    See MPI, 330
MicroSPARC, 118
microstate accounting, 64, 66
microtasking library, 442
million instructions per second (MIPS), 574
mmap, 214, 330, 422, 594
modulo-scheduling
    See software pipelining
MOESI cache coherence protocol, 564, 566, 569
mpf77, mpf90, mpcc, mpCC
    See MPI compilation scripts
MPI
    binding a process to a processor, 518
    bisection bandwidth, 503
    blocking and non-blocking functions, 495, 514
    chunk size for broadcast and reduction
        operations, 520
    collective operations, 519
    communication bandwidth, 502
    communication protocols, 503
    comparison with OpenMP and hybrid
        models, 534 to 537
    compilation scripts, 506
    connection initialization, 529
    cyclic message passing, 525
    dedicated system execution, 516
    diagnostic information, 515
    eager and rendezvous protocols, 523
    environment variables, 515 to 529

    I/O, 512 to 514
    LAM implementation, 345
    library, 367, 505
    message transfer time, 502
    MPICH implementation, 345
    packing messages, 498
    point to point communication, 523
    process yielding and coscheduling, 504, 518
    programming models, 488
    shared buffers, 524
    spawning and connecting processes, 509
MPI_BARRIER, 362
MPI_Recv, 378
MPI_Wtime, 361
MPI-2 features, 509, 512
mpinfo, 505
mprun, 376, 501
mpstat, 63, 91, 379, 381
MT safety
    See thread safety
multiple instruction multiple data (MIMD), 328
multiple instruction single data (MISD), 328
multiple program multiple data (MPMD), 323, 329,
    489
multiplication operation, 315
multi-processing models, 339 to 345
multithreading, 336 to 339
multithreading models, 331 to 339, 394 to 398
mutual exclusion (mutex) locks, 382, 383, 400, 413,
    417

N

NAS Parallel Benchmark, 468, 493
nested parallelism, 460
Netra server products, 15
netstat, 91
Newton method, 583
non-privileged trap, 71
non-uniform memory access architectures
    (NUMA), 323, 328
NP-complete, 295
NUMA
    See non-uniform memory access architecture

numerical stability, 318

O

OMP_DYNAMIC, 456
OMP_NUM_THREADS, 335, 454, 456
OMP_SCHEDULE, 454
OpenGL, 553
OpenMP
    atomic updates, 468
    barriers, 469
    comparison with MPI and hybrid models, 534 to 537
    comparison with P-threads, 478 to 479
    data scoping, 442, 466, 470 to 474
    environment variables, 441
    loop scheduling, 454
    ordered region, 469
    parallel region, 457, 460
    parallel sections, 457 to 460
    programming styles, 457 to 467
    SPMD style, 460 to 467
    support in Forte compilers, 334 to 336, 454 to 456
    synchronization, 467 to 469
optimized libraries, 226 to 229
optimizing code generator, 109
outlined function, 442

P

padding
    See array padding
page coloring, 256, 263 to 266
paging, 61
PARALLEL, 333, 335, 441, 444
parallel
    architectural models, 328
    efficiency, 325
    isoefficiency, 326
    programming models, 329
    region, 457, 460
    scalability, 324 to 327
    system, 324
Parallel Virtual Machine (PVM), 330

parallelism and concurrency, 352, 478
partial store order (PSO) model, 416
patchadd, 26
pbind, 379
PCI interface, 575
Performance Analyzer, 63, 79 to 83, 95, 320, 362 to 366
performance intstrumentation counters (PIC)
    See hardware counters
Performance Library
    See Sun Performance Library
performance measurements, 60
pflags, 85
physical memory (RAM), 245, 544, 546
ping-pong benchmark, 503, 526
pipeline model, 397, 490
pipeline stalls, 92
pipelining
    See software pipelining
pipelining of parallel tasks, 494, 499
pldd, 85
pmap, 84, 215
pointer alias analysis, 178 to 189, 208 to 209, 287 to 290
pool of threads, 442
position independent code, 213, 218
POSIX threads, 336 to 339, 399
prefetch and dispatch unit (PDU), 561
prefetch cache
    See caches, P-cache, 247
prefetch instruction, 111, 125, 149, 201, 272, 556
prefetching
    See data prefetching
prex, 368, 369
Prism, 22, 63, 367, 376 to 378, 503
proc file system, 84, 548
proc tools, 63, 84 to 86
process attributes, 399
processor sets, 353, 377
processor_info, 551
prof, 63, 74, 320
profile feedback, 109, 130, 144 to 148
Profiling tools, 384
profiling tools, 74 to 83, 238, 376

program counter (PC), 74, 80
prstat, 91
prtconf, 546
prtdiag, 61, 544
prun, 87
psradm, 548
psrinfo, 379, 386, 548
psrset, 379 to 380
pstack, 85, 517
pthread_join, 404
ptime, 64, 354

R

random access memory (RAM)
   See physical memory
RAW bypass, 127
read, 590
read-after-write, 125
READONLY qualifier, 449
real and imaginary parts, 317
reduction, 446, 449, 469
register window overflow, 132, 282 to 284
registers
   allocation, 110, 129, 144
   blocking, 294
   pressure, 195, 305
   spills, 180, 195, 295
   windows, 180, 282
relative scaling, 327
relative speedup, 324
relaxed memory order (RMO) model, 416
relocation, 218
Run Time Environment (RTE), 22
Runge-Kutta method, 457, 490
runtime linker, 212

S

S3L
   See Sun Scalable Scientific Subroutine Library
Sampling Collector, 79 to 83, 95, 362 to 366
sar, 91

SBus interface, 575
ScaLAPACK, 530, 533
scalar replacement, 135
scaled problem size speedup, 326
semaphores, 404, 430
servers
   See UltraSPARC servers
shared libraries, 85
shared memory, 330
shell limits, 444
showrev, 26, 549
signal handling, 478
SIGSEGV, 422
single instruction multiple data (SIMD), 228, 328
single instruction single data (SISD), 328
single program multiple data (SPMD), 323, 329,
   460 to 467, 489
single-to-double conversion, 142
size, 215
sockets, 330
software pipelining, 110, 111, 129, 192 to 199, 295,
   311
   initiation interval (II), 193
   stage count (SC), 193
Solaris
   developer version, 26
   Operating Environment, 17
   patches, 549
   system libraries, 18, 29, 213, 216, 220, 238, 367,
     373
   threads, 399
   tools, 31, 379 to 384
   tunables, 549
Solaris Developer Connection, 27, 369
sotruss, 87
source code verification tools, 32 to 36
SPARC V9 architecture, 11, 73, 122, 180
sparse matix operations, 479
spatial locality, 249
speculative load, 175 to 177
speedup of a parallel system, 324
spin barrier, 395
spin locks, 363, 421, 433, 481
spin wait, 444
stack, 214, 283, 422 to 427, 444

`stacksize` shell limit, 444
stair-stepping effect, 353, 451
standard counters, 96
standards conformance, 28 to 29
static data decomposition, 490
static linking, 213, 216 to 220
static random access memory (SRAM), 268
store barrier, 416
store instruction, 171
STREAM benchmark, 269, 475
strength reduction, 109, 169, 293, 314 to 318
`strip`, 552
structured grid partitioning, 491
Sun documentation, 27
Sun HPC ClusterTools, 22 to 23, 345, 367, 503, 531, 552
Sun Performance Library, 228, 249, 479 to 484, 530
    64-bit integer arguments, 482
    `SUNPERF` module, 483
    `use_threads`, 481
Sun Scalable Scientific Subroutine Library (S3L), 229, 530
    array descriptors, 533
    runtime error checking, 533
    thread safety, 533
Sun Technical Compute Farm (TCF), 16, 328, 501
SunIR
    See intermediate representation (IR)
superlinear speedup, 325, 466
SuperSPARC, 118
`swap`, 551
swapping, 61
symbol table, 107, 212, 221, 234, 552
symmetric multiprocessors (SMPs), 328
synchronization, 362, 395, 398, 400, 406, 413 to 422, 456, 465, 467 to 469, 478
`sysconf`, 550
`sysdef`, 549
`sysinfo`, 29, 551
system interface unit (SIU), 559
system libraries
    See Solaris system libraries
system monitoring tools, 89 to 91, 379 to 384

T

tail-call elimination, 129
task level parallelism, 329
`TASKCOMMON` directive, 448, 451
TCF
    See Sun Technical Compute Farm
`tcov`, 63, 77, 148, 320
temporal locality, 249, 295
`text` segment, 214
`thr_setconcurrency`, 404
thread library, 413, 507
    single-level implementation, 404
threads
    attributes, 402, 404
    bound, 372, 400, 404, 427
    creation, 427 to 437
    detached, 404
    joinable, 404
    POSIX standard, 399, 401
    safety, 479, 505, 533, 536
    Solaris models, 399, 401
    stack, 422 to 427, 441, 444
    thundering herds, 382
    unbound, 400, 404, 427
`TICK` register, 63, 65, 71
`time`, 63, 64
time constrained scaling, 327
`timex`, 63, 64
timing tools, 63 to 73, 354 to 362
`tmp` file system, 61, 596
TNF
    See trace normal form
total store order (TSO) model, 416
trace normal form (TNF), 63, 367 to 374, 505
    prex, 368, 369
    `TNF_PROBE`, 368
    `tnfdump`, 368
    `tnfmerge`, 369
    `tnftrace`, 369
    `tnfview`, 369
    `tnfxtract`, 368
tracing tools, 86 to 89
translation lookaside buffer (TLB), 92, 246, 250, 260, 556, 573
translation software buffer (TSB), 260

tree search, 325
tree structure algorithms, 478
`truss`, 86, 425
two dimensional bin packing, 295

U

Ultra port architecture (UPA) interconnect, 12, 563 to 564, 565, 567
UltraSPARC interconnect
  FirePlane, 12, 568 to 569
  Gigaplane, 12, 565
  Gigaplane XB, 12, 566 to 567
  UPA, 12, 563 to 564, 565, 567
UltraSPARC processors
  clock frequency ranges, 12
  UltraSPARC-I, 11, 92, 115, 194, 247, 555 to 556, 563, 572
  UltraSPARC-II, 11, 92, 115, 194, 247, 311, 555 to 556, 560, 563, 572
  UltraSPARC-IIe, 12, 562
  UltraSPARC-III, 11, 92, 115, 118, 148, 194, 202, 247, 279, 311, 557 to 560, 568, 572
  UltraSPARC-IIi, 11, 561
UltraSPARC servers, 14 to 16, 328, 565
UltraSPARC workstations, 13 to 14
`uname`, 61, 230, 234, 544, 549
uniform memory access (UMA), 328
Unix International (UI) threads
  See Solaris threads
unstructured grid partitioning, 493

V

`valloc`, 275, 281
VFFTPACK, 228, 479
virtual memory (VM), 246
Visual Instruction Set (VIS), 11, 118, 228, 270, 282, 328, 476, 557, 558
`vmstat`, 63, 89, 381
`volatile`, 421

W

weak symbol binding, 220
`whocalls`, 89
worker-crew model, 396, 490
workload distribution, 489
workpile model, 396
workstations
  See UltraSPARC workstations
write cache
  See caches, W-cache, 247